SIX RESTORATION PLAYS

RIVERSIDE EDITIONS

RIVERSIDE EDITIONS

UNDER THE GENERAL EDITORSHIP OF

Gordon N. Ray

SIX

RESTORATION PLAYS

EDITED BY

JOHN HAROLD WILSON

THE OHIO STATE UNIVERSITY

HOUGHTON MIFFLIN COMPANY

BOSTON • The Riverside Press Cambridge

CONTENTS

INTRODUCTION

The Background of Restoration Drama

BY JOHN HAROLD WILSON

WITH THE restoration of King Charles II on May 29, 1660, London turned from the austerities of puritanism to the pursuit of pleasure. Proscribed delights were once more permitted, and wanton youth could have its fling at music, dances, games, plays, and other, not-so-innocent, forms of merriment. Stage-plays were in immediate demand. Groups of actors — older men who had played before the closing of the theaters in 1642, and young men newly recruited — assembled and set to work in makeshift theaters. A few months after his return, the King licensed two companies: the King's Company, a troupe of older actors headed by Charles Hart and Michael Mohun and managed by a courtier, Thomas Killigrew; and the Duke's Company, a band of young men headed by Thomas Betterton and managed by the playwright-impresario Sir William Davenant. Within a few years both companies flourished in permanent theaters, the King's Company at the Theatre Royal in Bridges Street, near Drury Lane, and the Duke's Company at the Dorset Garden Theatre on the river bank, near the City.

Soon after their founding, both companies began to employ actresses. Thus, for the first time in the history of the English stage, women played the female roles formerly entrusted to boys. This daring innovation, while adding to the theatrical illusion of reality, had an unfortunate effect upon the development of the new drama. Many of the actresses, underpaid and constantly tempted by leering gentlemen with fat purses, became demi-mondaines, and playwrights were quick to capitalize upon their demi-reputations by writing provocative, erotic roles for them. A good share of the emphasis upon sex and sensuality in Restoration drama resulted from the introduction of women on the stage.

Unlike the great Elizabethan theaters, the new playhouses were small and intimate, seating only two or three hundred people.

The buildings were roofed over, and lighted by candles in chandeliers over the stage and in sconces about the walls. The half-oval apron, or fore-stage, upon which most of the action of a play took place, jutted well out into the pit. A proscenium arch with two wings, each pierced by two doors with windows above them, extended the width of the stage, cutting it almost in half. Behind the arch was an inner stage equipped with painted flats which slid in grooves to form scenes. The proscenium curtains parted at the beginning of a play and closed at the end. Musicians played before the curtain opened and between the acts. In the early Restoration the time for the daily performance (there were no plays on Sunday) was three or half past three o'clock in the afternoon. Toward the end of the century the time moved on to four, then five, and finally, in the early eighteenth century, to six o'clock.

The wits, beaux, and bullies of the Town sat on backless benches in the pit (2s 6d), talked, laughed, combed their periwigs, chaffed the vizard-masks (prostitutes), and bantered with the orange-girls, who stood with their backs to the stage, displaying oranges and seasonal fruits in baskets. Sometimes the bullies quarreled during a performance, drew their swords, and leaped upon the stage to settle the matter then and there. Royalty, fine ladies, and more sedate gentlemen occupied the side-boxes (4s), the lowest of a tier of galleries extending around three sides of the theater. Gentlemen standing in the pit leaned upon the rails of the side-boxes and entertained their ladies while the play went on unheeded. Clerks, timid country folk, and, rarely, a citizen or two, sat in the middle gallery (18d), and usually only servants climbed to the upper gallery (1s). There were no reserved seats; people who wished to be sure of places at a popular play sent their servants well in advance to hold them. There was no heat and little comfort, but much tinsel and splendor. There were scenes, machines, songs, dances, spectacles, and brilliant costumes which were theatrically effective but rarely historical.

At the beginning of the period the companies offered only revivals of old plays, the best of Shakespeare, Jonson, Beaumont and Fletcher, and other pre-Restoration dramatists. As time went on, new playwrights appeared; gradually the companies acquired repertories of modern plays, offering them alternately with revivals or modernized adaptations of Elizabethan plays. Some of the new playwrights were amateurs, gentlemen like the Duke of Buckingham, Sir Charles Sedley, Sir George Etherege, and William Wycherley, who wrote as much to display their wit and win favor at the Court of the theater-loving King Charles as to entertain the Town. But professional dramatists, men like Crowne, Davenant, Dryden, D'Urfey, Lee, Otway, Settle, and Shadwell, who lived by their pens and the uncertain rewards of patronage, provided the bulk of Restoration dramatic fare.

Players and playwrights were at the mercy of the surprisingly small theater-going public, a coterie of aristocratic, well-to-do, fashionable people ("the Town"), living for the most part in the western suburbs of London (outside "the City"), and closely attached to the Court. The godly and respectable London middle classes shunned the theaters as haunts of iniquity, and the lower classes preferred rougher forms of entertainment: bear-baiting, cock-fighting, sword-fighting, and the puppet-shows and rope-dancers of Bartholomew Fair. Consequently the potential audience for a play was so small that a dramatist was lucky if his play stayed on the board for three days successively — he got the net profit of the third performance. A popular play at one theater usually meant empty seats at the other. From 1660 to 1682 the two theaters competed bitterly for attendance; then the Duke's Company absorbed its declining rival, and for thirteen years the United Company provided sufficient dramatic entertainment for the Town. In 1695 Thomas Betterton took a dissident group to a theater in Lincoln's Inn Fields, founding a company which struggled along until a new amalgamation in 1708.

The courtiers, politicians, officers, wits, and ladies and gentlemen of leisure who made up the Restoration coterie considered the playhouses their private domain, and many attended as much to be seen in public, to show off a new suit or dress or mistress or lover, as to see a play. But many more were ardent lovers of drama, people of taste and judgment who could enjoy a good play in spite of the impertinent chatter and vain laughter of the empty-headed. In most respects the members of the coterie were united: in their strong royalism, with a corresponding hatred of Puritans and republicans; in their certainty that they alone were to the aristocratic manner born, and that all citizens, country bumpkins, foreigners, and would-be imitators were beyond the pale; in their conviction that they were rational, intellectual people, who could afford to be cynical about emotion, religious enthusiasm, and conventional morality; and in their enjoyment of sex-intrigue and their belief that love (as Dryden put it) was "the noblest frailty of the mind," while marriage was a mere concession to family necessity. Some of them had brought back from the Continent a taste for the overblown rhetoric and declamation of French tragedy and the polished brilliance of French comedy. They all loved wit, cleverness, fine language, dialectic debates, beauty and good dramatic construction. All but the most fastidious enjoyed also melodrama, torture, and blood, and rough, bawdy farce, larded with obscene jests. Restoration drama was written to please this audience.

It was written, furthermore, to the specifications of the actors. Most of the professional playwrights were under contract to one company or another, and were forced to fit their plays to the acting methods in vogue and to the abilities of the players. An actor emphasized emotion or thought by a variety of conventional gestures and poses. To demonstrate grief, he dropped his head, slumped his shoulders, and wiped his eyes; for joy, he stood erect, threw back his head, and laughed. He raised both hands to call Heaven to witness, and pointed downward with the right to show the way to Hell. He pointed to his heart to show he felt, and to his head to show he thought. He cringed in fear; knelt, both hands forward, in supplication; raised both arms, opened his mouth, and took a backward step in surprise; and folded his arms, dropped his head on one shoulder, and "stared fixedly" to indicate love. His voice had to be full and melodious, and in a "rant," a long passage of extravagant rhetoric, he tore a passion — and his lungs — to tatters. Each of the famous actors of the age — players like oratorical Thomas Betterton, heroic Charles Hart, villainous Samuel Sandford, dull-faced James Nokes, impudent Nell Gwyn, passionate Elizabeth Barry, and ingenuous Anne Bracegirdle — had an individual style which had to be taken into account by the playwright, in tragedy or comedy.

The commonest variety of light entertainment was the intrigue comedy, modeled originally upon the comedies of Beaumont and Fletcher. This consisted of a plot involving one or more cynical gallants who sought to seduce (or marry) a like number of brisk young ladies, and who had to overcome or circumvent a heavy father, an old husband, or a set of rivals. Fortified with a variety of fools, country bumpkins, braggarts, fops, and half-wits (all of whom provided broad physical comedy by their appearance and behavior in farcical situations), and spiced with erotic bedroom scenes, pretty actresses in breeches, and passages of *double entendre*, a merry intrigue comedy was sure to please the taste of the Town. Sometimes a setting in France, Spain, or Italy added a touch of variety. Notable writers of intrigue comedies were John Dryden, Aphra Behn, Thomas D'Urfey, and Edward Ravenscroft.

Writers of realistic comedies in the tradition of Ben Jonson claimed that their purpose was to inculcate morality by displaying "humors" — caricatures of folly and vice — upon the stage. Thomas Shadwell, one of the best of the "humors" writers, once attacked the popular comedy of intrigue, maintaining that its "fine people" were only "a swearing, drinking, whoring ruffian for a lover, and an impudent, ill-bred tomrig for a mistress," and that the chief study of intrigue writers was "bawdy and profaneness." The bawdy and profane appeared in Shadwell's comedies, too, but only, he insisted, for purposes of correction.

Upon the foundation of these two stock varieties of comedy, the writers usually hailed as the stars in the Restoration comic galaxy — Etherege, Wycherley, Congreve, and Farquhar — built their artistic structures. Since the plays of these four poets all contain varying amounts of social criticism, they are sometimes called social comedies; more often they are loosely classified as comedies of manners. However, such a play as Wycherley's *The Country Wife* is essentially comedy of satire, since its chief aim is to lash sexual hypocrisy while holding up to admiration the natural man, the libertine Horner. Etherege's *The Man of Mode* and Congreve's *The Way of the World* are properly called comedies of manners because the playwrights deal wittily with the manners of a sophisticated coterie very conscious of its superiority, while ridiculing those who deviate from the standard of social behavior presented for our admiration. Farquhar's *The Beaux' Stratagem*, a

transition play which has a little of everything, defies classifica-
tion. Basically an intrigue comedy, it has a little satire, a touch of
romance, a note of sentimentalism, much pleasant humor, and a
general air of good-natured gaiety.

None of these four comedies is a literal copy of the life and
manners of the age; the authors selected and refined their ma-
terials, presenting a picture of the smart set of the day not as it
really was but as it liked to imagine itself. In the hands of clever
actors, skilled at delivering witty repartee and badinage, and of
pretty actresses, impudent and alluring under the mellow glow of
the stage candles, the social comedies of the Restoration presented
a complete comic illusion. Some of them have not lost their charm
after the lapse of nearly three hundred years.

Serious drama, largely low tragedy or melodrama, dealt with the
antithesis of comedy. Romantic heroes, mighty in war but helpless
before their mistresses, true "slaves of love" in the tradition of
pastoral and heroic romance, pursued frigid heroines of incredible
purity. Oppressed by lecherous villains, the high-minded heroines
suffered nobly, clinging to virtue with one hand while clutching at
love with the other. The plot, which usually involved a wordy
conflict between love and honor, was set in a remote time and
place against a background of war or revolution, and the play was
garnished with rant and bombast, and with spectacular scenes of
battles, fires, shipwrecks, torture, madness, and massacres. Since
the plot rather than the characters determined the outcome, the
playwright could end the play as he chose, either in a welter of
gory deaths, or with the happy lovers clasped in each others' arms.
Thus Sir Robert Howard equipped his *The Vestal Virgin* (1664)
with two fifth acts — one sad and one happy — to be played on
alternate days!

Largely under the leadership of John Dryden, the rhymed
heroic play developed from this popular variety of melodrama. It
was called heroic because it was "an imitation, in little, of a
heroic poem," and because it was written in heroic (iambic pen-
tameter) couplets. This unusual, and often excellent, intellectual
poetic drama flourished, roughly, from 1665 to 1680. The master-
piece of its kind, Dryden's two-part *The Conquest of Granada*
(1670-71), was described by Mrs. John Evelyn, a witness of the

first performance, as "a play so full of ideas that the most refined romance I ever read is not to compare with it; love is made so pure, and valor so nice, that one would imagine it designed for an Utopia rather than our stage." Delivered in a kind of musical recitative by players strutting in high-heeled shoes, plumed hats, and rich costumes, and backed by elaborate scenic devices, the typical heroic play appealed to the eyes, the ears, and the minds of the Restoration intellectuals. A small faction of the coterie objected and, led by George Villiers, Duke of Buckingham, parodied the genre (and Dryden) in a famous burlesque, *The Rehearsal* (1671), without in the least affecting the vogue.

When all the changes possible had been rung on the heroic theme, the best writers of the age explored other fields. "Mad" Nat Lee found a vein of emotional excitement in stories taken from classical antiquity, and captured the Town with his wild, ranting tragedy, *The Rival Queen* (1677). John Dryden turned back to the Elizabethans for inspiration, and in his *All for Love* (1678) he produced the best, or at least the best-constructed, tragedy of the period. Thomas Otway, too, drew inspiration from Elizabethan drama, and developed somber themes of destructive passion and tender pathos, achieving his greatest success with *Venice Preserved* (1682). After these giants came a host of poetasters — Banks, Settle, Powell, Southerne, Mrs. Manley, and Mrs. Pix — and serious drama broke down, on the one hand, into sterile, passionless, neoclassical forms, and, on the other, into melodramas of over-stressed pathos, extravagant passions, and revolting horrors: mayhem, murder, rape, and incest. Toward the end of the century, dramatic opera, with foreign singers and dancers, began to usurp the place of tragedy.

By the beginning of the eighteenth century, the old Restoration coterie had effectively disappeared. The dominantly masculine audience of the earlier day had been softened by an increase in the number of ladies, whose tastes were for more decorous drama. Various reform movements were at work in the nation: societies for the reformation of morals and manners; bishops thundering against vice; legislators passing sumptuary laws; and an outwardly respectable Court setting an example quite different from that of merry King Charles. A symptom of the reforming spirit was the attack against the stage made by a clergyman, Jeremy Collier, in his *A Short View of the Immorality and Profaneness of the English Stage* (1698). Dramatic reform was in the air, and with it came moralizing and sentimentality. Pathetic "she-tragedy" replaced the tragedy of high-minded heroism, and the comedy of tears replaced the comedy of laughter. The Restoration, the age of wit and skepticism, was over.

See Leslie Hotson, *The Commonwealth and Restoration Stage*, 1928; Montague Summers, *The Restoration Theatre*, 1934; Kathleen M. Lynch, *The Social Mode of Restoration Comedy*, 1926; John Wilcox, *The Relation of Molière to Restoration Comedy*, 1938; Bonamy Dobrée, *Restoration Tragedy*, 1929; Allardyce Nicoll, *A History of Restoration Drama*, 4th ed. (revised), 1952; and John Harold Wilson, *All the King's Ladies: Actresses of the Restoration*, 1958.

THE COUNTRY-WIFE

A

COMEDY

Acted at the Theatre Royal

Written by MR. WYCHERLEY

Indignor quicquam reprehendi, non quia crasse
Compositum illepideve putetur, sed quia nuper:
Nec veniam Antiquis, sed honorem & praemia posci.
HORAT.[1]

LONDON:

Printed for Thomas Dring, at the Harrow, at the
Corner of Chancery-Lane in Fleet-street. *1675.*

---

[1] I am out of patience when anything is blamed, not because it is thought coarsely and inelegantly composed, but because it is new; when for the ancients not indulgence, but honor and rewards are demanded.
— Horace, *Epistles*, II, 1, 76-78.

THE COUNTRY WIFE

William Wycherley

WILLIAM WYCHERLEY (1640-1715) was an amateur playwright, one of "the mob of gentlemen who wrote with ease" in the reign of King Charles II. His first play, *Love in a Wood* (1671), brought him to the amatory attention of the Duchess of Cleveland, one of the King's cast-off mistresses, and into favor at Court. Thereafter he wrote *The Gentleman Dancing Master* (1672), *The Country Wife* (1675), and *The Plain Dealer* (1676). After 1676 Wycherley wrote no more plays. He married unwisely, fell out of favor at Court, spent seven years in prison for debt, and wasted the remainder of his life writing bad verse.

A convinced naturalist, Wycherley saw little of value in the sophisticated high society of Restoration London, with all its elegance and artificial manners. Like most of his fellows in the charmed circle of Court wits, the leaders of the Town in thought and fashion, he believed that libertinism was consistent with nature and therefore good; the only sin was sexual hypocrisy. He lived according to his convictions. Withal, Wycherley was a kindly, generous gentleman, sought out by a host of friends who called him (after the blunt hero of *The Plain Dealer*) "Manly" Wycherley.

In *The Country Wife* Wycherley ridiculed the sexual hypocrites, would-be wits, and witless fools who infested London Society. The chief objects of his satire are Lady Fidget, Mrs. Dainty Fidget, and Mrs. Squeamish ("the virtuous gang," as they called themselves), three canting trollops who had so much honor in their mouths that they had no room for it elsewhere; Sir Jasper Fidget, a witless City knight; Sparkish, a would-be wit; and Pinchwife, a jealous old keeper who married because he could never keep a wench to himself. The libertine Horner is held up to admiration as a true wit, a reasonable man who follows his nature and seduces ad lib, while despising his victims. Ironically he meets his match in Margery Pinchwife, a true child of nature. The comedy is a brutal picture of a decadent society in which virtuous Alithea stands alone as an almost unbelievable symbol of honor and good manners.

The Country Wife was first presented at the Theatre Royal in Bridges Street in January, 1675. The role of Horner, the witty prophet of a brave new world in which everyone belongs to everyone else, was brilliantly portrayed by Charles Hart, the leading actor of the King's Company, a man handsome enough to make sin dangerously attractive. Blonde, blue-eyed little Elizabeth Boutell, very elegant in breeches, played Margery Pinchwife, and Major Michael Mohun, a short, square-built actor with a genius for creating character, was grum Mr. Pinchwife. Mrs. Mary Knep, an excellent singer, played Lady Fidget, and facetious Joe Haines, a natural farceur with "a workaday, rough-hewn face," played Sparkish. The comedy was a considerable success and remained for many years a stock repertory piece. It has been frequently revived on the modern stage.

See *The Complete Works of William Wycherley*, ed. Montague Summers, 4 vols., 1924; *The Country Wife and The Plain Dealer*, ed. George B. Churchill, 1924; Willard Connely, *Brawny Wycherley*, 1930; and T. H. Fujimura, *The Restoration Comedy of Wit*, 1952, Chap. VI.

Dramatis Personae

MR. HORNER	MR. HART
MR. HARCOURT	MR. KYNASTON
MR. DORILANT	MR. LYDAL
MR. PINCHWIFE	MR. MOHUN
MR. SPARKISH	MR. HAINES
SIR JASPER FIDGET	MR. CARTWRIGHT
MRS. MARGERY PINCHWIFE	MRS. BOUTELL
MRS. ALITHEA	MRS. JAMES
MY LADY FIDGET	MRS. KNEP
MRS. DAINTY FIDGET	MRS. CORBET
MRS. SQUEAMISH	MRS. WYATT
OLD LADY SQUEAMISH	MRS. RUTTER

Waiters, Servants, and Attendants
A Boy
A Quack · MR. SHATTERELL
LUCY, *Alithea's Maid* · MRS. COREY

Scene: London

PROLOGUE

Spoken by Mr. Hart

Poets, like cudgelled bullies, never do
At first or second blow submit to you;
But will provoke you still, and ne'er have done,
Till you are weary first with laying on.
The late so baffled scribbler of this day,[1]
Though he stands trembling, bids me boldly say
What we before most plays are used to do,
For poets out of fear first draw on you;
In a fierce prologue the still pit defy,
And, ere you speak, like Kastril[2] give the lie.
But though our Bays's[3] battles oft I've fought,
And with bruised knuckles their dear conquests bought —
Nay, never yet fear'd odds upon the stage —
In prologue dare not hector with the age,
But would take quarter from your saving hands;
Though Bays within all yielding countermands,
Says you confederate wits no quarter give,
Therefore his play shan't ask you leave to live.
Well, let the vain rash fop, by huffing so,
Think to obtain the better terms of you;
But we, the actors, humbly will submit,
Now, and at any time, to a full pit.
Nay, often we anticipate your rage,
And murder poets for you on our stage.
We set no guards upon our tiring-room,
But when with flying colors there you come,
We patiently, you see, give up to you
Our poets, virgins, nay, our matrons, too.[4]

---

[1] Wycherley's *The Gentleman Dancing-Master* (1672) was not a success.

[2] A quarrelsome fellow in Jonson's *The Alchemist.*

[3] Bays was the name given to Dryden, the poet laureate, in Buckingham's *The Rehearsal*; here it seems to mean the author.

[4] Referring to the custom of gentlemen choosing their mistresses from the ranks of the women players.

ACT I

[HORNER's *lodging*]

Enter HORNER, *and* QUACK *following him at a distance*

HORNER. (*Aside*) A quack is as fit for a pimp as a midwife for a bawd; they are still but in their way both helpers of nature. — (*Aloud*) Well, my dear Doctor, hast thou done what I desired?

QUACK. I have undone you for ever with the women, and reported you throughout the whole town as bad as an eunuch, with as much trouble as if I had made you one in earnest.

HORNER. But have you told all the midwives you know, the orange wenches at the playhouses, the city husbands, and old fumbling keepers of this end of the town, for they'll be the readiest to report it?

QUACK. I have told all the chambermaids, waiting-women, tire-women, and old women of my acquaintance; nay, and whispered it as a secret to 'em, and to the whisperers of Whitehall; so that you need not doubt 'twill spread, and you will be as odious to the handsome young women as ——

HORNER. As the small-pox. Well ——

QUACK. And to the married women of this end of the town, as ——

HORNER. As the great ones;[1] nay, as their own husbands.

QUACK. And to the city dames, as aniseed Robin, of filthy and contemptible memory; and they will frighten their children with your name, especially their females.

HORNER. And cry, Horner's coming to carry you away. I am only afraid 'twill not be believed. You told 'em 'twas by an English-French disaster, and an English-French chirurgeon, who has given me at once not only a cure, but an antidote for the future against that damned malady, and that worse distemper, love, and all other women's evils?

QUACK. Your late journey into France has made it the more credible, and your being here a fortnight before you appeared in public looks as if you apprehended the shame, which I wonder you do not. Well, I have been hired by young gallants to belie 'em t'other way, but you are the first would be thought a man unfit for women.

HORNER. Dear Mr. Doctor, let vain rogues be contented only to be thought abler men than they are; generally 'tis all the pleasure they have, but mine lies another way.

[1] The great pox; i.e., venereal disease.

6

QUACK. You take, methinks, a very preposterous way to it, and as ridiculous as if we operators in physic should put forth bills to disparage our medicaments, with hopes to gain customers.

HORNER. Doctor, there are quacks in love as well as physic, who get but the fewer and worse patients for their boasting; a good name is seldom got by giving it one's self; and women no more than honor are compassed by bragging. Come, come, Doctor, the wisest lawyer never discovers the merits of his cause till the trial; the wealthiest man conceals his riches, and the cunning gamester his play. Shy husbands and keepers, like old rooks, are not to be cheated but by a new unpractised trick: false friendship will pass now no more than false dice upon 'em; no, not in the city.

Enter Boy

BOY. There are two ladies and a gentleman coming up.   [*Exit*]

HORNER. A pox! some unbelieving sisters of my former acquaintance, who, I am afraid, expect their sense should be satisfied of the falsity of the report. No — this formal fool and women!

Enter SIR JASPER FIDGET, LADY FIDGET, *and* MRS. DAINTY FIDGET

QUACK. His wife and sister.

SIR JASPER FIDGET. My coach breaking just now before your door, sir, I look upon as an occasional reprimand to me, sir, for not kissing your hands, sir, since your coming out of France, sir; and so my disaster, sir, has been my good fortune, sir; and this is my wife and sister, sir.

HORNER. What then, sir?

SIR JASPER FIDGET. My lady, and sister, sir. — Wife, this is Master Horner.

LADY FIDGET. Master Horner, husband!

SIR JASPER FIDGET. My lady, my Lady Fidget, sir.

HORNER. So, sir.

SIR JASPER FIDGET. Won't you be acquainted with her, sir? — (*Aside*) So, the report is true, I find, by his coldness or aversion to the sex; but I'll play the wag with him. — Pray salute my wife, my lady, sir.

HORNER. I will kiss no man's wife, sir, for him, sir; I have taken my eternal leave, sir, of the sex already, sir.

SIR JASPER FIDGET. (*Aside*) Ha! ha! ha! I'll plague him yet. —— Not know my wife, sir?

HORNER. I do know your wife, sir; she's a woman, sir, and consequently a monster, sir, a greater monster than a husband, sir.

SIR JASPER FIDGET. A husband! how, sir?

HORNER. So, sir; but I make no more cuckolds, sir.

(*makes horns*)

SIR JASPER FIDGET. Ha! ha! ha! Mercury! Mercury![2]

LADY FIDGET. Pray, Sir Jasper, let us be gone from this rude fellow.

MRS. DAINTY FIDGET. Who, by his breeding, would think he had ever been in France?

LADY FIDGET. Foh! he's but too much a French fellow, such as hate women of quality and virtue for their love to their husbands, Sir Jasper; a woman is hated by 'em as much for loving her husband as for loving their money. But pray, let's be gone.

HORNER. You do well, madam, for I have nothing that you came for; I have brought over not so much as a bawdy picture, new postures, nor the second part of the *Escole des Filles*;[3] nor ——

QUACK. (*Apart to* HORNER) Hold, for shame, sir! what d'ye mean? You'll ruin yourself for ever with the sex ——

SIR JASPER FIDGET. Ha! ha! ha! he hates women perfectly, I find.

MRS. DAINTY FIDGET. What pity 'tis he should!

LADY FIDGET. Ay, he's a base rude fellow for't. But affectation makes not a woman more odious to them than virtue.

HORNER. Because your virtue is your greatest affectation, madam.

LADY FIDGET. How, you saucy fellow! would you wrong my honor?

HORNER. If I could.

LADY FIDGET. How d'ye mean, sir?

SIR JASPER FIDGET. Ha! ha! ha! no, he can't wrong your Ladyship's honor, upon my honor; he, poor man — hark you in your ear a mere eunuch.

LADY FIDGET. O filthy French beast! foh! foh! why do we stay? let's be gone. I can't endure the sight of him.

SIR JASPER FIDGET. Stay but till the chairs come; they'll be here presently.

LADY FIDGET. No, no.

SIR JASPER FIDGET. Nor can I stay longer. 'Tis — let me see, a quarter and a half quarter of a minute past eleven. The council will be sat; I must away. Business must be preferred always before love and ceremony with the wise, Mr. Horner.

HORNER. And the impotent, Sir Jasper.

SIR JASPER FIDGET. Ay, ay, the impotent, Master Horner; ha! ha! ha!

LADY FIDGET. What, leave us with a filthy man alone in his lodgings?

SIR JASPER FIDGET. He's an innocent man now, you know. Pray stay, I'll hasten the chairs to you. —— Mr. Horner, your servant; I should be glad to see you at my house. Pray come and dine with me, and play at cards with my wife after dinner; you are fit for women at that game yet, ha! ha! — (*Aside*) 'Tis as much a husband's prudence

[2] Mercury was commonly used as a treatment for venereal disease.

[3] *L'Ecole des Filles* (1655), pornographic fiction.

to provide innocent diversion for a wife as to hinder her unlawful pleasures; and he had better employ her than let her employ herself. —— Farewell.

HORNER. Your servant, Sir Jasper.   *Exit* SIR JASPER

LADY FIDGET. I will not stay with him, foh! ——

HORNER. Nay, Madam, I beseech you stay, if it be but to see I can be as civil to ladies yet as they would desire.

LADY FIDGET. No, no, foh! you cannot be civil to ladies.

MRS. DAINTY FIDGET. You as civil as ladies would desire?

LADY FIDGET. No, no, no, foh! foh! foh!

         Exeunt LADY FIDGET *and* MRS. DAINTY FIDGET.

QUACK. Now, I think, I, or you yourself, rather, have done your business with the women.

HORNER. Thou art an ass. Don't you see already, upon the report and my carriage, this grave man of business leaves his wife in my lodgings, invites me to his house and wife, who before would not be acquainted with me out of jealousy?

QUACK. Nay, by this means you may be the more acquainted with the husbands, but the less with the wives.

HORNER. Let me alone; if I can but abuse the husbands, I'll soon disabuse the wives. Stay — I'll reckon you up the advantages I am like to have by my stratagem. First, I shall be rid of all my old acquaintances, the most insatiable sorts of duns, that invade our lodgings in a morning; and next to the pleasure of making a new mistress is that of being rid of an old one, and of all old debts. Love, when it comes to be so, is paid the most unwillingly.

QUACK. Well, you may be so rid of your old acquaintances; but how will you get any new ones?

HORNER. Doctor, thou wilt never make a good chemist, thou art so incredulous and impatient. Ask but all the young fellows of the town if they do not lose more time, like huntsmen, in starting the game, than in running it down. One knows not where to find 'em, who will or will not. Women of quality are so civil you can hardly distinguish love from good breeding, and a man is often mistaken; but now I can be sure she that shows an aversion to me loves the sport, as those women that are gone, whom I warrant to be right. And then the next thing is, your women of honor, as you call 'em, are only chary of their reputations, not their persons; and 'tis scandal they would avoid, not men. Now may I have, by the reputation of an eunuch, the privileges of one, and be seen in a lady's chamber in a morning as early as her husband; kiss virgins before their parents or lovers; and may be, in short, the *passe-partout*[4] of the town. Now, Doctor.

QUACK. Nay, now you shall be the doctor, and your process is so new that we do not know but it may succeed.

[4] Pass-key.

HORNER. Not so new neither; *probatum est*,[5] Doctor.

QUACK. Well, I wish you luck and many patients, whilst I go to mine.   *Exit*

Enter HARCOURT *and* DORILANT *to* HORNER

HARCOURT. Come, your appearance at the play yesterday has, I hope, hardened you for the future against the women's contempt and the men's raillery; and now you'll abroad as you were wont.

HORNER. Did I not bear it bravely?

DORILANT. With a most theatrical impudence, nay, more than the orange-wenches show there, or a drunken vizard-mask,[6] or a great-bellied actress; nay, or the most impudent of creatures, an ill poet; or what is yet more impudent, a second-hand critic.

HORNER. But what say the ladies? have they no pity?

HARCOURT. What ladies? The vizard-masks, you know, never pity a man when all's gone, though in their service.

DORILANT. And for the women in the boxes, you'd never pity them when 'twas in your power.

HARCOURT. They say 'tis pity but all that deal with common women should be served so.

DORILANT. Nay, I dare swear they won't admit you to play at cards with them, go to plays with 'em, or do the little duties which other shadows of men are wont to do for 'em.

HORNER. Who do you call shadows of men?

DORILANT. Half-men.

HORNER. What, boys?

DORILANT. Ay, your old boys, old *beaux garcons*,[7] who, like super-annuated stallions, are suffered to run, feed, and whinny with the mares as long as they live, though they can do nothing else.

HORNER. Well, a pox on love and wenching! Women serve but to keep a man from better company. Though I can't enjoy them, I shall you the more. Good fellowship and friendship are lasting, rational, and manly pleasures.

HARCOURT. For all that, give me some of those pleasures you call effeminate too; they help to relish one another.

HORNER. They disturb one another.

HARCOURT. No, mistresses are like books. If you pore upon them too much, they doze you, and make you unfit for company; but if used discreetly, you are the fitter for conversation by 'em.

DORILANT. A mistress should be like a little country retreat near the town; not to dwell in constantly, but only for a night and away, to taste the town the better when a man returns.

[5] It has been tried before.
[6] Prostitute.
[7] Dissipated fellows, playboys.

HORNER. I tell you, 'tis as hard to be a good fellow, a good friend, and a lover of women, as 'tis to be a good fellow, a good friend, and a lover of money. You cannot follow both, then choose your side. Wine gives you liberty, love takes it away.

DORILANT. Gad, he's in the right on't.

HORNER. Wine gives you joy; love, grief and tortures, besides the chirurgeon's.[8] Wine makes us witty; love, only sots. Wine makes us sleep; love breaks it.

DORILANT. By the world, he has reason, Harcourt.

HORNER. Wine makes ——

DORILANT. Ay, wine makes us — makes us princes; love makes us beggars, poor rogues, egad — and wine ——

HORNER. So, there's one converted. — No, no, love and wine, oil and vinegar.

HARCOURT. I grant it; love will still be uppermost.

HORNER. Come, for my part, I will have only those glorious manly pleasures of being very drunk and very slovenly.

Enter Boy

BOY. Mr. Sparkish is below, sir.   *[Exit]*

HARCOURT. What, my dear friend! a rogue that is fond of me, only I think, for abusing him.

DORILANT. No, he can no more think the men laugh at him than that women jilt him, his opinion of himself is so good.

HORNER. Well, there's another pleasure by drinking I thought not of — I shall lose his acquaintance, because he cannot drink; and you know 'tis a very hard thing to be rid of him, for he's one of those nauseous offerers at wit, who, like the worst fiddlers, run themselves into all companies.

HARCOURT. One that, by being in the company of men of sense, would pass for one.

HORNER. And may so to the short-sighted world, as a false jewel amongst true ones is not discerned at a distance. His company is as troublesome to us as a cuckold's when you have a mind to his wife's.

HARCOURT. No, the rogue will not let us enjoy one another, but ravishes our conversation, though he signifies no more to't than Sir Martin Mar-all's[9] gaping, and awkward thrumming upon the lute, does to his man's voice and music.

DORILANT. And to pass for a wit in town shows himself a fool every night to us, that are guilty of the plot.

HORNER. Such wits as he are, to a company of reasonable men, like rooks to the gamesters, who only fill a room at the table, but are so far

---

[8] The surgeon's painful treatment for venereal disease.

[9] Sir Martin Mar-all, in Dryden's play by that name (1667), pretended to serenade his mistress while his servant did the playing and singing.

from contributing to the play, that they only serve to spoil the fancy of those that do.

DORILANT. Nay, they are used like rooks too, snubbed, checked, and abused; yet the rogues will hang on.

HORNER. A pox on 'em, and all that force nature, and would be still what she forbids 'em! Affectation is her greatest monster.

HARCOURT. Most men are the contraries to that they would seem. Your bully, you see, is a coward with a long sword; the little humbly fawning physician, with his ebony cane, is he that destroys men.

DORILANT. The usurer, a poor rogue, possessed of mouldy bonds and mortgages; and we they call spendthrifts are only wealthy who lay out his money upon daily new purchases of pleasure.

HORNER. Ay, your arrantest cheat is your trustee or executor, your jealous man, the greatest cuckold, your churchman the greatest atheist, and your noisy pert rogue of a wit, the greatest fop, dullest ass, and worst company, as you shall see; for here he comes.

Enter SPARKISH *to them*

SPARKISH. How is't, sparks? how is't? Well, faith, Harry, I must rally thee a little, ha! ha! ha! upon the report in town of thee, ha! ha! ha! I can't hold i'faith; shall I speak?

HORNER. Yes; but you'll be so bitter then.

SPARKISH. Honest Dick and Frank here shall answer for me, I will not be extreme bitter, by the universe.

HARCOURT. We will be bound in ten-thousand-pound bond, he shall not be bitter at all.

DORILANT. Nor sharp, nor sweet.

HORNER. What, not downright insipid?

SPARKISH. Nay then, since you are so brisk, and provoke me, take what follows. You must know, I was discoursing and rallying with some ladies yesterday, and they happened to talk of the fine new signs in town.

HORNER. Very fine ladies, I believe.

SPARKISH. Said I, I know where the best new sign is. — Where? says one of the ladies. — In Covent Garden, I replied. —Said another, In what street? — In Russell Street, answered I. — Lord, says another, I'm sure there was ne'er a fine new sign there yesterday. — Yes, but there was, said I again, and it came out of France, and has been there a fortnight.

DORILANT. A pox! I can hear no more, prithee.

HORNER. No, hear him out; let him tune his crowd[10] a while.

HARCOURT. The worst music, the greatest preparation.

SPARKISH. Nay, faith, I'll make you laugh. — It cannot be, says a third lady. — Yes, yes, quoth I again. — Says a fourth lady ——

---

[10] Prepare; tune his fiddle. From Welsh *crwth* or *crowth*, a fiddle.

HORNER. Look to't, we'll have no more ladies.

SPARKISH. No — then mark, mark, now. Said I to the fourth, Did you never see Mr. Horner? he lodges in Russell Street, and he's a sign of a man, you know, since he came out of France; ha! ha! ha!

HORNER. But the devil take me if thine be the sign of a jest.

SPARKISH. With that they all fell a-laughing, till they bepissed themselves. What, but it does not move you, methinks? Well, I see one had as good go to law without a witness, as break a jest without a laugher on one's side. —— Come, come, sparks, but where do we dine? I have left at Whitehall an earl to dine with you.

DORILANT. Why, I thought thou hadst loved a man with a title better than a suit with a French trimming to't.

HARCOURT. Go to him again.

SPARKISH. No, sir, a wit to me is the greatest title in the world.

HORNER. But go dine with your earl, sir; he may be exceptious. We are your friends, and will not take it ill to be left, I do assure you.

HARCOURT. Nay, faith, he shall go to him.

SPARKISH. Nay, pray, gentlemen.

DORILANT. We'll thrust you out, if you won't; what, disappoint anybody for us?

SPARKISH. Nay, dear gentlemen, hear me.

HORNER. No, no, sir, by no means; pray go, sir.

SPARKISH. Why, dear rogues ——

DORILANT. No, no.   (*They all thrust him out of the room*)

ALL. Ha! ha! ha!

SPARKISH *returns*

SPARKISH. But, sparks, pray hear me. What, d'ye think I'll eat then with gay shallow fops and silent coxcombs? I think wit as necessary at dinner as a glass of good wine, and that's the reason I never have any stomach when I eat alone. — Come, but where do we dine?

HORNER. Even where you will.

SPARKISH. At Chateline's?

DORILANT. Yes, if you will.

SPARKISH. Or at the Cock?

DORILANT. Yes, if you please.

SPARKISH. Or at the Dog and Partridge? [11]

HORNER. Ay, if you have a mind to't; for we shall dine at neither.

SPARKISH. Pshaw! with your fooling we shall lose the new play; and I would no more miss seeing a new play the first day, than I would miss sitting in the wits' row. Therefore I'll go fetch my mistress, and away.

Exit

---

[11] Three popular taverns, in or near Covent Garden.

Manent HORNER, HARCOURT, DORILANT: *enter to them*
MR. PINCHWIFE

HORNER. Who have we here? Pinchwife?

PINCHWIFE. Gentlemen, your humble servant.

HORNER. Well, Jack, by thy long absence from the town, the grumness[12] of thy countenance, and the slovenliness of thy habit, I should give thee joy, should I not, of marriage?

PINCHWIFE. (*Aside*) Death! does he know I'm married too? I thought to have concealed it from him at least. —— My long stay in the country will excuse my dress; and I have a suit of law that brings me up to town, that puts me out of humor. Besides, I must give Sparkish to-morrow five thousand pound to lie with my sister.

HORNER. Nay, you country gentlemen, rather than not purchase, will buy anything; and he is a cracked title, if we may quibble. Well, but am I to give thee joy? I heard thou wert married.

PINCHWIFE. What then?

HORNER. Why, the next thing that is to be heard is, thou'rt a cuckold.

PINCHWIFE. (*Aside*) Insupportable name!

HORNER. But I did not expect marriage from such a whoremaster as you, one that knew the town so much, and women so well.

PINCHWIFE. Why, I have married no London wife.

HORNER. Pshaw! that's all one. That grave circumspection in marrying a country wife is like refusing a deceitful pampered Smithfield jade[13] to go and be cheated by a friend in the country.

PINCHWIFE. (*Aside*) A pox on him and his simile! —— At least we are a little surer of the breed there, know what her keeping has been, whether foiled[14] or unsound.

HORNER. Come, come, I have known a clap gotten in Wales; and there are cousins, justices' clerks, and chaplains in the country, I won't say coachmen. But she's handsome and young?

PINCHWIFE. (*Aside*) I'll answer as I should do. —— No, no; she has no beauty but her youth, no attraction but her modesty; wholesome, homely, and huswifely; that's all.

DORILANT. He talks as like a grazier as he looks.

PINCHWIFE. She's too awkward, ill-favoured, and silly to bring to town.

HARCOURT. Then methinks you should bring her to be taught breeding.

PINCHWIFE. To be taught! no, sir, I thank you. Good wives and private soldiers should be ignorant. [*Aside*] I'll keep her from your instructions, I warrant you.

12 Surliness.
13 The horse market at Smithfield was notorious.
14 Foundered.

HARCOURT. (*Aside*) The rogue is as jealous as if his wife were not ignorant.

HORNER. Why, if she be ill-favored, there will be less danger here for you than by leaving her in the country. We have such variety of dainties that we are seldom hungry.

DORILANT. But they have always coarse, constant, swingeing stomachs in the country.

HARCOURT. Foul feeders indeed!

DORILANT. And your hospitality is great there.

HARCOURT. Open house; every man's welcome.

PINCHWIFE. So, so, gentlemen.

HORNER. But prithee, why wouldst thou marry her? If she be ugly, ill-bred, and silly, she must be rich then.

PINCHWIFE. As rich as if she brought me twenty thousand pound out of this town; for she'll be as sure not to spend her moderate portion as a London baggage would be to spend hers, let it be what it would: so 'tis all one. Then, because she's ugly, she's the likelier to be my own; and being ill-bred, she'll hate conversation; and since silly and innocent, will not know the difference betwixt a man of one-and-twenty and one of forty.

HORNER. Nine — to my knowledge. But if she be silly, she'll expect as much from a man of forty-nine, as from him of one-and-twenty. But methinks wit is more necessary than beauty; and I think no young woman ugly, that has it, and no handsome woman agreeable without it.

PINCHWIFE. 'Tis my maxim, he's a fool that marries; but he's a greater that does not marry a fool. What is wit in a wife good for, but to make a man a cuckold?

HORNER. Yes, to keep it from his knowledge.

PINCHWIFE. A fool cannot contrive to make her husband a cuckold.

HORNER. No; but she'll club with a man that can and what is worse, if she cannot make her husband a cuckold, she'll make him jealous and pass for one; and then 'tis all one.

PINCHWIFE. Well, well, I'll take care for one. My wife shall make me no cuckold, though she had your help, Mr. Horner. I understand the town, sir.

DORILANT. (*Aside*) His help!

HARCOURT. (*Aside*) He's come newly to town, it seems, and has not heard how things are with him.

HORNER. But tell me, has marriage cured thee of whoring, which it seldom does?

HARCOURT. 'Tis more than age can do.

HORNER. No, the word is, I'll marry and live honest; but a marriage vow is like a penitent gamester's oath, and entering into bonds and penalties to stint himself to such a particular small sum at play for the future, which makes him but the more eager; and not being able to hold out, loses his money again, and his forfeit to boot.

DORILANT. Ay, ay, a gamester will be a gamester whilst his money lasts, and a whoremaster whilst his vigor.

HARCOURT. Nay, I have known 'em, when they are broke, and can lose no more, keep a-fumbling with the box in their hands to fool with only, and hinder other gamesters.

DORILANT. That had wherewithal to make lusty stakes.

PINCHWIFE. Well, gentlemen, you may laugh at me; but you shall never lie with my wife; I know the town.

HORNER. But prithee, was not the way you were in better? is not keeping better than marriage?

PINCHWIFE. A pox on't! the jades would jilt me, I could never keep a whore to myself.

HORNER. So, then, you only married to keep a whore to yourself. Well, but let me tell you, women, as you say, are like soldiers, made constant and loyal by good pay, rather than by oaths and covenants. Therefore I'd advise my friends to keep rather than marry, since too I find, by your example, it does not serve one's turn; for I saw you yesterday in the eighteen-penny place[15] with a pretty country wench.

PINCHWIFE. (Aside) How the devil! did he see my wife then? I sat there that she might not be seen. But she shall never go to a play again.

HORNER. What! dost thou blush at nine-and-forty for having been seen with a wench?

DORILANT. No, faith, I warrant 'twas his wife, which he seated there out of sight; for he's a cunning rogue, and understands the town.

HARCOURT. He blushes. Then 'twas his wife; for men are now more ashamed to be seen with them in public than with a wench.

PINCHWIFE. (Aside) Hell and damnation! I'm undone, since Horner has seen her, and they know 'twas she.

HORNER. But prithee, was it thy wife? She was exceedingly pretty; I was in love with her at that distance.

PINCHWIFE. You are like never to be nearer to her. Your servant, gentlemen. (Offers to go)

HORNER. Nay, prithee stay.

PINCHWIFE. I cannot; I will not.

HORNER. Come, you shall dine with us.

PINCHWIFE. I have dined already.

HORNER. Come, I know thou hast not. I'll treat thee, dear rogue; thou shalt spend none of thy Hampshire money to-day.

PINCHWIFE. (Aside) Treat me! So, he uses me already like his cuckold.

HORNER. Nay, you shall not go.

---

15 The middle gallery at the theater. Fashionable playgoers sat below, in the pit and boxes.

PINCHWIFE. I must; I have business at home.   *Exit*

HARCOURT. To beat his wife. He's as jealous of her as a Cheapside husband of a Covent Garden wife.[16]

HORNER. Why, 'tis as hard to find an old whoremaster without jealousy and the gout, as a young one without fear or the pox.

> As gout in age from pox in youth proceeds,
> So wenching past, then jealousy succeeds,
> The worst disease that love and wenching breeds.

                                                        Exeunt

ACT II

[SCENE I. *A room in* PINCHWIFE's *house*]

MRS. MARGERY PINCHWIFE *and* ALITHEA.
PINCHWIFE *peeping behind at the door*

MRS. PINCHWIFE. Pray, sister, where are the best fields and woods to walk in, in London?

ALITHEA. A pretty question! Why, sister, Mulberry Garden and St. James's Park; and, for close walks, the New Exchange.[1]

MRS. PINCHWIFE. Pray, sister, tell me why my husband looks so grum here in town, and keeps me up so close, and will not let me go a-walking, nor let me wear my best gown yesterday.

ALITHEA. Oh, he's jealous, sister.

MRS. PINCHWIFE. Jealous! what's that?

ALITHEA. He's afraid you should love another man.

MRS. PINCHWIFE. How should he be afraid of my loving another man, when he will not let me see any but himself?

ALITHEA. Did he not carry you yesterday to a play?

MRS. PINCHWIFE. Ay; but we sat amongst ugly people. He would not let me come near the gentry, who sat under us, so that I could not see 'em. He told me none but naughty women sat there, whom they toused and moused.[2] But I would have ventured, for all that.

ALITHEA. But how did you like the play?

MRS. PINCHWIFE. Indeed I was a-weary of the play, but I liked hugeously the actors. They are the goodliest, properest men, sister!

ALITHEA. Oh, but you must not like the actors, sister.

MRS. PINCHWIFE. Ay, how should I help it, sister? Pray, sister, when my husband comes in, will you ask leave for me to go a-walking?

ALITHEA. (*Aside*) A-walking! ha! ha! Lord, a country-gentlewoman's pleasure is the drudgery of a footpost; and she requires as much

---

[16] As a city merchant is of a wife taken from an aristocratic family.

[1] The Mulberry Garden was at the west end of St. James's Park. The New Exchange was a shopping arcade in the Strand.

[2] Tossed and tumbled; handled roughly.

airing as her husband's horses. —— But here comes your husband.
I'll ask, though I'm sure he'll not grant it.

MRS. PINCHWIFE. He says he won't let me go abroad for fear of
catching the pox.

ALITHEA. Fy! the small-pox you should say.

Enter PINCHWIFE to them

MRS. PINCHWIFE. O my dear, dear bud, welcome home! Why dost
thou look so fropish?[3] who has nangered thee?

PINCHWIFE. You're a fool.

(MRS. PINCHWIFE goes aside, and cries)

ALITHEA. Faith, so she is, for crying for no fault, poor tender creature!

PINCHWIFE. What, you would have her as impudent as yourself, as
arrant a jillflirt, a gadder, a magpie;[4] and to say all, a mere notorious
town-woman?

ALITHEA. Brother, you are my only censurer; and the honor of your
family shall sooner suffer in your wife there than in me, though I take
the innocent liberty of the town.

PINCHWIFE. Hark you, mistress, do not talk so before my wife. —
The innocent liberty of the town!

ALITHEA. Why, pray, who boasts of any intrigue with me? what
lampoon has made my name notorious? what ill women frequent my
lodgings? I keep no company with any women of scandalous reputations.

PINCHWIFE. No, you keep the men of scandalous reputations company.

ALITHEA. Where? would you not have me civil? answer 'em in a
box at the plays, in the drawing-room at Whitehall, in St. James's
Park, Mulberry Garden, or ——

PINCHWIFE. Hold, hold! Do not teach my wife where the men are
to be found; I believe she's the worse for your town-documents already.
I bid you keep her in ignorance, as I do.

MRS. PINCHWIFE. Indeed, be not angry with her, bud, she will tell
me nothing of the town, though I ask her a thousand times a day.

PINCHWIFE. Then you are very inqusitive to know, I find?

MRS. PINCHWIFE. Not I indeed, dear; I hate London. Our place-
house in the country is worth a thousand of't; would I were there again!

PINCHWIFE. So you shall, I warrant. But were you not talking of
plays and players when I came in? [*To* ALITHEA] You are her en-
courager in such discourses.

MRS. PINCHWIFE. No, indeed, dear; she chid me just now for liking
the playermen.

---

[3] Peevish.   [4] A chatterer.

PINCHWIFE. (*Aside*) Nay, if she be so innocent as to own to me her liking them, there is no hurt in't. —— Come, my poor rogue, but thou lik'st none better than me?

MRS. PINCHWIFE. Yes, indeed, but I do. The playermen are finer folks.

PINCHWIFE. But you love none better than me?

MRS. PINCHWIFE. You are mine own dear bud, and I know you. I hate a stranger.

PINCHWIFE. Ay, my dear, you must love me only, and not be like the naughty town-women, who only hate their husbands, and love every man else; love plays, visits, fine coaches, fine clothes, fiddles, balls, treats, and so lead a wicked town-life.

MRS. PINCHWIFE. Nay, if to enjoy all these things be a town-life, London is not so bad a place, dear.

ᵗ PINCHWIFE. How! if you love me, you must hate London.

ALITHEA. (*Aside*) The fool has forbid me discovering to her the pleasures of the town, and he is now setting her agog upon them himself.

MRS. PINCHWIFE. But, husband, do the town-women love the playermen too?

PINCHWIFE. Yes, I warrant you.

MRS. PINCHWIFE. Ay, I warrant you.

PINCHWIFE. Why, you do not, I hope?

MRS. PINCHWIFE. No, no, bud. But why have we no playermen in the country?

PINCHWIFE. Ha! — Mrs. Minx, ask me no more to go to a play.

MRS. PINCHWIFE. Nay, why love? I did not care for going; but when you forbid me, you make me, as 'twere, desire it.

ALITHEA. (*Aside*) So 'twill be in other things, I warrant.

MRS. PINCHWIFE. Pray let me go to a play, dear.

PINCHWIFE. Hold your peace, I wo' not.

MRS. PINCHWIFE. Why, love?

PINCHWIFE. Why, I'll tell you.

ALITHEA. (*Aside*) Nay, if he'll tell her, she'll give him more cause to forbid her that place.

MRS. PINCHWIFE. Pray why, dear?

PINCHWIFE. First, you like the actors; and the gallants may like you.

MRS. PINCHWIFE. What, a homely country girl! No, bud, nobody will like me.

PINCHWIFE. I tell you yes, they may.

MRS. PINCHWIFE. No, no, you jest — I won't believe; I will go.

PINCHWIFE. I tell you then, that one of the lewdest fellows in town, who saw you there, told me he was in love with you.

MRS. PINCHWIFE. Indeed! who, who, pray who was't?

PINCHWIFE. (*Aside*) I've gone too far, and slipped before I was aware; how overjoyed she is!

MRS. PINCHWIFE. Was it any Hampshire gallant, any of our neighbors? I promise you, I am beholden to him.

PINCHWIFE. I promise you, you lie; for he would but ruin you, as he has done hundreds. He has no other love for women but that; such as he look upon women, like basilisks, but to destroy 'em.

MRS. PINCHWIFE. Ay, but if he loves me, why should he ruin me? answer me to that. Methinks he should not, I would do him no harm.

ALITHEA. Ha! ha! ha!

PINCHWIFE. 'Tis very well; but I'll keep him from doing you any harm, or me either. But here comes company; get you in, get you in.

MRS. PINCHWIFE. But, pray, husband, is he a pretty gentleman that loves me?

PINCHWIFE. In, baggage, in. *Thrusts her in, shuts the door*

Enter SPARKISH *and* HARCOURT

What, all the lewd libertines of the town brought to my lodging by this easy coxcomb! 'Sdeath, I'll not suffer it.

SPARKISH. Here, Harcourt, do you approve my choice? —— Dear little rogue. I told you I'd bring you acquainted with all my friends, the wits and —— (HARCOURT *salutes her*)

PINCHWIFE. Ay, they shall know her, as well as you yourself will, I warrant you.

SPARKISH. This is one of those, my pretty rogue, that are to dance at your wedding to-morrow; and him you must bid welcome ever, to what you and I have.

PINCHWIFE. (*Aside*) Monstrous!

SPARKISH. Harcourt, how dost thou like her, faith? Nay, dear, do not look down; I should hate to have a wife of mine out of countenance at anything.

PINCHWIFE. (*Aside*) Wonderful!

SPARKISH. Tell me, I say, Harcourt, how dost thou like her? Thou hast stared upon her enough to resolve me.

HARCOURT. So infinitely well, that I could wish I had a mistress too, that might differ from her in nothing but her love and engagement to you.

ALITHEA. Sir, Master Sparkish has often told me that his acquaintance were all wits and railleurs, and now I find it.

SPARKISH. No, by the universe, madam, he does not rally now; you may believe him, I do assure you, he is the honestest, worthiest, true-hearted gentleman — a man of such perfect honor, he would say nothing to a lady he does not mean.

PINCHWIFE. (*Aside*) Praising another man to his mistress!

HARCOURT. Sir, you are so beyond expectation obliging, that ——

SPARKISH. Nay, egad, I am sure you do admire her extremely; I see't in your eyes. —— He does admire you, madam. —— By the world, don't you?

HARCOURT. Yes, above the world, or the most glorious part of it, her whole sex; and till now I never thought I should have envied you or any man about to marry, but you have the best excuse for marriage I ever knew.

ALITHEA. Nay, now, sir, I'm satisfied you are of the society of the wits and railleurs, since you cannot spare your friend, even when he is but too civil to you; but the surest sign is, since you are an enemy to marriage, for that I hear you hate as much as business or bad wine.

HARCOURT. Truly, madam, I never was an enemy to marriage till now, because marriage was never an enemy to me before.

ALITHEA. But why, sir, is marriage an enemy to you now? Because it robs you of your friend here? for you look upon a friend married as one gone into a monastery, that is, dead to the world.

HARCOURT. 'Tis indeed, because you marry him; I see, madam, you can guess my meaning. I do confess heartily and openly I wish it were in my power to break the match; by Heavens I would.

SPARKISH. Poor Frank!

ALITHEA. Would you be so unkind to me?

HARCOURT. No, no, 'tis not because I would be unkind to you.

SPARKISH. Poor Frank! no gad, 'tis only his kindness to me.

PINCHWIFE. (Aside) Great kindness to you indeed! Insensible fop, let a man make love to his wife to his face!

SPARKISH. Come, dear Frank, for all my wife there, that shall be, thou shalt enjoy me sometimes, dear rogue. By my honor, we men of wit condole for our deceased brother in marriage, as much as for one dead in earnest; I think that was prettily said of me, ha, Harcourt? —— But come, Frank, be not melancholy for me.

HARCOURT. No, I assure you, I am not melancholy for you.

SPARKISH. Prithee, Frank, dost think my wife that shall be there, a fine person?

HARCOURT. I could gaze upon her till I became as blind as you are.

SPARKISH. How as I am? how?

HARCOURT. Because you are a lover, and true lovers are blind, struck blind.

SPARKISH. True, true; but by the world, she has wit too, as well as beauty. Go, go with her into a corner, and try if she has wit; talk to her anything; she's bashful before me.

HARCOURT. Indeed if a woman wants wit in a corner, she has it nowhere.

ALITHEA. (Aside to SPARKISH) Sir, you dispose of me a little before your time ——

SPARKISH. Nay, nay, madam, let me have an earnest of your obedience, or — go, go, madam —— (HARCOURT courts ALITHEA aside)

PINCHWIFE. How, sir! if you are not concerned for the honor of a wife, I am for that of a sister; he shall not debauch her. Be a pander to your own wife! bring men to her! let 'em make love before your face! thrust 'em into a corner together, then leave 'em in private! is this your town wit and conduct?

SPARKISH. Ha! ha! ha! a silly wise rogue would make one laugh more than a stark fool, ha! ha! I shall burst. Nay, you shall not disturb 'em; I'll vex thee, by the world.

(Struggles with PINCHWIFE to keep him from HARCOURT and ALITHEA)

ALITHEA. The writings are drawn, sir, settlements made; 'tis too late, sir, and past all revocation.

HARCOURT. Then so is my death.

ALITHEA. I would not be unjust to him.

HARCOURT. Then why to me so?

ALITHEA. I have no obligation to you.

HARCOURT. My love.

ALITHEA. I had his before.

HARCOURT. You never had it; he wants, you see, jealousy, the only infallible sign of it.

ALITHEA. Love proceeds from esteem; he cannot distrust my virtue; besides, he loves me, or he would not marry me.

HARCOURT. Marrying you is no more sign of his love than bribing your woman, that he may marry you, is a sign of his generosity. Marriage is rather a sign of interest than love; and he that marries a fortune covets a mistress, not loves her. But if you take marriage for a sign of love, take it from me immediately.

ALITHEA. No, now you have put a scruple in my head; but in short, sir, to end our dispute, I must marry him; my reputation would suffer in the world else.

HARCOURT. No; if you do marry him, with your pardon, madam, your reputation suffers in the world, and you would be thought in necessity for a cloak.

ALITHEA. Nay, now you are rude, sir. —— Mr. Sparkish, pray come hither, your friend here is very troublesome, and very loving.

HARCOURT. (Aside to ALITHEA) Hold! hold! ——

PINCHWIFE. D'ye hear that?

SPARKISH. Why, d'ye think I'll seem to be jealous, like a country bumpkin?

PINCH. No, rather be a cuckold, like a credulous cit.

HARCOURT. Madam, you would not have been so little generous as to have told him.

ALITHEA. Yes, since you could be so little generous as to wrong him.

HARCOURT. Wrong him! no man can do't, he's beneath an injury; a bubble, a coward, a senseless idiot, a wretch so contemptible to all the world but you, that ——

ALITHEA. Hold, do not rail at him, for since he is like to be my husband, I am resolved to like him; nay, I think I am obliged to tell him you are not his friend. —— Master Sparkish, Master Sparkish!

SPARKISH. What, what? —— Now, dear rogue, has not she wit?

HARCOURT. (*Speaks surlily*) Not as much as I thought, and hoped she had.

ALITHEA. Mr. Sparkish, do you bring people to rail at you?

HARCOURT. Madam ——

SPARKISH. How! no; but if he does rail at me, 'tis but in jest, I warrant; what we wits do for one another, and never take any notice of it.

ALITHEA. He spoke so scurrilously of you, I had no patience to hear him; besides, he has been making love to me.

HARCOURT (*Aside*) True, damned tell-tale woman!

SPARKISH. Pshaw! to show his parts — we wits rail and make love often, but to show our parts; as we have no affections, so we have no malice, we ——

ALITHEA. He said you were a wretch below an injury ——

SPARKISH. Pshaw!

HARCOURT. (*Aside*) Damned, senseless, impudent, virtuous jade! Well, since she won't let me have her, she'll do as good, she'll make me hate her.

ALITHEA. A common bubble ——

SPARKISH. Pshaw!

ALITHEA. A coward ——

SPARKISH. Pshaw, pshaw!

ALITHEA. A senseless, drivelling idiot ——

SPARKISH. How! did he disparage my parts? Nay, then, my honor's concerned, I can't put up that, sir, by the world — brother, help me to kill him — (*Aside*) I may draw now, since we have the odds of him — 'tis a good occasion, too, before my mistress ——   (*Offers to draw*)

ALITHEA. Hold, hold!

SPARKISH. What, what?

ALITHEA. (*Aside*) I must not let 'em kill the gentleman neither, for his kindness to me. I am so far from hating him, that I wish my gallant had his person and understanding. Nay, if my honor ——

SPARKISH. I'll be thy death.

ALITHEA. Hold, hold! Indeed, to tell the truth, the gentleman said after all, that what he spoke was but out of friendship to you.

SPARKISH. How! say I am — I am a fool, that is no wit, out of friendship to me?

ALITHEA. Yes, to try whether I was concerned enough for you; and made love to me only to be satisfied of my virtue, for your sake.

HARCOURT. (*Aside*) Kind, however.

SPARKISH. Nay, if it were so, my dear rogue, I ask thee pardon; but why would not you tell me so, faith?

HARCOURT. Because I did not think on't, faith.

SPARKISH. Come, Horner does not come; Harcourt, let's be gone to the new play. — Come, madam.

ALITHEA. I will not go if you intend to leave me alone in the box and run into the pit, as you use to do.

SPARKISH. Pshaw! I'll leave Harcourt with you in the box to entertain you, and that's as good; if I sat in the box, I should be thought no judge but of trimmings. — Come away, Harcourt, lead her down.

(*Exeunt* SPARKISH, HARCOURT, *and* ALITHEA)

PINCHWIFE. Well, go thy ways, for the flower of the true town fops, such as spend their estates before they come to 'em, and are cuckolds before they're married. But let me go back to my own freehold. — How!

Enter MY LADY FIDGET, MRS. DAINTY FIDGET, *and* MRS. SQUEAMISH

LADY FIDGET. Your servant, sir; where is your lady? We are come to wait upon her to the new play.

PINCHWIFE. New play!

LADY FIDGET. And my husband will wait upon you presently.

PINCHWIFE. (*Aside*) Damn your civility. —— Madam, by no means; I will not see Sir Jasper here till I have waited upon him at home; nor shall my wife see you till she has waited upon your ladyship at your lodgings.

LADY FIDGET. Now we are here, sir?

PINCHWIFE. No, madam.

MRS. DAINTY FIDGET. Pray, let us see her.

MRS. SQUEAMISH. We will not stir till we see her.

PINCHWIFE. (*Aside*) A pox on you all! — (*Goes to the door, and returns*) She has locked the door, and is gone abroad.

LADY FIDGET. No, you have locked the door, and she's within.

MRS. DAINTY FIDGET. They told us below she was here.

PINCHWIFE. (*Aside*) Will nothing do? —— Well, it must out then. To tell you the truth, ladies, which I was afraid to let you know before, lest it might endanger your lives, my wife has just now the small-pox come out upon her; do not be frightened, but pray be gone, ladies; you shall not stay here in danger of your lives; pray get you gone, ladies.

LADY FIDGET. No, no, we have all had 'em.

MRS. SQUEAMISH. Alack, alack!

MRS. DAINTY FIDGET. Come, come, we must see how it goes with her; I understand the disease.

LADY FIDGET. Come!

PINCHWIFE. (*Aside*) Well, there is no being too hard for women at their own weapon, lying, therefore I'll quit the field. *Exit*

MRS. SQUEAMISH. Here's an example of jealousy!

LADY FIDGET. Indeed, as the world goes, I wonder there are no more jealous, since wives are so neglected.

MRS. DAINTY FIDGET. Pshaw! as the world goes, to what end should they be jealous?

LADY FIDGET. Foh! 'tis a nasty world.

MRS. SQUEAMISH. That men of parts, great acquaintance, and quality, should take up with and spend themselves and fortunes in keeping little playhouse creatures, foh!

LADY FIDGET. Nay, that women of understanding, great acquaintance, and good quality, should fall a-keeping too of little creatures, foh!

MRS. SQUEAMISH. Why, 'tis the men of quality's fault; they never visit women of honor and reputation as they used to do; and have not so much as common civility for ladies of our rank, but use us with the same indifference and ill-breeding as if we were all married to 'em.

LADY FIDGET. She says true; 'tis an arrant shame women of quality should be so slighted; methinks birth — birth should go for something; I have known men admired, courted, and followed for their titles only.

MRS. SQUEAMISH. Ay, one would think men of honor should not love, no more than marry, out of their own rank.

MRS. DAINTY FIDGET. Fy, fy, upon 'em! they are come to think cross breeding for themselves best, as well as for their dogs and horses.

LADY FIDGET. They are dogs and horses for't.

MRS. SQUEAMISH. One would think, if not for love, for vanity a little.

MRS. DAINTY FIDGET. Nay, they do satisfy their vanity upon us sometimes; and are kind to us in their report, tell all the world they lie with us.

LADY FIDGET. Damned rascals, that we should be only wronged by 'em! To report a man has had a person, when he has not had a person, is the greatest wrong in the whole world that can be done to a person.

MRS. SQUEAMISH. Well, 'tis an arrant shame noble persons should be so wronged and neglected.

LADY FIDGET. But still 'tis an arranter shame for a noble person to neglect her own honor, and defame her own noble person with little inconsiderable fellows, foh!

MRS. DAINTY FIDGET. I suppose the crime against our honor is the same with a man of quality as with another.

LADY FIDGET. How! no, sure, the man of quality is likest one's husband, and therefore the fault should be the less.

MRS. DAINTY FIDGET. But then the pleasure should be the less.

LADY FIDGET. Fy, fy, fy, for shame, sister! whither shall we ramble? Be continent in your discourse, or I shall hate you.

MRS. DAINTY FIDGET. Besides, an intrigue is so much the more notorious for the man's quality.

MRS. SQUEAMISH. 'Tis true, nobody takes notice of a private man, and therefore with him 'tis more secret; and the crime's the less when 'tis not known.

LADY FIDGET. You say true; i'faith, I think you are in the right on't; 'tis not an injury to a husband till it be an injury to our honors; so that a woman of honor loses no honor with a private person; and to say truth ——

MRS. DAINTY FIDGET. (*Apart to* MRS. SQUEAMISH) So, the little fellow is grown a private person — with her ——

LADY FIDGET. But still my dear, dear honor ——

Enter SIR JASPER, HORNER, *and* DORILANT

SIR JASPER FIDGET. Ay, my dear, dear of honor, thou hast still so much honor in thy mouth ——

HORNER. (*Aside*) That she has none elsewhere.

LADY FIDGET. Oh, what d'ye mean to bring in these upon us?

MRS. DAINTY FIDGET. Foh! these are as bad as wits.

MRS. SQUEAMISH. Foh!

LADY FIDGET. Let us leave the room.

SIR JASPER FIDGET. Stay, stay; faith, to tell you the naked truth ——

LADY FIDGET. Fy, Sir Jasper! do not use that word naked.

SIR JASPER FIDGET. Well, well, in short I have business at Whitehall, and cannot go to the play with you, therefore would have you go ——

LADY FIDGET. With those two to a play?

SIR JASPER FIDGET. No, not with t'other, but with Mr. Horner; there can be no more scandal to go with him than with Mr. Tattle, or Master Limberham.

LADY FIDGET. With that nasty fellow! no — no.

SIR JASPER FIDGET. Nay, prithee, dear, hear me.

(*Whispers to* LADY FIDGET)

HORNER. Ladies ——

(HORNER, DORILANT *drawing near* MRS. SQUEAMISH *and*
MRS. DAINTY FIDGET)

MRS. DAINTY FIDGET. Stand off.

MRS. SQUEAMISH. Do not approach us.

MRS. DAINTY FIDGET. You herd with the wits, you are obscenity all over.

MRS. SQUEAMISH. And I would as soon look upon a picture of Adam and Eve without fig-leaves as any of you, if I could help it; therefore keep off, and do not make us sick.

DORILANT. What a devil are these?

HORNER. Why, these are pretenders to honor, as critics to wit, only by censuring others; and as every raw, peevish, out-of-humored, affected, dull, tea-drinking, arithmetical fop, sets up for a wit by railing

at men of sense, so these for honor, by railing at the court, and ladies
of as great honor as quality.

SIR JASPER FIDGET. Come, Mr. Horner, I must desire you to go with
these ladies to the play, sir.

HORNER. I, sir?

SIR JASPER FIDGET. Ay, ay, come, sir.

HORNER. I must beg your pardon, sir, and theirs; I will not be seen
in women's company in public again for the world.

SIR JASPER FIDGET. Ha, ha, strange aversion!

MRS. SQUEAMISH. No, he's for women's company in private.

SIR JASPER FIDGET. He — poor man — he — ha! ha! ha!

MRS. DAINTY FIDGET. 'Tis a greater shame amongst lewd fellows to
be seen in virtuous women's company, than for the women to be seen
with them.

HORNER. Indeed, madam, the time was I only hated virtuous women,
but now I hate the other too; I beg your pardon, ladies.

LADY FIDGET. You are very obliging, sir, because we would not be
troubled with you.

SIR JASPER FIDGET. In sober sadness, he shall go.

DORILANT. Nay, if he wo' not, I am ready to wait upon the ladies,
and I think I am the fitter man.

SIR JASPER FIDGET. You, sir! no, I thank you for that. Master Horner
is a privileged man amongst the virtuous ladies, 'twill be a great while
before you are so; he! he! he! he's my wife's gallant; he! he! he! No,
pray withdraw, sir, for as I take it, the virtuous ladies have no business
with you.

DORILANT. And I am sure he can have none with them. 'Tis strange
a man can't come amongst virtuous women now, but upon the same
terms as men are admitted into the Great Turk's seraglio. But heavens
keep me from being an ombre[5] player with 'em! —— But where is
Pinchwife?   *Exit*

SIR JASPER FIDGET. Come, come, man; what, avoid the sweet society
of womankind? that sweet, soft, gentle, tame, noble creature, woman,
made for man's companion ——

HORNER. So is that soft, gentle, tame, and more noble creature a
spaniel, and has all their tricks; can fawn, lie down, suffer beating, and
fawn the more; barks at your friends when they come to see you, makes
your bed hard, gives you fleas, and the mange sometimes. And all the
difference is, the spaniel's the more faithful animal, and fawns but upon
one master.

SIR JASPER FIDGET. He! he! he!

MRS. SQUEAMISH. Oh, the rude beast!

MRS. DAINTY FIDGET. Insolent brute!

---

[5] A card game.

LADY FIDGET. Brute! stinking, mortified, rotten French wether, to dare ——

SIR JASPER FIDGET. Hold, an't please your ladyship. —— For shame, Master Horner! your mother was a woman — (*Aside*) Now shall I never reconcile 'em. —— (*Aside to* LADY FIDGET) Hark you, madam, take my advice in your anger. You know you often want one to make up your drolling pack of ombre players, and you may cheat him easily; for he's an ill gamester, and consequently loves play. Besides, you know you have but two old civil gentlemen (with stinking breaths too) to wait upon you abroad; take in the third into your service. The others are but crazy;[6] and a lady should have a supernumerary gentle-man-usher as a supernumerary coach-horse, lest sometimes you should be forced to stay at home.

LADY FIDGET. But are you sure he loves play and has money?

SIR JASPER FIDGET. He loves play as much as you, and has money as much as I.

LADY FIDGET. Then I am contented to make him pay for his scur-rility. (*Aside*) Money makes up in a measure all other wants in men. Those whom we cannot make hold for gallants, we make fine.[7]

SIR JASPER FIDGET. (*Aside*) So, so; now to mollify, to wheedle him. —— (*Aside to* HORNER) Master Horner, will you never keep civil com-pany? Methinks 'tis time now, since you are only fit for them. Come, come, man, you must e'en fall to visiting our wives, eating at our tables, drinking tea with our virtuous relations after dinner, dealing cards to 'em, reading plays and gazettes to 'em, picking fleas out of their shocks[8] for 'em, collecting receipts, new songs, women, pages, and footmen for 'em.

HORNER. I hope they'll afford me better employment, sir.

SIR JASPER FIDGET. He! he! he! 'tis fit you know your work before you come into your place. And since you are unprovided of a lady to flatter, and a good house to eat at, pray frequent mine, and call my wife mistress, and she shall call you gallant, according to the custom.

HORNER. Who, I?

SIR JASPER FIDGET. Faith, thou shalt for my sake; come, for my sake only.

HORNER. For your sake ——

SIR JASPER FIDGET. [*To* LADY FIDGET] Come, come, here's a game-ster for you; let him be a little familiar sometimes; nay, what if a little rude? Gamesters may be rude with ladies, you know.

LADY FIDGET. Yes; losing gamesters have a privilege with women.

HORNER. I always thought the contrary, that the winning gamester had most privilege with women; for when you have lost your money to a man, you'll lose anything you have — all you have, they say — and he may use you as he pleases.

---

[6] I.e., unsound, rickety.   [7] Pay.   [8] Poodles.

SIR JASPER FIDGET. He! he! he! well, win or lose, you shall have your liberty with her.

LADY FIDGET. As he behaves himself, and for your sake I'll give him admittance and freedom.

HORNER. All sorts of freedom, madam?

SIR JASPER FIDGET. Ay, ay, ay, all sorts of freedom thou canst take. And so go to her, begin thy new employment; wheedle her, jest with her, and be better acquainted one with another.

HORNER. (*Aside*) I think I know her already; therefore may venture with her my secret for hers.   (HORNER *and* LADY FIDGET *whisper*)

SIR JASPER FIDGET. Sister, cuz, I have provided an innocent playfellow for you there.

MRS. DAINTY FIDGET. Who, he?

MRS. SQUEAMISH. There's a playfellow, indeed!

SIR JASPER FIDGET. Yes, sure. What, he is good enough to play at cards, blindman's-buff, or the fool with, sometimes!

MRS. SQUEAMISH. Foh! we'll have no such playfellows.

MRS. DAINTY FIDGET. No, sir; you shan't choose playfellows for us, we thank you.

SIR JASPER FIDGET. Nay, pray hear me.   (*Whispering to them*)

LADY FIDGET. But, poor gentleman, could you be so generous, so truly a man of honor, as for the sakes of us women of honor, to cause yourself to be reported no man? No man! and to suffer yourself the greatest shame that could fall upon a man, that none might fall upon us women by your conversation? But, indeed, sir, as perfectly, perfectly the same man as before your going into France, sir? as perfectly, perfectly, sir?

HORNER. As perfectly, perfectly, madam. Nay, I scorn you should take my word; I desire to be tried only, madam.

LADY FIDGET. Well, that's spoken again like a man of honor: all men of honor desire to come to the test. But, indeed, generally you men report such things of yourselves, one does not know how or whom to believe; and it is come to that pass we dare not take your words no more than your tailor's, without some staid servant of yours be bound with you. But I have so strong a faith in your honor, dear, dear, noble sir, that I'd forfeit mine for yours, at any time, dear sir.

HORNER. No, madam, you should not need to forfeit it for me; I have given you security already to save you harmless, my late reputation being so well known in the world, madam.

LADY FIDGET. But if upon any future falling-out, or upon a suspicion of my taking the trust out of your hands to employ some other, you yourself should betray your trust, dear sir? I mean, if you'll give me leave to speak obscenely, you might tell, dear sir.

HORNER. If I did, nobody would believe me. The reputation of impotency is as hardly recovered again in the world as that of cowardice, dear madam.

LADY FIDGET. Nay, then, as one may say, you may do your worst, dear, dear sir.

SIR JASPER FIDGET. Come, is your ladyship reconciled to him yet? have you agreed on matters? For I must be gone to Whitehall.

LADY FIDGET. Why, indeed, Sir Jasper, Master Horner is a thousand, thousand times a better man than I thought him. Cousin Squeamish, sister Dainty, I can name him now. Truly, not long ago, you know, I thought his very name obscenity; and I would as soon have lain with him as have named him.

SIR JASPER FIDGET. Very likely, poor madam.

MRS. DAINTY FIDGET. I believe it.

MRS. SQUEAMISH. No doubt on't.

SIR JASPER FIDGET. Well, well — that your ladyship is as virtuous as any she, I know, and him all the town knows — he! he! he! Therefore, now you like him, get you gone to your business together; go, go to your business, I say, pleasure; whilst I go to my pleasure, business.

LADY FIDGET. Come, then, dear gallant.

HORNER. Come away, my dearest mistress.

SIR JASPER FIDGET. So, so; why, 'tis as I'd have it.   *Exit*

HORNER. And as I'd have it.

LADY FIDGET.

> Who for his business from his wife will run,
> Takes the best care to have her business done.

Exeunt omnes

ACT III

SCENE I. [A room in PINCHWIFE's house.]

Enter ALITHEA *and* MRS. PINCHWIFE.

ALITHEA. Sister, what ails you? You are grown melancholy.

MRS. PINCHWIFE. Would it not make any one melancholy to see you go every day fluttering abroad, whilst I must stay at home like a poor lonely sullen bird in a cage?

ALITHEA. Ay, sister, but you came young, and just from the nest to your cage, so that I thought you liked it, and could be as cheerful in't as others that took their flight themselves early, and are hopping abroad in the open air.

MRS. PINCHWIFE. Nay, I confess I was quiet enough till my husband told me what pure[1] lives the London ladies live abroad, with their dancing, meetings, and junketings, and dressed every day in their best

---

[1] Fine.

gowns; and I warrant you, play at nine-pins every day of the week, so they do.

Enter PINCHWIFE

PINCHWIFE. Come, what's here to do? You are putting the town-pleasures in her head, and setting her a-longing.

ALITHEA. Yes, after nine-pins. You suffer none to give her those longings you mean but yourself.

PINCHWIFE. I tell her of the vanities of the town like a confessor.

ALITHEA. A confessor! just such a confessor as he that, by forbidding a silly ostler to grease the horse's teeth, taught him to do't.

PINCHWIFE. Come, Mistress Flippant, good precepts are lost when bad examples are still before us; the liberty you take abroad makes her hanker after it, and out of humor at home. Poor wretch! she desired not to come to London; I would bring her.

ALITHEA. Very well.

PINCHWIFE. She has been this week in town, and never desired till this afternoon to go abroad.

ALITHEA. Was she not at a play yesterday?

PINCHWIFE. Yes, but she ne'er asked me; I was myself the cause of her going.

ALITHEA. Then if she ask you again, you are the cause of her asking, and not my example.

PINCHWIFE. Well, to-morrow night I shall be rid of you; and the next day, before 'tis light, she and I'll be rid of the town, and my dreadful apprehensions. —— Come, be not melancholy; for thou shalt go into the country after to-morrow, dearest.

ALITHEA. Great comfort!

MRS. PINCHWIFE. Pish! what d'ye tell me of the country for?

PINCHWIFE. How's this! what, pish at the country?

MRS. PINCHWIFE. Let me alone; I am not well.

PINCHWIFE. Oh, if that be all — what ails my dearest?

MRS. PINCHWIFE. Truly, I don't know; but I have not been well since you told me there was a gallant at the play in love with me.

PINCHWIFE. Ha! ——

ALITHEA. That's by my example too!

PINCH. Nay, if you are not well, but are so concerned because a lewd fellow chanced to lie, and say he liked you, you'll make me sick too.

MRS. PINCHWIFE. Of what sickness?

PINCHWIFE. Oh, of that which is worse than the plague, jealousy.

MRS. PINCHWIFE. Pish, you jeer! I'm sure there's no such disease in our receipt-book at home.

PINCHWIFE. No, thou never met'st with it, poor innocent. —— (*Aside*) Well, if thou cuckold me, 'twill be my own fault — for cuckolds and bastards are generally makers of their own fortune.

MRS. PINCHWIFE. Well, but pray, bud, let's go to a play to-night.

PINCHWIFE. 'Tis just done, she comes from it. But why are you so eager to see a play?

MRS. PINCHWIFE. Faith, dear, not that I care one pin for their talk there; but I like to look upon the playermen, and would see, if I could, the gallant you say loves me; that's all, dear bud.

PINCHWIFE. Is that all, dear bud?

ALITHEA. This proceeds from my example!

MRS. PINCHWIFE. But if the play be done, let's go abroad, however, dear bud.

PINCHWIFE. Come, have a little patience and thou shalt go into the country on Friday.

MRS. PINCHWIFE. Therefore I would see first some sights to tell my neighbors of. Nay, I will go abroad, that's once.

ALITHEA. I'm the cause of this desire too!

PINCHWIFE. But now I think on't, who, who was the cause of Horner's coming to my lodgings to-day? That was you.

ALITHEA. No, you, because you would not let him see your handsome wife out of your lodging.

MRS. PINCHWIFE. Why, O Lord! did the gentleman come hither to see me indeed?

PINCHWIFE. No, no. You are not cause of that damned question too, Mistress Alithea? — (*Aside*) Well, she's in the right of it. He is in love with my wife — and comes after her — 'tis so — but I'll nip his love in the bud, lest he should follow us into the country, and break his chariot-wheel near our house, on purpose for an excuse to come to't. But I think I know the town.

MRS. PINCHWIFE. Come, pray, bud, let's go abroad before 'tis late; for I will go, that's flat and plain.

PINCHWIFE. (*Aside*) So! the obstinacy already of a town-wife; and I must, whilst she's here, humor her like one. —— Sister, how shall we do, that she may not be seen or known?

ALITHEA. Let her put on her mask.

PINCHWIFE. Pshaw! a mask makes people but the more inquisitive, and is as ridiculous a disguise as a stage-beard; her shape, stature, habit will be known. And if we should meet with Horner, he would be sure to take acquaintance with us, must wish her joy, kiss her, talk to her, leer upon her, and the devil and all. No, I'll not use her to a mask; 'tis dangerous, for masks have made more cuckolds than the best faces that ever were known.

ALITHEA. How will you do then?

MRS. PINCHWIFE. Nay, shall we go? The Exchange will be shut, and I have a mind to see that.

PINCHWIFE. So — I have it — I'll dress her up in the suit we are to carry down to her brother, little Sir James; nay, I understand the town-

tricks. Come, let's go dress her. A mask! no — a woman masked, like
a covered dish, gives a man curiosity and appetite; when, it may be,
uncovered, 'twould turn his stomach; no, no.

ALITHEA. Indeed your comparison is something a greasy one: but I
had a gentle gallant used to say, "A beauty masked, like the sun in
eclipse, gathers together more gazers than if it shined out."   *Exeunt*

[SCENE II]

The Scene Changes to the New Exchange, [with CLASP, *a book-seller,
in his stall]*

Enter HORNER, HARCOURT, and DORILANT

DORILANT. Engaged to women, and not sup with us!

HORNER. Ay, a pox on 'em all!

HARCOURT. You were much a more reasonable man in the morning,
and had as noble resolutions against 'em as a widower of a week's
liberty.

DORILANT. Did I ever think to see you keep company with women
in vain?

HORNER. In vain! no — 'tis since I can't love 'em, to be revenged
on 'em.

HARCOURT. Now your sting is gone, you looked in the box amongst
all those women like a drone in the hive; all upon you, shoved and
ill-used by 'em all, and thrust from one side to t'other.

DORILANT. Yet he must be buzzing amongst 'em still, like other old
beetle-headed liquorish drones. Avoid 'em, and hate 'em, as they hate
you.

HORNER. Because I do hate 'em, and would hate 'em yet more, I'll
frequent 'em. You may see by marriage, nothing makes a man hate a
woman more than her constant conversation. In short, I converse with
'em, as you do with rich fools, to laugh at 'em and use 'em ill.

DORILANT. But I would no more sup with women unless I could lie
with 'em than sup with a rich coxcomb unless I could cheat him.

HORNER. Yes, I have known thee sup with a fool for his drinking;
if he could set out your hand[2] that way only, you were satisfied, and if
he were a wine-swallowing mouth, 'twas enough.

HARCOURT. Yes, a man drinks often with a fool, as he tosses with a
marker,[3] only to keep his hand in ure.[4] But do the ladies drink?

HORNER. Yes, sir; and I shall have the pleasure at least of laying 'em
flat with a bottle, and bring as much scandal that way upon 'em as
formerly t'other.

[2] If he could put a wine glass in your hand.
[3] A scorekeeper at gambling games.   [4] In practice.

HARCOURT. Perhaps you may prove as weak a brother amongst 'em that way as t'other.

DORILANT. Foh! drinking with women is as unnatural as scolding with 'em. But 'tis a pleasure of decayed fornicators, and the basest way of quenching love.

HARCOURT. Nay, 'tis drowning love, instead of quenching it. But leave us for civil women too!

DORILANT. Ay, when he can't be the better for 'em. We hardly pardon a man that leaves his friend for a wench, and that's a pretty lawful call.

HORNER. Faith, I would not leave you for 'em, if they would not drink.

DORILANT. Who would disappoint his company at Lewis's[5] for a gossiping?

HARCOURT. Foh! Wine and women, good apart, together as nauseous as sack and sugar. But hark you, sir, before you go, a little of your advice; an old maimed general, when unfit for action, is fittest for counsel. I have other designs upon women than eating and drinking with them; I am in love with Sparkish's mistress, whom he is to marry to-morrow. Now how shall I get her?

Enter SPARKISH, *looking about*

HORNER. Why, here comes one will help you to her.

HARCOURT. He! he, I tell you, is my rival, and will hinder my love.

HORNER. No; a foolish rival and a jealous husband assist their rival's designs, for they are sure to make their women hate them, which is the first step to their love for another man.

HARCOURT. But I cannot come near his mistress but in his company.

HORNER. Still the better for you; for fools are most easily cheated when they themselves are accessories, and he is to be bubbled of his mistress as of his money, the common mistress, by keeping him company.

SPARKISH. Who is that that is to be bubbled? Faith, let me snack; I han't met with a bubble since Christmas. 'Gad, I think bubbles are like their brother woodcocks, go out with the cold weather.

HARCOURT. (*Apart to* HORNER) A pox! he did not hear all, I hope.

SPARKISH. Come, you bubbling rogues you, where do we sup? —— Oh, Harcourt, my mistress tells me you have been making fierce love to her all the play long: ha! ha! But I ——

HARCOURT. I make love to her!

SPARKISH. Nay, I forgive thee, for I think I know thee, and I know her; but I am sure I know myself.

HARCOURT. Did she tell you so? I see all women are like these of the

---

[5] Unidentified, but presumably a tavern.

Exchange; who, to enhance the price of their commodities, report to their fond customers offers which were never made 'em.

HORNER. Ay, women are as apt to tell before the intrigue, as men after it, and so show themselves the vainer sex. But hast thou a mistress, Sparkish? 'Tis as hard for me to believe it as that thou ever hadst a bubble, as you bragged just now.

SPARKISH. Oh, your servant, sir; are you at your raillery, sir? But we were some of us beforehand with you to-day at the play. The wits were something bold with you, sir; did you not hear us laugh?

HORNER. Yes; but I thought you had gone to plays to laugh at the poet's wit, not at your own.

SPARKISH. Your servant, sir; no, I thank you. 'Gad, I go to a play as to a country treat; I carry my own wine to one, and my own wit to t'other, or else I'm sure I should not be merry at either. And the reason why we are so often louder than the players is because we think we speak more wit, and so become the poet's rivals in his audience; for to tell you the truth, we hate the silly rogues, nay, so much that we find fault even with their bawdy upon the stage, whilst we talk nothing else in the pit as loud.

HORNER. But why shouldst thou hate the silly poets? Thou hast too much wit to be one; and they, like whores, are only hated by each other; and thou dost scorn writing, I'm sure.

SPARKISH. Yes; I'd have you to know I scorn writing; but women, women, that make men do all foolish things, make 'em write songs too. Everybody does it. 'Tis even as common with lovers as playing with fans; and you can no more help rhyming to your Phyllis, than drinking to your Phyllis.

HARCOURT. Nay, poetry in love is no more to be avoided than jealousy.

DORILANT. But the poets damned your songs, did they?

SPARKISH. Damn the poets! they turned 'em into burlesque, as they call it. That burlesque is a hocus-pocus trick they have got, which, by the virtue of *Hictius doctius, topsy turvy,* they make a wise and witty man in the world, a fool upon the stage, you know not how; and 'tis therefore I hate 'em too, for I know not but it may be my own case; for they'll put a man into a play for looking asquint. Their predecessors were contented to make serving-men only their stage-fools; but these rogues must have gentlemen with a pox to 'em, nay, knights; and, indeed, you shall hardly see a fool upon the stage but he's a knight. And to tell you the truth, they have kept me these six years from being a knight in earnest, for fear of being knighted in a play, and dubbed a fool.

DORILANT. Blame 'em not, they must follow their copy, the age.

HARCOURT. But why shouldst thou be afraid of being in a play, who expose yourself every day in the playhouses, and at public places?

HORNER. 'Tis but being on the stage, instead of standing on a bench in the pit.

DORILANT. Don't you give money to painters to draw you like? and are you afraid of your pictures at length in a playhouse, where all your mistresses may see you?

SPARKISH. A pox! painters don't draw the small-pox or pimples in one's face. Come, damn all your silly authors whatever, all books and booksellers, by the world, and all readers, courteous or uncourteous!

HARCOURT. But who comes here, Sparkish?

Enter MR. PINCHWIFE *and his Wife in man's clothes,* ALITHEA, LUCY *her maid*

SPARKISH. Oh, hide me! There's my mistress too.

(SPARKISH *hides himself behind* HARCOURT)

HARCOURT. She sees you.

SPARKISH. But I will not see her. 'Tis time to go to Whitehall, and I must not fail the drawing-room.

HARCOURT. Pray, first carry me, and reconcile me to her.

SPARKISH. Another time. Faith, the king will have supped.

HARCOURT. Not with the worse stomach for thy absence. Thou art one of those fools that think their attendance at the king's meals as necessary as his physicians', when you are more troublesome to him than his doctors or his dogs.

SPARKISH. Pshaw! I know my interest, sir. Prithee hide me.

HORNER. Your servant, Pinchwife. —— What, he knows us not!

PINCHWIFE. (*To his wife aside*) Come along.

MRS. PINCHWIFE. Pray, have you any ballads? give me sixpenny worth.

CLASP. We have no ballads.

MRS. PINCHWIFE. Then give me "Covent Garden Drollery," and a play or two —— Oh, here's "Tarugo's Wiles," and "The Slighted Maiden"; I'll have them.[6]

PINCHWIFE. (*Apart to her*) No; plays are not for your reading. Come along; will you discover yourself?

HORNER. Who is that pretty youth with him, Sparkish?

SPARKISH. I believe his wife's brother, because he's something like her; but I never saw her but once.

HORNER. Extremely handsome; I have seen a face like it too. Let us follow 'em.   *Exeunt* PINCHWIFE, MRS. PINCHWIFE, ALITHEA, LUCY, HORNER, DORILANT *following them*

HARCOURT. Come, Sparkish, your mistress saw you, and will be

---

[6] *Covent Garden Drollery*, a collection of songs, was published in 1672; Sir Thomas St. Serfe's *Tarugo's Wiles*, a comedy, in 1668; Sir Robert Stapylton's *The Slighted Maid*, a comedy, in 1663.

angry you go not to her. Besides, I would fain be reconciled to her, which none but you can do, dear friend.

SPARKISH. Well, that's a better reason, dear friend. I would not go near her now for hers or my own sake; but I can deny you nothing; for though I have known thee a great while, never go, if I do not love thee as well as a new acquaintance.

HARCOURT. I am obliged to you indeed, dear friend. I would be well with her, only to be well with thee still; for these ties to wives usually dissolve all ties to friends. I would be contented she should enjoy you a-nights, but I would have you to myself a-days as I have had, dear friend.

SPARKISH. And thou shalt enjoy me a-days, dear, dear friend, never stir; and I'll be divorced from her, sooner than from thee. Come along.

HARCOURT. (*Aside*) So, we are hard put to't, when we make our rival our procurer; but neither she nor her brother would let me come near her now. When all's done, a rival is the best cloak to steal to a mistress under, without suspicion; and when we have once got to her as we desire, we throw him off like other cloaks.

Exit SPARKISH, *and* HARCOURT *following him*

Re-enter PINCHWIFE, MRS. PINCHWIFE *in man's clothes*

PINCHWIFE. (*To* ALITHEA) Sister, if you will not go, we must leave you. — (*Aside*) The fool her gallant and she will muster up all the young saunterers of this place, and they will leave their dear seam-stresses[7] to follow us. What a swarm of cuckolds and cuckold-makers are here! —— Come, let's be gone, Mistress Margery.

MRS. PINCHWIFE. Don't you believe that; I han't half my bellyfull of sights yet.

PINCH. Then walk this way.

MRS. PINCHWIFE. Lord, what a power of brave signs are here! stay — the Bull's-Head, the Ram's-Head, and the Stag's-Head, dear ——

PINCHWIFE. Nay, if every husband's proper sign here were visible, they would be all alike.

MRS. PINCHWIFE. What d'ye mean by that, bud?

PINCHWIFE. 'Tis no matter — no matter, bud.

MRS. PINCHWIFE. Pray tell me: nay, I will know.

PINCHWIFE. They would be all Bulls', Stags', and Rams'-heads.[8]

Exeunt MR. PINCHWIFE *and* MRS. PINCHWIFE

Re-enter SPARKISH, HARCOURT, ALITHEA, LUCY, *at t'other door*

SPARKISH. Come, dear madam, for my sake you shall be reconciled to him.

---

[7] The seamstresses who kept their shops in the New Exchange were notori-ously alluring.

[8] The play is on the horns, traditional sign of a cuckold.

ALITHEA. For your sake I hate him.

HARCOURT. That's something too cruel, madem, to hate me for his sake.

SPARKISH. Ay indeed, madam, too, too cruel to me, to hate my friend for my sake.

ALITHEA. I hate him because he is your enemy; and you ought to hate him too, for making love to me, if you love me.

SPARKISH. That's a good one! I hate a man for loving you! If he did love you, 'tis but what he can't help; and 'tis your fault, not his, if he admires you; I hate a man for being of my opinion? I'll ne'er do't, by the world!

ALITHEA. Is it for your honor, or mine, to suffer a man to make love to me, who am to marry you to-morrow?

SPARKISH. Is it for your honor, or mine, to have me jealous? That he makes love to you, is a sign you are handsome; and that I am not jealous, is a sign you are virtuous. That I think is for your honor.

ALITHEA. But 'tis your honor too I am concerned for.

HARCOURT. But why, dearest madam, will you be more concerned for his honor than he is himself? Let his honor alone, for my sake and his. He! he has no honor ——

SPARKISH. How's that?

HARCOURT. But what my dear friend can guard himself.

SPARKISH. Oh ho — that's right again.

HARCOURT. Your care of his honor argues his neglect of it, which is no honor to my dear friend here. Therefore once more, let his honor go which way it will, dear madam.

SPARKISH. Ay, ay; were it for my honor to marry a woman whose virtue I suspected, and could not trust her in a friend's hands?

ALITHEA. Are you not afraid to lose me?

HARCOURT. He afraid to lose you, madam! No, no — you may see how the most estimable and most glorious creature in the world is valued by him. Will you not see it?

SPARKISH. Right, honest Frank, I have that noble value for her that I cannot be jealous of her.

ALITHEA. You mistake him. He means, you care not for me, nor who has me.

SPARKISH. Lord, madam, I see you are jealous. Will you wrest a poor man's meaning from his words?

ALITHEA. You astonish me, sir, with your want of jealousy.

SPARKISH. And you make me giddy, madam, with your jealousy and fears, and virtue and honor. 'Gad, I see virtue makes a woman as troublesome as a little reading or learning.

ALITHEA. Monstrous!

LUCY. (Behind) Well, to see what easy husbands these women of quality can meet with! A poor chambermaid can never have such ladylike luck. Besides, he's thrown away upon her. She'll make no use of her fortune, her blessing, none to a gentleman, for a pure cuckold, for it requires good breeding to be a cuckold.

ALITHEA. I tell you then plainly, he pursues me to marry me.

SPARKISH. Pshaw.

HARCOURT. Come, madam, you see you strive in vain to make him jealous of me. My dear friend is the kindest creature in the world to me.

SPARKISH. Poor fellow.

HARCOURT. But his kindness only is not enough for me, without your favor, your good opinion, dear madam: 'tis that must perfect my happiness. Good gentleman, he believes all I say; would you would do so. Jealous of me! I would not wrong him nor you for the world.

SPARKISH. Look you there. Hear him, hear him, and do not walk away so.   (ALITHEA *walks carelessly to and fro*)

HARCOURT. I love you, madam, so ——

SPARKISH. How's that? Nay, now you begin to go too far indeed.

HARCOURT. So much, I confess, I say, I love you, that I would not have you miserable, and cast yourself away upon so unworthy and inconsiderable a thing as what you see here.

(*Clapping his hand on his breast, points at* SPARKISH)

SPARKISH. No, faith, I believe thou wouldst not; now his meaning is plain; but I knew before thou wouldst not wrong me, nor her.

HARCOURT. No, no, Heavens forbid the glory of her sex should fall so low, as into the embraces of such a contemptible wretch, the last of mankind — my dear friend here — I injure him!

(*Embracing* SPARKISH)

ALITHEA. Very well.

SPARKISH. No, no, dear friend, I knew it. —— Madam, you see he will rather wrong himself than me, in giving himself such names.

ALITHEA. Do you not understand him yet?

SPARKISH. Yes, how modestly he speaks of himself, poor fellow!

ALITHEA. Methinks he speaks impudently of yourself, since — before yourself too; insomuch that I can no longer suffer his scurrilous abusiveness to you, no more than his love to me.   (*Offers to go*)

SPARKISH. Nay, nay, madam, pray stay — his love to you! Lord, madam, has he not spoke yet plain enough?

ALITHEA. Yes, indeed, I should think so.

SPARKISH. Well then, by the world, a man can't speak civilly to a woman now, but presently⁹ she says he makes love to her. Nay, madam, you shall stay, with your pardon, since you have not yet understood him, till he has made an *éclaircissement*¹⁰ of his love to you, that is, what kind of love it is. Answer to thy catechism, friend; do you love my mistress here?

---

⁹ Immediately.   ¹⁰ Explanation.

HARCOURT. Yes, I wish she would not doubt it.

SPARKISH. But how do you love her?

HARCOURT. With all my soul.

ALITHEA. I thank him, methinks he speaks plain enough now.

SPARKISH. (*To* ALITHEA) You are out still. —— But with what kind of love, Harcourt?

HARCOURT. With the best and truest love in the world.

SPARKISH. Look you there then, that is with no matrimonal love, I'm sure.

ALITHEA. How's that? do you say matrimonial love is not best?

SPARKISH. 'Gad, I went too far ere I was aware. But speak for thyself, Harcourt, you said you would not wrong me nor her.

HARCOURT. No, no, madam, e'en take him for Heaven's sake ——

SPARKISH. Look you there, madam.

HARCOURT. Who should in all justice be yours, he that loves you most. (*Claps his hand on his breast*)

ALITHEA. Look you there, Mr. Sparkish, who's that?

SPARKISH. Who should it be? —— Go on, Harcourt.

HARCOURT. Who loves you more than women titles, or fortune fools.
(*Points at* SPARKISH)

SPARKISH. Look you there, he means me still, for he points at me.

ALITHEA. Ridiculous!

HARCOURT. Who can only match your faith and constancy in love.

SPARKISH. Ay.

HARCOURT. Who knows, if it be possible, how to value so much beauty and virtue.

SPARKISH. Ay.

HARCOURT. Whose love can no more be equalled in the world, than that heavenly form of yours.

SPARKISH. No.

HARCOURT. Who could no more suffer a rival than your absence, and yet could no more suspect your virtue than his own constancy in his love to you.

SPARKISH. No.

HARCOURT. Who, in fine, loves you better than his eyes, that first made him love you.

SPARKISH. Ay —— Nay, madam, faith, you shan't go till ——

ALITHEA. Have a care, lest you make me stay too long.

SPARKISH. But till he has saluted you; that I may be assured you are friends, after his honest advice and declaration. Come, pray, madam, be friends with him.

[*Re-*]*enter* PINCHWIFE, MRS. PINCHWIFE

ALITHEA. You must pardon me, sir, that I am not yet so obedient to you.

PINCHWIFE. What, invite your wife to kiss men? Monstrous! Are you not ashamed? I will never forgive you.

SPARKISH. Are you not ashamed that I should have more confidence in the chastity of your family than you have? You must not teach me; I am a man of honor, sir, though I am frank and free; I am frank, sir ——

PINCHWIFE. Very frank, sir, to share your wife with your friends.

SPARKISH. He is an humble, menial friend, such as reconciles the differences of the marriage bed; you know man and wife do not always agree; I design him for that use, therefore would have him well with my wife.

PINCHWIFE. A menial friend! — you will get a great many menial friends, by showing your wife as you do.

SPARKISH. What then? It may be I have a pleasure in't, as I have to show fine clothes at a playhouse the first day, and count money before poor rogues.

PINCHWIFE. He that shows his wife or money will be in danger of having them borrowed sometimes.

SPARKISH. I love to be envied, and would not marry a wife that I alone could love; loving alone is as dull as eating alone. Is it not a frank age? and I am a frank person; and to tell you the truth, it may be I love to have rivals in a wife; they make her seem to a man still but as a kept mistress; and so good night, for I must to Whitehall. —— Madam, I hope you are now reconciled to my friend; and so I wish you a good night, madam, and sleep if you can; for to-morrow you know I must visit you early with a canonical gentleman. Good night, dear Harcourt. *Exit* SPARKISH

HARCOURT. Madam, I hope you will not refuse my visit to-morrow, if it should be earlier with a canonical gentleman than Mr. Sparkish's.

PINCHWIFE. This gentlewoman is yet under my care, therefore you must yet forbear your freedom with her, sir.

(*Coming between* ALITHEA *and* HARCOURT)

HARCOURT. Must, sir?

PINCHWIFE. Yes, sir, she is my sister.

HARCOURT. 'Tis well she is, sir — for I must be her servant, sir. —— Madam ——

PINCHWIFE. Come away, sister, we had been gone if it had not been for you, and so avoided these lewd rake-hells, who seem to haunt us.

Enter HORNER, DORILANT *to them*

HORNER. How now, Pinchwife!

PINCHWIFE. Your servant.

HORNER. What! I see a little time in the country makes a man turn wild and unsociable, and only fit to converse with his horses, dogs, and his herds.

PINCHWIFE. I have business, sir, and must mind it; your business is pleasure; therefore you and I must go different ways.

HORNER. Well, you may go on, but this pretty young gentleman —— (*Takes hold of* MRS. PINCHWIFE)

HARCOURT. The lady ——

DORILANT. And the maid ——

HORNER. Shall stay with us; for I suppose their business is the same with ours, pleasure.

PINCHWIFE. (*Aside*) 'Sdeath, he knows her, she carries it so sillily! Yet if he does not, I should be more silly to discover it first.

ALITHEA. Pray, let us go, sir.

PINCHWIFE. Come, come ——

HORNER. (*To* MRS. PINCHWIFE) Had you not rather stay with us? —— Prithee, Pinchwife, who is this pretty young gentleman?

PINCHWIFE. One to whom I'm a guardian. — (*Aside*) I wish I could keep her out of your hands.

HORNER. Who is he? I never saw anything so pretty in all my life.

PINCHWIFE. Pshaw! do not look upon him so much, he's a poor bashful youth; you'll put him out of countenance. —— Come away, brother. (*Offers to take her away*)

HORNER. Oh, your brother!

PINCHWIFE. Yes, my wife's brother. —— Come, come, she'll stay supper for us.

HORNER. I thought so, for he is very like her I saw you at the play with, whom I told you I was in love with.

MRS. PINCHWIFE. (*Aside*) O jeminy! is this he that was in love with me? I am glad on't, I vow, for he's a curious fine gentleman, and I love him already, too. — (*To* PINCHWIFE) Is this he, bud?

PINCHWIFE. (*To his wife*) Come away, come away.

HORNER. Why, what haste are you in? Why won't you let me walk with him?

PINCHWIFE. Because you'll debauch him; he's yet young and innocent, and I would not have him debauched for anything in the world. — (*Aside*) How she gazes on him! the devil!

HORNER. Harcourt, Dorilant, look you here, this is the likeness of that dowdy he told us of, his wife; did you ever see a lovelier creature? The rogue has reason to be jealous of his wife, since she is like him, for she would make all that see her in love with her.

HARCOURT. And, as I remember now, she is as like him here as can be.

DORILANT. She is indeed very pretty, if she be like him.

HORNER. Very pretty? a very pretty condemnation! — she is a glorious creature, beautiful beyond all things I ever beheld.

PINCHWIFE. So, so.

HARCOURT. More beautiful than a poet's first mistress of imagination.

HORNER. Or another man's last mistress of flesh and blood.

MRS. PINCHWIFE. Nay, now you jeer, sir; pray don't jeer me.

PINCHWIFE. Come, come. — (*Aside*) By Heavens, she'll discover herself!

HORNER. I speak of your sister, sir.

PINCHWIFE. Ay, but saying she was handsome, if like him, made him blush. — (*Aside*) I am upon a rack!

HORNER. Methinks he is so handsome he should not be a man.

PINCHWIFE. (*Aside*) Oh, there 'tis out! he has discovered her! I am not able to suffer any longer. — (*To his wife*) Come, come away, I say.

HORNER. Nay, by your leave, sir, he shall not go yet. (*Aside to them*) Harcourt, Dorilant, let us torment this jealous rogue a little.

HARCOURT. ⎫
　　　　　　⎬ How?
DORILANT. ⎭

HORNER. I'll show you.

PINCHWIFE. Come, pray let him go, I cannot stay fooling any longer; I tell you his sister stays supper for us.

HORNER. Does she? Come then, we'll all go sup with her and thee.

PINCHWIFE. No, now I think on't, having stayed so long for us, I warrant she's gone to bed. — (*Aside*) I wish she and I were well out of their hands. —— Come, I must rise early to-morrow, come.

HORNER. Well then, if she be gone to bed, I wish her and you a good night. But pray, young gentleman, present my humble service to her.

MRS. PINCHWIFE. Thank you heartily, sir.

PINCHWIFE. (*Aside*) 'Sdeath she will discover herself yet in spite of me. —— He is something more civil to you, for your kindness to his sister, than I am, it seems.

HORNER. Tell her, dear sweet little gentleman, for all your brother there, that you have revived the love I had for her at first sight in the playhouse.

MRS. PINCHWIFE. But did you love her indeed, and indeed?

PINCHWIFE. (*Aside*) So, so. —— Away, I say.

HORNER. Nay, stay. —— Yes, indeed, and indeed, pray do you tell her so, and give her this kiss from me.　　　　　　(*Kisses her*)

PINCHWIFE. (*Aside*) O Heavens! what do I suffer? Now 'tis too plain he knows her, and yet ——

HORNER. And this, and this ——　　　　　　(*Kisses her again*)

MRS. PINCHWIFE. What do you kiss me for? I am no woman.

PINCHWIFE. (*Aside*) So, there, 'tis out. —— Come, I cannot, nor will stay any longer.

HORNER. Nay, they shall send your lady a kiss too. Here, Harcourt, Dorilant, will you not?   (*They kiss her*)

PINCHWIFE. (*Aside*) How! do I suffer this? Was I not accusing another just now for this rascally patience, in permitting his wife to be kissed before his face? Ten thousand ulcers gnaw away their lips. —— Come, come.

HORNER. Good night, dear little gentleman; madam, good night; farewell, Pinchwife. — (*Apart to* HARCOURT *and* DORILANT) Did not I tell you I would raise his jealous gall?

Exeunt HORNER, HARCOURT, *and* DORILANT

PINCHWIFE. So, they are gone at last; stay, let me see first if the coach be at this door.   *Exit*

HORNER, HARCOURT, DORILANT *return*

HORNER. What, not gone yet? Will you be sure to do as I desired you, sweet sir?

MRS. PINCHWIFE. Sweet sir, but what will you give me then?

HORNER. Anything. Come away into the next walk.

Exit, haling away MRS. PINCHWIFE

ALITHEA. Hold! hold! what d'ye do?

LUCY. Stay, stay, hold ——

HARCOURT. Hold, madam, hold, let him present him — he'll come presently; nay, I will never let you go till you answer my question.

(ALITHEA, LUCY, *struggling with* HARCOURT *and* DORILANT)

LUCY. For God's sake, sir, I must follow 'em.

DORILANT. No, I have something to present you with too, you shan't follow them.

PINCHWIFE *returns*

PINCHWIFE. Where? — how — what's become of? — gone! — whither?

LUCY. He's only gone with the gentleman, who will give him something, an't please your worship.

PINCHWIFE. Something! — give him something, with a pox! — where are they?

ALITHEA. In the next walk only, brother.

PINCHWIFE. Only, only! where, where?

Exit PINCHWIFE *and returns presently,*
then goes out again

HARCOURT. What's the matter with him? Why so much concerned? But, dearest madam ——

ALITHEA. Pray let me go, sir; I have said and suffered enough already.

HARCOURT. Then you will not look upon, nor pity, my sufferings?

ALITHEA. To look upon 'em, when I cannot help 'em, were cruelty, not pity; therefore, I will never see you more.

HARCOURT. Let me then, madam, have my privilege of a banished lover, complaining or railing, and giving you but a farewell reason why, if you cannot condescend to marry me, you should not take that wretch, my rival.

ALITHEA. He only, not you, since my honor is engaged so far to him, can give me a reason why I should not marry him; but if he be true, and what I think him to me, I must be so to him. Your servant, sir.

HARCOURT. Have women only constancy when 'tis a vice, and, like Fortune, only true to fools?

DORILANT. (*To* LUCY, *who struggles to get from him*) Thou shalt not stir, thou robust creature; you see, I can deal with you, therefore you should stay the rather, and be kind.

Enter PINCHWIFE

PINCHWIFE. Gone, gone, not to be found! quite gone! ten thousand plagues go with 'em! which way went they?

ALITHEA. But into t'other walk, brother.

LUCY. Their business will be done presently sure, an't please your worship; it can't be long in doing, I'm sure on't.

ALITHEA. Are they not there?

PINCHWIFE. No, you know where they are, you infamous wretch, eternal shame of your family, which you do not dishonor enough yourself, you think, but you must help her to do it too, thou legion of bawds!

ALITHEA. Good brother ——

PINCHWIFE. Damned, damned sister!

ALITHEA. Look you here, she's coming.

Enter MRS. PINCHWIFE *in man's clothes, running, with her hat under her arm, full of oranges and dried fruit,* HORNER *following*

MRS. PINCHWIFE. O dear bud, look you here what I have got, see!

PINCHWIFE. (*Aside, rubbing his forehead*)[11] And what I have got here too, which you can't see.

MRS. PINCHWIFE. The fine gentleman has given me better things yet.

PINCHWIFE. Has he so? — (*Aside*) Out of breath and colored! — I must hold yet.

HORNER. I have only given your little brother an orange, sir.

PINCHWIFE. (*To* HORNER) Thank you, sir. — (*Aside*) You have only squeezed my orange, I suppose, and given it me again; yet I must have a city patience. — (*To his wife*) Come, come away.

MRS. PINCHWIFE. Stay, till I have put up my fine things, bud.

---

[11] Where he feels the cuckold's horns sprouting.

Enter SIR JASPER FIDGET

SIR JASPER FIDGET. O, Master Horner, come, come, the ladies stay for you; your mistress, my wife, wonders you make not more haste to her.

HORNER. I have stayed this half hour for you here, and 'tis your fault I am not now with your wife.

SIR JASPER FIDGET. But, pray, don't let her know so much; the truth on't is, I was advancing a certain project to his majesty about — I'll tell you.

HORNER. No, let's go, and hear it at your house. — Good night, sweet little gentleman; one kiss more, you'll remember me now, I hope. (*Kisses her*)

DORILANT. What, Sir Jasper, will you separate friends? He promised to sup with us, and if you take him to your house, you'll be in danger of our company too.

SIR JASPER FIDGET. Alas! gentlemen, my house is not fit for you; there are none but civil women there, which are not for your turn. He, you know, can bear with the society of civil women now, ha! ha! ha! besides, he's one of my family — he's — he! he! he!

DORILANT. What is he?

SIR JASPER FIDGET. Faith, my eunuch, since you'll have it; he! he! he! *Exeunt* SIR JASPER FIDGET *and* HORNER

DORILANT. I rather wish thou wert his or my cuckold. Harcourt, what a good cuckold is lost there for want of a man to make him one! Thee and I cannot have Horner's privilege, who can make use of it.

HARCOURT. Ay, to poor Horner 'tis like coming to an estate at three-score, when a man can't be the better for't.

PINCHWIFE. Come.

MRS. PINCHWIFE. Presently, bud.

DORILANT. Come, let us go too. — (*To* ALITHEA) Madam, your servant. — (*To* LUCY) Good night, strapper.

HARCOURT. Madam, though you will not let me have a good day or night, I wish you one; but dare not name the other half of my wish.

ALITHEA. Good night, sir, for ever.

MRS. PINCHWIFE. I don't know where to put this here, dear bud, you shall eat it; nay, you shall have part of the fine gentleman's good things, or treat, as you call it, when we come home.

PINCHWIFE. Indeed, I deserve it, since I furnished the best part of it. (*Strikes away the orange*)

> The gallant treats presents, and gives the ball,
> But 'tis the absent cuckold pays for all.

ACT IV

SCENE I. *In* PINCHWIFE'S *house in the morning*

[Enter] LUCY, ALITHEA *dressed in new clothes*

LUCY. Well, madam, now have I dressed you, and set you out with so many ornaments, and spent upon you ounces of essence and pulvillio;[1] and all this for no other purpose but as people adorn and perfume a corpse for a stinking second-hand grave; such, or as bad, I think Master Sparkish's bed.

ALITHEA. Hold your peace.

LUCY. Nay, madam, I will ask you the reason why you should banish poor Master Harcourt for ever from your sight; how could you be so hard-hearted?

ALITHEA. 'Twas because I was not hard-hearted.

LUCY. No, no; 'twas stark love and kindness, I warrant.

ALITHEA. It was so; I would see him no more because I love him.

LUCY. Hey day, a very pretty reason!

ALITHEA. You do not understand me.

LUCY. I wish you may yourself.

ALITHEA. I was engaged to marry, you see, another man, whom my justice will not suffer me to deceive or injure.

LUCY. Can there be a greater cheat or wrong done to a man than to give him your person without your heart? I should make a conscience of it.

ALITHEA. I'll retrieve it for him after I am married a while.

LUCY. The woman that marries to love better will be as much mistaken as the wencher that marries to live better. No, madam, marrying to increase love is like gaming to become rich; alas! you only lose what little stock you had before.

ALITHEA. I find by your rhetoric you have been bribed to betray me.

LUCY. Only by his merit, that has bribed your heart, you see, against your word and rigid honor. But what a devil is this honor! 'tis sure a disease in the head, like the megrim or falling-sickness,[2] that always hurries people away to do themselves mischief. Men lose their lives by it; women, what's dearer to 'em, their love, the life of life.

ALITHEA. Come, pray talk you no more of honor, nor Master Harcourt; I wish the other would come to secure my fidelity to him and his right in me.

LUCY. You will marry him then?

ALITHEA. Certainly; I have given him already my word, and will my hand too, to make it good, when he comes.

---

[1] Perfumed powder.

[2] Migraine or epilepsy.

LUCY. Well, I wish I may never stick pin more, if he be not an arrant natural[3] to t'other fine gentleman.

ALITHEA. I own he wants the wit of Harcourt, which I will dispense withal for another want he has, which is want of jealousy, which men of wit seldom want.

LUCY. Lord, madam, what should you do with a fool to your husband? You intend to be honest, don't you? Then that husbandly virtue, credulity, is thrown away upon you.

ALITHEA. He only that could suspect my virtue should have cause to do it; 'tis Sparkish's confidence in my truth that obliges me to be so faithful to him.

LUCY. You are not sure his opinion may last.

ALITHEA. I am satisfied 'tis impossible for him to be jealous after the proofs I have had of him. Jealousy in a husband — Heaven defend me from it! it begets a thousand plagues to a poor woman, the loss of her honor, her quiet, and her ——

LUCY. And her pleasure.

ALITHEA. What d'ye mean, impertinent?

LUCY. Liberty is a great pleasure, madam.

ALITHEA. I say, loss of her honor, her quiet, nay, her life sometimes; and what's as bad almost, the loss of this town; that is, she is sent into the country, which is the last ill-usage of a husband to a wife, I think.

LUCY. (Aside) Oh, does the wind lie there? —— Then of necessity, madam, you think a man must carry his wife into the country, if he be wise. The country is as terrible, I find, to our young English ladies, as a monastery to those abroad; and, on my virginity, I think they would rather marry a London jailer than a high sheriff of a county, since neither can stir from his employment. Formerly women of wit married fools for a great estate, a fine seat, or the like; but now 'tis for a pretty seat only in Lincoln's Inn Fields, St. James's Fields, or the Pall Mall.

Enter to them SPARKISH, *and* HARCOURT, *dressed like a Parson*

SPARKISH. Madam, your humble servant, a happy day to you, and to us all.

HARCOURT. Amen.

ALITHEA. Who have we here?

SPARKISH. My chaplain, faith —— O madam, poor Harcourt remembers his humble service to you; and, in obedience to your last commands, refrains coming into your sight.

ALITHEA. Is not that he?

SPARKISH. No, fy, no; but to show that he ne'er intended to hinder

[3] A fool.

our match, has sent his brother here to join our hands. When I get me a wife, I must get her a chaplain, according to the custom; this is his brother, and my chaplain.

ALITHEA. His brother!

LUCY. (*Aside*) And your chaplain, to preach in your pulpit then —

ALITHEA. His brother!

SPARKISH. Nay, I knew you would not believe it. —— I told you, sir, she would take you for your brother Frank.

ALITHEA. Believe it!

LUCY. (*Aside*) His brother! ha! ha!   ha! He has a trick left still, it seems.

SPARKISH. Come, my dearest, pray let us go to church before the canonical hour is past.[4]

ALITHEA. For shame, you are abused still.

SPARKISH. By the world, 'tis strange now you are so incredulous.

ALITHEA. 'Tis strange you are so credulous.

SPARKISH. Dearest of my life, hear me. I tell you this is Ned Harcourt of Cambridge, by the world; you see he has a sneaking college look. 'Tis true he's something like his brother Frank; and they differ from each other no more than in their age, for they were twins.

LUCY. Ha! ha! he!

ALITHEA. Your servant, sir; I cannot be so deceived, though you are. But come, let's hear, how do you know what you affirm so confidently?

SPARKISH. Why, I'll tell you all. Frank Harcourt coming to me this morning to wish me joy, and present his service to you, I asked him if he could help me to a parson. Whereupon he told me he had a brother in town who was in orders; and he went straight away, and sent him, you see there, to me.

ALITHEA. Yes, Frank goes and puts on a black coat, then tells you he is Ned; that's all you have for't.

SPARKISH. Pshaw! pshaw! I tell you, by the same token, the midwife put her garter about Frank's neck, to know 'em asunder, they were so like.

ALITHEA. Frank tells you this too?

SPARKISH. Ay, and Ned there too; nay, they are both in a story.

ALITHEA. So, so; very foolish.

SPARKISH. Lord, if you won't believe one, you had best try him by your chambermaid there; for chambermaids must needs know chaplains from other men, they are so used to 'em.

LUCY. Let's see; nay, I'll be sworn he has the canonical smirk, and the filthy clammy palm of a chaplain.

ALITHEA. Well, most reverend doctor, pray let us make an end of this fooling.

[4] According to ecclesiastical law, marriages could be performed only between 8 A.M. and noon.

HARCOURT. With all my soul, divine heavenly creature, when you please.

ALITHEA. He speaks like a chaplain indeed.

SPARKISH. Why, was there not soul, divine, heavenly, in what he said?

ALITHEA. Once more, most impertinent black coat, cease your persecution, and let us have a conclusion of this ridiculous love.

HARCOURT. (Aside) I had forgot; I must suit my style to my coat, or I wear it in vain.

ALITHEA. I have no more patience left; let us make once an end of this troublesome love, I say.

HARCOURT. So be it, seraphic lady, when your honor shall think it meet and convenient so to do.

SPARKISH. 'Gad, I'm sure none but a chaplain could speak so, I think.

ALITHEA. Let me tell you, sir, this dull trick will not serve your turn; though you delay our marriage, you shall not hinder it.

HARCOURT. Far be it from me, munificent patroness, to delay your marriage; I desire nothing more than to marry you presently, which I might do, if you yourself would; for my noble, good-natured, and thrice generous patron here would not hinder it.

SPARKISH. No, poor man, not I, faith.

HARCOURT. And now, madam, let me tell you plainly nobody else shall marry you. By Heavens! I'll die first, for I'm sure I should die after it.

LUCY. How his love has made him forget his function, as I have seen it in real parsons!

ALITHEA. That was spoken like a chaplain too? Now you understand him, I hope.

SPARKISH. Poor man, he takes it heinously to be refused; I can't blame him, 'tis putting an indignity upon him, not to be suffered; but you'll pardon me, madam, it shan't be; he shall marry us; come away, pray, madam.

LUCY. Ha! ha! he! more ado! 'tis late.

ALITHEA. Invincible stupidity! I tell you, he would marry me as your rival, not as your chaplain.

SPARKISH. Come, come, madam. (Pulling her away)

LUCY. I pray, madam, do not refuse this reverend divine the honor and satisfaction of marrying you; for I dare say he has set his heart upon't, good doctor.

ALITHEA. What can you hope or design by this?

HARCOURT. [Aside] I could answer her, a reprieve for a day only, often revokes a hasty doom. At worst, if she will not take mercy on me, and let me marry her, I have at least the lover's second pleasure, hindering my rival's enjoyment, though but for a time.

SPARKISH. Come, madam, 'tis e'en twelve o'clock, and my mother charged me never to be married out of the canonical hours. Come, come; Lord, here's such a deal of modesty, I warrant, the first day.

LUCY. Yes, an't please your worship, married women show all their modesty the first day, because married men show all their love the first day.

Exeunt SPARKISH, ALITHEA, HARCOURT, *and* LUCY

SCENE II. *The Scene changes to a Bedchamber, where appear*
PINCHWIFE *and* MRS. PINCHWIFE

PINCHWIFE. Come, tell me, I say.

MRS. PINCHWIFE. Lord! han't I told it an hundred times over?

PINCHWIFE (*Aside*) I would try, if in the repetition of the ungrateful tale, I could find her altering it in the least circumstance; for if her story be false, she is so too. —— Come, how was't, baggage?

MRS. PINCHWIFE. Lord, what pleasure you take to hear it, sure!

PINCHWIFE. No, you take more in telling it, I find; but speak, how was't?

MRS. PINCHWIFE. He carried me up into the house next to the Exchange.

PINCHWIFE. So, and you two were only in the room!

MRS. PINCHWIFE. Yes, for he sent away a youth that was there, for some dried fruits and China orange,.

PINCHWIFE. Did he so? Damn him for it — and for ——

MRS. PINCHWIFE. But presently came up the gentlewoman of the house.

PINCHWIFE. Oh, 'twas well she did; but what did he do whilst the fruit came?

MRS. PINCHWIFE. He kissed me an hundred times, and told me he fancied he kissed my fine sister, meaning me, you know, whom he said he loved with all his soul, and bid me be sure to tell her so, and to desire her to be at her window, by eleven of the clock this morning, and he would walk under at that time.

PINCHWIFE. (*Aside*) And he was as good as his word, very punctual; a pox reward him for't.

MRS. PINCHWIFE. Well, and he said if you were not within, he would come up to her, meaning me, you know, bud, still.

PINCHWIFE. (*Aside*) So — he knew her certainly; but for this confession, I am obliged to her simplicity. —— But what, you stood very still when he kissed you?

MRS. PINCHWIFE. Yes, I warrant you; would you have had me discover myself?

PINCHWIFE. But you told me he did some beastliness to you, as you call it; what was't?

MRS. PINCHWIFE. Why, he put ——

PINCHWIFE. What?

MRS. PINCHWIFE. Why, he put the tip of his tongue between my lips, and so mousled[5] me — and I said, I'd bite it.

PINCHWIFE. An eternal canker seize it, for a dog!

MRS. PINCHWIFE. Nay, you need not be so angry with him neither, for to say truth, he has the sweetest breath I ever knew.

PINCHWIFE. The devil! you were satisfied with it then, and would do it again?

MRS. PINCHWIFE. Not unless he should force me.

PINCHWIFE. Force you, changeling![6] I tell you, no woman can be forced.

MRS. PINCHWIFE. Yes, but she may sure, by such a one as he, for he's a proper, goodly, strong man; 'tis hard, let me tell you, to resist him.

PINCHWIFE. (*Aside*) So, 'tis plain she loves him, yet she has not love enough to make her conceal it from me; but the sight of him will increase her aversion for me and love for him, and that love instruct her how to deceive me and satisfy him, all idiot as she is. Love! 'twas he gave women first their craft, their art of deluding. Out of Nature's hands they came plain, open, silly, and fit for slaves, as she and Heaven intended 'em; but damned Love — well — I must strangle that little monster whilst I can deal with him. —— Go fetch pen, ink, and paper out of the next room.

MRS. PINCHWIFE. Yes, bud.

PINCHWIFE. Why should women have more invention in love than men? It can only be because they have more desires, more soliciting passions, more lust, and more of the devil.

MRS. PINCHWIFE *returns*

Come, minx, sit down and write.

MRS. PINCHWIFE. Ay, dear bud, but I can't do't very well.

PINCHWIFE. I wish you could not at all.

MRS. PINCHWIFE. But what should I write for?

PINCHWIFE. I'll have you write a letter to your lover.

MRS. PINCHWIFE. O Lord, to the fine gentleman a letter!

PINCHWIFE. Yes, to the fine gentleman.

MRS. PINCHWIFE. Lord, you do but jeer; sure you jest.

PINCHWIFE. I am not so merry; come, write as I bid you.

MRS. PINCHWIFE. What, do you think I am a fool?

PINCHWIFE. (*Aside*) She's afraid I would not dictate any love to him, therefore she's unwilling. —— But you had best begin.

---

[5] Muzzled, teased.
[6] Half-wit.

MRS. PINCHWIFE. Indeed, and indeed, but I won't, so I won't.

PINCHWIFE. Why?

MRS. PINCHWIFE. Because he's in town; you may send for him if you will.

PINCHWIFE. Very well, you would have him brought to you; is it come to this? I say, take the pen and write, or you'll provoke me.

MRS. PINCHWIFE. Lord, what d'ye make a fool of me for? Don't I know that letters are never writ but from the country to London, and from London into the country? Now he's in town, and I am in town too; therefore I can't write to him, you know.

PINCHWIFE. (*Aside*) So, I am glad it is no worse; she is innocent enough yet. —— Yes, you may, when your husband bids you, write letters to people that are in town.

MRS. PINCHWIFE. Oh, may I so? then I'm satisfied.

PINCHWIFE. Come, begin (*Dictates*) — "Sir" ——

MRS. PINCHWIFE. Shan't I say, "Dear Sir"? You know one says always something more than bare "Sir."

PINCHWIFE. Write as I bid you, or I will write whore with this penknife in your face.

MRS. PINCHWIFE. Nay, good bud (*She writes*) — "Sir" ——

PINCHWIFE. "Though I suffered last night your nauseous, loathed kisses and embraces" —— Write!

MRS. PINCHWIFE. Nay, why should I say so? You know I told you he had a sweet breath.

PINCHWIFE. Write!

MRS. PINCHWIFE. Let me but put out "loathed."

PINCHWIFE. Write, I say!

MRS. PINCHWIFE. Well then.   (*Writes*)

PINCHWIFE. Let's see, what have you writ? — (*Takes the paper and reads*) "Though I suffered last night your kisses and embraces" —— Thou impudent creature! where is "nauseous" and "loathed"?

MRS. PINCHWIFE. I can't abide to write such filthy words.

PINCHWIFE. Once more write as I'd have you, and question it not, or I will spoil thy writing with this. I will stab out those eyes that cause my mischief.   (*Holds up the penknife*)

MRS. PINCHWIFE. O Lord! I will.

PINCHWIFE. So — so — let's see now. — (*Reads*) "Though I suffered last night your nauseous, loathed kisses and embraces" — go on — "yet I would not have you presume that you shall ever repeat them" — so ——   (*She writes*)

MRS. PINCHWIFE. I have writ it.

PINCHWIFE. On, then — "I then concealed myself from your knowledge, to avoid your insolencies." ——   (*She writes*)

MRS. PINCHWIFE. So ——

PINCHWIFE. "The same reason, now I am out of your hands" ——

(*She writes*)

MRS. PINCHWIFE. So ——

PINCHWIFE. "Makes me own to you my unfortunate, though innocent frolic, of being in man's clothes" —— (*She writes*)

MRS. PINCHWIFE. So ——

PINCHWIFE. "That you may for evermore cease to pursue her, who hates and detests you" —— (*She writes on*)

MRS. PINCHWIFE. So-h —— (*Sighs*)

PINCHWIFE. What, do you sigh? — "detests you — as much as she loves her husband and her honor."

MRS. PINCHWIFE. I vow, husband, he'll ne'er believe I should write such a letter.

PINCHWIFE. What, he'd expect a kinder from you? Come, now your name only.

MRS. PINCHWIFE. What, shan't I say "Your most faithful humble servant till death"?

PINCHWIFE. No, tormenting fiend! — (*Aside*) Her style, I find, would be very soft. —— Come, wrap[7] it up now, whilst I go fetch wax and a candle; and write on the backside, "For Mr. Horner."

Exit PINCHWIFE

MRS. PINCHWIFE. "For Mr. Horner." — So, I am glad he has told me his name. Dear Mr. Horner! But why should I send thee such a letter that will vex thee, and make thee angry with me? — Well, I will not send it. —— Ay, but then my husband will kill me — for I see plainly he won't let me love Mr. Horner — but what care I for my husband? I won't, so I won't, send poor Mr. Horner such a letter —— But then my husband — but oh, what if I writ at bottom my husband made me write it? —— Ay, but then my husband would see't — Can one have no shift? Ah, a London woman would have had a hundred presently. Stay — what if I should write a letter, and wrap it up like this, and write upon't too? Ay, but then my husband would see't — I don't know what to do. — But yet evads[8] I'll try, so I will — for I will not send this letter to poor Mr. Horner, come what will on't.

"Dear, sweet Mr. Horner" — (*She writes and repeats what she hath writ*) — so — "my husband would have me send you a base, rude, unmannerly letter; but I won't" — so — "and would have me forbid you loving me; but I won't" — so — "and would have me say to you, I hate you, poor Mr. Horner; but I won't tell a lie for him" — there — "for I'm sure if you and I were in the country at cards together" — so — "I could not help treading on your toe under the table" — so — "or rubbing knees with you, and staring in your face, till you saw me" —

---

[7] Letters were not sent in envelopes, but folded several times and sealed with wax.

[8] In faith.

very well — "and then looking down, and blushing for an hour together" — so — "but I must make haste before my husband come; and
now he has taught me to write letters, you shall have longer ones from
me, who am, dear, dear, poor, dear Mr. Horner, your most humble
friend, and servant to command till death. — Margery Pinchwife."

Stay, I must give him a hint at bottom — so — now wrap it up just
like t'other — so — now write "For Mr. Horner" — But oh now, what
shall I do with it? for here comes my husband.

Enter PINCHWIFE

PINCHWIFE. (*Aside*) I have been detained by a sparkish coxcomb,
who pretended a visit to me; but I fear 'twas to my wife —— What,
have you done?

MRS. PINCHWIFE. Ay, ay, bud, just now.

PINCHWIFE. Let's see't; what d'ye tremble for? what, you would not
have it go?

MRS. PINCHWIFE. Here — (*Aside*) No, I must not give him that; so
I had been served if I had given him this.

(*He opens and reads the first letter*)

PINCHWIFE. Come, where's the wax and seal?

MRS. PINCHWIFE. (*Aside*) Lord, what shall I do now? Nay, then I
have it —— Pray let me see't. Lord, you think me so arrant a fool I
cannot seal a letter; I will do't, so I will.

(*Snatches the letter from him, changes it for the other, seals it,
and delivers it to him*)

PINCHWIFE. Nay, I believe you will learn that, and other things too,
which I would not have you.

MRS. PINCHWIFE. So, han't I done it curiously?[9] — (*Aside*) I think
I have; there's my letter going to Mr. Horner, since he'll needs have
me send letters to folks.

PINCHWIFE. 'Tis very well; but I warrant you would not have it go
now?

MRS. PINCHWIFE. Yes, indeed, but I would, bud, now.

PINCHWIFE. Well, you are a good girl then. Come, let me lock you
up in your chamber till I come back; and be sure you come not within
three strides of the window when I am gone, for I have a spy in the
street. — (*Exit* MRS. PINCHWIFE, PINCHWIFE *locks the door.*) At
least, 'tis fit she think so. If we do not cheat women, they'll cheat us,
and fraud may be justly used with secret enemies, of which a wife is
the most dangerous; and he that has a handsome one to keep, and a
frontier town, must provide against treachery, rather than open force.
Now I have secured all within, I'll deal with the foe without, with
false intelligence. (*Holds up the letter*)   *Exit*

---

[9] Cleverly.

SCENE III. *The Scene changes to* HORNER's *lodging*

[*Enter*] QUACK *and* HORNER

QUACK. Well, sir, how fadges[10] the new design? Have you not the luck of all your brother projectors, to deceive only yourself at last?

HORNER. No, good domine doctor, I deceive you, it seems, and others too; for the grave matrons, and old, rigid husbands think me as unfit for love as they are; but their wives, sisters, and daughters know, some of 'em, better things already.

QUACK. Already!

HORNER. Already, I say. Last night I was drunk with half-a-dozen of your civil persons, as you call 'em, and people of honor, and so was made free of their society and dressing-rooms for ever hereafter; and am already come to the privileges of sleeping upon their pallets, warming smocks, tying shoes and garters, and the like, doctor, already, already, doctor.

QUACK. You have made use of your time, sir.

HORNER. I tell thee, I am now no more interruption to 'em when they sing, or talk, bawdy, than a little squab[11] French page who speaks no English.

QUACK. But do civil persons and women of honor drink, and sing bawdy songs?

HORNER. Oh, amongst friends, amongst friends. For your bigots in honor are just like those in religion; they fear the eye of the world more than the eye of Heaven, and think there is no virtue but railing at vice, and no sin but giving scandal. They rail at a poor little kept player, and keep themselves some young modest pulpit comedian[12] to be privy to their sins in their closets, not to tell 'em of them in their chapels.

QUACK. Nay, the truth on't is, priests, amongst the women now, have quite got the better of us lay-confessors, physicians.

HORNER. And they are rather their patients; but ——

Enter MY LADY FIDGET, *looking about her*

Now we talk of women of honor, here comes one. Step behind the screen there, and but observe if I have not particular privileges with the women of reputation already, doctor, already.   (QUACK *retires*)

LADY FIDGET. Well, Horner, am not I a woman of honor? You see, I'm as good as my word.

HORNER. And you shall see, madam, I'll not be behindhand with you in honor; and I'll be as good as my word too, if you please but to withdraw into the next room.

[10] Succeeds.   [11] Plump.   [12] A chaplain.

LADY FIDGET. But first, my dear sir, you must promise to have a care of my dear honor.

HORNER. If you talk a word more of your honor, you'll make me incapable to wrong it. To talk of honor in the mysteries of love, is like talking of Heaven or the Deity in an operation of witchcraft just when you are employing the devil; it makes the charm impotent.

LADY FIDGET. Nay, fy! let us not be smutty. But you talk of mysteries and bewitching to me; I don't understand you.

HORNER. I tell you, madam, the word money in a mistress's mouth, at such a nick of time, is not a more disheartening sound to a younger brother, than that of honor to an eager lover like myself.

LADY FIDGET. But you can't blame a lady of my reputation to be chary.

HORNER. Chary! I have been chary of it already, by the report I have caused of myself.

LADY FIDGET. Ay, but if you should ever let other women know that dear secret, it would come out. Nay, you must have a great care of your conduct; for my acquaintance are so censorious (oh, 'tis a wicked, censorious world, Mr. Horner!), I say, are so censorious and detracting that perhaps they'll talk to the prejudice of my honor, though you should not let them know the dear secret.

HORNER. Nay, madam, rather than they shall prejudice your honor, I'll prejudice theirs; and, to serve you, I'll lie with 'em all, make the secret their own, and then they'll keep it. I am a Machiavel in love, madam.

LADY FIDGET. Oh, no, sir, not that way.

HORNER. Nay, the devil take me if censorious women are to be silenced any other way.

LADY FIDGET. A secret is better kept, I hope, by a single person than a multitude; therefore pray do not trust anybody else with it, dear, dear Mr. Horner.　　　　　　　　　　　　　　(*Embracing him*)

Enter SIR JASPER FIDGET

SIR JASPER FIDGET. How now!

LADY FIDGET. (*Aside*) Oh my husband! — prevented — and what's almost as bad, found with my arms about another man — that will appear too much — what shall I say? —— Sir Jasper, come hither. I am trying if Mr. Horner were ticklish, and he's as ticklish as can be. I love to torment the confounded toad; let you and I tickle him.

SIR JASPER FIDGET. No, your ladyship will tickle him better without me, I suppose. But is this your buying china? I thought you had been at the china-house.

HORNER. (*Aside*) China-house; that's my cue, I must take it. —— A pox! can't you keep your impertinent wives at home? Some men are troubled with the husbands, but I with the wives; but I'd have you to know, since I cannot be your journeyman by night, I will not be your drudge by day, to squire your wife about, and be your man of straw, or scarecrow only to pies and jays, that would be nibbling at your forbidden fruit; I shall be shortly the hackney[13] gentleman-usher of the town.

SIR JASPER FIDGET. (*Aside*) He! he! he! poor fellow, he's in the right on't, faith. To squire women about for other folks is as ungrateful an employment as to tell money for other folks. —— He! he! he! be'n't angry, Horner.

LADY FIDGET. No, 'tis I have more reason to be angry, who am left by you to go abroad indecently alone; or, what is more indecent, to pin myself upon such ill-bred people of your acquaintance as this is.

SIR JASPER FIDGET. Nay, prithee, what has he done?

LADY FIDGET. Nay, he has done nothing.

SIR JASPER FIDGET. But what d'ye take ill, if he has done nothing?

LADY FIDGET. Ha! ha! ha! faith, I can't but laugh, however; why, d'ye think the unmannerly toad would come down to me to the coach? I was fain to come up to fetch him, or go without him, which I was resolved not to do; for he knows china very well, and has himself very good, but will not let me see it lest I should beg some; but I will find it out, and have what I came for yet.

Exit LADY FIDGET, *followed by* HORNER *to the door*

HORNER. (*Apart to* LADY FIDGET) Lock the door, madam. So, she has got into my chamber and locked me out. Oh the impertinency of womankind! Well, Sir Jasper, plain-dealing is a jewel; if ever you suffer your wife to trouble me again here she shall carry you home a pair of horns, by my lord mayor she shall; though I cannot furnish you myself, you are sure, yet I'll find a way.

SIR JASPER FIDGET. Ha! ha! he! — (*Aside*) At my first coming in, and finding her arms about him, tickling him it seems, I was half jealous, but now I see my folly. —— He! he! he! poor Horner.

HORNER. Nay, though you laugh now, 'twill be my turn ere long. Oh, women, more impertinent, more cunning, and more mischievous than their monkeys, and to me almost as ugly! — Now is she throwing my things about and rifling all I have; but I'll get in to her the back way, and so rifle her for it.

SIR JASPER FIDGET. Ha! ha! ha! poor angry Horner.

HORNER. Stay here a little, I'll ferret her out to you presently, I warrant. *Exit at t'other door*

(SIR JASPER *calls through the door to his wife; she answers from within*)

SIR JASPER FIDGET. Wife! my Lady Fidget! wife! he is coming in to you the back way.

LADY FIDGET. Let him come and welcome, which way he will.

[13] A hired drudge.

SIR JASPER FIDGET. He'll catch you, and use you roughly, and be too strong for you.

LADY FIDGET. Don't you trouble yourself, let him if he can.

QUACK. (*Behind*) This indeed I could not have believed from him, nor any but my own eyes.

Enter MRS. SQUEAMISH

MRS. SQUEAMISH. Where's this woman-hater, this toad, this ugly, greasy, dirty sloven?

SIR JASPER FIDGET. [*Aside*] So, the women all will have him ugly; methinks he is a comely person, but his wants make his form contemptible to 'em; and 'tis e'en as my wife said yesterday, talking of him, that a proper handsome eunuch was as ridiculous a thing as a gigantic coward.

MRS. SQUEAMISH. Sir Jasper, your servant. Where is the odious beast?

SIR JASPER FIDGET. He's within in his chamber, with my wife; she's playing the wag with him.

MRS. SQUEAMISH. Is she so? and he's a clownish beast, he'll give her no quarter, he'll play the wag with her again, let me tell you. Come, let's go help her. — What, the door's locked?

SIR JASPER FIDGET. Ay, my wife locked it.

MRS. SQUEAMISH. Did she so? Let us break it open then.

SIR JASPER FIDGET. No, no; he'll do her no hurt.

MRS. SQUEAMISH. No. — (*Aside*) But is there no other way to get in to 'em? Whither goes this? I will disturb 'em.

Exit MRS. SQUEAMISH *at another door*

Enter OLD LADY SQUEAMISH

OLD LADY SQUEAMISH. Where is this harlotry, this impudent baggage, this rambling tomrigg?[14] O Sir Jasper, I'm glad to see you here; did you not see my vile grandchild come in hither just now?

SIR JASPER FIDGET. Yes.

OLD LADY SQUEAMISH. Ay, but where is she then? where is she? Lord, Sir Jasper, I have e'en rattled myself to pieces in pursuit of her. But can you tell what she makes here? They say below, no woman lodges here.

SIR JASPER FIDGET. No.

OLD LADY SQUEAMISH. No! what does she here then? Say, if it be not a woman's lodging, what makes she here? But are you sure no woman lodges here?

SIR JASPER FIDGET. No, nor no man neither; this is Mr. Horner's lodging.

OLD LADY SQUEAMISH. Is it so, are you sure?

14 Tom-boy.

SIR JASPER FIDGET. Yes, yes.

OLD LADY SQUEAMISH. So; then there's no hurt in't, I hope. But where is he?

SIR JASPER FIDGET. He's in the next room with my wife.

OLD LADY SQUEAMISH. Nay, if you trust him with your wife, I may with my Biddy. They say he's a merry harmless man now, e'en as harmless a man as ever came out of Italy with a good voice,[15] and as pretty, harmless company for a lady as a snake without his teeth.

SIR JASPER FIDGET. Ay, ay, poor man.

Enter MRS. SQUEAMISH

MRS. SQUEAMISH. I can't find 'em. —— Oh, are you here, grandmother? I followed, you must know, my Lady Fidget hither; 'tis the prettiest lodging, and I have been staring on the prettiest pictures ——

Enter LADY FIDGET *with a piece of china in her hand,*
and HORNER *following*

LADY FIDGET. And I have been toiling and moiling for the prettiest piece of china, my dear.

HORNER. Nay, she has been too hard for me, do what I could.

MRS. SQUEAMISH. O Lord, I'll have some china too. Good Mr. Horner, don't think to give other people china, and me none; come in with me too.

HORNER. Upon my honor, I have none left now.

MRS. SQUEAMISH. Nay, nay, I have known you deny your china before now, but you shan't put me off so. Come.

HORNER. This lady had the last there.

LADY FIDGET. Yes, indeed, madam, to my certain knowledge, he has no more left.

MRS. SQUEAMISH. Oh, but it may be he may have some you could not find.

LADY FIDGET. What, d'ye think if he had had any left, I would not have had it too? for we women of quality never think we have china enough.

HORNER. Do not take it ill, I cannot make china for you all, but I will have a roll-waggon[16] for you too, another time.

MRS. SQUEAMISH. Thank you, dear toad.

LADY FIDGET. (*To* HORNER *aside*) What do you mean by that promise?

HORNER. (*Apart to* LADY FIDGET) Alas, she has an innocent, literal understanding.

---

[15] A eunuch.

[16] Usually defined as a low-wheeled wagon. More probably it was the name of a dish or tray for rolls.

OLD LADY SQUEAMISH. Poor Mr. Horner! he has enough to do to please you all, I see.

HORNER. Ay, madam, you see how they use me.

OLD LADY SQUEAMISH. Poor gentleman, I pity you.

HORNER. I thank you, madam. I could never find pity but from such reverend ladies as you are; the young ones will never spare a man.

MRS. SQUEAMISH. Come, come, beast, and go dine with us; for we shall want a man at ombre after dinner.

HORNER. That's all their use of me, madam, you see.

MRS. SQUEAMISH. Come, sloven, I'll lead you, to be sure of you.

(*Pulls him by the cravat*)

OLD LADY SQUEAMISH. Alas, poor man, how she tugs him! Kiss, kiss her; that's the way to make such women quiet.

HORNER. No, madam, that remedy is worse than the torment; they know I dare suffer anything rather than do it.

OLD LADY SQUEAMISH. Prithee kiss her, and I'll give you her picture in little,[17] that you admired so last night; prithee do.

HORNER. Well, nothing but that could bribe me. I love a woman only in effigy and good painting, as much as I hate them. I'll do't, for I could adore the devil well painted.   (*Kisses* MRS. SQUEAMISH)

MRS. SQUEAMISH. Foh, you filthy toad! nay, now I've done jesting.

OLD LADY SQUEAMISH. Ha! ha! ha! I told you so.

MRS. SQUEAMISH. Foh! a kiss of his ——

SIR JASPER FIDGET. Has no more hurt in't than one of my spaniel's.

MRS. SQUEAMISH. Nor no more good neither.

QUACK. (*Behind*) I will now believe anything he tells me.

Enter PINCHWIFE

LADY FIDGET. O Lord, here's a man! Sir Jasper, my mask, my mask! I would not be seen here for the world.

SIR JASPER FIDGET. What, not when I am with you?

LADY FIDGET. No, no, my honor — let's be gone.

MRS. SQUEAMISH. O grandmother, let us be gone; make haste, make haste, I know not how he may censure us.

LADY FIDGET. Be found in the lodging of anything like a man! — Away.

Exeunt SIR JASPER FIDGET, LADY FIDGET, OLD LADY SQUEAMISH, MRS. SQUEAMISH

QUACK. (*Behind*) What's here? another cuckold? he looks like one, and none else sure have any business with him.

HORNER. Well, what brings my dear friend hither?

PINCHWIFE. Your impertinency.

HORNER. My impertinency! — Why, you gentlemen that have got

[17] A miniature.

handsome wives think you have a privilege of saying anything to your friends, and are as brutish as if you were our creditors.

PINCHWIFE. No, sir, I'll ne'er trust you any way.

HORNER. But why not, dear Jack? Why diffide[18] in me thou know'st so well?

PINCHWIFE. Because I do know you so well.

HORNER. Han't I been always thy friend, honest Jack, always ready to serve thee, in love or battle, before thou wert married, and am so still?

PINCHWIFE. I believe so; you would be my second now, indeed.

HORNER. Well then, dear Jack, why so unkind, so grum, so strange to me? Come, prithee, kiss me, dear rogue. Gad, I was always, I say, and am still as much thy servant as ——

PINCHWIFE. As I am yours, sir. What, you would send a kiss to my wife, is that it?

HORNER. So, there 'tis — a man can't show his friendship to a married man, but presently he talks of his wife to you. Prithee, let thy wife alone, and let thee and I be all one, as we were wont. What, thou art as shy of my kindness as a Lombard Street alderman of a courtier's civility at Locket's![19]

PINCHWIFE. But you are overkind to me, as kind as if I were your cuckold already; yet I must confess you ought to be kind and civil to me, since I am so kind, so civil to you, as to bring you this. Look you there, sir.   (*Delivers him a letter*)

HORNER. What is't?

PINCHWIFE. Only a love letter, sir.

HORNER. From whom? — how! this is from your wife — hum — and hum ——   (*Reads*)

PINCHWIFE. Even from my wife, sir; am I not wondrous kind and civil to you now too? — (*Aside*) But you'll not think her so.

HORNER. (*Aside*) Ha! is this a trick of his or hers?

PINCHWIFE. The gentleman's surprised I find. — What, you expected a kinder letter?

HORNER. No faith, not I, how could I?

PINCHWIFE. Yes, yes, I'm sure you did. A man so well made as you are must needs be disappointed if the women declare not their passion at first sight or opportunity.

HORNER. (*Aside*) But what should this mean? Stay, the postscript. — (*Reads aside*) "Be sure you love me, whatsoever my husband says to the contrary, and let him not see this, lest he should come home and pinch me, or kill my squirrel." — It seems he knows not what the letter contains.

PINCHWIFE. Come, ne'er wonder at it so much.

18 Mistrust me.
19 Locket's tavern at Charing Cross, frequented by wits and courtiers.

HORNER. Faith, I can't help it.

PINCHWIFE. Now, I think I have deserved your infinite friendship and kindness, and have showed myself sufficiently an obliging kind friend and husband; am I not so, to bring a letter from my wife to her gallant?

HORNER. Ay, the devil take me, art thou, the most obliging, kind friend and husband in the world, ha! ha!

PINCHWIFE. Well, you may be merry, sir; but in short I must tell you, sir, my honor will suffer no jesting.

HORNER. What dost thou mean?

PINCHWIFE. Does the letter want a comment? Then, know, sir, though I have been so civil a husband as to bring you a letter from my wife, to let you kiss and court her to my face, I will not be a cuckold, sir, I will not.

HORNER. Thou art mad with jealousy. I never saw thy wife in my life but at the play yesterday, and I know not if it were she or no. I court her, kiss her!

PINCHWIFE. I will not be a cuckold, I say; there will be danger in making me a cuckold.

HORNER. Why, wert thou not well cured of thy last clap?

PINCHWIFE. I wear a sword.

HORNER. It should be taken from thee, lest thou shouldst do thyself a mischief with it; thou art mad, man.

PINCHWIFE. As mad as I am, and as merry as you are, I must have more reason from you ere we part. I say again, though you kissed and courted last night my wife in man's clothes, as she confesses in her letter ——

HORNER. (*Aside*) Ha!

PINCHWIFE. Both she and I say you must not design it again, for you have mistaken your woman, as you have done your man.

HORNER. (*Aside*) Oh — I understand something now —— Was that thy wife? Why wouldst thou not tell me 'twas she? Faith, my freedom with her was your fault, not mine.

PINCHWIFE. (*Aside*) Faith, so 'twas.

HORNER. Fy! I'd never do't to a woman before her husband's face, sure.

PINCHWIFE. But I had rather you should do't to my wife before my face, than behind my back; and that you shall never do.

HORNER. No — you will hinder me.

PINCHWIFE. If I would not hinder you, you see by her letter she would.

HORNER. Well, I must acquiesce then, and be contented with what she writes.

PINCHWIFE. I'll assure you 'twas voluntarily writ; I had no hand in't, you may believe me.

HORNER. I do believe thee, faith.

PINCHWIFE. And believe her too, for she's an innocent creature, has no dissembling in her; and so fare you well, sir.

HORNER. Pray, however, present my humble service to her, and tell her I will obey her letter to a tittle, and fulfill her desires, be what they will, or with what difficulty soever I do't; and you shall be no more jealous of me, I warrant her, and you.

PINCHWIFE. Well then, fare you well; and play with any man's honor but mine, kiss any man's wife but mine, and welcome.   *Exit*

HORNER. Ha! ha! ha! — Doctor.

QUACK. It seems he has not heard the report of you, or does not believe it.

HORNER. Ha! ha! — now, doctor, what think you?

QUACK. Pray let's see the letter — hum — (*Reads the letter*) — "for — dear — love you ——"

HORNER. I wonder how she could contrive it! What say'st thou to't? 'Tis an original.[20]

QUACK. So are your cuckolds, too, originals, for they are like no other common cuckolds, and I will henceforth believe it not impossible for you to cuckold the Grand Signior[21] amidst his guards of eunuchs, that I say.

HORNER. And I say for the letter, 'tis the first love letter that ever was without flames, darts, fates, destinies, lying and dissembling in't.

Enter SPARKISH *pulling in* MR. PINCHWIFE

SPARKISH. Come back, you are a pretty brother-in-law, neither go to church nor to dinner with your sister bride!

PINCHWIFE. My sister denies her marriage, and you see is gone away from you dissatisfied.

SPARKISH. Pshaw! upon a foolish scruple that our parson was not in lawful orders, and did not say all the common prayer; but 'tis her modesty only I believe. But let women be never so modest the first day, they'll be sure to come to themselves by night, and I shall have enough of her then. In the meantime, Harry Horner, you must dine with me. I keep my wedding at my aunt's in the Piazza.[22]

HORNER. Thy wedding! What stale maid has lived to despair of a husband, or what young one of a gallant?

SPARKISH. Oh, your servant, sir — this gentleman's sister then, —no stale maid.

HORNER. I'm sorry for't.

PINCHWIFE. (*Aside*) How comes he so concerned for her?

SPARKISH. You sorry for't? Why, do you know any ill by her?

[20] Singular or eccentric person.
[21] The Sultan of Turkey.
[22] In Covent Garden.

HORNER. No, I know none but by thee; 'tis for her sake, not yours, and another man's sake that might have hoped, I thought.

SPARKISH. Another man! another man! What is his name?

HORNER. Nay, since 'tis past, he shall be nameless. — (*Aside*) Poor Harcourt! I am sorry thou hast missed her.

PINCHWIFE. (*Aside*) He seems to be much troubled at the match.

SPARKISH. Prithee, tell me —— Nay, you shan't go, brother.

PINCHWIFE. I must of necessity, but I'll come to you to dinner.

Exit

SPARKISH. But, Harry, what, have I a rival in my wife already? But with all my heart, for he may be of use to me hereafter; for though my hunger is now my sauce, and I can fall on heartily without, the time will come when a rival will be as good sauce for a married man to a wife, as an orange to veal.

HORNER. O thou damned rogue! thou hast set my teeth on edge with thy orange.

SPARKISH. Then let's to dinner — there I was with you again. Come.

HORNER. But who dines with thee?

SPARKISH. My friends and relations, my brother Pinchwife, you see, of your acquaintance.

HORNER. And his wife?

SPARKISH. No, 'gad, he'll ne'er let her come amongst us good fellows; your stingy country coxcomb keeps his wife from his friends, as he does his little firkin of ale for his own drinking, and a gentleman can't get a smack on't; but his servants, when his back is turned, broach it at their pleasures, and dust it away, ha! ha! ha! — 'Gad, I'm witty, I think, considering I was married to-day, by the world; but come ——

HORNER. No, I will not dine with you, unless you can fetch her too.

SPARKISH. Pshaw! what pleasure canst thou have with women now, Harry?

HORNER. My eyes are not gone; I love a good prospect yet, and will not dine with you unless she does too; go fetch her, therefore, but do not tell her husband 'tis for my sake.

SPARKISH. Well, I'll go try what I can do; in the meantime, come away to my aunt's lodging; 'tis in the way to Pinchwife's.

HORNER. The poor woman has called for aid, and stretched forth her hand, doctor; I cannot but help her over the pale out of the briars.

Exeunt SPARKISH, HORNER, QUACK

SCENE IV. *The Scene changes to* PINCHWIFE's *house*

MRS. PINCHWIFE *alone, leaning on her elbow. A table, pen, ink, and paper*

MRS. PINCHWIFE. Well, 'tis e'en so, I have got the London disease they call love; I am sick of my husband, and for my gallant. I have heard this distemper called a fever, but methinks 'tis liker an ague; for when I think of my husband, I tremble, and am in a cold sweat, and have inclinations to vomit; but when I think of my gallant, dear Mr. Horner, my hot fit comes, and I am all in a fever indeed; and, as in other fevers, my own chamber is tedious to me, and I would fain be removed to his, and then methinks I should be well. Ah, poor Mr. Horner! Well, I cannot, will not stay here; therefore I'll make an end of my letter to him, which shall be a finer letter than my last, because I have studied it like anything. Oh, sick, sick! (*Takes the pen and writes*)

Enter PINCHWIFE, *who, seeing her writing, steals softly behind her, and, looking over her shoulder, snatches the paper from her*

PINCHWIFE. What, writing more letters?

MRS. PINCHWIFE. O Lord, bud, why d'ye fright me so?

(*She offers to run out; he stops her, and reads*)

PINCHWIFE. How's this? nay, you shall not stir, madam; — "Dear, dear, dear Mr. Horner" — very well — I have taught you to write letters to good purpose — but let's see't. "First, I am to beg your pardon for my boldness in writing to you, which I'd have you to know I would not have done, had you not said first you loved me so extremely, which if you do, you will never suffer me to lie in the arms of another man whom I loathe, nauseate, and detest." — Now you can write these filthy words. But what follows? — "Therefore, I hope you will speedily find some way to free me from this unfortunate match, which was never, I assure you, of my choice, but I'm afraid 'tis already too far gone; however, if you love me, as I do you, you will try what you can do; but you must help me away before to-morrow, or else, alas! I shall be for ever out of your reach, for I can defer no longer our — our ——" (*The letter concludes.*) what is to follow "our"? — speak, what? Our journey into the country I suppose — Oh woman, damned woman! and Love, damned Love, their old tempter! for this is one of his miracles; in a moment he can make those blind that could see, and those see that were blind, those dumb that could speak, and those prattle who were dumb before; nay, what is more than all, make these dough-baked, senseless, indocile animals, women, too hard for us, their politic lords and rulers, in a moment. But make an end of your letter, and then I'll make an end of you thus, and all my plagues together.

(*Draws his sword*)

MRS. PINCHWIFE. O Lord, O Lord, you are such a passionate man, bud!

Enter SPARKISH

SPARKISH. How now, what's here to do?

PINCHWIFE. This fool here now!

SPARKISH. What, drawn upon your wife? You should never do that, but at night in the dark, when you can't hurt her. This is my sister-in-law, is it not? ay, faith, e'en our country Margery (*Pulls aside her hand-kerchief*); one may know her. Come, she and you must go dine with me; dinner's ready, come. But where's my wife? Is she not come home yet? Where is she?

PINCHWIFE. Making you a cuckold; 'tis that they all do, as soon as they can.

SPARKISH. What, the wedding-day? No, a wife that designs to make a cully[23] of her husband will be sure to let him win the first stake of love, by the world. But come, they stay dinner for us; come, I'll lead down our Margery.

MRS. PINCHWIFE. No — Sir, go, we'll follow you.

SPARKISH. I will not wag without you.

PINCHWIFE (*Aside*) This coxcomb is a sensible torment to me amidst the greatest in the world.

SPARKISH. Come, come, Madam Margery.

PINCHWIFE. No; I'll lead her my way: what, would you treat your friends with mine, for want of your own wife? — (*Leads her to t'other door, and locks her in and returns*) I am contented my rage should take breath ——

SPARKISH. (*Aside*) I told Horner this.

PINCHWIFE. Come now.

SPARKISH. Lord, how shy you are of your wife! But let me tell you, brother, we men of wit have amongst us a saying that cuckolding, like the small-pox, comes with a fear; and you may keep your wife as much as you will out of danger of infection, but if her constitution incline her to't, she'll have it sooner or later, by the world, say they.

PINCHWIFE. (*Aside*) What a thing is a cuckold, that every fool can make him ridiculous! —— Well, sir — but let me advise you, now you are come to be concerned, because you suspect the danger, not to neglect the means to prevent it, especially when the greatest share of the malady will light upon your own head, for

> Hows'e'er the kind wife's belly comes to swell,
> The husband breeds[24] for her, and first is ill.

---

23 Dupe, gull.
24 I.e., sprouts horns.

ACT V

SCENE I. MR. PINCHWIFE'S *house*

Enter MR. PINCHWIFE *and* MRS. PINCHWIFE.

A table and candle

PINCHWIFE. Come, take the pen and make an end of the letter, just as you intended; if you are false in a tittle, I shall soon perceive it, and punish you with this as you deserve. — (*Lays his hand on his sword*) Write what was to follow — let's see — "You must make haste, and help me away before to-morrow, or else I shall be for ever out of your reach, for I can defer no longer our" — What follows "our"?

MRS. PINCHWIFE. Must all out, then, bud? — Look you there, then.   (MRS. PINCHWIFE *takes the pen and writes*)

PINCHWIFE. Let's see — "For I can defer no longer our — wedding — Your slighted Alithea." — What's the meaning of this? my sister's name to't? Speak, unriddle.

MRS. PINCHWIFE. Yes, indeed, bud.

PINCHWIFE. But why her name to't? Speak — speak, I say.

MRS. PINCHWIFE. Ay, but you'll tell her then again. If you would not tell her again ——

PINCHWIFE. I will not — I am stunned, my head turns round. — Speak.

MRS. PINCHWIFE. Won't you tell her, indeed, and indeed?

PINCHWIFE. No; speak, I say.

MRS. PINCHWIFE. She'll be angry with me; but I had rather she should be angry with me than you, bud; and, to tell you the truth, 'twas she made me write the letter, and taught me what I should write.

PINCHWIFE. (*Aside*) Ha! I thought the style was somewhat better than her own. —— But how could she come to you to teach you, since I had locked you up alone?

MRS. PINCHWIFE. Oh, through the keyhole, bud.

PINCHWIFE. But why should she make you write a letter for her to him, since she can write herself?

MRS. PINCHWIFE. Why, she said because — for I was unwilling to do it ——

PINCHWIFE. Because what — because?

MRS. PINCHWIFE. Because, lest Mr. Horner should be cruel, and refuse her; or vain afterwards, and show the letter, she might disown it, the hand not being hers.

PINCHWIFE. (*Aside*) How's this? Ha! — then I think I shall come to myself again. This changeling could not invent this lie, but if she

could, why should she? she might think I should soon discover it. —
Stay — now I think on't too, Horner said he was sorry she had married
Sparkish; and her disowning her marriage to me makes me think she
has evaded it for Horner's sake. Yet why should she take this course?
But men in love are fools; women may well be so —— But hark you,
madam, your sister went out in the morning, and I have not seen her
within since.

MRS. PINCHWIFE. Alack-a-day, she has been crying all day above, it
seems, in a corner.

PINCHWIFE. Where is she? Let me speak with her.

MRS. PINCHWIFE. (*Aside*) O Lord, then he'll discover all! —— Pray
hold, bud; what, d'ye mean to discover me? She'll know I have told
you then. Pray, bud, let me talk with her first.

PINCHWIFE. I must speak with her, to know whether Horner ever
made her any promise, and whether she be married to Sparkish or no.

MRS. PINCHWIFE. Pray, dear bud, don't, till I have spoken with her,
and told her that I have told you all; for she'll kill me else.

PINCHWIFE. Go then, and bid her come out to me.

MRS. PINCHWIFE. Yes, yes, bud.

PINCHWIFE. Let me see ——

MRS. PINCHWIFE. (*Aside*) I'll go, but she is not within to come to
him. I have just got time to know of Lucy, her maid, who first set me
on work, what lie I shall tell next; for I am e'en at my wit's end.

Exit

PINCHWIFE. Well, I resolve it, Horner shall have her. I'd rather give
him my sister than lend him my wife; and such an alliance will prevent
his pretensions to my wife, sure. I'll make him of kin to her, and then
he won't care for her.

MRS. PINCHWIFE *returns*

MRS. PINCHWIFE. O Lord, bud! I told you what anger you would
make me with my sister.

PINCHWIFE. Won't she come hither?

MRS. PINCHWIFE. No, no. Alack-a-day, she's ashamed to look you in
the face, and she says, if you go in to her, she'll run away downstairs,
and shamefully go herself to Mr. Horner, who has promised her marriage, she says; and she will have no other, so she won't.

PINCHWIFE. Did he so? — promise her marriage! — then she shall
have no other. Go tell her so; and if she will come and discourse with
me a little concerning the means, I will about it immediately. Go. —
(*Exit* MRS. PINCHWIFE) His estate is equal to Sparkish's, and his ex-
traction as much better than his as his parts are; but my chief reason
is I'd rather be akin to him by the name of brother-in-law than that of
cuckold.

Enter MRS. PINCHWIFE

Well, what says she now?

MRS. PINCHWIFE. Why, she says she would only have you lead her to Horner's lodging; with whom she first will discourse the matter before she talks with you, which yet she cannot do; for alack, poor creature, she says she can't so much as look you in the face, therefore she'll come to you in a mask. And you must excuse her if she make you no answer to any question of yours, till you have brought her to Mr. Horner; and if you will not chide her, nor question her, she'll come out to you immediately.

PINCHWIFE. Let her come. I will not speak a word to her, nor require a word from her.

MRS. PINCHWIFE. Oh, I forgot; besides, she says she cannot look you in the face, though through a mask; therefore would desire you to put out the candle.

PINCHWIFE. I agree to all. Let her make haste. — There, 'tis out. — (*Puts out the candle. Exit* MRS. PINCHWIFE) My case is something better; I'd rather fight with Horner for not lying with my sister, than for lying with my wife; and of the two, I had rather find my sister too forward than my wife. I expected no other from her free education, as she calls it, and her passion for the town. Well, wife and sister are names which make us expect love and duty, pleasure and comfort; but we find 'em plagues and torments, and are equally, though differently, troublesome to their keeper, for we have as much ado to get people to lie with our sisters as to keep 'em from lying with our wives.

Enter MRS. PINCHWIFE *masked, and in hoods and scarfs, and a night-gown* [1] *and petticoat of* ALITHEA'S, *in the dark*

What, are you come, sister? let us go then. — But first let me lock up my wife. Mrs. Margery, where are you?

MRS. PINCHWIFE. Here, bud.

PINCHWIFE. Come hither, that I may lock you up; get you in. — (*Locks the door*) Come, sister, where are you now?

(MRS. PINCHWIFE *gives him her hand; but when he lets her go, she steals softly on t'other side of him, and is led away by him for his sister,* ALITHEA)

SCENE II. *The Scene changes to* HORNER'S *lodging*

QUACK, HORNER

QUACK. What, all alone? not so much as one of your cuckolds here, nor one of their wives! They use to take their turns with you, as if they were to watch you.

[1] Dressing-gown.

HORNER. Yes, it often happens that a cuckold is but his wife's spy, and is more upon family duty when he is with her gallant abroad, hindering his pleasure, than when he is at home with her playing the gallant. But the hardest duty a married woman imposes upon a lover is keeping her husband company always.

QUACK. And his fondness wearies you almost as soon as hers.

HORNER. A pox! keeping a cuckold company, after you have had his wife, is as tiresome as the company of a country squire to a witty fellow of the town, when he has got all his money.

QUACK. And as at first a man makes a friend of the husband to get the wife, so at last you are fain to fall out with the wife to be rid of the husband.

HORNER. Ay, most cuckold-makers are true courtiers, when once a poor man has cracked his credit for 'em, they can't abide to come near him.

QUACK. But at first, to draw him in, are so sweet, so kind, so dear! just as you are to Pinchwife. But what becomes of that intrigue with his wife?

HORNER. A pox! he's as surly as an alderman that has been bit; and since he's so coy, his wife's kindness is in vain, for she's a silly innocent.

QUACK. Did she not send you a letter by him?

HORNER. Yes; but that's a riddle I have not yet solved. Allow the poor creature to be willing, she is silly too, and he keeps her up so close ——

QUACK. Yes, so close, that he makes her but the more willing, and adds but revenge to her love; which two, when met, seldom fail of satis-fying each other one way or other.

HORNER. What! here's the man we are talking of, I think.

Enter MR. PINCHWIFE, *leading in his wife masked, muffled,*
and in her sister's gown

Pshaw!

QUACK. Bringing his wife to you is the next thing to bringing a love letter from her.

HORNER. What means this?

PINCHWIFE. The last time, you know, sir, I brought you a letter; now, you see, a mistress; I think you'll say I am a civil man to you.

HORNER. Ay, the devil take me, will I say thou art the civilest man I ever met with; and I have known some. I fancy I understand thee now better than I did the letter. But, hark thee, in thy ear ——

PINCHWIFE. What?

HORNER. Nothing but the usual question, man: is she sound, on thy word?

PINCHWIFE. What, you take her for a wench, and me for a pimp?

HORNER. Pshaw! wench and pimp, paw[2] words; I know thou art an honest fellow, and hast a great acquaintance among the ladies, and perhaps hast made love for me, rather than let me make love to thy wife.

PINCHWIFE. Come, sir, in short, I am for no fooling.

HORNER. Nor I neither; therefore prithee, let's see her face presently. Make her show, man; art thou sure I don't know her?

PINCHWIFE. I am sure you do know her.

HORNER. A pox! why dost thou bring her to me then?

PINCHWIFE. Because she's a relation of mine ——

HORNER. Is she, faith, man? then thou art still more civil and obliging, dear rogue.

PINCHWIFE. Who desired me to bring her to you.

HORN. Then she is obliging, dear rogue.

PINCHWIFE. You'll make her welcome for my sake, I hope.

HORNER. I hope she is handsome enough to make herself welcome. Prithee, let her unmask.

PINCHWIFE. Do you speak to her; she would never be ruled by me.

HORNER. Madam —— (MRS. PINCHWIFE *whispers to* HORNER) She says she must speak with me in private. Withdraw, prithee.

PINCHWIFE. (*Aside*) She's unwilling, it seems, I should know all her undecent conduct in this business. —— Well then, I'll leave you together, and hope when I am gone, you'll agree; if not, you and I shan't agree, sir.

HORNER. What means the fool? if she and I agree 'tis no matter what you and I do. (*Whispers to* MRS. PINCHWIFE, *who makes signs with her hand for him[3] to be gone*)

PINCHWIFE. In the meantime I'll fetch a parson, and find out Sparkish and disabuse him. You would have me fetch a parson, would you not? Well then — now I think I am rid of her, and shall have no more trouble with her. Our sisters and daughters, like usurers' money, are safest when put out; but our wives, like their writings, never safe but in our closets under lock and key.   *Exit*

Enter Boy

BOY. Sir Jasper Fidget, sir, is coming up.   [*Exit*]

HORNER. Here's the trouble of a cuckold now we are talking of. A pox on him! has he not enough to do to hinder his wife's sport, but he must other women's too? — Step in here, madam.

                                        Exit MRS. PINCHWIFE

Enter SIR JASPER FIDGET

SIR JASPER FIDGET. My best and dearest friend.

HORNER. (*Aside to* QUACK) The old style, doctor. —— Well, be short, for I am busy. What would your impertinent wife have now?

---

[2] Improper, naughty.   [3] I.e., Pinchwife.

SIR JASPER FIDGET. Well guessed, i'faith; for I do come from her.

HORNER. To invite me to supper! Tell her, I can't come; go.

SIR JASPER FIDGET. Nay, now you are out, faith; for my lady, and the whole knot of the virtuous gang, as they call themselves, are resolved upon a frolic of coming to you tonight in masquerade, and are all dressed already.

HORNER. I shan't be at home.

SIR JASPER FIDGET. [*Aside*] Lord, how churlish he is to women! —— Nay, prithee don't disappoint 'em; they'll think 'tis my fault; prithee don't. I'll send in the banquet and the fiddles. But make no noise on't; for the poor virtuous rogues would not have it known, for the world, that they go a-masquerading; and they would come to no man's ball but yours.

HORNER. Well, well — get you gone; and tell 'em, if they come, 'twill be at the peril of their honor and yours.

SIR JASPER FIDGET. He! he! he! — we'll trust you for that; farewell.

Exit

HORNER.

> Doctor, anon you too shall be my guest,
> But now I'm going to a private feast.   *Exeunt*

SCENE III. *The Scene changes to the Piazza of Covent Garden*

SPARKISH, PINCHWIFE

SPARKISH. (*With the letter*[4] *in his hand*) But who would have thought a woman could have been false to me? By the world, I could not have thought it.

PINCHWIFE. You were for giving and taking liberty; she has taken it only, sir, now you find in that letter. You are a frank person, and so is she, you see there.

SPARKISH. Nay, if this be her hand — for I never saw it.

PINCHWIFE. 'Tis no matter whether that be her hand or no; I am sure this hand, at her desire, led her to Mr. Horner, with whom I left her just now, to go fetch a parson to 'em at their desire too, to deprive you of her for ever; for it seems yours was but a mock marriage.

SPARKISH. Indeed, she would needs have it that 'twas Harcourt himself, in a parson's habit, that married us; but I'm sure he told me 'twas his brother Ned.

PINCHWIFE. Oh, there 'tis out; and you were deceived, not she; for you are such a frank person. But I must be gone. — You'll find her at Mr. Horner's. Go, and believe your eyes.   *Exit*

SPARKISH. Nay, I'll to her, and call her as many crocodiles, sirens, harpies, and other heathenish names as a poet would do a mistress who

---

[4] I.e., the letter Mrs. Pinchwife had signed with Alithea's name.

had refused to hear his suit, nay more, his verses on her. — But stay, is not that she following a torch at t'other end of the Piazza? and from Horner's certainly — 'tis so.

Enter ALITHEA *following a torch, and* LUCY *behind*

You are well met, madam, though you don't think so. What, you have made a short visit to Mr. Horner. But I suppose you'll return to him presently; by that time the parson can be with him.

ALITHEA. Mr. Horner and the parson, sir!

SPARKISH. Come, madam, no more dissembling, no more jilting; for I am no more a frank person.

ALITHEA. How's this?

LUCY. (*Aside*) So, 'twill work, I see.

SPARKISH. Could you find out no easy country fool to abuse? none but me, a gentleman of wit and pleasure about the town? But it was your pride to be too hard for a man of parts, unworthy false woman! false as a friend that lends a man money to lose; false as dice, who undo those that trust all they have to 'em.

LUCY. (*Aside*) He has been a great bubble, by his similes, as they say.

ALITHEA. You have been too merry, sir, at your wedding-dinner, sure.

SPARKISH. What, d'ye mock me too?

ALITHEA. Or you have been deluded.

SPARKISH. By you.

ALITHEA. Let me understand you.

SPARKISH. Have you the confidence — I should call it something else, since you know your guilt — to stand my just reproaches? You did not write an impudent letter to Mr. Horner? who I find now has clubbed with you in deluding me with his aversion for women, that I might not, forsooth, suspect him for my rival.

LUCY. (*Aside*) D'ye think the gentleman can be jealous now, madam?

ALITHEA. I write a letter to Mr. Horner!

SPARKISH. Nay, madam, do not deny it. Your brother showed it me just now; and told me likewise, he left you at Horner's lodging to fetch a parson to marry you to him, and I wish you joy, madam, joy, joy; and to him, too, much joy; and to myself more joy, for not marrying you.

ALITHEA. (*Aside*) So, I find my brother would break off the match; and I can consent to't, since I see this gentleman can be made jealous. —— O Lucy, by his rude usage and jealousy, he makes me almost afraid I am married to him. Art thou sure 'twas Harcourt himself, and no parson, that married us?

SPARKISH. No, madam, I thank you. I suppose that was a contrivance too of Mr. Horner's and yours, to make Harcourt play the parson; but I would as little as you have him one now, no, not for the world.

For shall I tell you another truth? I never had any passion for you till now, for now I hate you. 'Tis true, I might have married your portion, as other men of parts of the town do sometimes; and so, your servant. And to show my unconcernedness, I'll come to your wedding, and resign you with as much joy as I would a stale wench to a new cully; nay, with as much joy as I would after the first night, if I had been married to you. There's for you; and so your servant, servant.   *Exit*

ALITHEA. How was I deceived in a man!

LUCY. You'll believe then a fool may be made jealous now? For that easiness in him that suffers him to be led by a wife, will likewise permit him to be persuaded against her by others.

ALITHEA. But marry Mr. Horner! my brother does not intend it, sure; if I thought he did, I would take thy advice, and Mr. Harcourt for my husband. And now I wish that if there be any overwise woman of the town, who, like me, would marry a fool for fortune, liberty, or title, first, that her husband may love play, and be a cully to all the town but her, and suffer none but Fortune to be mistress of his purse; then, if for liberty, that he may send her into the country under the conduct of some huswifely mother-in-law; and if for title, may the world give 'em none but that of cuckold.

LUCY. And for her greater curse, madam, may he not deserve it.

ALITHEA. Away, impertinent! Is not this my old Lady Lanterlu's?[5]

LUCY. Yes, madam. — (*Aside*) And here I hope we shall find Mr. Harcourt.   *Exeunt*

SCENE IV. *The Scene changes again to* HORNER's *lodging. A table, banquet, and bottles*

[*Enter*] HORNER, LADY FIDGET, MRS. DAINTY FIDGET, MRS. SQUEAMISH

HORNER. (*Aside*) A pox! they are come too soon — before I have sent back my new mistress. All I have now to do is to lock her in, that they may not see her.

LADY FIDGET. That we may be sure of our welcome, we have brought our entertainment with us, and are resolved to treat thee, dear toad.

MRS. DAINTY FIDGET. And that we may be merry to purpose, have left Sir Jasper and my old Lady Squeamish quarreling at home at backgammon.

MRS. SQUEAMISH. Therefore let us make use of our time, lest they should chance to interrupt us.

LADY FIDGET. Let us sit then.

HORNER. First, that you may be private, let me lock this door and that, and I'll wait upon you presently.

---

[5] Lanterloo was an old card game.

LADY FIDGET. No, sir, shut 'em only, and your lips for ever; for we must trust you as much as our women.

HORNER. You know all vanity's killed in me; I have no occasion for talking.

LADY FIDGET. Now, ladies, supposing we had drank each of us our two bottles, let us speak the truth of our hearts.

MRS. DAINTY FIDGET and MRS. SQUEAMISH. Agreed.

LADY FIDGET. By this brimmer,[6] for truth is nowhere else to be found. —(Aside to HORNER) not in thy heart, false man!

HORNER. (Aside to LADY FIDGET) You have found me a true man, I'm sure.

LADY FIDGET. (Aside to HORNER) Not every way. —— But let us sit and be merry. (LADY FIDGET sings)

1

Why should our damned tyrants oblige us to live
On the pittance of pleasure which they only give?
     We must not rejoice
     With wine and with noise;
In vain we must wake in a dull bed alone,
Whilst to our warm rival, the bottle, they're gone.
     Then lay aside charms,
     And take up these arms.[7]

2

'Tis wine only gives 'em their courage and wit;
Because we live sober, to men we submit.
     If for beauties you'd pass,
     Take a lick of the glass,
'Twill mend your complexions, and when they are gone,
    The best red we have is the red of the grape.
Then, sisters, lay't on,
     And damn a good shape.

MRS. DAINTY FIDGET. Dear brimmer! Well, in token of our openness and plain-dealing, let us throw our masks over our heads.

HORNER. So, 'twill come to the glasses anon.[8]

MRS. SQUEAMISH. Lovely brimmer! let me enjoy him first.

LADY FIDGET. No, I never part with a gallant till I've tried him. Dear brimmer! that makest our husbands short-sighted.

MRS. DAINTY FIDGET. And our bashful gallants bold.

---

[6] A glass or cup filled to the brim with wine.
[7] The glasses.
[8] Alluding to the custom of drinking toasts and flinging away the empty glasses.

MRS. SQUEAMISH. And, for want of a gallant, the butler lovely in our eyes. —— Drink, eunuch.

LADY FIDGET. Drink, thou representative of a husband. — Damn a husband!

MRS. DAINTY FIDGET. And, as it were a husband, an old keeper.[9]

MRS. SQUEAMISH. And an old grandmother.

HORNER. And an English bawd, and a French chirurgeon.[10]

LADY FIDGET. Ay, we have all reason to curse 'em.

HORNER. For my sake, ladies?

LADY FIDGET. No, for our own; for the first spoils all young gallants' industry.

MRS. DAINTY FIDGET. And the other's art makes 'em bold only with common women.

MRS. SQUEAMISH. And rather run the hazard of the vile distemper amongst them, than of a denial amongst us.

MRS. DAINTY FIDGET. The filthy toads choose mistresses now as they do stuffs, for having been fancied and worn by others.

MRS. SQUEAMISH. For being common and cheap.

LADY FIDGET. Whilst women of quality, like the richest stuffs, lie untumbled, and unasked for.

HORNER. Ay, neat, and cheap, and new, often they think best.

MRS. DAINTY FIDGET. No, sir, the beasts will be known by a mistress longer than by a suit.

MRS. SQUEAMISH. And 'tis not for cheapness neither.

LADY FIDGET. No; for the vain fops will take up druggets[11] and embroider 'em. But I wonder at the depraved appetites of witty men; they use to be out of the common road, and hate imitation. Pray tell me, beast, when you were a man, why you rather chose to club[12] with a multitude in a common house for an entertainment than to be the only guest at a good table.

HORNER. Why, faith, ceremony and expectation are unsufferable to those that are sharp bent. People always eat with the best stomach at an ordinary,[13] where every man is snatching for the best bit.

LADY FIDGET. Though he get a cut over the fingers. — But I have heard people eat most heartily of another man's meat, that is, what they do not pay for.

HORNER. When they are sure of their welcome and freedom; for ceremony in love and eating is as ridiculous as in fighting; falling on briskly is all should be done on those occasions.

LADY FIDGET. Well then, let me tell you, sir, there is nowhere more freedom than in our houses; and we take freedom from a young person

---

[9] Of mistresses.　　　　[11] Cheap woolen goods.

[10] Surgeon.　　　　　　[12] Take shares.

[13] A tavern. Bawdy house is understood.

as a sign of good breeding; and a person may be as free as he pleases with us, as frolic, as gamesome, as wild as he will.

HORNER. Han't I heard you all declaim against wild men?

LADY FIDGET. Yes; but for all that, we think wildness in a man as desirable a quality as in a duck or rabbit; a tame man! foh!

HORNER. I know not, but your reputations frightened me as much as your faces invited me.

LADY FIDGET. Our reputation! Lord, why should you not think that we women make use of our reputation, as you men of yours, only to deceive the world with less suspicion? Our virtue is like the stateman's religion, the Quaker's word, the gamester's oath, and the great man's honor — but to cheat those that trust us.

MRS. SQUEAMISH. And that demureness, coyness, and modesty that you see in our faces in the boxes at plays, is as much a sign of a kind woman, as a vizard-mask[14] in the pit.

MRS. DAINTY FIDGET. For, I assure you, women are least masked when they have the velvet vizard on.

LADY FIDGET. You would have found us modest women in our denials only.

MRS. SQUEAMISH. Our bashfulness is only the reflection of the men's.

MRS. DAINTY FIDGET. We blush when they are shamefaced.

HORNER. I beg your pardon, ladies, I was deceived in you devilishly. But why that mighty pretense to honor?

LADY FIDGET. We have told you; but sometimes 'twas for the same reason you men pretend business often, to avoid ill company, to enjoy the better and more privately those you love.

HORNER. But why would you ne'er give a friend a wink then?

LADY FIDGET. Faith, your reputation frightened us as much as ours did you, you were so notoriously lewd.

HORNER. And you so seemingly honest.

LADY FIDGET. Was that all that deterred you?

HORNER. And so expensive — you allow freedom, you say ——

LADY FIDGET. Ay, ay.

HORNER. That I was afraid of losing my little money, as well as my little time, both which my other pleasures required.

LADY FIDGET. Money! foh! you talk like a little fellow now; do such as we expect money?

HORNER. I beg your pardon, madam, I must confess, I have heard that great ladies, like great merchants, set but the higher prices upon what they have, because they are not in necessity of taking the first offer.

MRS. DAINTY FIDGET. Such as we make sale of our hearts?

MRS. SQUEAMISH. We bribed for our love? foh!

14 Prostitute.

HORNER. With your pardon, ladies, I know, like great men in offices, you seem to exact flattery and attendance only from your followers; but you have receivers[15] about you, and such fees to pay a man is afraid to pass your grants.[16] Besides, we must let you win at cards, or we lose your hearts; and if you make an assignation, 'tis at a gold-smith's, jeweller's, or china-house, where for your honor you deposit to him, he must pawn his to the punctual cit,[17] and so paying for what you take up, pays for what he takes up.

MRS. DAINTY FIDGET. Would you not have us assured of our gallants' love?

MRS. SQUEAMISH. For love is better known by liberality than by jealousy.

LADY FIDGET. For one may be dissembled, the other not. — (*Aside*) But my jealousy can be no longer dissembled, and they are telling ripe. —— Come, here's to our gallants in waiting,[18] whom we must name, and I'll begin. This is my false rogue.   (*Claps him on the back*)

MRS. SQUEAMISH. How!

HORNER. So, all will out now.

MRS. SQUEAMISH. (*Aside to* HORNER) Did you not tell me 'twas for my sake only you reported yourself no man?

MRS. DAINTY FIDGET. (*Aside to* HORNER) Oh, wretch! did you not swear to me, 'twas for my love and honor you passed for that thing you do?

HORNER. So, so.

LADY FIDGET. Come, speak, ladies, this is my false villain.

MRS. SQUEAMISH. And mine too.

MRS. DAINTY FIDGET. And mine.

HORNER. Well then, you are all three my false rogues too, and there's an end on't.

LADY FIDGET. Well then, there's no remedy; sister sharers, let us not fall out, but have a care of our honor. Though we get no presents, no jewels of him, we are savers of our honor, the jewel of most value and use, which shines yet to the world unsuspected, though it be counterfeit.

HORNER. Nay, and is e'en as good as if it were true, provided the world think so; for honor, like beauty now, only depends on the opinion of others.

LADY FIDGET. Well, Harry Common, I hope you can be true to three. Swear; but 'tis to no purpose to require your oath, for you are as often forsworn as you swear to new women.

HORNER. Come, faith, madam, let us e'en pardon one another; for all the difference I find betwixt we men and you women, we forswear ourselves at the beginning of an amour; you as long as it lasts.

---

[15] Bribe collectors; i.e., servants.   [17] Citizen, shopkeeper.
[16] Accept your favors.   [18] In service.

Enter SIR JASPER FIDGET, *and* OLD LADY SQUEAMISH

SIR JASPER FIDGET. Oh, my Lady Fidget, was this your cunning, to come to Mr. Horner without me? But you have been nowhere else, I hope.

LADY FIDGET. No, Sir Jasper.

OLD LADY SQUEAMISH. And you came straight hither, Biddy?

MRS. SQUEAMISH. Yes, indeed, lady grandmother.

SIR JASPER FIDGET. 'Tis well, 'tis well; I knew when once they were thoroughly acquainted with poor Horner, they'd ne'er be from him. You may let her masquerade it with my wife and Horner, and I warrant her reputation safe.

Enter Boy

BOY. O sir, here's the gentleman come, whom you bid me not suffer to come up without giving you notice, with a lady too, and other gentlemen.

HORNER. Do you all go in there, whilst I send 'em away; and, boy, do you desire 'em to stay below till I come, which shall be immediately.

Exeunt SIR JASPER, [OLD] LADY SQUEAMISH, LADY FIDGET,
MRS. DAINTY, MRS. SQUEAMISH

BOY. Yes, sir. *Exit*

(*Exit* HORNER *at t'other door, and
returns with* MRS. PINCHWIFE)

HORNER. You would not take my advice, to be gone home before your husband came back; he'll now discover all. Yet pray, my dearest, be persuaded to go home, and leave the rest to my management; I'll let you down the back way.

MRS. PINCHWIFE. I don't know the way home, so I don't.

HORNER. My man shall wait upon you.

MRS. PINCHWIFE. No, don't you believe that I'll go at all; what, are you weary of me already?

HORNER. No, my life, 'tis that I may love you long, 'tis to secure my love, and your reputation with your husband; he'll never receive you again else.

MRS. PINCHWIFE. What care I? d'ye think to frighten me with that? I don't intend to go to him again; you shall be my husband now.

HORNER. I cannot be your husband, dearest, since you are married to him.

MRS. PINCHWIFE. Oh, would you make me believe that? Don't I see every day, at London here, women leave their first husbands, and go and live with other men as their wives? Pish, pshaw! you'd make me angry, but that I love you so mainly.

HORNER. So, they are coming up — In again, in, I hear 'em. — (*Exit* MRS. PINCHWIFE) Well, a silly mistress is like a weak place, soon got, soon lost, a man has scarce time for plunder; she betrays her husband first to her gallant, and then her gallant to her husband.

Enter PINCHWIFE, ALITHEA, HARCOURT,
SPARKISH, LUCY, *and a Parson*

PINCHWIFE. Come, madam, 'tis not the sudden change of your dress, the confidence of your asseverations, and your false witness there, shall persuade me I did not bring you hither just now; here's my witness, who cannot deny it, since you must be confronted. —— Mr. Horner, did not I bring this lady to you just now?

HORNER. (*Aside*) Now must I wrong one woman for another's sake — but that's no new thing with me, for in these cases I am still on the criminal's side against the innocent.

ALITHEA. Pray speak, sir.

HORNER (*Aside*) It must be so. I must be impudent, and try my luck; impudence uses to be too hard for truth.

PINCHWIFE. What, are you studying an evasion or excuse for her! Speak, sir.

HORNER. No, faith, I am something backward only to speak in women's affairs or disputes.

PINCHWIFE. She bids you speak.

ALITHEA. Ah, pray, sir, do, pray satisfy him.

HORNER. Then truly, you did bring that lady to me just now.

PINCHWIFE. Oh ho!

ALITHEA. How, sir?

HARCOURT. How, Horner?

ALITHEA. What mean you, sir? I always took you for a man of honor.

HORNER. (*Aside*) Ay, so much a man of honor, that I must save my mistress, I thank you, come what will on't.

SPARKISH. So, if I had had her, she'd have made me believe the moon had been made of a Christmas pie.[19]

LUCY. (*Aside*) Now could I speak, if I durst, and solve the riddle, who am the author of it.

ALITHEA. O unfortunate woman! A combination against my honor! which most concerns me now, because you share in my disgrace, sir, and it is your censure, which I must now suffer, that troubles me, not theirs.

HARCOURT. Madam, then have no trouble, you shall now see 'tis possible for me to love too, without being jealous; I will not only believe your innocence myself, but make all the world believe it. — (*Apart to* HORNER) Horner, I must now be concerned for this lady's honor.

HORNER. And I must be concerned for a lady's honor too.

[19] Usually a mince-pie.

HARCOURT. This lady has her honor, and I will protect it.

HORNER. My lady has not her honor, but has given it me to keep, and I will preserve it.

HARCOURT. I understand you not.

HORNER. I would not have you.

MRS. PINCHWIFE. (*Peeping in behind*) What's the matter with 'em all?

PINCHWIFE. Come, come, Mr. Horner, no more disputing; here's the parson, I brought him not in vain.

HARCOURT. No, sir, I'll employ him, if this lady please.

PINCHWIFE. How! what d'ye mean?

SPARKISH. Ay, what does he mean?

HORNER. Why, I have resigned your sister to him; he has my consent.

PINCHWIFE. But he has not mine, sir; a woman's injured honor, no more than a man's, can be repaired or satisfied by any but him that first wronged it; and you shall marry her presently, or ——

(*Lays his hand on his sword*)

Enter to them MRS. PINCHWIFE

MRS. PINCHWIFE. (*Aside*) O Lord, they'll kill poor Mr. Horner! Besides, he shan't marry her whilst I stand by and look on; I'll not lose my second husband so.

PINCHWIFE. What do I see?

ALITHEA. My sister in my clothes!

SPARKISH. Ha!

MRS. PINCHWIFE. (*To* MR. PINCHWIFE) Nay, pray now don't quarrel about finding work for the parson; he shall marry me to Mr. Horner; for now, I believe, you have enough of me.

HORNER. (*Aside*) Damned, damned loving changeling!

MRS. PINCHWIFE. Pray, sister, pardon me for telling so many lies of you.

HORNER. I suppose the riddle is plain now.

LUCY. No, that must be my work. —— Good sir, hear me.

(*Kneels to* MR. PINCHWIFE, *who stands doggedly with his hat over his eyes*)

PINCHWIFE. I will never hear women again, but make 'em all silent thus —— (*Offers to draw upon his wife*)

HORNER. No, that must not be.

PINCHWIFE. You then shall go first, 'tis all one to me.

(*Offers to draw on* HORNER, *stopped by* HARCOURT)

HARCOURT. Hold!

Enter SIR JASPER FIDGET, LADY FIDGET, [OLD] LADY SQUEAMISH,
MRS. DAINTY FIDGET, MRS. SQUEAMISH

SIR JASPER FIDGET. What's the matter? what's the matter? pray, what's the matter, sir? I beseech you communicate, sir.

PINCHWIFE. Why, my wife has communicated, sir, as your wife may have done too, sir, if she knows him, sir.

SIR JASPER FIDGET. Pshaw, with him! ha! ha! he!

PINCHWIFE. D'ye mock me, sir? A cuckold is a kind of a wild beast; have a care, sir.

SIR JASPER FIDGET. No, sure, you mock me, sir. He cuckold you! it can't be, ha! ha! he! why, I'll tell you, sir —— (*Offers to whisper*)

PINCHWIFE. I tell you again, he has whored my wife, and yours too, if he knows her, and all the women he comes near; 'tis not his dissembling, his hypocrisy, can wheedle me.

SIR JASPER FIDGET. How! does he dissemble? is he a hypocrite? Nay, then — how — wife — sister, is he a hypocrite?

OLD LADY SQUEAMISH. A hypocrite! a dissembler! Speak, young harlotry, speak, how?

SIR JASPER FIDGET. Nay, then — Oh my head too! — Oh thou libidinous lady!

OLD LADY SQUEAMISH. Oh thou harloting harlotry! hast thou done't then?

SIR JASPER FIDGET. Speak, good Horner, art thou a dissembler, a rogue? hast thou ——

HORNER. Soh!

LUCY. (*Apart to* HORNER) I'll fetch you off, and her too, if she will but hold her tongue.

HORNER. (*Apart to* LUCY) Can'st thou? I'll give thee ——

LUCY. (*To* MR. PINCHWIFE) Pray have but patience to hear me, sir, who am the unfortunate cause of all this confusion. Your wife is innocent, I only culpable; for I put her upon telling you all these lies concerning my mistress, in order to the breaking off the match between Mr. Sparkish and her, to make way for Mr. Harcourt.

SPARKISH. Did you so, eternal rotten tooth? Then, it seems, my mistress was not false to me, I was only deceived by you. Brother, that should have been, now man of conduct, who is a frank person now, to bring your wife to her lover, ha?

LUCY. I assure you, sir, she came not to Mr. Horner out of love, for she loves him no more ——

MRS. PINCHWIFE. Hold, I told lies for you, but you shall tell none for me, for I do love Mr. Horner with all my soul, and nobody shall say me nay; pray, don't you go to make poor Mr. Horner believe to the contrary; 'tis spitefully done of you, I'm sure.

HORNER. (*Aside to* MRS. PINCHWIFE) Peace, dear idiot.

MRS. PINCHWIFE. Nay, I will not peace.

PINCHWIFE. Not till I make you.

Enter DORILANT, QUACK

DORILANT. Horner, your servant; I am the doctor's guest, he must excuse our intrusion.

QUACK. But what's the matter, gentlemen? for Heaven's sake, what's the matter?

HORNER. Oh, 'tis well you are come. 'Tis a censorious world we live in; you may have brought me a reprieve, or else I had died for a crime I never committed, and these innocent ladies had suffered with me; therefore, pray satisfy these worthy, honorable, jealous gentlemen — that —— (*Whispers*)

QUACK. Oh, I understand you; is that all? —— Sir Jasper, by Heavens, and upon the word of a physician, sir ——

(*Whispers to* SIR JASPER)

SIR JASPER FIDGET. Nay, I do believe you truly. —— Pardon me, my virtuous lady, and dear of honor.

OLD LADY SQUEAMISH. What, then all's right again?

SIR JASPER FIDGET. Ay, ay, and now let us satisfy him too.

(*They whisper with* MR. PINCHWIFE)

PINCHWIFE. An eunuch! Pray, no fooling with me.

QUACK. I'll bring half the chirurgeons in town to swear it.

PINCHWIFE. They! — they'll swear a man that bled to death through his wounds died of an apoplexy.

QUACK. Pray, hear me, sir — why, all the town has heard the report of him.

PINCHWIFE. But does all the town believe it?

QUACK. Pray, inquire a little, and first of all these.

PINCHWIFE. I'm sure when I left the town, he was the lewdest fellow in't.

QUACK. I tell you, sir, he has been in France since; pray, ask but these ladies and gentlemen, your friend Mr. Dorilant. Gentlemen and ladies, han't you all heard the late sad report of poor Mr. Horner?

ALL THE LADIES. Ay, ay, ay.

DORILANT. Why, thou jealous fool, dost thou doubt it? he's an arrant French capon.

MRS. PINCHWIFE. 'Tis false, sir, you shall not disparage poor Mr. Horner, for to my certain knowledge ——

LUCY. Oh, hold!

MRS. SQUEAMISH. (*Aside to* LUCY) Stop her mouth!

LADY FIDGET. (*To* PINCHWIFE) Upon my honor, sir, 'tis as true ——

MRS. DAINTY FIDGET. D'ye think we would have been seen in his company?

MRS. SQUEAMISH. Trust our unspotted reputations with him?

LADY FIDGET. (*Aside to* HORNER) This you get, and we too, by trusting your secret to a fool.

HORNER. Peace, madam. — (*Aside to* QUACK) Well, doctor, is not this a good design, that carries a man on unsuspected, and brings him off safe?

PINCHWIFE. (*Aside*) Well, if this were true — but my wife ——
                              (DORILANT *whispers with* MRS. PINCHWIFE)

ALITHEA. Come, brother, your wife is yet innocent, you see; but have a care of too strong an imagination, lest, like an over-concerned timorous gamester, by fancying an unlucky cast, it should come. Women and fortune are truest still to those that trust 'em.

LUCY. And any wild thing grows but the more fierce and hungry for being kept up, and more dangerous to the keeper.

ALITHEA. There's doctrine for all husbands, Mr. Harcourt.

HARCOURT. I edify, madam, so much, that I am impatient till I am one.

DORILANT. And I edify so much by example, I will never be one.

SPARKISH. And because I will not disparage my parts, I'll ne'er be one.

HORNER. And I, alas! can't be one.

PINCHWIFE. But I must be one — against my will to a country wife, with a country murrain[20] to me!

MRS. PINCHWIFE. (*Aside*) And I must be a country wife still too, I find; for I can't, like a city one, be rid of my musty husband, and do what I list.[21]

HORNER. Now, sir, I must pronounce your wife innocent, though I blush whilst I do it; and I am the only man by her now exposed to shame, which I will straight drown in wine, as you shall your suspicion; and the ladies' troubles we'll divert with a ballet. —— Doctor, where are your maskers?

LUCY. Indeed, she's innocent, sir, I am her witness; and her end of coming out was but to see her sister's wedding; and what she has said to your face of her love to Mr. Horner was but the usual innocent revenge on a husband's jealousy — was it not, madam, speak?

MRS. PINCH. (*Aside to* LUCY *and* HORNER) Since you'll have me tell more lies —— Yes, indeed, bud.

PINCHWIFE.
For my own sake fain I would all believe;
Cuckolds, like lovers, should themselves deceive.
But —— (*Sighs*) his honor is least safe (too late I find)
Who trusts it with a foolish wife or friend.

[20] A cattle-plague; a curse.
[21] Please.

A Dance of Cuckolds

HORNER.
Vain fops but court and dress, and keep a pother,
To pass for women's men with one another;
But he who aims by woman to be prized,
First by the men, you see, must be despised.

EPILOGUE

Spoken by Mrs. Knep

Now you the vigorous, who daily here
O'er vizard-mask in public domineer,
And what you'd do to her, if in place where;
Nay, have the confidence to cry, "Come out!"
Yet when she says, "Lead on," you are not stout;
But to your well-dressed brother straight turn round,
And cry, "Pox on her, Ned, she can't be sound!"
Then slink away, a fresh one to engage,
With so much seeming heat and loving rage,
You'd frighten listening actress on the stage,
Till she at last has seen you huffing come,
And talk of keeping in the tiring-room,
Yet cannot be provoked to lead her home.
Next, you Falstaffs of fifty, who beset
Your buckram[1] maidenheads, which your friends get,
And whilst to them you of achievements boast,
They share the booty, and laugh at your cost.
In fine, you essenced boys, both old and young,
Who would be thought so eager, brisk, and strong,
Yet do the ladies, not their husbands, wrong;
Whose purses for your manhood make excuse,
And keep your Flanders mares[2] for show, not use;
Encouraged by our woman's man today,
A Horner's part may vainly think to play;
And may intrigues so bashfully disown,
That they may doubted be by few or none;
May kiss the cards at picquet, ombre, loo,
And so be thought to kiss the lady, too;
But, gallants, have a care, faith, what you do.
The world, which to no man his due will give,
You by experience know you can deceive,
And men may still believe you vigorous;
But then we women — there's no cozening[3] us.

[1] Fictitious. See *Henry IV, Part 1*, II, iv.
[2] Mistresses (fat, over-fed horses).   [3] Deceiving.

THE MAN OF MODE

or, Sr FOPLING FLUTTER

A

COMEDY

Acted at the Duke's Theatre

By GEORGE ETHEREGE, ESQ.

Licensed,
June 3,
1676.

ROGER L'ESTRANGE

LONDON:

*Printed by J. Macock, for Henry Herringman, at the
Sign of the Blew Anchor in the Lower Walk
of the New Exchange, 1676.*

THE MAN OF MODE

or, SIR FOPLING FLUTTER

Sir George Etherege

"GENTLE GEORGE" ETHEREGE (1635-1692) wrote only three plays: *The Comical Revenge* (1664), *She Would if She Could* (1668), and *The Man of Mode* (1676). As a gentleman-pensioner of the Duke of York and one of the circle of Court Wits, he knew intimately the manners of the flippant, idle people so brilliantly described in his comedies. In character he was not unlike his own rakish heroes. Eventually, capitalizing upon his reputation as a wit, he married a rich widow, bought a knighthood, and, in 1685 (partly to escape from his wife), he managed to get himself appointed Envoy to Ratisbon, in Germany. After the Revolution of 1689 he followed James II to France and ended his days in elegant exile at Paris.

Although tradition has it that many of the characters in *The Man of Mode* were drawn from life, such identifications cannot be trusted. Dorimant may have been intended to represent the witty Earl of Rochester, and his affair with Harriet may be a far-off echo of the wooing of Elizabeth Malet, a Somersetshire heiress who became Rochester's wife. On the other hand it is more likely that Dorimant was intended as an archetypical Restoration gentleman, a genteel libertine who warred against women as much to feed his ego as to satisfy his appetite, and left a trail of broken hearts and ruined reputations along his triumphal way. The identification of Medley with Sir Charles Sedley, another of the Court Wits, rests only upon the similarity of name sounds, and the linking of Sir Fopling Flutter with Sir George Hewitt breaks down completely upon a study of Hewitt's character and reputation. In short, the characters are composites, representatives of a small, homogeneous, urbane society which lived only for pleasure, valued wit and good manners above morality, distrusted passion, and rejected with laughter those who, like Sir Fopling, strove to pass as to the manner born.

The Man of Mode was first presented at the Dorset Garden Theatre in March, 1676, by a brilliant troupe of players headed by the great Thomas Betterton. His deep "grumbling" voice and impressive manner gave strength and dignity to the role of Dorimant. His wife, pretty

Mrs. Mary Betterton, played Bellinda. Mr. William Smith, a versatile actor, played Sir Fopling, and established for all time a pattern of invincible foppery. The comedian Anthony Leigh brought his roguish leers to the role of Old Bellair, and his wife, Mrs. Elinor Leigh, added many comic touches to the character of countrified Lady Woodvill. Although John Downes, prompter at the Dorset Garden Theatre, listed Mrs. Elizabeth Barry as Mrs. Loveit, it is more likely that Mrs. Barry succeeded to the role only after beautiful Mrs. Mary Lee, noted for her success in passionate roles, left the stage in 1685. Probably Mrs. Norris played Lady Townley, and witty Elizabeth Currer was the original Harriet. "This comedy," wrote Downes, "being well clothed and well acted, got a great deal of money." It was frequently revived.

See *The Works of Sir George Etherege*, ed. H.F.B. Brett-Smith, 2 vols., 1927; Bonamy Dobrée, *Restoration Comedy*, 1924; R. G. Howarth, "Untraced Quotations in Etherege," *Notes & Queries*, June 30, 1945; Arthur Sherbo, "Sir Fopling Flutter and Beau Hewitt," *Modern Language Notes*, LXIV, 1949; John Wain, "Restoration Comedy and its Modern Critics," *Essays in Criticism*, VI, October, 1956.

Dramatis Personae

MR. DORIMANT	MR. BETTERTON [1]
MR. MEDLEY	MR. HARRIS
OLD BELLAIR	MR. LEIGH
YOUNG BELLAIR	MR. JEVON
SIR FOPLING FLUTTER	MR. SMITH
LADY TOWNLEY	
EMILIA	MRS. TWIFORD
MRS. LOVEIT	MRS. BARRY
BELLINDA	MRS. BETTERTON
LADY WOODVILL and	MRS. LEIGH
HARRIET, her daughter	

BUSY
PERT } Waiting women

A Shoemaker
An Orange-woman
Three Slovenly Bullies
Two Chair-men
MR. SMIRK, a Parson
HANDY, a Valet de Chambre
Pages, Footmen, &c.

SCENE: LONDON

[1] The cast is from John Downes, *Roscius Anglicanus* (ed. Montague Summers, 1928), p. 36.

PROLOGUE

By Sir Carr Scroope, Baronet [1]

Like dancers on the ropes poor poets fare,
Most perish young, the rest in danger are;
This (one would think) should make our authors wary,
But, gamester-like, the giddy fools miscarry.
A lucky hand or two so tempts 'em on,
They cannot leave off play till they're undone.
With modest fears a muse does first begin,
Like a young wench newly enticed to sin;
But tickled once with praise, by her good will,
The wanton fool would never more lie still.
'Tis an old mistress you'll meet here tonight,
Whose charms you once have looked on with delight;
But now of late such dirty drabs have known ye,[2]
A muse o' the better sort's ashamed to own [ye].
Nature well drawn, and wit, must now give place
To gaudy nonsense and to dull grimace;
Nor is it strange that you should like so much
That kind of wit, for most of yours is such.
But I'm afraid that while to France we go,
To bring you home fine dresses, dance, and show,
The stage, like you, will but more foppish grow.
Of foreign wares, why should we fetch the scum,[3]
When we can be so richly served at home?
For, Heav'n be thanked, 'tis not so wise an age
But your own follies may supply the stage.
Though often plowed, there's no great fear the soil
Should barren grow by the too frequent toil;
While at your doors are to be daily found
Such loads of dunghill to manure the ground.
'Tis by your follies that we players thrive,
As the physicians by diseases live;
And as each year some new distemper[4] reigns,
Whose friendly poison helps t'increase their gains,
So among you there starts up every day
Some new, unheard-of fool for us to play.
Then for your own sakes be not too severe,
Nor what you all admire at home, damn here.
Since each is fond of his own ugly face,
Why should you, when we hold it, break the glass?

[1] A lesser number of the circle of Court Wits.
[2] Both theaters had recently presented wild farces and spectacular plays with music and dancing.
[3] Possibly a veiled allusion to the king's French mistress, Louise Keroualle, Duchess of Portsmouth.
[4] Disease.

ACT I

SCENE I. *A dressing-room. A table covered with a toilet; clothes laid ready*

Enter DORIMANT *in his gown and slippers, with a note in his hand, made up, repeating verses*

DORIMANT.
> Now for some ages had the pride of Spain
> Made the sun shine on half the world in vain.[1]

(*Then looking on the note*) "For Mrs. Loveit" — What a dull, insipid thing is a billet-doux written in cold blood, after the heat of the business is over! It is a tax upon good nature which I have here been laboring to pay, and have done it, but with as much regret as ever fanatic paid the Royal Aid or church duties. 'Twill have the same fate, I know, that all my notes to her have had of late; 'twill not be thought kind enough. 'Faith, women are i'the right when they jealously examine our letters, for in them we always first discover our decay of passion. — Hey! Who waits?

Enter HANDY

HANDY. Sir ——

DORIMANT. Call a footman.

HANDY. None of 'em are come yet.

DORIMANT. Dogs! Will they ever lie snoring abed till noon?

HANDY. 'Tis all one, sir; if they're up, you indulge 'em so they're ever poaching after whores all the morning.

DORIMANT. Take notice henceforward who's wanting in his duty, the next clap he gets, he shall rot for an example. — What vermin are those chattering without?

HANDY. Foggy Nan, the orange-woman, and Swearing Tom, the shoemaker.

DORIMANT. Go, call in that over-grown jade with the flasket of guts before her; fruit is refreshing in a morning.   *Exit* HANDY
                                                                                                      (*Reads*)

> It is not that I love you less.[2]
> Than when before your feet I lay —

---

[1] From Waller's "Of a War with Spain, and Fight at Sea."
[2] Waller, "The Self-Banished."

Enter ORANGE-WOMAN [*and* HANDY]

How now, double-tripe, what news do you bring?

ORANGE-WOMAN. News! Here's the best fruit has come to town t'year; gad, I was up before four o'clock this morning and bought all the choice i'the market.

DORIMANT. The nasty refuse of your shop.

ORANGE-WOMAN. You need not make mouths at it; I assure you, 'tis all culled ware.

DORIMANT. The citizens buy better on a holiday in their walk to Totnam.[3]

ORANGE-WOMAN. Good or bad, 'tis all one; I never knew you commend anything. Lord! would the ladies had heard you talk of 'em as I have done! (*Sets down the fruit*) Here, bid your man give me an angel.[4]

DORIMANT. [*To* HANDY] Give the bawd her fruit again.

ORANGE-WOMAN. Well, on my conscience, there never was the like of you! — God's my life, I had almost forgot to tell you there is a young gentlewoman lately come to town with her mother, that is so taken with you.

DORIMANT. Is she handsome?

ORANGE-WOMAN. Nay, gad, there are few finer women, I tell you but so — and a hugeous fortune, they say. — Here, eat this peach. It comes from the stone; 'tis better than any Newington y'have tasted.

DORIMANT. (*Taking the peach*) This fine woman, I'll lay my life, is some awkward, ill-fashioned country toad who, not having above four dozen of black hairs on her head, has adorned her baldness with a large, white fruz,[5] that she may look sparkishly in the forefront of the King's box at an old play.

ORANGE-WOMAN. Gad, you'd change your note quickly if you did but see her.

DORIMANT. How came she to know me?

ORANGE-WOMAN. She saw you yesterday at the *Change*.[6] She told me you came and fooled with the woman at the next shop.

DORIMANT. I remember there was a mask observed me, indeed. Fooled, did she say?

ORANGE-WOMAN. Aye; I vow she told me twenty things you said, too, and acted with her head and with her body so like you —

Enter MEDLEY

MEDLEY. Dorimant, my life, my joy, my darling sin! how dost thou?

---

[3] Tottenham, frequented by the lower middle class.
[4] A gold coin worth about 10 shillings.
[5] Frizz of curled hair.
[6] The New Exchange, a fashionable shopping center in the Strand.

ORANGE-WOMAN. Lord, what a filthy trick these men have got of kissing one another! (*She spits*)

MEDLEY. Why do you suffer this cartload of scandal to come near you and make your neighbors think you so improvident to need a bawd?

ORANGE-WOMAN. Good, now we shall have it, you did but want him to help you! — [*To* DORIMANT] Come, pay me for my fruit.

MEDLEY. Make us thankful for it, huswife, bawds are as much out of fashion as gentlemen-ushers; none but old formal ladies use the one, and none but foppish old stagers employ the other. Go, you are an insignificant brandy bottle.

DORIMANT. Nay, there you wrong her; three quarts of Canary is her business.

ORANGE-WOMAN. What you please, gentlemen.

DORIMANT. To him! give him as good as he brings.

ORANGE-WOMAN. Hang him, there is not such another heathen in the town again, except it be the shoemaker without.

MEDLEY. I shall see you hold up your hand at the bar next sessions for murder, huswife; that shoemaker can take his oath you are in fee with the doctors to sell green fruit to the gentry, that the crudities may breed diseases.

ORANGE-WOMAN. Pray give me my money.

DORIMANT. Not a penny! When you bring the gentlewoman hither you spoke of, you shall be paid.

ORANGE-WOMAN. The gentlewoman! the gentlewoman may be as honest as your sisters, for aught I know. Pray, pay me, Mr. Dorimant, and do not abuse me so; I have an honester way of living — you know it.

MEDLEY. Was there ever such a resty bawd!

DORIMANT. Some jade's tricks she has, but she makes amends when she's in good humor. [*To the* ORANGE WOMAN] Come, tell me the lady's name and Handy shall pay you.

ORANGE-WOMAN. I must not; she forbid me.

DORIMANT. That's a sure sign she would have you.

MEDLEY. Where does she live?

ORANGE-WOMAN. They lodge at my house.

MEDLEY. Nay, then she's in a hopeful way.

ORANGE-WOMAN. Good Mr. Medley, say your pleasure of me, but take heed how you affront my house! — God's my life, in a hopeful way!

DORIMANT. Prithee, peace! What kind of woman's the mother?

ORANGE-WOMAN. A goodly, grave gentlewoman. Lord, how she talks against the young men o' the town! As for your part, she thinks you an arrant devil; should she see you, on my conscience she would look if you had not a cloven foot.

DORIMANT. Does she know me?

ORANGE-WOMAN. Only by hearsay; a thousand horrid stories have been told her of you, and she believes 'em all.

MEDLEY. By the character this should be the famous Lady Woodvill and her daughter Harriet.

ORANGE-WOMAN. The devil's in him for guessing, I think.

DORIMANT. Do you know 'em?

MEDLEY. Both very well; the mother's a great admirer of the forms and civility of the last age.

DORIMANT. An antiquated beauty may be allowed to be out of humor at the freedoms of the present. This is a good account of the mother; pray, what is the daughter?

MEDLEY. Why, first, she's an heiress vastly rich.

DORIMANT. And handsome?

MEDLEY. What alteration a twelvemonth may have bred in her I know not, but a year ago she was the beautifullest creature I ever saw: a fine, easy, clean shape; light brown hair in abundance; her features regular; her complexion clear and lively; large, wanton eyes; but above all, a mouth that has made me kiss it a thousand times in imagination; teeth white and even, and pretty, pouting lips, with a little moisture ever hanging on them, that look like the Provence rose fresh on the bush, ere the morning sun has quite drawn up the dew.

DORIMANT. Rapture! mere⁷ rapture!

ORANGE-WOMAN. Nay, gad, he tells you true, she's a delicate creature.

DORIMANT. Has she wit?

MEDLEY. More than is usual in her sex, and as much malice. Then she's as wild as you would wish her, and has a demureness in her looks that makes it so surprising.

DORIMANT. Flesh and blood cannot hear this and not long to know her.

MEDLEY. I wonder what makes her mother bring her up to town; an old doting keeper cannot be more jealous of his mistress.

ORANGE-WOMAN. She made me laugh yesterday; there was a judge came to visit 'em, and the old man she told me did so stare upon her, and when he saluted her, smacked so heartily. Who would think it of 'em?

MEDLEY. God a-mercy!⁸ Judge!

DORIMANT. Do 'em right; the gentlemen of the long robe⁹ have not been wanting by their good examples to countenance the crying sin o' the nation.

MEDLEY. Come, on with your trappings; 'tis later than you imagine.

DORIMANT. Call in the shoemaker, Handy.

ORANGE-WOMAN. Good Mr. Dorimant, pay me. Gad, I had rather

---

⁷ Pure.   ⁸ "Well done!"   ⁹ Lawyers.

give you my fruit than stay to be abused by that foul-mouthed rogue; what you gentlemen say, it matters not much, but such a dirty fellow does one more disgrace.

DORIMANT. Give her ten shillings — and be sure you tell the young gentlewoman I must be acquainted with her.

ORANGE-WOMAN. Now do you long to be tempting this pretty creature? Well, heavens mend you!

MEDLEY. Farewell, bog!

[*Exeunt*] ORANGE-WOMAN *and* HANDY

Dorimant, when did you see your *pis-aller*,[10] as you call her — Mrs. Loveit?

DORIMANT. Not these two days.

MEDLEY. And how stand affairs between you?

DORIMANT. There has been great patching of late, much ado; we make a shift to hang together.

MEDLEY. I wonder how her mighty spirit bears it.

DORIMANT. Ill enough, on all conscience; I never knew so violent a creature.

MEDLEY. She's the most passionate in her love and the most extravagant in her jealousy of any woman I ever heard of. What note is that?

DORIMANT. An excuse I am going to send her for the neglect I am guilty of.

MEDLEY. Prithee, read it.

DORIMANT. No; but if you will take the pains, you may.

MEDLEY. (*Reads*) "I never was a lover of business, but now I have a just reason to hate it, since it has kept me these two days from seeing you. I intend to wait upon you in the afternoon, and in the pleasure of your conversation forget all I have suffered during this tedious absence."

This business of yours, Dorimant, has been with a vizard[11] at the playhouse; I have had an eye on you. If some malicious body should betray you, this kind note would hardly make your peace with her.

DORIMANT. I desire no better.

MEDLEY. Why, would her knowledge of it oblige you?

DORIMANT. Most infinitely; next to the coming to a good understanding with a new mistress, I love a quarrel with an old one. But the devil's in't! There has been such a calm in my affairs of late, I have not had the pleasure of making a woman so much as break her fan, to be sullen, or forswear herself, these three days.

MEDLEY. A very great misfortune. Let me see; I love mischief well enough to forward this business myself. I'll about it presently, and though I know the truth of what you've done will set her a-raving, I'll

10 Makeshift.
11 Masked woman.

heighten it a little with invention, leave her in a fit o' the mother,[12] and be here again before y'are ready.

DORIMANT. Pray stay; you may spare yourself the labor. The business is undertaken already by one who will manage it with as much address, and I think with a little more malice than you can.

MEDLEY. Who i'the devil's name can this be!

DORIMANT. Why, the vizard — that very vizard you saw me with.

MEDLEY. Does she love mischief so well as to betray herself to spite another?

DORIMANT. Not so neither, Medley. I will make you comprehend the mystery. This mask, for a farther confirmation of what I have been these two days swearing to her, made me yesterday at the playhouse make her a promise before her face utterly to break off with Loveit, and, because she tenders my reputation and would not have me do a barbarous thing, has contrived a way to give me a handsome occasion.

MEDLEY. Very good.

DORIMANT. She intends about an hour before me, this afternoon, to make Loveit a visit and, having the privilege by reason of a professed friendship between them, to talk of her concerns.

MEDLEY. Is she a friend?

DORIMANT. Oh, an intimate friend!

MEDLEY. Better and better; pray, proceed.

DORIMANT. She means insensibly to insinuate a discourse of me and artificially[13] to raise her jealousy to such a height that, transported with the first motions of her passion, she shall fly upon me with all the fury imaginable as soon as ever I enter. The quarrel being thus happily begun, I am to play my part, confess and justify all my roguery, swear her impertinence and ill-humor makes her intolerable, tax her with the next fop that comes into my head, and in a huff march away, slight her and leave her to be taken by whosoever thinks it worth his time to lie down before her.

MEDLEY. This vizard is a spark and has a genius that makes her worthy of yourself, Dorimant.

Enter HANDY, *the* SHOEMAKER, *and* FOOTMAN

DORIMANT. You rogue there, who sneak like a dog that has flung down a dish, if you do not mend your waiting, I'll uncase[14] you and turn you loose to the wheel of fortune. — Handy, seal this and let him run with it presently.   *Exit* FOOTMAN

MEDLEY. Since you're resolved on a quarrel, why do you send her this kind note?

DORIMANT. To keep her at home in order to the business. (*To the* SHOEMAKER) How now, you drunken sot?

[12] Hysterics.   [13] Artfully.
[14] Strip you of your livery.

SHOEMAKER. 'Zbud, you have no reason to talk; I have not had a bottle of sack of yours in my belly this fortnight.

MEDLEY. The orange-woman says your neighbors take notice what a heathen you are, and design to inform a bishop and have you burned for an atheist.

SHOEMAKER. Damn her, dunghill, if her husband does not remove her, she stinks so, the parish intends to indict him for a nuisance.

MEDLEY. I advise you like a friend — reform your life. You have brought the envy of the world upon you by living above yourself. Whoring and swearing are vices too genteel for a shoemaker.

SHOEMAKER. 'Zbud, I think you men of quality will grow as unreasonable as the women. You would ingross[15] the sins of the nation; poor folks can no sooner be wicked but they're railed at by their betters.

DORIMANT. Sirrah, I'll have you stand i'the pillory for this libel.

SHOEMAKER. Some of you deserve it, I'm sure; there are so many of 'em, that our journeymen nowadays, instead of harmless ballads, sing nothing but your damned lampoons.

DORIMANT. Our lampoons, you rogue?

SHOEMAKER. Nay, good master, why should not you write your own commentaries as well as Caesar?

MEDLEY. The rascal's read, I perceive.

SHOEMAKER. You know the old proverb — ale and history.[16]

DORIMANT. Draw on my shoes, sirrah.

SHOEMAKER. [*Does so*] Here's a shoe!

DORIMANT. — sits with more wrinkles than there are in an angry bully's forehead!

SHOEMAKER. 'Zbud, as smooth as your mistress's skin does upon her! So; strike your foot in home. 'Zbud, if e'er a monsieur of 'em all make more fashionable ware, I'll be content to have my ears whipped off with my own paring knife.

MEDLEY. And served up in a ragout instead of coxcombs to a company of French shoemakers for a collation.

SHOEMAKER. Hold, hold! Damn em, caterpillars, let 'em feed upon cabbage. Come master, your health this morning! next my heart now.

DORIMANT. Go, get you home and govern your family better! Do not let your wife follow you to the alehouse, beat your whore, and lead you home in triumph.

SHOEMAKER. 'Zbud, there's never a man i'the town lives more like a gentleman with his wife than I do. I never mind her motions, she never inquires into mine; we speak to one another civilly, hate one

---

[15] Monopolize.

[16] This may be a reference to a line in Bishop Corbet's "Iter Boreale," "mine host was full of ale and history" (Howarth).

another heartily, and because 'tis vulgar to lie and soak together,[17] we have each of us our several settle-bed.

DORIMANT. Give him half a crown.

MEDLEY. Not without he will promise to be bloody drunk.

SHOEMAKER. "Tope's"[18] the word i'the eye of the world. For my master's honor, Robin!

DORIMANT. Do not debauch my servants, sirrah.

SHOEMAKER. I only tip him the wink; he knows an alehouse from a hovel.   *Exit* SHOEMAKER

DORIMANT. [*To* HANDY] My clothes, quickly.

MEDLEY. Where shall we dine to-day?

Enter YOUNG BELLAIR

DORIMANT. Where you will; here comes a good third man.

YOUNG BELLAIR. Your servant, gentlemen.

MEDLEY. Gentle sir, how will you answer this visit to your honorable mistress? 'Tis not her interest you should keep company with men of sense who will be talking reason.

YOUNG BELLAIR. I do not fear her pardon, do you but grant me yours for my neglect of late.

MEDLEY. Though you've made us miserable by the want of your good company, to show you I am free from all resentment, may the beautiful cause of our misfortune give you all the joys happy lovers have shared ever since the world began.

YOUNG BELLAIR. You wish me in heaven, but you believe me on my journey to hell.

MEDLEY. You have a good strong faith, and that may contribute much towards your salvation. I confess I am but of an untoward constitution, apt to have doubts and scruples, and in love they are no less distracting than in religion. Were I so near marriage, I should cry out by fits as I ride in my coach, "Cuckold, cuckold!" with no less fury than the mad fanatic does "glory!" in Bethlem.[19]

YOUNG BELLAIR. Because religion makes some run mad, must I live an atheist?

MEDLEY. Is it not great indiscretion for a man of credit, who may have money enough on his word, to go and deal with Jews, who for little sums make men enter into bonds and give judgments?

YOUNG BELLAIR. Preach no more on this text. I am determined, and there is no hope of my conversion.

DORIMANT. (*To* HANDY, *who is fiddling about him*) Leave your un-

[17] Get drunk.

[18] To tope meant to get drunk, but the implication is that the term is less vulgar than "bloody drunk."

[19] Bethlehem Hospital, where the insane were confined.

necessary fiddling; a wasp that's buzzing about a man's nose at dinner is not more troublesome than thou art.

HANDY. You love to have your clothes hang just, sir.

DORIMANT. I love to be well dressed, sir, and think it no scandal to my understanding.

HANDY. Will you use the essence or orange-flower water?

DORIMANT. I will smell as I do today, no offence to the ladies' noses.

HANDY. Your pleasure, sir.   [*Exit* HANDY]

DORIMANT. That a man's excellency should lie in neatly tying of a ribband or a cravat! How careful's nature in furnishing the world with necessary coxcombs!

YOUNG BELLAIR. That's a mighty pretty suit of yours, Dorimant.

DORIMANT. I am glad't has your approbation.

YOUNG BELLAIR. No man in town has a better fancy in his clothes than you have.

DORIMANT. You will make me have an opinion of my genius.

MEDLEY. There is a great critic, I hear, in these matters lately arrived piping hot from Paris.

YOUNG BELLAIR. Sir Fopling Flutter, you mean?

MEDLEY. The same.

YOUNG BELLAIR. He thinks himself the pattern of modern gallantry.

DORIMANT. He is indeed the pattern of modern foppery.

MEDLEY. He was yesterday at the play, with a pair of gloves up to his elbows, and a periwig more exactly curled than a lady's head newly dressed for a ball.

YOUNG BELLAIR. What a pretty lisp he has!

DORIMANT. Ho! that he affects in imitation of the people of quality of France.

MEDLEY. His head stands, for the most part, on one side, and his looks are more languishing than a lady's when she lolls at stretch in her coach or leans her head carelessly against the side of a box i'the playhouse.

DORIMANT. He is a person indeed of great acquired follies.

MEDLEY. He is like many others, beholding to his education for making him so eminent a coxcomb. Many a fool had been lost to the world had their indulgent parents wisely bestowed neither learning nor good breeding on 'em.

YOUNG BELLAIR. He has been, as the sparkish word is, "brisk upon the ladies" already. He was yesterday at my Aunt Townley's and gave Mrs. Loveit a catalogue of his good qualities under the character of a complete gentleman, who, according to Sir Fopling, ought to dress well, dance well, fence well, have a genius for love letters, an agreeable voice for a chamber, be very amorous, something discreet, but not overconstant.

MEDLEY. Pretty ingredients to make an accomplished person!

DORIMANT. I am glad he pitched upon Loveit.

YOUNG BELLAIR. How so?

DORIMANT. I wanted a fop to lay to her charge, and this is as pat as may be.

YOUNG BELLAIR. I am confident she loves no man but you.

DORIMANT. The good fortune were enough to make me vain, but that I am in my nature modest.

YOUNG BELLAIR. Hark you, Dorimant. — With your leave, Mr. Medley; 'tis only a secret concerning a fair lady.

MEDLEY. Your good breeding, sir, gives you too much trouble; you might have whispered without all this ceremony.

YOUNG BELLAIR (*To* DORIMANT) How stand your affairs with Bellinda of late?

DORIMANT. She's a little jilting baggage.

YOUNG BELLAIR. Nay, I believe her false enough, but she's ne'er the worse for your purpose; she was with you yesterday in a disguise at the play.

DORIMANT. There we fell out and resolved never to speak to one another more.

YOUNG BELLAIR. The occasion?

DORIMANT. Want of courage to meet me at the place appointed. These young women apprehend loving as much as the young men do fighting, at first; but once entered, like them too, they all turn bullies straight.

Enter HANDY *to* BELLAIR

HANDY. Sir, your man without desires to speak with you.

YOUNG BELLAIR. Gentlemen, I'll return immediately.

Exit BELLAIR

MEDLEY. A very pretty fellow this.

DORIMANT. He's handsome, well bred, and by much the most tolerable of all the young men that do not abound in wit.

MEDLEY. Ever well dressed, always complaisant, and seldom impertinent. You and he are grown very intimate, I see.

DORIMANT. It is our mutual interest to be so: it makes the women think the better of his understanding, and judge more favorably of my reputation; it makes him pass upon some for a man of very good sense, and I upon others for a very civil person.

MEDLEY. What was that whisper?

DORIMANT. A thing which he would fain have known, but I did not think it fit to tell him; it might have frighted him from his honorable intentions of marrying.

MEDLEY. Emilia, give her her due, has the best reputation of any young woman about the town who has beauty enough to provoke detraction. Her carriage is unaffected, her discourse modest — not at all censorious nor pretending, like the counterfeits of the age.

DORIMANT. She's a discreet maid, and I believe nothing can corrupt her but a husband.

MEDLEY. A husband?

DORIMANT. Yes, a husband. I have known many a woman make a difficulty of losing a maidenhead, who have afterwards made none of making a cuckold.

MEDLEY. This prudent consideration, I am apt to think, has made you confirm poor Bellair in the desperate resolution he has taken.

DORIMANT. Indeed, the little hope I found there was of her, in the state she was in, has made me by my advice contribute something towards the changing of her condition.

Enter YOUNG BELLAIR

Dear Bellair! By heavens, I thought we had lost thee; men in love are never to be reckoned on when we would form a company.

YOUNG BELLAIR. Dorimant, I am undone; my man has brought the most surprising news i'the world.

DORIMANT. Some strange misfortune has befallen your love?

YOUNG BELLAIR. My father came to town last night and lodges i'the very house where Emilia lies.

MEDLEY. Does he know it is with her you are in love?

YOUNG BELLAIR. He knows I love, but knows not whom, without some officious sot has betrayed me.

DORIMANT. Your Aunt Townley is your confidant and favors the business.

YOUNG BELLAIR. I do not apprehend any ill office from her. I have received a letter, in which I am commanded by my father to meet him at my aunt's this afternoon. He tells me farther he has made a match for me and bids me resolve to be obedient to his will or expect to be disinherited.

MEDLEY. Now's your time, Bellair. Never had lover such an opportunity of giving a generous proof of his passion.

YOUNG BELLAIR. As how, I pray?

MEDLEY. Why, hang an estate, marry Emilia out of hand, and provoke your father to do what he threatens. 'Tis but despising a coach, humbling yourself to a pair of goloshes, being out of countenance when you meet your friends, pointed at and pitied wherever you go by all the amorous fops that know you, and your fame will be immortal.

YOUNG BELLAIR. I could find it in my heart to resolve not to marry at all.

DORIMANT. Fie, fie, that would spoil a good jest and disappoint the well-natured town of an occasion of laughing at you.

YOUNG BELLAIR. The storm I have so long expected hangs o'er my head and begins to pour down upon me. I am on the rack and can have no rest till I'm satisfied in what I fear. — Where do you dine?

DORIMANT. At Long's or Locket's.[20]

MEDLEY. At Long's let it be.

YOUNG BELLAIR. I'll run and see Emilia and inform myself how matters stand. If my misfortunes are not so great as to make me unfit for company, I'll be with you.　　　　　　　　　　*Exit* BELLAIR

Enter a Footman with a letter

FOOTMAN. (*To* DORIMANT) Here's a letter, sir.

DORIMANT. The superscription's right: "For Mr. Dorimant."

MEDLEY. Let's see — the very scrawl and spelling of a true-bred whore.

DORIMANT. I know the hand; the style is admirable, I assure you.

MEDLEY. Prithee, read it.

DORIMANT. (*Reads*) "I told a you you dud not love me, if you dud, you wou'd have seen me again ere now. I have no money and am very Mallicolly. Pray send me a Guynie to see the Operies. Your Servant to Command, Molly."

MEDLEY. Pray, let the whore have a favorable answer, that she may spark it in a box and do honor to her profession.

DORIMANT. She shall, and perk up i'the face of quality. — Is the coach at the door?

HANDY. You did not bid me send for it. (HANDY *offers to go out*)

DORIMANT. Eternal blockhead! Hey, sot —

HANDY. Did you call me, sir?

DORIMANT. I hope you have no just exception to the name, sir?

HANDY. I have sense, sir.

DORIMANT. Not so much as a fly in winter. How did you come, Medley?

MEDLEY. In a chair.

FOOTMAN. You may have a hackney coach if you please, sir.

DORIMANT. I may ride the elephant if I please, sir. Call another chair and let my coach follow to Long's.　　　　　*Exeunt, singing*

Be calm, ye great parents, etc.

ACT II

SCENE I. [LADY TOWNLEY'S *house*]

Enter LADY TOWNLEY *and* EMILIA

LADY TOWNLEY. I was afraid, Emilia, all had been discovered.

EMILIA. I tremble with the apprehension still.

20 Two fashionable taverns.

LADY TOWNLEY. That my brother should take lodgings i'the very house where you lie!

EMILIA. 'Twas lucky we had timely notice to warn the people to be secret. He seems to be a mighty good-humored old man.

LADY TOWNLEY. He ever had a notable smirking way with him.

EMILIA. He calls me "rogue," tells me he can't abide me, and does so be-pat me.

LADY TOWNLEY. On my word, you are much in his favor then!

EMILIA. He has been very inquisitive, I am told, about my family, my reputation, and my fortune.

LADY TOWNLEY. I am confident he does not i'the least suspect you are the woman his son's in love with.

EMILIA. What should make him, then, inform himself so particularly of me?

LADY TOWNLEY. He was always of a very loving temper himself; it may be he has a doting fit upon him — who knows?

EMILIA. It cannot be!

Enter YOUNG BELLAIR

LADY TOWNLEY. Here comes my nephew. Where did you leave your father?

YOUNG BELLAIR. Writing a note within. Emilia, this early visit looks as if some kind jealousy would not let you rest at home.

EMILIA. The knowledge I have of my rival gives me a little cause to fear your constancy.

YOUNG BELLAIR. My constancy! I vow —

EMILIA. Do not vow. Our love is frail as is our life and full as little in our power; and are you sure you shall outlive this day?

YOUNG BELLAIR. I am not; but when we are in perfect health, 'twere an idle thing to fright ourselves with the thoughts of sudden death.

LADY TOWNLEY. Pray, what has passed between you and your father i'the garden?

YOUNG BELLAIR. He's firm in his resolution, tells me I must marry Mrs. Harriet, or swears he'll marry himself and disinherit me. When I saw I could not prevail with him to be more indulgent, I dissembled an obedience to his will, which has composed his passion and will give us time, and I hope, opportunity, to deceive him.

Enter OLD BELLAIR *with a note in his hand*

LADY TOWNLEY. Peace, here he comes!

OLD BELLAIR. Harry, take this and let your man carry it for me to Mr. Fourbe's[1] chamber — my lawyer i'the Temple.

[*Exit* YOUNG BELLAIR]

(*To* EMILIA) Neighbor, a dod, I am glad to see thee here. — Make

---

[1] From *fourbe*, a cheat.

much of her, sister; she's one of the best of your acquaintance. I like her countenance and her behavior well; she has a modesty that is not common i'this age — a dod, she has!

LADY TOWNLEY. I know her value, brother, and esteem her accordingly.

OLD BELLAIR. Advise her to wear a little more mirth in her face; a dod, she's too serious.

LADY TOWNLEY. The fault is very excusable in a young woman.

OLD BELLAIR. Nay, a dod, I like her ne'er the worse. A melancholy beauty has her charms. I love a pretty sadness in a face, which varies now and then, like changeable colors, into a smile.

LADY TOWNLEY. Methinks you speak very feelingly, brother.

OLD BELLAIR. I am but five and fifty, sister, you know, an age not altogether unsensible. — (*To* EMILIA) Cheer up, sweetheart! I have a secret to tell thee may chance to make thee merry. We three will make collation together anon; i'the meantime, mum, I can't abide you! Go, I can't abide you. —

Enter YOUNG BELLAIR

Harry, come! You must along with me to my Lady Woodvill's. — I am going to slip the boy at a mistress.

YOUNG BELLAIR. At a wife, sir, you would say.

OLD BELLAIR. You need not look so glum, sir; a wife is no curse when she brings the blessing of a good estate with her. But an idle town flirt, with a painted face, a rotten reputation, and a crazy fortune, a dod! is the devil and all, and such a one I hear you are in league with.

YOUNG BELLAIR. I cannot help detraction, sir.

OLD BELLAIR. Out! 'A pize[2] o' their breeches, there are keeping-fools enough for such flaunting baggages, and they are e'en too good for 'em (*To* EMILIA) Remember 'night — Go; you're a rogue, you're a rogue! — Fare you well, fare you well! — Come, come, come along, sir! *Exeunt* OLD *and* YOUNG BELLAIR

LADY TOWNLEY. On my word, the old man comes on apace. I'll lay my life he's smitten.

EMILIA. This is nothing but the pleasantness of his humor.

LADY TOWNLEY. I know him better than you. Let it work; it may prove lucky.

Enter a Page

PAGE. Madam, Mr. Medley has sent to know whether a visit will not be troublesome this afternoon.

LADY TOWNLEY. Send him word his visits never are so. [*Exit Page*]

EMILIA. He's a very pleasant man.

LADY TOWNLEY. He's a very necessary man among us women; he's

2 Pox (?).

not scandalous i'the least, perpetually contriving to bring good company together, and always ready to stop up a gap at ombre.[3] Then, he knows all the little news o'the town.

EMILIA. I love to hear him talk o'the intrigues. Let 'em be never so dull in themselves, he'll make 'em pleasant i'the relation.

LADY TOWNLEY. But he improves things so much one can take no measure of the truth from him. Mr. Dorimant swears a flea or a maggot is not made more monstrous by a magnifying glass than a story is by his telling it.

Enter MEDLEY

EMILIA. Hold, here he comes.

LADY TOWNLEY. Mr. Medley.

MEDLEY. Your servant, madam.

LADY TOWNLEY. You have made yourself a stranger of late.

EMILIA. I believe you took a surfeit of ombre last time you were here.

MEDLEY. Indeed, I had my belly full of that termagant, Lady Dealer. There never was so insatiable a carder,[4] an old gleeker[5] never loved to sit to't like her. I have played with her now at least a dozen times till she's worn out all her fine complexion and her tower[6] would keep in curl no longer.

LADY TOWNLEY. Blame her not, poor woman, she loves nothing so well as a black ace.[7]

MEDLEY. The pleasure I have seen her in when she has had hope in drawing for a matadore.

EMILIA. 'Tis as pretty sport to her as persuading masks off is to you, to make discoveries.

LADY TOWNLEY. Pray, where's your friend Mr. Dorimant?

MEDLEY. Soliciting his affairs; he's a man of great employment — has more mistresses now depending than the most eminent lawyer in England has causes.

EMILIA. Here has been Mrs. Loveit so uneasy and out of humor these two days.

LADY TOWNLEY. How strangely love and jealousy rage in that poor woman!

MEDLEY. She could not have picked out a devil upon earth so proper to torment her; h'as made her break a dozen or two fans already, tear half a score points in pieces, and destroy hoods and knots without number.

---

[3] A card game.
[4] Card-player.
[5] Player of gleek, a card game.
[6] A front of false hair.
[7] A high trump, one of three "matadores" in ombre.

LADY TOWNLEY. We heard of a pleasant serenade he gave her t'other night.

MEDLEY. A Danish serenade with kettledrums and trumpets.

EMILIA. Oh, barbarous!

MEDLEY. What! You are of the number of the ladies whose ears are grown so delicate since our operas you can be charmed with nothing but *flûtes douces* and French hautboys.[8]

EMILIA. Leave your raillery, and tell us is there any new wit come forth — songs or novels?

MEDLEY. A very pretty piece of gallantry, by an eminent author, called *The Diversions of Brussels*,[9] very necessary to be read by all old ladies who are desirous to improve themselves at questions and commands, blindman's buff, and the like fashionable recreations.

EMILIA. Oh, ridiculous!

MEDLEY. Then there is *The Art of Affectation*, written by a late beauty of quality, teaching you how to draw up your breasts, stretch out your neck, to thrust out your breech, to play with your head, to toss up your nose, to bite your lips, to turn up your eyes, to speak in a silly, soft tone of a voice, and use all the foolish French words that will infallibly make your person and conversation charming, with a short apology at the latter end in the behalf of young ladies who notoriously wash and paint though they have naturally good complexions.

EMILIA. What a deal of stuff you tell us!

MEDLEY. Such as the town affords, madam. The Russians, hearing the great respect we have for foreign dancing, have lately sent over some of their best balladines,[10] who are now practising a famous ballet which will be suddenly danced at the Bear Garden.[11]

LADY TOWNLEY. Pray forbear your idle stories, and give us an account of the state of love as it now stands.

MEDLEY. Truly, there have been some revolutions in those affairs — great chopping and changing among the old, and some new lovers whom malice, indiscretion, and misfortune have luckily brought into play.

LADY TOWNLEY. What think you of walking into the next room and sitting down before you engage in this business?

MEDLEY. I wait upon you, and I hope (though women are commonly unreasonable) by the plenty of scandal I shall discover, to give you very good content, ladies.   *Exeunt*

[8] Oboes.

[9] Medley's books are imaginary.

[10] Ballet dancers.

[11] Where ordinarily bears were baited!

SCENE II. [MISTRESS LOVEIT's *lodgings*]

Enter MRS. LOVEIT *and* PERT, MRS. LOVEIT *putting up a letter, then pulling out a pocket-glass and looking in it*

MRS. LOVEIT. Pert.

PERT. Madam?

MRS. LOVEIT. I hate myself, I look so ill to-day.

PERT. Hate the wicked cause on't, that base man Mr. Dorimant, who makes you torment and vex yourself continually.

MRS. LOVEIT. He is to blame, indeed.

PERT. To blame to be two days without sending, writing, or coming near you, contrary to his oath and covenant! 'Twas to much purpose to make him swear! I'll lay my life there's not an article but he has broken — talked to the vizards i'the pit, waited upon the ladies from the boxes to their coaches, gone behind the scenes, and fawned upon those little insignificant creatures, the players. 'Tis impossible for a man of his inconstant temper to forbear, I'm sure.

MRS. LOVEIT. I know he is a devil, but he has something of the angel yet undefaced in him, which makes him so charming and agreeable that I must love him, be he never so wicked.

PERT. I little thought, madam, to see your spirit tamed to this degree, who banished poor Mr. Lackwit but for taking up another lady's fan in your presence.

MRS. LOVEIT. My knowing of such odious fools contributes to the making of me love Dorimant the better.

PERT. Your knowing of Mr. Dorimant, in my mind, should rather make you hate all mankind.

MRS. LOVEIT. So it does — besides himself.

PERT. Pray, what excuse does he make in his letter?

MRS. LOVEIT. He has had business.

PERT. Business in general terms would not have been a current excuse for another. A modish man is always very busy when he is in pursuit of a new mistress.

MRS. LOVEIT. Some fop has bribed you to rail at him. He had business, I will believe it, and will forgive him.

PERT. You may forgive him anything, but I shall never forgive him his turning me into ridicule, as I hear he does.

MRS. LOVEIT. I perceive you are of the number of those fools his wit had made his enemies.

PERT. I am of the number of those he's pleased to rally, madam, and if we may believe Mr. Wagfan and Mr. Caperwell, he sometimes makes merry with yourself, too, among his laughing companions.

MRS. LOVEIT. Blockheads are as malicious to witty men as ugly women are to the handsome; 'tis their interest, and they make it their business to defame 'em.

PERT. I wish Mr. Dorimant would not make it his business to defame you.

MRS. LOVEIT. Should he, I had rather be made infamous by him than owe my reputation to the dull discretion of those fops you talk of.

Enter BELLINDA

— Bellinda! (*Running to her*)

BELLINDA. My dear!

MRS. LOVEIT. You have been unkind of late.

BELLINDA. Do not say unkind, say unhappy.

MRS. LOVEIT. I could chide you. Where have you been these two days?

BELLINDA. Pity me rather, my dear, where I have been so tired with two or three country gentlewomen, whose conversation has been more unsufferable than a country fiddle.

MRS. LOVEIT. Are they relations?

BELLINDA. No; Welsh acquaintance I made when I was last year at St. Winifred's. They have asked me a thousand questions of the modes and intrigues of the town, and I have told 'em almost as many things for news that hardly were so when their gowns were in fashion.

MRS. LOVEIT. Provoking creatures! How could you endure 'em?

BELLINDA. (*Aside*) Now to carry on my plot. Nothing but love could make me capable of so much falsehood. 'Tis time to begin, lest Dorimant should come before her jealousy has stung her. (*Laughs, and then speaks on*) I was yesterday at a play with 'em, where I was fain to show 'em the living, as the man at Westminster does the dead: "That is Mrs. Such-a-one, admired for her beauty; that is Mr. Such-a-one, cried up for a wit; that is sparkish Mr. Such-a-one, who keeps reverend Mrs. Such-a-one, and there sits fine Mrs. Such-a-one who was lately cast off by my Lord Such-a-one."

MRS. LOVEIT. Did you see Dorimant there?

BELLINDA. I did, and imagine you were with him and have no mind to own it.

MRS. LOVEIT. What should make you think so?

BELLINDA. A lady masked in a pretty *déshabillé*, whom Dorimant entertained with more respect than the gallants do a common vizard.

MRS. LOVEIT. (*Aside*) Dorimant at the play entertaining a mask! Oh, heavens!

BELLINDA. (*Aside*) Good!

MRS. LOVEIT. Did he stay all the while?

BELLINDA. 'Till the play was done and then led her out, which confirms me it was you.

MRS. LOVEIT. Traitor!

PERT. Now you may believe he had business, and you may forgive him, too.

MRS. LOVEIT. Ingrateful, perjured man!

BELLINDA. You seem so much concerned, my dear, I fear I have told you unawares what I had better have concealed for your quiet.

MRS. LOVEIT. What manner of shape had she?

BELLINDA. Tall and slender. Her motions were very genteel; certainly she must be some person of condition.

MRS. LOVEIT. Shame and confusion be ever in her face when she shows it!

BELLINDA. I should blame your discretion for loving that wild man, my dear, but they say he has a way so bewitching that few can defend their hearts who know him.

MRS. LOVEIT. I will tear him from mine or die i'the attempt.

BELLINDA. Be more moderate.

MRS. LOVEIT. Would I had daggers, darts, or poisoned arrows in my breast, so I could but remove the thoughts of him from thence!

BELLINDA. Fie, fie! your transports are too violent, my dear; this may be but an accidental gallantry, and 'tis likely ended at her coach.

PERT. Should it proceed farther, let your comfort be, the conduct Mr. Dorimant affects will quickly make you know your rival, ten to one let you see her ruined, her reputation exposed to the town — a happiness none will envy her but yourself, madam.

MRS. LOVEIT. Whoe'er she be, all the harm I wish her is, may she love him as well as I do and may he give her as much cause to hate him.

PERT. Never doubt the latter end of your curse, madam.

MRS. LOVEIT. May all the passions that are raised by neglected love — jealousy, indignation, spite, and thirst of revenge — eternally rage in her soul as they do now in mine. (*Walks up and down with a distracted air*)

Enter a Page

PAGE. Madam, Mr. Dorimant —

MRS. LOVEIT. I will not see him.

PAGE. I told him you were within, madam.

MRS. LOVEIT. Say you lied — say I'm busy; shut the door — say anything!

PAGE. He's here, madam.

Enter DORIMANT

DORIMANT.
> They taste of death who do at heaven arrive,[12]
> But we this paradise approach alive.

[12] From Waller's "Of Her Chamber."

(*To* MRS. LOVEIT) What, dancing The Galloping Nag[13] without a fiddle? (*Offers to catch her by the hand. She flings away and walks on,* [*he*] *pursuing her*) I fear this restlessness of the body, madam, proceeds from an unquietness of the mind. What unlucky accident puts you out of humor? A point ill washed, knots spoiled i'the making up, hair shaded awry, or some other little mistake in setting you in order?

PERT. A trifle, in my opinion, sir, more inconsiderable than any you mention.

DORIMANT. O Mrs. Pert! I never knew you sullen enough to be silent; come, let me know the business.

PERT. The business, sir, is the business that has taken you up these two days. How have I seen you laugh at men of business, and now to become a man of business yourself!

DORIMANT. We are not masters of our own affections; our inclinations daily alter. Now we love pleasure, and anon we shall dote on business. Human frailty will have it so, and who can help it?

MRS. LOVEIT. Faithless, inhuman, barbarous man —

DORIMANT. Good! Now the alarm strikes. —

MRS. LOVEIT. — without sense of love, of honor, or of gratitude, tell me, for I will know, what devil masked she was you were with at the play yesterday?

DORIMANT. Faith, I resolved as much as you, but the devil was obstinate and would not tell me.

MRS. LOVEIT. False in this as in your vows to me! You do know.

DORIMANT. The truth is, I did all I could to know.

MRS. LOVEIT. And dare you own it to my face? Hell and furies! (*Tears her fan in pieces*)

DORIMANT. Spare your fan, madam; you are growing hot and will want it to cool you.

MRS. LOVEIT. Horror and distraction seize you! Sorrow and remorse gnaw your soul, and punish all your perjuries to me — (*Weeps*)

DORIMANT.

> So thunder breaks the cloud in twain
> And makes a passage for the rain.[14]

(*Turning to* BELLINDA) Bellinda, you are the devil that have raised this storm; you were at the play yesterday and have been making discoveries to your dear.

BELLINDA. You're the most mistaken man i' the world.

DORIMANT. It must be so, and here I vow revenge; resolve to pursue and persecute you more impertinently than ever any loving fop did his

[13] A country dance.
[14] See "An Elegie . . . for Apostrophel," attributed to Matthew Roydon, in *The Phoenix Nest* (1593), ed. Hyder Rollins, 1931.

mistress, hunt you i'the park, trace you i'the Mall,[15] dog you in every visit you make, haunt you at the plays and i'the drawing-room, hang my nose in your neck and talk to you whether you will or no, and ever look upon you with such dying eyes till your friends grow jealous of me, send you out of town, and the world suspect your reputation. (*In a lower voice*) — At my Lady Townley's when we go from hence. (*He looks kindly on* BELLINDA)

BELLINDA. I'll meet you there.

DORIMANT. Enough.

MRS. LOVEIT. Stand off! (*Pushing* DORIMANT *away*) You sha' not stare upon her so.

DORIMANT. Good; there's one made jealous already.

MRS. LOVEIT. Is this the constancy you vowed?

DORIMANT. Constancy at my years? 'Tis not a virtue in season; you might as well expect the fruit the autumn ripens i'the spring.

MRS. LOVEIT. Monstrous principle!

DORIMANT. Youth has a long journey to go, madam; should I have set up my rest at the first inn I lodged at, I should never have arrived at the happiness I now enjoy.

MRS. LOVEIT. Dissembler, damned dissembler!

DORIMANT. I am so, I confess. Good nature and good manners corrupt me. I am honest in my inclinations, and would not, wer't not to avoid offence, make a lady a little in years believe I think her young — willfully mistake art for nature — and seem as fond of a thing I am weary of as when I doted on't in earnest.

MRS. LOVEIT. False man!

DORIMANT. True woman!

MRS. LOVEIT. Now you begin to show yourself.

DORIMANT. Love gilds us over and makes us show fine things to one another for a time, but soon the gold wears off and then again the native brass appears.

MRS. LOVEIT. Think on your oaths, your vows, and protestations, perjured man!

DORIMANT. I made 'em when I was in love.

MRS. LOVEIT. And therefore ought they not to bind? Oh, impious!

DORIMANT. What we swear at such a time may be a certain proof of a present passion, but to say truth, in love there is no security to be given for the future.

MRS. LOVEIT. Horrid and ingrateful! Begone, and never see me more!

DORIMANT. I am not one of those troublesome coxcombs who, because they were once well received, take the privilege to plague a woman with their love ever after. I shall obey you, madam, though I

---

[15] A walk in St. James's Park.

do myself some violence. (*He offers to go and* MRS. LOVEIT *pulls him back*)

MRS. LOVEIT. Come back! You sha' not go! Could you have the ill-nature to offer it?

DORIMANT. When love grows diseased, the best thing we can do is to put it to a violent death. I cannot endure the torture of a ling'ring and consumptive passion.

MRS. LOVEIT. Can you think mine sickly?

DORIMANT. Oh, 'tis desperately ill. What worse symptoms are there than your being always uneasy when I visit you, your picking quarrels with me on slight occasions, and in my absence kindly listening to the impertinences of every fashionable fool that talks to you?

MRS. LOVEIT. What fashionable fool can you lay to my charge?

DORIMANT. Why, the very cock-fool of all those fools — Sir Fopling Flutter.

MRS. LOVEIT. I never saw him in my life but once.

DORIMANT. The worse woman you, at first sight to put on all your charms, to entertain him with that softness in your voice, and all that wanton kindness in your eyes you so notoriously affect when you design a conquest.

MRS. LOVEIT. So damned a lie did never malice yet invent. Who told you this?

DORIMANT. No matter. That ever I should love a woman that can dote on a senseless caper, a tawdry French ribband, and a formal cravat!

MRS. LOVEIT. You make me mad.

DORIMANT. A guilty conscience may do much. Go on — be the game-mistress o' the town, and enter all our young fops as fast as they come from travel.

MRS. LOVEIT. Base and scurrilous!

DORIMANT. A fine mortifying reputation 'twill be for a woman of your pride, wit, and quality!

MRS. LOVEIT. This jealousy's a mere pretense, a cursed trick of your own devising. — I know you.

DORIMANT. Believe it and all the ill of me you can, I would not have a woman have the least good thought of me, that can think well of Fopling. Farewell! Fall to, and much good may do you with your coxcomb.

MRS. LOVEIT. Stay! Oh stay! and I will tell you all!

DORIMANT. I have been told too much already.   *Exit* DORIMANT

MRS. LOVEIT. Call him again!

PERT. E'en let him go — a fair riddance.

MRS. LOVEIT. Run, I say! Call him again! I will have him called!

PERT. The devil should call him away first, were it my concern.

Exit PERT

BELLINDA. He's frighted me from the very thoughts of loving men. For heaven's sake, my dear, do not discover what I told you! I dread his tongue as much as you ought to have done his friendship.

Enter PERT

PERT. He's gone, madam.

MRS. LOVEIT. Lightning blast him!

PERT. When I told him you desired him to come back, he smiled, made a mouth at me, flung into his coach, and said —

MRS. LOVEIT. What did he say?

PERT. "Drive away!" and then repeated verses.

MRS. LOVEIT. Would I had made a contract to be a witch when first I entertained this greater devil — monster — barbarian! I could tear myself in pieces. Revenge — nothing but revenge can ease me! Plague, war, famine, fire — all that can bring universal ruin and misery on mankind, with joy I'd perish to have you in my power but this moment! *Exit* MRS. LOVEIT

PERT. Follow, madam; leave her not in this outrageous passion! (PERT *gathers up the things*)

BELLINDA. He's given me the proof which I desired of his love, but 'tis a proof of his ill-nature too. I wish I had not seen him use her so.

> I sigh to think that Dorimant may be
> One day as faithless and unkind to me.

Exeunt

ACT III

SCENE I. LADY WOODVILL's *lodgings*

Enter HARRIET *and* BUSY, *her woman*

BUSY. Dear madam, let me set that curl in order.

HARRIET. Let me alone; I will shake 'em all out of order.

BUSY. Will you never leave this wildness?

HARRIET. Torment me not.

BUSY. Look! there's a knot falling off.

HARRIET. Let it drop.

BUSY. But one pin, dear madam.

HARRIET. How do I daily suffer under thy officious fingers!

BUSY. Ah, the difference that is between you and my Lady Dapper! How uneasy she is if the least thing be amiss about her.

HARRIET. She is indeed most exact; nothing is ever wanting to make her ugliness remarkable.

BUSY. Jeering people say so.

HARRIET. Her powdering, painting, and her patching never fail in public to draw the tongues and eyes of all the men upon her.

BUSY. She is, indeed, a little too pretending.

HARRIET. That women should set up for beauty as much in spite of nature as some men have done for wit!

BUSY. I hope without offence one may endeavor to make one's self agreeable.

HARRIET. Not when 'tis impossible. Women then ought to be no more fond of dressing than fools should be of talking; hoods and modesty, masks and silence — things that shadow and conceal — they should think of nothing else.

BUSY. Jesu! Madam, what will your mother think is become of you? For heaven's sake go in again!

HARRIET. I won't.

BUSY. This is the extravagant'st thing that ever you did in your life, to leave her and a gentleman who is to be your husband.

HARRIET. My husband! Hast thou so little wit to think I spoke what I meant when I overjoyed her in the country with a low curtsey and "What you please, madam; I shall ever be obedient"?

BUSY. Nay, I know not, you have so many fetches.[1]

HARRIET. And this was one to get her up to London — nothing else, I assure thee.

BUSY. Well, the man, in my mind, is a fine man.

HARRIET. The man indeed wears his clothes fashionably and has a pretty, negligent way with him, very courtly and much affected; he bows, and talks, and smiles so agreeably, as he thinks.

BUSY. I never saw anything so genteel.

HARRIET. Varnished over with good breeding, many a blockhead makes a tolerable show.

BUSY. I wonder you do not like him.

HARRIET. I think I might be brought to endure him, and that is all a reasonable woman should expect in a husband; but there is duty i'the case, and like the haughty Merab[2] I

> Find much aversion in my stubborn mind,

which

> Is bred by being promised and designed.

BUSY. I wish you do not design your own ruin! I partly guess your inclinations, madam — that Mr. Dorimant —

HARRIET. Leave your prating, and sing some foolish song or other.

BUSY. I will; the song you love so well ever since you saw Mr. Dorimant. [*Sings*]

[1] Tricks.

[2] See I Samuel xiv:49; xviii, 17-19. The verses are paraphrased from Cowley's *Davideis*, Bk. III, lines 705-6.

SONG

When first Amintas charmed my heart,
My heedless sheep began to stray;
The wolves soon stole the greatest part,
And all will now be made a prey.

Ah, let not love your thoughts possess,
'Tis fatal to a shepherdess;
The dang'rous passion you must shun,
Or else like me be quite undone.

HARRIET. Shall I be paid down by a covetous parent for a purchase? I need no land; no, I'll lay myself out all in love. It is decreed —

Enter YOUNG BELLAIR

YOUNG BELLAIR. What generous resolution are you making, madam?

HARRIET. Only to be disobedient, sir.

YOUNG BELLAIR. Let me join hands with you in that —

HARRIET. With all my heart. I never thought I should have given you mine so willingly. Here I, Harriet —

YOUNG BELLAIR. And I, Harry —

HARRIET. Do solemnly protest —

YOUNG BELLAIR. And vow —

HARRIET. That I with you —

YOUNG BELLAIR. And I with you —

BOTH. Will never marry.

HARRIET. A match!

YOUNG BELLAIR. And no match! How do you like this indifference now?

HARRIET. You expect I should take it ill, I see.

YOUNG BELLAIR. 'Tis not unnatural for you women to be a little angry; you miss a conquest, though you would slight the poor man were he in your power.

HARRIET. There are some, it may be, have an eye like Bart'lomew[3] — big enough for the whole fair; but I am not of the number, and you may keep your gingerbread. 'Twill be more acceptable to the lady whose dear image it wears, sir.

YOUNG BELLAIR. But I confess, madam, you came a day after the fair.

HARRIET. You own, then, you are in love?

YOUNG BELLAIR. I do.

HARRIET. The confidence is generous, and in return I could almost find in my heart to let you know my inclinations.

YOUNG BELLAIR. Are you in love?

[3] At Bartholomew Fair, held annually in Smithfield, gingerbread was a popular dainty.

HARRIET. Yes, with this dear town, to that degree I can scarce endure the country in landscapes and hangings.

YOUNG BELLAIR. What a dreadful thing 'twould be to be hurried back to Hampshire!

HARRIET. Ah, name it not!

YOUNG BELLAIR. As for us, I find we shall agree well enough. Would we could do something to deceive the grave people!

HARRIET. Could we delay their quick proceeding, 'twere well. A reprieve is a good step towards the getting of a pardon.

YOUNG BELLAIR. If we give over the game, we are undone. What think you of playing it on booty? [4]

HARRIET. What do you mean?

YOUNG BELLAIR. Pretend to be in love with one another! 'twill make some dilatory excuses we may feign, pass the better.

HARRIET. Let us do't, if it be but for the dear pleasure of dissembling.

YOUNG BELLAIR. Can you play your part?

HARRIET. I know not what it is to love, but I have made pretty remarks by being now and then where lovers meet. Where did you leave their gravities?

YOUNG BELLAIR. I'th' next room! Your mother was censuring our modern gallant.

Enter OLD BELLAIR *and* LADY WOODVILL

HARRIET. Peace! Here they come; I will lean against this wall and look bashfully down upon my fan, while you, like an amorous spark, modishly entertain me.

LADY WOODVILL (*To* OLD BELLAIR) Never go about to excuse 'em; come, come, it was not so when I was a young woman.

OLD BELLAIR. A dod, they're something disrespectful —

LADY WOODVILL. Quality was then considered and not rallied by every fleering fellow.

OLD BELLAIR. Youth will have its jest — a dod, it will.

LADY WOODVILL. 'Tis good breeding now to be civil to none but players and Exchange women;[5] they are treated by 'em as much above their condition as others are below theirs.

OLD BELLAIR. Out! A pize on 'em; talk no more! The rogues ha' got an ill habit of preferring beauty no matter where they find it.

LADY WOODVILL. See your son and my daughter; they have improved their acquaintance since they were within.

OLD BELLAIR. A dod, methinks they have! Let's keep back and observe.

[4] Dishonest collusion.

[5] Shopkeepers in the New Exchange, considered to be ladies of easy virtue.

YOUNG BELLAIR. [*To* HARRIET] Now for a look and gestures that may persuade 'em I am saying all the passionate things imaginable —

HARRIET. Your head a little more on one side. Ease yourself on your left leg and play with your right hand.

YOUNG BELLAIR. Thus, is it not?

HARRIET. Now set your right leg firm on the ground, adjust your belt, then look about you.

YOUNG BELLAIR. A little exercising will make me perfect.

HARRIET. Smile, and turn to me again very sparkish.

YOUNG BELLAIR. Will you take your turn and be instructed?

HARRIET. With all my heart!

YOUNG BELLAIR. At one motion play your fan, roll your eyes, and then settle a kind look upon me.

HARRIET. So.

YOUNG BELLAIR. Now spread your fan, look down upon it, and tell the sticks with a finger!

HARRIET. Very modish!

YOUNG BELLAIR. Clap your hand up to your bosom, hold down your gown, shrug a little, draw up your breasts, and let 'em fall again gently, with a sigh or two, etc.

HARRIET. By the good instructions you give, I suspect you for one of those malicious observers who watch people's eyes, and from innocent looks make scandalous conclusions.

YOUNG BELLAIR. I know some, indeed, who out of mere love to mischief are as vigilant as jealousy itself, and will give you an account of every glance that passes at a play and i'th' Circle.[6]

HARRIET. 'Twill not be amiss now to seem a little pleasant.

YOUNG BELLAIR. Clap your fan, then, in both your hands, snatch it to your mouth, smile, and with a lively motion fling your body a little forwards. So — now spread it; fall back on the sudden, cover your face with it and break out into loud laughter. Take up! look grave and fall a-fanning of yourself. — Admirably well acted!

HARRIET. I think I am pretty apt at these matters.

OLD BELLAIR. [*To* LADY WOODVILL] A dod, I like this well!

LADY WOODVILL. This promises something.

OLD BELLAIR. Come! there is love i'th' case — a dod there is, or will be. [*To* HARRIET] What say you, young lady?

YOUNG BELLAIR. All in good time, sir; you expect we should fall to and love as gamecocks fight, as soon as we are set together? A dod, y'are unreasonable!

OLD BELLAIR. A dod, sirrah, I like thy wit well.

Enter a Servant

SERVANT. The coach is at the door, madam.

[6] I.e., in Hyde Park.

OLD BELLAIR. Go, get you and take the air together.

LADY WOODVILL. Will not you go with us?

OLD BELLAIR. Out, a pize! A dod, I ha' business and cannot. We shall meet at night at my sister Townley's.

YOUNG BELLAIR. (*Aside*) He's going to Emilia. I overheard him talk of a collation.   *Exeunt*

SCENE II. [LADY TOWNLEY'S *drawing-room*]

Enter LADY TOWNLEY, EMILIA, *and* MR. MEDLEY

LADY TOWNLEY. I pity the young lovers we last talked of, though to say truth their conduct has been so indiscreet they deserve to be unfortunate.

MEDLEY. You've had an exact account, from the great lady i'th' box down to the little orange wench.

EMILIA. You're a living libel, a breathing lampoon. I wonder you are not torn in pieces.

MEDLEY. What think you of setting up an office of intelligence for these matters? The project may get money.

LADY TOWNLEY. You would have great dealings with country ladies.

MEDLEY. More than Muddiman[7] has with their husbands.

Enter BELLINDA

LADY TOWNLEY. Bellinda, what has been become of you? We have not seen you here of late with your friend Mrs. Loveit.

BELLINDA. Dear creature, I left her but now so sadly afflicted!

LADY TOWNLEY. With her old distemper, jealousy?

MEDLEY. Dorimant has played her some new prank.

BELLINDA. Well, that Dorimant is certainly the worst man breathing.

EMILIA. I once thought so.

BELLINDA. And do you not think so still?

EMILIA. No, indeed!

BELLINDA. Oh, Jesu!

EMILIA. The town does him a great injury, and I will never believe what it says of a man I do not know, again, for his sake.

BELLINDA. You make me wonder.

LADY TOWNLEY. He's a very well-bred man.

BELLINDA. But strangely ill-natured.

EMILIA. Then, he's a very witty man.

BELLINDA. But a man of no principles.

MEDLEY. Your man of principles is a very fine thing, indeed.

[7] Henry Muddiman (1629-92), a commercial writer of "news-letters."

BELLINDA. To be preferred to men of parts by women who have regard to their reputation and quiet. Well, were I minded to play the fool, he should be the last man I'd think of.

MEDLEY. He has been the first in many ladies' favors, though you are so severe, madam.

LADY TOWNLEY. What he may be for a lover, I know not; but he's a very pleasant acquaintance, I am sure.

BELLINDA. Had you seen him use Mrs. Loveit as I have done, you would never endure him more —

EMILIA. What, he has quarreled with her again?

BELLINDA. Upon the slightest occasion; he's jealous of Sir Fopling.

LADY TOWNLEY. She never saw him in her life but yesterday, and that was here.

EMILIA. On my conscience, he's the only man in town that's her aversion. How horribly out of humor she was all the time he talked to her!

BELLINDA. And somebody has wickedly told him —

EMILIA. Here he comes.

Enter DORIMANT

MEDLEY. Dorimant! you are luckily come to justify yourself. — Here's a lady —

BELLINDA. Has a word or two to say to you from a disconsolate person.

DORIMANT. You tender your reputation too much, I know, madam, to whisper with me before this good company.

BELLINDA. To serve Mrs. Loveit I'll make a bold venture.

DORIMANT. Here's Medley — the very spirit of scandal.

BELLINDA. No matter!

EMILIA. 'Tis something you are unwilling to hear, Mr. Dorimant.

LADY TOWNLEY. Tell him, Bellinda, whether he will or no.

BELLINDA. (*Aloud*) Mrs. Loveit —

DORIMANT. Softly! these are laughers; you do not know 'em.

BELLINDA. (*To* DORIMANT *apart*) In a word, you've made me hate you, which I thought you never could have done.

DORIMANT. In obeying your commands.

BELLINDA. 'Twas a cruel part you played. How could you act it?

DORIMANT. Nothing is cruel to a man who could kill himself to please you. Remember five o'clock tomorrow morning!

BELLINDA. I tremble when you name it.

DORIMANT. Be sure you come!

BELLINDA. I sha' not.

DORIMANT. Swear you will!

BELLINDA. I dare not.

DORIMANT. Swear, I say!

BELLINDA. By my life — by all the happiness I hope for —

DORIMANT. You will.

BELLINDA. I will!

DORIMANT. Kind!

BELLINDA. I am glad I've sworn. I vow, I think I should ha' failed you else!

DORIMANT. Surprisingly kind! In what temper did you leave Loveit?

BELLINDA. Her raving was prettily over, and she began to be in a brave way of defying you and all your works. Where have you been since you went from thence?

DORIMANT. I looked in at the play.

BELLINDA. I have promised, and must return to her again.

DORIMANT. Persuade her to walk in the Mall this evening.

BELLINDA. She hates the place and will not come.

DORIMANT. Do all you can to prevail with her.

BELLINDA. For what purpose?

DORIMANT. Sir Fopling will be here anon; I'll prepare him to set upon her there before me.

BELLINDA. You persecute her too much, but I'll do all you'll ha' me.

DORIMANT. (*Aloud*) Tell her plainly 'tis grown too dull a business; I can drudge no longer.

EMILIA. There are afflictions in love, Mr. Dorimant.

DORIMANT. You women make 'em, who are commonly as unreasonable in that as you are at play. Without the advantage be on your side, a man can never quietly give over when he's weary.

MEDLEY. If you would play without being obliged to complaisance, Dorimant, you should play in public places.

DORIMANT. Ordinaries [8] were a very good thing for that, but gentlemen do not of late frequent 'em. The deep play is now in private houses.   (BELLINDA *offering to steal away*)

LADY TOWNLEY. Bellinda, are you leaving us so soon?

BELLINDA. I am to go to the Park with Mrs. Loveit, madam.

Exit BELLINDA

LADY TOWNLEY. This confidence will go nigh to spoil this young creature.

MEDLEY. 'Twill do her good, madam. Young men who are bred up under practising lawyers prove the abler counsel when they come to be called to the bar themselves.

DORIMANT. The town has been very favorable to you this afternoon, my Lady Townley; you used to have an *embarras* [9] of chairs and coaches at your door, an uproar of footmen in your hall, and a noise of fools above here.

LADY TOWNLEY. Indeed, my house is the general rendezvous, and

[8] Taverns.
[9] Blockade.

next to the playhouse is the common refuge of all the young, idle people.

EMILIA. Company is a very good thing, madam, but I wonder you do not love it a little more chosen.

LADY TOWNLEY. 'Tis good to have an universal taste; we should love wit, but for variety be able to divert ourselves with the extravagancies of those who want it.

MEDLEY. Fools will make you laugh.

EMILIA. For once or twice, but the repetition of their folly after a visit or two grows tedious and unsufferable.

LADY TOWNLEY. You are a little too delicate, Emilia.

Enter a Page

PAGE. Sir Fopling Flutter, madam, desires to know if you are to be seen.

LADY TOWNLEY. Here's the freshest fool in town, and one who has not cloyed you yet. — Page!

PAGE. Madam?

LADY TOWNLEY. Desire him to walk up.

DORIMANT. Do not you fall on him, Medley, and snub him. Soothe him up in his extravagance; he will show the better.

MEDLEY. You know I have a natural indulgence for fools and need not this caution, sir.

Enter SIR FOPLING FLUTTER *with his Page after him*

SIR FOPLING. Page, wait without. (*To* LADY TOWNLEY) Madam, I kiss your hands. I see yesterday was nothing of chance; the *belles assemblées*[10] form themselves here every day. (*To* EMILIA) Lady, your servant. — Dorimant, let me embrace thee! Without lying, I have not met with any of my acquaintance who retain so much of Paris as thou dost — the very air thou hadst when the marquise mistook thee i'th' Tuileries and cried, "Hey, Chevalier!" and then begged thy pardon.

DORIMANT. I would fain wear in fashion as long as I can, sir; 'tis a thing to be valued in men as well as baubles.

SIR FOPLING. Thou art a man of wit and understands[t] the town. Prithee, let thee and I be intimate; there is no living without making some good man the confidant of our pleasures.

DORIMANT. 'Tis true! but there is no man so improper for such a business as I am.

SIR FOPLING. Prithee, why hast thou so modest an opinion of thyself?

DORIMANT. Why, first, I could never keep a secret in my life; and then, there is no charm so infallibly makes me fall in love with a

10 Fashionable gatherings.

woman as my knowing a friend loves her. — I deal honestly with you.

SIR FOPLING. Thy humor's very gallant, or let me perish! I knew a French count so like thee!

LADY TOWNLEY. Wit, I perceive, has more power over you than beauty, Sir Fopling, else you would not have let this lady stand so long neglected.

SIR FOPLING. (*To* EMILIA) A thousand pardons, madam; some civilities due of course upon the meeting a long absent friend. The *éclat* of so much beauty, I confess, ought to have charmed me sooner.

EMILIA. The *brillant* of so much good language, sir, has much more power than the little beauty I can boast.

SIR FOPLING. I never saw anything prettier than this high work on your *point d'Espagne*.[11]

EMILIA. 'Tis not so rich as *point de Venise*.

SIR FOPLING. Not altogether, but looks cooler and is more proper for the season. — Dorimant, is not that Medley?

DORIMANT. The same, sir.

SIR FOPLING. Forgive me, sir; in this *embarras* of civilities I could not come to have you in my arms sooner. You understand an equipage the best of any man in town, I hear.

MEDLEY. By my own you would not guess it.

SIR FOPLING. There are critics who do not write, sir.

MEDLEY. Our peevish poets will scarce allow it.

SIR FOPLING. Damn 'em, they'll allow no man wit who does not play the fool like themselves and show it! Have you taken notice of the *gallesh*[12] I brought over?

MEDLEY. Oh, yes! It has quite another air than the English makes.

SIR FOPLING. 'Tis as easily known from an English tumbril as an Inns-of-Court man[13] is from one of us.

DORIMANT. True; there is a *bel air*[14] in *galleshes* as well as men.

MEDLEY. But there are few so delicate to observe it.

SIR FOPLING. The world is generally very *grossier*[15] here, indeed.

LADY TOWNLEY. He's very fine.

EMILIA. Extreme proper.

SIR FOPLING. A slight suit I made to appear in at my first arrival — not worthy your consideration, ladies.

DORIMANT. The pantaloon is very well mounted.

SIR FOPLING. The tassels are new and pretty.

MEDLEY. I never saw a coat better cut.

SIR FOPLING. It makes me show long-waisted, and, I think, slender.

DORIMANT. That's the shape our ladies dote on.

[11] Point lace, Spanish or Venetian.
[12] Calèche, carriage.   [14] Fine style.
[13] Law student or lawyer.   [15] Gross, coarse.

MEDLEY. Your breech, though, is a handful too high, in my eye, Sir Fopling.

SIR FOPLING. Peace, Medley, I have wished it lower a thousand times, but a pox on't! 'twill not be.

LADY TOWNLEY. His gloves are well fringed, large, and graceful.

SIR FOPLING. I was always eminent for being *bien ganté*.[16]

EMILIA. He wears nothing but what are originals of the most famous hands in Paris.

SIR FOPLING. You are in the right, madam.

LADY TOWNLEY. The suit?

SIR FOPLING. Barroy.[17]

EMILIA. The garniture?

SIR FOPLING. Le Gras.

MEDLEY. The shoes?

SIR FOPLING. Piccar.

DORIMANT. The periwig?

SIR FOPLING. Chedreux.

LADY TOWNLEY. } The gloves?
EMILIA.

SIR FOPLING. Orangerie![18] You know the smell, ladies. Dorimant, I could find in my heart for an amusement to have a gallantry with some of our English ladies.

DORIMANT. 'Tis a thing no less necessary to confirm the reputation of your wit than a duel will be to satisfy the town of your courage.

SIR FOPLING. Here was a woman yesterday —

DORIMANT. Mistress Loveit?

SIR FOPLING. You have named her!

DORIMANT. You cannot pitch on a better for your purpose.

SIR FOPLING. Prithee, what is she?

DORIMANT. A person of quality, and one who has a rest[19] of reputation enough to make the conquest considerable; besides, I hear she likes you, too.

SIR FOPLING. Methoughts she seemed, though, very reserved and uneasy all the time I entertained her.

DORIMANT. Grimace and affectation! You will see her i'th' Mall tonight.

SIR FOPLING. Prithee, let thee and I take the air together.

DORIMANT. I am engaged to Medley, but I'll meet you at Saint James's and give you some information upon the which you may regulate your proceedings.

SIR FOPLING. All the world will be in the Park to-night. Ladies,

---

16 Well gloved.
17 Sir Fopling names a series of fashionable Parisian tradesmen.
18 I.e., gloves scented with essence of orange.
19 Remnant.

'twere pity to keep so much beauty longer within doors and rob the Ring[20] of all those charms that should adorn it. — Hey, page!

Enter Page

See that all my people be ready.　　　　　　([Page] *goes out again*)
— Dorimant, *a revoir*.[21]　　　　　　　　　[*Exit* SIR FOPLING]

MEDLEY. A fine, mettled coxcomb.

DORIMANT. Brisk and insipid.

MEDLEY. Pert and dull.

EMILIA. However you despise him, gentlemen, I'll lay my life he passes for a wit with many.

DORIMANT. That may very well be; Nature has her cheats, stums[22] a brain, and puts sophisticate dulness often on the tasteless multitude for true wit and good humor. Medley, come.

MEDLEY. I must go a little way; I will meet you i'the Mall.

DORIMANT. I'll walk through the Garden thither. — (*To the women*) We shall meet anon and bow.

LADY TOWNLEY. Not to-night. We are engaged about a business the knowledge of which may make you laugh hereafter.

MEDLEY. Your servant, ladies.

DORIMANT. "A revoir," as Sir Fopling says.

　　　　　　　　　　　　　　Exeunt DORIMANT *and* MEDLEY

LADY TOWNLEY. The old man will be here immediately.

EMILIA. Let's expect him i'th' garden —

LADY TOWNLEY. Go! you are a rogue.

EMILIA. I can't abide you.　　　　　　　　　　　　*Exeunt*

SCENE III. *The Mall*

Enter HARRIET *and* YOUNG BELLAIR, *she pulling him*

HARRIET. Come along.

YOUNG BELLAIR. And leave your mother?

HARRIET. Busy will be sent with a hue and cry after us, but that's no matter.

YOUNG BELLAIR. 'Twill look strangely in me.

HARRIET. She'll believe it a freak of mine and never blame your manners.

YOUNG BELLAIR. What reverend acquaintance is that she has met?

HARRIET. A fellow-beauty of the last king's time, though by the ruins you would hardly guess it.　　　　　　　　*Exeunt*

---

[20] In Hyde Park.

[21] Sir Fopling constantly mispronounces French phrases.

[22] Revives, as wine is re-fermented by the addition of stum, or must.

Enter DORIMANT *and crosses the stage*
Enter YOUNG BELLAIR *and* HARRIET

YOUNG BELLAIR. By this time your mother is in a fine taking.

HARRIET. If your friend Mr. Dorimant were but here now, that she might find me talking with him!

YOUNG BELLAIR. She does not know him, but dreads him, I hear, of all mankind.

HARRIET. She concludes if he does but speak to a woman, she's undone — is on her knees every day to pray Heaven defend me from him.

YOUNG BELLAIR. You do not apprehend him so much as she does?

HARRIET. I never saw anything in him that was frightful.

YOUNG BELLAIR. On the contrary, have you not observed something extreme delightful in his wit and person?

HARRIET. He's agreeable and pleasant, I must own; but he does so much affect being so, he displeases me.

YOUNG BELLAIR. Lord, madam! all he does and says is so easy and so natural!

HARRIET. Some men's verses seem so to the unskillful, but labor i'the one and affectation in the other to the judicious plainly appear.

YOUNG BELLAIR. I never heard him accused of affectation before.

Enter DORIMANT *and stares upon her*

HARRIET. It passes on the easy town, who are favorably pleased in him to call it humor.   *Exeunt* YOUNG BELLAIR *and* HARRIET

DORIMANT. 'Tis she! it must be she — that lovely hair, that easy shape, those wanton eyes, and all those melting charms about her mouth which Medley spoke of! I'll follow the lottery and put in for a prize with my friend Bellair.   *Exit* DORIMANT *repeating*

> In love the victors from the vanquished fly;
> They fly that wound, and they pursue that die.[23]

Enter YOUNG BELLAIR *and* HARRIET; *and after them,*
DORIMANT *standing at a distance*

YOUNG BELLAIR. Most people prefer Hyde Park to this place.

HARRIET. It has the greater reputation, I confess; but I abominate the dull diversions there — the formal bows, the affected smiles, the silly by-words and amorous tweers[24] in passing. Here one meets with a little conversation now and then.

YOUNG BELLAIR. These conversations have been fatal to some of your sex, madam.

[23] From Waller's "To a Friend, of the Different Success of their Loves."
[24] Leers.

HARRIET. It may be so; because some who want temper have been undone by gaming, must others who have it wholly deny themselves the pleasure of play?

DORIMANT. (*Coming up gently and bowing to her*) Trust me, it were unreasonable, madam.

HARRIET. (*She starts and looks grave*) Lord, who's this?

YOUNG BELLAIR. Dorimant!

DORIMANT. [*Aside*] Is this the woman your father would have you marry?

YOUNG BELLAIR. It is.

DORIMANT. Her name?

YOUNG BELLAIR. Harriet.

DORIMANT. I am not mistaken; she's handsome.

YOUNG BELLAIR. Talk to her; her wit is better than her face. We were wishing for you but now.

DORIMANT (*To* HARRIET) Overcast with seriousness o'the sudden! A thousand smiles were shining in that face but now; I never saw so quick a change of weather.

HARRIET. (*Aside*) I feel as great a change within; but he shall never know it.

DORIMANT. You were talking of play, madam. Pray, what may be your stint?

HARRIET. A little harmless discourse in public walks, or at most an appointment in a box, bare faced, at the playhouse. You are for masks and private meetings, where women engage for all they are worth, I hear.

DORIMANT. I have been used to deep play, but I can make one at small game when I like my gamester well.

HARRIET. And be so unconcerned you'll ha' no pleasure in't.

DORIMANT. Where there is a considerable sum to be won, the hope of drawing people in makes every trifle considerable.

HARRIET. The sordidness of men's natures, I know, makes 'em willing to flatter and comply with the rich, though they are sure never to be the better for 'em.

DORIMANT. 'Tis in their power to do us good, and we despair not but at some time or other they may be willing.

HARRIET. To men who have fared in this town like you, 'twould be a great mortification to live on hope. Could you keep a Lent for a mistress?

DORIMANT. In expectation of a happy Easter and, though time be very precious, think forty days well lost to gain your favor.

HARRIET. Mr. Bellair, let us walk; 'tis time to leave him. Men grow dull when they begin to be particular.

DORIMANT. You're mistaken; flattery will not ensue, though I know you're greedy of the praises of the whole Mall.

HARRIET. You do me wrong.

DORIMANT. I do not. As I followed you, I observed how you were pleased when the fops cried, "She's handsome — very handsome! By God, she is!" and whispered aloud your name. The thousand several forms you put your face into, then, to make yourself more agreeable! How wantonly you played with your head, flung back your locks, and looked smilingly over your shoulder at 'em!

HARRIET. I do not go begging the men's, as you do the ladies', good liking, with a sly softness in your looks and a gentle slowness in your bows as you pass 'em — as thus, sir. (*Acts him*) Is not this like you?

Enter LADY WOODVILL *and* BUSY

YOUNG BELLAIR. Your mother, madam. (*Pulls* HARRIET; *she composes herself*)

LADY WOODVILL. Ah, my dear child Harriet!

BUSY. Now she is so pleased with finding her again she cannot chide her.

LADY WOODVILL. Come away!

DORIMANT. 'Tis now but high Mall, madam — the most entertaining time of the evening.

HARRIET. I would fain see that Dorimant, mother, you so cry out of for a monster; he's in the Mall, I hear.

LADY WOODVILL. Come away then! The plague is here and you should dread the infection.

YOUNG BELLAIR. You may be misinformed of the gentleman.

LADY WOODVILL. Oh, no! I hope you do not know him. He is the prince of all the devils in the town — delights in nothing but in rapes and riots!

DORIMANT. If you did but hear him speak, madam!

LADY WOODVILL. Oh, he has a tongue, they say, would tempt the angels to a second fall.

Enter SIR FOPLING *with his equipage, six Footmen and a Page*

SIR FOPLING. Hey! Champagne, Norman, La Rose, La Fleur, La Tour, La Verdure! — Dorimant —

LADY WOODVILL. Here, here he is among this rout! — He names him! Come away, Harriet; come away!

Exeunt LADY WOODVILL, HARRIET, BUSY, *and* YOUNG BELLAIR

DORIMANT. This fool's coming has spoiled all. She's gone, but she has left a pleasing image of herself behind that wanders in my soul — it must not settle there.

SIR FOPLING. What reverie is this? Speak, man!

DORIMANT.

Snatched from myself, how far behind
Already I behold the shore![25]

Enter MEDLEY

MEDLEY. Dorimant, a discovery! I met with Bellair.

DORIMANT. You can tell me no news, sir; I know all.

MEDLEY. How do you like the daughter?

DORIMANT. You never came so near truth in your life as you did in her description.

MEDLEY. What think you of the mother?

DORIMANT. Whatever I think of her, she thinks very well of me, I find.

MEDLEY. Did she know you?

DORIMANT. She did not; whether she does now or no, I know not. Here was a pleasant scene towards, when in came Sir Fopling mustering up his equipage, and at the latter end named me and frightened her away.

MEDLEY. Loveit and Bellinda are not far off; I saw 'em alight at St. James's.

DORIMANT. Sir Fopling! Hark you, a word or two. (*Whispers*) Look you do not want assurance.

SIR FOPLING. I never do on these occasions.

DORIMANT. Walk on; we must not be seen together. Make your advantage of what I have told you. The next turn you will meet the lady.

SIR FOPLING. Hey! Follow me all!

Exit SIR FOPLING *and his equipage*

DORIMANT. Medley, you shall see good sport anon between Loveit and this Fopling.

MEDLEY. I thought there was something toward, by that whisper.

DORIMANT. You know a worthy principle of hers?

MEDLEY. Not to be so much as civil to a man who speaks to her in the presence of him she professes to love.

DORIMANT. I have encouraged Fopling to talk to her to-night.

MEDLEY. Now you are here, she will go nigh to beat him.

DORIMANT. In the humor she's in, her love will make her do some very extravagant thing, doubtless.

MEDLEY. What was Bellinda's business with you at my Lady Townley's?

DORIMANT. To get me to meet Loveit here in order to an *éclaircissement*.[26] I made some difficulty of it and have prepared this encounter to make good my jealousy.

MEDLEY. Here they come!

[25] Waller, "Of Loving at First Sight."
[26] Explanation, clarification.

Enter MRS. LOVEIT, BELLINDA, *and* PERT

DORIMANT. I'll meet her and provoke her with a deal of dumb civility in passing by, then turn short and be behind her when Sir Fopling sets upon her —

> See how unregarded now
> That piece of beauty passes.[27]

Exeunt DORIMANT *and* MEDLEY

BELLINDA. How wonderful respectfully he bowed!

PERT. He's always over-mannerly when he has done a mischief.

BELLINDA. Methought, indeed, at the same time he had a strange, despising countenance.

PERT. The unlucky look, he thinks, becomes him.

BELLINDA. I was afraid you would have spoken to him, my dear.

MRS. LOVEIT. I would have died first. He shall no more find me the loving fool he has done.

BELLINDA. You love him still?

MRS. LOVEIT. No!

PERT. I wish you did not.

MRS. LOVEIT. I do not, and I will have you think so. What made you hale me to this odious place, Bellinda?

BELLINDA. I hate to be hulched up[28] in a coach; walking is much better.

MRS. LOVEIT. Would we could meet Sir Fopling now!

BELLINDA. Lord, would you not avoid him?

MRS. LOVEIT. I would make him all the advances that may be.

BELLINDA. That would confirm Dorimant's suspicion, my dear.

MRS. LOVEIT. He is not jealous; but I will make him so, and be revenged a way he little thinks on.

BELLINDA. (*Aside*) If she should make him jealous, that may make him fond of her again. I must dissuade her from it. — Lord, my dear, this will certainly make him hate you.

MRS. LOVEIT. 'Twill make him uneasy, though he does not care for me. I know the effects of jealousy on men of his proud temper.

BELLINDA. 'Tis a fantastic remedy; its operations are dangerous and uncertain.

MRS. LOVEIT. 'Tis the strongest cordial we can give to dying love. It often brings it back when there's no sign of life remaining. But I design not so much the reviving his, as my revenge.

Enter SIR FOPLING *and his equipage*

SIR FOPLING. Hey! Bid the coachman send home four of his horses and bring the coach to Whitehall; I'll walk over the Park. — Madam,

---

[27] Suckling, *Sonnet I.*   [28] Huddled up.

the honor of kissing your fair hand is a happiness I missed this afternoon at my Lady Townley's.

MRS. LOVEIT. You were very obliging, Sir Fopling, the last time I
saw you there.

SIR FOPLING. The preference was due to your wit and beauty. —
Madam, your servant; there never was so sweet an evening.

BELLINDA. 'T has drawn all the rabble of the town hither.

SIR FOPLING. 'Tis pity there's not an order made that none but the
beau monde should walk here.

MRS. LOVEIT. 'Twould add much to the beauty of the place. See
what a sort of nasty fellows are coming.

Enter four ill-fashioned fellows, singing:

'Tis not for kisses alone. etc.[29]

MRS. LOVEIT. Fo! Their periwigs are scented with tobacco so
strong —

SIR FOPLING. It overcomes our pulvilio[30] — methinks I smell the
coffee-house they come from.

FIRST MAN. Dorimant's convenient,[31] Madam Loveit.

SECOND MAN. I like the oily buttock[32] with her.

THIRD MAN. What spruce prig[33] is that?

FIRST MAN. A caravan[34] lately come from Paris.

SECOND MAN. Peace! they smoke.[35]   [*They sing again*]

There's something else to be done, etc.

All of them coughing; exeunt singing

Enter DORIMANT *and* MEDLEY

DORIMANT. They're engaged.

MEDLEY. She entertains him as if she liked him!

DORIMANT. Let us go forward — seem earnest in discourse and show
ourselves; then you shall see how she'll use him.

BELLINDA. Yonder's Dorimant, my dear.

MRS. LOVEIT. I see him. (*Aside*) He comes insulting, but I will
disappoint him in his expectation. (*To* SIR FOPLING) I like this
pretty, nice humor of yours, Sir Fopling. With what a loathing eye
he looked upon those fellows!

SIR FOPLING. I sat near one of 'em at a play to-day and was almost
poisoned with a pair of cordovan gloves he wears.

---

[29] This and the singers' exit line are from a popular song, "Tell me no more
you love," printed in *The Last and Best Edition of New Songs*, 1677.
[30] Scented powder.   [33] Fop, coxcomb.
[31] Mistress.   [34] Dupe, bubble.
[32] Smooth-looking wench.   [35] Observe, suspect.

MRS. LOVEIT. Oh, filthy cordovan! How I hate the smell! (*Laughs in a loud, affected way*)

SIR FOPLING. Did you observe, madam, how their cravats hung loose an inch from their neck[s] and what a frightful air it gave 'em?

MRS. LOVEIT. Oh, I took particular notice of one that is always spruced up with a deal of dirty sky-colored ribband.

BELLINDA. That's one of the walking flageolets[36] who haunt the Mall o'nights.

MRS. LOVEIT. Oh, I remember him; he's a hollow tooth enough to spoil the sweetness of an evening.

SIR FOPLING. I have seen the tallest walk the streets with a dainty pair of boxes[37] neatly buckled on.

MRS. LOVEIT. And a little foot-boy at his heels, pocket-high, with a flat cap, a dirty face —

SIR FOPLING. And a snotty nose.

MRS. LOVEIT. Oh, odious! — There's many of my own sex with that Holborn equipage trig to Gray's Inn Walks[38] and now and then travel hither on a Sunday.

MEDLEY. She takes no notice of you.

DORIMANT. Damn her! I am jealous of a counterplot!

MRS. LOVEIT. Your liveries are the finest, Sir Fopling — Oh, that page! that page is the prettili'st dressed — they are all Frenchmen?

SIR FOPLING. There's one damned English blockhead among 'em; you may know him by his mien.

MRS. LOVEIT. Oh, that's he — that's he! What do you call him?

SIR FOPLING. Hey — I know not what to call him —

FOOTMAN. John Trott, madam.

SIR FOPLING. Oh, unsufferable! Trott, Trott, Trott! There's nothing so barbarous as the names of our English servants. What countryman are you, sir?

FOOTMAN. Hampshire, sir.

SIR FOPLING. Then Hampshire be your name. Hey, Hampshire!

MRS. LOVEIT. Oh, that sound, that sound becomes the mouth of a man of quality!

MEDLEY. Dorimant, you look a little bashful on the matter.

DORIMANT. She dissembles better than I thought she could have done.

MEDLEY. You have tempted her with too luscious a bait. She bites at the coxcomb.

DORIMANT. She cannot fall from loving me to that.

MEDLEY. You begin to be jealous in earnest.

[36] Possibly an itinerant flageolet player.
[37] Patterns or clogs; some kind of overshoes.
[38] Many women followed by ill-dressed pages trot to the Gardens of Gray's Inn.

DORIMANT. Of one I do not love —

MEDLEY. You did love her.

DORIMANT. The fit has long been over —

MEDLEY. But I have known men fall into dangerous relapses when they found a woman inclining to another.

DORIMANT. (*To himself*) He guesses the secret of my heart! I am concerned but dare not show it, lest Bellinda should mistrust all I have done to gain her.

BELLINDA. (*Aside*) I have watched his look and find no alteration there. Did he love her, some signs of jealousy would have appeared.

DORIMANT. [*To* MRS. LOVEIT] I hope this happy evening, madam, has reconciled you to the scandalous Mall. We shall have you now hankering here again —

MRS. LOVEIT. Sir Fopling, will you walk?

SIR FOPLING. I am all obedience, madam.

MRS. LOVEIT. Come along then, and let's agree to be malicious on all the ill-fashioned things we meet.

SIR FOPLING. We'll make a critique on the whole Mall, madam.

MRS. LOVEIT. Bellinda, you shall engage —

BELLINDA. To the reserve of our friends, my dear.

MRS. LOVEIT. [*To* SIR FOPLING] No, no exceptions.

SIR FOPLING. We'll sacrifice all to our diversion —

MRS. LOVEIT. All — all —

SIR FOPLING. All.

BELLINDA. All? Then let it be.

Exeunt SIR FOPLING, MRS. LOVEIT, BELLINDA,
and PERT, *laughing*

MEDLEY. Would you had brought some more of your friends, Dorimant, to have been witnesses of Sir Fopling's disgrace and your triumph.

DORIMANT. 'Twere unreasonable to desire you not to laugh at me; but pray, do not expose me to the town this day or two.

MEDLEY. By that time you have hope to have regained your credit?

DORIMANT. I know she hates Fopling and only makes use of him in hope to work on me again. Had it not been for some powerful considerations which will be removed to-morrow morning, I had made her pluck off this mask and show the passion that lies panting under.

Enter a Footman

MEDLEY. Here comes a man from Bellair with news of your last adventure.

DORIMANT. I am glad he sent him. I long to know the consequence of our parting.

FOOTMAN. Sir, my master desires you to come to my Lady Town-

ley's presently and bring Mr. Medley with you. My Lady Woodvill
and her daughter are there.

MEDLEY. Then all's well, Dorimant.

FOOTMAN. They have sent for the fiddles and mean to dance. He
bid me tell you, sir, the old lady does not know you, and would have
you own yourself to be Mr. Courtage. They are all prepared to receive
you by that name.

DORIMANT. That foppish admirer of quality, who flatters the very
meat at honorable tables and never offers love to a woman below a
lady-grandmother?

MEDLEY. You know the character you are to act, I see.

DORIMANT. This is Harriet's contrivance — wild, witty, lovesome,
beautiful, and young! — Come along, Medley.

MEDLEY. This new woman would well supply the loss of Loveit.

DORIMANT. That business must not end so; before to-morrow's sun
is set I will revenge and clear it.

> And you and Loveit, to her cost, shall find,
> I fathom all the depths of womankind.

Exeunt

ACT IV

[SCENE I. LADY TOWNLEY's *drawing-room*]

The scene opens with the fiddles playing a country dance.

Enter DORIMANT, LADY WOODVILL, YOUNG BELLAIR *and* MRS. HARRIET,
OLD BELLAIR *and* EMILIA, MR. MEDLEY *and* LADY TOWNLEY, *as
having just ended the dance*

OLD BELLAIR. So, so, so — a smart bout! a very smart bout, a dod!

LADY TOWNLEY. How do you like Emilia's dancing, brother?

OLD BELLAIR. Not at all — not at all!

LADY TOWNLEY. You speak not what you think, I am sure.

OLD BELLAIR. No matter for that; go, bid her dance no more. It
don't become her — it don't become her! Tell her I say so. (*Aside*)
A dod, I love her!

DORIMANT. (*To* LADY WOODVILL) All people mingle nowadays,
madam, and in public places women of quality have the least respect
showed 'em.

LADY WOODVILL. I protest you say the truth, Mr. Courtage.

DORIMANT. Forms and ceremonies, the only things that uphold
quality and greatness, are now shamefully laid aside and neglected.

LADY WOODVILL. Well, this is not the women's age. Let 'em think what they will, lewdness is the business now; love was the business in my time.

DORIMANT. The women, indeed, are little beholding to the young men of this age; they're generally only dull admirers of themselves, and make their court to nothing but their periwigs and cravats, and would be more concerned for the disordering of 'em, tho' on a good occasion, than a young maid would be for the tumbling of her head or handkercher.[1]

LADY WOODVILL. I protest you hit 'em.

DORIMANT. They are very assiduous to show themselves at Court, well dressed, to the women of quality, but their business is with the stale mistresses of the town, who are prepared to receive their lazy addresses by industrious old lovers who have cast 'em off and made 'em easy.

HARRIET. [*To* MEDLEY] He fits my mother's humor so well, a little more and she'll dance a kissing dance with him anon.

MEDLEY. Dutifully observed, madam.

DORIMANT. [*To* LADY WOODVILL] They pretend to be great critics in beauty. By their talk you would think they liked no face, and yet can dote on an ill one if it belong to a laundress or a tailor's daughter. They cry, "A woman's past her prime at twenty, decayed at four-and-twenty, and unsufferable at thirty."

LADY WOODVILL. Unsufferable at thirty! That they are in the wrong, Mr. Courtage, at five-and-thirty, there are living proofs enough to convince 'em.

DORIMANT. Aye, madam. There's Mrs. Setlooks, Mrs. Droplip, and my Lady Loud; show me among all our opening buds a face that promises so much beauty as the remains of theirs.

LADY WOODVILL. The depraved appetite of this vicious age tastes nothing but green fruit, and loathes it when 'tis kindly[2] ripened.

DORIMANT. Else so many deserving women, madam, would not be so untimely neglected.

LADY WOODVILL. I protest, Mr. Courtage, a dozen such good men as you would be enough to atone for that wicked Dorimant and all the under debauchees of the town. (HARRIET, EMILIA, YOUNG BELLAIR, MEDLEY, and LADY TOWNLEY *break out into laughter*) — What's the matter here?

MEDLEY. A pleasant mistake, madam, that a lady has made, occasions a little laughter.

OLD BELLAIR. Come, come; you keep 'em idle! They are impatient till the fiddles play again.

DORIMANT. You are not weary, madam?

LADY WOODVILL. One dance more! I cannot refuse you, **Mr.**

[1] A scarf worn over the décolletage of her gown.
[2] Naturally.

Courtage. (*They dance. After the dance* OLD BELLAIR, *singing and dancing, up to* EMILIA)

EMILIA. You are very active, sir.

OLD BELLAIR. A dod, sirrah! when I was a young fellow I could ha' capered up to my woman's gorget.

DORIMANT. [*To* LADY WOODVILL] You are willing to rest yourself, madam?

LADY TOWNLEY. [*To* MEDLEY] We'll walk into my chamber and sit down.

MEDLEY. Leave us Mr. Courtage; he's a dancer, and the young ladies are not weary yet.

LADY WOODVILL. We'll send him out again.

HARRIET. If you do not quickly, I know where to send for Mr. Dorimant.

LADY WOODVILL. This girl's head, Mr. Courtage, is ever running on that wild fellow.

DORIMANT. 'Tis well you have got her a good husband, madam; that will settle it.

Exeunt LADY TOWNLEY, LADY WOODVILL, *and* DORIMANT

OLD BELLAIR. (*To* EMILIA) A dod, sweetheart, be advised and do not throw thyself away on a young, idle fellow.

EMILIA. I have no such intention, sir.

OLD BELLAIR. Have a little patience! Thou shalt have the man I spake of. A dod, he loves thee and will make a good husband — but no words —

EMILIA. But, sir —

OLD BELLAIR. No answer — out a pize, peace! and think on't.

Enter DORIMANT

DORIMANT. Your company is desired within, sir.

OLD BELLAIR. I go, I go! Good Mr. Courtage, fare you well! — (*To* EMILIA) Go, I'll see you no more!

EMILIA. What have I done, sir?

OLD BELLAIR. You are ugly! you are ugly! —is she not, Mr. Courtage?

EMILIA. Better words or I shan't abide you.

OLD BELLAIR. Out a pize; a dod, what does she say? Hit her a pat for me there.   *Exit* OLD BELLAIR

MEDLEY. You have charms for the whole family.

DORIMANT. You'll spoil all with some unseasonable jest, Medley.

MEDLEY. You see I confine my tongue and am content to be a bare spectator, much contrary to my nature.

EMILIA. Methinks, Mr. Dorimant, my Lady Woodvill is a little fond of you.

DORIMANT. Would her daughter were!

MEDLEY. It may be you may find her so. Try her — you have an opportunity.

DORIMANT. And I will not lose it. Bellair, here's a lady has something to say to you.

YOUNG BELLAIR. I wait upon her. Mr. Medley, we have both business with you.

DORIMANT. Get you all together then. (*To* HARRIET) That demure curtsey is not amiss in jest, but do not think in earnest it becomes you.

HARRIET. Affectation is catching, I find — from your grave bow I got it.

DORIMANT. Where had you all that scorn and coldness in your look?

HARRIET. From nature, sir; pardon my want of art. I have not learnt those softnesses and languishings which now in faces are so much in fashion.

DORIMANT. You need 'em not; you have a sweetness of your own if you would but calm your frowns and let it settle.

HARRIET. My eyes are wild and wandering like my passions, and cannot yet be tied to rules of charming.

DORIMANT. Women, indeed, have commonly a method of managing those messengers of love. Now they will look as if they would kill, and anon they will look as if they were dying. They point and rebate[3] their glances, the better to invite us.

HARRIET. I like this variety well enough, but hate the set face that always looks as if it would say, "Come, love me" — a woman who at plays makes the *doux yeux*[4] to a whole audience and at home cannot forbear 'em to her monkey.

DORIMANT. Put on a gentle smile and let me see how well it will become you.

HARRIET. I am sorry my face does not please you as it is, but I shall not be complaisant and change it.

DORIMANT. Though you are obstinate, I know 'tis capable of improvement and shall do you justice, madam, if I chance to be at Court when the critics of the circle pass their judgment; for thither you must come.

HARRIET. And expect to be taken in pieces, have all my features examined, every motion censured, and on the whole be condemned to be but pretty, or a beauty of the lowest rate. What think you?

DORIMANT. The women, nay, the very lovers who belong to the drawing-room, will maliciously allow you more than that. They always grant what is apparent, that they may the better be believed when they name concealed faults they cannot easily be disproved in.

HARRIET. Beauty runs as great a risk exposed at Court as wit does on the stage, where the ugly and the foolish all are free to censure.

[3] Blunt.
[4] Amorous glances.

DORIMANT. (*Aside*) I love her and dare not let her know it; I fear she has an ascendant o'er me and may revenge the wrongs I have done her sex. (*To her*) Think of making a party, madam, love will engage.

HARRIET. You make me start! I did not think to have heard of love from you!

DORIMANT. I never knew what 'twas to have a settled ague yet, but now and then have had irregular fits.

HARRIET. Take heed; sickness after long health is commonly more violent and dangerous.

DORIMANT. (*Aside*) I have took the infection from her, and feel the disease now spreading in me. (*To her*) Is the name of love so frightful that you dare not stand it?

HARRIET. 'Twill do little execution out of your mouth on me, I'm sure.

DORIMANT. It has been fatal —

HARRIET. To some easy women, but we are not all born to one destiny. I was informed you use to laugh at love and not make it.

DORIMANT. The time has been, but now I must speak —

HARRIET. If it be on that idle subject, I will put on my serious look, turn my head carelessly from you, drop my lip, let my eyelids fall and hang half o'er my eyes — thus — while you buzz a speech of an hour long in my ear, and I answer never a word. Why do you not begin?

DORIMANT. That the company may take notice how passionately I make advances of love! And how disdainfully you receive 'em.

HARRIET. When your love's grown strong enough to make you bear being laughed at, I'll give you leave to trouble me with it; till when pray forbear, sir.

Enter SIR FOPLING *and others in masks*

DORIMANT. What's here — masquerades?

HARRIET. I thought that foppery had been left off, and people might have been in private with a fiddle.

DORIMANT. 'Tis endeavored to be kept on foot still by some who find themselves the more acceptable the less they are known.

YOUNG BELLAIR. This must be Sir Fopling.

MEDLEY. This extraordinary habit shows it.

YOUNG BELLAIR. What are the rest?

MEDLEY. A company of French rascals whom he picked up in Paris and has brought over to be his dancing equipage on these occasions. Make him own himself; a fool is very troublesome when he presumes he is incognito.

SIR FOPLING. (*To* HARRIET) Do you know me?

HARRIET. Ten to one but I guess at you.

SIR FOPLING. Are you women as fond of a vizard as we men are?

HARRIET. I am very fond of a vizard that covers a face I do not like, sir.

YOUNG BELLAIR. Here are no masks, you see, sir, but those which came with you. This was intended a private meeting; but because you look like a gentleman, if you will discover yourself and we know you to be such, you shall be welcome.

SIR FOPLING. *(Pulling off his mask)* Dear Bellair!

MEDLEY. Sir Fopling! How came you hither?

SIR FOPLING. Faith, as I was coming late from Whitehall, after the King's *couchée*,[5] one of my people told me he had heard fiddles at my Lady Townley's, and —

DORIMANT. You need not say any more, sir.

SIR FOPLING. Dorimant, let me kiss thee.

DORIMANT. Hark you, Sir Fopling —   *(Whispers)*

SIR FOPLING. Enough, enough, Courtage. — A pretty kind of young woman that, Medley. I observed her in the Mall — more *éveillée*[6] than our English women commonly are. Prithee, what is she?

MEDLEY. The most noted *coquetté* in town. Beware of her.

SIR FOPLING. Let her be what she will, I know how to take my measures. In Paris the mode is to flatter the *prudè*, laugh at the *faux-prudè*, make serious love to the *demi-prudè*, and only rally with the *coquetté*.[7] — Medley, what think you?

MEDLEY. That for all this smattering of the mathematics, you may be out in your judgment at tennis.

SIR FOPLING. What a *coq-à-l'âne*[8] is this? I talk of women and thou answer'st tennis.

MEDLEY. Mistakes will be for want of apprehension.

SIR FOPLING. I am very glad of the acquaintance I have with this family.

MEDLEY. My lady truly is a good woman.

SIR FOPLING. Ah, Dorimant — Courtage, I would say — would thou hadst spent the last summer in Paris with me! When thou wert there, La Corneus and Sallyes[9] were the only habitués we had: a comedian would have been a *boné fortune*.[10] No stranger ever passed his time so well as I did some months before I came over. I was well received in a dozen families where all the women of quality used to visit; I have intrigues to tell thee more pleasant than ever thou read'st in a novel.

HARRIET. Write 'em, sir, and oblige us women. Our language wants such little stories.

---

[5] Evening reception.
[6] Sprightly.
[7] False French: the prudish, the pseudo-prudish, and the half-prudish. Sir Fopling seems to think it necessary to accent every final e.
[8] Lot of nonsense.
[9] Possibly Mesdames Corneul and Selles, two literary ladies.
[10] Stroke of good luck.

SIR FOPLING. Writing, madam, 's a mechanic part of wit. A gentle-man should never go beyond a song or a billet.

HARRIET. Bussy was a gentleman.

SIR FOPLING. Who, d'Ambois? [11]

MEDLEY. Was there ever such a brisk blockhead?

HARRIET. Not d'Ambois, sir, but Rabutin — he who writ the loves of France.

SIR FOPLING. That may be, madam; many gentlemen do things that are below 'em. Damn your authors, Courtage; women are the prettiest things we can fool away our time with.

HARRIET. I hope ye have wearied yourself to-night at Court, sir, and will not think of fooling with anybody here.

SIR FOPLING. I cannot complain of my fortune, there, madam. — Dorimant —

DORIMANT. Again!

SIR FOPLING. Courtage — a pox on't! I have something to tell thee. When I had made my court within, I came out and flung myself upon the mat under the state [12] i'th' outward room, i'th' midst of half a dozen beauties who were withdrawn "to jeer among themselves," as they called it.

DORIMANT. Did you know em?

SIR FOPLING. Not one of 'em, by heavens! — not I; but they were all your friends.

DORIMANT. How are you sure of that?

SIR FOPLING. Why, we laughed at all the town — spared nobody but yourself. They found me a man for their purpose.

DORIMANT. I know you are malicious, to your power.

SIR FOPLING. And faith, I had occasion to show it, for I never saw more gaping fools at a ball or on a birthday. [13]

DORIMANT. You learned who the women were?

SIR FOPLING. No matter; they frequent the drawing-room.

DORIMANT. And entertain themselves pleasantly at the expense of all the fops who come there.

SIR FOPLING. That's their bus'ness. Faith, I sifted 'em, and find they have a sort of wit among them — Ah, filthy! (*Pinches a tallow candle*)

DORIMANT. Look, he has been pinching the tallow candle.

SIR FOPLING. How can you breathe in a room where there's grease frying! Dorimant, thou art intimate with my lady; advise her for her own sake and the good company that comes hither, to burn wax lights.

---

[11] Sir Fopling confuses Bussy d'Ambois, hero of Chapman's play with that name, with Roger de Rabutin, Comte de Bussy, author of *Histoire Amoureuse des Gaules.*

[12] Canopy.

[13] A celebration of the King's birthday.

HARRIET. What are these masquerades who stand so obsequiously at a distance?

SIR FOPLING. A set of balladines whom I picked out of the best in France and brought over with a *flute-douce* or two — my servants. They shall entertain you.

HARRIET. I had rather see you dance yourself, Sir Fopling.

SIR FOPLING. And I had rather do it — all the company knows it — but madam —

MEDLEY. Come, come, no excuses, Sir Fopling.

SIR FOPLING. By heavens, Medley —

MEDLEY. Like a woman I find you must be struggled with, before one brings you to what you desire.

HARRIET. (*Aside*) Can he dance?

EMILIA. And fence and sing too, if you'll believe him.

DORIMANT. He has no more excellence in his heels than in his head. He went to Paris a plain, bashful English blockhead, and is returned a fine undertaking French fop.

MEDLEY. I cannot prevail.

SIR FOPLING. Do not think it want of complaisance, madam.

HARRIET. You are too well bred to want that, Sir Fopling. I believe it want of power.

SIR FOPLING. By heavens, and so it is! I have sat up so damned late and drunk so cursed hard since I came to this lewd town, that I am fit for nothing but low dancing now — a *corant*, a *bourrée*, or a *menuet*.[14] But St. André[15] tells me, if I will but be regular, in one month I shall rise again. (*Endeavors at a caper*) — Pox on this debauchery!

EMILIA. I have heard your dancing much commended.

SIR FOPLING. It had the good fortune to please in Paris. I was judged to rise within an inch as high as the basqué[16] in an entry I danced there.

HARRIET. [*To* EMILIA] I am mightily taken with this fool; let us sit. — Here's a seat, Sir Fopling.

SIR FOPLING. At your feet, madam; I can be nowhere so much at ease. — By your leave, gown.

HARRIET.
EMILIA. } Ah, you'll spoil it!

SIR FOPLING. No matter; my clothes are my creatures. I make 'em to make my court to you ladies. Hey! (*Dance*) *Qu'on commencè*[17] — to an English dancer, English motions. I was forced to entertain this fellow, one of my set miscarrying. — Oh, horrid! Leave your damned manner of dancing and put on the French air. Have you not

---

[14] All stately dances.
[15] A famous French dancing master.
[16] *Basque*; the skirt of a coat.
[17] Begin.

a pattern before you? — Pretty well! — imitation in time may bring him to something.

> *After the dance, enter* OLD BELLAIR, LADY WOODVILL, *and*
> LADY TOWNLEY

OLD BELLAIR. Hey, a dod, what have we here — a mumming?

LADY WOODVILL. Where's my daughter — Harriet?

DORIMANT. Here, here, madam! I know not but under these disguises there may be dangerous sparks; I gave the young lady warning.

LADY WOODVILL. Lord! I am so obliged to you, Mr. Courtage.

HARRIET. Lord, how you admire this man!

LADY WOODVILL. What have you to except against him?

HARRIET. He's a fop.

LADY WOODVILL. He's not a Dorimant — a wild extravagant fellow of the times.

HARRIET. He's a man made up of forms and commonplaces sucked out of the remaining lees of the last age.

LADY WOODVILL. He's so good a man that, were you not engaged —

LADY TOWNLEY. You'll have but little night to sleep in.

LADY WOODVILL. Lord, 'tis perfect day.

DORIMANT. (*Aside*) The hour is almost come I appointed Bellinda, and I am not so foppishly in love here to forget. I am flesh and blood yet.

LADY TOWNLEY. I am very sensible, madam.

LADY WOODVILL. Lord, madam!

HARRIET. Look! in what a struggle is my poor mother yonder!

YOUNG BELLAIR. She has much ado to bring out the compliment.

DORIMANT. She strains hard for it.

HARRIET. See, see! her head tottering, her eyes staring, and her under lip trembling —

DORIMANT. Now — now she's in the very convulsions of her civility. (*Aside*) 'Sdeath, I shall lose Bellinda! I must fright her hence; she'll be an hour in this fit of good manners else. (*To* LADY WOODVILL) Do you not know Sir Fopling, madam?

LADY WOODVILL. I have seen that face — Oh, heavens! 'tis the same we met in the Mall! How came he here?

DORIMANT. A fiddle, in this town, is a kind of fop-call; no sooner it strikes up but the house is besieged with an army of masquerades straight.

LADY WOODVILL. Lord! I tremble, Mr. Courtage! For certain, Dorimant is in the company.

DORIMANT. I cannot confidently say he is not. You had best be gone. I will wait upon you; your daughter is in the hands of Mr. Bellair.

LADY WOODVILL. I'll see her before me. — Harriet, come away.

YOUNG BELLAIR. Lights! lights!

LADY TOWNLEY. Light, down there!

OLD BELLAIR. A dod, it needs not —

DORIMANT. [*To the* SERVANT *entering*] Call my Lady Woodvill's coach to the door quickly.

> [*Exeunt* YOUNG BELLAIR, HARRIET, LADY TOWNLEY,
> LADY WOODVILL, *and* DORIMANT]

OLD BELLAIR. Stay, Mr. Medley. Let the young fellows do that duty; we will drink a glass of wine together. 'Tis good after dancing. — What mumming spark is that?   [*Points at* SIR FOPLING]

MEDLEY. He is not to be comprehended in few words.

SIR FOPLING. Hey, La Tour!

MEDLEY. Whither away, Sir Fopling?

SIR FOPLING. I have business with Courtage.

MEDLEY. He'll but put the ladies into their coach and come up again.

OLD BELLAIR. In the meantime I'll call for a bottle. *Exit* OLD BELLAIR

Enter YOUNG BELLAIR

MEDLEY. Where's Dorimant?

YOUNG BELLAIR. Stol'n home. He has had business waiting him there all this night, I believe, by an impatience I observed in him.

MEDLEY. Very likely; 'tis but dissembling drunkenness, railing at his friends, and the kind soul will embrace the blessing and forget the tedious expectation.

SIR FOPLING. I must speak with him before I sleep.

YOUNG BELLAIR. [*To* MEDLEY] Emilia and I are resolved on that business.

MEDLEY. Peace, here's your father.

Enter OLD BELLAIR *and a Butler with a bottle of wine*

OLD BELLAIR. The women are all gone to bed. — Fill, boy. Mr. Medley, begin a health.

MEDLEY. (*Whispers*) To Emilia!

OLD BELLAIR. Out a pize! she's a rogue and I'll not pledge you.

MEDLEY. I know you will.

OLD BELLAIR. A dod, drink it then!

SIR FOPLING. Let us have the new bacchic.

OLD BELLAIR. A dod, that is a hard word. What does it mean, sir?

MEDLEY. A catch or drinking song.

OLD BELLAIR. Let us have it then.

SIR FOPLING. Fill the glasses round and draw up in a body. Hey, music!   (*They sing*)

The pleasures of love and the joys of good wine
To perfect our happiness, wisely we join.
We to beauty all day
Give the sovereign sway
And her favorite nymphs devoutly obey.
At the plays we are constantly making our court,
And when they are ended we follow the sport
To the Mall and the Park,
Where we love till 'tis dark.
Then sparkling champagne
Puts an end to their reign;
It quickly recovers
Poor languishing lovers;
Makes us frolic and gay, and drowns all our sorrow.
But alas! we relapse again on the morrow.
  Let every man stand
  With his glass in his hand,
And briskly discharge at the word of command:
  Here's a health to all those
  Whom to-night we depose!
Wine and beauty by turns great souls should inspire;
Present all together — and now, boys, give fire!

            [*They drink*]

OLD BELLAIR. A dod! a pretty business and very merry.

SIR FOPLING. Hark you, Medley, let's you and I take the fiddles and go waken Dorimant.

MEDLEY. We shall do him a courtesy, if it be as I guess. For after the fatigue of this night he'll quickly have his belly full and be glad of an occasion to cry, "Take away, Handy!"

YOUNG BELLAIR. I'll go with you, and there we'll consult about affairs, Medley.

OLD BELLAIR. (*Looks on his watch*) A dod, 'tis six o'clock!

SIR FOPLING. Let's away then.

OLD BELLAIR. Mr. Medley, my sister tells me you are an honest man — and a dod, I love you. Few words and hearty — that's the way with old Harry, old Harry.

SIR FOPLING. [*To his Servants*] Light your flambeaux. Hey!

OLD BELLAIR. What does the man mean?

MEDLEY. 'Tis day, Sir Fopling.

SIR FOPLING. No matter; our serenade will look the greater.

            Exeunt omnes

SCENE II. DORIMANT's *lodging. A table, a candle, a toilet, etc.;*
      HANDY, *tying up linen*

   Enter DORIMANT *in his gown, and* BELLINDA

DORIMANT. Why will you be gone so soon?

BELLINDA. Why did you stay out so late?

DORIMANT. Call a chair, Handy. — What makes you tremble so?

BELLINDA. I have a thousand fears about me. Have I not been seen, think you?

DORIMANT. By nobody but myself and trusty Handy.

BELLINDA. Where are all your people?

DORIMANT. I have dispersed 'em all on sleeveless[18] errands. What does that sigh mean?

BELLINDA. Can you be so unkind to ask me? (*Sighs*) Well — were it to do again —

DORIMANT. We should do it, should we not?

BELLINDA. I think we should — the wickeder man you, to make me love you so well. — Will you be discreet now?

DORIMANT. I will.

BELLINDA. You cannot.

DORIMANT. Never doubt it.

BELLINDA. I will not expect it.

DORIMANT. You do me wrong.

BELLINDA. You have no more power to keep the secret than I had not to trust you with it.

DORIMANT. By all the joys I have had and those I keep in store —

BELLINDA. — You'll do for my sake, what you never did before.

DORIMANT. By that truth thou hast spoken, a wife shall sooner betray herself to her husband —

BELLINDA. Yet I had rather you should be false in this than in another thing you promised me.

DORIMANT. What's that?

BELLINDA. That you would never see Loveit more but in public places — in the Park, at Court, and plays.

DORIMANT. 'Tis not likely a man should be fond of seeing a damned old play when there is a new one acted.

BELLINDA. I dare not trust your promise.

DORIMANT. You may —

BELLINDA. This does not satisfy me. You shall swear you never will see her more.

DORIMANT. I will, a thousand oaths. By all —

BELLINDA. Hold! You shall not, now I think on't better.

DORIMANT. I will swear!

BELLINDA. I shall grow jealous of the oath and think I owe your truth to that, not to your love.

DORIMANT. Then, by my love; no other oath I'll swear.

Enter HANDY

HANDY. Here's a chair.

BELLINDA. Let me go.

18 Pointless.

DORIMANT. I cannot.

BELLINDA. Too willingly, I fear.

DORIMANT. Too unkindly feared. When will you promise me again?

BELLINDA. Not this fortnight.

DORIMANT. You will be better than your word.

BELLINDA. I think I shall. Will it not make you love me less? (*Starting; fiddles without*) — Hark, what fiddles are these?

DORIMANT. Look out, Handy.   *Exit* HANDY *and returns*

HANDY. Mr. Medley, Mr. Bellair, and Sir Fopling; they are coming up.

DORIMANT. How got they in?

HANDY. The door was open for the chair.

BELLINDA. Lord, let me fly!

DORIMANT. Here! here down the back stairs! I'll see you into your chair.

BELLINDA. No, no! Stay and receive 'em. — And be sure you keep your word and never see Loveit more. Let it be a proof of your kindness.

DORIMANT. It shall. — Handy, direct her. (*Kissing her hand*) Everlasting love go along with thee.   *Exeunt* BELLINDA *and* HANDY

Enter YOUNG BELLAIR, MEDLEY, *and* SIR FOPLING

YOUNG BELLAIR. Not abed yet?

MEDLEY. You have had an irregular fit, Dorimant.

DORIMANT. I have.

YOUNG BELLAIR. And is it off already?

DORIMANT. Nature has done her part, gentlemen; when she falls kindly to work, great cures are effected in little time, you know.

SIR FOPLING. We thought there was a wench in the case, by the chair that waited. Prithee, make us a confidancé.[19]

DORIMANT. Excuse me.

SIR FOPLING. Lè sagè[20] Dorimant! — Was she pretty?

DORIMANT. So pretty she may come to keep her coach and pay parish duties if the good humor of the age continue.

MEDLEY. And be of the number of the ladies kept by public-spirited men for the good of the whole town.

SIR FOPLING. Well said, Medley.

                    (SIR FOPLING *dancing by himself*)

YOUNG BELLAIR. See Sir Fopling dancing!

DORIMANT. You are practising and have a mind to recover, I see.

SIR FOPLING. Prithee, Dorimant, why hast thou not a glass hung up here? A room is the dullest thing without one.

YOUNG BELLAIR. Here is company to entertain you.

[19] Faire une confidance: to tell a secret.
[20] Sage: discreet.

SIR FOPLING. But I mean in case of being alone. In a glass a man may entertain himself —

DORIMANT. The shadow of himself, indeed.

SIR FOPLING. — correct the errors of his motions and his dress.

MEDLEY. I find, Sir Fopling, in your solitude you remember the saying of the wise man, and study yourself.

SIR FOPLING. 'Tis the best diversion in our retirements. Dorimant, thou art a pretty fellow and wear'st thy clothes well, but I never saw thee have a handsome cravat. Were they made up like mine, they'd give another air to thy face. Prithee, let me send my man to dress thee but one day. By heavens, an Englishman cannot tie a ribbon.

DORIMANT. They are something clumsy fisted —

SIR FOPLING. I have brought over the prettiest fellow that ever spread a toilet. He served some time under Merille, the greatest *genie* in the world for a *valet-de-chambré*.

DORIMANT. What, he who formerly belonged to the Duke of Candale?

SIR FOPLING. The same, and got him his immortal reputation.

DORIMANT. Y' have a very fine brandenburg[21] on, Sir Fopling.

SIR FOPLING. It serves to wrap me up after the fatigue of a ball.

MEDLEY. I see you often in it, with your periwig tied up.

SIR FOPLING. We should not always be in a set dress; 'tis more *en cavalier*[22] to appear now and then in a *deshabillée*.

MEDLEY. Pray, how goes your business with Loveit?

SIR FOPLING. You might have answered yourself in the Mall last night. Dorimant, did you not see the advances she made me? I have been endeavoring at a song.

DORIMANT. Already!

SIR FOPLING. 'Tis my *coup d'essai*[23] in English — I would fain have thy opinion of it.

DORIMANT. Let's see it.

SIR FOPLING. Hey, page, give me my song. — Bellair, here; thou hast a pretty voice — sing it.

YOUNG BELLAIR. Sing it yourself, Sir Fopling.

SIR FOPLING. Excuse me.

YOUNG BELLAIR. You learnt to sing in Paris.

SIR FOPLING. I did — of Lambert,[24] the greatest master in the world. But I have his own fault, a weak voice, and care not to sing out of a *ruelle*.[25]

DORIMANT. A *ruelle* is a pretty cage for a singing fop, indeed.

---

[21] Morning gown.
[22] Fashionable.
[23] First attempt.
[24] Michel Lambert (1610-96), a French court musician.
[25] A lady's bedchamber.

YOUNG BELLAIR. (*Reads the song*)

> How charming Phyllis is, how fair!
> Ah, that she were as willing
> To ease my wounded heart of care,
> And make her eyes less killing.
> I sigh, I sigh, I languish now,
> And love will not let me rest;
> I drive about the Park and bow,
> Still as I meet my dearest.

SIR FOPLING. Sing it! sing it, man; it goes to a pretty new tune which I am confident was made by Baptiste.[26]

MEDLEY. Sing it yourself, Sir Fopling; he does not know the tune.

SIR FOPLING. I'll venture.   (SIR FOPLING *sings*)

DORIMANT. Aye, marry! now 'tis something. I shall not flatter you, Sir Fopling; there is not much thought in't, but 'tis passionate and well turned.

MEDLEY. After the French way.

SIR FOPLING. That I aimed at. Does it not give you a lively image of the thing? Slap! down goes the glass,[27] and thus we are at it.

DORIMANT. It does, indeed. I perceive, Sir Fopling, you'll be the very head of the sparks who are lucky in compositions of this nature.

Enter SIR FOPLING's *Footman*

SIR FOPLING. La Tour, is the bath ready?

FOOTMAN. Yes, sir.

SIR FOPLING. *Adieu don[c], mes chers.*[28]   *Exit* SIR FOPLING

MEDLEY. When have you your revenge on Loveit, Dorimant?

DORIMANT. I will but change my linen and about it.

MEDLEY. The powerful considerations which hindered, have been removed then?

DORIMANT. Most luckily this morning. You must alone with me; my reputation lies at stake there.

MEDLEY. I am engaged to Bellair.

DORIMANT. What's your business?

MEDLEY. Ma-tri-mony, an't like you.

DORIMANT. It does not, sir.

YOUNG BELLAIR. It may in time, Dorimant. What think you of Mrs. Harriet?

DORIMANT. What does she think of me?

YOUNG BELLAIR. I am confident she loves you.

DORIMANT. How does it appear?

YOUNG BELLAIR. Why, she's never well but when she's talking of

[26] Jean Baptiste Lully, musician and composer at the court of Louis XIV.
[27] The coach window.
[28] Goodbye then, my friends.

you — but then, she finds all the faults in you she can. She laughs at all who commend you — but then, she speaks ill of all who do not.

DORIMANT. Women of her temper betray themselves by their over-cunning. I had once a growing quarrel with a lady who would always quarrel with me when I came to see her, and yet was never quiet if I stayed a day from her.

YOUNG BELLAIR. My father is in love with Emilia.

DORIMANT. That is a good warrant for your proceedings. Go on and prosper; I must to Loveit. Medley, I am sorry you cannot be a witness.

MEDLEY. Make her meet Sir Fopling again in the same place and use him ill before me.

DORIMANT. That may be brought about, I think. I'll be at your aunt's anon and give you joy, Mr. Bellair.

YOUNG BELLAIR. You had not best think of Mrs. Harriet too much; without church security there's no taking up there.

DORIMANT. I may fall into the snare, too. But —

> The wise will find a difference in our fate;
> You wed a woman, I a good estate.

Exeunt

SCENE III. [*The street before* MRS. LOVEIT'S *house*]

Enter the chair with BELLINDA; *the men set it down and open it.*
BELLINDA *starting*

BELLINDA. (*Surprised*) Lord, where am I? — in the Mall! Whither have you brought me?

FIRST CHAIRMAN. You gave us no directions, madam.

BELLINDA. (*Aside*) The fright I was in made me forget it.

FIRST CHAIRMAN. We use to carry a lady from the Squire's hither.

BELLINDA. (*Aside*) This is Loveit['s]; I am undone if she sees me. — Quickly, carry me away!

FIRST CHAIRMAN. Whither, an't like your honor?

BELLINDA. Ask no questions —

Enter LOVEIT'S *Footman*

FOOTMAN. Have you seen my lady, madam?

BELLINDA. I am just come to wait upon her.

FOOTMAN. She will be glad to see you, madam. She sent me to you this morning to desire your company, and I was told you went out by five o'clock.

BELLINDA. (*Aside*) More and more unlucky!

FOOTMAN. Will you walk in, madam?

BELLINDA. I'll discharge my chair and follow. Tell your mistress I am here. (*Exit* FOOTMAN) Take this (*Gives the Chairmen money*), and if ever you should be examined, say you took me up in the Strand over against the Exchange, as you will answer it to Mr. Dorimant.

CHAIRMEN. We will, an't like your honor.   *Exeunt Chairmen*

BELLINDA. Now to come off, I must on —

> In confidence and lies some hope is left;
> 'Twere hard to be found out in the first theft.

Exit BELLINDA

ACT V

SCENE II. [MISTRESS LOVEIT's *lodgings*]

Enter MRS. LOVEIT *and* PERT, *her woman*

PERT. Well, in my eyes Sir Fopling is no such despicable person.

MRS. LOVEIT. You are an excellent judge.

PERT. He's as handsome a man as Mr. Dorimant, and as great a gallant.

MRS. LOVEIT. Intolerable! Is't not enough I submit to his impertinences but I must be plagued with yours, too?

PERT. Indeed, madam —

MRS. LOVEIT. 'Tis false, mercenary malice —

Enter her Footman

FOOTMAN. Mrs. Bellinda, madam —

MRS. LOVEIT. What of her?

FOOTMAN. She's below.

MRS. LOVEIT. How came she?

FOOTMAN. In a chair; Ambling Harry brought her.

MRS. LOVEIT. He bring her? His chair stands near Dorimant's door and always brings me from thence. — Run and ask him where he took her up. Go! There is no truth in friendship neither. Women, as well as men, all are false, or all are so to me, at least.

PERT. You are jealous of her, too?

MRS. LOVEIT. You had best tell her I am. 'Twill become the liberty you take of late. This fellow's bringing of her, her going out by five o'clock — I know not what to think.

Enter BELLINDA

Bellinda, you are grown an early riser, I hear.

BELLINDA. Do you not wonder, my dear, what made me abroad so soon?

MRS. LOVEIT. You do not use to be so.

BELLINDA. The country gentlewomen I told you of (Lord, they have the oddest diversions!) would never let me rest till I promised to go with them to the market this morning to eat fruit and buy nosegays.

MRS. LOVEIT. Are they so fond of a filthy nosegay?

BELLINDA. They complain of the stinks of the town, and are never well but when they have their noses in one.

MRS. LOVEIT. There are essences and sweet waters.

BELLINDA. Oh, they cry out upon perfumes, they are unwholesome; one of 'em was falling into a fit with the smell of these *nerolii*.[1]

MRS. LOVEIT. Methinks in compliance you should have had a nosegay, too.

BELLINDA. Do you think, my dear, I could be so loathsome, to trick myself up with carnations and stock gillyflowers? I begged their pardon and told them I never wore anything but orange flowers and tuberose. That which made me willing to go, was a strange desire I had to eat some fresh nectarines.

MRS. LOVEIT. And had you any?

BELLINDA. The best I ever tasted.

MRS. LOVEIT. Whence came you now?

BELLINDA. From their lodgings, where I crowded out of a coach and took a chair to come and see you, my dear.

MRS. LOVEIT. Whither did you send for that chair?

BELLINDA. 'Twas going by empty.

MRS. LOVEIT. Where do these countrywomen lodge, I pray?

BELLINDA. In the Strand over against the Exchange.

PERT. The place is never without a nest of 'em. They are always, as one goes by, fleering in balconies or staring out of windows.

Enter Footman

MRS. LOVEIT. (*To the Footman*) Come hither!   (*Whispers*)

BELLINDA. (*Aside*) This fellow by her order has been questioning the chairmen. I threatened 'em with the name of Dorimant; if they should have told the truth, I am lost forever.

MRS. LOVEIT. — In the Strand, said you?

FOOTMAN. Yes, madam; over against the Exchange.

Exit Footman

MRS. LOVEIT. She's innocent, and I am much to blame.

BELLINDA. (*Aside*) I am so frighted my countenance will betray me.

MRS. LOVEIT. Bellinda, what makes you look so pale?

BELLINDA. Want of my usual rest and jolting up and down so long in an odious hackney.

Footman returns

FOOTMAN. Madam, Mr. Dorimant.

---

[1] Essence of orange-flowers.

MRS. LOVEIT. What makes him here?

BELLINDA. (*Aside*) Then I am betrayed, indeed. He's broken his word and I love a man that does not care for me!

MRS. LOVEIT. Lord, you faint, Bellinda!

BELLINDA. I think I shall — such an oppression here on the sudden.

PERT. She has eaten too much fruit I warrant you.

MRS. LOVEIT. Not unlikely.

PERT. 'Tis that lies heavy on her stomach.

MRS. LOVEIT. Have her into my chamber, give her some surfeit water, and let her lie down a little.

PERT. Come, madam, I was a strange devourer of fruit when I was young — so ravenous —

Exeunt BELLINDA *and* PERT *leading her off*

MRS. LOVEIT. Oh, that my love would be but calm awhile, that I might receive this man with all the scorn and indignation he deserves!

Enter DORIMANT

DORIMANT. Now for a touch of Sir Fopling to begin with. — Hey, page, give positive order that none of these people stir. Let the canaille[2] wait as they should do. Since noise and nonsense have such powerful charms,

> I, that I may successful prove,
> Transform myself to what you love.[3]

MRS. LOVEIT. If that would do, you need not change from what you are. You can be vain and loud enough.

DORIMANT. But not with so good a grace as Sir Fopling — "Hey, Hampshire!" — "Oh, that sound, that sound becomes the mouth of a man of quality!"

MRS. LOVEIT. Is there a thing so hateful as a senseless mimic?

DORIMANT. He's a great grievance to all who, like yourself, madam, love to play the fool in quiet.

MRS. LOVEIT. A ridiculous animal, who has more of the ape than the ape has of the man in him!

DORIMANT. I have as mean an opinion of a sheer mimic as yourself; yet were he all ape, I should prefer him to the gay, the giddy, brisk, insipid, noisy fool you dote on.

MRS. LOVEIT. Those noisy fools, however you despise 'em, have good qualities which weigh more (or ought at least) with us women than all the pernicious wit you have to boast of.

DORIMANT. That I may hereafter have a just value for their merit, pray, do me the favor to name 'em.

MRS. LOVEIT. You'll despise 'em as the dull effects of ignorance

---

[2] The vulgar herd.
[3] Waller, "To the Mutable Fair."

and vanity; yet I care not if I mention some. First, they really admire us, while you at best but flatter us well.

DORIMANT. Take heed! Fools can dissemble, too.

MRS. LOVEIT. They may, but not so artificially as you. There is no fear they should deceive us! Then, they are assiduous, sir; they are ever offering us their service, and always waiting on our will.

DORIMANT. You owe that to their excessive idleness. They know not how to entertain themselves at home, and find so little welcome abroad they are fain to fly to you who countenance 'em, as a refuge against the solitude they would be otherwise condemned to.

MRS. LOVEIT. Their conversation, too, diverts us better.

DORIMANT. Playing with your fan, smelling to your gloves, commending your hair, and taking notice how 'tis cut and shaded after the new way —

MRS. LOVEIT. Were it sillier than you can make it, you must allow 'tis pleasanter to laugh at others than to be laughed at ourselves, though never so wittily. Then, though they want skill to flatter us, they flatter themselves so well they save us the labor. We need not take that care and pains to satisfy 'em of our love, which we so often lose on you.

DORIMANT. They commonly, indeed, believe too well of themselves, and always better of you than you deserve.

MRS. LOVEIT. You are in the right. They have an implicit faith in us which keeps 'em from prying narrowly into our secrets and saves us the vexatious trouble of clearing doubts which your subtle and causeless jealousies every moment raise.

DORIMANT. There is an inbred falsehood in women, which inclines 'em still to them whom they may most easily deceive.

MRS. LOVEIT. The man who loves above his quality does not suffer more from the insolent impertinence of his mistress than the woman who loves above her understanding does from the arrogant presumptions of her friend.

DORIMANT. You mistake the use of fools; they are designed for properties,[4] and not for friends. You have an indifferent stock of reputation left yet. Lose it all like a frank gamester on the square; 'twill then be time enough to turn rook and cheat it up again on a good, substantial bubble.[5]

MRS. LOVEIT. The old and the ill-favored are only fit for properties, indeed, but the young and handsome fools have met with kinder fortunes.

DORIMANT. They have — to the shame of your sex be it spoken! 'Twas this, the thought of this, made me by a timely jealousy endeavor to prevent the good fortune you are providing for Sir Fopling. But against a woman's frailty all our care is vain.

[4] Dupes, to be deceived and used.
[5] Dupe or victim of a sharper.

MRS. LOVEIT. Had I not with a dear experience bought the knowledge of your falsehood, you might have fooled me yet. This is not the first jealousy you have feigned, to make a quarrel with me, and get a week to throw away on some such unknown, inconsiderable slut as you have been lately lurking with at plays.

DORIMANT. Women, when they would break off with a man, never want th' address to turn the fault on him.

MRS. LOVEIT. You take a pride of late in using me ill, that the town may know the power you have over me, which now (as unreasonably as yourself) expects that I (do me all the injuries you can) must love you still.

DORIMANT. I am so far from expecting that you should, I begin to think you never did love me.

MRS. LOVEIT. Would the memory of it were so wholly worn out in me that I did doubt it, too! What made you come to disturb my growing quiet?

DORIMANT. To give you joy of your growing infamy.

MRS. LOVEIT. Insupportable! Insulting devil! This from you, the only author of my shame! This from another had been but justice; but from you, 'tis a hellish and inhuman outrage. What have I done?

DORIMANT. A thing that puts you below my scorn, and makes my anger as ridiculous as you have made my love.

MRS. LOVEIT. I walked last night with Sir Fopling.

DORIMANT. You did, madam; and you talked and laughed aloud, "Ha, ha, ha!" — Oh, that laugh! that laugh becomes the confidence of a woman of quality.

MRS. LOVEIT. You who have more pleasure in the ruin of a woman's reputation than in the endearments of her love, reproach me not with yourself — and I defy you to name the man can lay a blemish on my fame.

DORIMANT. To be seen publicly so transported with the vain follies of that notorious fop, to me is an infamy below the sin of prostitution with another man.

MRS. LOVEIT. Rail on! I am satisfied in the justice of what I did; you had provoked me to't.

DORIMANT. What I did was the effect of a passion whose extravagancies you have been willing to forgive.

MRS. LOVEIT. And what I did was the effect of a passion you may forgive if you think fit.

DORIMANT. Are you so indifferent grown?

MRS. LOVEIT. I am.

DORIMANT. Nay, then 'tis time to part. I'll send you back your letters you have so often asked for. — I have two or three of 'em about me.

MRS. LOVEIT. Give 'em me.

DORIMANT. You snatch as if you thought I would not. There! and may the perjuries in 'em be mine if e'er I see you more. (*Offers to go; she catches him*)

MRS. LOVEIT. Stay!

DORIMANT. I will not.

MRS. LOVEIT. You shall.

DORIMANT. What have you to say?

MRS. LOVEIT. I cannot speak it yet.

——DORIMANT. Something more in commendation of the fool? — Death, I want patience; let me go!

MRS. LOVEIT. I cannot. (*Aside*) I can sooner part with the limbs that hold him. — I hate that nauseous fool; you know I do.

DORIMANT. Was it the scandal you were fond of then?

MRS. LOVEIT. Y'had raised my anger equal to my love — a thing you ne'er could do before, and in revenge I did — I know not what I did. Would you would not think on't any more!

DORIMANT. Should I be willing to forget it, I shall be daily minded of it; 'twill be a commonplace for all the town to laugh at me, and Medley, when he is rhetorically drunk, will ever be declaiming on it in my ears.

MRS. LOVEIT. 'Twill be believed a jealous spite. Come, forget it.

DORIMANT. Let me consult my reputation; you are too careless of it. (*Pauses*) You shall meet Sir Fopling in the Mall again to-night.

MRS. LOVEIT. What mean you?

DORIMANT. I have thought on it, and you must. 'Tis necessary to justify my love to the world. You can handle a coxcomb as he deserves when you are not out of humor, madam.

MRS. LOVEIT. Public satisfaction for the wrong I have done you? This is some new device to make me more ridiculous.

DORIMANT. Hear me!

MRS. LOVEIT. I will not.

DORIMANT. You will be persuaded.

MRS. LOVEIT. Never!

DORIMANT. Are you so obstinate?

MRS. LOVEIT. Are you so base?

DORIMANT. You will not satisfy my love?

MRS. LOVEIT. I would die to satisfy that; but I will not, to save you from a thousand racks, do a shameless thing to please your vanity.

DORIMANT. Farewell, false woman!

MRS. LOVEIT. Do — go!

DORIMANT. You will call me back again.

MRS. LOVEIT. Exquisite fiend, I knew you came but to torment me!

Enter BELLINDA *and* PERT

DORIMANT. (*Surprised*) Bellinda here!

BELLINDA. (*Aside*) He starts and looks pale! The sight of me has touched his guilty soul.

PERT. 'Twas but a qualm, as I said — a little indigestion; the surfeit water did it, madam, mixed with a little *mirabilis*.[6]

DORIMANT. I am confounded, and cannot guess how she came hither!

MRS. LOVEIT. 'Tis your fortune, Bellinda, ever to be here when I am abused by this prodigy of ill-nature.

BELLINDA. I am amazed to find him here. How has he the face to come near you?

DORIMANT. (*Aside*) Here is fine work towards! I never was at such a loss before.

BELLINDA. One who makes a public profession of breach of faith and gratitude — I loathe the sight of him.

DORIMANT. [*Aside*] There is no remedy; I must submit to their tongues now, and some other time bring myself off as well as I can.

BELLINDA. Other men are wicked; but then, they have some sense of shame! He is never well but when he triumphs — nay, glories to a woman's face in his villainies.

MRS. LOVEIT. You are in the right, Bellinda, but methinks your kindness for me makes you concern yourself too much with him.

BELLINDA. It does indeed, my dear. His barbarous carriage to you yesterday made me hope you ne'er would see him more, and the very next day to find him here again, provokes me strangely. But because I know you love him, I have done.

DORIMANT. You have reproached me handsomely, and I deserve it for coming hither; but —

PERT. You must expect it, sir. All women will hate you for my lady's sake.

DORIMANT. Nay, if she begins too, 'tis time to fly; I shall be scolded to death else. (*Aside to* BELLINDA) I am to blame in some circumstances, I confess; but as to the main, I am not so guilty as you imagine. [*Aloud*] I shall seek a more convenient time to clear myself.

MRS. LOVEIT. Do it now. What impediments are here?

DORIMANT. I want time, and you want temper.

MRS. LOVEIT. These are weak pretenses.

DORIMANT. You were never more mistaken in your life; and so farewell.   (DORIMANT *flings off*)

MRS. LOVEIT. Call a footman, Pert, quickly; I will have him dogged.

PERT. I wish you would not, for my quiet and your own.

MRS. LOVEIT. I'll find out the infamous cause of all our quarrels, pluck her mask off, and expose her bare-faced to the world!

BELLINDA. (*Aside*) Let me but escape this time, I'll never venture more.

[6] Aqua mirabilis, made of spirits of wine and spices.

MRS. LOVEIT. Bellinda, you shall go with me.

BELLINDA. I have such a heaviness hangs on me with what I did this morning, I would fain go home and sleep, my dear.

MRS. LOVEIT. Death! and eternal darkness! I shall never sleep again. Raging fevers seize the world and make mankind as restless as I am!   *Exit* MRS. LOVEIT

BELLINDA. I knew him false and helped to make him so. Was not her ruin enough to fright me from the danger? It should have been, but love can take no warning.   *Exit* BELLINDA

SCENE II. LADY TOWNLEY's *house*

Enter MEDLEY, YOUNG BELLAIR, LADY TOWNLEY, EMILIA, *and*
[SMIRK, a] *Chaplain*

MEDLEY. Bear up, Bellair, and do not let us see that repentance in thine we daily do in married faces.

LADY TOWNLEY. This marriage will strangely surprise my brother when he knows it.

MEDLEY. Your nephew ought to conceal it for a time, madam. Since marriage has lost its good name, prudent men seldom expose their own reputations till 'tis convenient to justify their wives.

OLD BELLAIR (*Without*) Where are you all there? Out! a dod, will nobody hear?

LADY TOWNLEY. My brother! Quickly, Mr. Smirk, into this closet; you must not be seen yet!   (SMIRK *goes into the closet*)

Enter OLD BELLAIR *and* LADY TOWNLEY's *Page*

OLD BELLAIR. Desire Mr. Fourbe to walk into the lower parlor; I will be with him presently. (*To* YOUNG BELLAIR) Where have you been, sir, you could not wait on me to-day?

YOUNG BELLAIR. About a business.

OLD BELLAIR. Are you so good at business? A dod, I have a business too, you shall dispatch out of hand, sir. — Send for a parson, sister; my Lady Woodvill and her daughter are coming.

LADY TOWNLEY. What need you huddle up things thus?

OLD BELLAIR. Out a pize! youth is apt to play the fool, and 'tis not good it should be in their power.

LADY TOWNLEY. You need not fear your son.

OLD BELLAIR. H'has been idling this morning, and a dod, I do not like him. (*To* EMILIA) How dost thou do, sweetheart?

EMILIA. You are very severe, sir — married in such haste.

OLD BELLAIR. Go to, thou'rt a rogue, and I will talk with thee anon. Here's my Lady Woodvill come.

Enter LADY WOODVILL, HARRIET, *and* BUSY

Welcome, madam; Mr. Fourbe's below with the writings.

LADY WOODVILL. Let us down and make an end then.

OLD BELLAIR. Sister, show us the way. (*To* YOUNG BELLAIR, *who is talking to* HARRIET) Harry, your business lies not there yet. Excuse him till we have done, lady, and then, a dod, he shall be for thee. Mr. Medley, we must trouble you to be a witness.

MEDLEY. I luckily came for that purpose, sir.

Exeunt OLD BELLAIR, YOUNG BELLAIR, LADY TOWNLEY,
and LADY WOODVILL

BUSY. What will you do, madam?

HARRIET. Be carried back and mewed up in the country again — run away here — anything rather than be married to a man I do not care for! Dear Emilia, do thou advise me.

EMILIA. Mr. Bellair is engaged, you know.

HARRIET. I do, but know not what the fear of losing an estate may fright him to.

EMILIA. In the desperate condition you are in, you should consult with some judicious man. What think you of Mr. Dorimant?

HARRIET. I do not think of him at all.

BUSY. She thinks of nothing else, I am sure.

EMILIA. How fond your mother was of Mr. Courtage!

HARRIET. Because I contrived the mistake to make a little mirth, you believe I like the man.

EMILIA. Mr. Bellair believes you love him.

HARRIET. Men are seldom in the right when they guess at a woman's mind. Would she whom he loves, loved him no better!

BUSY (*Aside*) That's e'en well enough, on all conscience.

EMILIA. Mr. Dorimant has a great deal of wit.

HARRIET. And takes a great deal of pains to show it.

EMILIA. He's extremely well fashioned.

HARRIET. Affectedly grave, or ridiculously wild and apish.

BUSY. You defend him still against your mother!

HARRIET. I would not, were he justly rallied, but I cannot hear anyone undeservedly railed at.

EMILIA. Has your woman learned the song you were so taken with?

HARRIET. I was fond of a new thing; 'tis dull at a second hearing.

EMILIA. Mr. Dorimant made it.

BUSY. She knows it, madam, and has made me sing it at least a dozen times this morning.

HARRIET. Thy tongue is as impertinent as thy fingers.

EMILIA. You have provoked her.

BUSY. 'Tis but singing the song and I shall appease her.

EMILIA. Prithee, do.

HARRIET. She has a voice will grate your ears worse than a cat-call, and dresses so ill she's scarce fit to trick up a yeoman's daughter on a holiday. (BUSY *sings*)

SONG

BY SIR C. S.[7]

As Amoret with Phyllis sat,
One evening on the plain,
And saw the charming Strephon wait
To tell the nymph his pain;

The threat'ning danger to remove,
She whispered in her ear,
"Ah, Phyllis, if you would not love,
This shepherd do not hear!

"None ever had so strange an art,
His passion to convey
Into a list'ning virgin's heart,
And steal her soul away.

"Fly, fly betimes, for fear you give
Occasion for your fate."
"In vain," said she; "in vain I strive!
Alas, 'tis now too late."

Enter DORIMANT

DORIMANT.   Music so softens and disarms the mind —

HARRIET.   That not one arrow does resistance find.[8]

DORIMANT. Let us make use of the lucky minute, then.

HARRIET. (*Aside, turning from* DORIMANT) My love springs with my blood into my face; I dare not look upon him yet.

DORIMANT. What have we here? the picture of a celebrated beauty giving audience in public to a declared lover?

HARRIET. Play the dying fop and make the piece complete, sir.

DORIMANT. What think you if the hint were well improved? The whole mystery of making love pleasantly designed and wrought in a suit of hangings?[9]

HARRIET. 'Twere needless to execute fools in effigy who suffer daily in their own persons.

DORIMANT. (*Aside to* EMILIA) Mrs. Bride, for such I know this happy day has made you —

EMILIA. [*Aside*] Defer the formal joy you are to give me, and mind your business with her. (*Aloud*) Here are dreadful preparations, Mr. Dorimant — writings sealing, and a parson sent for.

DORIMANT. To marry this lady?

7 The song is probably by Sir Carr Scroope, who wrote the prologue.
8 Waller, "Of my Lady Isabella playing on the lute."
9 A set of tapestry wall hangings.

BUSY. Condemned she is, and what will become of her I know not, without you generously engage in a rescue.

DORIMANT. In this sad condition, madam, I can do no less than offer you my service.

HARRIET. The obligation is not great; you are the common sanctuary for all young women who run from their relations.

DORIMANT. I have always my arms open to receive the distressed, but I will open my heart and receive you where none yet did ever enter. You have filled it with a secret; might I but let you know it —

HARRIET. Do not speak it if you would have me believe it. Your tongue is so famed for falsehood, 'twill do the truth an injury.

(*Turns away her head*)

DORIMANT. Turn not away, then, but look on me and guess it.

HARRIET. Did you not tell me there was no credit to be given to faces? — that women nowadays have their passions as much at will as they have their complexions, and put on joy and sadness, scorn and kindness, with the same ease they do their paint and patches? Are they the only counterfeits?

DORIMANT. You wrong your own while you suspect my eyes. By all the hope I have in you, the inimitable color in your cheeks is not more free from art than are the sighs I offer.

HARRIET. In men who have been long hardened in sin, we have reason to mistrust the first signs of repentance.

DORIMANT. The prospect of such a heaven will make me persevere and give you marks that are infallible.

HARRIET. What are those?

DORIMANT. I will renounce all the joy I have in friendship and in wine, sacrifice to you all the interest I have in other women —

HARRIET. Hold! Though I wish you devout, I would not have you turn fanatic. Could you neglect these a while and make a journey into the country?

DORIMANT. To be with you, I could live there and never send one thought to London.

HARRIET. Whate'er you say, I know all beyond Hyde Park's a desert to you, and that no gallantry can draw you farther.

DORIMANT. That has been the utmost limit of my love; but now my passion knows no bounds, and there's no measure to be taken of what I'll do for you from anything I ever did before.

HARRIET. When I hear you talk thus in Hampshire, I shall begin to think there may be some little truth enlarged upon.

DORIMANT. Is this all? — Will you not promise me —

HARRIET. I hate to promise; what we do then is expected from us and wants much of the welcome it finds when it surprises.

DORIMANT. May I not hope?

HARRIET. That depends on you and not on me, and 'tis to no purpose to forbid it.   (*Turns to* BUSY)

BUSY. Faith, madam, now I perceive the gentleman loves you, too; e'en let him know your mind and torment yourselves no longer.

HARRIET. Dost think I have no sense of modesty?

BUSY. Think, if you lose this you may never have another opportunity.

HARRIET. May he hate me (a curse that frights me when I speak it), if ever I do a thing against the rules of decency and honor.

DORIMANT (*To* EMILIA) I am beholding to you for your good intentions, madam.

EMILIA. I thought the concealing of our marriage from her might have done you better service.

DORIMANT. Try her again.

EMILIA. What have you resolved, madam? The time draws near.

HARRIET. To be obstinate and protest against this marriage.

Enter LADY TOWNLEY *in haste*

LADY TOWNLEY. (*To* EMILIA) Quickly! quickly! let Mr. Smirk out of the closet.   (SMIRK *comes out of the closet*)

HARRIET. A parson! Had you laid him in here?

DORIMANT. I knew nothing of him.

HARRIET. Should it appear you did, your opinion of my easiness may cost you dear.

Enter OLD BELLAIR, YOUNG BELLAIR, MEDLEY, *and* LADY WOODVILL

OLD BELLAIR. Out a pize! the canonical hour[10] is almost past. Sister, is the man of God come?

LADY TOWNLEY. He waits your leisure.

OLD BELLAIR. [*To* SMIRK] By your favor, sir. — A dod, a pretty spruce fellow! What may we call him?

LADY TOWNLEY. Mr. Smirk — my Lady Bigot's chaplain.

OLD BELLAIR. A wise woman; a dod, she is. The man will serve for the flesh as well as the spirit. [*To* SMIRK] Please you, sir, to commission a young couple to go to bed together a-God's name. — Harry!

YOUNG BELLAIR. Here, sir.

OLD BELLAIR. Out a pize! Without your mistress in your hand?

SMIRK. Is this the gentleman?

OLD BELLAIR. Yes, sir.

SMIRK. Are you not mistaken, sir?

OLD BELLAIR. A dod, I think not, sir.

SMIRK. Sure, you are, sir!

---

[10] The canonical hours for marriage were from eight in the morning until noon.

OLD BELLAIR. You look as if you would forbid the banns, Mr. Smirk. I hope you have no pretension to the lady?

SMIRK. Wish him joy, sir; I have done the good office to-day already.

OLD BELLAIR. Out a pize! What do I hear?

LADY TOWNLEY. Never storm, brother; the truth is out.

OLD BELLAIR. How say you, sir? Is this your wedding day?

YOUNG BELLAIR. It is, sir.

OLD BELLAIR. And a dod, it shall be mine too. (*To* EMILIA) Give me your hand, sweetheart. — What dost thou mean? Give me thy hand, I say. (EMILIA *kneels and* YOUNG BELLAIR)

LADY TOWNLEY. Come, come! give her your blessing. This is the woman your son loved and is married to.

OLD BELLAIR. Ha! cheated! cozened! and by your contrivance, sister!

LADY TOWNLEY. What would you do with her? She's a rogue and you can't abide her.

MEDLEY. Shall I hit her a pat for you, sir?

OLD BELLAIR. [*Flinging away*] A dod, you are all rogues, and I never will forgive you.

LADY TOWNLEY. Whither? Whither away?

MEDLEY. Let him go and cool awhile.

LADY WOODVILL. (*To* DORIMANT) Here's a business broke out now, Mr. Courtage; I am made a fine fool of.

DORIMANT. You see the old gentleman knew nothing of it.

LADY WOODVILL. I find he did not. I shall have some trick put upon me if I stay in this wicked town any longer. — Harriet! Dear child, where art thou? I'll into the country straight.

OLD BELLAIR. A dod, madam, you shall hear me first.

Enter MRS. LOVEIT *and* BELLINDA

MRS. LOVEIT. Hither my man dogged him.

BELLINDA. Yonder he stands, my dear.

MRS. LOVEIT. I see him, (*Aside*) and with him the face that has undone me. Oh, that I were but where I might throw out the anguish of my heart! Here, it must rage within and break it.

LADY TOWNLEY. Mrs. Loveit! Are you afraid to come forward?

MRS. LOVEIT. I was amazed to see so much company here in the morning. The occasion sure is extraordinary.

DORIMANT. (*Aside*) Loveit and Bellinda! The devil owes me a shame to-day and I think never will have done paying it.

MRS. LOVEIT. Married! dear Emilia! How am I transported with the news!

HARRIET. (*To* DORIMANT) I little thought Emilia was the woman Mr. Bellair was in love with. I'll chide her for not trusting me with the secret.

DORIMANT. How do you like Mrs. Loveit?

HARRIET. She's a famed mistress of yours, I hear.

DORIMANT. She has been on occasion.

OLD BELLAIR. (*To* LADY WOODVILL) A dod, madam, I cannot help it.

LADY WOODVILL. You need make no more apologies, sir.

EMILIA. (*To* MRS. LOVEIT) The old gentleman's excusing himself to my Lady Woodvill.

MRS. LOVEIT. Ha, ha, ha! I never heard of anything so pleasant!

HARRIET. (*To* DORIMANT) She's extremely overjoyed at something.

DORIMANT. At nothing. She is one of those hoiting[11] ladies who gaily fling themselves about and force a laugh when their aching hearts are full of discontent and malice.

MRS. LOVEIT. O Heaven! I was never so near killing myself with laughing — Mr. Dorimant, are you a brideman?

LADY WOODVILL. Mr. Dorimant! — Is this Mr. Dorimant, madam?

MRS. LOVEIT. If you doubt it, your daughter can resolve you, I suppose.

LADY WOODVILL. I am cheated too — basely cheated!

OLD BELLAIR. Out a pize! what's here? More knavery yet?

LADY WOODVILL. Harriet! On my blessing, come away, I charge you!

HARRIET. Dear mother, do but stay and hear me.

LADY WOODVILL. I am betrayed and thou art undone, I fear.

HARRIET. Do not fear it; I have not, nor never will, do anything against my duty. Believe me, dear mother — do!

DORIMANT. (*To* MRS. LOVEIT) I had trusted you with this secret but that I knew the violence of your nature would ruin my fortune — as now unluckily it has. I thank you, madam.

MRS. LOVEIT. She's an heiress, I know, and very rich.

DORIMANT. To satisfy you, I must give up my interest wholly to my love. Had you been a reasonable woman, I might have secured 'em both and been happy.

MRS. LOVEIT. You might have trusted me with anything of this kind — you know you might. Why did you go under a wrong name?

DORIMANT. The story is too long to tell you now. Be satisfied, this is the business; this is the mask has kept me from you.

BELLINDA. (*Aside*) He's tender of my honor though he's cruel to my love.

MRS. LOVEIT. Was it no idle mistress, then?

DORIMANT. Believe me, a wife to repair the ruins of my estate that needs it.

MRS. LOVEIT. The knowledge of this makes my grief hang lighter on my soul, but I shall never more be happy.

DORIMANT. Bellinda!

[11] Romping.

BELLINDA. Do not think of clearing yourself with me; it is impossible. Do all men break their words thus?

DORIMANT. Th'extravagant words they speak in love. 'Tis as unreasonable to expect we should perform all we promise then, as do all we threaten when we are angry. When I see you next —

BELLINDA. Take no notice of me, and I shall not hate you.

DORIMANT. How came you to Mrs. Loveit?

BELLINDA. By a mistake the chairmen made, for want of my giving them directions.

DORIMANT. 'Twas a pleasant one. We must meet again.

BELLINDA. Never!

DORIMANT. Never?

BELLINDA. When we do, may I be as infamous as you are false.

LADY TOWNLEY. Men of Mr. Dorimant's character always suffer in the general opinion of the world.

MEDLEY. You can make no judgment of a witty man from common fame, considering the prevailing faction, madam.

OLD BELLAIR. A dod, he's in the right.

MEDLEY. Besides, 'tis a common error among women to believe too well of them they know, and too ill of them they don't.

OLD BELLAIR. A dod, he observes well.

LADY TOWNLEY. Believe me, madam, you will find Mr. Dorimant as civil a gentleman as you thought Mr. Courtage.

HARRIET. If you would but know him better —

LADY WOODVILL. You have a mind to know him better? Come away! You shall never see him more.

HARRIET. Dear mother, stay!

LADY WOODVILL. I won't be consenting to your ruin.

HARRIET. Were my fortune in your power —

LADY WOODVILL. Your person is.

HARRIET. Could I be disobedient, I might take it out of yours and put it into his.

LADY WOODVILL. 'Tis that you would be at? — You would marry this Dorimant?

HARRIET. I cannot deny it; I would, and never will marry any other man.

LADY WOODVILL. Is this the duty that you promised?

HARRIET. But I will never marry him against your will.

LADY WOODVILL. (*Aside*) She knows the way to melt my heart. (*Aloud*) Upon yourself light your undoing!

MEDLEY. (*To* OLD BELLAIR) Come, sir, you have not the heart any longer to refuse your blessing.

OLD BELLAIR. A dod, I ha' not. — Rise, and God bless you both! Make much of her, Harry; she deserves thy kindness. (*To* EMILIA) A dod, sirrah, I did not think it had been in thee!

Enter SIR FOPLING *and his Page*

SIR FOPLING. 'Tis a damned windy day. Hey, page, is my periwig right?

PAGE. A little out of order, sir.

SIR FOPLING. Pox o' this apartment! It wants an antechamber to adjust oneself in. (*To* MRS. LOVEIT) Madam, I came from your house, and your servants directed me hither.

MRS. LOVEIT. I will give order hereafter they shall direct you better.

SIR FOPLING. The great satisfaction I had in the Mall last night has given me much disquiet since.

MRS. LOVEIT. 'Tis likely to give me more than I desire.

SIR FOPLING. What the devil makes her so reserved? — Am I guilty of an indiscretion, madam?

MRS. LOVEIT. You will be — of a great one — if you continue your mistake, sir.

SIR FOPLING. Something puts you out of humor.

MRS. LOVEIT. The most foolish, inconsiderable thing that ever did.

SIR FOPLING. Is it in my power?

MRS. LOVEIT. — To hang or drown it. Do one of 'em and trouble me no more.

SIR FOPLING. So fieré? Serviteur, madam.[12] — Medley, where's Dorimant?

MEDLEY. Methinks the lady has not made you those advances to-day she did last night, Sir Fopling.

SIR FOPLING. Prithee, do not talk of her!

MEDLEY. She would be a *bonne fortune*.

SIR FOPLING. Not to me at present.

MEDLEY. How so?

SIR FOPLING. An intrigue now would be but a temptation to me to throw away that vigor on one, which I mean shall shortly make my court to the whole sex in a ballet.

MEDLEY. Wisely considered, Sir Fopling.

SIR FOPLING. No woman is worth the loss of a cut in a caper.

MEDLEY. Not when 'tis so universally designed.

LADY WOODVILL. Mr. Dorimant, everyone has spoke so much in your behalf that I can no longer doubt but I was in the wrong.

MRS. LOVEIT. There's nothing but falsehood and impertinence in this world! All men are villains or fools; take example from my misfortunes, Bellinda; if thou wouldst be happy, give thyself wholly up to goodness.

HARRIET. (*To* MRS. LOVEIT) Mr. Dorimant has been your God Almighty long enough; 'tis time to think of another.

[12] So haughty? Your servant, madam.

MRS. LOVEIT. Jeered by her! — I will lock myself up in my house and never see the world again.

HARRIET. A nunnery is the more fashionable place for such a retreat, and has been the fatal consequence of many a *belle passion*.[13]

MRS. LOVEIT. Hold, heart, till I get home! Should I answer, 'twould make her triumph greater. (*Is going out*)

DORIMANT. Your hand, Sir Fopling —

SIR FOPLING. Shall I wait upon you, madam?

MRS. LOVEIT. Legion of fools, as many devils take thee!

Exit MRS. LOVEIT

MEDLEY. Dorimant, I pronounce thy reputation clear; and henceforward when I would know anything of woman, I will consult no other oracle.

SIR FOPLING. Stark mad, by all that's handsome! — Dorimant, thou hast engaged me in a pretty business.

DORIMANT. I have not leisure now to talk about it.

OLD BELLAIR. Out a pize! what does this man of mode do here again?

LADY TOWNLEY. He'll be an excellent entertainment within, brother, and is luckily come to raise the mirth of the company.

LADY WOODVILL. Madam, I take my leave of you.

LADY TOWNLEY. What do you mean, madam?

LADY WOODVILL. To go this afternoon part of my way to Hartley —

OLD BELLAIR. A dod, you shall stay and dine first! Come, we will all be good friends, and you shall give Mr. Dorimant leave to wait upon you and your daughter in the country.

LADY WOODVILL. If his occasions bring him that way, I have now so good an opinion of him, he shall be welcome.

HARRIET. To a great rambling, lone house that looks as it were not inhabited, the family's so small. There you'll find my mother, an old lame aunt, and myself, sir, perched up on chairs at a distance in a great parlor, sitting moping like three or four melancholy birds in a spacious volery.[14] Does not this stagger your resolution?

DORIMANT. Not at all, madam. The first time I saw you you left me with the pangs of love upon me, and this day my soul has quite given up her liberty.

HARRIET. This is more dismal than the country! Emilia, pity me, who am going to that sad place. Methinks I hear the hateful noise of rooks already — *Kaw, kaw, kaw!* There's music in the worst cry in London, "My dill and cowcumbers to pickle!"[15]

OLD BELLAIR. Sister, knowing of this matter, I hope you have provided us some good cheer.

LADY TOWNLEY. I have, brother, and the fiddles, too.

---

13 Love affair.   14 Aviary.
15 A street-vendor's cry.

OLD BELLAIR. Let 'em strike up, then; the young lady shall have a
dance before she departs.   (*Dance*)
(*After the dance*) — So! Now we'll in and make this an arrant wedding-day.   (*To the pit*)

> And if these honest gentlemen rejoice,
> A dod, the boy has made a happy choice.

Exeunt omnes

THE EPILOGUE

By Mr. Dryden

Most modern wits such monstrous fools have shown,
They seemed not of Heaven's making, but their own.
Those nauseous harlequins in farce may pass,
But there goes more to a substantial ass;
Something of man must be exposed to view,
That, gallants, they may more resemble you.
Sir Fopling is a fool so nicely writ,
The ladies would mistake him for a wit,
And when he sings, talks loud, and cocks,[1] would cry,
"I vow, methinks he's pretty company!"
So brisk, so gay, so traveled, so refined,
As he took pains to graft upon his kind.[2]
True fops help nature's work and go to school,
To file and finish God A'mighty's fool.
Yet none Sir Fopling him, or him, can call;
He's knight o'th' shire,[3] and represents ye all.
From each he meets, he culls whate'er he can;
Legion's his name, a people in a man.
His bulky folly gathers as it goes,
And, rolling o'er you, like a snowball grows.
His various modes, from various fathers follow;
One taught the toss,[4] and one the new French wallow;[5]
His sword-knot, this; his cravat, this, designed;
And this, the yard-long snake[6] he twirls behind.
From one the sacred periwig he gained,
Which wind ne'er blew, nor touch of hat profaned.
Another's diving bow he did adore,
Which with a shog[7] casts all his hair before,
Till he with full decorum brings it back,
And rises with a water spaniel's shake.
As for his songs (the ladies' sheer delight),
Those sure he took from most of you who write.
Yet every man is safe from what he feared,
For no one fool is hunted from the herd.

---

[1] Struts and cocks his hat.   [2] To improve his natural folly.
[3] A member of Parliament, hence a representative, a type.
[4] Toss of the head.   [5] Fashionable rolling gait.
[6] Tail of his wig.   [7] A jerk, shake.

ALL FOR LOVE

or, THE WORLD WELL LOST

A

TRAGEDY

As it is Acted at the Theatre-Royal;
And Written in Imitation of Shakespeare's Stile

By JOHN DRYDEN, *Servant to His Majesty*

Facile est verbum aliquod ardens (ut ita dicam) notare: idque
restinctis animorum incendis irridere.   CICERO[1]

IN THE SAVOY:

Printed by Tho. Newcomb, *for* Henry Herringman, *at the*
Blew Anchor *in the* Lower Walk *of the*
New-Exchange. *1678.*

---

[1] It is easy to note some glowing word, if I may say so, and to laugh at it
when the fires of the mind are cooled.
        — Cicero, *Orator ad M. Brutum,* VIII, 27-29.

ALL FOR LOVE

or, The World Well Lost

John Dryden

IN THE COURSE of his long professional career, John Dryden (1631-1700) wrote, alone or in collaboration, some twenty-eight plays — comedies, tragedies, tragicomedies, and operas. Poet, playwright, satirist, translator, critic, and essayist, Dryden achieved fame in his own day as the greatest English man of letters. In his old age, when he was the arbiter of Will's Coffee-house, the world of learning and literature gave him its homage.

Generally recognized as his greatest play, *All for Love* (1678) inevitably invites comparison with Shakespeare's *Antony and Cleopatra* (1607). But comparisons are odious; although Dryden professed to write "in imitation of Shakespeare's style," his tragedy is not a mere alteration or adaptation of Shakespeare's. Its simple structure, clear-cut images, and sinewy blank verse differ sharply from the infinite variety, rich allusiveness, and flowing music of the great original. Dryden wrote for a new age with values quite unlike those of the Elizabethans. To please the new taste he had to observe neo-classic decorum and the unities of time, place, and action. Therefore he took his famous lovers at the climax of their lives, that last day in Alexandria when their world crashed in chaos. Dryden's Antony is magnificently heroic; torn between love and honor (as represented by Cleopatra and Ventidius), he ends with neither and goes grandly to his death. Cleopatra is no coquette, no serpent of the Nile, but the embodiment of woman in love, lost to reason and sunk in passion; for a love such as hers the world could, indeed, be well lost. Defeat, foreshadowed in the earliest scenes, becomes inevitable as the closely organized plot moves inexorably to its climax. In the stormy sea of Restoration heroic rant and bombast, *All for Love* stands like a steady beacon of sound judgment and good dramaturgy.

Although Dryden had written *All for Love* before midsummer, 1677, its production at the Theatre Royal in Bridges Street was postponed until December. By that time, bad management, quarrels, and desertions had sadly weakened the King's Company. Charles Hart and Michael Mohun, somewhat handicapped by age and illness, gave their usual impressive performances as Antony and Ventidius respectively, but young and comparatively inexperienced actors played the lesser male characters. Because of the shortage of experienced actresses, Katherine Corey, a comedienne who usually took "old woman" parts, played Octavia, and blonde Betty Boutell, an ingénue, somewhat incongruously played Cleopatra, a role originally designed for dark, passionate Rebecca Marshall, who had deserted to the Duke's Company. (In later productions Elizabeth Barry played the leading role so successfully as to earn the nickname of "the renowned Cleopatra.") In spite of acting difficulties, the play was a success, and it remained a stock theatrical piece until well into the eighteenth century.

See *The Dramatic Works of John Dryden*, ed. Montague Summers, 1932; Hazelton Spencer, *Shakespeare Improved*, 1927; Bonamy Dobrée, *Restoration Tragedy*, 1929 ; F. R. Leavis, "Antony and Cleopatra and All for Love," *Scrutiny*, V (September, 1936); and M. E. Prior, *The Language of Tragedy*, 1947, Chap. III.

Dramatis Personae

MARK ANTONY	MR. HART
VENTIDIUS, *his General*	MR. MOHUN
DOLABELLA, *his Friend*	MR. CLARKE
ALEXAS, *the Queen's Eunuch*	MR. GOODMAN
SERAPION, *Priest of Isis*	MR. GRIFFIN
MYRIS, *another Priest*	MR. COYSH
Servants to Antony	
CLEOPATRA, *Queen of Egypt*	MRS. BOUTELL
OCTAVIA, *Antony's Wife*	MRS. COREY
CHARMION	*Cleopatra's Maids*	
IRAS	
Antony's two little Daughters	

SCENE: ALEXANDRIA

PROLOGUE

What flocks of critics hover here today,
As vultures wait on armies for their prey,
All gaping for the carcass of a play!
With croaking notes they bode some dire event,
And follow dying poets by the scent.
Ours gives himself for gone; y'have watched your time!
He fights this day unarmed — without his rhyme —
And brings a tale which often has been told,
As sad as Dido's and almost as old.
His hero, whom you wits his bully call,
Bates of his mettle[1] and scarce rants at all.
He's somewhat lewd, but a well-meaning mind;
Weeps much, fights little, but is wond'rous kind;
In short, a pattern and companion fit
For all the keeping tonies[2] of the pit.
I could name more: a wife, and mistress too,
Both (to be plain) too good for most of you;
The wife well-natured, and the mistress true.

    Now, poets, if your fame has been his care,
Allow him all the candor you can spare.
A brave man scorns to quarrel once a day,
Like Hectors,[3] in at every petty fray.
Let those find fault whose wit's so very small,
They've need to show that they can think at all.
Errors, like straws, upon the surface flow;
He who would search for pearls must dive below.
Fops may have leave to level all they can,
As pigmies would be glad to lop a man.
Half-wits are fleas, so little and so light,
We scarce could know they live but that they bite.
But as the rich, when tired with daily feasts,
For change become their next poor tenant's guests,
Drink hearty draughts of ale from plain brown bowls,
And snatch the homely rasher from the coals,
So you, retiring from much better cheer,
For once may venture to do penance here.
And since that plenteous autumn now is past,
Whose grapes and peaches have indulged your taste,
Take in good part, from our poor poet's board,
Such rivelled[4] fruits as winter can afford.

---

[1] Blunts his edge; abates his bombast.
[2] Dissolute fools (with a play on Antony).
[3] Bullies; street-brawlers.
[4] Shriveled.

ACT I

scene i. *The Temple of Isis*

Enter serapion, myris, *Priests of Isis*

serapion. Portents and prodigies are grown so frequent
That they have lost their name. Our fruitful Nile
Flowed ere the wonted season with a torrent
So unexpected and so wondrous fierce
That the wild deluge overtook the haste
Even of the hinds that watched it. Men and beasts
Were borne above the tops of trees that grew
On th' utmost margin of the water-mark.
Then, with so swift an ebb the flood drove backward,
It slipt from underneath the scaly herd:
Here monstrous phocae[1] panted on the shore;
Forsaken dolphins there with their broad tails
Lay lashing the departing waves; hard by 'em,
Sea-horses, floundering in the slimy mud,
Tossed up their heads, and dashed the ooze about them.

Enter alexas *behind them*

myris. Avert these omens, Heaven!
serapion. Last night, between the hours of twelve and one,
In a lone aisle of the temple while I walked,
A whirlwind rose that with a violent blast
Shook all the dome; the doors around me clapped;
The iron wicket that defends the vault
Where the long race of Ptolemies is laid
Burst open and disclosed the mighty dead.
From out each monument, in order placed,
An armèd ghost starts up: the boy-king[2] last
Reared his inglorious head. A peal of groans
Then followed, and a lamentable voice
Cried, "Egypt is no more!" My blood ran back,
My shaking knees against each other knocked;
On the cold pavement down I fell entranced,
And so unfinished left the horrid scene.

[1] Seals.
[2] Cleopatra's dead brother.

ALEXAS. (*Showing himself*) And dreamed you this? or did invent the
    story
To frighten our Egyptian boys withal,
And train them up betimes in fear of priesthood?
    SERAPION. My lord, I saw you not,
Nor meant my words should reach your ears; but what
I uttered was most true.
    ALEXAS.   A foolish dream,
Bred from the fumes of indigested feasts
And holy luxury.
    SERAPION.   I know my duty;
This goes no farther.
    ALEXAS.   'Tis not fit it should,
Nor would the times now bear it, were it true.
All southern, from yon hills, the Roman camp
Hangs o'er us black and threatening like a storm
Just breaking on our heads.
    SERAPION. Our faint Egyptians pray for Antony;
But in their servile hearts they own Octavius.
    MYRIS. Why then does Antony dream out his hours,
And tempts not fortune for a noble day
Which might redeem what Actium lost?
    ALEXAS. He thinks 'tis past recovery.
    SERAPION.   Yet the foe
Seems not to press the siege.
    ALEXAS.   Oh, there's the wonder.
Maecenas and Agrippa, who can most
With Caesar, are his foes. His wife Octavia,
Driven from his house, solicits her revenge;
And Dolabella, who was once his friend,
Upon some private grudge now seeks his ruin;
Yet still war seems on either side to sleep.
    SERAPION. 'Tis strange that Antony, for some days past,
Has not beheld the face of Cleopatra,
But here in Isis' temple lives retired,
And makes his heart a prey to black despair.
    ALEXAS. 'Tis true; and we much fear he hopes by absence
To cure his mind of love.
    SERAPION.   If he be vanquished
Or make his peace, Egypt is doomed to be
A Roman province, and our plenteous harvests
Must then redeem the scarceness of their soil.
While Antony stood firm, our Alexandria
Rivaled proud Rome (dominion's other seat),
And Fortune, striding like a vast Colossus,

Could fix an equal foot of empire here.

ALEXAS. Had I my wish, these tyrants of all nature
Who lord it o'er mankind, should perish — perish
Each by the other's sword; but, since our will
Is lamely followed by our power, we must
Depend on one, with him to rise or fall.

SERAPION. How stands the queen affected?

ALEXAS.   Oh, she dotes,
She dotes, Serapion, on this vanquished man,
And winds herself about his mighty ruins;
Whom would she yet forsake, yet yield him up,
This hunted prey, to his pursuer's hands,
She might preserve us all; but 'tis in vain —
This changes my designs, this blasts my counsels,
And makes me use all means to keep him here,
Whom I could wish divided from her arms
Far as the earth's deep center. Well, you know
The state of things; no more of your ill omens
And black prognostics; labor to confirm
The people's hearts.

      Enter VENTIDIUS, *talking aside with a Gentleman of* ANTONY'S

SERAPION. These Romans will o'erhear us.
But who's that stranger? By his warlike port,
His fierce demeanor, and erected look,
He's of no vulgar note.

ALEXAS.   Oh, 'tis Ventidius,
Our emperor's great lieutenant in the East,
Who first showed Rome that Parthia could be conquered.
When Antony returned from Syria last,
He left this man to guard the Roman frontiers.

SERAPION. You seem to know him well.

ALEXAS. Too well. I saw him in Cilicia first,
When Cleopatra there met Antony.
A mortal foe he was to us and Egypt.
But — let me witness to the worth I hate —
A braver Roman never drew a sword;
Firm to his prince, but as a friend, not slave.
He ne'er was of his pleasures; but presides
O'er all his cooler hours and morning counsels;
In short, the plainness, fierceness, rugged virtue
Of an old true-stamped Roman lives in him.
His coming bodes I know not what of ill
To our affairs. Withdraw, to mark him better;
And I'll acquaint you why I sought you here,

And what's our present work.
> (*They withdraw to a corner of the stage; and* VENTIDIUS, *with the other, comes forward to the front*)

VENTIDIUS.   Not see him, say you?
I say I must and will.
    GENTLEMAN.   He has commanded,
On pain of death, none should approach his presence.
    VENTIDIUS. I bring him news will raise his drooping spirits,
Give him new life.
    GENTLEMAN.   He sees not Cleopatra.
    VENTIDIUS. Would he had never seen her!
    GENTLEMAN. He eats not, drinks not, sleeps not, has no use
Of anything but thought; or, if he talks,
'Tis to himself, and then 'tis perfect raving.
Then he defies the world, and bids it pass;
Sometimes he gnaws his lip and curses loud
The boy Octavius; then he draws his mouth
Into a scornful smile and cries, "Take all,
The world's not worth my care."
    VENTIDIUS.   Just, just his nature.
Virtue's his path; but sometimes 'tis too narrow
For his vast soul; and then he starts out wide,
And bounds into a vice that bears him far
From his first course and plunges him in ills;
But when his danger makes him find his fault,
Quick to observe, and full of sharp remorse,
He censures eagerly his own misdeeds,
Judging himself with malice to himself,
And not forgiving what as man he did,
Because his other parts are more than man.
He must not thus be lost.
> (ALEXAS *and the Priests come forward*)

    ALEXAS. You have your full instructions, now advance;
Proclaim your orders loudly.
    SERAPION. Romans, Egyptians, hear the queen's command!
Thus Cleopatra bids: Let labor cease;
To pomp and triumphs give this happy day
That gave the world a lord: 'tis Antony's.
Live, Antony; and Cleopatra, live!
Be this the general voice sent up to heaven,
And every public place repeat this echo.
    VENTIDIUS. (*Aside*) Fine pageantry!
    SERAPION.   Set out before your doors
The images of all your sleeping fathers,
With laurels crowned; with laurels wreathe your posts

And strew with flowers the pavement; let the priests
Do present[3] sacrifice; pour out the wine
And call the gods to join with you in gladness.

    VENTIDIUS. Curse on the tongue that bids this general joy!
Can they be friends of Antony, who revel
When Antony's in danger? Hide, for shame,
You Romans, your great grandsires' images,
For fear their souls should animate their marbles,
To blush at their degenerate progeny.

    ALEXAS. A love which knows no bounds to Antony
Would mark the day with honors when all heaven
Labored for him, when each propitious star
Stood wakeful in his orb to watch that hour
And shed his better influence. Her own birthday
Our queen neglected like a vulgar fate
That passed obscurely by.

    VENTIDIUS.   Would it had slept,
Divided far from his, till some remote
And future age had called it out, to ruin
Some other prince, not him!

    ALEXAS.   Your emperor,
Though grown unkind, would be more gentle than
T' upbraid my queen for loving him too well.

    VENTIDIUS. Does the mute sacrifice upbraid the priest?
He knows him not his executioner.
Oh, she has decked his ruin with her love,
Led him in golden bands to gaudy slaughter,
And made perdition pleasing. She has left him
The blank of what he was.
I tell thee, eunuch, she has quite unmanned him.
Can any Roman see and know him now,
Thus altered from the lord of half mankind,
Unbent, unsinewed, made a woman's toy,
Shrunk from the vast extent of all his honors,
And cramped within a corner of the world?
O Antony!
Thou bravest soldier and thou best of friends!
Bounteous as nature; next to nature's God!
Couldst thou but make new worlds, so wouldst thou give 'em,
As bounty were thy being; rough in battle
As the first Romans when they went to war;
Yet, after victory, more pitiful
Than all their praying virgins left at home!

---

[3] Immediate.

ALEXAS. Would you could add to those more shining virtues,
His truth to her who loves him.
VENTIDIUS.   Would I could not!
But wherefore waste I precious hours with thee?
Thou art her darling mischief, her chief engine,
Antony's other fate. Go, tell thy queen
Ventidius is arrived to end her charms.
Let your Egyptian timbrels play alone,
Nor mix effeminate sounds with Roman trumpets.
You dare not fight for Antony; go pray,
And keep your coward's holiday in temples.
                              Exeunt ALEXAS, SERAPION

[Enter a second] Gentleman of MARK ANTONY
SECOND GENTLEMAN. The emperor approaches and commands
On pain of death that none presume to stay.
FIRST GENTLEMAN. I dare not disobey him.
                              (*Going out with the other*)
VENTIDIUS.   Well, I dare.
But I'll observe him first unseen, and find
Which way his humor drives. The rest I'll venture.   (*Withdraws*)

Enter ANTONY, *walking with a disturbed motion before he speaks*
ANTONY. They tell me 'tis my birthday, and I'll keep it
With double pomp of sadness.
'Tis what the day deserves which gave me breath.
Why was I raised the meteor of the world,
Hung in the skies and blazing as I travelled,
Till all my fires were spent, and then cast downward
To be trod out by Caesar?
VENTIDIUS. (*Aside*)   On my soul,
'Tis mournful, wondrous mournful!
ANTONY.   Count thy gains.
Now, Antony, wouldst thou be born for this?
Glutton of fortune, thy devouring youth
Has starved thy wanting age.
VENTIDIUS. (*Aside*)   How sorrow shakes him!
So now the tempest tears him up by the roots,
And on the ground extends the noble ruin.
ANTONY. (*Having thrown himself down*) Lie there, thou shadow
     of an emperor;
The place thou pressest on thy mother earth
Is all thy empire now; now it contains thee;
Some few days hence, and then 'twill be too large,
When thou'rt contracted in thy narrow urn,

Shrunk to a few cold ashes. Then Octavia
(For Cleopatra will not live to see it),
Octavia then will have thee all her own,
And bear thee in her widowed hand to Caesar;
Caesar will weep, the crocodile will weep,
To see his rival of the universe
Lie still and peaceful there. I'll think no more on't.
    Give me some music; look that it be sad.
I'll soothe my melancholy till I swell
And burst myself with sighing. —   (*Soft music*)
'Tis somewhat to my humor. Stay, I fancy
I'm now turned wild, a commoner of nature;
Of all forsaken and forsaking all,
Live in a shady forest's sylvan scene,
Stretched at my length beneath some blasted oak,
I lean my head upon the mossy bark
And look just of a piece as I grew from it;
My uncombed locks, matted like mistletoe,
Hang o'er my hoary face; a murm'ring brook
Runs at my foot.
    VENTIDIUS. [*Aside*] Methinks I fancy
Myself there, too.
    ANTONY.   The herd come jumping by me,
And, fearless, quench their thirst while I look on,
And take me for their fellow-citizen.[4]
More of this image, more it lulls my thoughts.   (*Soft music again*)
    VENTIDIUS. I must disturb him; I can hold no longer.
                              (*Stands before him*)
    ANTONY. (*Starting up*) Art thou Ventidius?
    VENTIDIUS.   Are you Antony?
I'm liker what I was than you to him
I left you last.
    ANTONY.   I'm angry.
    VENTIDIUS.   So am I.
    ANTONY. I would be private. Leave me.
    VENTIDIUS.   Sir, I love you,
And therefore will not leave you.
    ANTONY.   Will not leave me!
Where have you learned that answer? Who am I?
    VENTIDIUS. My emperor; the man I love next Heaven;
If I said more, I think 'twere scarce a sin —
You're all that's good and good-like.
    ANTONY .   All that's wretched.
You will not leave me then?

    [4] See *As You Like It*, II, i.

VENTIDIUS.   'Twas too presuming
To say I would not; but I dare not leave you,
And 'tis unkind in you to chide me hence
So soon, when I so far have come to see you.

ANTONY. Now thou hast seen me, art thou satisfied?
For, if a friend, thou hast beheld enough;
And, if a foe, too much.

VENTIDIUS. (*Weeping*) Look, emperor, this is no common dew.
I have not wept this forty years; but now
My mother comes afresh into my eyes;
I cannot help her softness.

ANTONY. By heaven, he weeps! poor, good old man, he weeps!
The big round drops course one another down
The furrows of his cheeks. — Stop 'em, Ventidius,
Or I shall blush to death; they set my shame,
That caused 'em, full before me.

VENTIDIUS.
                        I'll do my best.

ANTONY. Sure, there's contagion in the tears of friends —
See, I have caught it, too. Believe me, 'tis not
For my own griefs, but thine. — Nay, father!

VENTIDIUS.   Emperor!

ANTONY. Emperor! Why, that's the style of victory;
The conqu'ring soldier, red with unfelt wounds,
Salutes his general so; but never more
Shall that sound reach my ears.

VENTIDIUS.   I warrant you.

ANTONY. Actium, Actium! Oh! —

VENTIDIUS.   It sits too near you.

ANTONY. Here, here it lies, a lump of lead by day,
And, in my short, distracted, nightly slumbers,
The hag that rides my dreams.

VENTIDIUS. Out with it; give it vent.

ANTONY.   Urge not my shame.
I lost a battle.

VENTIDIUS. So has Julius done.

ANTONY. Thou favor'st me, and speak'st not half thou think'st;
For Julius fought it out, and lost it fairly,
But Antony —

VENTIDIUS. Nay, stop not.

ANTONY.   Antony,
(Well, thou wilt have it), like a coward fled,
Fled while his soldiers fought; fled first, Ventidius.
Thou long'st to curse me, and I give thee leave.
I know thou cam'st prepared to rail.

VENTIDIUS.   I did.

ANTONY. I'll help thee. — I have been a man, Ventidius.

VENTIDIUS. Yes, and a brave one; but —

ANTONY.   I know thy meaning.
But I have lost my reason, have disgraced
The name of soldier with inglorious ease.
In the full vintage of my flowing honors,
Sat still, and saw it pressed by other hands.
Fortune came smiling to my youth, and wooed it,
And purple greatness met my ripened years.
When first I came to empire, I was borne
On tides of people crowding to my triumphs —
The wish of nations! and the willing world
Received me as its pledge of future peace.
I was so great, so happy, so beloved,
Fate could not ruin me, till I took pains,
And worked against my fortune, chid her from me,
And turned her loose; yet still she came again.
My careless days and my luxurious nights
At length have wearied her, and now she's gone,
Gone, gone, divorced for ever. Help me, soldier,
To curse this madman, this industrious fool,
Who labored to be wretched. Pr'ythee, curse me.

VENTIDIUS. No.

ANTONY.   Why?

VENTIDIUS.   You are too sensible already
Of what you've done, too conscious of your failings;
And, like a scorpion, whipped by others first
To fury, sting yourself in mad revenge.
I would bring balm and pour it in your wounds,
Cure your distempered mind and heal your fortunes.

ANTONY. I know thou would'st.

VENTIDIUS.   I will.

ANTONY.   Ha, ha, ha, ha!

VENTIDIUS. You laugh.

ANTONY.   I do, to see officious love
Give cordials to the dead.

VENTIDIUS. You would be lost, then?

ANTONY.   I am.

VENTIDIUS. I say you are not. Try your fortune.

ANTONY. I have, to th' utmost. Dost thou think me desperate
Without just cause? No, when I found all lost
Beyond repair, I hid me from the world,
And learned to scorn it here; which now I do

So heartily, I think it is not worth
The cost of keeping.
    VENTIDIUS.   Caesar thinks not so.
He'll thank you for the gift he could not take.
You would be killed like Tully, would you? Do,
Hold out your throat to Caesar, and die tamely.
    ANTONY. No, I can kill myself; and so resolve.
    VENTIDIUS. I can die with you, too, when time shall serve,
But fortune calls upon us now to live,
To fight, to conquer.
    ANTONY.   Sure, thou dream'st, Ventidius.
    VENTIDIUS. No; 'tis you dream. You sleep away your hours
In desperate sloth, miscalled philosophy.
Up, up, for honor's sake! Twelve legions wait you
And long to call you chief. By painful journeys
I led them, patient both of heat and hunger,
Down from the Parthian marches to the Nile.
'Twill do you good to see their sunburnt faces,
Their scarred cheeks, and chopped[5] hands.
        There's virtue in 'em.
They'll sell those mangled limbs at dearer rates
Than yon trim bands can buy.
    ANTONY.   Where left you them?
    VENTIDIUS. I said in Lower Syria.
    ANTONY.   Bring them hither;
There may be life in these.
    VENTIDIUS.   They will not come.
    ANTONY. Why didst thou mock my hopes with promised aids,
To double my despair? They're mutinous.
    VENTIDIUS. Most firm and loyal.
    ANTONY.   Yet they will not march
To succor me. O trifler!
    VENTIDIUS.   They petition
You would make haste to head them.
    ANTONY.   I'm besieged.
    VENTIDIUS. There's but one way shut up.
        How came I hither?
    ANTONY. I will not stir.
    VENTIDIUS.   They would perhaps desire
A better reason.
    ANTONY.   I have never used
My soldiers to demand a reason of
My actions. Why did they refuse to march?

[5] Chapped.

VENTIDIUS. They said they would not fight for Cleopatra.

ANTONY. What was't they said?

VENTIDIUS. They said they would not fight for Cleopatra.
Why should they fight, indeed, to make her conquer,
And make you more a slave? to gain you kingdoms
Which, for a kiss at your next midnight feast,
You'll sell to her? Then she new-names her jewels
And calls this diamond such or such a tax;
Each pendant in her ear shall be a province.

ANTONY. Ventidius, I allow your tongue free license
On all my other faults; but, on your life,
No word of Cleopatra. She deserves
More worlds than I can lose.

VENTIDIUS.   Behold, you powers,
To whom you have intrusted humankind!
See Europe, Afric, Asia, put in balance,
And all weighed down by one light, worthless woman!
I think the gods are Antonies and give,
Like prodigals, this nether world away
To none but wasteful hands.

ANTONY.   You grow presumptuous.

VENTIDIUS. I take the privilege of plain love to speak.

ANTONY. Plain love! plain arrogance, plain insolence!
Thy men are cowards, thou, an envious traitor,
Who, under seeming honesty, hast vented
The burden of thy rank, o'erflowing gall.
O that thou wert my equal, great in arms
As the first Caesar was, that I might kill thee
Without a stain to honor!

VENTIDIUS.   You may kill me;
You have done more already, — called me traitor.

ANTONY. Art thou not one?

VENTIDIUS.   For showing you yourself,
Which none else durst have done? But had I been
That name which I disdain to speak again,
I needed not have sought your abject fortunes,
Come to partake your fate, to die with you.
What hindered me t' have led my conquering eagles
To fill Octavius' bands? I could have been
A traitor then, a glorious, happy traitor,
And not have been so called.

ANTONY.   Forgive me, soldier;
I've been too passionate.

VENTIDIUS.   You thought me false;
Thought my old age betrayed you. Kill me, sir,

Pray, kill me. Yet you need not; your unkindness
Has left your sword no work.
          ANTONY.   I did not think so.
I said it in my rage. Pr'ythee, forgive me.
Why didst thou tempt my anger by discovery
Of what I would not hear?
          VENTIDIUS.   No prince but you
Could merit that sincerity I used,
Nor durst another man have ventured it;
But you, ere love misled your wandering eyes,
Were sure the chief and best of human race,
Framed in the very pride and boast of nature;
So perfect that the gods who formed you wondered
At their own skill, and cried, "A lucky hit
Has mended our design." Their envy hindered,
Else you had been immortal, and a pattern,
When Heaven would work for ostentation's sake
To copy out again.
          ANTONY.   But Cleopatra —
Go on, for I can bear it now.
          VENTIDIUS.   No more.
          ANTONY. Thou dar'st not trust my passion, but thou may'st;
Thou only lov'st, the rest have flattered me.
          VENTIDIUS. Heaven's blessing on your heart for that kind word!
May I believe you love me? Speak again.
          ANTONY. Indeed I do. Speak this, and this, and this. (*Hugging him*)
Thy praises were unjust, but I'll deserve them,
And yet mend all. Do with me what thou wilt;
Lead me to victory! Thou know'st the way.
          VENTIDIUS. And will you leave this —
          ANTONY.   Pr'ythee, do not curse her,
And I will leave her; though Heaven knows I love
Beyond life, conquest, empire, all but honor;
But I will leave her.
          VENTIDIUS.   That's my royal master;
And shall we fight?
          ANTONY.   I warrant thee, old soldier.
Thou shalt behold me once again in iron;
And at the head of our old troops that beat
The Parthians, cry aloud, "Come, follow me!"
          VENTIDIUS. Oh, now I hear my emperor! In that word
Octavius fell. Gods, let me see that day,
And, if I have ten years behind, take all;
I'll thank you for th' exchange.
          ANTONY.   O Cleopatra!

VENTIDIUS. Again?

ANTONY.   I've done. In that last sigh, she went.
Caesar shall know what 'tis to force a lover
From all he holds most dear.

VENTIDIUS.   Methinks you breathe
Another soul. Your looks are more divine;
You speak a hero, and you move a god.

ANTONY. Oh, thou hast fired me! My soul's up in arms,
And mans each part about me. Once again
That noble eagerness of fight has seized me,
That eagerness with which I darted upward
To Cassius' camp. In vain the steepy hill
Opposed my way; in vain a war of spears
Sung round my head and planted all my shield;
I won the trenches while my foremost men
Lagged on the plain below.

VENTIDIUS.   Ye gods, ye gods,
For such another hour!

ANTONY.   Come on, my soldier!
Our hearts and arms are still the same. I long
Once more to meet our foes, that thou and I,
Like time and death, marching before our troops,
May taste fate[6] to them, mow them out a passage,
And, entering where the foremost squadrons yield,
Begin the noble harvest of the field.   **Exeunt**

[6] Act as tasters of their fate.

ACT II

SCENE I.

Enter CLEOPATRA, IRAS, and ALEXAS

CLEOPATRA. What shall I do or whither shall I turn?
Ventidius has o'ercome, and he will go.

ALEXAS. He goes to fight for you.

CLEOPATRA. Then he would see me ere he went to fight.
Flatter me not. If once he goes, he's lost,
And all my hopes destroyed.

ALEXAS.   Does this weak passion
Become a mighty queen?

CLEOPATRA.   I am no queen.
Is this to be a queen, to be besieged
By yon insulting Roman, and to wait
Each hour the victor's chain? These ills are small;

For Antony is lost, and I can mourn
For nothing else but him. Now come, Octavius,
I have no more to lose! Prepare thy bands;
I'm fit to be a captive; Antony
Has taught my mind the fortune of a slave.

    IRAS. Call reason to assist you.

    CLEOPATRA.   I have none,
And none would have. My love's a noble madness,
Which shows the cause deserved it. Moderate sorrow
Fits vulgar love, and for a vulgar man,
But I have loved with such transcendent passion,
I soared, at first, quite out of reason's view,
And now am lost above it. No, I'm proud
'Tis thus. Would Antony could see me now!
Think you he would not sigh? Though he must leave me,
Sure, he would sigh, for he is noble-natured,
And bears a tender heart. I know him well.
Ah, no, I know him not; I knew him once,
But now 'tis past.

    IRAS.   Let it be past with you.
Forget him, madam.

    CLEOPATRA.   Never, never, Iras.
He once was mine; and once, though now 'tis gone,
Leaves a faint image of possession still.

    ALEXAS. Think him unconstant, cruel, and ungrateful.

    CLEOPATRA. I cannot. If I could, those thoughts were vain.
Faithless, ungrateful, cruel though he be,
I still must love him.

Enter CHARMION

Now, what news, my Charmion?

Will he be kind? And will he not forsake me?
Am I to live, or die? — nay, do I live?
Or am I dead? For when he gave his answer,
Fate took the word, and then I lived or died.

    CHARMION. I found him, madam —

    CLEOPATRA.   A long speech preparing?
If thou bring'st comfort, haste, and give it me,
For never was more need.

    IRAS.   I know he loves you.

    CLEOPATRA. Had he been kind, her eyes had told me so
Before her tongue could speak it. Now she studies
To soften what he said; but give me death
Just as he sent it, Charmion, undisguised,
And in the words he spoke.

CHARMION.   I found him, then,
Encompassed round, I think, with iron statues;
So mute, so motionless his soldiers stood,
While awfully he cast his eyes about
And every leader's hopes or fears surveyed.
Methought he looked resolved, and yet not pleased.
When he beheld me struggling in the crowd,
He blushed, and bade make way.
       ALEXAS.   There's comfort yet.
       CHARMION. Ventidius fixed his eyes upon my passage
Severely, as he meant to frown me back,
And sullenly gave place. I told my message,
Just as you gave it, broken and disordered;
I numbered in it all your sighs and tears,
And while I moved your pitiful request,
That you but only begged a last farewell,
He fetched an inward groan; and every time
I named you, sighed as if his heart were breaking,
But shunned my eyes and guiltily looked down.
He seemed not now that awful Antony
Who shook an armed assembly with his nod;
But, making show as he would rub his eyes,
Disguised and blotted out a falling tear.
       CLEOPATRA. Did he then weep? And was I worth a tear?
If what thou hast to say be not as pleasing,
Tell me no more, but let me die contented.
       CHARMION. He bid me say, he knew himself so well,
He could deny you nothing if he saw you;
And therefore —
       CLEOPATRA. Thou wouldst say, he would not see me?
       CHARMION. And therefore begged you not to use a power
Which he could ill resist; yet he should ever
Respect you as he ought.
       CLEOPATRA.   Is that a word
For Antony to use to Cleopatra?
O that faint word, *respect!* how I disdain it!
Disdain myself for loving, after it!
He should have kept that word for cold Octavia.
Respect is for a wife. Am I that thing,
That dull, insipid lump, without desires,
And without power to give them?
       ALEXAS.   You misjudge;
You see through love, and that deludes your sight,
As what is straight seems crooked through the water.
But I, who bear my reason undisturbed,

Can see this Antony, this dreaded man,
A fearful slave who fain would run away,
And shuns his master's eyes. If you pursue him,
My life on 't, he still drags a chain along
That needs must clog his flight.
  CLEOPATRA.   Could I believe thee! —
  ALEXAS. By every circumstance I know he loves,
True, he's hard pressed by int'rest and by honor;
Yet he but doubts and parleys and casts out
Many a long look for succor.
  CLEOPATRA.   He sends word
He fears to see my face.
  ALEXAS.   And would you more?
He shows his weakness who declines the combat,
And you must urge your fortune. Could he speak
More plainly? To my ears the message sounds —
"Come to my rescue, Cleopatra, come;
Come, free me from Ventidius — from my tyrant;
See me and give me a pretense to leave him!"
I hear his trumpets. This way he must pass.
Please you, retire a while; I'll work him first,
That he may bend more easy.
  CLEOPATRA.   You shall rule me;
But all, I fear, in vain.

                              Exit with CHARMION *and* IRAS
  ALEXAS.   I fear so, too,
Though I concealed my thoughts, to make her bold,
But 'tis our utmost means, and fate befriend it!   (*Withdraws*)

Enter Lictors with fasces, one bearing the eagle; then enter ANTONY
     with VENTIDIUS, *followed by other commanders*

  ANTONY. Octavius is the minion of blind chance
But holds from virtue nothing.
  VENTIDIUS.   Has he courage?
  ANTONY. But just enough to season him from coward.
Oh, 'tis the coldest youth upon a charge,
The most deliberate fighter! If he ventures
(As in Illyria once, they say, he did,
To storm a town), 'tis when he cannot choose;
When all the world have fixed their eyes upon him,
And then he lives on that for seven years after;
But at a close revenge he never fails.
  VENTIDIUS. I heard you challenged him.
  ANTONY.   I did, Ventidius.
What think'st thou was his answer? 'Twas so tame! —

He said he had more ways than one to die;
I had not.

    VENTIDIUS. Poor!

    ANTONY.   He has more ways than one,
But he would choose them all before that one.

    VENTIDIUS. He first would choose an ague or a fever.

    ANTONY. No; it must be an ague, not a fever;
He has not warmth enough to die by that.

    VENTIDIUS. Or old age and a bed.

    ANTONY.   Ay, there's his choice,
He would live like a lamp to the last wink,
And crawl upon the utmost verge of life.
O Hercules! Why should a man like this,
Who dares not trust his fate for one great action,
Be all the care of Heaven? Why should he lord it
O'er fourscore thousand men, of whom each one
Is braver than himself?

    VENTIDIUS.   You conquered for him.
Philippi knows it; there you shared with him
That empire which your sword made all your own.

    ANTONY. Fool that I was, upon my eagle's wings
I bore this wren till I was tired with soaring,
And now he mounts above me.
Good heavens, is this — is this the man who braves me?
Who bids my age make way? Drives me before him
To the world's ridge and sweeps me off like rubbish?

    VENTIDIUS. Sir, we lose time; the troops are mounted all.

    ANTONY. Then give the word to march.
I long to leave this prison of a town,
To join thy legions, and in open field
Once more to show my face. Lead, my deliverer.

Enter ALEXAS

    ALEXAS. Great emperor,
In mighty arms renowned above mankind,
But in soft pity to th' oppressed, a god,
This message sends the mournful Cleopatra
To her departing lord.

    VENTIDIUS.   Smooth sycophant!

    ALEXAS. A thousand wishes and ten thousand prayers,
Millions of blessings wait you to the wars;
Millions of sighs and tears she sends you, too,
And would have sent
As many parting kisses to your lips,
But those, she fears, have wearied you already.

VENTIDIUS (*Aside*) False crocodile!

ALEXAS. And yet she begs not now you would not leave her;
That were a wish too mighty for her hopes,
Too presuming
For her low fortune and your ebbing love;
That were a wish for her more prosperous days,
Her blooming beauty and your growing kindness.

ANTONY. (*Aside*) Well, I must man it out. — What would the
queen?

ALEXAS. First, to these noble warriors who attend
Your daring courage in the chase of fame, —
Too daring and too dangerous for her quiet, —
She humbly recommends all she holds dear,
All her own cares and fears, — the care of you.

VENTIDIUS. Yes, witness Actium.

ANTONY.   Let him speak, Ventidius.

ALEXAS. You, when his matchless valor bears him forward
With ardor too heroic, on his foes,
Fall down, as she would do, before his feet;
Lie in his way and stop the paths of death.
Tell him this god is not invulnerable,
That absent Cleopatra bleeds in him,
And, that you may remember her petition,
She begs you wear these trifles as a pawn
Which, at your wished return, she will redeem
                          (*Gives jewels to the commanders*)
With all the wealth of Egypt.
This to the great Ventidius she presents,
Whom she can never count her enemy,
Because he loves her lord.

VENTIDIUS.   Tell her, I'll none on't;
I'm not ashamed of honest poverty;
Not all the diamonds of the east can bribe
Ventidius from his faith. I hope to see
These and the rest of all her sparkling store
Where they shall more deservingly be placed.

ANTONY. And who must wear 'em then?

VENTIDIUS.   The wronged Octavia.

ANTONY. You might have spared that word.

VENTIDIUS.   And he, that bribe.

ANTONY. But have I no remembrance?

ALEXAS.   Yes, a dear one;
Your slave the queen —

ANTONY.   My mistress.

ALEXAS.   Then your mistress;
Your mistress would, she says, have sent her soul,
But that you had long since; she humbly begs
This ruby bracelet, set with bleeding hearts,
The emblems of her own, may bind your arm.

(Presenting a bracelet)

VENTIDIUS. Now, my best lord, in honor's name, I ask you,
For manhood's sake and for your own dear safety,
Touch not these poisoned gifts,
Infected by the sender; touch 'em not;
Myriads of bluest plagues lie underneath them,
And more than aconite has dipped the silk.

ANTONY. Nay, now you grow too cynical, Ventidius;
A lady's favors may be worn with honor.
What, to refuse her bracelet! On my soul,
When I lie pensive in my tent alone,
'Twill pass the wakeful hours of winter nights
To tell these pretty beads upon my arm,
To count for every one a soft embrace,
A melting kiss at such and such a time,
And now and then the fury of her love
When — And what harm's in this?

ALEXAS.   None, none, my lord,
But what's to her, that now 'tis past for ever.

ANTONY. *(Going to tie it)* We soldiers are so awkward — help me
    tie it.

ALEXAS. In faith, my lord, we courtiers, too, are awkward
In these affairs; so are all men indeed,
Even I, who am not one. But shall I speak?

ANTONY. Yes, freely.

ALEXAS.   Then, my lord, fair hands alone
Are fit to tie it; she who sent it can.

VENTIDIUS. Hell! death! this eunuch pander ruins you.
You will not see her?

(ALEXAS whispers an attendant, who goes out)

ANTONY.   But to take my leave.

VENTIDIUS. Then I have washed an Aethiop. You're undone;
You're in the toils; you're taken; you're destroyed;
Her eyes do Caesar's work.

ANTONY.   You fear too soon.
I'm constant to myself; I know my strength;
And yet she shall not think me barbarous neither,
Born in the depths of Afric. I'm a Roman,
Bred to the rules of soft humanity.
A guest, and kindly used, should bid farewell.

VENTIDIUS. You do not know
How weak you are to her, how much an infant;
You are not proof against a smile or glance;
A sigh will quite disarm you.
 ANTONY.   See, she comes!
Now you shall find your error. — Gods, I thank you.
I formed the danger greater than it was,
And now 'tis near, 'tis lessened.
 VENTIDIUS.   Mark the end yet.

    Enter CLEOPATRA, CHARMION, *and* IRAS

 ANTONY. Well, madam, we are met.
 CLEOPATRA.   Is this a meeting?
Then, we must part?
 ANTONY.   We must.
 CLEOPATRA.   Who says we must?
 ANTONY. Our own hard fates.
 CLEOPATRA.   We make those fates ourselves.
 ANTONY. Yes, we have made them; we have loved each other
Into our mutual ruin.
 CLEOPATRA. The gods have seen my joys with envious eyes;
I have no friends in heaven, and all the world,
As 'twere the business of mankind to part us,
Is armed against my love. Even you yourself
Join with the rest; you, you are armed against me.
 ANTONY. I will be justified in all I do
To late posterity, and therefore hear me.
If I mix a lie
With any truth, reproach me freely with it;
Else, favor me with silence.
 CLEOPATRA.   You command me,
And I am dumb.
 VENTIDIUS. [*Aside*] I like this well; he shows authority.
 ANTONY. That I derive my ruin
From you alone —
 CLEOPATRA.   O heavens! I ruin you!
 ANTONY. You promised me your silence, and you break it
Ere I have scarce begun.
 CLEOPATRA.   Well, I obey you.
 ANTONY. When I beheld you first, it was in Egypt.
Ere Caesar saw your eyes, you gave me love,
And were too young to know it; that I settled
Your father in his throne was for your sake;
I left th' acknowledgment for time to ripen.
Caesar stepped in and with a greedy hand

Plucked the green fruit ere the first blush of red,
Yet cleaving to the bough. He was my lord,
And was, beside, too great for me to rival.
But I deserved you first, though he enjoyed you.
When, after, I beheld you in Cilicia,
An enemy to Rome, I pardoned you.

CLEOPATRA. I cleared myself —

ANTONY.   Again you break your promise.
I loved you still and took your weak excuses,
Took you into my bosom, stained by Caesar,
And not half mine. I went to Egypt with you,
And hid me from the business of the world,
Shut out inquiring nations from my sight
To give whole years to you.

VENTIDIUS. (*Aside*) Yes, to your shame be't spoken.

ANTONY.   How I loved,
Witness, ye days and nights and all your hours
That danced away with down upon your feet,
As all your business were to count my passion!
One day passed by and nothing saw but love;
Another came and still 'twas only love.
The suns were wearied out with looking on,
And I untired with loving.
I saw you every day, and all the day;
And every day was still but as the first,
So eager was I still to see you more.

VENTIDIUS. 'Tis all too true.

ANTONY.   Fulvia, my wife, grew jealous,
As she indeed had reason; raised a war
In Italy to call me back.

VENTIDIUS.   But yet
You went not.

ANTONY.   While within your arms I lay,
The world fell moldering from my hands each hour,
And left me scarce a grasp — I thank your love for't.

VENTIDIUS. Well pushed: that last was home.

CLEOPATRA.   Yet may I speak?

ANTONY. If I have urged a falsehood, yes; else, not.
Your silence says I have not. Fulvia died
(Pardon, you gods, with my unkindness died);
To set the world at peace I took Octavia,
This Caesar's sister; in her pride of youth
And flower of beauty did I wed that lady,
Whom, blushing, I must praise, because I left her.
You called; my love obeyed the fatal summons.

This raised the Roman arms; the cause was yours,
I would have fought by land where I was stronger;
You hindered it; yet, when I fought at sea,
Forsook me fighting; and (O stain to honor!
O lasting shame!) I knew not that I fled,
But fled to follow you.
  VENTIDIUS. What haste she made to hoist her purple sails!
And, to appear magnificent in flight,
Drew half our strength away.
  ANTONY.   All this you caused.
And would you multiply more ruins on me?
This honest man, my best, my only friend,
Has gathered up the shipwreck of my fortunes;
Twelve legions I have left, my last recruits,
And you have watched the news, and bring your eyes
To seize them, too. If you have aught to answer,
Now speak, you have free leave.
  ALEXAS. (*Aside*) She stands confounded.
Despair is in her eyes.
  VENTIDIUS. Now lay a sigh i'th' way to stop his passage;
Prepare a tear and bid it for his legions;
'Tis like they shall be sold.
  CLEOPATRA. How shall I plead my cause when you, my judge,
Already have condemned me? Shall I bring
The love you bore me for my advocate?
That now is turned against me, that destroys me;
For love, once past, is, at the best, forgotten,
But oft'ner sours to hate. 'Twill please my lord
To ruin me, and therefore I'll be guilty.
But could I once have thought it would have pleased you,
That you would pry, with narrow searching eyes,
Into my faults, severe to my destruction,
And watching all advantages with care
That serve to make me wretched? Speak, my lord,
For I end here. Though I deserve this usage,
Was it like you to give it?
  ANTONY.   Oh, you wrong me
To think I sought this parting or desired
To accuse you more than what will clear myself
And justify this breach.
  CLEOPATRA.   Thus low I thank you,
And, since my innocence will not offend,
I shall not blush to own it.
  VENTIDIUS. (*Aside*)   After this,
I think she'll blush at nothing.

CLEOPATRA.   You seem grieved
(And therein you are kind) that Caesar first
Enjoyed my love, though you deserved it better.
I grieve for that, my lord, much more than you;
For, had I first been yours, it would have saved
My second choice: I never had been his,
And ne'er had been but yours. But Caesar first,
You say, possessed my love. Not so, my lord.
He first possessed my person; you, my love.
Caesar loved me, but I loved Antony.
If I endured him after, 'twas because
I judged it due to the first name of men,
And, half constrained, I gave as to a tyrant
What he would take by force.

VENTIDIUS.   O Siren! Siren!
Yet grant that all the love she boasts were true,
Has she not ruined you? I still urge that,
The fatal consequence.

CLEOPATRA.   The consequence, indeed,
For I dare challenge him, my greatest foe,
To say it was designed. 'Tis true I loved you,
And kept you far from an uneasy wife, —
Such Fulvia was.
Yes, but he'll say you left Octavia for me; —
And can you blame me to receive that love
Which quitted such desert for worthless me?
How often have I wished some other Caesar,
Great as the first, and as the second, young,
Would court my love to be refused for you!

VENTIDIUS. Words, words; but Actium, sir; remember Actium.

CLEOPATRA. Even there I dare his malice. True, I counseled
To fight at sea, but I betrayed you not.
I fled, but not to the enemy. 'Twas fear.
Would I had been a man, not to have feared!
For none would then have envied me your friendship,
Who envy me your love.

ANTONY.   We're both unhappy.
If nothing else, yet our ill fortune parts us.
Speak; would you have me perish by my stay?

CLEOPATRA. If, as a friend, you ask my judgment, go;
If as a lover, stay. If you must perish —
'Tis a hard word — but stay.

VENTIDIUS. See now th' effects of her so boasted love!
She strives to drag you down to ruin with her;
But could she 'scape without you, oh, how soon

Would she let go her hold and haste to shore
And never look behind!

CLEOPATRA.   Then judge my love by this.

(*Giving Antony a writing*)

Could I have borne
A life or death, a happiness or woe
From yours divided, this had given me means.

ANTONY. By Hercules, the writing of Octavius!
I know it well; 'tis that proscribing hand,
Young as it was, that led the way to mine
And left me but the second place in murder. —
See, see, Ventidius! here he offers Egypt,
And joins all Syria to it as a present,
So, in requital, she forsake my fortunes
And join her arms with his.

CLEOPATRA.   And yet you leave me!
You leave me, Antony; and yet I love you,
Indeed I do. I have refused a kingdom;
That's a trifle;
For I could part with life, with anything,
But only you. Oh, let me die but with you!
Is that a hard request?

ANTONY.   Next living with you,
'Tis all that Heaven can give.

ALEXAS. (*Aside*) He melts; we conquer.

CLEOPATRA. No; you shall go. Your interest calls you hence;
Yes, your dear interest pulls too strong for these
Weak arms to hold you here.   (*Takes his hand*)
Go; leave me, soldier
(For you're no more a lover), leave me dying;
Push me, all pale and panting, from your bosom,
And, when your march begins, let one run after,
Breathless almost for joy, and cry, "She's dead."
The soldiers shout; you then perhaps may sigh
And muster all your Roman gravity.
Ventidius chides; and straight your brow clears up,
As I had never been.

ANTONY.   Gods, 'tis too much —
Too much for man to bear.

CLEOPATRA.   What is't for me, then,
A weak, forsaken woman and a lover? —
Here let me breathe my last. Envy me not
This minute in your arms. I'll die apace,
As fast as e'er I can, and end your trouble.

ANTONY. Die! Rather let me perish; loosened nature
Leap from its hinges! Sink the props of heaven,
And fall the skies to crush the nether world!
My eyes, my soul, my all!   (*Embraces her*)
   VENTIDIUS.   And what's this toy
In balance with your fortune, honor, fame?
   ANTONY. What is't, Ventidius? It outweighs 'em all;
Why, we have more than conquered Caesar now.
My queen's not only innocent, but loves me.
This, this is she who drags me down to ruin!
"But could she 'scape without me, with what haste
Would she let slip her hold and make to shore
And never look behind!"
Down on thy knees, blasphemer as thou art,
And ask forgiveness of wronged innocence.
   VENTIDIUS. I'll rather die than take it. Will you go?
   ANTONY. Go! Whither? Go from all that's excellent!
Faith, honor, virtue, all good things forbid
That I should go from her who sets my love
Above the price of kingdoms. Give, you gods,
Give to your boy, your Caesar,
This rattle of a globe to play withal,
This gewgaw world, and put him cheaply off.
I'll not be pleased with less than Cleopatra.
   CLEOPATRA. She's wholly yours. My heart's so full of joy
That I shall do some wild extravagance
Of love in public, and the foolish world,
Which knows not tenderness, will think me mad.
   VENTIDIUS. O women! women! women! all the gods
Have not such power of doing good to man
As you of doing harm.
   ANTONY.   Our men are armed.   *Exit*
Unbar the gate that looks to Caesar's camp.
I would revenge the treachery he meant me;
And long security makes conquest easy.
I'm eager to return before I go,
For all the pleasures I have known beat thick
On my remembrance. — How I long for night!
That both the sweets of mutual love may try,
And once triumph o'er Caesar [ere] we die.   *Exeunt*

ACT III

SCENE I.

At one door enter CLEOPATRA, CHARMION, IRAS, and ALEXAS, a train of
Egyptians; at the other, ANTONY and Romans. The entrance on
both sides is prepared by music; the trumpets first sounding on
ANTONY's part, then answered by timbrels, etc., on CLEOPATRA's.
CHARMION and IRAS hold a laurel wreath betwixt them. A dance
of Egyptians. After the ceremony CLEOPATRA crowns ANTONY

ANTONY. I thought how those white arms would fold me in,
And strain me close and melt me into love;
So pleased with that sweet image, I sprung forwards,
And added all my strength to every blow.
    CLEOPATRA. Come to me, come, my soldier, to my arms!
You've been too long away from my embraces,
But, when I have you fast and all my own,
With broken murmurs and with amorous sighs
I'll say you were unkind, and punish you,
And mark you red with many an eager kiss.
    ANTONY. My brighter Venus!
    CLEOPATRA.   O my greater Mars!
    ANTONY. Thou join'st us well, my love!
Suppose me come from the Phlegraean plains[1]
Where gasping giants lay, cleft by my sword,
And mountain-tops pared off each other blow
To bury those I slew. Receive me, goddess!
Let Caesar spread his subtle nets, like Vulcan;
In thy embraces I would be beheld
By heaven and earth at once;
And make their envy what they meant their sport.
Let those who took us blush; I would love on
With awful state, regardless of their frowns,
As their superior god.
There's no satiety of love in thee:
Enjoyed, thou still art new; perpetual spring
Is in thy arms; the ripened fruit but falls,
And blossoms rise to fill its empty place,
And I grow rich by giving.[2]

[1] In Macedonia, scene of the battle between the Gods and the Titans.
[2] See *Antony and Cleopatra*, II, ii, 240-243.

Enter VENTIDIUS, *and stands apart*

ALEXAS. Oh, now the danger's past, your general comes!
He joins not in your joys, nor minds your triumphs;
But with contracted brows looks frowning on,
As envying your success.

    ANTONY. Now, on my soul, he loves me; truly loves me;
He never flattered me in any vice,
But awes me with his virtue. Even this minute
Methinks, he has a right of chiding me.—
Lead to the temple—I'll avoid his presence;
It checks too strong upon me.

                                Exeunt the rest.
                       (*As* ANTONY *is going,* VENTIDIUS *pulls*
                                him by the robe)

VENTIDIUS.   Emperor!
    ANTONY. (*Looking back*) 'Tis the old argument. I pr'ythee, spare me.
    VENTIDIUS. But this one hearing, emperor.
    ANTONY.   Let go
My robe; or, by my father Hercules—
    VENTIDIUS. By Hercules his father, that's yet greater,
I bring you somewhat you would wish to know.
    ANTONY. Thou see'st we are observed; attend me here,
And I'll return.   *Exit*
    VENTIDIUS. I'm waning in his favor, yet I love him;
I love this man who runs to meet his ruin;
And sure the gods, like me, are fond of him.
His virtues lie so mingled with his crimes,
As would confound their choice to punish one
And not reward the other.

Enter ANTONY

ANTONY.   We can conquer,
You see, without your aid.
We have dislodged their troops;
They look on us at distance and, like curs
'Scaped from the lion's paw, they bay far off,
And lick their wounds and faintly threaten war.
Five thousand Romans with their faces upward
Lie breathless on the plain.
    VENTIDIUS.   'Tis well; and he
Who lost them could have spared ten thousand more.
Yet if, by this advantage, you could gain
An easier peace while Caesar doubts the chance
Of arms—

ANTONY.   Oh, think not on't, Ventidius!
The boy pursues my ruin, he'll no peace;
His malice is considerate in advantage.
Oh, he's the coolest murderer! so staunch,
He kills, and keeps his temper.
    VENTIDIUS.   Have you no friend
In all his army who has power to move him?
Maecenas, or Agrippa, might do much.
    ANTONY.   They're both too deep in Caesar's interests.
We'll work it out by dint of sword, or perish.
    VENTIDIUS.   Fain I would find some other.
    ANTONY.   Thank thy love.
Some four or five such victories as this
Will save thy further pains.
    VENTIDIUS.   Expect no more—Caesar is on his guard.
I know, sir, you have conquered against odds,
But still you draw supplies from one poor town,
And of Egyptians. He has all the world,
And at his back nations come pouring in
To fill the gaps you make. Pray, think again,
    ANTONY.   Why dost thou drive me from myself, to search
For foreign aids?—to hunt my memory,
And range all o'er a waste and barren place
To find a friend? The wretched have no friends.—
Yet I had one, the bravest youth of Rome,
Whom Caesar loves beyond the love of women;
He could resolve his mind as fire does wax,
From that hard, rugged image melt him down,
And mold him in what softer form he pleased.
    VENTIDIUS.   Him would I see—that man of all the world;
Just such a one we want.
    ANTONY.   He loved me, too;
I was his soul; he lived not but in me.
We were so closed within each other's breasts,
The rivets were not found that joined us first.
That does not reach us yet; we were so mixed
As meeting streams, both to ourselves were lost;
We were one mass; we could not give or take
But from the same, for he was I, I he.
    VENTIDIUS.   (*Aside*) He moves as I would wish him.
    ANTONY.   After this
I need not tell his name.—Twas Dolabella.
    VENTIDIUS.   He's now in Caesar's camp.
    ANTONY.   No matter where,
Since he's no longer mine. He took unkindly

That I forbade him Cleopatra's sight,
Because I feared he loved her. He confessed
He had a warmth which, for my sake, he stifled,
For 'twere impossible that two, so one,
Should not have loved the same. When he departed,
He took no leave, and that confirmed my thoughts.

    VENTIDIUS. It argues that he loved you more than her,
Else he had stayed. But he perceived you jealous,
And would not grieve his friend. I know he loves you.

    ANTONY. I should have seen him, then, ere now.

    VENTIDIUS.   Perhaps
He has thus long been laboring for your peace.

    ANTONY. Would he were here!

    VENTIDIUS.   Would you believe he loved you?
I read your answer in your eyes—you would.
Not to conceal it longer, he has sent
A messenger from Caesar's camp with letters.

    ANTONY. Let him appear.

    VENTIDIUS.   I'll bring him instantly.

                Exit VENTIDIUS, [*and*] *re-enters immediately*
                                  with DOLABELLA

    ANTONY. 'Tis he himself! himself, by holy friendship!
                      (*Runs to embrace him*)
Art thou returned at last, my better half?
Come, give me all myself! Let me not live,
If the young bridegroom, longing for his night,
Was ever half so fond!

    DOLABELLA. I must be silent, for my soul is busy
About a nobler work: she's new come home,
Like a long-absent man, and wanders o'er
Each room, a stranger to her own, to look
If all be safe.

    ANTONY.   Thou hast what's left of me;
For I am now so sunk from what I was,
Thou find'st me at my lowest water-mark.
The rivers that ran in and raised my fortunes
Are all dried up, or take another course;
What I have left is from my native spring.
I've still a heart that swells in scorn of fate
And lifts me to my banks.

    DOLABELLA. Still you are lord of all the world to me.

    ANTONY. Why, then I yet am so; for thou art all.
If I had any joy when thou wert absent,
I grudged it to myself; methought I robbed
Thee of thy part. But, O my Dolabella!

Thou hast beheld me other than I am.
Hast thou not seen my morning chambers filled
With sceptred slaves who waited to salute me?
With eastern monarchs who forgot the sun
To worship my uprising?—menial kings
Ran coursing up and down my palace-yard,
Stood silent in my presence, watched my eyes,
And at my least command all started out
Like racers to the goal.
    DOLABELLA.   Slaves to your fortune.
    ANTONY. Fortune is Caesar's now; and what am I?
    VENTIDIUS. What you have made yourself; I will not flatter.
    ANTONY. Is this friendly done?
    DOLABELLA. Yes; when his end is so, I must join with him;
Indeed, I must; and yet you must not chide;
Why am I else your friend?
    ANTONY.   Take heed, young man,
How thou upbraid'st my love. The queen has eyes,
And thou, too, hast a soul. Canst thou remember
When,swelled with hatred, thou beheld'st her first,
As accessary to thy brother's death?
    DOLABELLA. Spare my remembrance; 'twas a guilty day,
And still the blush hangs here.
    ANTONY.   To clear herself[3]
For sending him no aid, she came from Egypt.
Her galley down the silver Cydnos rowed,
The tackling silk, the streamers waved with gold;
The gentle winds were lodged in purple sails;
Her nymphs, like Nereids, round her couch were placed,
Where she, another sea-born Venus, lay.
    DOLABELLA. No more; I would not hear it.
    ANTONY.   Oh, you must!
She lay, and leant her cheek upon her hand,
And cast a look so languishingly sweet
As if, secure of all beholders' hearts,
Neglecting, she could take them. Boys like Cupids
Stood fanning with their painted wings the winds
That played about her face; but if she smiled,
A darting glory seemed to blaze abroad,
That men's desiring eyes were never wearied,
But hung upon the object. To soft flutes
The silver oars kept time; and while they played,
The hearing gave new pleasure to the sight,
And both, to thought. 'Twas heaven or somewhat more;

[3] See *Antony and Cleopatra*, II, ii, 196-223.

For she so charmed all hearts, that gazing crowds
Stood panting on the shore, and wanted breath
To give their welcome voice.
Then, Dolabella, where was then thy soul?
Was not thy fury quite disarmed with wonder?
Didst thou not shrink behind me from those eyes
And whisper in my ear "Oh, tell her not
That I accused her of my brother's death?"

DOLABELLA. And should my weakness be a plea for yours?
Mine was an age when love might be excused,
When kindly warmth, and when my springing youth,
Made it a debt to nature. Yours—

VENTIDIUS.   Speak boldly.
Yours, he would say, in your declining age,
When no more heat was left but what you forced,
When all the sap was needful for the trunk,
When it went down, then you constrained the course,
And robbed from nature to supply desire;
In you (I would not use so harsh a word)
'Tis but plain dotage.

ANTONY.   Ha!
DOLABELLA.   'Twas urged too home.—
But yet the loss was private that I made;
'Twas but myself I lost. I lost no legions;
I had no world to lose, no people's love.

ANTONY. This from a friend?
DOLABELLA.   Yes, Antony, a true one;
A friend so tender that each word I speak
Stabs my own heart before it reach your ear.
Oh, judge me not less kind because I chide!
To Caesar I excuse you.

ANTONY.   O ye gods!
Have I then lived to be excused to Caesar?

DOLABELLA. As to your equal.
ANTONY.   Well, he's but my equal;
While I wear this, he never shall be more.

DOLABELLA. I bring conditions from him.
ANTONY.   Are they noble?
Methinks thou shouldst not bring them else; yet he
Is full of deep dissembling; knows no honor
Divided from his interest. Fate mistook him,
For nature meant him for an usurer;
He's fit indeed to buy, not conquer, kingdoms.

VENTIDIUS. Then, granting this,
What power was theirs who wrought so hard a temper

To honorable terms?

    ANTONY. It was my Dolabella, or some god.

    DOLABELLA. Nor I, nor yet Maecenas, nor Agrippa;
They were your enemies, and I, a friend,
Too weak alone; yet 'twas a Roman's deed.

    ANTONY. 'Twas like a Roman done; show me that man
Who has preserved my life, my love, my honor;
Let me but see his face.

    VENTIDIUS.   That task is mine,
And, Heaven, thou know'st how pleasing   *Exit* VENTIDIUS.

    DOLABELLA.   You'll remember
To whom you stand obliged?

    ANTONY.   When I forget it,
Be thou unkind, and that's my greatest curse.
My queen shall thank him, too.

    DOLABELLA.   I fear she will not.

    ANTONY. But she shall do't—the queen, my Dolabella!
Hast thou not still some grudgings of thy fever?

    DOLABELLA. I would not see her lost.

    ANTONY.   When I forsake her,
Leave me, my better stars! for she has truth
Beyond her beauty. Caesar tempted her,
At no less price than kingdoms, to betray me,
But she resisted all; and yet thou chid'st me
For loving her too well. Could I do so?

Re-enter VENTIDIUS *with* OCTAVIA, *leading*
ANTONY's *two little Daughters*

    DOLABELLA. Yes; there's my reason.

    ANTONY.   Where?—Octavia there!
                                     (*Starting back*)

    VENTIDIUS. What—is she poison to you?—a disease?
Look on her, view her well, and those she brings.
Are they all strangers to yours eyes? has nature
No secret call, no whisper they are yours?

    DOLABELLA. For shame, my lord, if not for love, receive them
With kinder eyes. If you confess a man,
Meet them, embrace them, bid them welcome to you.
Your arms should open, even without your knowledge,
To clasp them in; your feet should turn to wings,
To bear you to them; and your eyes dart out
And aim a kiss ere you could reach the lips.

    ANTONY. I stood amazed to think how they came hither.

    VENTIDIUS. I sent for 'em; I brought 'em in, unknown
To Cleopatra's guards.

DOLABELLA. Yet are you cold?

OCTAVIA. Thus long I have attended for my welcome,
Which, as a stranger, sure I might expect.
Who am I?

ANTONY. Caesar's sister.

OCTAVIA. That's unkind.
Had I been nothing more than Caesar's sister,
Know, I had still remained in Caesar's camp.
But your Octavia, your much injured wife,
Though banished from your bed, driven from your house,
In spite of Caesar's sister, still is yours.
'Tis true, I have a heart disdains your coldness,
And prompts me not to seek what you should offer;
But a wife's virtue still surmounts that pride.
I come to claim you as my own; to show
My duty first; to ask, nay beg, your kindness.
Your hand, my lord; 'tis mine, and I will have it. *(Taking his hand)*

VENTIDIUS. Do, take it; thou deserv'st it.

DOLABELLA. On my soul,
And so she does; she's neither too submissive,
Nor yet too haughty; but so just a mean
Shows, as it ought, a wife and Roman too.

ANTONY. I fear, Octavia, you have begged my life.

OCTAVIA. Begged it, my lord?

ANTONY. Yes, begged it, my ambassadress;
Poorly and basely begged it of your brother.

OCTAVIA. Poorly and basely I could never beg.
Nor could my brother grant.

ANTONY. Shall I, who, to my kneeling slave, could say,
"Rise up and be a king," shall I fall down
And cry, "Forgive me, Caesar?" Shall I set
A man, my equal, in the place of Jove,
As he could give me being? No—that word
"Forgive" would choke me up
And die upon my tongue.

DOLABELLA. You shall not need it.

ANTONY. I will not need it. Come, you've all betrayed me—
My friend too!—to receive some vile conditions.
My wife has bought me with her prayers and tears,
And now I must become her branded slave.
In every peevish mood she will upbraid
The life she gave; if I but look awry,
She cries, "I'll tell my brother."

OCTAVIA. My hard fortune
Subjects me still to your unkind mistakes.

But the conditions I have brought are such
You need not blush to take; I love your honor,
Because 'tis mine. It never shall be said
Octavia's husband was her brother's slave.
Sir, you are free—free, even from her you loathe;
For, though my brother bargains for your love,
Makes me the price and cément of your peace,
I have a soul like yours; I cannot take
Your love as alms, nor beg what I deserve.
I'll tell my brother we are reconciled;
He shall draw back his troops, and you shall march
To rule the East. I may be dropped at Athens—
No matter where. I never will complain,
But only keep the barren name of wife,
And rid you of the trouble.

    VENTIDIUS. Was ever such a strife of sullen honor!
Both scorn to be obliged.

    DOLABELLA. Oh, she has touched him in the tenderest part;
See how he reddens with despite and shame,
To be outdone in generosity!

    VENTIDIUS. See how he winks! how he dries up a tear,
That fain would fall!

    ANTONY. Octavia, I have heard you, and must praise
The greatness of your soul;
But cannot yield to what you have proposed,
For I can ne'er be conquered but by love,
And you do all for duty. You would free me,
And would be dropped at Athens; was't not so?

    OCTAVIA. It was, my lord.

    ANTONY.   Then I must be obliged
To one who loves me not; who, to herself,
May call me thankless and ungrateful man.—
I'll not endure it—no.

    VENTIDIUS. (*Aside*) I am glad it pinches there.

    OCTAVIA. Would you triumph o'er poor Octavia's virtue?
That pride was all I had to bear me up;
That you might think you owed me for your life,
And owed it to my duty, not my love.
I have been injured, and my haughty soul
Could brook but ill the man who slights my bed.

    ANTONY. Therefore you love me not.

    OCTAVIA.   Therefore, my lord,
I should not love you.

    ANTONY. Therefore you would leave me?

    OCTAVIA. And therefore I should leave you — if I could.

DOLABELLA. Her soul's too great, after such injuries,
To say she loves; and yet she lets you see it.
Her modesty and silence plead her cause.

ANTONY. O Dolabella, which way shall I turn?
I find a secret yielding in my soul;
But Cleopatra, who would die with me,
Must she be left? Pity pleads for Octavia,
But does it not plead more for Cleopatra?

VENTIDIUS. Justice and pity both plead for Octavia;
For Cleopatra, neither.
One would be ruined with you, but she first
Had ruined you; the other, you have ruined,
And yet she would preserve you.
In everything their merits are unequal.

ANTONY. O my distracted soul!

OCTAVIA. Sweet Heaven, compose it!—
Come, come, my lord, if I can pardon you,
Methinks you should accept it. Look on these—
Are they not yours? or stand they thus neglected
As they are mine? Go to him, children, go;
Kneel to him, take him by the hand, speak to him,
For you may speak and he may own you, too,
Without a blush—and so he cannot all
His children. Go, I say, and pull him to me,
And pull him to yourselves from that bad woman.
You, Agrippina, hang upon his arms,
And you, Antonia, clasp about his waist.
If he will shake you off, if he will dash you
Against the pavement, you must bear it, children,
For you are mine, and I was born to suffer.

(*Here the Children go to him, etc.*)

VENTIDIUS. Was ever sight so moving?—Emperor!

DOLABELLA.   Friend!

OCTAVIA. Husband!

BOTH CHILDREN.   Father!

ANTONY. I am vanquished. Take me,
Octavia—take me, children—share me all.   (*Embracing them*)
I've been a thriftless debtor to your loves,
And run out much, in riot, from your stock,
But all shall be amended.

OCTAVIA.   O blest hour!

DOLABELLA. O happy change!

VENTIDIUS.   My joy stops at my tongue,
But it has found two channels here for one,
And bubbles out above.

ANTONY. (*To Octavia*) This is thy triumph. Lead me where thou
    wilt,
Even to thy brother's camp.
    OCTAVIA.   All there are yours.

Enter ALEXAS *hastily*

ALEXAS. The queen, my mistress, sir, and yours—
ANTONY. 'Tis past.—
Octavia, you shall stay this night. Tomorrow
Caesar and we are one.

Exit, leading OCTAVIA; DOLABELLA *and
the Children follow*

VENTIDIUS. There's news for you! Run, my officious eunuch,
Be sure to be the first—haste forward!
Haste, my dear eunuch, haste!   *Exit*
    ALEXAS. This downright fighting fool, this thick-skulled hero,
This blunt, unthinking instrument of death,
With plain, dull virtue has outgone my wit.
Pleasure forsook my earliest infancy;
The luxury of others robbed my cradle,
And ravished thence the promise of a man.
Cast out from nature, disinherited
Of what her meanest children claim by kind,
Yet greatness kept me from contempt. That's gone.
Had Cleopatra followed my advice,
Then he had been betrayed who now forsakes.
She dies for love, but she has known its joys.
Gods, is this just that I, who know no joys,
Must die because she loves?

Enter CLEOPATRA, CHARMION, IRAS, [*and*] *train*

O madam, I have seen what blasts my eyes!
Octavia's here.
    CLEOPATRA. Peace with that raven's note.
I know it, too, and now am in
The pangs of death.
    ALEXAS.   You are no more a queen—
Egypt is lost.
    CLEOPATRA. What tell'st thou me of Egypt?
My life, my soul is lost! Octavia has him!—
O fatal name to Cleopatra's love!
My kisses, my embraces now are hers,
While I—But thou hast seen my rival. Speak—
Does she deserve this blessing? Is she fair?
Bright as a goddess? and is all perfection

Confined to her?—It is. Poor I was made
Of that coarse matter which, when she was finished,
The gods threw by for rubbish.
    ALEXAS. She's indeed a very miracle.
    CLEOPATRA. Death to my hopes, a miracle!
    ALEXAS. (*Bowing*)   A miracle—
I mean, of goodness; for in beauty, madam,
You make all wonders cease.
    CLEOPATRA.   I was too rash.
Take this in part of recompense. But, oh!   (*Giving a ring*)
I fear thou flatter'st me.
    CHARMION.   She comes! She's here!
    IRAS. Fly, madam, Caesar's sister!
    CLEOPATRA. Were she the sister of the thunderer Jove,
And bore her brother's lightning in her eye,
Thus would I face my rival.
(*Meets* OCTAVIA *with* VENTIDIUS. OCTAVIA *bears up to her. Their trains
    come up on either side*)
    OCTAVIA. I need not ask if you are Cleopatra,
Your haughty carriage—
    CLEOPATRA.   Shows I am a queen.
Nor need I ask you who you are.
    OCTAVIA.   A Roman;
A name that makes and can unmake a queen.
    CLEOPATRA. Your lord, the man who serves me, is a Roman.
    OCTAVIA. He was a Roman, till he lost that name
To be a slave in Egypt; but I come
To free him thence.
    CLEOPATRA. Peace, peace, my lover's Juno.
When he grew weary of that household clog,
He chose my easier bonds.
    OCTAVIA.   I wonder not
Your bonds are easy. You have long been practised
In that lascivious art. He's not the first
For whom you spread your snares: let Caesar witness.
    CLEOPATRA. I loved not Caesar; 'twas but gratitude
I paid his love. The worst your malice can
Is but to say the greatest of mankind
Has been my slave. The next, but far above him
In my esteem, is he whom law calls yours,
But whom his love made mine.
    OCTAVIA. (*Coming up closer to her*) I would view nearer
That face which has so long usurped my right,
To find the inevitable charms that catch
Mankind so sure, that ruined my dear lord.

CLEOPATRA. Oh, you do well to search, for had you known
But half these charms, you had not lost his heart.

OCTAVIA. Far be their knowledge from a Roman lady —
Far from a modest wife! Shame of our sex,
Dost thou not blush to own those black endearments
That make sin pleasing?

CLEOPATRA.   You may blush, who want them.
If bounteous nature, if indulgent heaven
Have given me charms to please the bravest man,
Should I not thank them? Should I be ashamed,
And not be proud? I am, that he has loved me.
And when I love not him, heaven change this face
For one like that.

OCTAVIA. Thou lov'st him not so well.

CLEOPATRA. I love him better, and deserve him more.

OCTAVIA. You do not—cannot. You have been his ruin.
Who made him cheap at Rome but Cleopatra?
Who made him scorned abroad but Cleopatra?
At Actium, who betrayed him? Cleopatra!
Who made his children orphans, and poor me
A wretched widow? Only Cleopatra.

CLEOPATRA. Yet she who loves him best is Cleopatra.
If you have suffered, I have suffered more.
You bear the specious title of a wife
To gild your cause and draw the pitying world
To favor it. The world contemns poor me,
For I have lost my honor, lost my fame,
And stained the glory of my royal house,
And all to bear the branded name of mistress.
There wants but life, and that, too, I would lose
For him I love.

OCTAVIA.   Be't so, then; take thy wish.

Exit with her train

CLEOPATRA. And 'tis my wish,
Now he is lost for whom alone I lived.
My sight grows dim, and every object dances
And swims before me in the maze of death.
My spirits, while they were opposed, kept up;
They could not sink beneath a rival's scorn,
But now she's gone, they faint.

ALEXAS.   Mine have had leisure
To recollect their strength and furnish counsel
To ruin her, who else must ruin you.

CLEOPATRA.   Vain promiser!
Lead me, my Charmion; nay, your hand, too, Iras.

My grief has weight enough to sink you both.
Conduct me to some solitary chamber,
And draw the curtains round;
Then leave me to myself, to take alone
My fill of grief.
There I till death will his unkindness weep,
As harmless infants moan themselves asleep.

Exeunt

ACT IV

SCENE I

[Enter] ANTONY *[and]* DOLABELLA

DOLABELLA. Why would you shift it from yourself on me?
Can you not tell her you must part?
    ANTONY.   I cannot.
I could pull out an eye and bid it go,
And t'other should not weep. O Dolabella,
How many deaths are in this word, *Depart!*
I dare not trust my tongue to tell her so—
One look of hers would thaw me into tears,
And I should melt till I were lost again.
    DOLABELLA. Then let Ventidius—
He's rough by nature.
    ANTONY. Oh, he'll speak too harshly;
He'll kill her with the news. Thou, only thou!
    DOLABELLA. Nature has cast me in so soft a mould
That but to hear a story feigned for pleasure,
Of some sad lover's death moistens my eyes,
And robs me of my manhood. I should speak
So faintly, with such fear to grieve her heart,
She'd not believe it earnest.
    ANTONY.   Therefore—therefore
Thou, only thou art fit. Think thyself me,
And when thou speak'st (but let it first be long),
Take off the edge from every sharper sound,
And let our parting be as gently made
As other loves begin. Wilt thou do this?
    DOLABELLA. What you have said so sinks into my soul
That, if I must speak, I shall speak just so.
    ANTONY. I leave you then to your sad task.
Farewell!
I sent her word to meet you.   (*Goes to the door and comes back*)
                             I forgot.

Let her be told I'll make her peace with mine.
Her crown and dignity shall be preserved,
If I have power with Caesar.—Oh, be sure
To think on that!
    DOLABELLA.   Fear not, I will remember.
                (ANTONY *goes again to the door and comes back*)
    ANTONY. And tell her, too, how much I was constrained;
I did not this but with extremest force.
Desire her not to hate my memory,
For I still cherish hers;—insist on that.
    DOLABELLA. Trust me, I'll not forget it.
    ANTONY.   Then that's all.
                  (*Goes out and returns again*)
Wilt thou forgive my fondness this once more?
Tell her, though we shall never meet again,
If I should hear she took another love,
The news would break my heart.—Now I must go,
For every time I have returned, I feel
My soul more tender, and my next command
Would be to bid her stay, and ruin both.

                                            Exit

    DOLABELLA. Men are but children of a larger growth;
Our appetites as apt to change as theirs,
And full as craving, too, and full as vain;
And yet the soul, shut up in her dark room,
Viewing so clear abroad, at home sees nothing;
But like a mole in earth, busy and blind,
Works all her folly up and casts it outward
To the world's open view. Thus I discovered,
And blamed, the love of ruined Antony,   .
Yet wish that I were he, to be so ruined.

                Enter VENTIDIUS *above*
    VENTIDIUS. Alone, and talking to himself? concerned, too?
Perhaps my guess is right; he loved her once,
And may pursue it still.
    DOLABELLA.   O friendship! friendship!
Ill canst thou answer this; and reason, worse.
Unfaithful in the attempt; hopeless to win;
And, if I win, undone; mere madness all.
And yet the occasion's fair. What injury
To him, to wear the robe which he throws by?
    VENTIDIUS. None, none at all. This happens as I wish,
To ruin her yet more with Antony.

Enter CLEOPATRA, *talking with* ALEXAS;
CHARMION, IRAS *on the other side*

DOLABELLA. She comes! What charms have sorrow on that face!
Sorrow seems pleased to dwell with so much sweetness;
Yet, now and then, a melancholy smile
Breaks loose like lightning in a winter's night,
And shows a moment's day.

    VENTIDIUS. If she should love him, too— her eunuch there!
That porc'pisce[1] bodes ill weather. Draw, draw nearer,
Sweet devil, that I may hear.

    ALEXAS.   Believe me; try

                  (DOLABELLA *goes over to* CHARMION *and*
                  IRAS; *seems to talk with them*)

To make him jealous; jealousy is like
A polished glass held to the lips when life's in doubt;
If there be breath, 'twill catch the damp, and show it.

    CLEOPATRA. I grant you, jealousy's a proof of love,
But 'tis a weak and unavailing medicine;
It puts out the disease, and makes it show,
But has no power to cure.

    ALEXAS. 'Tis your last remedy, and strongest, too.
And then this Dolabella—who so fit
To practise on? He's handsome, valiant, young,
And looks as he were laid for nature's bait
To catch weak women's eyes.
He stands already more than half suspected
Of loving you. The least kind word or glance
You give this youth will kindle him with love;
Then, like a burning vessel set adrift,
You'll send him down amain before the wind
To fire the heart of jealous Antony.

    CLEOPATRA. Can I do this? Ah, no. My love's so true
That I can neither hide it where it is,
Nor show it where it is not. Nature meant me
A wife—a silly, harmless, household dove,
Fond without art, and kind without deceit;
But Fortune, that has made a mistress of me,
[Has] thrust me out to the wide world, unfurnished
Of falsehood to be happy.

    ALEXAS.   Force yourself.
The event will be, your lover will return
Doubly desirous to possess the good
Which once he feared to lose.

    [1] Porcus pisces; porpoise.

CLEOPATRA.   I must attempt it,

                                                    Exit ALEXAS

But oh, with what regret!

                        (*She comes up to* DOLABELLA)

VENTIDIUS. So, now the scene draws near; they're in my reach.

CLEOPATRA. (*To* DOLABELLA) Discoursing with my women! Might
    not I

Share in your entertainment?

CHARMION.   You have been

The subject of it, madam.

CLEOPATRA.   How! and how?

IRAS. Such praises of your beauty!

CLEOPATRA.   Mere poetry.

Your Roman wits, your Gallus and Tibullus;

Have taught you this from Cytheris and Delia.

DOLABELLA. Those Roman wits have never been in Egypt;

Cytheris and Delia else had been unsung.

I, who have seen—had I been born a poet,

Should choose a nobler name.

CLEOPATRA.   You flatter me.

But 'tis your nation's vice. All of your country

Are flatterers, and all false. Your friend's like you.

I'm sure he sent you not to speak these words.

DOLABELLA. No, madam, yet he sent me —

CLEOPATRA.   Well, he sent you —

DOLABELLA. Of a less pleasing errand.

CLEOPATRA.   How less pleasing?

Less to yourself, or me?

DOLABELLA.   Madam, to both.

For you must mourn, and I must grieve to cause it.

CLEOPATRA. You, Charmion, and your fellow, stand at distance —

(*Aside*) Hold up, my spirits.—Well, now your mournful matter,

For I'm prepared—perhaps can guess it, too.

DOLABELLA. I wish you would, for 'tis a thankless office

To tell ill news; and I, of all your sex,

Most fear displeasing you.

CLEOPATRA.   Of all your sex

I soonest could forgive you if you should.

VENTIDIUS. Most delicate advances!

    Woman! woman!

Dear, damned, inconstant sex!

CLEOPATRA.   In the first place,

I am to be forsaken. Is't not so?

DOLABELLA. I wish I could not answer to that question.

CLEOPATRA. Then pass it o'er, because it troubles you;

I should have been more grieved another time.
Next, I'm to lose my kingdom—Farewell, Egypt!
Yet, is there any more?

    DOLABELLA.   Madam, I fear
Your too deep sense of grief has turned your reason.

    CLEOPATRA. No, no, I'm not run mad; I can bear fortune,
And love may be expelled by other love,
As poisons are by poisons.

    DOLABELLA.   You o'erjoy me, madam,
To find your griefs so moderately borne.
You've heard the worst; all are not false like him.

    CLEOPATRA. No. Heaven forbid they should.

    DOLABELLA.   Some men are constant.

    CLEOPATRA. And constancy deserves reward, that's certain.

    DOLABELLA. Deserves it not, but give it leave to hope.

    VENTIDIUS. I'll swear thou hast my leave. I have enough.—
But how to manage this! Well, I'll consider.   *Exit*

    DOLABELLA. I came prepared
To tell you heavy news—news which, I thought,
Would fright the blood from your pale cheeks to hear,
But you have met it with a cheerfulness
That makes my task more easy; and my tongue,
Which on another's message was employed,
Would gladly speak its own.

    CLEOPATRA.   Hold, Dolabella.
First tell me, were you chosen by my lord?
Or sought you this employment?

    DOLABELLA. He picked me out; and, as his bosom friend,
He charged me with his words.

    CLEOPATRA.   The message then
I know was tender, and each accent smooth,
To mollify that rugged word, *Depart*.

    DOLABELLA. Oh, you mistake. He chose the harshest words;
With fiery eyes and with contracted brows
He coined his face in the severest stamp;
And fury shook his fabric like an earthquake;
He heaved for vent, and burst like bellowing Aetna.
In sounds scarce human—"Hence, away, for ever,
Let her begone, the blot of my renown,
And bane of all my hopes!

               (*All the time of this speech* CLEOPATRA
                   seems more and more concerned till
                         she sinks quite down)

Let her be driven as far as men can think
From man's commèrce! she'll poison to the center."

CLEOPATRA. Oh, I can bear no more!

DOLABELLA. Help, help!—O wretch! O cursèd, cursèd wretch!
What have I done!

CHARMION.   Help, chafe her temples, Iras.

IRAS. Bend, bend her forward quickly.

CHARMION.   Heaven be praised,
She comes again.

CLEOPATRA. Oh, let him not approach me.
Why have you brought me back to this loathed being,
The abode of falsehood, violated vows,
And injured love? For pity, let me go;
For, if there be a place of long repose,
I'm sure I want it. My disdainful lord
Can never break that quiet, nor awake
The sleeping soul with hollowing in my tomb
Such words as fright her hence.—Unkind, unkind!

DOLABELLA. (*Kneeling*) Believe me, 'tis against myself I speak.
That sure deserves belief—I injured him:
My friend ne'er spoke those words. Oh, had you seen
How often he came back, and every time
With something more obliging and more kind
To add to what he said; what dear farewells;
How almost vanquished by his love he parted,
And leaned to what unwillingly he left!
I, traitor as I was, for love of you
(But what can you not do, who made me false?)
I forged that lie; for whose forgiveness kneels
This self-accused, self-punished criminal.

CLEOPATRA. With how much ease believe we what we wish!
Rise, Dolabella; if you have been guilty,
I have contributed, and too much love
Has made me guilty too.
The advance of kindness which I made was feigned
To call back fleeting love by jealousy,
But 'twould not last. Oh, rather let me lose
Than so ignobly trifle with his heart!

DOLABELLA. I find your breast fenced round from human reach,
Transparent as a rock of solid crystal,
Seen through, but never pierced. My friend, my friend!
What endless treasure hast thou thrown away,
And scattered, like an infant, in the ocean,
Vain sums of wealth, which none can gather thence!

CLEOPATRA. Could you not beg
An hour's admittance to his private ear?
Like one who wanders through long barren wilds,

And yet foreknows no hospitable inn
Is near to succor hunger, eats his fill
Before his painful march,
So would I feed a while my famished eyes
Before we part, for I have far to go,
If death be far, and never must return.

                [Enter] VENTIDIUS *with* OCTAVIA, *behind*

VENTIDIUS. From hence you may discover — Oh, sweet, sweet!
Would you, indeed? The pretty hand in earnest?
    DOLABELLA. I will, for this reward.

                  (*Takes her hand*)

                          Draw it not back,
'Tis all I e'er will beg.
    VENTIDIUS.   They turn upon us.
    OCTAVIA. What quick eyes has guilt!
    VENTIDIUS. Seem not to have observed them, and go on.

                      (*They enter*)

    DOLABELLA. Saw you the emperor, Ventidius?
    VENTIDIUS.   No.
I sought him, but I heard that he was private,
None with him but Hipparchus, his freedman.
    DOLABELLA. Know you his business?
    VENTIDIUS.   Giving him instructions
And letters to his brother Caesar.
    DOLABELLA.   Well,
He must be found.

              Exeunt DOLABELLA *and* CLEOPATRA
    OCTAVIA.   Most glorious impudence!
    VENTIDIUS. She looked, methought,
As she would say, "Take your old man, Octavia,
Thank you, I'm better here." Well, but what use
Make we of this discovery?
    OCTAVIA.   Let it die.
    VENTIDIUS. I pity Dolabella. But she's dangerous;
Her eyes have power beyond Thessalian charms
To draw the moon from heaven; for eloquence,
The sea-green Syrens taught her voice their flatt'ry;
And while she speaks, night steals upon the day,
Unmarked of those that hear. Then she's so charming
Age buds at sight of her, and swells to youth;
The holy priests gaze on her when she smiles,
And with heaved hands, forgetting gravity,
They bless her wanton eyes. Even I, who hate her,
With a malignant joy behold such beauty,

And while I curse, desire it. Antony
Must needs have some remains of passion still,
Which may ferment into a worse relapse
It now not fully cured. I know, this minute,
With Caesar he's endeavoring her peace.
    OCTAVIA. You have prevailed:——But for a further purpose

                                        (*Walks off*)

I'll prove how he will relish this discovery.
What, make a strumpet's peace! it swells my heart;
It must not, shall not be.
    VENTIDIUS.   His guards appear.
Let me begin, and you shall second me.

                    Enter ANTONY

    ANTONY. Octavia, I was looking you, my love.
What, are your letters ready? I have given
My last instructions.
    OCTAVIA.   Mine, my lord, are written.
    ANTONY. Ventidius.   (*Drawing him aside*)
    VENTIDIUS.   My lord?
    ANTONY.   A word in private.—
When saw you Dolabella?
    VENTIDIUS.   Now, my lord,
He parted hence; and Cleopatra with him.
    ANTONY. Speak softly.—'Twas by my command he went
To bear my last farewell.
    VENTIDIUS. (*Aloud*)   It looked indeed
Like your farewell.
    ANTONY.   More softly. —My farewell?
What secret meaning have you in those words
Of "my farewell?" He did it by my order.
    VENTIDIUS. (*Aloud*) Then he obeyed your order. I suppose
You bid him do it with all gentleness,
All kindness, and all—love.
    ANTONY.   How she mourned,
The poor forsaken creature!
    VENTIDIUS. She took it as she ought; she bore your parting
As she did Caesar's, as she would another's,
Were a new love to come.
    ANTONY. (*Aloud*)   Thou dost belie her;
Most basely and maliciously belie her.
    VENTIDIUS. I thought not to displease you; I have done.
    OCTAVIA. (*Coming up*) You seem disturbed, my lord.
    ANTONY.   A very trifle.
Retire, my love.

VENTIDIUS.   It was indeed a trifle.
He sent—
ANTONY. (*Angrily*) No more. Look how thou disobey'st me;
Thy life shall answer it.
OCTAVIA.   Then 'tis no trifle.
VENTIDIUS. (*To Octavia*) 'Tis less—a very nothing. You too saw it,
As well as I, and therefore 'tis no secret.
ANTONY. She saw it!
VENTIDIUS.   Yes. She saw young Dolabella—
ANTONY. Young Dolabella!
VENTIDIUS.   Young, I think him young,
And handsome too, and so do others think him.
But what of that? He went by your command,
Indeed, 'tis probable, with some kind message,
For she received it graciously; she smiled;
And then he grew familiar with her hand,
Squeezed it, and worried it with ravenous kisses;
She blushed, and sighed, and smiled, and blushed again;
At last she took occasion to talk softly,
And brought her cheek up close, and leaned on his;
At which, he whispered kisses back on hers;
And then she cried aloud that constancy
Should be rewarded.
OCTAVIA.   This I saw and heard.
ANTONY. What woman was it whom you heard and saw
So playful with my friend? Not Cleopatra?
VENTIDIUS. Even she, my lord.
ANTONY.   My Cleopatra?
VENTIDIUS. Your Cleopatra;
Dolabella's Cleopatra;
Every man's Cleopatra.
ANTONY.   Thou liest.
VENTIDIUS. I do not lie, my lord.
Is this so strange? Should mistresses be left,
And not provide against a time of change?
You know she's not much used to lonely nights.
ANTONY. I'll think no more on't.
I know 'tis false, and see the plot betwixt you.—
You needed not have gone this way, Octavia.
What harms it you that Cleopatra's just?
She's mine no more. I see, and I forgive.
Urge it no further, love.
OCTAVIA.   Are you concerned
That she's found false?
ANTONY.   I should be, were it so,

For though 'tis past, I would not that the world
Should tax my former choice, that I loved one
Of so light note, but I forgive you both.

VENTIDIUS. What has my age deserved that you should think
I would abuse your ears with perjury?
If Heaven be true, she's false.

ANTONY.   Though heaven and earth
Should witness it, I'll not believe her tainted.

VENTIDIUS. I'll bring you, then, a witness
From hell to prove her so.—Nay, go not back,

                    (Seeing ALEXAS *just entering, and starting back*)
For stay you must and shall.

ALEXAS.   What means my lord?

VENTIDIUS. To make you do what most you hate,—speak truth.
You are of Cleopatra's private counsel,
Of her bed-counsel, her lascivious hours;
Are conscious of each nightly change she makes,
And watch her, as Chaldaeans do the moon,
Can tell what signs she passes through, what day.

ALEXAS. My noble lord!

VENTIDIUS.   My most illustrious pander,
No fine set speech, no cadence, no turned periods,
But a plain homespun truth is what I ask:
I did myself o'erhear your queen make love
To Dolabella. Speak. For I will know
By your confession what more passed betwixt them;
How near the business draws to your employment;
And when the happy hour.

ANTONY. Speak truth, Alexas; whether it offend
Or please Ventidius, care not. Justify
Thy injured queen from malice. Dare his worst.

OCTAVIA. (*Aside*) See how he gives him courage! how he fears
To find her false! and shuts his eyes to truth,
Willing to be misled!

ALEXAS. As far as love may plead for woman's frailty,
Urged by desert and greatness of the lover,
So far, divine Octavia, may my queen
Stand even excused to you for loving him
Who is your lord; so far, from brave Ventidius,
May her past actions hope a fair report.

ANTONY. 'Tis well, and truly spoken. Mark, Ventidius.

ALEXAS. To you, most noble emperor, her strong passion
Stands not excused, but wholly justified.
Her beauty's charms alone, without her crown,

From Ind and Meroë[2] drew the distant vows
Of sighing kings; and at her feet were laid
The sceptres of the earth exposed on heaps,
To choose where she would reign.
She thought a Roman only could deserve her,
And of all Romans only Antony;
And, to be less than wife to you, disdained
Their lawful passion.
    ANTONY.   'Tis but truth.
    ALEXAS. And yet, though love and your unmatched desert
Have drawn her from the due regard of honor,
At last Heaven opened her unwilling eyes
To see the wrongs she offered fair Octavia,
Whose holy bed she lawlessly usurped.
The sad effects of this improsperous war
Confirmed those pious thoughts.
    VENTIDIUS. (*Aside*)   Oh, wheel you there?
Observe him now; the man begins to mend,
And talk substantial reason.—Fear not, eunuch,
The emperor has given thee leave to speak.
    ALEXAS. Else had I never dared to offend his ears
With what the last necessity has urged
On my forsaken mistress; yet I must not
Presume to say her heart is wholly altered.
    ANTONY. No, dare not for thy life, I charge thee dare not
Pronounce that fatal word!
    OCTAVIA. (*Aside*) Must I bear this? Good Heaven, afford me
      patience!
    VENTIDIUS. On, sweet eunuch; my dear half-man, proceed.
    ALEXAS. Yet Dolabella
Has loved her long. He, next my god-like lord,
Deserves her best; and should she meet his passion,
Rejected as she is by him she loved—
    ANTONY. Hence from my sight! for I can bear no more.
Let furies drag thee quick to hell; let all
The longer damned have rest; each torturing hand
Do thou employ till Cleopatra comes;
Then join thou too, and help to torture her!
             Exit ALEXAS, *thrust out by* ANTONY
    OCTAVIA. 'Tis not well,
Indeed, my lord, 'tis much unkind to me,
To show this passion, this extreme concernment
For an abandoned, faithless prostitute.

    [2] Upper Egypt.

ANTONY. Octavia, leave me. I am much disordered.
Leave me, I say.

OCTAVIA.   My lord!

ANTONY.   I bid you leave me.

VENTIDIUS. Obey him, madam. Best withdraw a while,
And see how this will work.

OCTAVIA. Wherein have I offended you, my lord,
That I am bid to leave you? Am I false
Or infamous? Am I a Cleopatra?
Were I she,
Base as she is, you would not bid me leave you,
But hang upon my neck, take slight excuses,
And fawn upon my falsehood.

ANTONY.   'Tis too much,
Too much, Octavia. I am pressed with sorrows
Too heavy to be borne, and you add more.
I would retire and recollect what's left
Of man within, to aid me.

OCTAVIA.   You would mourn
In private for your love, who has betrayed you.
You did but half return to me; your kindness
Lingered behind with her. I hear, my lord,
You make conditions for her,
And would include her treaty. Wondrous proofs
Of love to me!

ANTONY.   Are you my friend, Ventidius?
Or are you turned a Dolabella too,
And let this Fury loose?

VENTIDIUS.   Oh, be advised,
Sweet madam, and retire.

OCTAVIA. Yes, I will go, but never to return.
You shall no more be haunted with this Fury.
My lord, my lord, love will not always last
When urged with long unkindness and disdain.
Take her again whom you prefer to me;
She stays but to be called. Poor cozened man!
Let a feigned parting give her back your heart,
Which a feigned love first got; for injured me,
Though my just sense of wrongs forbid my stay,
My duty shall be yours.
To the dear pledges of our former love
My tenderness and care shall be transferred,
And they shall cheer, by turns, my widowed nights.
So, take my last farewell, for I despair
To have you whole, and scorn to take you half.

VENTIDIUS. I combat Heaven, which blasts my best designs;
My last attempt must be to win her back;
But oh! I fear in vain.   *Exit*

ANTONY. Why was I framed with this plain, honest heart,
Which knows not to disguise its griefs and weakness,
But bears its workings outward to the world?
I should have kept the mighty anguish in,
And forced a smile at Cleopatra's falsehood.
Octavia had believed it, and had stayed.
But I am made a shallow-forded stream,
Seen to the bottom; all my clearness scorned,
And all my faults exposed.—See where he comes

Enter DOLABELLA

Who has profaned the sacred name of friend,
And worn it into vileness!
With how secure a brow, and specious form,
He gilds the secret villain! Sure that face
Was meant for honesty, but Heaven mismatched it,
And furnished treason out with nature's pomp
To make its work more easy.

DOLABELLA.   O my friend!

ANTONY. Well, Dolabella, you performed my message?

DOLABELLA. I did, unwillingly.

ANTONY.   Unwillingly?
Was it so hard for you to bear our parting?
You should have wished it.

DOLABELLA.   Why?

ANTONY.   Because you love me.
And she received my message with as true,
With as unfeigned a sorrow as you brought it?

DOLABELLA. She loves you, even to madness.

ANTONY.   Oh, I know it.
You, Dolabella, do not better know
How much she loves me. And should I
Forsake this beauty? This all-perfect creature?

DOLABELLA. I could not, were she mine.

ANTONY.   And yet you first
Persuaded me. How come you altered since?

DOLABELLA. I said at first I was not fit to go;
I could not hear her sighs and see her tears,
But pity must prevail. And so perhaps
It may again with you, for I have promised
That she should take her last farewell. And see,
She comes to claim my word.

Enter CLEOPATRA

ANTONY.   False Dolabella!

DOLABELLA. What's false, my lord?

ANTONY.   Why, Dolabella's false,
And Cleopatra's false—both false and faithless.
Draw near, you well-joined wickedness, you serpents
Whom I have in my kindly bosom warmed,
Till I am stung to death.

DOLABELLA.   My lord, have I
Deserved to be thus used?

CLEOPATRA.   Can Heaven prepare
A newer torment? Can it find a curse
Beyond our separation?

ANTONY.   Yes, if fate
Be just, much greater. Heaven should be ingenious
In punishing such crimes. The rolling stone
And gnawing vulture were slight pains, invented
When Jove was young, and no examples known
Of mighty ills. But you have ripened sin
To such a monstrous growth 'twill pose the gods
To find an equal torture. Two, two such!—
Oh, there's no farther name,—two such! to me,
To me, who locked my soul within your breasts,
Had no desires, no joys, no life, but you.
When half the globe was mine, I gave it you
In dowry with my heart; I had no use,
No fruit of all, but you. A friend and mistress
Was what the world could give. O Cleopatra!
O Dolabella! how could you betray
This tender heart which with an infant fondness
Lay lulled betwixt your bosoms and there slept,
Secure of injured faith?

DOLABELLA.   If she has wronged you,
Heaven, hell, and you, revenge it.

ANTONY.   If she wronged me!
Thou wouldst evade thy part of guilt. But swear
Thou lov'st not her.

DOLABELLA.   Not so as I love you.

ANTONY. Not so? Swear, swear, I say, thou dost not love her.

DOLABELLA. No more than friendship will allow.

ANTONY.   No more?
Friendship allows thee nothing. Thou art perjured —
And yet thou didst not swear thou lov'd'st her not,
But not so much, no more. O trifling hypocrite,

Who dar'st not own to her, thou dost not love,
Nor own to me, thou dost. Ventidius heard it;
Octavia saw it.

    CLEOPATRA.   They are enemies.

    ANTONY. Alexas is not so. He, he confessed it;
He, who, next hell, best knew it, he avowed it.
Why do I seek a proof beyond yourself?

                                           (*TO* DOLABELLA)

You, whom I sent to bear my last farewell,
Returned to plead her stay.

    DOLBELLA.   What shall I answer?
If to have loved be guilt, then I have sinned;
But if to have repented of that love
Can wash away my crime, I have repented.
Yet, if I have offended past forgiveness,
Let not her suffer. She is innocent.

    CLEOPATRA. Ah, what will not a woman do who loves?
What means will she refuse to keep that heart
Where all her joys are placed? 'Twas I encouraged,
'Twas I blew up the fire that scorched his soul,
To make you jealous, and by that regain you.
But all in vain. I could not counterfeit;
In spite of all the dams, my love broke o'er,
And drowned my heart again; fate took the occasion,
And thus one minute's feigning has destroyed
My whole life's truth.

    ANTONY.   Thin cobweb arts of falsehood,
Seen, and broke through at first

    DOLABELLA.   Forgive your mistress.

    CLEOPATRA. Forgive your friend.

    ANTONY.   You have convinced[3]yourselves.
You plead each other's cause. What witness have you
That you but meant to raise my jealousy?

    CLEOPATRA. Ourselves, and Heaven.

    ANTONY. Guilt witnesses for guilt. Hence, love and friendship!
You have no longer place in human breasts;
These two have driven you out. Avoid my sight!
I would not kill the man whom I have loved,
And cannot hurt the woman. But avoid me,
I do not know how long I can be tame,
For, if I stay one minute more, to think
How I am wronged, my justice and revenge
Will cry so loud within me that my pity
Will not be heard for either.

    [3] Convicted.

DOLABELLA.   Heaven has but
Our sorrow for our sins, and then delights
To pardon erring man. Sweet mercy seems
Its darling attribute, which limits justice
As if there were degrees in infinite,
And infinite would rather want perfection
Than punish to extent.
ANTONY.   I can forgive
A foe, but not a mistress and a friend.
Treason is there in its most horrid shape
Where trust is greatest, and the soul, resigned,
Is stabbed by its own guards. I'll hear no more.—
Hence from my sight forever!
CLEOPATRA.   How? Forever?
I cannot go one moment from your sight,
And must I go forever?
My joys, my only joys, are centered here.
What place have I to go to? My own kingdom?
That I have lost for you. Or to the Romans?
They hate me for your sake. Or must I wander
The wide world o'er, a helpless, banished woman,
Banished for love of you—banished from you?
Aye, there's the banishment! Oh, hear me, hear me
With strictest justice, for I beg no favor,
And if I have offended you, then kill me,
But do not banish me.
ANTONY.   I must not hear you.
I have a fool within me takes your part,
But honor stops my ears.
CLEOPATRA.   For pity hear me!
Would you cast off a slave who followed you?
Who crouched beneath your spurn?—He has no pity!
See if he gives one tear to my departure,
One look, one kind farewell. O iron heart!
Let all the gods look down and judge betwixt us,
If he did ever love!
ANTONY.   No more.—Alexas!
DOLABELLA. A perjured villain!
ANTONY. (*To* CLEOPATRA)   Your Alexas, yours.
CLEOPATRA. Oh, 'twas his plot, his ruinous design,
T' engage you in my love by jealousy.
Hear him. Confront him with me. Let him speak.
ANTONY. I have, I have.
CLEOPATRA.   And if he clear me not—
ANTONY. Your creature! one who hangs upon your smiles!

Watches your eye to say or to unsay
Whate'er you please! I am not to be moved.
   CLEOPATRA. Then must we part? Farewell, my cruel lord!
Th' appearance is against me, and I go,
Unjustified, forever from your sight.
How I have loved, you know; how yet I love,
My only comfort is, I know myself.
I love you more, even now you are unkind,
Than when you loved me most; so well, so truly
I'll never strive against it but die pleased
To think you once were mine.
   ANTONY. Good heaven, they weep at parting!
Must I weep too? That calls them innocent.
I must not weep. And yet I must, to think
That I must not forgive.—
Live, but live wretched; 'tis but just you should,
Who made me so. Live from each other's sight.
Let me not hear, you meet. Set all the earth
And all the seas betwixt your sundered loves;
View nothing common but the sun and skies.
Now, all take several ways;
And each your own sad fate, with mine, deplore;
That you were false, and I could trust no more.

Exeunt severally

ACT V

SCENE I

[Enter] CLEOPATRA, CHARMION, [and] IRAS

   CHARMION. Be juster, Heaven; such virtue punished thus
Will make us think that chance rules all above,
And shuffles with a random hand the lots
Which man is forced to draw.
   CLEOPATRA. I could tear out these eyes that gained his heart,
And had not power to keep it. O the curse
Of doting on, even when I find it dotage!
Bear witness, gods, you heard him bid me go;
You whom he mocked with imprecating vows
Of promised faith!—I'll die! I will not bear it.
You may hold me—
                (*She pulls out her dagger, and they hold her*)
But I can keep my breath; I can die inward,
And choke this love.

Enter ALEXAS

IRAS.   Help, O Alexas, help!
The queen grows desperate; her soul struggles in her
With all the agonies of love and rage,
And strives to force its passage.

CLEOPATRA.   Let me go.
Art thou there, traitor!—Oh,
Oh, for a little breath, to vent my rage!
Give, give me way, and let me loose upon him.

ALEXAS. Yes, I deserve it for my ill-timed truth.
Was it for me to prop
The ruins of a falling majesty?
To place myself beneath the mighty flaw,
Thus to be crushed and pounded into atoms
By its o'erwhelming weight? 'Tis too presuming
For subjects to preserve that wilful power
Which courts its own destruction.

CLEOPATRA.   I would reason
More calmly with you. Did not you o'errule
And force my plain, direct, and open love
Into these crooked paths of jealousy?
Now, what's the event? Octavia is removed,
But Cleopatra's banished. Thou, thou villain,
[Hast] pushed my boat to open sea, to prove
At my sad cost, if thou canst steer it back.
It can not be; I'm lost too far; I'm ruined!—
Hence, thou imposter, traitor, monster, devil!—
I can no more. Thou, and my griefs, have sunk
Me down so low that I want voice to curse thee.

ALEXAS. Suppose some shipwrecked seaman near the shore,
Dropping and faint with climbing up the cliff;
If, from above, some charitable hand
Pull him to safety, hazarding himself
To draw the other's weight, would he look back
And curse him for his pains?   The case is yours;
But one step more, and you have gained the height.

CLEOPATRA. Sunk, never more to rise.

ALEXAS. Octavia's gone, and Dolabella banished.
Believe me, madam, Antony is yours.
His heart was never lost, but started off
To jealousy, love's last retreat and covert,
Where it lies hid in shades, watchful in silence,
And listening for the sound that calls it back.
Some other, any man ('tis so advanced)

May perfect this unfinished work, which I
(Unhappy only to myself) have left
So easy to his hand.

    CLEOPATRA. Look well thou do't; else—

    ALEXAS. Else what your silence threatens.—Anthony
Is mounted up the Pharos, from whose turret
He stands surveying our Egyptian galleys
Engaged with Caesar's fleet. Now death or conquest!
If the first happen, fate acquits my promise;
If we o'ercome, the conqueror is yours.

                                    (*A distant shout within*)

    CHARMION. Have comfort, madam. Did you mark that shout?

                                   (*Second shout nearer*)

    IRAS. Hark! they redouble it.

    ALEXAS.   'Tis from the port.
The loudness shows it near. Good news, kind heavens!

    CLEOPATRA. Osiris make it so!

Enter SERAPION

    SERAPION.   Where, where's the queen?

    ALEXAS. How frightfully the holy coward stares
As if not yet recovered of the assault,
When all his gods and, what's more dear to him,
His offerings were at stake!

    SERAPION.   O horror, horror!
Egypt has been; our latest hour is come;
The queen of nations from her ancient seat
Is sunk forever in the dark abyss;
Time has unrolled her glories to the last,
And now closed up the volume.

    CLEOPATRA.   Be more plain.
Say whence thou comest, though fate is in thy face,
Which from thy haggard eyes looks wildly out,
And threatens ere thou speakest.

    SERAPION.   I came from Pharos—
From viewing (spare me, and imagine it)
Our land's last hope, your navy—

    CLEOPATRA.   Vanquished?

    SERAPION.   No.
They fought not.

    CLEOPATRA.   Then they fled!

    SERAPION.   Nor that. I saw,
With Antony, your well-appointed fleet
Row out; and thrice he waved his hand on high,
And thrice with cheerful cries they shouted back.

'Twas then false Fortune like a fawning strumpet
About to leave the bankrupt prodigal,
With a dissembled smile would kiss at parting,
And flatter to the last; the well-timed oars
Now dipt from every bank, now smoothly run
To meet the foe; and soon indeed they met,
But not as foes.   In few, we saw their caps
On either side thrown up. The Egyptian galleys,
Received like friends, passed through and fell behind
The Roman rear. And now they all come forward,
And ride within the port.

    CLEOPATRA.   Enough, Serapion.
I've heard my doom.—This needed not, you gods:
When I lost Antony, your work was done.
'Tis but superfluous malice.—Where's my lord?
How bears he this last blow?

    SERAPION. His fury can not be expressed by words.
Thrice he attempted headlong to have fallen
Full on his foes, and aimed at Caesar's galley;
Withheld, he raves on you; cries he's betrayed.
Should he now find you—

    ALEXAS.   Shun him. Seek your safety
Till you can clear your innocence.

    CLEOPATRA.   I'll stay.

    ALEXAS. You must not. Haste you to your monument,
While I make speed to Caesar.

    CLEOPATRA.   Caesar! No,
I have no business with him.

    ALEXAS.   I can work him
To spare your life, and let this madman perish.

    CLEOPATRA. Base, fawning wretch! wouldst thou betray him too?
Hence from my sight! I will not hear a traitor.
'Twas thy design brought all this ruin on us.—
Serapion, thou art honest. Counsel me—
But haste, each moment's precious.

    SERAPION. Retire. You must not yet see Antony.
He who began this mischief,
'Tis just he tempt the danger. Let him clear you;
And, since he offered you his servile tongue,
To gain a poor precarious life from Caesar
Let him expose that fawning eloquence,
And speak to Antony.

    ALEXAS.   O heaven! I dare not;
I meet my certain death.

    CLEOPATRA.   Slave, thou deservest it.—

Not that I fear my lord, will I avoid him;
I know him noble. When he banished me,
And thought me false, he scorned to take my life;
But I'll be justified, and then die with him.

ALEXAS. O pity me, and let me follow you!

CLEOPATRA. To death, if thou stir hence. Speak if thou canst
Now for thy life which basely thou wouldst save,
While mine I prize at—this. Come, good Serapion.

Exeunt CLEOPATRA, SERAPION, CHARMION, *and* IRAS

ALEXAS. O that I less could fear to lose this being,
Which, like a snowball in my coward hand,
The more 'tis grasped, the faster melts away.
Poor reason! what a wretched aid art thou!
For still, in spite of thee,
These two long lovers, soul and body, dread
Their final separation. Let me think;
What can I say to save myself from death,
No matter what becomes of Cleopatra?

ANTONY. (*Within*) Which way? where?

VENTIDIUS. (*Within*) This leads to the monument.

ALEXAS. Ah me! I hear him; yet I'm unprepared,
My gift of lying's gone;
And this court-devil, which I so oft have raised,
Forsakes me at my need. I dare not stay,
Yet can not far go hence.   *Exit*

Enter ANTONY *and* VENTIDIUS

ANTONY. O happy Caesar! thou hast men to lead!
Think not 'tis thou hast conquered Antony,
But Rome has conquered Egypt. I'm betrayed.

VENTIDIUS. Curse on this treacherous train!
Their soil and heaven infect them all with baseness,
And their young souls come tainted to the world
With the first breath they draw.

ANTONY. The original villain sure no god created;
He was a bastard of the sun by Nile,
Aped into man; with all his mother's mud[1]
Crusted about his soul.

VENTIDIUS.   The nation is
One universal traitor, and their queen
The very spirit and extract of them all.

ANTONY. Is there yet left
A possibility of aid from valor?
Is there one god unsworn to my destruction?

----

[1] I.e., bred by the sun from the mud of the Nile.

The least unmortgaged hope? for, if there be,
Methinks I can not fall beneath the fate
Of such a boy as Caesar.
The world's one half is yet in Antony,
And from each limb of it that's hewed away,
The soul comes back to me.
    VENTIDIUS.   There yet remain
Three legions in the town. The last assault
Lopt off the rest. If death be your design—
As I must wish it now—these are sufficient
To make a heap about us of dead foes,
An honest pile for burial.
    ANTONY.   They're enough.
We'll not divide our stars, but, side by side,
Fight emulous, and with malicious eyes
Survey each other's acts, so every death
Thou giv'st, I'll take on me as a just debt,
And pay thee back a soul.
    VENTIDIUS. Now you shall see I love you. Not a word
Of chiding more. By my few hours of life,
I am so pleased with this brave Roman fate
That I would not be Caesar to outlive you.
When we put off this flesh and mount together,
I shall be shown to all the ethereal crowd,—
"Lo, this is he who died with Antony!"
    ANTONY. Who knows but we may pierce through all their troops,
And reach my veterans yet? 'tis worth the 'tempting
To o'erleap this gulf of fate,
And leave our wondering destinies behind.

                Enter ALEXAS, *trembling*
    VENTIDIUS. See, see, that villain!
See Cleopatra stamped upon that face
With all her cunning, all her arts of falsehood!
How she looks out through those dissembling eyes!
How he has set his count'nance for deceit,
And promises a lie before he speaks!
(*Drawing*) Let me dispatch him first.
    ALEXAS.   O spare me, spare me!
    ANTONY. Hold He's not worth your killing.—On thy life,
Which thou may'st keep because I scorn to take it,
No syllable to justify thy queen.
Save thy base tongue its office.
    ALEXAS.   Sir, she's gone

Where she shall never be molested more
By love, or you.

    ANTONY.   Fled to her Dolabella!
Die, traitor! I revoke my promise! die!   *(Going to kill him)*
    ALEXAS. O hold! she is not fled.

    ANTONY.   She is. My eyes
Are open to her falsehood; my whole life
Has been a golden dream of love and friendship;
But, now I wake, I'm like a merchant roused
From soft repose to see his vessel sinking,
And all his wealth cast o'er. Ingrateful woman!
Who followed me but as the swallow summer,
Hatching her young ones in my kindly beams,
Singing her flatteries to my morning wake;
But now my winter comes, she spreads her wings,
And seeks the spring of Caesar.

    ALEXAS.   Think not so:
Her fortunes have in all things mixed with yours.
Had she betrayed her naval force to Rome,
How easily might she have gone to Caesar,
Secure by such a bribe.

    VENTIDIUS.   She sent it first,
To be more welcome after.

    ANTONY.   'Tis too plain,
Else would she have appeared to clear herself.

    ALEXAS. Too fatally she has. She could not bear
To be accused by you, but shut herself
Within her monument, looked down and sighed,
While from her unchanged face the silent tears
Dropped, as they had not leave, but stole their parting.
Some undistinguished words she inly murmured;
At last she raised her eyes, and, with such looks
As dying Lucrece cast—

    ANTONY.   My heart forebodes—

    VENTIDIUS. All for the best;—go on.

    ALEXAS.   She snatched her poniard,
And, ere we could prevent the fatal blow,
Plunged it within her breast, then turned to me:
"Go, bear my lord," said she, "my last farewell,
And ask him if he yet suspect my faith."
More she was saying, but death rushed betwixt.
She half pronounced your name with her last breath,
And buried half within her.

    VENTIDIUS.   Heaven be praised!

ANTONY. Then art thou innocent, my poor dear love?
And art thou dead?
O those two words! their sound should be divided;
Hadst thou been false, and died; or hadst thou lived,
And hadst been true—But innocence and death!
This shows not well above. Then what am I,
The murderer of this truth, this innocence!
Thoughts can not form themselves in words so horrid
As can express my guilt!

VENTIDIUS. Is't come to this? The gods have been too gracious,
And thus you thank 'em for't!

ANTONY. (*To* ALEXAS)   Why stayest thou here?
Is it for thee to spy upon my soul
And see its inward mourning? Get thee hence.
Thou art not worthy to behold what now
Becomes a Roman emperor to perform.

ALEXAS. (*Aside*) He loves her still:
His grief betrays it. Good! the joy to find
She's yet alive completes the reconcilement.
I've saved myself and her. But, oh! the Romans!
Fate comes too fast upon my wit,
Hunts me too hard, and meets me at each double.   *Exit*

VENTIDIUS. Would she had died a little sooner, though,
Before Octavia went; you might have treated;
Now 'twill look tame, and would not be received.
Come, rouse yourself, and let's die warm together.

ANTONY. I will not fight: there's no more work for war.
The business of my angry hours is done.

VENTIDIUS. Caesar is at your gates.

ANTONY.   Why, let him enter;
He's welcome now.

VENTIDIUS. What lethargy has crept into your soul?

ANTONY. 'Tis but a scorn of life, and just desire
To free myself from bondage.

VENTIDIUS.   Do it bravely.

ANTONY. I will; but not by fighting. O Ventidius!
What should I fight for now?—my queen is dead.
I was but great for her; my power, my empire,
Were but my merchandise to buy her love,
And conquered kings, my factors. Now she's dead,
Let Caesar take the world,—
An empty circle since the jewel's gone
Which made it worth my strife; my being's nauseous;
For all the bribes of life are gone away.

VENTIDIUS. Would you be taken?

ANTONY.   Yes, I would be taken,
But as a Roman ought,—dead, my Ventidius.
For I'll convey my soul from Caesar's reach,
And lay down life myself. 'Tis time the world
Should have a lord, and know whom to obey.
We two have kept its homage in suspense,
And bent the globe, on whose each side we trod,
Till it was dinted inwards. Let him walk
Alone upon't; I'm weary of my part.
My torch is out; and the world stands before me
Like a black desert at th' approach of night.
I'll lay me down and stray no farther on.
    VENTIDIUS. I could be grieved,
But that I'll not outlive you. Choose your death,
For I have seen him in such various shapes,
I care not which I take—I'm only troubled,
The life I bear is worn to such a rag,
'Tis scarce worth giving. I could wish, indeed,
We threw it from us with a better grace;
That, like two lions taken in the toils,
We might at least thrust out our paws and wound
The hunters that inclose us.
    ANTONY.   I have thought on it.
Ventidius, you must live.
    VENTIDIUS.   I must not, sir.
    ANTONY. Wilt thou not live to speak some good of me?
To stand by my fair fame and guard the approaches
From the ill tongues of men?
    VENTIDIUS.   Who shall guard mine
For living after you?
    ANTONY.   Say I command it.
    VENTIDIUS. If we die well, our deaths will speak themselves,
And need no living witness.
    ANTONY.   Thou hast loved me,
And fain I would reward thee. I must die.
Kill me, and take the merit of my death
To make thee friends with Caesar.
    VENTIDIUS.   Thank your kindness.
You said I loved you; and in recompense
You bid me turn a traitor.—Did I think
You would have used me thus?—that I should die
With a hard thought of you?
    ANTONY.   Forgive me, Roman.
Since I have heard of Cleopatra's death,
My reason bears no rule upon my tongue,

But lets my thoughts break all at random out.
I've thought better; do not deny me twice.
    VENTIDIUS. By Heaven, I will not.
Let it not be to outlive you.
    ANTONY.   Kill me first,
And then die thou; for 'tis but just thou serve
Thy friend before thyself.
    VENTIDIUS.   Give me your hand.
We soon shall meet again. Now farewell, emperor!—   (*Embrace*)
Methinks that word's too cold to be my last:
Since death sweeps all distinctions, farewell, friend!
That's all—
I will not make a business of a trifle;
And yet I can not look on you and kill you;
Pray turn your face.
    ANTONY.   I do. Strike home, be sure.
    VENTIDIUS. Home as my sword will reach.   (*Kills himself*)
    ANTONY. Oh, thou mistak'st;
That wound was none of thine; give it me back;
Thou robb'st me of my death.
    VENTIDIUS.   I do, indeed;
But think 'tis the first time I e'er deceived you,
If that may plead my pardon.—And you, gods,
Forgive me if you will; for I die perjured
Rather than kill my friend.   (*Dies*)
    ANTONY. Farewell! Ever my leader, even in death!
My queen and thou have got the start of me,
And I'm the lag of honor.—Gone so soon?
Is death no more? he used him carelessly,
With a familiar kindness; ere he knocked,
Ran to the door and took him in his arms,
As who should say, "You're welcome at all hours,
A friend need give no warning." Books had spoiled him,
For all the learn'd are cowards by profession.
'Tis not worth
My farther thought; for death, for aught I know,
Is but to think no more. Here's to be satisfied.   (*Falls on his sword*)
I've missed my heart. O unperforming hand!
Thou never couldst have erred in a worse time.
My fortune jades me to the last; and death,
Like a great man, takes state, and makes me wait
For my admittance—

                             (*Trampling within*)
                         Some, perhaps, from Caesar

If he should find me living, and suspect
That I played booty[2] with my life! I'll mend
My work ere they can reach me.   (*Rises upon his knees*)

          Enter CLEOPATRA, CHARMION, [*and*] IRAS

CLEOPATRA. Where is my lord? where is he?
CHARMION.   There he lies,
And dead Ventidius by him.
     CLEOPATRA. My fear were prophets; I am come too late.
                                        (*Runs to him*)
O that accursed Alexas!
     ANTONY.   Art thou living?
Or am I dead before I knew, and thou
The first kind ghost that meets me?
     CLEOPATRA.   Help me seat him.
Send quickly, send for help!
                              (*They place him in a chair*)
     ANTONY.   I am answered.
We live both. Sit thee down, my Cleopatra;
I'll make the most I can of life, to stay
A moment more with thee.
     CLEOPATRA.   How is it with you?
     ANTONY. 'Tis as with a man
Removing in a hurry; all packed up,
But one dear jewel that his haste forgot;
And he, for that, returns upon the spur;
So I come back for thee.
     CLEOPATRA. Too long, you heavens, you have been cruel to me;
Now show your mended faith, and give me back
His fleeting life!
     ANTONY.   It will not be, my love;
I keep my soul by force.
Say but, thou are not false.
     CLEOPATRA.   'Tis now too late
To say I'm true: I'll prove it, and die with you.
Unknown to me, Alexas feigned my death,
Which, when I knew, I hasted to prevent
This fatal consequence. My fleet betrayed
Both you and me.
     ANTONY.   And Dolabella—
     CLEOPATRA.   Scarce
Esteemed before he loved; but hated now.
     ANTONY. Enough. My life's not long enough for more.
Thou say'st thou wilt come after: I believe thee,
     2 Shammed suicide to gain pity.

For I can now believe whate'er thou sayest,
That we may part more kindly.

    CLEOPATRA.   I will come.
Doubt not, my life, I'll come, and quickly too;
Caesar shall triumph o'er no part of thee.

    ANTONY. But grieve not, while thou stay'st,
My last disastrous times.
Think we have had a clear and glorious day,
And Heaven did kindly to delay the storm
Just till our close of evening. Ten years' love,
And not a moment lost, but all improved
To the utmost joys,—what ages have we lived!
And now to die each other's; and, so dying,
While hand in hand we walk in groves below,
Whole troops of lovers' ghosts shall flock about us,
And all the train be ours.

    CLEOPATRA. Your words are like the notes of dying swans,
Too sweet to last. Were there so many hours
For your unkindness, and not one for love?

    ANTONY. No, not a minute.—This one kiss—more worth
Than all I leave to Caesar.   (*Dies*)

    CLEOPATRA.   O tell me so again,
And take ten thousand kisses for that word.
My lord, my lord! Speak, if you yet have being;
Sign to me, if you can not speak; or cast
One look! Do anything that shows you live.

    IRAS. He's gone too far to hear you,
And this you see, a lump of senseless clay,
The leavings of a soul.

    CHARMION.   Remember, madam,
He charged you not to grieve.

    CLEOPATRA.   And I'll obey him.
I have not loved a Roman not to know
What should become his wife—his wife, my Charmion!
For 'tis to that high title I aspire,
And now I'll not die less. Let dull Octavia
Survive to mourn him, dead. My nobler fate
Shall knit our spousals with a tie too strong
For Roman laws to break.

    IRAS.   Will you then die?

    CLEOPATRA. Why shouldst thou make that question?

    IRAS. Caesar is merciful.

    CLEOPATRA.   Let him be so
To those that want his mercy. My poor lord
Made no such covenant with him to spare me

When he was dead. Yield me to Caesar's pride?
What! to be led in triumph through the streets,
A spectacle to base plebian eyes,
While some dejected friend of Antony's
Close in a corner, shakes his head, and mutters
A secret curse on her who ruined him?
I'll none of that.

    CHARMION.   Whatever you resolve,
I'll follow, even to death.

    IRAS.   I only feared
For you, but more should fear to live without you.

    CLEOPATRA. Why, now, 'tis as it should be. Quick, my friends,
Dispatch. Ere this, the town's in Caesar's hands.
My lord looks down concerned, and fears my stay,
Lest I should be surprised.
Keep him not waiting for his love too long.
You, Charmion, bring my crown and richest jewels;
With them, the wreath of victory I made
(Vain augury!) for him who now lies dead.
You, Iras, bring the cure of all our ills.

    IRAS. The aspics, madam?

    CLEOPATRA.   Must I bid you twice?

                         (*Exeunt* CHARMION *and* IRAS)
'Tis sweet to die when they would force life on me,
To rush into the dark abode of death,
And seize him first. If he be like my love,
He is not frightful, sure.
We're now alone in secrecy and silence;
And is not this like lovers? I may kiss
These pale, cold lips; Octavia does not see me.
And oh! 'tis better far to have him thus
Than see him in her arms.—Oh, welcome, welcome!

              Enter CHARMION [*and*] IRAS

    CHARMION. What must be done?

    CLEOPATRA.   Short ceremony, friends,
But yet it must be decent. First, this laurel
Shall crown my hero's head; he fell not basely,
Nor left his shield behind him.—Only thou
Couldst triumph o'er thyself; and thou alone
Wert worthy so to triumph.

    CHARMION.   To what end
These ensigns of your pomp and royalty?

    CLEOPATRA. Dull that thou art! why, 'tis to meet my love
As when I saw him first on Cydnos' bank,
All sparkling, like a goddess; so adorned,

I'll find him once again. My second spousals
Shall match my first in glory. Haste, haste, both,
And dress the bride of Antony.

    CHARMION.   —'Tis done.

    CLEOPATRA. Now seat me by my lord. I claim this place,
For I must conquer Caesar, too, like him,
And win my share o' th' world.—Hail, you dear relics
Of my immortal love!
O let no impious hand remove you hence,
But rest for ever here! Let Egypt give
His death that peace which it denied his life.—
Reach me the casket.

    IRAS.   Underneath the fruit
The aspic lies.

    CLEOPATRA. Welcome, thou kind deceiver!

                       (Putting aside the leaves)
Thou best of thieves, who, with an easy key,
Dost open life and, unperceived by us,
Even steal us from ourselves, discharging so
Death's dreadful office better than himself,
Touching our limbs so gently into slumber
That Death stands by, deceived by his own image,
And thinks himself but sleep.

    SERAPION. (*Within*)   The queen, where is she?
The town is yielded, Caesar's at the gates.

    CLEOPATRA. He comes too late to invade the rights of death.
Haste, bare my arm, and rouse the serpent's fury.

             (Holds out her arm, and draws it back)
Coward flesh,
Wouldst thou conspire with Caesar to betray me
As thou wert none of mine? I'll force thee to 't,
And not be sent by him,
But bring, myself, my soul to Antony.

         (Turns aside, and then shows her arm bloody)
Take hence. The work is done.

    SERAPION. (*Within*)   Break ope the door
And guard the traitor well.

    CHARMION.   The next is ours.

    IRAS. Now, Charmion, to be worthy
Of our great queen and mistress.

                   (They apply the aspics)
    CLEOPATRA. Already, death, I feel thee in my veins.
I go with such a will to find my lord
That we shall quickly meet.
A heavy numbness creeps through every limb,

And now 'tis at my head. My eyelids fall,
And my dear love is vanished in a mist.—
Where shall I find him—where? O turn me to him,
And lay me on his breast!—Caesar, thy worst.
Now part us, if thou canst.   (*Dies*)
                                   (IRAS *sinks down at her feet, and dies;*
                                   CHARMION *stands behind her chair, as*
                                                        dressing her head)

                    Enter SERAPION, *two Priests,* ALEXAS, *bound, Egyptians*
      PRIEST.   Behold, Serapion,
What havoc death has made!
      SERAPION.   'Twas what I feared.—
Charmion, is this well done?
      CHARMION. Yes, 'tis well done, and like a queen, the last
Of her great race. I follow her.   (*Sinks down* [*and*] *dies*)
      ALEXAS.   'Tis true,
She has done well. Much better thus to die
Than live to make a holiday in Rome.
      SERAPION. See, see how the lovers sit in state together,
As they were giving laws to half mankind!
Th' impression of a smile, left in her face,
Shows she died pleased with him for whom she lived,
And went to charm him in another world.
Caesar's just entering; grief has now no leisure.
Secure that villain as our pledge of safety
To grace the imperial triumph.—Sleep, blest pair,
Secure from human chance, long ages out,
While all the storms of fate fly o'er your tomb;
And fame to late posterity shall tell,
No lovers lived so great or died so well.
                                                        Exeunt

EPILOGUE

Poets, like disputants when reasons fail,
Have one sure refuge left—and that's to rail.
Fop, coxcomb, fool, are thundered through the pit;
And this is all their equipage of wit.
We wonder how the devil this difference grows
Betwixt our fools in verse, and yours in prose;
For, 'faith, the quarrel rightly understood,
'Tis civil war with their own flesh and blood.
The threadbare author hates the gaudy coat;
And swears at the gilt coach, but swears afoot;
For 'tis observed of every scribbling man,
He grows a fop as fast as e'er he can;
Prunes up, and asks his oracle, the glass,
If pink or purple best become his face.
For our poor wretch, he neither rails nor prays; ⎤
Nor likes your wit just as you like his plays;   ⎬
He has not yet so much of Mr. Bayes.[1]   ⎦
He does his best; and if he can not please,
Would quickly sue out his *writ of ease*.[2]
Yet, if he might his own grand jury call,
By the fair sex he begs to stand or fall.
Let Caesar's power the men's ambition move,
But grace you him who lost the world for love!
Yet if some antiquated lady say,
The last age is not copied in his play;
Heaven help the man who for that face must drudge,
Which only has the wrinkles of a judge.
Let not the young and beauteous join with those;
For should you raise such numerous hosts of foes,
Young wits and sparks he to his aid must call;
'Tis more than one man's work to please you all.

[1] See Buckingham's *The Rehearsal*, a satire on Dryden.
[2] Certificate of discharge.

VENICE PRESERV'D

or, A PLOT DISCOVERED

A
TRAGEDY

As it is Acted at the Duke's Theatre

Written *by* THOMAS OTWAY

LONDON:

Printed for Jos. Hindmarsh at the Sign of the
Black Bull, over against the Royal
Exchange in Cornhill. 1682.

VENICE PRESERVED

OR, A PLOT DISCOVERED

Thomas Otway

WHEN POVERTY forced young Thomas Otway (1652-1685) to leave Oxford without taking a degree, he drifted to London and tried his hand at acting, with very little success. As a playwright he did much better; after his first play, *Alcibiades* (1675), failed, he hit his stride and quickly became one of the foremost writers of his generation. Early in his career as a dramatist he fell violently in love with the actress Elizabeth Barry (at that time the Earl of Rochester's protégée and mistress). The frustration of his hopeless passion discolored the remainder of his short life. He idealized Mrs. Barry in his most passionate heroines, creating for her some of her greatest roles. It is said, however, that her rejection of his love drove him to dissipation and (in 1678) to a short period of service in the English army in Flanders—the Foreign Legion of his day. A sensitive, unhappy man, Otway lived always in the bitterness of poverty, despite the great success of some of his plays. He died, probably of a fever, at the age of thirty-three, leaving ten plays to posterity, among them two first-rate tragedies, *The Orphan* (1680) and *Venice Preserved* (1682).

Although *Venice Preserved* reflects contemporary politics, those reflections must not be over-stressed. As a good Tory, Otway took delight in satirizing the great Whig leader, Anthony Ashley Cooper, Earl of Shaftesbury, as the senator Antonio (who represented Shaftesbury's public function as a member of Parliament), and as the conspirator Renault (who represented his secret role as leader of what the Tories considered a Whig plot). But there is no parallel to be drawn between England in 1682 and the Venice of 1616 pictured in Otway's source, Saint-Réal's novel, *Le Conjuration des Espagnolles contre la République de Venise* (1674). The central theme of the play has nothing to do with politics. It is the problem of a noble Venetian, Jaffier, who makes a series of unwise decisions, beginning with his elopement with Belvidera, and who finds himself at last in a tragic dilemma which forces him to choose between his honor, as represented by Pierre, and his humanity, or love, as represented by Belvidera. Although there are weaknesses of plot and characterization, and Otway's tragic vision is too often clouded by sentiment, the play is excellent theater, full of bravura passages and scenes of intense emotion. It is a good example of Restoration baroque, a high tragedy which narrowly misses greatness.

Venice Preserved was produced at the Dorset Garden Theatre in February, 1682. Mrs. Barry played the distressed Belvidera with such pathos that her audience dissolved in tears. Betterton scored a new triumph as Jaffier, and William Smith was properly impressive as Pierre. Two comedians, burly Anthony Leigh and lively Elizabeth Currer, played the "doting cully" Antonio and the "rampant courtesan" Aquilina so brilliantly that, as the eighteenth-century stage historian, Thomas Davies, remarked, "the applause was as loud as the triumphant Tories, for so they were at that time, could bestow." The play remained a stock theatrical piece for nearly two centuries.

See The Works of Thomas Otway, ed. J. C. Ghosh, 2 vols., 1932; John Robert Moore, "Contemporary Satire in Otway's Venice Preserved," Publications of the Modern Language Association, XLIII (March 1928); Bonamy Dobrée, Restoration Tragedy, 1929; Roswell G. Ham, Otway and Lee, 1931; and Aline M. Taylor, Next to Shakespeare, 1950.

Dramatis Personae

DUKE OF VENICE	MR. D. WILLIAMS
PRIULI, *father to Belvidera, a senator*	MR. BOWMAN
ANTONIO, *a fine speaker in the Senate*	MR. LEIGH

JAFFEIR		MR. BETTERTON
PIERRE		MR. SMITH
RENAULT		MR. WILTSHIRE
BEDAMAR		MR. GILLO
SPINOSA		MR. PERCIVAL
THEODORE		
ELIOT		
REVILLIDO	*Conspirators*	
DURAND		
MEZZANA		
BRAINVEIL		
TERNON		
BRABE		
RETROSI		

BELVIDERA	MRS. BARRY
AQUILINA	MRS. CURRER

Two Women, attendants on Belvidera
Two Women, servants to Aquilina
The Council of Ten
Officer, Guards, Friar, Executioner, and Rabble

Scene: Venice

PROLOGUE

In these distracted times, when each man dreads
The bloody stratagems of busy heads;
When we have feared three years [1] we know not what, ⎤
Till witnesses begin to die o'th' rot, ⎟
What made our poet meddle with a plot? ⎦
Was't that he fancied, for the very sake
And name of plot, his trifling play might take?
For there's not in't one inch-board evidence, [2]
But 'tis, he says, to reason plain and sense,
And that he thinks a plausible defense.
Were truth by sense and reason to be tried,
Sure all our swearers might be laid aside.
No, of such tools our author has no need,
To make his plot, or make his play succeed;
He, of black bills, [3] has no prodigious tales,
Or Spanish pilgrims cast ashore in Wales; [4]
Here's not one murdered magistrate at least, [5]
Kept rank like ven'son for a city feast,
Grown four days stiff, the better to prepare
And fit his pliant limbs to ride in chair.
Yet here's an army raised, though underground,
But no man seen, nor one commission found.
Here is a traitor too, [6] that's very old,
Turbulent, subtle, mischievous, and bold,
Bloody, revengeful, and to crown his part,
Loves fumbling with a wench with all his heart;
Till after having many changes passed,
In spite of age (thanks heaven) is hanged at last.
Next is a senator [7] that keeps a whore;
In Venice none a higher office bore;
To lewdness every night the lecher ran—
Show me, all London, such another man;
Match him at Mother Cresswold's [8] if you can.
O Poland, Poland! [9] had it been thy lot
T'have heard in time of this Venetian plot,
Thou surely chosen hadst one king from thence,
And honored them as thou hast England since.

[1] Since the disclosure of the so-called "Popish Plot" in October, 1678.

[2] Hard-sworn, as through an inch-thick board.

[3] Halberds supposedly distributed in preparation for a rising.

[4] Irish soldiers disguised as Spaniards.

[5] The body of Sir Edmund Berry Godfrey was discovered on October 17, on Primrose Hill, near London. Presumably he had been murdered elsewhere and brought to the scene in a sedan-chair.

[6] Renault.

[7] Antonio. Presumed to be a satire on the Whig leader, Anthony Ashley Cooper, Earl of Shaftesbury.

[8] More commonly, Cresswell, a notorious procuress.

[9] Shaftesbury had once aspired to the elective throne of Poland.

ACT I

SCENE I

Enter PRIULI and JAFFEIR

PRIULI. No more! I'll hear no more; begone and leave.

JAFFEIR. Not hear me! by my sufferings, but you shall!
My lord, my lord! I'm not that abject wretch
You think me. Patience! where's the distance throws
Me back so far, but I may boldly speak
In right, though proud oppression will not hear me!

PRIULI. Have you not wronged me?

JAFFEIR. Could my nature e'er
Have brooked injustice or the doing wrongs,
I need not now thus low have bent myself,
To gain a hearing from a cruel father!
Wronged you?

PRIULI. Yes! wronged me, in the nicest point,
The honor of my house; you have done me wrong.
You may remember (for I now will speak,
And urge its baseness) when you first came home
From travel, with such hopes as made you looked on
By all men's eyes, a youth of expectation;
Pleased with your growing virtue, I received you,
Courted, and sought to raise you to your merits.
My house, my table, nay, my fortune, too,
My very self, was yours; you might have used me
To your best service. Like an open friend,
I treated, trusted you, and thought you mine;
When in requital of my best endeavors,
You treacherously practised to undo me,
Seduced the weakness of my age's darling,
My only child, and stole her from my bosom.
Oh, Belvidera!

JAFFEIR. 'Tis to me you owe her;
Childless you had been else, and in the grave,
Your name extinct, nor no more Priuli heard of.
You may remember, scarce five years are past
Since in your brigandine you sailed to see

The Adriatic wedded by our Duke,
And I was with you. Your unskilful pilot
Dashed us upon a rock. When to your boat
You made for safety, entrèd first yourself.
The affrighted Belvidera following next,
As she stood trembling on the vessel side,
Was by a wave washed off into the deep;
When instantly I plunged into the sea,
And buffeting the billows to her rescue,
Redeemed her life with half the loss of mine.
Like a rich conquest in one hand I bore her,
And with the other dashed the saucy waves
That thronged and pressed to rob me of my prize.
I brought her, gave her to your despairing arms.
Indeed you thanked me, but a nobler gratitude
Rose in her soul; for from that hour she loved me,
Till for her life she paid me with herself.

    PRIULI. You stole her from me! Like a thief you stole her,
At dead of night; that cursèd hour you chose
To rifle me of all my heart held dear.
May all your joys in her prove false like mine;
A sterile fortune and a barren bed
Attend you both; continual discord make
Your days and nights bitter and grievous; still
May the hard hand of a vexatious need
Oppress and grind you, till at last you find
The curse of disobedience all your portion.

    JAFFEIR. Half of your curse you have bestowed in vain;
Heav'n has already crowned our faithful loves
With a young boy, sweet as his mother's beauty.
May he live to prove more gentle than his grandsire,
And happier than his father!

    PRIULI.   Rather live
To bait thee for his bread and din your ears
With hungry cries, whilst his unhappy mother
Sits down and weeps in bitterness of want.

    JAFFEIR. You talk as if it would please you.

    PRIULI.   'Twould, by heaven!
Once she was dear indeed; the drops that fell
From my sad heart when she forgot her duty,
The fountain of my life was not so precious.
But she is gone; and if I am a man,
I will forget her.

    JAFFEIR. Would I were in my grave.

PRIULI. And she, too, with thee;
For, living here, you're but my curs'd remembrancers
   I once was happy.

JAFFEIR. You use me thus because you know my soul
Is fond of Belvidera. You perceive
My life feeds on her, therefore thus you treat me.
Oh! could my soul ever have known satiety!
Were I that thief, the doer of such wrongs
As you upbraid me with, what hinders me
But I might send her back to you with contumely,
And court my fortune where she would be kinder!

PRIULI. You dare not do't.—

JAFFEIR. Indeed, my lord, I dare not.
My heart, that awes me, is too much my master.
Three years are past since first our vows were plighted,
During which time, the world must bear me witness,
I have treated Belvidera like your daughter,
The daughter of a senator of Venice;
Distinction, place, attendance, and observance
Due to her birth, she always has commanded.
Out of my little fortune I have done this,
Because (though hopeless e'er to win your nature)
The world might see I loved her for herself,
Not as the heiress of the great Priuli.—

PRIULI. No more!

JAFFEIR. Yes! all, and then adieu forever!
There's not a wretch that lives on common charity
But's happier than me. For I have known
The luscious sweets of plenty; every night
Have slept with soft content about my head,
And never waked but to a joyful morning;
Yet now must fall like a full ear of corn,
Whose blossom 'scaped, yet's withered in the ripening.

PRIULI. Home, and be humble; study to retrench.
Discharge the lazy vermin of thy hall,
Those pageants of thy folly;
Reduce the glittering trappings of thy wife
To humble weeds, fit for thy little state.
Then to some suburb cottage both retire;
Drudge to feed loathsome life; get brats, and starve—
Home, home, I say! *Exit* PRIULI

JAFFEIR. Yes, if my heart would let me—
This proud, this swelling heart. Home I would go,
But that my doors are hateful to my eyes,
Filled and dammed up with gaping creditors,

Watchful as fowlers when their game will spring.
I have now not fifty ducats in the world;
Yet still I am in love, and pleased with ruin.
O Belvidera! oh, she's my wife—
And we will bear our wayward fate together,
But ne'er know comfort more.

Enter PIERRE

PIERRE.   My friend, good morrow!
How fares the honest partner of my heart?
—What, melancholy? not a word to spare me?
      JAFFEIR. I'm thinking, Pierre, how that damned starving quality
Called honesty, got footing in the world.
      PIERRE. Why, pow'rful villainy first set it up,
For its own ease and safety; honest men
Are the soft, easy cushions on which knaves
Repose and fatten. Were all mankind villains,
They'd starve each other; lawyers would want practice,
Cut-throats rewards; each man would kill his brother
Himself; none would be paid or hanged for murder.
Honesty was a cheat invented first
To bind the hands of bold deserving rogues,
That fools and cowards might sit safe in power,
And lord it uncontrolled above their betters.
      JAFFEIR. Then honesty is but a notion?
      PIERRE.   Nothing else;
Like wit, much talked of, not to be defined.
He that pretends to most, too, has least share in't;
'Tis a ragged virtue. Honesty!—no more on't.
      JAFFEIR. Sure, thou art honest!
      PIERRE.   So indeed men think me.
But they're mistaken, Jaffeir; I am a rogue
As well as they—
A fine, gay, bold-faced villain, as thou seest me.
'Tis true, I pay my debts when they're contracted;
I steal from no man; would not cut a throat
To gain admission to a great man's purse,
Or a whore's bed. I'd not betray my friend,
To get his place or fortune. I scorn to flatter
A blown-up fool above me, or crush the wretch beneath me.
Yet, Jaffeir, for all this, I am a villain!
      JAFFEIR. A villain—
      PIERRE.   Yes, a most notorious villain
To see the suff'rings of my fellow creatures,
And own myself a man; to see our senators

Cheat the deluded people with a show
Of liberty, which yet they ne'er must taste of!
They say by them our hands are free from fetters;
Yet whom they please they lay in basest bonds;
Bring whom they please to infamy and sorrow;
Drive us like wracks down the rough tide of power,
Whilst no hold's left to save us from destruction.
All that bear this are villains; and I one,
Not to rouse up at the great call of nature,
And check the growth of these domestic spoilers,
That makes us slaves and tell us 'tis our charter.

    JAFFEIR. O Aquilina! Friend, to lose such beauty,
The dearest purchase of thy noble labors!
She was thy right by conquest, as by love.

    PIERRE. O Jaffeir! I'd so fixed my heart upon her
That wheresoe'er I framed a scheme of life
For time to come, she was my only joy
With which I wished to sweeten future cares.
I fancied pleasures, none but one that loves
And dotes as I did, can imagine like 'em.
When in the extremity of all these hopes,
In the most charming hour of expectation,
Then when our eager wishes soar the highest,
Ready to stoop and grasp the lovely game,
A haggard owl, a worthless kite of prey,
With his foul wings sailed in and spoiled my quarry.

    JAFFEIR. I know the wretch, and scorn him as thou hat'st him.

    PIERRE. Curse on the common good that's so protected,
Where every slave that heaps up wealth enough
To do much wrong, becomes a lord of right!
I, who believed no ill could e'er come near me,
Found in the embraces of my Aquilina
A wretched, old, but itching senator;
A wealthy fool, that had bought out my title,
A rogue that uses beauty like a lambskin,
Barely to keep him warm. That filthy cuckoo, too,
Was in my absence crept into my nest,
And spoiling all my brood of noble pleasure.

    JAFFEIR. Didst thou not chase him thence?

    PIERRE.   I did, and drove
The rank old bearded Hirco [1] stinking home.
The matter was complained of in the Senate;
I, summoned to appear, and censured basely,

---

[1] *Hircus*, a he-goat, a lecher, in this case Antonio. Shaftesbury, the model for Antonio, was constantly accused of libertinism.

For violating something they call "privilege"—
This was the recompense of my service.
Would I'd been rather beaten by a coward!
A soldier's mistress, Jaffeir, 's his religion;
When that's profaned, all other ties are broken;
That even dissolves all former bonds of service,
And from that hour I think myself as free
To be the foe as ere the friend of Venice.
Nay, dear Revenge, whene'er thou call'st I am ready.

JAFFEIR. I think no safety can be here for virtue,
And grieve, my friend, as much as thou to live
In such a wretched state as this of Venice,
Where all agree to spoil the public good,
And villains fatten with the brave man's labors.

PIERRE. We have neither safety, unity, nor peace,
For the foundation's lost of common good;
Justice is lame as well as blind amongst us;
The laws (corrupted to their ends that make 'em)
Serve but for instruments of some new tyranny,
That every day starts up t'enslave us deeper.
Now could this glorious cause but find out friends
To do it right! O Jaffeir! then mightst thou
Not wear these seals of woe upon thy face;
The proud Priuli should be taught humanity,
And learn to value such a son as thou art.
I dare not speak! But my heart bleeds this moment.

JAFFEIR. Curs'd be the cause, though I thy friend be part on't!
Let me partake the troubles of thy bosom,
For I am used to misery, and perhaps
May find a way to sweeten't to thy spirit.

PIERRE. Too soon it will reach thy knowledge—
JAFFEIR.   Then from thee
Let it proceed. There's virtue in thy friendship
Would make the saddest tale of sorrow pleasing,
Strengthen my constancy, and welcome ruin.

PIERRE. Then thou art ruined!
JAFFEIR.   That I long since knew;
I and ill fortune have been long acquaintance.

PIERRE. I passed this very moment by thy doors,
And found them guarded by a troop of villains;
The sons of public rapine were destroying;
They told me, by the sentene of the law,
They had commission to seize all thy fortune—
Nay, more, Priuli's cruel hand hath signed it.
Here stood a ruffian with a horrid face

Lording it o'er a pile of massy plate
Tumbled into a heap for public sale.
There was another making villainous jests
At thy undoing. He had ta'en possession
Of all thy ancient, most domestic ornaments,
Rich hangings intermixed and wrought with gold;
The very bed which on thy wedding night
Received thee to the arms of Belvidera,
The scene of all thy joys, was violated
By the coarse hands of filthy dungeon villains,
And thrown amongst the common lumber.

    JAFFEIR. Now thanks, Heaven—
    PIERRE. Thank Heaven! for what?
    JAFFEIR.   That I'm not worth a ducat.
    PIERRE. Curse thy dull stars and the worse fate of Venice!
Where brothers, friends, and fathers, all are false;
Where there's no trust, no truth; where innocence
Stoops under vile oppression, and vice lords it.
Hadst thou but seen, as I did, how at last
Thy beauteous Belvidera, like a wretch
That's doomed to banishment, came weeping forth,
Shining through tears, like April suns in showers
That labor to o'ercome the cloud that loads 'em;
Whilst two young virgins, on whose arms she leaned,
Kindly looked up, and at her grief grew sad,
As if they catched the sorrows that fell from her.
Even the lewd rabble that were gathered round
To see the sight, stood mute when they beheld her,
Governed their roaring throats, and grumbled pity.
I could have hugged the greasy rogues; they pleased me.

    JAFFEIR. I thank thee for this story from my soul,
Since now I know the worst that can befall me.
Ah, Pierre! I have a heart that could have borne
The roughest wrong my fortune could have done me;
But when I think what Belvidera feels,
The bitterness her tender spirit tastes of,
I own myself a coward. Bear my weakness,
If throwing thus my arms about thy neck,
I play the boy and blubber in thy bosom.
Oh, I shall drown thee with my sorrows!

    PIERRE.   Burn!
First burn, and level Venice to thy ruin!
What! Starve like beggar's brats in frosty weather
Under a hedge, and whine ourselves to death!
Thou, or thy cause, shall never want assistance

Whilst I have blood or fortune fit to serve thee.
Command my heart: thou art every way its master.
 JAFFEIR. No! There's a secret pride in bravely dying.
 PIERRE. Rats die in holes and corners, dogs run mad;
Man knows a braver remedy for sorrow—
Revenge! the attribute of gods. They stamped it
With their great image on our natures. Die!
Consider well the cause that calls upon thee,
And if thou'rt base enough, die then; remember
Thy Belvidera suffers. Belvidera!
Die—damn first! What, be decently interred
In a church-yard, and mingle thy brave dust
With stinking rogues that rot in dirty winding sheets—
Surfeit-slain fools, the common dung o'th' soil?
 JAFFEIR. Oh!
 PIERRE.   Well said! out with't; swear a little—
 JAFFEIR. Swear!
By sea and air! by earth, by heaven and hell,
I will revenge my Belvidera's tears!
Hark thee, my friend: Pruili—is—a senator!
 PIERRE. A dog!
 JAFFEIR.   Agreed.
 PIERRE.   Shoot him.
 JAFFEIR.   With all my heart.
No more. Where shall we meet at night?
 PIERRE.   I'll tell thee;
On the Rialto every night at twelve
I take my evening's walk of meditation;
There we two will meet, and talk of precious
Mischief—
 JAFFEIR. Farewell.
 PIERRE.   At twelve.
 JAFFEIR.   At any hour; my plagues
Will keep me waking.

          Exit PIERRE
     Tell me why, good Heaven,
Thou mad'st me what I am, with all the spirit,
Aspiring thoughts, and elegant desires
That fill the happiest man? Ah! rather why
Didst thou not form me sordid as my fate,
Base-minded, dull, and fit to carry burdens?
Why have I sense to know the curse that's on me?
Is this just dealing, Nature?—Belvidera!

Enter BELVIDERA [*with Attendants*]

Poor Belvidera!

BELVIDERA.   Lead me, lead me, my virgins,
To that kind voice!—My lord, my love, my refuge!
Happy my eyes when they behold thy face;
My heavy heart will leave its doleful beating
At sight of thee, and bound with sprightful joys.
Oh, smile, as when our loves were in their spring,
And cheer my fainting soul!

JAFFEIR.   As when our loves
Were in their spring? has then my fortune changed?
Art thou not Belvidera, still the same—
Kind, good, and tender, as my arms first found thee?
If thou art altered, where shall I have harbor?
Where ease my loaded heart? oh! where complain?

BELVIDERA. Does this appear like change, or love decaying,
When thus I throw myself into thy bosom
With all the resolution of a strong truth?
Beats not my heart as 'twould alarm thine
To a new charge of bliss? I joy more in thee
Than did thy mother when she hugged thee first,
And blessed the gods for all her travail past.

JAFFEIR. Can there in woman be such glorious faith?
Sure, all ill stories of thy sex are false.
Oh, woman! lovely woman! Nature made thee
To temper man; we had been brutes without you.
Angels are painted fair, to look like you;
There's in you all that we believe of heaven—
Amazing brightness, purity, and truth,
Eternal joy and everlasting love.

BELVIDERA. If love be treasure, we'll be wondrous rich;
I have so much, my heart will surely break with't.
Vows cannot express it. When I would declare
How great's my joy, I'm dumb with the big thought;
I swell, and sigh, and labor with my longing.
O lead me to some desert wide and wild,
Barren as our misfortunes, where my soul
May have its vent; where I may tell aloud
To the high heavens and every list'ning planet,
With what a boundless stock my bosom's fraught;
Where I may throw my eager arms about thee,
Give loose to love with kisses, kindling joy,
And let off all the fire that's in my heart.

JAFFEIR. O Belvidera! double I am a beggar—
Undone by fortune, and in debt to thee.
Want! worldly want! that hungry, meager fiend
Is at my heels, and chases me in view.
Canst thou bear cold and hunger? Can these limbs,
Framed for the tender offices of love,
Endure the bitter gripes of smarting poverty?
When banished by our miseries abroad,
(As suddenly we shall be) to seek out
(In some far climate where our names are strangers)
For charitable succor; wilt thou then,
When in a bed of straw we shrink together,
And the bleak winds shall whistle round our heads,
Wilt thou then talk thus to me? Wilt thou then
Hush my cares thus, and shelter me with love?
    BELVIDERA. Oh, I will love thee, even in madness love thee.
Though my distracted senses should forsake me,
I'd find some intervals when my poor heart
Should 'suage itself, and be let loose to thine.
Though the bare earth be all our resting-place,
Its roots our food, some clift our habitation,
I'll make this arm a pillow for thy head;
And as thou sighing li'st, and swelled with sorrow,
Creep to thy bosom, pour the balm of love
Into thy soul, and kiss thee to thy rest;
Then praise our God, and watch thee till the morning.
    JAFFEIR. Hear this, you heavens, and wonder how you made her!
Reign, reign, ye monarchs that divide the world!
Busy rebellion ne'er will let you know
Tranquility and happiness like mine.
Like gaudy ships, th'obsequious billows fall
And rise again, to lift you in your pride;
They wait but for a storm and then devour you;
I, in my private bark already wrecked,
Like a poor merchant driven on unknown land,
That had by chance packed up his choicest treasure
In one dear casket, and saved only that,
        Since I must wander further on the shore,
        Thus hug my little, but my precious store;
        Resolved to scorn, and trust my fate no more.
                          Exeunt

ACT II

[SCENE I. AQUILINA'S *house*]

Enter PIERRE *and* AQUILINA

AQUILINA. By all thy wrongs, thou'rt dearer to my arms
Than all the wealth of Venice; prithee, stay
And let us love tonight.
    PIERRE.   No; there's fool,
There's fool about thee. When a woman sells
Her flesh to fools, her beauty's lost to me;
They leave a taint, a sully where th'ave passed;
There's such a baneful quality about 'em,
Even spoils complexions with their own nauseousness.
They infect all they touch; I cannot think
Of tasting any thing a fool has palled.
    AQUILINA. I loathe and scorn that fool thou mean'st, as much
Or more than thou canst. But the beast has gold
That makes him necessary; power too,
To qualify my character, and poise me
Equal with peevish virtue, that beholds
My liberty with envy! In their hearts,
Are loose as I am; but an ugly power
Sits in their faces, and frights pleasures from 'em.
    PIERRE. Much good may't do you, madam, with your senator.
    AQUILINA. My senator! why, canst thou think that wretch
E'er filled thy Aquilina's arms with pleasure?
Think'st thou, because I sometimes give him leave
To foil himself at what he is unfit for,
Because I force myself to endure and suffer him,
Think'st thou I love him? No, by all the joys
Thou ever gav'st me, his presence is my penance;
The worst thing an old man can be's a lover—
A mere *memento mori* to poor woman.
I never lay by his decrepit side
But all that night I pondered on my grave.
    PIERRE. Would he were well sent thither!
    AQUILINA.   That's my wish, too,
For then, my Pierre, I might have cause with pleasure
To play the hypocrite. Oh! how I could weep
Over the dying dotard, and kiss him too,
In hopes to smother him quite; then, when the time
Was come to pay my sorrows at his funeral,

(For he has already made me heir to treasures
Would make me out-act a real widow's whining)
How could I frame my face to fit my mourning!
With wringing hands attend him to his grave;
Fall swooning on his hearse; take mad possession
Even of the dismal vault where he lay buried;
There like the Ephesian matron dwell, till thou,
My lovely soldier, comest to my deliverance;
Then throwing up my veil, with open arms
And laughing eyes, run to new dawning joy.

    PIERRE. No more! I have friends to meet me here tonight,
And must be private. As you prize my friendship,
Keep up your coxcomb: Let him not pry nor listen
Nor fisk[1] about the house as I have seen him,
Like a tame mumping[2] squirrel with a bell on.
Curs will be abroad to bite him, if you do.

    AQUILINA. What friends to meet? may I not be of your council?

    PIERRE. How! a woman ask questions out of bed?
Go to your senator, ask him what passes
Amongst his brethren; he'll hide nothing from you.
But pump not me for politics. No more!
Give order that whoever in my name
Comes here, receive admittance; so, good night.

    AQUILINA. Must we ne'er meet again? Embrace no more?
Is love so soon and utterly forgotten?

    PIERRE. As you henceforward treat your fool, I'll think on't.

    AQUILINA. [*Aside*] Cursed be all fools, and doubly cursed myself,
The worst of fools. I die if he forsakes me;
And how to keep him, heaven or hell instruct me.

                           Exeunt

SCENE [II.] *The Rialto*

Enter JAFFEIR

    JAFFEIR. I am here; and thus, the shades of night around me,
I look as if all hell were in my heart,
And I in hell. Nay, surely, 'tis so with me;
For every step I tread methinks some fiend
Knocks at my breast, and bids it not be quiet.
I've heard how desperate wretches like myself
Have wandered out at this dead time of night
To meet the foe of mankind in his walk;

---

[1] Frisk, run.   [2] Nibbling.

Sure, I'm so curs'd that, though of heaven forsaken,
No minister of darkness cares to tempt me.
Hell! Hell! why sleepest thou?

Enter PIERRE

PIERRE.   [*Aside*] Sure, I have stayed too long;
The clock has struck, and I may lose my proselyte.
—Speak, who goes there?
JAFFEIR.   A dog that comes to howl
At yonder moon. What's he that asks the question?
PIERRE. A friend to dogs, for they are honest creatures,
And ne'er betray their masters; never fawn
On any that they love not. Well met, friend.
—Jaffeir!
JAFFEIR. The same. O Pierre! thou art come in season:
I was just going to pray.
PIERRE.   Ah, that's mechanic;[3]
Priests make a trade on't, and yet starve by't, too.
No praying; it spoils business, and time's precious.
Where's Belvidera?
JAFFEIR.   For a day or two
I've lodged her privately, till I see farther
What fortune will do with me. Prithee, friend,
If thou wouldst have me fit to hear good counsel,
Speak not of Belvidera—
PIERRE.   Speak not of her?
JAFFEIR. Oh, no!
PIERRE.   Nor name her? May be I wish her well.
JAFFEIR. Whom well?
PIERRE.   Thy wife, thy lovely Belvidera.
I hope a man may wish his friend's wife well
And no harm done!
JAFFEIR.   Y'are merry, Pierre!
PIERRE. I am so.
Thou shalt smile too, and Belvidera smile;
We'll all rejoice.   [*Offering gold*]
                 Here's something to buy pins;
Marriage is chargeable.
JAFFEIR.   [*Aside*] I but half wished
To see the devil, and he's here already.
—Well!
What must this buy: rebellion, murder, treason?
Tell me which way I must be damned for this.

[3] Commonplace, vulgar.

PIERRE. When last we parted, we had no qualms like these,
But entertained each other's thoughts like men
Whose souls were well acquainted. Is the world
Reformed since our last meeting? What new miracles
Have happened? Has Priuli's heart relented?
Can he be honest?

JAFFEIR.　　　　　　　Kind heaven! let heavy curses
Gall his old age! cramps, achès, rack his bones,
And bitterest disquiet wring his heart!
Oh, let him live till life become his burden;
Let him groan under't long, linger an age
In the worst agonies and pangs of death,
And find its ease but late!

PIERRE.　　　　　　　Nay, couldst thou not
As well, my friend, have stretched the curse to all
The Senate round as to one single villain?

JAFFEIR. But curses stick not. Could I kill with cursing,
By heaven, I know not thirty heads in Venice
Should not be blasted! Senators should rot
Like dogs on dunghills, but their wives and daughters
Die of their own diseases. O for a curse
To kill with!

PIERRE.　　　Daggers, daggers, are much better.

JAFFEIR. Ha!

PIERRE.　　　　Daggers.

JAFFEIR.　　But where are they?

PIERRE.　　　　　　　　　　Oh, a thousand
May be disposed in honest hands in Venice.

JAFFEIR. Thou talk'st in clouds.

PIERRE.　　　　　　　　　But yet a heart half wronged
As thine has been, would find the meaning, Jaffeir.

JAFFEIR. A thousand daggers, all in honest hands,
And have not I a friend will stick one here?

PIERRE. Yes, if I thought thou wert not to be cherished
To a nobler purpose, I'd be that friend.
But thou hast better friends—friends whom thy wrongs
Have made thy friends—friends worthy to be called so.
I'll trust thee with a secret; there are spirits
This hour at work. But as thou art a man
Whom I have picked and chosen from the world,
Swear that thou wilt be true to what I utter;
And when I have told thee that which only gods
And men like gods are privy to, then swear
No chance or change shall wrest it from thy bosom.

JAFFEIR. When thou wouldst bind me, is there need of oaths?
(Green-sickness girls lose maiden-heads with such counters!) [4]
For thou art so near my heart that thou mayst see
Its bottom, sound its strength and firmness to thee.
Is coward, fool, or villain in my face?
If I seem none of these, I dare believe
Thou wouldst not use me in a little cause,
For I am fit for honor's toughest task,
Nor ever yet found fooling was my province;
And for a villainous, inglorious enterprise,
I know thy heart so well, I dare lay mine
Before thee, set it to what point thou wilt.
    PIERRE. Nay, it's a cause thou wilt be fond of, Jaffeir,
For it is founded on the noblest basis—
Our liberties, our natural inheritance.
There's no religion, no hypocrisy in't;
We'll do the business, and ne'er fast and pray for't;
Openly act a deed the world shall gaze
With wonder at, and envy when 'tis done.
    JAFFEIR. For liberty!
    PIERRE.   For liberty, my friend!
Thou shalt be freed from base Priuli's tyranny,
And thy sequestred fortunes healed again.
I shall be freed from opprobrious wrongs
That press me now and bend my spirit downward.
All Venice free, and every growing merit
Succeed to its just right; fools shall be pulled
From wisdom's seat—those baleful, unclean birds,
Those lazy owls, who (perched near fortune's top)
Sit only watchful with their heavy wings
To cuff down new-fledged virtues, that would rise
To nobler heights, and make the grove harmonious.
    JAFFEIR. What can I do?
    PIERRE.   Canst thou not kill a senator?
    JAFFEIR. Were there one wise or honest, I could kill him
For herding with that nest of fools and knaves.
By all my wrongs, thou talk'st as if revenge
Were to be had, and the brave story warms me.
    PIERRE. Swear then!
    JAFFEIR.   I do, by all those glittering stars
And yond great ruling planet of the night!
By all good powers above, and ill below,
By love and friendship, dearer than my life,
No pow'r or death shall make me false to thee!

    [4] False coins, tokens made of base metal.

PIERRE. Here we embrace, and I'll unlock my heart.
A council's held hard by, where the destruction
Of this great empire's hatching; there I'll lead thee!
But be a man, for thou art to mix with men
Fit to disturb the peace of all the world,
And rule it when it's wildest.
     JAFFEIR.   I give thee thanks
For this kind warning. Yes, I will be a man,
And charge thee, Pierre, whene'er thou see'st my fears
Betray me less, to rip this heart of mine
Out of my breast, and show it for a coward's.
Come, let's begone, for from this hour I chase
All little thoughts, all tender human follies
Out of my bosom. Vengeance shall have room—
Revenge!
     PIERRE. And liberty!
     JAFFEIR.   Revenge! revenge—

                                    Exeunt

[SCENE III.] *The scene changes to* AQUILINA'S
house, the Greek courtesan

Enter RENAULT

RENAULT. Why was my choice ambition[5] the worst ground
A wretch can build on? It's indeed at distance
A good prospect, tempting to the view;
The height delights us, and the mountain top
Looks beautiful, because it's nigh to heaven.
But we ne'er think how sandy's the foundation,
What storm will batter, and what tempest shake us!
—Who's there?

Enter SPINOSA

SPINOSA.   Renault, good morrow! for by this time
I think the scale of night has turned the balance
And weighs up morning. Has the clock struck twelve?
     RENAULT. Yes, clocks will go as they are set. But man,
Irregular man's ne'er constant, never certain.
I've spent at least three precious hours of darkness
In waiting dull attendance; 'tis the curse
Of diligent virtue to be mixed, like mine,
With giddy tempers, souls but half resolved.

    [5] Shaftesbury's soaring ambition seems to be hit at here.

SPINOSA. Hell seize that soul amongst us it can frighten.
RENAULT. What's then the cause that I am here alone?
Why are we not together?

Enter ELIOT

—O sir, welcome!
You are an Englishman: when treason's hatching
One might have thought you'd not have been behindhand.
In what whore's lap have you been lolling?
Give but an Englishman his whore and ease,
Beef and a sea-coal fire,[6] he's yours forever.
ELIOT. Frenchman, you are saucy.
RENAULT.   How!

Enter BEDAMAR the ambassador, THEODORE, BRAINVEIL, DURAND, BRABE, REVILLIDO, MEZZANA, TERNON, RETROSI, Conspirators

BEDAMAR. At difference?—fy!
Is this a time for quarrels? Thieves and rogues
Fall out and brawl. Should men of your high calling,
Men separated by the choice of providence
From this gross heap of mankind, and set here
In this great assembly as in one great jewel,
T'adorn the bravest purpose it e'er smiled on—
Should you like boys wrangle for trifles?
RENAULT.   Boys!
BEDAMAR. Renault, thy hand!
RENAULT.   I thought I'd given my heart
Long since to every man that mingles here,
But grieve to find it trusted with such tempers,
That can't forgive my froward age its weakness.
BEDAMAR. Eliot, thou once hadst virtue; I have seen
Thy stubborn temper bend with godlike goodness,
Not half thus courted. 'Tis thy nation's glory,
To hug the foe that offers brave alliance.
Once more embrace, my friends—we'll all embrace.
United thus, we are the mighty engine
Must twist this rooted empire from its basis!
Totters it not already?
ELIOT.   Would it were tumbling.
BEDAMAR. Nay, it shall down; this night we seal its ruin.

Enter PIERRE

—O Pierre! thou art welcome!
Come to my breast, for by its hopes thou look'st

[6] Coal brought to London by sea.

Lovelily dreadful, and the fate of Venice
Seems on thy sword already. Oh, my Mars!
The poets that first feigned a god of war
Sure prophesied of thee.
    PIERRE.   Friends! was not Brutus,
(I mean that Brutus who in open senate
Stabbed the first Caesar that usurped the world)
A gallant man?
    RENAULT.   Yes, and Catiline too,
Though story wronged his fame; for he conspired
To prop the reeling glory of his country.
His cause was good.
    BEDAMAR.   And ours as much above it
As, Renault, thou art superior to Cethegus [7]
Or Pierre to Cassius.
    PIERRE.   Then to what we aim at.
When do we start? or must we talk forever?
    BEDAMAR. No, Pierre, the deed's near birth.
Fate seems to have set
The business up and given it to our care.
I hope there's not a heart nor hand amongst us
But is firm and ready.
    ALL. All! We'll die with Bedamar.
    BEDAMAR.   O men,
Matchless as will your glory be hereafter!
The game is for a matchless prize, if won;
If lost, disgraceful ruin.
    RENAULT.   What can lose it?
The public stock's a beggar; one Venetian
Trusts not another. Look into their stores
Of general safety: empty magazines,
A tattered fleet, a murmuring unpaid army,
Bankrupt nobility, a harassed commonalty,
A factious, giddy, and divided senate
Is all the strength of Venice. Let's destroy it.
Let's fill their magazines with arms to awe them,
Man out their fleet, and make their trade maintain it;
Let loose the murmuring army on their masters,
To pay themselves with plunder; lop their nobles
To the base roots, whence most of 'em first sprung;
Enslave the rout, whom smarting will make humble;
Turn out their droning senate, and possess
That seat of empire which our souls were framed for.

   [7] A leading member of Catiline's conspiracy.

PIERRE. Ten thousand men are armèd at your nod,
Commanded all by leaders fit to guide
A battle for the freedom of the world;
This wretched state has starved them in its service,
And by your bounty quickened, they're resolved
To serve your glory and revenge their own.
They've all their different quarters in this city,
Watch for th'alarm, and grumble 'tis so tardy.

BEDAMAR. I doubt not, friend, but thy unwearied diligence
Has still kept waking, and it shall have ease.
After this night it is resolved we meet
No more, till Venice own us for her lords.

PIERRE. How lovely the Adriatic whore,
Dressed in her flames, will shine!—devouring flames,
Such as shall burn her to the watery bottom
And hiss in her foundation!

BEDAMAR. Now if any
Amongst us that owns this glorious cause
Have friends or interest he'd wish to save,
Let it be told. The general doom is sealed,
But I'd forego the hopes of a world's empire,
Rather than wound the bowels of my friend.

PIERRE. I must confess you there have touched my weakness.
I have a friend; hear it, such a friend!
My heart was ne'er shut to him. Nay, I'll tell you.
He knows the very business of this hour,
But he rejoices in the cause and loves it.
W'have changed a vow to live and die together,
And he's at hand to ratify it here.

RENAULT. How! all betrayed?

PIERRE. No—I've dealt nobly with you.
I've brought my all into the public stock;
I had but one friend, and him I'll share amongst you!
Receive and cherish him; or if, when seen
And searched, you find him worthless, as my tongue
Has lodged this secret in his faithful breast,
To ease your fears I wear a dagger here
Shall rip it out again and give you rest.
—Come forth, thou only good I e'er could boast of!

Enter JAFFEIR *with a dagger*

BEDAMAR. His presence bears the show of manly virtue.

JAFFEIR. I know you'll wonder all, that thus uncalled
I dare approach this place of fatal councils;
But I am amongst you, and by heaven it glads me

To see so many virtues thus united
To restore justice and dethrone oppression.
Command this sword, if you would have it quiet,
Into this breast; but if you think it worthy
To cut the throats of reverend rogues in robes,
Send me into the curs'd, assembled Senate;
It shrinks not, tho' I meet a father there.
Would you behold this city flaming? Here's
A hand shall bear a lighted torch at noon
To the arsenal, and set its gates on fire.

 RENAULT. You talk this well, sir.

 JAFFEIR.   Nay—by heaven, I'll do this!
Come, come, I read distrust in all your faces,
You fear me a villain, and indeed it's odd
To hear a stranger talk thus at first meeting,
Of matters that have been so well debated;
But I come ripe with wrongs as you with councils.
I hate this Senate, am a foe to Venice,
A friend to none but men resolved like me
To push on mischief. Oh, did you but know me,
I need not talk thus!

 BEDAMAR.   Pierre!—I must embrace him;
My heart beats to this man as if it knew him.

 RENAULT. [*Aside*] I never loved these huggers.

 JAFFEIR.   Still I see
The cause delights me not. Your friends survey me
As I were dang'rous—but I come armed
Against all doubts, and to your trust will give
A pledge worth more than all the world can pay for.
—My Belvidera! Ho! my Belvidera!

 BEDAMAR. What wonder next?

 JAFFEIR.   Let me entreat you,
As I have henceforth hopes to call ye friends,
That all but the ambassador, this
Grave guide of councils, with my friend that owns me,
Withdraw awhile to spare a woman's blushes.

     Exeunt all but BEDAMAR, RENAULT, JAFFEIR, PIERRE

 BEDAMAR. Pierre, whither will this ceremony lead us?

 JAFFEIR. My Belvidera! Belvidera!

      Enter BELVIDERA

 BELVIDERA.   Who?
Who calls so loud at this late, peaceful hour?
That voice was wont to come in gentler whispers,
And fill my ears with the soft breath of love.

Thou hourly image of my thoughts, where art thou?

JAFFEIR. Indeed, 'tis late.

BELVIDERA.   Oh! I have slept, and dreamt,
And dreamt again. Where hast thou been, thou loiterer?
Though my eyes closed, my arms have still been opened,
Stretched every way betwixt my broken slumbers,
To search if thou wert come to crown my rest.
There's no repose without thee. Oh the day
Too soon will break, and wake us to our sorrow;
Come, come to bed, and bid thy cares good night.

JAFFEIR. O Belvidera! we must change the scene
In which the past delights of life were tasted.
The poor sleep little; we must learn to watch
Our labors late, and early every morning.
Midst winter frosts, thin clad and fed with sparing,
Rise to our toils, and drudge away the day.

BELVIDERA. Alas! where am I? whither is't you lead me?
Methinks I read distraction in your face,
Something less gentle than the fate you tell me!
You shake and tremble too! your blood runs cold!
Heavens, guard my love, and bless his heart with patience.

JAFFEIR. That I have patience, let our fate bear witness,
Who has ordained it so that thou and I
(Thou the divinest good man e'er possessed,
And I the wretched'st of the race of man)
This very hour, without one tear, must part.

BELVIDERA. Part! must we part? Oh! am I then forsaken?
Will my love cast me off? have my misfortunes
Offended him so highly that he'll leave me?
Why drag you from me? whither are you going?
My dear! my life! my love!

JAFFEIR.   Oh, friends!

BELVIDERA. Speak to me.

JAFFEIR.   Take her from my heart,
She'll gain such hold else, I shall ne'er get loose.
I charge thee take her, but with tender'st care,
Relieve her troubles, and assuage her sorrows.

RENAULT. Rise, madam! and command amongst your servants,

JAFFEIR. To you, sirs, and your honors, I bequeath her,
And with her this. When I prove unworthy—   (Gives a dagger)
You know the rest—then strike it to her heart;
And tell her, he who three whole happy years
Lay in her arms and each kind night repeated
The passionate vows of still increasing love,
Sent that reward for all her truth and sufferings.

BELVIDERA. Nay, take my life, since he has sold it cheaply;
Or send me to some distant clime your slave;
But let it be far off, lest my complainings
Should reach his guilty ears, and shake his peace.

JAFFEIR. No, Belvidera, I've contrived thy honor;
Trust to my faith, and be but Fortune kind
To me, as I'll preserve that faith unbroken,
When next we meet, I'll lift thee to a height
Shall gather all the gazing world about thee
To wonder what strange virtue placed thee there.
But if we ne'er meet more—

BELVIDERA.   Oh, thou unkind one,
Never meet more! Have I deserved this from you?
Look on me, tell me, tell me, speak, thou dear deceiver,
Why am I separated from thy love?
If I am false, accuse me; but if true,
Don't, prithee, don't in poverty forsake me,
But pity the sad heart that's torn with parting.
Yet hear me! yet recall me—

> *Exeunt* RENAULT, BEDAMAR, and BELVIDERA

JAFFEIR.   O my eyes,
Look not that way, but turn yourselves awhile
Into my heart, and be weaned altogether!
—My friend,, where art thou?

PIERRE.   Here, my honor's brother.

JAFFEIR. Is Belvidera gone?

PIERRE.   Renault has led her
Back to her own apartment. But, by heaven!
Thou must not see her more till our work's over.

JAFFEIR. No.

PIERRE.   Not for your life.

JAFFEIR.   O Pierre, wert thou but she,
How I could pull thee down into my heart,
Gaze on thee till my eye-strings cracked with love,
Till all my sinews with its fire extended,
Fixed me upon the rack of ardent longing;
Then swelling, sighing, raging to be blest,
Come like a panting turtle[8] to thy breast;
On thy soft bosom, hovering, bill and play,
Confess the cause why last I fled away;
>   Own 'twas a fault, but swear to give it o'er,
>   And never follow false ambition more.

> *Exeunt ambo*

---

[8] Turtle-dove.

ACT III

[SCENE I. AQUILINA's house]

Enter AQUILINA *and her Maid*

AQUILINA. Tell him I am gone to bed; tell him I am not at home; tell him I've better company with me, or anything; tell him in short I will not see him, the eternal troublesome, vexatious fool! He's worse company than an ignorant physician. I'll not be disturbed at these unseasonable hours!

MAID. But, madam, he's here already, just entered the doors.

AQUILINA. Turn him out again, you unnecessary, useless, giddy-brained ass! If he will not begone, set the house afire and burn us both. I'd rather meet a toad in my dish than that old hideous animal in my chamber to-night.

Enter ANTONIO

ANTONIO. Nacky, Nacky, Nacky—how dost do, Nacky? Hurry durry. I am come, little Nacky; past eleven a-clock, a late hour; time in all conscience to go to bed, Nacky—Nacky, did I say? Aye, Nacky; Aquilina, lina, lina, quilina, quilina, quilina, Aquilina, Naquilina, Naquilina, Acky, Acky, Nacky, Nacky, queen Nacky—come, let's to bed—you fubbs, you pugg, you—you little puss—purree tuzzey—I am a senator.

AQUILINA. You are a fool, I am sure.

ANTONIO. May be so, too, sweetheart. Never the worse senator for all that. Come Nacky, Nacky, let's have a game at rump, Nacky.

AQUILINA. You would do well, signior, to be troublesome here no longer, but leave me to myself, be sober, and go home, sir.

ANTONIO. Home, Madonna!

AQUILINA. Aye, home, sir. Who am I?

ANTONIO. Madonna, as I take it you are my—you are—thou art my little Nicky Nacky—that's all!

AQUILINA. I find you are resolved to be troublesome; and so to make short of the matter in few words, I hate you, detest you, loathe you, I am weary of you, sick of you—hang you, you are an old, silly, impertinent, impotent, solicitous coxcomb, crazy in your head and lazy in your body, love to be meddling with everything, and if you had not money, you are good for nothing.

ANTONIO. Good for nothing! Hurry durry, I'll try that presently. Sixty-one years old,[1] and good for nothing; that's brave! (*To the Maid*) —Come, come, come, Mistress Fiddle-faddle, turn you out for a season.

---

[1] Shaftesbury too was about sixty-one.

Go, turn out, I say, it is our will and pleasure to be private some moments—out, out when you are bid to! (*Puts her out and locks the door*)—Good for nothing, you say?

AQUILINA. Why, what are you good for?

ANTONIO. In the first place, madam, I am old, and consequently very wise, very wise, Madonna, d'e mark that? In the second place take notice, if you please, that I am a senator, and when I think fit can make speeches,[2] Madonna. Hurry durry, I can make a speech in the Senate-house now and then—would make your hair stand on end, Madonna.

AQUILINA. What care I for your speeches in the Senate-house? If you would be silent here, I should thank you.

ANTONIO. Why, I can make speeches to thee, too, my lovely Madonna; for example: My cruel fair one (*Takes out a purse of gold, and at every pause shakes it*), since it is my fate that you should with your servant angry prove; tho' late at night—I hope 'tis not too late with this to gain reception for my love.—There's for thee, my little Nicky Nacky—take it, here take it—I say take it, or I'll throw it at your head. How now, rebel!

AQUILINA. Truly, my illustrious senator, I must confess your honor is at present most profoundly eloquent, indeed.

ANTONIO. Very well; come now, let's sit down and think upon't a little. Come sit, I say—sit down by me a little, my Nicky Nacky, hah —(*Sits down*) Hurry durry—"good for nothing!"

AQUILINA. No, sir; if you please, I can know my distance, and stand.

ANTONIO. Stand! How, Nacky up, and I down? Nay, then, let me exclaim with the poet,

> Show me a case more pitiful who can,
> A standing woman and a falling man.

Hurry durry—not sit down!—See this, ye gods.—You won't sit down?

AQUILINA. No, sir.

ANTONIO. Then look you now, suppose me a bull, a Basan-bull, the bull of bulls, or any bull. Thus up I get and with my brows thus bent —I broo, I say I broo, I broo, I broo. You won't sit down, will you? —I broo—   (*Bellows like a bull, and drives her about*)

AQUILINA. Well, sir, I must endure this. (*She sits down*) Now your honor has been a bull, pray what beast will your worship please to be next?

ANTONIO. Now I'll be a senator again, and thy lover, little Nicky Nacky! (*He sits by her*) Ah, toad, toad, toad, toad! spit in my face a little, Nacky—spit in my face, prithee, spit in my face, never so little. Spit but a little bit—spit, spit, spit, spit when you are bid, I say; do,

---

[2] Shaftesbury was famed as an orator in the House of Lords.

prithee, spit—now, now, now, spit. What, you won't spit, will you? then I'll be a dog.

AQUILINA. A dog, my lord?

ANTONIO. Aye, a dog — and I'll give thee this t'other purse to let me be a dog — and to use me like a dog a little. Hurry durry — I will — here 'tis. (*Gives the purse*)

AQUILINA. Well, with all my heart. But let me beseech your dog-ship to play your tricks over as fast as you can, that you may come to stinking the sooner and be turned out of doors as you deserve.

ANTONIO. Aye, aye — no matter for that — that shan't move me. (*He gets under the table*) Now, bough waugh waugh, bough waugh —
(*Barks like a dog*)

AQUILINA. Hold, hold, hold, sir. I beseech you, what is't you do? If curs bite, they must be kicked, sir. — Do you see, kicked thus?

ANTONIO. Aye, with all my heart. Do kick, kick on; now I am under the table, kick again — kick harder — harder yet, bough waugh waugh, waugh, bough — 'odd, I'll have a snap at thy shins — bough waugh wough, waugh, bough! — 'Odd, she kicks bravely. —

AQUILINA. Nay, then, I'll go another way to work with you; and I think here's an instrument fit for the purpose. (*Fetches a whip and bell*) — What, bite your mistress, sirrah! out, out of doors, you dog, to kennel and be hanged — bite your mistress by the legs, you rogue!
(*She whips him*)

ANTONIO. Nay, prithee, Nacky, now thou art too loving! Hurry durry, 'odd! I'll be a dog no longer.

AQUILINA. Nay, none of your fawning and grinning, but be gone, or here's the discipline! What, bite your mistress by the legs, you mongrel? Out of doors — hout hout, to kennel, sirrah! go!

ANTONIO. This is very barbarous usage, Nacky, very barbarous. Look you, I will not go — I will not stir from the door; that I resolve — hurry durry — what, shut me out? (*She whips him out*)

AQUILINA. Aye, and if you come here any more to-night, I'll have my footmen lug you, you cur. What, bite your poor mistress Nacky, sirrah?

Enter Maid

MAID. Heavens, Madam! what's the matter?
(*He howls at the door like a dog*)

AQUILINA. Call my footmen hither presently.

Enter two Footmen

MAID. They are here already, madam; the house is all alarmed with a strange noise that nobody knows what to make of.

AQUILINA. Go, all of you, and turn that troublesome beast in the next room out of my house — if I ever see him within these walls

again without my leave for his admittance, you sneaking rogues, I'll
have you poisoned all — poisoned like rats! Every corner of the
house shall stink of one of you; go! and learn hereafter to know my
pleasure. So now for my Pierre:

> Thus when godlike lover was displeased,
> We sacrifice our fool and he's appeased.

Exeunt

[SCENE II. The same]

Enter BELVIDERA.

BELVIDERA. I'm sacrificed! I am sold! betrayed to shame!
Inevitable ruin has inclosed me!
No sooner was I to my bed repaired,
To weigh, and (weeping) ponder my condition,
But the old hoary wretch to whose false care
My peace and honor was entrusted, came
(Like Tarquin) ghastly with infernal lust.
O thou Roman Lucrece!
Thou couldst find friends to vindicate thy wrong!
I never had but one, and he's proved false;
He that should guard my virtue has betrayed it —
Left me! undone me! Oh, that I could hate him!
Where shall I go? oh, whither, whither wander?

Enter JAFFEIR

JAFFEIR. Can Belvidera want a resting place
When these poor arms are open to receive her?
Oh, 'tis in vain to struggle with desires
Strong as my love to thee; for every moment
I am from thy sight, the heart within my bosom
Moans like a tender infant in its cradle,
Whose nurse had left it. Come, and with the songs
Of gentle love persuade it to its peace.
BELVIDERA. I fear the stubborn wanderer will not own me;
'Tis grown a rebel to be ruled no longer,
Scorns the indulgent bosom that first lulled it,
And like a disobedient child disdains
The soft authority of Belvidera.
JAFFEIR. There was a time —
BELVIDERA.   Yes, yes, there was a time
When Belvidera's tears, her cries, and sorrows
Were not despised; when if she chanced to sigh,
Or look but sad — there was indeed a time

When Jaffeir would have ta'en her in his arms,
Eased her declining head upon his breast,
And never left her till he found the cause.
But let her now weep seas,
Cry till she rend the earth, sigh till she burst
Her heart asunder; still he bears it all,
Deaf as the wind, and as the rocks unshaken.

    JAFFEIR. Have I been deaf? am I that rock unmoved,
Against whose root tears beat and sighs are sent
In vain? have I beheld thy sorrows calmly?
Witness against me, heavens; have I done this?
Then bear me in a whirlwind back again,
And let that angry dear one ne'er forgive me!
Oh, thou too rashly censur'st of my love!
Couldst thou but think how I have spent this night,
Dark and alone, no pillow to my head,
Rest in my eyes, nor quiet in my heart,
Thou wouldst not, Belvidera, sure thou wouldst not
Talk to me thus, but like a pitying angel
Spreading thy wings, come settle on my breast
And hatch warm comfort there ere sorrows freeze it.

    BELVIDERA. Why, then, poor mourner, in what baleful corner
Hast thou been talking with that witch, the Night?
On what cold stone hast thou been stretched along,
Gathering the grumbling winds about thy head,
To mix with theirs the accents of thy woes?
Oh, now I find the cause my love forsakes me!
I am no longer fit to bear a share
In his concernments; my weak, female virtue
Must not be trusted; 'tis too frail and tender.

    JAFFEIR. O Portia! Portia! what a soul was thine!

    BELVIDERA. That Portia was a woman, and when Brutus,
Big with the fate of Rome (Heaven guard thy safety!),
Concealed from her the labors of his mind,
She let him see her blood was great as his,
Flowed from a spring as noble, and a heart
Fit to partake his troubles, as his love.
Fetch, fetch that dagger back, the dreadful dower
Thou gav'st last night in parting with me. Strike it
Here to my heart, and as the blood flows from it,
Judge if it run not pure as Cato's daughter's.

    JAFFEIR. Thou art too good, and I indeed unworthy —
Unworthy so much virtue. Teach me how
I may deserve such matchless love as thine,
And see with what attention I'll obey thee.

BELVIDERA. Do not despise me: that's the all I ask.

JAFFEIR. Despise thee! hear me —

BELVIDERA.　　　　　　　　　　Oh, thy charming tongue
Is but too well acquainted with my weakness;
Knows, let it name but love, my melting heart
Dissolves within my breast, till with closed eyes
I reel into thy arms and all's forgotten.

JAFFEIR. What shall I do?

BELVIDERA. Tell me! be just, and tell me
Why dwells that busy cloud upon thy face?
Why am I made a stranger? why that sigh,
And I not know the cause? why, when the world
Is wrapped in rest, why chooses then my love
To wander up and down in horrid darkness,
Loathing his bed and these desiring arms?
Why are these eyes bloodshot with tedious watching?
Why starts he now? and looks as if he wished
His fate were finished? Tell me, ease my fears,
Lest when we next time meet I want the power
To search into the sickness of thy mind,
But talk as wildly then as thou look'st now.

JAFFEIR. O Belvidera!

BELVIDERA. Why was I last night delivered to a villain?

JAFFEIR. Hah, a villain!

BELVIDERA. Yes! to a villain! Why at such an hour
Meets that assembly all made up of wretches
That look as hell had drawn 'em into league?
Why, I in this hand, and in that a dagger,
Was I delivered with such dreadful ceremonies?
"To you, sirs, and to your honor I bequeath her,
And with her this. Whene'er I prove unworthy —
You know the rest—then strike it to her heart?"
Oh! why's that rest concealed from me? Must I
Be made the hostage of a hellish trust?
For such I know I am; that's all my value!
But by the love and loyalty I owe thee,
I'll free thee from the bondage of these slaves;
Straight to the Senate, tell 'em all I know,
All that I think, all that my fears inform me.

JAFFEIR. Is this the Roman virtue? this the blood
That boasts its purity with Cato's daughter?
Would she have e'er betrayed her Brutus?

BELVIDERA.　　　　　　　　　　No.
For Brutus trusted her; wert thou so kind,
What would not Belvidera suffer for thee!

JAFFEIR. I shall undo myself and tell thee all
BELVIDERA. Look not upon me as I am, a woman,
But as a bone,[3] thy wife, thy friend, who long
Has had admission to thy heart, and there
Studied the virtues of thy gallant nature.
Thy constancy, thy courage, and thy truth
Have been my daily lesson. I have learnt them,
Am bold as thou, can suffer or despise
The worst of fates for thee, and with thee share them.
JAFFEIR. Oh you divinest powers! look down and hear
My prayers! instruct me to reward this virtue! —
Yet think a little ere thou tempt me further,
Think I've a tale to tell will shake thy nature,
Melt all this boasted constancy thou talk'st of
Into vile tears and despicable sorrows:
Then if thou shouldst betray me — !
BELVIDERA.   Shall I swear?
JAFFEIR. No, do not swear. I would not violate
Thy tender nature with so rude a bond;
But as thou hop'st to see me live my days
And love thee long, lock this within thy breast.
I've bound myself by all the strictest sacraments,
Divine and human —
BELVIDERA.   Speak!
JAFFEIR.   To kill thy father —
BELVIDERA. My father!
JAFFEIR.   Nay, the throats of the whole senate
Shall bleed, my Belvidera. He amongst us
That spares his father, brother, or his friend,
Is damned. How rich and beauteous will the face
Of ruin look, when these wide streets run blood;
I and the glorious partners of my fortune
Shouting, and striding o'er the prostrate dead,
Still to new waste; whil'st thou, far off in safety
Smiling, shall see the wonders of our daring;
And when night comes, with praise and love receive me.
BELVIDERA. Oh!
JAFFEIR.   Have a care, and shrink not, even in thought,
For if thou dost —
BELVIDERA.   I know it — thou wilt kill me.
Do, strike thy sword into this bosom. Lay me
Dead on the earth, and then thou wilt be safe.
Murder my father! though his cruel nature
Has persecuted me to my undoing,

[3] See Genesis ii:23.

Driven me to basest wants, can I behold him
With smiles of vengeance, butchered in his age?
The sacred fountain of my life destroyed?
And canst thou shed the blood that gave me being?
Nay, be a traitor too, and sell thy country?
Can thy great heart descend so vilely low,
Mix with hired slaves, bravoes, and common stabbers,
Nose-slitters, alley-lurking villains? join
With such a crew, and take a ruffian's wages,
To cut the throats of wretches as they sleep?

    JAFFEIR. Thou wrong'st me, Belvidera! I've engaged
With men of souls, fit to reform the ills
Of all mankind. There's not a heart amongst them
But's stout as death, yet honest as the nature
Of man first made, ere fraud and vice were fashions.

    BELVIDERA. What's he to whose curs'd hands last night thou gav'st
      me?
Was that well done? Oh! I could tell a story
Would rouse thy lion heart out of its den,
And make it rage with terrifying fury.

    JAFFEIR. Speak on, I charge thee!
    BELVIDERA.   O my love! if e'er
Thy Belvidera's peace deserved thy care,
Remove me from this place! Last night, last night!

    JAFFEIR. Distract me not, but give me all the truth.

    BELVIDERA. No sooner wert thou gone, and I alone,
Left in the power of that old son of mischief;
No sooner was I lain on my sad bed,
But that vile wretch approached me; loose, unbuttoned,
Ready for violation. Then my heart
Throbbed with its fears. Oh, how I wept and sighed,
And shrunk and trembled; wished in vain for him
That should protect me. Thou, alas, wert gone!

    JAFFEIR. Patience, sweet Heaven! till I make vengeance sure.

    BELVIDERA. He drew the hideous dagger forth thou gav'st him,
And with upbraiding smiles he said, "Behold it;
This is the pledge of a false husband's love."
And in my arms then pressed, and would have clasped me;
But with my cries I scared his coward heart,
Till he withdrew and muttered vows to hell.
These are thy friends! with these thy life, thy honor,
Thy love — all's staked, and all will go to ruin.

    JAFFEIR. No more. I charge thee keep this secret close.
Clear up thy sorrows, look as if thy wrongs
Were all forgot, and treat him like a friend,

As no complaint were made. No more; retire,
Retire, my life, and doubt not of my honor;
I'll heal its failings and deserve thy love.

BELVIDERA. Oh, should I part with thee, I fear thou wilt
In anger leave me, and return no more.

JAFFEIR. Return no more! I would not live without thee
Another night, to purchase the creation.

BELVIDERA. When shall we meet again?

JAFFEIR.   Anon at twelve!
I'll steal myself to thy expecting arms,
Come like a travelled dove and bring thee peace.

BELVIDERA. Indeed!

JAFFEIR.   By all our loves!

BELVIDERA.   'Tis hard to part;
But sure, no falsehood e'er looked so fairly.
Farewell. — Remember twelve!

Exit BELVIDERA

JAFFEIR.   Let heaven forget me
When I remember not thy truth, thy love.
How curs'd is my condition, tossed and jostled
From every corner; Fortune's common fool,
The jest of rogues, an instrumental ass
For villains to lay loads of shame upon,
And drive about just for their ease and scorn!

Enter PIERRE

PIERRE. Jaffeir!

JAFFEIR.   Who calls?

PIERRE.   A friend, that could have wished
T'have found thee otherwise employed. What, hunt
A wife on the dull foil![4] sure, a stanch husband
Of all hounds is the dullest! Wilt thou never,
Never be weaned from caudles and confections?
What feminine tale has thou been listening to,
Of unaired shirts, catarrhs, and tooth-ache got
By thin-soled shoes? Damnation! that a fellow
Chosen to be a sharer in the destruction
Of a whole people, should sneak thus in corners
To ease his fulsome lusts and fool his mind.

JAFFEIR. May not a man, then, trifle out an hour
With a kind woman and not wrong his calling?

PIERRE. Not in a cause like ours.

JAFFEIR.   Then, friend, our cause
Is in a damned condition; for I'll tell thee,

    [4] Trail of a hunted animal.

That canker-worm called lechery has touched it;
'Tis tainted vilely. Wouldst thou think it? Renault
(That mortified, old, withered, winter rogue)
Loves simple fornication like a priest.
I found him out for watering at my wife;
He visited her last night like a kind guardian.
Faith, she has some temptations, that's the truth on't.

    PIERRE. He durst not wrong his trust!

    JAFFEIR.   'Twas something late, though,
To take the freedom of a lady's chamber.

    PIERRE. Was she in bed?

    JAFFEIR.   Yes, faith, in virgin sheets
White as her bosom, Pierre, dished neatly up,
Might tempt a weaker appetite to taste.
Oh, how the old fox stunk, I warrant thee,
When the rank fit was on him!

    PIERRE.   Patience guide me!
He used no violence?

    JAFFEIR.   No, no! out on't, violence!
Played with her neck, brushed her with his gray beard,
Struggled and towzled, tickled her till she squeaked a little,
Maybe, or so — but not a jot of violence —

    PIERRE. Damn him!

    JAFFEIR.   Aye, so say I; but hush, no more on't!
All hitherto is well, and I believe
Myself no monster[5] yet, tho' no man knows
What fate he's born to. Sure, 'tis near the hour
We all should meet for our concluding orders.
Will the ambassador be here in person?

    PIERRE. No. He has sent commission to that villain, Renault,
To give the executing charge.
I'd have thee be a man if possible,
And keep thy temper; for a brave revenge
Ne'er comes too late.

    JAFFEIR.   Fear not; I am cool as patience.
Had he completed my dishonor, rather
Than hazard the success our hopes are ripe for,
I'd bear it all with mortifying virtue.

    PIERRE. He's yonder, coming this way through the hall;
His thoughts seem full.

    JAFFEIR.   Prithee retire, and leave me
With him alone. I'll put him to some trial,
See how his rotten part will bear the touching.

    PIERRE. Be careful then.   *Exit* PIERRE

[5] Cuckold.

JAFFEIR.   Nay, never doubt, but trust me.
What, be a devil? take a damning oath
For shedding native blood? can there be a sin
In merciful repentance? Oh, this villain!

Enter RENAULT

RENAULT. Perverse and peevish! What a slave is man!
To let his itching flesh thus get the better of him!
Dispatch the tool, her husband — that were well.
— Who's there?
JAFFEIR.   A man.
RENAULT.   My friend, my near ally!
The hostage of your faith, my beauteous charge,
Is very well.
JAFFEIR.   Sir, are you sure of that?
Stands she in perfect health? beats her pulse even?
Neither too hot nor cold?
RENAULT.   What means that question?
JAFFEIR. Oh, women have fantastic constitutions,
Inconstant as their wishes, always wavering,
And ne'er fixed. Was it not boldly done
Even at first sight to trust the thing I loved
(A tempting treasure too!) with youth so fierce
And vigorous as thine? But thou art honest.
RENAULT. Who dares accuse me?
JAFFEIR.   Curs'd be him that doubts
Thy virtue! I have tried it, and declare,
Were I to choose a guardian of my honor,
I'd put it into thy keeping; for I know thee.
RENAULT. Know me!
JAFFEIR.   Aye, know thee. There's no falsehood in
   thee.
Thou look'st just as thou art. Let us embrace.
Now wouldst thou cut my throat or I cut thine?
RENAULT. You dare not do't.
JAFFEIR.   You lie, sir.
RENAULT.   How!
JAFFEIR.   No more.
'Tis a base world, and must reform, that's all.

Enter SPINOSA, THEODORE, ELIOT, REVILLIDO, DURAND, BRAINVEIL,
   and the rest of the Conspirators.

RENAULT. Spinosa! Theodore!
SPINOSA.   The same.
RENAULT.   You are welcome!

SPINOSA.   You are trembling, sir.

RENAULT.   'Tis a cold night, indeed, and I
    am aged,
Full of decay and natural infirmities.
We shall be warm, my friend, I hope tomorrow.

PIERRE *re-enters*

PIERRE. (*Aside*) 'Twas not well done; thou shouldst have stroked
    him
And not have galled him.

JAFFEIR. (*Aside*)   Damn him, let him chew on't!
Heaven! where am I? beset with cursèd fiends,
That wait to damn me. What a devil's man
When he forgets his nature! — Hush, my heart.

RENAULT. My friends, 'tis late; are we assembled all?
Where's Theodore?

THEODORE.   At hand.

RENAULT.   Spinosa?

SPINOSA.   Here.

RENAULT. Brainveil?

BRAINVEIL.   I am ready.

RENAULT.   Durand and Brabe?

DURAND.   Command us;
We are both prepared!

RENAULT.   Mezzana, Revillido,
Ternon, Retrosi; oh, you are men, I find,
Fit to behold your fate and meet her summons.
To-morrow's rising sun must see you all
Decked in your honors! Are the soldiers ready?

OMNES. All, all.

RENAULT. You, Durand, with your thousand must possess
St. Mark's. You, captain, know your charge already;
'Tis to secure the Ducal Palace. You,
Brabe, with a hundred more must gain the Secque.[6]
With the like number, Brainveil, to the Procuralle.[7]
Be all this done with the least tumult possible,
Till in each place you post sufficient guards;
Then sheathe your swords in every breast you meet.

JAFFEIR. (*Aside*) Oh, reverend cruelty! damned, bloody villain!

RENAULT. During this execution, Durand, you
Must in the midst keep your battalia fast.
And, Theodore, be sure to plant the cannon
That may command the streets; whilst Revillido,

[6] The Mint.
[7] The residences of the nine Procurators of Venice.

Mezzana, Ternon and Retrosi, guard you.
This done, we'll give the general alarm,
Apply petards, and force the Ars'nal gates;
Then fire the city round in several places,
Or with our cannon (if it dare resist)
Batter't to ruin. But above all I charge you,
Shed blood enough; spare neither sex nor age,
Name nor condition. If there live a senator
After to-morrow, tho' the dullest rogue
That e'er said nothing, we have lost our ends.
If possible, let's kill the very name
Of senator, and bury it in blood.

    JAFFEIR. (*Aside*) Merciless, horrid slave! — Aye, blood enough!
Shed blood enough, old Renault. How thou charm'st me!

    RENAULT. But one thing more, and then farewell till fate
Join us again or separate us ever.
First, let's embrace; Heaven knows who next shall thus
Wing ye together. But let's all remember
We wear no common cause upon our swords.
Let each man think that on his single virtue
Depends the good and fame of all the rest —
Eternal honor or perpetual infamy.
Let's remember through what dreadful hazards
Propitious Fortune hitherto has led us,
How often on the brink of some discovery
Have we stood tottering, and yet still kept our ground
So well, the busiest searchers ne'er could follow
Those subtle tracks which puzzled all suspicion.
—You droop, sir!

    JAFFEIR.   No; with a most profound attention
I've heard it all, and wonder at thy virtue.

    RENAULT. Though there be yet few hours 'twixt them and ruin,
Are not the Senate lulled in full security,
Quiet and satisfied, as fools are always?
Never did so profound repose forerun
Calamity so great! Nay, our good fortune
Has blinded the most piercing of mankind,
Strengthened the fearfullest, charmed the most suspectful,
Confounded the most subtle; for we live,
We live, my friends, and quickly shall our life
Prove fatal to these tyrants. Let's consider
That we destroy oppression, avarice,
A people nursed up equally with vices
And loathsome lusts which Nature most abhors,
And such as without shame she cannot suffer.

JAFFEIR. (*Aside*) O Belvidera, take me to thy arms,
And show me where's my peace, for I've lost it.   *Exit* JAFFEIR

RENAULT. Without the least remorse, then, let's resolve
With fire and sword t'exterminate these tyrants;
And when we shall behold those cursed tribunals,
Stained by the tears and sufferings of the innocent,
Burning with flames rather from heaven than ours,
The raging, furious, and unpitying soldier
Pulling his reeking dagger from the bosoms
Of gasping wretches; death in every quarter,
With all that sad disorder can produce,
To make a spectacle of horror — then,
Then let's call to mind, my dearest friends,
That there is nothing pure upon the earth;
That the most valued things have most allays;[8]
And that in change of all those vile enormities
Under whose weight this wretched country labors,
The means are only in our hands to crown them.

PIERRE. And may those powers above that are propitious
To gallant minds, record this cause and bless it.

RENAULT. Thus happy, thus secure of all we wish for,
Should there, my friends, be found amongst us one
False to this glorious enterprise, what fate,
What vengeance were enough for such a villain?

ELIOT. Death here without repentance, hell hereafter.

RENAULT. Let that be my lot if as here I stand
Lifted by fate amongst her darling sons,
Though I had only one brother, dear by all
The strictest ties of nature; though one hour
Had given us birth, one fortune fed our wants,
One only love, and that but of each other,
Still filled our minds: could I have such a friend
Joined in this cause, and had but ground to fear
Meant foul play, may this right hand drop from me,
If I'd not hazard all my future peace,
And stab him to the heart before you. Who
Would do less? wouldst not thou, Pierre, the same?

PIERRE. You have singled me, sir, out for this hard question,
As if 'twere started only for my sake!
Am I the thing you fear? Here, here's my bosom;
Search it with all your swords! Am I a traitor?

RENAULT. No, but I fear your late commended friend
Is little less. Come, sirs, 'tis now no time
To trifle with our safety. Where's this Jaffeir?

8 Alloys.

SPINOSA. He left the room just now in strange disorder.

RENAULT. Nay, there is danger in him; I observed him
During the time I took for explanation;
He was transported from most deep attention
To a confusion which he could not smother.
His looks grew full of sadness and surprise,
All which betrayed a wavering spirit in him,
That labored with reluctancy and sorrow.
What's requisite for safety must be done
With speedy execution; he remains
Yet in our power. I for my own part wear
A dagger.

PIERRE. Well?

RENAULT. And I could wish it —

PIERRE. Where?

RENAULT. Buried in his heart.

PIERRE. Away! w'are yet all friends!
No more of this; 'twill breed ill blood amongst us!

SPINOSA. Let us all draw our swords, and search the house,
Pull him from the dark hole where he sits brooding
O'er his cold fears, and each man kill his share of him.

PIERRE. Who talks of killing? Who's he'll shed the blood
That's dear to me? — Is't you? — or you? — or you, sir
What, not one speak? how you stand gaping all
On your grave oracle, your wooden god there!
Yet not a word? (*To* RENAULT) Then, sir, I'll tell you a secret:
Suspicion's but at best a coward's virtue!

RENAULT. A coward — (*Handles his sword*)

PIERRE. Put, put up thy sword, old man,
Thy hand shakes at it. Come, let's heal this breach,
I am too hot. We yet may live friends.

SPINOSA. Till we are safe, our friendship cannot be so.

PIERRE. Again! Who's that?

SPINOSA. 'Twas I.

THEODORE. And I.

REVILLIDO. And I.

ELIOT. And all.

RENAULT. Who are on my side?

SPINOSA. Every honest sword.
Let's die like men and not be sold like slaves.

PIERRE. One such word more, by heaven, I'll to the Senate
And hang ye all, like dogs in clusters!
Why peep your coward swords half out their shells?
Why do you not all brandish them like mine?
You fear to die, and yet dare talk of killing.

RENAULT. Go to the Senate and betray us! Hasten,
Secure thy wretched life; we fear to die
Less than thou darest be honest.
　　　PIERRE.　　　　　　　　　　That's rank falsehood!
Fear'st not thou death? fie, there's a knavish itch
In that salt blood, an utter foe to smarting.
Had Jaffeir's wife proved kind, he had still been true.
Foh — how that stinks?
Thou die! thou kill my friend! — or thou — or thou
— Or thou, with that lean, withered, wretched face!
Away! disperse all to your several charges,
And meet to-morrow where your honor calls you;
I'll bring that man whose blood you so much thirst for,
And you shall see him venture for you fairly.
— Hence, hence, I say　　　　　　　*Exit* RENAULT *angrily*
　　　SPINOSA.　　　　　　　I fear we've been to blame,
And done too much.
　　　THEODORE. 'Twas too far urged against the man you loved.
　　　REVILLIDO. Here, take our swords and crush 'em with your feet.
　　　SPINOSA. Forgive us, gallant friend.
　　　PIERRE.　　　　　　　　　Nay, now y'have found
The way to melt and cast me as you will,
I'll fetch this friend and give him to your mercy;
Nay, he shall die if you will take him from me.
For your repose I'll quit my heart's jewel,
But would not have him torn away by villains.
And spiteful villainy.
　　　SPINOSA.　　　　　　No, may you both
Forever live and fill the world with fame!
　　　PIERRE. Now you are too kind. Whence rose all this discord?
Oh, what a dangerous precipice have we 'scaped!
How near a fall was all we had long been building!
What an eternal blot had stained our glories,
If one, the bravest and the best of men,
Had fall'n a sacrifice to rash suspicion,
Butchered by those whose cause he came to cherish!
Oh, could you know him all as I have known him,
How good he is, how just, how true, how brave,
You would not leave this place till you had seen him,
Humbled yourselves before him, kissed his feet,
And gained remission for the worst of follies.
　　　　　Come but to-morrow, all your doubts shall end,
　　　　　And to your loves me better recommend,
　　　　　That I've preserved your fame, and saved my friend.
　　　　　　　　　　　　　　　　　Exeunt omnes

ACT IV

[SCENE I. *A street*]

Enter JAFFEIR *and* BELVIDERA

JAFFEIR. Where dost thou lead me? Every step I move,
Methinks I tread upon some mangled limb
Of a racked friend. O, my dear charming ruin!
Where are we wand'ring?
    BELVIDERA.   To eternal honor;
To do a deed shall chronicle thy name
Among the glorious legends of those few
That have saved sinking nations. Thy renown
Shall be the future song of all the virgins
Who by thy piety have been preserved
From horrid violation. Every street
Shall be adorned with statues to thy honor.
And at thy feet this great inscription written:
Remember him that propped the fall of Venice.
    JAFFEIR. Rather, remember him who after all
The sacred bonds of oaths and holier friendship
In fond compassion to a woman's tears,
Forgot his manhood, virtue, truth, and honor,
To sacrifice the bosom that relieved him.
Why wilt thou damn me?
    BELVIDERA.   O inconstant man!
How will you promise? how will you deceive?
Do, return back, replace me in my bondage,
Tell all thy friends how dangerously thou lov'st me,
And let thy dagger do its bloody office.
Oh, that kind dagger, Jaffeir, how 'twill look
Stuck through my heart, drenched in my blood to th'hilts,
Whilst these poor dying eyes shall with their tears
No more torment thee! Then thou wilt be free.
Or if thou think'st it nobler, let me live
Till I'm a victim to the hateful lust
Of that infernal devil, that old fiend
That's damned himself and would undo mankind.
Last night, my love!
    JAFFEIR.   Name, name it not again.
It shows a beastly image to my fancy
Will wake me into madness. Oh, the villain!

That durst approach such purity as thine
On terms so vile! Destruction, swift destruction
Fall on my coward head, and make my name
The common scorn of fools if I forgive him!
If I forgive him! If I not revenge
With utmost rage, and most unstaying fury,
Thy sufferings, thou dear darling of my life, love!
    BELVIDERA. Delay no longer then, but to the Senate;
And tell the dismal'st story e'er was uttered.
Tell 'em what bloodshed, rapines, desolations,
Have been prepared — how near's the fatal hour!
Save thy poor country; save the reverend blood
Of all its nobles, which to-morrow's dawn
Must else see shed. Save the poor, tender lives
Of all those little infants which the swords
Of murderers are whetting for this moment.
Think thou already hear'st their dying screams,
Think that thou seest their sad, distracted mothers
Kneeling before thy feet, and begging pity,
With torn, dishevelled hair and streaming eyes,
Their naked, mangled breasts besmeared with blood,
And even the milk with which their fondled babes
Softly they hushed, dropping in anguish from 'em.
Think thou seest this, and then consult thy heart.
    JAFFEIR. Oh!
    BELVIDERA. Think too, if thou lose this present minute,
What miseries the next day bring upon thee.
Imagine all the horrors of that night,
Murder and rapine, waste and desolation,
Confusedly ranging. Think what then may prove
My lot! The ravisher may then come safe,
And 'midst the terror of the public ruin
Do a damned deed — perhaps to lay a train
May catch thy life; then there will be revenge,
The dear revenge that's due to such a wrong?
    JAFFEIR. By all heaven's powers, prophetic truth dwells in thee;
For every word thou speak'st strikes through my heart
Like a new light, and shows it how't has wandered.
Just what th'hast made me, take me, Belvidera,
And lead me to the place where I'm to say
This bitter lesson; where I must betray
My truth, my virtue, constancy, and friends.
Must I betray my friends? Ah, take me quickly,
Secure me well before that thought's renewed.
If I relapse once more, all's lost forever.

BELVIDERA. Hast thou a friend more dear than Belvidera?

JAFFEIR. No, th'art my soul itself, wealth, friendship, honor;
All present joys, and earnest of all future,
Are summed in thee. Methinks, when in thy arms
Thus leaning on thy breast, one minute's more
Than a long thousand years of vulgar hours.
Why was such happiness not given me pure?
Why dashed with cruel wrongs, and bitter wantings?
Come, lead me forward now like a tame lamb
To sacrifice; thus in his fatal garlands,
Decked fine, and pleased, the wanton skips and plays,
    Trots by the enticing, flattering priestess' side,
    And much transported with his little pride,
    Forgets his dear companions of the plain
    Till by her, bound, he's on the altar lain;
    Yet then too hardly bleats, such pleasure's in the pain.

Enter Officer and Six Guards

OFFICER. Stand! Who goes there?

BELVIDERA.   Friends.

JAFFEIR. Friends, Belvidera! Hide me from my friends.
By heaven, I'd rather see the face of hell
Than meet the man I love.

OFFICER.   But what friends are you?

BELVIDERA. Friends to the Senate and the state of Venice.

OFFICER. My orders are to seize on all I find
At this late hour, and bring 'em to the Council,
Who now are sitting.

JAFFEIR.   Sir, you shall be obeyed.
Hold, brutes, stand off! none of your paws upon me!
Now the lot's cast, and, Fate, do what thou wilt.

Exeunt guarded

SCENE [II.] *The Senate-house*

Where appear sitting, the DUKE OF VENICE,
PRIULI, ANTONIO, *and eight other Senators*

DUKE. Antony, Priuli, senators of Venice,
Speak; why are we assembled here this night?
What have you to inform us of, concerns
The state of Venice, honor, or its safety?

PRIULI. Could words express the story I have to tell you,
Fathers, these tears were useless— these sad tears

That fall from my old eyes; but there is cause
We all should weep, tear off these purple robes,
And wrap ourselves in sack-cloth, sitting down
On the sad earth, and cry aloud to heaven.
Heaven knows if yet there be an hour to come
Ere Venice be no more!
    ALL SENATORS.   How!
    PRIULI.   Nay, we stand
Upon the very brink of gaping ruin.
Within this city's formed a dark conspiracy
To massacre us all, our wives and children,
Kindred and friends, our palaces and temples
To lay in ashes—nay, the hour, too, fixed;
The swords, for aught I know, drawn even this moment,
And the wild waste begun. From unknown hands
I had this warning. But if we are men,
Let's not be tamely butchered, but do something
That may inform the world in after ages,
Our virtue was not ruined, though we were.
(*A noise without* "Room, room, make room for some prisoners!")
    2D SENATOR. Let's raise the city!

Enter Officer and Guard

    PRIULI. Speak there—what disturbance?
    OFFICER. Two prisoners have the guard seized in the streets,
Who say they come to inform this reverend Senate
About the present danger.
    ALL.   Give 'em entrance—

Enter JAFFEIR *and* BELVIDERA, *guarded*

Well, who are you?
    JAFFEIR.   A villain.
    ANTONIO.   Short and pithy.
The man speaks well.
    JAFFEIR.   Would every man that hears me
Would deal so honestly, and own his title.
    DUKE. 'Tis rumored that a plot has been contrived
Against this state; that you have a share in't, too.
If you are a villain, to redeem your honor,
Unfold the truth and be restored with mercy.
    JAFFEIR. Think not that I to save my life come hither—
I know its value better—but in pity
To all those wretches whose unhappy dooms
Are fixed and sealed. You see me here before you,
The sworn and covenanted foe of Venice.

But use me as my dealings may deserve,
And I may prove a friend.
DUKE.   The slave capitulates.
Give him the tortures.
JAFFEIR.   That you dare not do;
Your fears won't let you, nor the longing itch
To hear a story which you dread the truth of—
Truth which the fear of smart shall ne'er get from me.
Cowards are scared with threat'nings. Boys are whipped
Into confessions; but a steady mind
Acts of itself, ne'er asks the body counsel.
"Give him the tortures!" Name but such a thing
Again, by heaven, I'll shut these lips forever.
Not all your racks, your engines, or your wheels
Shall force a groan away—that you may guess at.
ANTONIO. A bloody-minded fellow, I'll warrant;
A damned bloody-minded fellow.
DUKE. Name your conditions.
JAFFEIR.   For myself, full pardon,
Besides the lives of two and twenty friends   (*Delivers a list*)[1]
Whose names are here enrolled. Nay, let their crimes
Be ne'er so monstrous, I must have the oaths
And sacred promise of this reverend council,
That in a full assembly of the Senate
The thing I ask be ratified. Swear this,
And I'll unfold the secrets of your danger.
ALL. We'll swear.
DUKE.   Propose the oath.
JAFFEIR.   By all the hopes
Ye have of peace and happiness hereafter,
Swear!
ALL.   We all swear.
JAFFEIR.   To grant me what I've asked,
Ye swear.
ALL.   We swear.
JAFFEIR.   And as ye keep the oath,
May you and your posterity be blest
Or curs'd forever.
ALL.   Else be curs'd forever!
JAFFEIR. (*Delivers another paper*) Then here's the list, and with't
the full disclose of all that threatens you.—Now, Fate, thou hast caught
me.

---

[1] This stage direction must be a mistake, since Jaffeir delivers the list some
twelve lines later. Probably at this point he displayed the list.

ANTONIO. Why, what a dreadful catalogue of cut-throats is here!
I'll warrant you not one of these fellows but has a face like a lion. I dare
not so much as read their names over.

DUKE. Give orders that all dilligent search be made
To seize these men; their characters are public.
The paper intimates their rendezvous
To be at the house of a famed Grecian courtesan
Called Aquilina; see that place secured.

ANTONIO. [Aside] What! My Nicky Nacky, Hurry Durry, Nicky
Nacky in the plot? I'll make a speech.
Most noble senators,
What headlong apprehension drives you on,
Right noble, wise, and truly solid senators,
To violate the laws and right of nations?
The lady is a lady of renown.
'Tis true, she holds a house of fair reception,
And though I say't myself, as many more
Can say as well as I—

2D SENATOR.   My lord, long speeches
Are frivolous here when dangers are so near us.
We all well know your interest in that lady;
The world talks loud on't.

ANTONIO.   Verily, I have done.
I say no more.

DUKE.   But, since he has declared
Himself concerned, pray, captain, take great caution
To treat the fair one as becomes her character,
And let her bed-chamber be searched with decency.
You, Jaffeir, must with patience bear till morning
To be our prisoner.

JAFFEIR.   [Aside] Would the chains of death
Had bound me fast ere I had known this minute!
I've done a deed will make my story hereafter
Quoted in competition with all ill ones.
The history of my wickedness shall run
Down through the low traditions of the vulgar,
And boys be taught to tell the tale of Jaffeir.

DUKE. Captain, withdraw your prisoner.

JAFFEIR.   Sir, if possible,
Lead me where my own thoughts themselves may lose me;
Where I may doze out what I've left of life,
Forget myself and this day's guilt and falsehood.
Cruel remembrance, how shall I appease thee!

                                                   Exit guarded
(*Noise without* "More traitors; room, room, make room there!")

DUKE. How's this? Guards—
Where are our guards? Shut up the gates; the treason's
Already at our doors!

Enter Officer

OFFICER.   My lords, more traitors—
Seized in the very act of consultation;
Furnished with arms and instruments of mischief.
Bring in the prisoners.

Enter PIERRE, RENAULT, THEODORE, ELIOT, REVILLIDO *and other*
Conspirators, in fetters, guarded

PIERRE.   You, my lords, and fathers
(As you are pleased to call yourselves) of Venice,
If you sit here to guide the course of justice,
Why these disgraceful chains upon the limbs
That have so often labored in your service?
Are these the wreaths of triumphs ye bestow
On those that bring you conquests home and honors?

DUKE. Go on; you shall be heard, sir.

ANTONIO. And be hanged too, I hope.

PIERRE. Are these the trophies I've deserved for fighting
Your battles with confederated powers,
When winds and seas conspired to overthrow you,
And brought the fleets of Spain to your own harbors?
When you, great Duke, shrunk trembling in your palace,
And saw your wife, th'Adriatic, ploughed
Like a lewd whore by bolder prows than yours—
Stepped not I forth, and taught your loose Venetians
The task of honor and the way to greatness,
Raised you from your capitulating fears,
To stipulate the terms of sued-for peace—
And this my recompense! If I am a traitor,
Produce my charge; or show the wretch that's base enough
And brave enough to tell me I am a traitor.

DUKE. Know you one Jaffeir?

(*All the Conspirators murmur*)
PIERRE.   Yes, and know his virtue.
His justice, truth, his general worth and sufferings
From a hard father, taught me first to love him.

Enter JAFFEIR, *guarded*

DUKE. See him brought forth.

PIERRE.   [*Aside*] My friend, too, bound? nay then
Our fate has conquered us, and we must fall.
—Why droops the man whose welfare's so much mine

They're but one thing? These reverend tyrants, Jaffeir,
Call us traitors; art thou one, my brother?
    JAFFEIR. To thee I am the falsest, veriest slave
That e'er betrayed a generous, trusting friend,
And gave up honor to be sure of ruin.
All our fair hopes which morning was to have crowned,
Has this curs'd tongue o'erthrown.
    PIERRE.   So! Then all's over.
Venice has lost her freedom; I, my life.
No more. Farewell!
    DUKE.   Say, will you make confession
Of your vile deeds and trust the Senate's mercy?
    PIERRE. Curs'd be your Senate; curs'd your constitution.
The curse of growing factions and division
Still vex your councils, shake your public safety,
And make the robes of government you wear
Hateful to you as these base chains to me!
    DUKE. Pardon, or death?
    PIERRE.   Death—honorable death!
    RENAULT. Death's the best thing we ask or you can give.
    ALL CONSPIRATORS. No shameful bonds, but honorable death!
    DUKE. Break up the council. Captain, guard your prisoners.
Jaffeir, y'are free, but these must wait for judgment.
                  Exeunt all the Senators [*and* BELVIDERA]
    PIERRE. Come, where's my dungeon? Lead me to my straw.
It will not be the first time I've lodged hard
To do your Senate service.
    JAFFEIR.   Hold one moment!
    PIERRE. Who's he disputes the judgment of the Senate?
Presumptuous rebel—on—   (*Strikes* JAFFEIR)
    JAFFEIR.   By heaven, you stir not.
I must be heard, I must have leave to speak!
Thou hast disgraced me, Pierre, by a vile blow.
Had not a dagger done thee nobler justice?
But use me as thou wilt, thou canst not wrong me,
For I am fallen beneath the basest injuries;
Yet look upon me with an eye of mercy,
With pity and with charity behold me;
Shut not thy heart against a friend's repentance,
But as there dwells a god-like nature in thee,
Listen with mildness to my supplications.
    PIERRE. What whining monk art thou? what holy cheat
That wouldst encroach upon my credulous ears,
And cant'st thus vilely? Hence! I know thee not.
Dissemble and be nasty. Leave me, hypocrite.

JAFFEIR. Not know me, Pierre?

PIERRE.   No, know thee not. What art thou?

JAFFEIR. Jaffeir, thy friend, thy once loved, valued friend,
Though now deserv'dly scorned, and used most hardly.

PIERRE. Thou Jaffeir! thou my once loved, valued friend!
By heavens, thou li'st! The man so called, my friend,
Was generous, honest, faithful, just and valiant,
Noble in mind, and in his person lovely,
Dear to my eyes and tender to my heart;
But thou, a wretched, base, false, worthless coward,
Poor, even in soul, and loathsome in thy aspect,
All eyes must shun thee, and all hearts detest thee.
Prithee avoid, nor longer cling thus round me
Like something baneful that my nature's chilled at.

JAFFEIR. I have not wronged thee—by these tears I have not!
But still am honest, true, and hope, too, valiant;
My mind still full of thee; therefore, still noble.
Let not thy eyes then shun me, nor thy heart
Detest me utterly. Oh, look upon me!
Look back and see my sad, sincere submission!
How my heart swells, as even 'twould burst my bosom,
Fond of its goal, and laboring to be at thee!
What shall I do, what say to make thee hear me?

PIERRE. Hast thou not wronged me? dar'st thou call thyself
Jaffeir, that once loved, valued friend of mine,
And swear thou hast not wronged me? Whence these chains?
Whence this vile death, which I may meet this moment?
Whence this dishonor but from thee, thou false one?

JAFFEIR. —All's true; yet grant one thing, and I've done asking.

PIERRE. What's that?

JAFFEIR.   To take thy life on such conditions
The Council have proposed. Thou and thy friends
May yet live long, and to be better treated.

PIERRE. Life! Ask my life? Confess? Record myself
A villain for the privilege to breathe
And carry up and down this cursèd city
A discontented and repining spirit,
Burdensome to itself, a few years longer,
To lose, it may be, at last in a lewd quarrel
For some new friend, treacherous and false as thou art?
No, this vile world and I have long been jangling,
And cannot part on better terms than now,
When only men like thee are fit to live in't.

JAFFEIR. By all that's just—

PIERRE.   Swear by some other powers,
For thou hast broke that sacred oath too lately.

JAFFEIR. Then by that hell I merit, I'll not leave thee
Till to thyself, at least, thou'rt reconciled,
However thy resentments deal with me.

PIERRE. Not leave me?

JAFFEIR.   No, thou shalt not force me from thee.
Use me reproachfully, and like a slave;
Tread on me, buffet me, heap wrongs on wrongs
On my poor head, I'll bear it all with patience
Shall weary out thy most unfriendly cruelty,
Lie at thy feet and kiss 'em though they spurn me
Till, wounded by my sufferings, thou relent,
Aud raise me to thy arms with dear forgiveness.

PIERRE. Art thou not—

JAFFEIR.   What?

PIERRE.   A traitor?

JAFFEIR.   Yes.

PIERRE.   A villain?

JAFFEIR. Granted.

PIERRE.   A coward—a most scandalous coward,
Spiritless, void of honor, one who has sold
Thy everlasting fame for shameless life?

JAFFEIR. All, all, and more—much more. My faults are numberless.

PIERRE. And wouldst thou have me live on terms like thine?
Base as thou art false?

JAFFEIR.   No, 'tis to me that's granted;
The safety of thy life was all I aimed at,
In recompense for faith and trust so broken.

PIERRE. I scorn it more because preserved by thee.
And as, when first my foolish heart took pity
On thy misfortunes, sought thee in thy miseries,
Relieved thy wants, and raised thee from thy state
Of wretchedness in which thy fate had plunged thee,
To rank thee in my list of noble friends,
All I received in surety for thy truth,
Were unregarded oaths—and this, this dagger,
Given with a worthless pledge thou since hast stol'n:
So I restore it back to thee again,
Swearing by all those powers which thou hast violated,
Never from this curs'd hour to hold communion,
Friendship, or interest with thee, though our years
Were to exceed those limited the world.
Take it—farewell!—for now I owe thee nothing.

JAFFEIR. Say thou wilt live, then.

PIERRE. For my life, dispose it
Just as thou wilt, because 'tis what I'm tired with.
JAFFEIR. O Pierre!
PIERRE. No more.
JAFFEIR. My eyes won't lose the sight of thee,
But languish after thine and ache with gazing.
PIERRE. Leave me.—Nay, then—thus, thus, I throw thee from me,
And curses, great as is thy falsehood, catch thee! *Exit*
JAFFEIR. Amen.—He's gone, my father, friend, preserver,
And here's the portion he has left me. (*Holds the dagger up*)
This dagger, well remembrèd—with this dagger
I gave a solemn vow of dire importance,
Parted with this and Belvidera together.
Have a care, Mem'ry, drive that thought no farther.
No, I'll esteem it as a friend's last legacy,
Treasure it up in this wretched bosom,
Where it may grow acquainted with my heart,
That when they meet, they start not from each other.
—So; now for thinking. A blow; called traitor, villain,
Coward, dishonorable coward—fogh!
Oh, for a long, sound sleep, and so forget it!
Down, busy devil—

Enter BELVIDERA

BELVIDERA. Whither shall I fly?
Where hide me and my miseries together?
Where's now the Roman constancy I boasted?
Sunk into trembling fears and desperation!
Not daring to look up to that dear face
Which used to smile even on my faults, but down
Bending these miserable eyes to earth,
Must move in penance, and implore much mercy.
JAFFEIR. Mercy! Kind heaven has surely endless stores
Hoarded for thee of blessings yet untasted;
Let wretches loaded hard with guilt as I am,
Bow [with] the weight, and groan beneath the burden,
Creep with a remnant of that strength th'have left
Before the footstool of that heaven th'have injured.
O Belvidera! I'm the wretched'st creature
E'er crawled on earth! Now if thou hast virtue, help me;
Take me into thy arms, and speak the words of peace
To my divided soul that wars within me,
And raises every sense to my confusion.
By heaven, I am tottering to the very brink
Of peace, and thou art all the hold I've left.

BELVIDERA. Alas! I know thy sorrows are most mighty.
I know th'hast cause to mourn—to mourn, my Jaffeir,
With endless cries, and never-ceasing wailings.
Th'hast lost—
　　JAFFEIR.　　　　Oh, I have lost what can't be counted!
My friend, too, Belvidera, that dear friend,
Who, next to thee, was all my health rejoiced in,
Has used me like a slave—shamefully used me.
'Twould break thy pitying heart to hear the story.
What shall I do? resentment, indignation,
Love, pity, fear, and mem'ry how I've wronged him,
Distract my quiet with the very thought on't,
And tear my heart to pieces in my bosom.
　　BELVIDERA. What has he done?
　　JAFFEIR.　　　　　　　Thou'dst hate me should I tell thee
　　BELVIDERA. Why?
　　JAFFEIR. Oh, he has used me—! Yet, by heaven, I bear it!
He has used me, Belvidera—but first swear
That when I've told thee, thou wilt not loathe me utterly,
Though vilest blots and stains appear upon me;
But still at least with charitable goodness,
Be near me in the pangs of my affliction—
Not scorn me, Belvidera, as he has done.
　　BELVIDERA. Have I then e'er been false that now I'm doubted?
Speak, what's the cause I'm grown into distrust?
Why thought unfit to hear my love's complainings?
　　JAFFEIR. Oh!
　　BELVIDERA. Tell me.
　　JAFFEIR.　　　　　Bear my failings, for they are many.
O my dear angel! In that friend I've lost
All my soul's peace; for every thought of him
Strikes my sense hard, and deads in it my brains.
Wouldst thou believe it—
　　BELVIDERA.　　　　Speak.
　　JAFFEIR.　　　　　　　Before we parted,
Ere yet his guards had led him to his prison,
Full of severest sorrows for his suff'rings,
With eyes o'erflowing and a bleeding heart,
Humbling myself almost beneath my nature,
As at his feet I kneeled and sued for mercy,
Forgetting all our friendship, all the dearness
In which w'have lived so many years together,
With a reproachful hand he dashed a blow—
He struck me, Belvidera, by heaven, he struck me,
Buffeted, called me traitor, villain, coward!—

Am I a coward? am I a villain? Tell me:
Th'art the best judge, and mad'st me, if I am so.
Damnation—coward!

    BELVIDERA.   Oh! forgive him, Jaffeir!
And if his sufferings wound thy heart already,
What will they do tomorrow

    JAFFEIR.   Hah!

    BELVIDERA.   Tomorrow,
When thou shalt see him stretched in all the agonies
Of a tormenting and a shameful death,
His bleeding bowels, and his broken limbs,
Insulted o'er by a vile, butchering villain;
What will thy heart do then? Oh, sure 'twill stream
Like my eyes now.

    JAFFEIR.   What means thy dreadful story?
Death, and tomorrow? broken limbs and bowels?
Insulted o'er by a vile butchering villain?
By all my fears, I shall start out to madness
With barely guessing if the truth's hid longer.

    BELVIDERA. The faithless senators, 'tis they've decreed it.
They say, according to our friends' request,
They shall have death, and not ignoble bondage;
Declare their promised mercy all as forfeited,
False to their oaths, and deaf to intercession.
Warrants are passed for public death tomorrow.

    JAFFEIR. Death! doomed to die! condemned unheard! unpleaded!

    BELVIDERA. Nay, cruel'st racks and torments are preparing,
To force confessions from their dying pangs.
Oh, do not look so terribly upon me!
How your lips shake, and all your face disordered!
What means my love?

    JAFFEIR. Leave me! I charge thee, leave me. Strong temptations
Wake in my heart.

    BELVIDERA.   For what?

    JAFFEIR.   No more, but leave me.

    BELVIDERA. Why?

    JAFFEIR. Oh! by heaven, I love thee with that fondness,
I would not have thee stay a moment longer
Near these curs'd hands. Are they not cold upon thee?

                       (*Pulls the dagger half out of his bosom
                           and puts it back again*)

    BELVIDERA. No, everlasting comfort's in thy arms,
To lean thus on thy breast is softer ease
Than downy pillows decked with leaves of roses.

JAFFEIR. Alas, thou think'st not of the thorns 'tis filled with:
Fly ere they gall thee. There's a lurking serpent
Ready to leap and sting thee to thy heart.
Art thou not terrified?
    BELVIDERA.   No.
    JAFFEIR.   Call to mind
What thou hast done, and whither thou hast brought me.
    BELVIDERA. Hah!
    JAFFEIR.   Where's my friend? my friend, thou smiling
        mischief?
Nay, shrink not, now 'tis too late. Thou shouldst have fled
When thy guilt first had cause, for dire revenge
Is up and raging for my friend. He groans—
Hark, how he groans! His screams are in my ears
Already; see, th'have fixed him on the wheel,
And now they tear him.—Murder! perjured Senate!
Murder—Oh!—hark thee, trait'ress, thou hast done this;
Thanks to thy tears and false persuading love.
How her eyes speak! O thou bewitching creature!
                              (*Fumbling for his dagger*)
Madness cannot hurt thee. Come, thou little trembler,
Creep, even into my heart, and there lie safe;
'Tis thy own citadel.—Hah—yet stand off!
Heaven must have justice, and my broken vows
Will sink me else beneath its reaching mercy.
I'll wink and then 'tis done—
    BELVIDERA.   What means the lord
Of me, my life and love? What's in thy bosom
Thou grasp'st at so? Nay, why am I thus treated?
                    [*Jaffeir draws the dagger; offers to stab her*]
What wilt thou do?—Ah, do not kill me, Jaffeir!
Pity these panting breasts and trembling limbs
That used to clasp thee when thy looks were milder—
That yet hang heavy on my unpurged soul;
And plunge it not into eternal darkness.
    JAFFEIR. No, Belvidera, when we parted last,
I gave this dagger with thee as in trust
To be thy portion if I e'er proved false.
On such condition was my truth believed;
But now 'tis forfeited and must be paid for.
                              (*Offers to stab her again*)
    BELVIDERA. (*Kneeling*) Oh, mercy!
    JAFFEIR.   Nay, no struggling.
    BELVIDERA. (*Leaps upon his neck and kisses him*)
        Now then kill me!

While thus I cling about thy cruel neck,
Kiss thy revengeful lips and die in joys
Greater than any I can guess hereafter.
    JAFFEIR. I am, I am a coward. Witness't, heaven,
Witness it, earth, and every being, witness!
'Tis but one blow; yet—by immortal love,
I cannot longer bear a thought to harm thee!
                (*He throws away the dagger and embraces her*)
The seal of providence is sure upon thee,
And thou wert born for yet unheard-of wonders.
Oh, thou wert either born to save or damn me!
By all the power that's given thee o'er my soul,
By thy resistless tears and conquering smiles,
By the victorious love that still waits on thee,
Fly to thy cruel father. Save my friend,
Or all our future quiet's lost forever.
Fall at his feet; cling round his reverend knees;
Speak to him with thy eyes, and with thy tears
Melt his hard heart, and wake dead nature in him.
Crush him in th'arms, and torture him with thy softness;
          Nor, till thy prayers are granted, set him free,
          But conquer him, as thou hast vanquished me.

                                  Exeunt ambo

ACT V

[SCENE I. *A street*]

Enter PRIULI, *solus*

    PRIULI. Why, cruel heaven, have my unhappy days
Been lengthened to this sad one? Oh! dishonor
And deathless infamy is fallen upon me.
Was it my fault? Am I a traitor? No.
But then, my only child, my daughter, wedded;
There my best blood runs foul, and a disease
Incurable has seized upon my memory,
To make it rot and stink to after ages.
Curs'd be the fatal minute when I got her;
Or would that I'd been anything but man,
And raised an issue which would ne'er have wronged me.
The miserablest creatures (man excepted)
Are not the less esteemed though their posterity
Degenerate from the virtues of their fathers;
The vilest beasts are happy in their offsprings,

While only man gets traitors, whores, and villains.
Curs'd be the name, and some swift blow from fate
Lay his head deep, where mine may be forgotten!

Enter BELVIDERA *in a long mourning veil*

BELVIDERA. He's there—my father, my inhuman father,
That, for three years, has left an only child
Exposed to all the outrages of fate
And cruel ruin.—Oh!—
PRIULI.   What child of sorrow
Art thou, that com'st thus wrapped in weeds of sadness,
And mov'st as if thy steps were towards a grave?
BELVIDERA. A wretch who from the very top of happiness
Am fallen into the lowest depths of misery,
And want your pitying hand to raise me up again.
PRIULI. Indeed, thou talk'st as thou hadst tasted sorrows.
Would I could help thee.
BELVIDERA.   'Tis greatly in your power.
The world, too, speaks you charitable, and I,
Who ne'er asked alms before, in that dear hope
Am come a-begging to you, sir.
PRIULI.   For what?
BELVIDERA. Oh, well regard me! Is this voice a strange one?
Consider, too, when beggars once pretend
A case like mine, no little will content 'em.
PRIULI. What wouldst thou beg for?
BELVIDERA.   Pity and forgiveness.
                              (*Throws up her veil*)
By the kind tender names of child and father,
Hear my complaints, and take me to your love.
PRIULI. My daughter!
BELVIDERA.   Yes, your daughter, by a mother
Virtuous and noble, faithful to your honor,
Obedient to your will, kind to your wishes,
Dear to your arms. By all the joys she gave you,
When in her blooming years she was your treasure,
Look kindly on me; in my face behold
The lineaments of hers y'have kissed so often,
Pleading the cause of your poor cast-off child.
PRIULI. Thou art my daughter.
BELVIDERA.   Yes—and y'have oft told me
With smiles of love and chaste, paternal kisses,
I'd much resemblance of my mother.
PRIULI.   Oh!
Hadst thou inherited her matchless virtues,

I'd been too bless'd.

BELVIDERA.   Nay, do not call to memory
My disobedience, but let pity enter
Into your heart, and quite deface the impression;
For could you think how mine's perplexed, what sadness,
Fears, and despairs distract the peace within me,
Oh, you would take me in your dear, dear arms,
Hover with strong compassion o'er your young one,
To shelter me with a protecting wing
From the black gathered storm that's just, just breaking!

PRIULI. Don't talk thus.

BELVIDERA.   Yes, I must; and you must hear too.
I have a husband—

PRIULI.   Damn him!

BELVIDERA.   Oh, do not curse him!
He would not speak so hard a word towards you
On any terms, [howe'er] he deal with me.

PRIULI. Hah! what means my child?

BELVIDERA. Oh, there's but this short moment
'Twixt me and fate. Yet send me not with curses
Down to my grave; afford me one kind blessing
Before we part! Just take me in your arms
And recommend me with a prayer to heaven,
That I may die in peace. And when I'm dead—

PRIULI. How my soul's catched!

BELVIDERA.   Lay me, I beg you, lay me
By the dear ashes of my tender mother.
She would have pitied me, had fate yet spared her.

PRIULI. By heaven, my aching heart forebodes much mischief.
Tell me thy story, for I'm still thy father.

BELVIDERA. No, I'm contented.

PRIULI.   Speak.

BELVIDERA.   No matter

PRIULI.   Tell me.
By yon blest heaven, my heart runs o'er with fondness.

BELVIDERA. Oh!

PRIULI.   Utter't.

BELVIDERA.   Oh, my husband, my dear husband
Carries a dagger in his once kind bosom,
To pierce the heart of your poor Belvidera.

PRIULI. Kill thee!

BELVIDERA.   Yes, kill me. When he passed his faith
And covenant against your state and Senate,
He gave me up as hostage for his truth,
With me a dagger and a dire commission,

Whene'er he failed, to plunge it through this bosom.
I learnt the danger, chose the hour of love
T'attempt his heart, and bring it back to honor.
Great love prevailed and blessed me with success.
He came, confessed, betrayed his dearest friends
For promised mercy. Now they're doomed to suffer,
Galled with remembrance of what then was sworn
If they are lost, he vows t'appease the gods
With this poor life, and make my blood th'atonement.

 PRIULI. Heavens!

 BELVIDERA.   Think you saw what passed at our last parting;
Think you beheld him like a raging lion,
Pacing the earth, and tearing up his steps,
Fate in his eyes, and roaring with the pain
Of burning fury; think you saw his one hand
Fixed on my throat, while the extended other
Grasped a keen, threat'ning dagger. Oh, 'twas thus
We last embraced; when, trembling with revenge,
He dragged me to the ground, and at my bosom
Presented horrid death, cried out, "My friends—
Where are my friends?" swore, wept, raged, threatened, loved—
For he yet loved, and that dear love preserved me
To this last trial of a father's pity.
I fear not death, but cannot bear a thought
That that dear hand should do th' unfriendly office.
If I was ever then your care, now hear me;
Fly to the Senate, save the promised lives
Of his dear friends, ere mine be made the sacrifice.

 PRIULI. Oh, my heart's comfort!

 BELVIDERA.   Will you not, my father?
Weep not, but answer me.

 PRIULI.   By heaven, I will!
Not one of 'em but what shall be immortal.
Canst thou forgive me all my follies past?
I'll henceforth be indeed a father; never,
Never more thus expose, but cherish thee,
Dear as the vital warmth that feeds my life,
Dear as these eyes that weep in fondness o'er thee.
Peace to thy heart! Farewell.

 BELVIDERA.   Go, and remember,
'Tis Belvidera's life her father pleads for.

              Exeunt severally

       Enter ANTONIO

ANTONIO. Hum, hum, hah. Signior Priuli, my lord Priuli, my lord, my lord, my lord.—How we lords love to call one another by our titles.—My lord, my lord, my lord—Pox on him, I am a lord as well as he. And so let him fiddle.—I'll warrant him he's gone to the Senate-house, and I'll be there too, soon enough for somebody. Odd!—here's a tickling speech about the plot. I'll prove there's a plot with a vengeance—would I had it without book. Let me see—"Most reverend senators, That there is a plot, surely by this time, no man that hath eyes or understanding in his head will presume to doubt; 'tis as plain as the light in the cowcumber"—no—hold there—cowcumber does not come in yet—"'tis as plain as the light in the sun, or as the man in the moon, even at noonday. It is, indeed, a pumpkin-plot, which, just as it was mellow, we have gathered; and now we have gathered it, prepared, and dressed it, shall we throw it like a pickled cowcumber out at the window? No! That it is not only a bloody, horrid, execrable, damnable, and audacious plot, but it is, as I may so say, a saucy plot; and we all know, most reverend fathers, that what is sauce for a goose is sauce for a gander: therefore, I say, as those blood-thirsty ganders of the conspiracy would have destroyed us geese of the Senate, let us make haste to destroy them. So I humbly move for hanging"—Hah, hurry durry—I think this will do—though I was something out, at first, about the sun and the cowcumber.

Enter AQUILINA

AQUILINA. Good morrow, senator.

ANTONIO. Nacky, my dear Nacky; morrow, Nacky. Odd, I am very brisk, very merry, very pert, very jovial—ha-a-a-a-a—kiss me, Nacky. How dost thou do, my little Tory, rory strumpet? Kiss me, I say, hussy, kiss me.

AQUILINA. "Kiss me, Nacky!" Hang you, sir coxcomb! hang you, sir!

ANTONIO. Hayty, tayty, is it so indeed, with all my heart, faith— (Sings) Hey then, up go we,[1] faith—hey then, up go we, dum dum derum dump.

AQUILINA. Signior.

ANTONIO. Madonna.

AQUILINA. Do you intend to die in your bed?

ANTONIO. About threescore years hence, much may be done, my dear.

AQUILINA. You'll be hanged, signior.

ANTONIO. Hanged, sweetheart? Prithee, be quiet. Hanged, quoth-a, that's a merry conceit, with all my heart. Why, thou jok'st, Nacky; thou art given to joking, I'll swear. Well, I protest, Nacky—nay, I must protest, and will protest that I love joking dearly, man. And I love thee for joking, and I'll kiss thee for joking, and touse thee for joking—and odd, I have a devilish mind to take thee aside about that

---

[1] A popular Whig song.

business for joking, too—odd, I have! and (Sings) *Hey then, up go
we, dum dum derum dump.*

AQUILINA. (*Draws a dagger*) See you this, sir?

ANTONIO. O laud, a dagger! O laud! it is naturally my aversion! I
cannot endure the sight on't; hide it, for heaven's sake! I cannot look
that way till it be gone—hide it, hide it, oh, oh, hide it!

AQUILINA. Yes, in your heart I'll hide it.

ANTONIO. My heart! What, hide a dagger in my heart's blood!

AQUILINA. Yes, in thy heart—thy throat, thou pampered devil!
Thou hast helped to spoil my peace, and Ill have vengeance
On thy curs'd life for all the bloody Senate,
The perjured, faithless Senate. Where's my lord,
My happiness, my love, my god, my hero?
Doomed by thy accursed tongue, amongst the rest,
T'a shameful wrack? By all the rage that's in me,
I'll be whole years in murdering thee!

ANTONIO. Why, Nacky, wherefore so passionate? What have I done?
What's the matter, my dear Nacky? Am not I thy love, thy happiness,
thy lord, thy hero, thy senator, and everything in the world, Nacky?

AQUILINA. Thou! Thinkst thou, thou art fit to meet my joys—
To bear the eager clasps of my embraces?
Give me my Pierre, or—

ANTONIO. Why, he's to be hanged, little Nacky—trussed up for
treason, and so forth, child.

AQUILINA. Thou li'st! stop down thy throat that hellish sentence,
Or 'tis thy last. Swear that my love shall live,
Or thou art dead!

ANTONIO.   Ah-h-h.

AQUILINA.   Swear to recall his doom—
Swear at my feet, and tremble at my fury.

ANTONIO. I do. [*Aside*] Now, if she would but kick a little bit—one
kick now, ah-h-h-h.

AQUILINA. Swear, or—

ANTONIO.   I do, by these dear fragrant foots and little
toes, sweet as—e-e-e-e, my Nacky, Nacky, Nacky.

AQUILINA. How!

ANTONIO. Nothing but untie thy shoestring a little, faith and troth;
that's all—that's all, as I hope to live, Nacky, that's all.

AQUILINA. Nay, then—

ANTONIO.   Hold, hold! thy love, thy lord, thy hero
Shall be preserved and safe.

AQUILINA.   Or may this poniard
Rust in thy heart!

ANTONIO.   With all my soul.

AQUILINA.   Farewell—

Exit AQUILINA

ANTONIO. Adieu.   Why, what a bloodyminded, inveterate, termagant strumpet have I been plagued with! Oh-h-h, yet more! nay, then,
I die, I die—I am dead already.   (*Stretches himself out*)

[SCENE II. *A street near* PRIULI'S *house*]

Enter JAFFEIR

JAFFEIR. Final destruction seize on all the world!
Bend down, ye heavens, and shutting round this earth,
Crush the vile globe into its first confusion;
Scorch it with elemental flames to one curs'd cinder,
And all us little creepers in't, called men,
Burn, burn to nothing. But let Venice burn
Hotter than all the rest; here kindle hell
Ne'er to extinguish, and let souls hereafter
Groan here, in all those pains which mine feels now.

Enter BELVIDERA

BELVIDERA. (*Meeting him*) My life—
JAFFEIR.   (*Turning from her*) My plague—
BELVIDERA.   Nay, then I see my ruin,
If I must die!
JAFFEIR.   No, Death's this day too busy;
Thy father's ill-timed mercy came too late.
I thank thee for thy labors, tho', and him, too,
But all my poor, betrayed, unhappy friends
Have summons to prepare for fate's black hour;
And yet I live.
BELVIDERA.   Then be the next my doom.
I see thou hast passed my sentence in thy heart,
And I'll no longer weep or plead against it;
But with the humblest, most obedient patience
Meet thy dear hands, and kiss 'em when they wound me.
Indeed I am willing, but I beg thee do it
With some remorse; and where thou giv'st the blow,
View me with eyes of a relenting love,
And show me pity, for 'twill sweeten justice.
JAFFEIR. Show pity to thee!
BELVIDERA.   Yes, and when thy hands,
Charged with my fate, come trembling to the deed,
As thou hast done a thousand, thousand dear times
To this poor breast when kinder rage has brought thee,
When our stinged hearts have leaped to meet each other,

And melting kisses sealed our lips together,
When joys have left me gasping in thy arms,
So let my death come now, and I'll not shrink from't.
 JAFFEIR. Nay, Belvidera, do not fear my cruelty,
Nor let the thoughts of death perplex thy fancy;
But answer me to what I shall demand,
With a firm temper and unshaken spirit.
 BELVIDERA. I will when I've done weeping —
 JAFFEIR.   Fie, no more on't!
How long is't since the miserable day
We wedded first —
 BELVIDERA.   Oh-h-h.
 JAFFEIR.   Nay, keep in thy tears,
Lest they unman me, too.
 BELVIDERA.   Heaven knows I cannot;
The words you utter sound so very sadly,
These streams will follow —
 JAFFEIR.   Come, I'll kiss 'em dry, then.
 BELVIDERA. But was't a miserable day?
 JAFFEIR.   A curs'd one.
 BELVIDERA. I thought it otherwise, and you've oft sworn
In the transporting hours of warmest love,
When sure you spoke the truth, you've sworn you blessed it.
 JAFFEIR. 'Twas a rash oath.
 BELVIDERA.   Then why am I not curs'd too?
 JAFFEIR. No, Belvidera; by th'eternal truth,
I dote with too much fondness.
 BELVIDERA.   Still so kind!
Still then do you love me?
 JAFFEIR.   Nature, in her workings,
Inclines not with more ardor to creation
Than I do now towards thee; man ne'er was bless'd
Since the first pair first met, as I have been.
 BELVIDERA. Then sure you will not curse me.
 JAFFEIR.   No, I'll bless thee;
I came on purpose, Belvidera, to bless thee.
'Tis now, I think, three years w'have lived together.
 BELVIDERA. And may no fatal minute ever part us
Till, reverend grown for age and love, we go
Down to one grave as our last bed, together;
There sleep in peace till an eternal morning.
 JAFFEIR. (Sighing) When will that be?
 BELVIDERA.   I hope long ages hence.
 JAFFEIR. Have I not hitherto (I beg thee tell me
Thy very fears) used thee with tender'st love?

Did e'er my soul rise up in wrath against thee?
Did I e'er frown when Belvidera smiled,
Or, by the least unfriendly word, betray
A bating passion? Have I ever wronged thee?
  BELVIDERA. No.
  JAFFEIR.   Has my heart, or have my eyes e'er wand'rèd
To any other woman?
  BELVIDERA.   Never, never —
I were the worst of false ones, should I accuse thee.
I own I've been too happy, bless'd above
My sex's charter.
  JAFFEIR. Did I not say I came to bless thee?
  BELVIDERA. Yes.
  JAFFEIR.   Then hear me, bounteous heaven!
Pour down your blessings on this beauteous head,
Where everlasting sweets are always springing.
With a continual giving hand, let peace,
Honor, and safety always hover round her;
Feed her with plenty; let her eyes ne'er see
A sight of sorrow, nor her heart know mourning;
Crown all her days with joy, her nights with rest
Harmless as her own thoughts, and prop her virtue
To bear the loss of one that too much loved,
And comfort her with patience in our parting.
  BELVIDERA. How — parting, parting!
  JAFFEIR.   Yes, forever parting.
I have sworn, Belvidera, by yon heaven
That best can tell how much I lose to leave thee,
We part this hour forever.
  BELVIDERA.   Oh, call back
Your cruel blessings; stay with me and curse me!
  JAFFEIR. No, 'tis resolved.
  BELVIDERA.   Then hear me, too, just heaven!
Pour down your curses on this wretched head
With never-ceasing vengeance; let despair,
Danger, or infamy—nay all, surround me;
Starve me with wantings; let my eyes ne'er see
A sight of comfort, nor my heart know peace;
But dash my days with sorrow, nights with horrors
Wild as my own thoughts now, and let loose fury
To make me mad enough for what I lose,
If I must lose him. — If I must! — I will not.
Oh, turn and hear me!
  JAFFEIR.   Now hold, heart, or never!
  BELVIDERA. By all the tender days we've lived together,

By all our charming nights, and joys that crowned 'em,
Pity my sad condition — speak, but speak!
    JAFFEIR. Oh-h-h!
    BELVIDERA.   By these arms that now cling round thy neck,
By this dear kiss and by ten thousand more,
By these poor streaming eyes —
    JAFFEIR.   Murder! unhold me.
By th'immortal destiny that doomed me   (*Draws his dagger*)
To this curs'd minute, I'll not live one longer.
Resolve to let me go or see me fall —
    BELVIDERA. Hold, sir; be patient.   (*Passing-bell tolls*)
    JAFFEIR.   Hark, the dismal bell
Tolls out for death! I must attend its call, too;
For my poor friend, my dying Pierre, expects me.
He sent a message to require I'd see him
Before he died, and take his last forgiveness.
Farewell forever.   (*Going out, looks back at her*)
    BELVIDERA.   Leave thy dagger with me;
Bequeath me something. — Not one kiss at parting?
O my poor heart, when wilt thou break?
    JAFFEIR.   Yet stay!
We have a child, as yet a tender infant.
Be a kind mother to him when I am gone;
Breed him in virtue and the paths of honor,
But let him never know his father's story.
I charge thee guard him from the wrongs my fate
May do his future fortune or his name.
Now — nearer yet —   (*Approaching each other*)
            Oh, that my arms were riveted
Thus round thee ever! — But my friends, my oath! (*Kisses her*)
This and no more.
    BELVIDERA.   Another, sure another,
For that poor little one you've ta'en care of;
I'll give't him truly.
    JAFFEIR.   [*Kissing her*] So! — now farewell.
    BELVIDERA.   Forever?
    JAFFEIR. Heaven knows, forever; all good angels guard thee.
                           (*Exit*)

    BELVIDERA. All ill ones sure had charge of me this moment.
Curs'd be my days, and doubly curs'd my nights,
Which I must now mourn out in widowed tears.
Blasted be every herb and fruit and tree;
Curs'd be the rain that falls upon the earth,
And may the general curse reach man and beast.
Oh, give me daggers, fire, or water!

How I could bleed, how burn, how drown, the waves
Huzzing and booming round my sinking head,
Till I descended to the peaceful bottom!
Oh, there's all quiet; here, all rage and fury!
The air's too thin, and pierces my weak brain.
I long for thick, substantial sleep. Hell, hell,
Burst from the center, rage and roar aloud
If thou art half so hot, so mad as I am.

Enter PRIULI *and Servants*

Who's there?
PRIULI.   Run, seize and bring her safely home.

(*They seize her*)

Guard her as you would life. Alas, poor creature!
BELVIDERA. What? To my husband then conduct me quickly.
Are all things ready? Shall we die most gloriously?
Say not a word of this to my old father.
Murmuring streams, soft shades, and springing flowers,
Lutes, laurels, seas of milk, and ships of amber.   *Exeunt*

SCENE [III] *opening, discovers a scaffold and a wheel prepared for the
executing of* PIERRE; *then enter Officers,* PIERRE, *and Guards,
a Friar, Executioner, and a great Rabble*

OFFICER. Room, room there! Stand all by; make room for the
prisoner.
PIERRE. My friend not come yet?
FATHER.   Why are you so obstinate?
PIERRE. Why you so troublesome, that a poor wretch
Cannot die in peace,
But you, like ravens, will be croaking round him?
FATHER. Yet heaven —
PIERRE.   I tell thee, heaven and I are friends.
I ne'er broke peace with't yet by cruel murders,
Rapine, or perjury, or vile deceiving;
But lived in moral justice towards all men,
Nor am a foe to the most strong believers,
Howe'er my own short-sighted faith confine me.
FATHER. But an all-seeing Judge —
PIERRE.   You say my conscience
Must be mine accuser. I have searched that conscience,
And finds no records there of crimes that scare me.
FATHER. 'Tis strange you should want faith.

PIERRE.   You want to lead
My reason blindfold, like a hampered lion,
Checked of its nobler vigor, then when baited
Down to obedient tameness, make it couch,
And show strange tricks which you call signs of faith.
So silly souls are gulled and you get money.
Away, no more! — Captain, I would hereafter
This fellow wrote no lies of my conversion
Because he has crept upon my troubled hours.

Enter JAFFEIR

JAFFEIR. Hold. Eyes, be dry; heart, strengthen me to bear
This hideous sight, and humble me to take
The last forgiveness of a dying friend,
Betrayed by my vile falsehood to his ruin! —
O Pierre!
PIERRE.   Yet nearer.
JAFFEIR.   Crawling on my knees,
And prostrate on the earth, let me approach thee.
How shall I look up to thy injured face,
That always used to smile with friendship on me?
It darts an air of so much manly virtue,
That I, methinks, look little in thy sight,
And stripes are fitter for me than embraces.
PIERRE. Dear to my arms, though thou hast undone my fame,
I cannot forget to love thee. Prithee, Jaffeir,
Forgive that filthy blow my passion dealt thee;
I am now preparing for the land of peace,
And fain would have the charitable wishes
Of all good men, like thee, to bless my journey.
JAFFEIR. Good! I am the vilest creature, worse than e'er
Suffered the shameful fate thou art going to taste of.
Why was I sent for to be used thus kindly?
Call, call me villain, as I am; describe
The foul complexion of my hateful deeds.
Lead me to the rack, and stretch me in thy stead;
I've crimes enough to give it its full load,
And do it credit. Thou wilt but spoil the use on't,
And honest men hereafter bear its figure
About 'em as a charm from treacherous friendship.
OFFICER. The time grows short. Your friends are dead already.
JAFFEIR. Dead!
PIERRE. Yes, dead, Jaffeir; they've all died like men, too,
Worthy their character.
JAFFEIR.   And what must I do?

PIERRE. O Jaffeir!

JAFFEIR.   Speak aloud thy burdened soul,
And tell thy troubles to thy tortured friend.

PIERRE. Friend! Couldst thou yet be a friend, a generous friend,
I might hope comfort from thy noble sorrows.
Heaven knows I want a friend.

JAFFEIR.   And I a kind one,
That would not thus scorn my repenting virtue,
Or think, when he's to die, my thoughts are idle.

PIERRE. No! Live, I charge thee, Jaffeir.

JAFFEIR.   Yes, I will live,
But it shall be to see thy fall revenged
At such a rate as Venice long shall groan for.

PIERRE. Wilt thou?

JAFFEIR.   I will, by heaven!

PIERRE.   Then still thou'rt noble,
And I forgive thee. Oh — yet — shall I trust thee?

JAFFEIR. No; I've been false already.

PIERRE.   Dost thou love me?

JAFFEIR. Rip up my heart, and satisfy thy doubtings.

PIERRE. (*He weeps*) Curse on this weakness!

JAFFEIR.   Tears! Amazement! Tears!
I never saw thee melted thus before.
And know there's something lab'ring in thy bosom
That must have vent; though I'm a villain, tell me.

PIERRE. (*Pointing to the wheel*) Seest thou that engine?

JAFFEIR. Why?

PIERRE. Is't fit a soldier who has lived with honor,
Fought nations' quarrels, and been crowned with conquest,
Be exposed a common carcass on a wheel?

JAFFEIR. Hah!

PIERRE.   Speak! is't fitting?

JAFFEIR.   Fitting?

PIERRE.   Yes, is't fitting?

JAFFEIR. What's to be done?

PIERRE.   I'd have thee undertake
Something that's noble, to preserve my memory
From the disgrace that's ready to attaint it.

OFFICER. The day grows late, sir.

PIERRE.   I'll make haste — O Jaffeir,
Though thou'st betrayed me, do me some way justice.

JAFFEIR. No more of that. Thy wishes shall be satisfied.
I have a wife, and she shall bleed; my child, too,
Yield up his little throat, and all t'appease thee —

                              (*Going away,* PIERRE *holds him*)

PIERRE. No, this —　　　　　　　　(*He whispers* JAFFEIR)
　　　　— no more!
JAFFEIR.　　　　　　　Hah! is't then so?
PIERRE.　　　　　　　　　　　　　Most certainly.
JAFFEIR. I'll do't.
PIERRE.　　　　　Remember!
OFFICER.　　　　　　　Sir.
PIERRE.　　　　　　　　　　Come, now I'm ready.
　　　　　　(*He and* JAFFEIR *ascend the scaffold*)
Captain, you should be a gentleman of honor;
Keep off the rabble, that I may have room
To entertain my fate, and die with decency.
Come!
　　　　　(*Takes off his gown. Executioner prepares to bind him*)
FATHER. Son!
PIERRE.　　　Hence, tempter!
OFFICER.　　　　　　　Stand off, priest!
PIERRE. I thank you, sir.　　　　　　(*To* JAFFEIR)
　　　　　You'll think on't?
JAFFEIR. 'Twon't grow stale before to-morrow.
PIERRE. Now, Jaffeir! now I am going. Now —
　　　　　　(*Executioners having bound him*)
JAFFEIR. Have at thee,
Thou honest heart. Then — here —　　(*Stabs him*)
— And this is well, too.　　　(*Then stabs himself*)
FATHER.　　　　　　Damnable deed!
PIERRE. Now thou hast indeed been faithful.
This was done nobly. — We have deceived the Senate.
JAFFEIR. Bravely.
PIERRE. Ha, ha, ha — Oh, oh —　　　　　(*Dies*)
JAFFEIR.　　　　　　Now, ye curs'd rulers,
Thus of the blood y'have shed I make libation,
And sprinkle't mingling. May it rest upon you,
And all your race. Be henceforth peace a stranger
Within your walls; let plagues and famine waste
Your generations. — Oh, poor Belvidera!
Sir, I have a wife; bear this[2] in safety to her —
A token that with my dying breath I blest her,
And the dear little infant left behind me.
I am sick — I am quiet —　　　　(JAFFEIR *dies*)
OFFICER.　　　　Bear this news to the Senate,
And guard their bodies till there's farther order.
Heaven grant I die so well —　　(*Scene shuts upon them*)

　　[2] The dagger, evidently the one he had earlier offered with Belvidera as a pledge of his good faith.

[SCENE IV. A *room in* PRIULI'S *house*]

Soft music. Enter BELVIDERA *distracted, led by two of her* Women,
PRIULI, *and Servants*

PRIULI. Strengthen her heart with patience, pitying heaven.

BELVIDERA. Come, come, come, come, come! Nay, come to bed,
Prithee, my love. The winds! — hark, how they whistle!
And the rain beats; oh, how the weather shrinks me!
You are angry now; who cares? pish, no indeed.
Choose then. I say you shall not go, you shall not!
Whip your ill nature; get you gone then! — (JAFFEIR's *Ghost rises*)
                                                                Oh,
Are you returned? See, father, here he's come again!
Am I to blame to love him? Oh, thou dear one,   (*Ghost sinks*)
Why do you fly me? Are you angry still, then?
Jaffeir! where art thou? — Father, why do you thus?
Stand off, don't hide him from me! He's here somewhere.
Stand off, I say! — What, gone? Remember't, tyrant!
I may revenge myself for this trick one day.
I'll do't — I'll do't. Renault's a nasty fellow.
Hang him, hang him, hang him!

         Enter Officer and others. Officer whispers PRIULI

PRIULI. News — what news?

OFFICER.   Most sad, sir.
Jaffeir, upon the scaffold, to prevent
A shameful death, stabbed Pierre, and next himself.
Both fell together.

PRIULI.   — Daughter —
         (*The Ghosts of* JAFFEIR *and* PIERRE *rise together, both bloody*)
BELVIDERA.   Hah, look there!
My husband bloody, and his friend, too! — Murder!
Who has done this? Speak to me, thou sad vision;
On these poor trembling knees I beg it.   (*Ghosts sink*)
                                        Vanished —
Here they went down. Oh, I'll dig, dig the den up.
You shan't delude me thus. — Hoa, Jaffeir, Jaffeir!
Peep up and give me but a look. — I have him!
I've got him, father; oh, now how I'll smuggle him!
My love! my dear! my blessing! help me, help me!
They have hold on me, and drag me to the bottom!
Nay — now they pull so hard — farewell —   (*She dies*)

MAID.   She's dead —
Breathless and dead.
    PRIULI.   Then guard me from the sight on't.
Lead me into some place that's fit for mourning,
Where the free air, light, and the cheerful sun
May never enter. Hang it round with black;
Set up one taper that may last a day —
As long as I've to live; and there all leave me,
        Sparing no tears when you this tale relate,
        But bid all cruel fathers dread my fate.
                                Exeunt omnes

EPILOGUE

The text is done, and now for application,
And when that's ended, pass your approbation.
Though the conspiracy's prevented here,
Methinks I see another hatching there;
And there's a certain faction fain would sway,　⎫
If they had strength enough, and damn this play.　⎬
But this the author bade me boldly say:　　　　　⎭
If any take his plainness in ill part,
He's glad on't from the bottom of his heart.
Poets in honor of the truth should write,
With the same spirit brave men for it fight;
And though against him causeless hatreds rise,　⎫
And daily where he goes of late he spies　　　　⎬
The scowls of sullen and revengeful eyes,　　　⎭
'Tis what he knows with much contempt to bear,
And serves a cause too good to let him fear.
He fears no poison from an incensed drab,
No ruffian's five-foot-sword, nor rascal's stab,
Nor any other snares of mischief laid,
Not a Rose-alley cudgel-ambuscade,[1]
From any private cause where malice reigns,
Or general pique all blockheads have to brains.
Nothing shall daunt his pen when truth does call,
No, not the picture-mangler at Guildhall.[2]
The rebel-tribe,[3] of which that vermin's one,
Have now set forward and their course begun;
And while that prince's figure they deface,
　　As they before had massacred his name,
Durst their base fears but look him in the face,
　　They'd use his person as they've used his fame;
A face in which such lineaments they read
Of that great martyr's[4] whose rich blood they shed,
That their rebellious hate they still retain,
And in his son would murder him again.
With indignation then, let each brave heart
Rouse and unite to take his injured part;
Till royal love and goodness call him home,[5]
And songs of triumph meet him as he come;
Till heaven his honor and our peace restore,
And villains never wong his virtue more.

---

[1] In December, 1679, Dryden was beaten in Rose Alley on his way home from Will's Coffee-house. The identity of his assailants was never discovered.

[2] A rascal who slashed the Duke of York's picture; presumably a Whig.

[3] The Whigs.

[4] Charles I.

[5] The Duke of York had been sent to Scotland in October, 1680. He returned in March, 1682.

THE WAY OF THE WORLD

A
COMEDY

As it is Acted at the Theatre in
Lincoln's-Inn-Fields, by His Majesty's Servants

Written by Mr. Congreve

Audire est operae pretium, procedere recte
Qui maechis non vultis —
                                  Hor. Sat. 2. 1. I.
— Metuat doti deprensa. —
                                  Ibid.[1]

LONDON:

Printed for Jacob Tonson, within Gray's-Inn-Gate
next Gray's-Inn-Lane. 1700.

---

[1] O you that do not wish well to the proceedings of adulterers, it is worth
your while to hear how they are hampered on all sides. — Caught in the act,
the woman fears for her dowry.   — Horace, *Satires,* II, 1, 37-38, 131.

THE WAY OF THE WORLD

William Congreve

AFTER THE PRODUCTION of his first comedy, *The Old Batchelor*, in 1693, William Congreve (1670-1729), a refugee from the study of law at the Middle Temple, was acclaimed as one of the leading playwrights of the decade. His popularity grew with each succeeding play: *The Double Dealer* (1693), *Love for Love* (1695), and *The Mourning Bride*, a tragedy (1697). But when he came to write *The Way of the World* (1700), Congreve refused to truckle any longer to the debased taste of the time, which was all for farce, show, and sex. Instead he wrote to please himself, to satisfy his own high standards of art. He was so disappointed by the unfavorable reception of his comedy (which "had but moderate success") that he vowed to write no more plays. Although, as a share-holder, he continued his association with the theater, he kept his promise. A succession of government posts gave him a meager living, and, in his last years, some measure of affluence. He never married; however, it is noteworthy that he left the bulk of his personal estate to the beautiful Henrietta, Duchess of Marlborough — perhaps so that it would pass eventually to her daughter Mary. Congreve was too discreet to assert his paternity by leaving his estate to Mary directly.

The Way of the World is now generally accepted as the greatest English comedy of manners (or of wit). It is more than an exercise in style, more than an exhibition of witty virtuosity. Beneath the sparkle of simile and the sting of epigram lie tenderness and human understanding. Congreve's people play the game according to the rules of polite society, and banter and jest with the light insouciance of true sophisticates, but they remain always struggling human beings; we can sympathize even with the villains, the false wits, and the half-wits. Congreve's intellectual brilliance is never divorced from compassion.

The Way of the World was produced in March, 1700, at the New Theatre in Lincoln's Inn Fields. Aging Thomas Betterton turned over the leading role of Mirabell to dashing Jack Verbruggen, and devoted his own talents and long experience to the task of making Fainall a credible villain. The delightful coquette, Mrs. Millamant, was designed for and brilliantly played by Mrs. Anne Bracegirdle, with whom the dramatist had long been in love. (The gossips insisted that his love was returned, and that the famous "Virgin" actress had no right to her title.) Mrs. Elinor Leigh brought her long career to a stunning climax in the role of languishing Lady Wishfort, and Elizabeth Barry played Mrs. Marwood with her usual fire and passion. The other roles were adequately sustained by experienced players, who were taxed to the utmost to keep up with the rapid exchange of witty dialogue and the swift flow of events.

See *The Complete Works of William Congreve*, ed. Montague Summers, 1923; Bonamy Dobrée, *William Congreve, a Conversation between Swift and Gay*, 1929; John C. Hodges, *William Congreve the Man*, 1941; and K. M. Lynch, *A Congreve Gallery*, 1951.

Dramatis Personae

FAINALL, *in love with Mrs. Marwood*	MR. BETTERTON
MIRABELL, *in love with Mrs. Millamant*	MR. VERBRUGGEN
WITWOUD } *followers of Mrs. Millamant*	MR. BOWEN
PETULANT }	MR. BOWMAN
SIR WILFULL WITWOUD, *half brother to Witwoud and nephew to Lady Wishfort*	MR. UNDERHILL
WAITWELL, *servant to Mirabell*	MR. BRIGHT
LADY WISHFORT, *enemy to Mirabell for having falsely pretended love to her*	MRS. LEIGH
MRS. MILLAMANT, *a fine lady, niece to Lady Wishfort, and loves Mirabell*	MRS. BRACEGIRDLE
MRS. MARWOOD, *friend to Mr. Fainall, and likes Mirabell*	MRS. BARRY
MRS. FAINALL, *daughter to Lady Wishfort and wife to Fainall, formerly friend to Mirabell*	
FOIBLE, *woman to Lady Wishfort*	MRS. BOWMAN
MINCING, *woman to Mrs. Millamant*	MRS. WILLIS
Dancers, Footmen, and Attendants	MRS. PRINCE

Scene: London

PROLOGUE

Spoken by Mr. Betterton

Of those few fools who with ill stars are cursed,
Sure scribbling fools, called poets, fare the worst;
For they're a sort of fools which Fortune makes,
And after she has made 'em fools, forsakes.
With Nature's oafs 'tis quite a different case,
For Fortune favors all her idiot-race;
In her own nest the cuckoo-eggs we find,
O'er which she broods to hatch the changeling-kind.[1]
No portion for her own she has to spare,
So much she dotes on her adopted care.
    Poets are bubbles,[2] by the town drawn in,
Suffered at first some trifling stakes to win;
But what unequal hazards do they run!
Each time they write they venture all they've won;
The squire that's buttered[3] still, is sure to be undone.
This author heretofore has found your favor,
But pleads no merit from his past behavior;
To build on that might prove a vain presumption,
Should grants to poets made admit resumption;[4]
And in Parnassus he must lose his seat,
If that be found a forfeited estate.
    He owns, with toil he wrought the following scenes,
But, if they're naught, ne'er spare him for his pains;
Damn him the more; have no commiseration
For dullness on mature deliberation.
He swears he'll not resent one hissed-off scene,
Nor, like those peevish wits, his play maintain,
Who, to assert their sense, your taste arraign.
Some plot we think he has, and some new thought;
Some humor, too, no farce — but that's a fault.
Satire, he thinks, you ought not to expect;
For so reformed a town who dares correct?
To please this time has been his sole pretense;
He'll not instruct, lest it should give offense.
Should he by chance a knave or fool expose,
That hurts none here; sure, here are none of those.
In short, our play shall (with your leave to show it)
Give you one instance of a passive poet,
Who to your judgments yields all resignation;
So save or damn after your own discretion.

---

[1] The cuckoo was famous for laying its eggs in the nests of other birds. "Changeling" means (1) one child substituted for another, and (2) an idiot.
[2] Dupes or gulls, cheated by gamesters.
[3] Persuaded to pyramid his bets.
[4] I.e., capable of being taken back.

ACT I

SCENE I. A chocolate-house

MIRABELL and FAINALL [rising from cards]
BETTY waiting

MIRABELL. You are a fortunate man, Mr. Fainall!

FAINALL. Have we done?

MIRABELL. What you please. I'll play on to entertain you.

FAINALL. No, I'll give you your revenge another time, when you are not so indifferent; you are thinking of something else now, and play too negligently. The coldness of a losing gamester lessens the pleasure of the winner. I'd no more play with a man that slighted his ill fortune than I'd make love to a woman who undervalued the loss of her reputation.

MIRABELL. You have a taste extremely delicate, and are for refining on your pleasures.

FAINALL. Prithee, why so reserved? Something has put you out of humor.

MIRABELL. Not at all. I happen to be grave to-day, and you are gay; that's all.

FAINALL. Confess, Millamant and you quarrelled last night after I left you; my fair cousin has some humors that would tempt the patience of a stoic. What, some coxcomb came in, and was well received by her, while you were by?

MIRABELL. Witwoud and Petulant; and what was worse, her aunt, your wife's mother, my evil genius; or to sum up all in her own name, my old Lady Wishfort came in.

FAINALL. Oh, there it is then! She has a lasting passion for you, and with reason. — What, then my wife was there?

MIRABELL. Yes, and Mrs. Marwood, and three or four more, whom I never saw before. Seeing me, they all put on their grave faces, whispered one another; then complained aloud of the vapors[1] and after fell into a profound silence.

FAINALL. They had a mind to be rid of you.

MIRABELL. For which reason I resolved not to stir. At last the good old lady broke through her painful taciturnity with an invective against long visits. I would not have understood her, but Millamant joining

[1] The blues, tedium.

324

in the argument, I rose, and with a constrained smile, told her I thought nothing was so easy as to know when a visit began to be troublesome. She reddened, and I withdrew without expecting her reply.

FAINALL. You were to blame to resent what she spoke only in compliance with her aunt.

MIRABELL. She is more mistress of herself than to be under the necessity of such a resignation.

FAINALL. What! though half her fortune depends upon her marrying with my lady's approbation?

MIRABELL. I was then in such a humor that I should have been better pleased if she had been less discreet.

FAINALL. Now I remember, I wonder not they were weary of you; last night was one of their cabal nights. They have 'em three times a week, and meet by turns at one another's apartments, where they come together like the coroner's inquest, to sit upon the murdered reputations of the week. You and I are excluded, and it was once proposed that all the male sex should be excepted; but somebody moved that, to avoid scandal, there might be one man of the community, upon which motion Witwoud and Petulant were enrolled members.

MIRABELL. And who may have been the foundress of this sect? My Lady Wishfort, I warrant, who publishes her detestation of mankind, and, full of the vigor of fifty-five, declares for a friend and ratafia;[2] and let posterity shift for itself, she'll breed no more.

FAINALL. The discovery of your sham addresses to her, to conceal your love to her niece, has provoked this separation; had you dissembled better, things might have continued in the state of nature.

MIRABELL. I did as much as man could, with any reasonable conscience; I proceeded to the very last act of flattery with her, and was guilty of a song in her commendation. Nay, I got a friend to put her into a lampoon and compliment her with the imputation of an affair with a young fellow, which I carried so far that I told her the malicious town took notice that she was grown fat of a sudden; and when she lay in of a dropsy, persuaded her she was reported to be in labor. The devil's in't, if an old woman is to be flattered further, unless a man should endeavor downright personally to debauch her; and that my virtue forbade me. But for the discovery of this amour I am indebted to your friend, or your wife's friend, Mrs. Marwood.

FAINALL. What should provoke her to be your enemy, unless she has made you advances which you have slighted? Women do not easily forgive omissions of that nature.

MIRABELL. She was always civil to me till of late. I confess I am not one of those coxcombs who are apt to interpret a woman's good

[2] A cordial flavored with the kernels of peach, cherry, apricot, or almond.

manners to her prejudice, and think that she who does not refuse 'em everything, can refuse 'em nothing.

FAINALL. You are a gallant man, Mirabell; and though you may have cruelty enough not to satisfy a lady's longing, you have too much generosity not to be tender of her honor. Yet you speak with an indifference which seems to be affected and confesses you are conscious of a negligence.

MIRABELL. You pursue the argument with a distrust that seems to be unaffected and confesses you are conscious of a concern for which the lady is more indebted to you than is your wife.

FAINALL. Fie, fie, friend! If you grow censorious I must leave you.— I'll look upon the gamesters in the next room.

MIRABELL. Who are they?

FAINALL. Petulant and Witwoud. — [*To* BETTY] Bring me some chocolate.   [*Exit* FAINALL]

MIRABELL. Betty, what says your clock?

BETTY. Turned of the last canonical hour,[3] sir.

MIRABELL. How pertinently the jade answers me! — (*Looking on his watch*) — Ha? almost one o'clock! — Oh, y'are come!

Enter a Servant

Well, is the grand affair over? You have been something tedious.

SERVANT. Sir, there's such coupling at Pancras[4] that they stand behind one another, as 'twere in a country dance. Ours was the last couple to lead up, and no hopes appearing of dispatch — besides, the parson growing hoarse, we were afraid his lungs would have failed before it came to our turn; so we drove round to Duke's Place[5] and there they were riveted in a trice.

MIRABELL. So, so! You are sure they are married?

SERVANT. Married and bedded, sir; I am witness.

MIRABELL. Have you the certificate?

SERVANT. Here it is, sir.

MIRABELL. Has the tailor brought Waitwell's clothes home, and the new liveries?

SERVANT. Yes, sir.

MIRABELL. That's well. Do you go home again, d'ye hear, and adjourn the consummation till further orders. Bid Waitwell shake his ears, and Dame Partlet[6] rustle up her feathers and meet me at one o'clock by Rosamond's Pond,[7] that I may see her before she returns to her lady; and as you tender your ears be secret.   [*Exit Servant*]

---

[3] Hour of legal marriage.
[4] St. Pancras Church, where marriages could be performed at any time without a special license.
[5] Where St. James's Church was situated.
[6] The wife of Chantecleer in the fable of the cock and the fox.
[7] In St. James's Park.

Re-enter FAINALL

FAINALL. Joy of your success, Mirabell; you look pleased.

MIRABELL. Aye; I have been engaged in a matter of some sort of mirth, which is not yet ripe for discovery. I am glad this is not a cabal night.   I wonder, Fainall, that you, who are married and of consequence should be discreet, will suffer your wife to be of such a party.

FAINALL. Faith, I am not jealous. Besides, most who are engaged are women and relations; and for the men, they are of a kind too contemptible to give scandal.

MIRABELL. I am of another opinion. The greater the coxcomb, always the more the scandal; for a woman who is not a fool, can have but one reason for associating with a man who is one.

FAINALL. Are you jealous as often as you see Witwoud entertained by Millamant?

MIRABELL. Of her understanding I am, if not of her person.

FAINALL. You do her wrong; for, to give her her due, she has wit.

MIRABELL. She has beauty enough to make any man think so; and complaisance enough not to contradict him who shall tell her so.

FAINALL. For a passionate lover, methinks you are a man somewhat too discerning in the failings of your mistress.

MIRABELL. And for a discerning man, somewhat too passionate a lover; for I like her with all her faults—nay, like her for her faults. Her follies are so natural, or so artful, that they become her; and those affectations which in another woman would be odious, serve but to make her more agreeable. I'll tell thee, Fainall, she once used me with that insolence, that in revenge I took her to pieces, sifted her, and separated her failings; I studied 'em, and got 'em by rote. The catalogue was so large that I was not without hopes one day or other to hate her heartily; to which end I so used myself to think of 'em that at length, contrary to my design and expectation, they gave me every hour less and less disturbance, till in a few days it became habitual to me to remember 'em without being displeased. They are now grown as familiar to me as my own frailties, and, in all probability, in a little time longer I shall like 'em as well.

FAINALL. Marry her, marry her! Be half as well acquainted with her charms as you are with her defects, and my life on't, you are your own man again.

MIRABELL. Say you so?

FAINALL. Aye, aye, I have experience: I have a wife, and so forth.

Enter Messenger

MESSENGER. Is one Squire Witwoud here?

BETTY. Yes, what's your business?

MESSENGER. I have a letter for him from his brother Sir Wilfull, which I am charged to deliver into his own hands.

BETTY. He's in the next room, friend—that way.

[*Exit Messenger*]

MIRABELL. What, is the chief of that noble family in town—Sir Wilfull Witwoud?

FAINALL. He is expected today. Do you know him?

MIRABELL. I have seen him; he promises to be an extraordinary person. I think you have the honor to be related to him.

FAINALL. Yes; he is half-brother to this Witwoud by a former wife, who was sister to my Lady Wishfort, my wife's mother. If you marry Millamant, you must call cousins too.

MIRABELL. I had rather be his relation than his acquaintance.

FAINALL. He comes to town in order to equip himself for travel.

MIRABELL. For travel! Why, the man that I mean is above forty.

FAINALL. No matter for that; 'tis for the honor of England, that all Europe should know we have blockheads of all ages.

MIRABELL. I wonder there is not an act of parliament to save the credit of the nation, and prohibit the exportation of fools.

FAINALL. By no means; 'tis better as 'tis. 'Tis better to trade with a little loss, than to be quite eaten up with being overstocked.

MIRABELL. Pray, are the follies of this knight-errant and those of the squire his brother anything related?

FAINALL. Not at all; Witwoud grows by the knight, like a medlar grafted on a crab. One will melt in your mouth, and t'other set your teeth on edge; one is all pulp, and the other all core.

MIRABELL. So one will be rotten before he be ripe, and the other will be rotten without ever being ripe at all.

FAINALL. Sir Wilfull is an odd mixture of bashfulness and obstinacy. —But when he's drunk, he's as loving as the monster in *The Tempest*,[8] and much after the same manner. To give t'other his due, he has something of good nature, and does not always want wit.

MIRABELL. Not always; but as often as his memory fails him, and his commonplace of comparisons. He is a fool with a good memory and some few scraps of other folks' wit. He is one whose conversation can never be approved; yet it is now and then to be endured. He has indeed one good quality—he is not exceptious; for he so passionately affects the reputation of understanding raillery, that he will construe an affront into a jest, and call downright rudeness and ill language, satire and fire.

FAINALL. If you have a mind to finish his picture, you have an opportunity to do it at full length.—Behold the original!

[8] Sycorax or Caliban in the Davenant-Dryden version of *The Tempest*, 1670.

Enter WITWOUD

WITWOUD. Afford me your compassion, my dears! Pity me, Fainall! Mirabell, pity me!

MIRABELL. I do, from my soul.

FAINALL. Why, what's the matter?

WITWOUD. No letters for me, Betty?

BETTY. Did not the messenger bring you one but now, sir?

WITWOUD. Aye, but no other?

BETTY. No, sir.

WITWOUD. That's hard, that's very hard. —A messenger, a mule, a beast of burden! He has brought me a letter from the fool my brother, as heavy as a panegyric in a funeral sermon, or a copy of commendatory verses from one poet to another. And what's worse, 'tis as sure a fore-runner of the author as an epistle dedicatory.

MIRABELL. A fool,—and your brother, Witwoud!

WITWOUD. Aye, aye, my half-brother. My half-brother he is, no nearer, upon honor.

MIRABELL. Then 'tis possible he may be but half a fool.

WITWOUD. Good, good, Mirabell, *le drôle!*[9] Good, good; hang him, don't let's talk of him.—Fainall, how does your lady? Gad, I say anything in the world to get this fellow out of my head. I beg pardon that I should ask a man of pleasure and the town, a question at once so foreign and domestic. But I talk like an old maid at a marriage; I don't know what I say. But she's the best woman in the world.

FAINALL. 'Tis well you don't know what you say, or else your com-mendation would go near to make me either vain or jealous.

WITWOUD. No man in town lives well with a wife but Fainall.— Your judgment, Mirabell?

MIRABELL. You had better step and ask his wife if you would be credibly informed.

WITWOUD. Mirabell?

MIRABELL. Aye?

WITWOUD. My dear, I ask ten thousand pardons—gad, I have forgot what I was going to say to you!

MIRABELL. I thank you heartily, heartily.

WITWOUD. No, but prithee, excuse me—my memory is such a memory.

MIRABELL. Have a care of such apologies, Witwoud; for I never knew a fool but he affected to complain either of the spleen or his memory.

FAINALL. What have you done with Petulant?

WITWOUD. He's reckoning his money—my money it was. I have no luck to-day.

[9] The comic.

FAINALL. You may allow him to win of you at play, for you are sure to be too hard for him at repartee. Since you monopolize the wit that is between you, the fortune must be his, of course.

MIRABELL. I don't find that Petulant confesses the superiority of wit to be your talent, Witwoud.

WITWOUD. Come, come, you are malicious now, and would breed debates.—Petulant's my friend, and a very honest fellow, and a very pretty fellow, and has a smattering—faith and troth, a pretty deal of an odd sort of a small wit. Nay, I'll do him justice. I'm his friend, I won't wrong him.—And if he had any judgment in the world, he would not be altogether contemptible. Come, come, don't detract from the merits of my friend.

FAINALL. You don't take your friend to be over-nicely bred?

WITWOUD. No, no, hang him, the rogue has no manners at all, that I must own—no more breeding than a bumbaily[19] that I grant you—'tis pity, faith; the fellow has fire and life.

MIRABELL. What, courage?

WITWOUD. Hum, faith I don't know as to that; I can't say as to that. Yes, faith, in a controversy, he'll contradict anybody.

MIRABELL. Though 'twere a man whom he feared, or a woman whom he loved?

WITWOUD. Well, well, he does not always think before he speaks— we have all our failings. You're too hard upon him—you are, faith. Let me excuse him. I can defend most of his faults, except one or two. One he has, that's the truth on't; if he were my brother, I could not acquit him—that, indeed, I could wish were otherwise.

MIRABELL. Aye, marry, what's that, Witwoud?

WITWOUD. O pardon me!—Expose the infirmities of my friend?— No, my dear, excuse me there.

FAINALL. What! I warrant he's unsincere, or 'tis some such trifle.

WITWOUD. No, no, what if he be? 'Tis no matter for that; his wit will excuse that. A wit should no more be sincere than a woman constant; one argues a decay of parts, as t'other of beauty.

MIRABELL. Maybe you think him too positive?

WITWOUD. No, no, his being positive is an incentive to argument, and keeps up conversation.

FAINALL. Too illiterate?

WITWOUD. That? That's his happiness; his want of learning gives him the more opportunities to show his natural parts.

MIRABELL. He wants words?

WITWOUD. Aye, but I like him for that, now; for his want of words gives me the pleasure very often to explain his meaning.

FAINALL. He's impudent?

WITWOUD. No, that's not it.

---

10 Colloquialism for bailiff.

MIRABELL. Vain?

WITWOUD. No.

MIRABELL. What! He speaks unseasonable truths sometimes, because he has not wit enough to invent an evasion?

WITWOUD. Truths! ha! ha! ha! No, no; since you will have it—I mean, he never speaks truth at all—that's all. He will lie like a chambermaid, or a woman of quality's porter. Now, that is a fault.

Enter Coachman

COACHMAN. Is Master Petulant here, mistress?

BETTY. Yes.

COACHMAN. Three gentlewomen in the coach would speak with him.

FAINALL. O brave Petulant!—three!

BETTY. I'll tell him.

COACHMAN. You must bring two dishes of chocolate and a glass of cinnamon-water.[11]

[*Exit Coachman*]

WITWOUD. That should be for two fasting strumpets, and a bawd troubled with wind. Now you may know what the three are.

MIRABELL. You are very free with your friend's acquaintance.

WITWOUD. Aye, aye, friendship without freedom is as dull as love without enjoyment, or wine without toasting. But to tell you a secret, these are trulls whom he allows coach-hire, and something more by the week, to call on him once a day at public places.

MIRABELL. How!

WITWOUD. You shall see he won't go to 'em, because there's no more company here to take notice of him.—Why, this is nothing to what he used to do; before he found out this way, I have known him call for himself.

FAINALL. Call for himself! What dost thou mean?

WITWOUD. Mean! Why, he would slip you out of this chocolate-house just when you had been talking to him; as soon as your back was turned—whip, he was gone!—then trip to his lodging, clap on a hood and scarf and a mask, slap into a hackney-coach, and drive hither to the door again in a trice, where he would send in for himself, that is, I mean—call for himself, wait for himself; nay, and what's more, not finding himself, sometimes leave a letter for himself.

MIRABELL. I confess this is something extraordinary.—I believe he waits for himself now, he is so long a-coming.—Oh! I ask his pardon.

Enter PETULANT

BETTY. Sir, the coach stays.

PETULANT. Well, well; I come.—'Sbud,[12] a man had as good be a

---

[11] A drink made by distilling spirits with cinnamon and sugar.

[12] A contraction of 'sbodikins, "God's dear body."

professed midwife as a professed whoremaster, at this rate! To be knocked up and raised at all hours, and in all places! Pox on 'em, I won't come!—D'ye hear, tell 'em I won't come—let 'em snivel and cry their hearts out.

FAINALL. You are very cruel, Petulant.

PETULANT. All's one, let it pass. I have a humor to be cruel.

MIRABELL. I hope they are not persons of condition that you use at this rate.

PETULANT. Condition! condition's a dried fig if I am not in humor! —By this hand, if they were your—a—a—your what-d'ye-call-'ems themselves, they must wait or rub off, if I want appetite.

MIRABELL. What-d'ye-call-'ems! What are they, Witwoud?

WITWOUD. Empresses, my dear: by your what-d'ye-call-'ems he means sultana queens.

PETULANT. Aye, Roxolanas.[13]

MIRABELL. Cry you mercy.

FAINALL. Witwoud says they are—

PETULANT. What does he say th' are?

WITWOUD. I? Fine ladies, I say.

PETULANT. Pass on, Witwoud.—Hark'ee, by this light, his relations —two co-heiresses, his cousins, and an old aunt who loves caterwauling better than a conventicle.

WITWOUD. Ha, ha, ha! I had a mind to see how the rogue would come off.—Ha, ha, ha! Gad, I can't be angry with him if he had said they were my mother and my sisters.

MIRABELL. No?

WITWOUD. No; the rogue's wit and readiness of invention charm me. Dear Petulant!

BETTY. They are gone, sir, in great anger.

PETULANT. Enough; let 'em trundle. Anger helps complexion— saves paint.

FAINALL. This continence is all dissembled; this is in order to have something to brag of the next time he makes court to Millamant and swear he has abandoned the whole sex for her sake.

MIRABELL. Have you not left off your impudent pretensions there yet? I shall cut your throat some time or other, Petulant, about that business.

PETULANT. Aye, aye, let that pass—there are other throats to be cut.

MIRABELL. Meaning mine, sir?

PETULANT. Not I—I mean nobody—I know nothing. But there are uncles and nephews in the world—and they may be rivals—what then? All's one for that.

[13] For a famous Roxolana, see Davenant's The Siege of Rhodes.

MIRABELL. How! Hark'ee, Petulant, come hither—explain, or I shall call your interpreter.

PETULANT. Explain? I know nothing. Why, you have an uncle, have you not, lately come to town, and lodges by my Lady Wishfort's?

MIRABELL. True.

PETULANT. Why, that's enough—you and he are not friends; and if he should marry and have a child you may be disinherited, ha?

MIRABELL. Where hast thou stumbled upon all this truth?

PETULANT. All's one for that; why, then, say I know something.

MIRABELL. Come, thou art an honest fellow, Petulant, and shalt make love to my mistress; thou sha't, faith. What hast thou heard of my uncle?

PETULANT. I? Nothing, I. If throats are to be cut, let swords clash! snug's the word; I shrug and am silent.

MIRABELL. Oh, raillery, raillery! Come, I know thou art in the women's secrets.—What, you're a cabalist; I know you stayed at Millamant's last night after I went. Was there any mention made of my uncle or me? Tell me. If thou hadst but good nature equal to thy wit, Petulant, Tony Witwoud, who is now thy competitor in fame, would show as dim by thee as a dead whiting's eye by a pearl of orient; he would no more be seen by thee than Mercury is by the sun.
Come, I'm sure thou wo't tell me.

PETULANT. If I do, will you grant me common sense then, for the future?

MIRABELL. Faith, I'll do what I can for thee, and I'll pray that Heaven may grant it thee in the meantime.

PETULANT. Well, hark'ee.   [MIRABELL and PETULANT *talk apart*]

FAINALL. [*To* WITWOUD] Petulant and you both will find Mirabell as warm a rival as a lover.

WITWOUD. Pshaw! pshaw! that she laughs at Petulant is plain. And for my part, but that it is almost a fashion to admire her, I should—hark'ee—to tell you a secret, but let it go no further—between friends, I shall never break my heart for her.

FAINALL. How!

WITWOUD. She's handsome; but she's a sort of an uncertain woman.

FAINALL. I thought you had died for her.

WITWOUD. Umh—no—

FAINALL. She has wit.

WITWOUD. 'Tis what she will hardly allow anybody else. Now, demme! I should hate that, if she were as handsome as Cleopatra. Mirabell is not so sure of her as he thinks for.

FAINALL. Why do you think so?

WITWOUD. We stayed pretty late there last night, and heard something of an uncle to Mirabell, who is lately come to town—and is between him and the best part of his estate. Mirabell and he are at some distance, as my Lady Wishfort has been told; and you know she hates Mirabell worse than a Quaker hates a parrot, or than a fishmonger hates a hard frost. Whether this uncle has seen Mrs. Millamant or not, I cannot say, but there were items of such a treaty being in embryo; and if it should come to life, poor Mirabell would be in some sort unfortunately fobbed,[14] i'faith.

FAINALL. 'Tis impossible Millamant should hearken to it.

WITWOUD. Faith, my dear, I can't tell; she's a woman, and a kind of humorist.[15]

MIRABELL. [*To* PETULANT] And this is the sum of what you could collect last night?

PETULANT. The quintessence. Maybe Witwoud knows more, he stayed longer. Besides, they never mind him; they say anything before him.

MIRABELL. I thought you had been the greatest favorite.

PETULANT. Aye, *tête-à-tête*, but not in public, because I make remarks.

MIRABELL. Do you?

PETULANT. Aye, aye; pox, I'm malicious, man! Now, he's soft, you know; they are not in awe of him—the fellow's well-bred; he's what you call a—what-d'ye-call-'em, a fine gentleman.—But he's silly withal.

MIRABELL. I thank you. I know as much as my curiosity requires.— Fainall, are you for the Mall?[16]

FAINALL. Aye, I'll take a turn before dinner.

WITWOUD. Aye, we'll all walk in the Park; the ladies talked of being there.

MIRABELL. I thought you were obliged to watch for your brother Sir Wilfull's arrival.

WITWOUD. No, no; he comes to his aunt's, my Lady Wishfort. Pox on him! I shall be troubled with him, too; what shall I do with the fool?

PETULANT. Beg him for his estate, that I may beg you afterwards, and so have but one trouble with you both.

WITWOUD. Oh, rare Petulant! Thou art as quick as fire in a frosty morning. Thou shalt to the Mall with us, and we'll be very severe.

PETULANT. Enough! I'm in a humor to be severe.

MIRABELL. Are you? Pray then, walk by yourselves; let not us be accessory to your putting the ladies out of countenance with your senseless ribaldry, which you roar out aloud as often as they pass by you; and when you have made a handsome woman blush, then you think you have been severe.

PETULANT. What, what? Then let 'em either show their innocence

14 Cheated. The uncle is fictitious.
15 Whimsical person.
16 In St. James's Park.

by not understanding what they hear, or else show their discretion by
not hearing what they would not be thought to understand.

MIRABELL. But hast not thou then sense enough to know that thou
oughtest to be most ashamed thyself when thou hast put another out of
countenance?

PETULANT. Not I, by this hand!—I always take blushing either for
a sign of guilt or ill breeding.

MIRABELL. I confess you ought to think so. You are in the right,
that you may plead the error of your judgment in defence of your
practice.

Where modesty's ill manners, 'tis but fit
That impudence and malice pass for wit.

Exeunt

ACT II

SCENE I. *St. James's Park*

Enter MRS. FAINALL *and* MRS. MARWOOD

MRS. FAINALL. Aye, aye, dear Marwood, if we will be happy, we
must find the means in ourselves and among ourselves. Men are ever
in extremes—either doting or averse. While they are lovers, if they
have fire and sense, their jealousies are insupportable; and when they
cease to love—(we ought to think at least) they loathe; they look
upon us with horror and distaste; they meet us like the ghosts of what
we were, and as from such, fly from us.

MRS. MARWOOD. True, 'tis an unhappy circumstance of life that
love should ever die before us, and that the man so often should outlive
the lover. But say what you will, 'tis better to be left than never to
have been loved. To pass our youth in dull indifference, to refuse the
sweets of life because they once must leave us, is as preposterous as to
wish to have been born old because we one day must be old. For my
part, my youth may wear and waste, but it shall never rust in my
possession.

MRS. FAINALL. Then it seems you dissemble an aversion to mankind
only in compliance to my mother's humor?

MRS. MARWOOD. Certainly. To be free; I have no taste of those
insipid dry discourses with which our sex of force must entertain themselves apart from men. We may affect endearments to each other,
profess eternal friendships, and seem to dote like lovers; but 'tis not
in our natures long to persevere. Love will resume his empire in our
breasts, and every heart, or soon or late, receive and readmit him as
its lawful tyrant.

MRS. FAINALL. Bless me, how have I been deceived? Why, you profess a libertine.

MRS. MARWOOD. You see my friendship by my freedom. Come, be as sincere; acknowledge that your sentiments agree with mine.

MRS. FAINALL. Never!

MRS. MARWOOD. You hate mankind?

MRS. FAINALL. Heartily, inveterately.

MRS. MARWOOD. Your husband?

MRS. FAINALL. Most transcendently; aye, though I say it, meritoriously.

MRS. MARWOOD. Give me your hand upon it.

MRS. FAINALL. There.

MRS. MARWOOD. I join with you; what I have said has been to try you.

MRS. FAINALL. Is it possible? Dost thou hate those vipers, men?

MRS. MARWOOD. I have done hating 'em, and am now come to despise 'em; the next thing I have to do is eternally to forget 'em.

MRS. FAINALL. There spoke the spirit of an Amazon, a Penthesilea![1]

MRS. MARWOOD. And yet I am thinking sometimes to carry my aversion further.

MRS. FAINALL. How?

MRS. MARWOOD. Faith, by marrying; if I could but find one that loved me very well and would be thoroughly sensible of ill usage, I think I should do myself the violence of undergoing the ceremony.

MRS. FAINALL. You would not make him a cuckold?

MRS. MARWOOD. No; but I'd make him believe I did, and that's as bad.

MRS. FAINALL. Why had not you as good do it?

MRS. MARWOOD. Oh, if he should ever discover it, he would then know the worst and be out of his pain; but I would have him ever to continue upon the rack of fear and jealousy.

MRS. FAINALL. Ingenious mischief! would thou wert married to Mirabell.

MRS. MARWOOD. Would I were!

MRS. FAINALL. You change color.

MRS. MARWOOD. Because I hate him.

MRS. FAINALL. So do I, but I can hear him named. But what reason have you to hate him in particular?

MRS. MARWOOD. I never loved him; he is, and always was, insufferably proud.

MRS. FAINALL. By the reason you give for your aversion, one would think it dissembled; for you have laid a fault to his charge, of which his enemies must acquit him.

---

[1] Queen of the Amazons at the time of the Trojan War.

MRS. MARWOOD. Oh, then it seems you are one of his favorable enemies! Methinks you look a little pale—and now you flush again.

MRS. FAINALL. Do I? I think I am a little sick o' the sudden.

MRS. MARWOOD. What ails you?

MRS. FAINALL. My husband. Don't you see him? He turned short upon me unawares, and has almost overcome me.

Enter FAINALL *and* MIRABELL

MRS. MARWOOD. Ha, ha, ha! He comes opportunely for you.

MRS. FAINALL. For you, for he has brought Mirabell with him.

FAINALL. [*To* MRS. FAINALL] My dear!

MRS. FAINALL. My soul!

FAINALL. You don't look well to-day, child.

MRS. FAINALL. D'ye think so?

MIRABELL. He is the only man that does, madam.

MRS. FAINALL. The only man that would tell me so, at least, and the only man from whom I could hear it without mortification.

FAINALL. Oh, my dear, I am satisfied of your tenderness; I know you cannot resent anything from me, especially what is an effect of my concern.

MRS. FAINALL. Mr. Mirabell, my mother interrupted you in a pleasant relation last night; I would fain hear it out.

MIRABELL. The persons concerned in that affair have yet a tolerable reputation. I am afraid Mr. Fainall will be censorious.

MRS. FAINALL. He has a humor more prevailing than his curiosity, and will willingly dispense with the hearing of one scandalous story, to avoid giving an occasion to make another by being seen to walk with his wife. This way, Mr. Mirabell, and I dare promise you will oblige us both.   *Exeunt* MRS. FAINALL *and* MIRABELL

FAINALL. Excellent creature! Well, sure if I should live to be rid of my wife, I should be a miserable man.

MRS. MARWOOD. Aye?

FAINALL. For having only that one hope, the accomplishment of it, of consequence, must put an end to all my hopes; and what a wretch is he who must survive his hopes! Nothing remains when that day comes but to sit down and weep like Alexander when he wanted other worlds to conquer.

MRS. MARWOOD. Will you not follow 'em?

FAINALL. Faith, I think not.

MRS. MARWOOD. Pray, let us; I have a reason.

FAINALL. You are not jealous?

MRS. MARWOOD. Of whom?

FAINALL. Of Mirabell.

MRS. MARWOOD. If I am, is it inconsistent with my love to you that I am tender of your honor?

FAINALL. You would intimate, then, as if [there] were a fellow-feeling between my wife and him.

MRS. MARWOOD. I think she does not hate him to that degree she would be thought.

FAINALL. But he, I fear, is too insensible.

MRS. MARWOOD. It may be you are deceived.

FAINALL. It may be so. I do not now begin to apprehend it.

MRS. MARWOOD. What?

FAINALL. That I have been deceived, madam, and you are false.

MRS. MARWOOD. That I am false! What mean you?

FAINALL. To let you know I see through all your little arts.—Come, you both love him, and both have equally dissembled your aversion. Your mutual jealousies of one another have made you clash till you have both struck fire. I have seen the warm confession reddening on your cheeks and sparkling from your eyes.

MRS. MARWOOD. You do me wrong.

FAINALL. I do not. 'Twas for my ease to oversee and willfully neglect the gross advances made him by my wife, that by permitting her to be engaged, I might continue unsuspected in my pleasures and take you oftener to my arms in full security. But could you think, because the nodding husband would not wake, that e'er the watchful lover slept?

MRS. MARWOOD. And wherewithal can you reproach me?

FAINALL. With infidelity, with loving another—with love of Mirabell.

MRS. MARWOOD. 'Tis false! I challenge you to show an instance that can confirm your groundless accusation. I hate him!

FAINALL. And wherefore do you hate him? He is insensible, and your resentment follows his neglect. An instance!—the injuries you have done him are a proof—your interposing in his love. What cause had you to make discoveries of his pretended passion?—to undeceive the credulous aunt, and be the officious obstacle of his match with Millamant?

MRS. MARWOOD. My obligations to my lady urged me. I had professed a friendship to her, and could not see her easy nature so abused by that dissembler.

FAINALL. What, was it conscience then? Professed a friendship! Oh, the pious friendships of the female sex!

MRS. MARWOOD. More tender, more sincere, and more enduring than all the vain and empty vows of men, whether professing love to us or mutual faith to one another.

FAINALL. Ha, ha, ha! You are my wife's friend, too.

MRS. MARWOOD. Shame and ingratitude! Do you reproach me? You, you upbraid me? Have I been false to her, through strict fidelity to you, and sacrificed my friendship to keep my love inviolate? And have you the baseness to charge me with the guilt, unmindful of the merit? To you it should be meritorious that I have been vicious; and do you reflect that guilt upon me which should lie buried in your bosom?

FAINALL. You misinterpret my reproof. I meant but to remind you of the slight account you once could make of strictest ties when set in competition with your love to me.

MRS. MARWOOD. 'Tis false; you urged it with deliberate malice! 'Twas spoke in scorn, and I never will forgive it.

FAINALL. Your guilt, not your resentment, begets your rage. If yet you loved, you could forgive a jealousy; but you are stung to find you are discovered.

MRS. MARWOOD. It shall be all discovered.—You too shall be discovered; be sure you shall. I can but be exposed.—If I do it myself I shall prevent your baseness.

FAINALL. Why, what will you do?

MRS. MARWOOD. Disclose it to your wife; own what has passed between us.

FAINALL. Frenzy!

MRS. MARWOOD. By all my wrongs I'll do't!—I'll publish to the world the injuries you have done me, both in my fame and fortune! With both I trusted you,—you bankrupt in honor, as indigent of wealth.

FAINALL. Your fame I have preserved. Your fortune has been bestowed as the prodigality of your love would have it, in pleasures which we both have shared. Yet, had not you been false, I had ere this repaid it. 'Tis true. Had you permitted Mirabell with Millamant to have stolen their marriage, my lady had been incensed beyond all means of reconcilement; Millamant had forfeited the moiety of her fortune, which then would have descended to my wife—and wherefore did I marry but to make lawful prize of a rich widow's wealth, and squander it on love and you?

MRS. MARWOOD. Deceit and frivolous pretence!

FAINALL. Death, am I not married? What's pretence? Am I not imprisoned, fettered? Have I not a wife?—nay, a wife that was a widow, a young widow, a handsome widow; and would be again a widow, but that I have a heart of proof, and something of a constitution to bustle through the ways of wedlock and this world! Will you yet be reconciled to truth and me?

MRS. MARWOOD. Impossible. Truth and you are inconsistent—I hate you, and shall forever.

FAINALL. For loving you?

MRS. MARWOOD. I loathe the name of love after such usage; and next to the guilt with which you would asperse me, I scorn you most. Farewell!

FAINALL. Nay, we must not part thus.

MRS. MARWOOD. Let me go.

FAINALL. Come, I'm sorry.

MRS. MARWOOD. I care not—let me go—break my hands, do! I'd leave 'em to get loose.

FAINALL. I would not hurt you for the world. Have I no other hold to keep you here?

MRS. MARWOOD. Well, I have deserved it all.

FAINALL. You know I love you.

MRS. MARWOOD. Poor dissembling!—Oh, that—well, it is not yet—

FAINALL. What? What is it not? What is it not yet? It is not yet too late—

MRS. MARWOOD. No, it is not yet too late—I have that comfort.

FAINALL. It is, to love another.

MRS. MARWOOD. But not to loathe, detest, abhor mankind, myself, and the whole treacherous world.

FAINALL. Nay, this is extravagance!—Come, I ask your pardon— no tears—I was to blame, I could not love you and be easy in my doubts. Pray, forbear—I believe you; I'm convinced I've done you wrong, and any way, every way will make amends. I'll hate my wife yet more, damn her! I'll part with her, rob her of all she's worth, and we'll retire somewhere—anywhere—to another world. I'll marry thee—be pacified— 'Sdeath, they come! Hide your face, your tears.—You have a mask; wear it a moment. This way, this way—be persuaded.   *Exeunt*

Enter MIRABELL *and* MRS. FAINALL.

MRS. FAINALL. They are here yet.

MIRABELL. They are turning into the other walk.

MRS. FAINALL. While I only hated my husband, I could bear to see him; but since I have despised him, he's too offensive.

MIRABELL. Oh, you should hate with prudence.

MRS. FAINALL. Yes, for I have loved with indiscretion.

MIRABELL. You should have just so much disgust for your husband as may be sufficient to make you relish your lover.

MRS. FAINALL. You have been the cause that I have loved without bounds, and would you set limits to that aversion of which you have been the occasion? Why did you make me marry this man?

MIRABELL. Why do we daily commit disagreeable and dangerous actions? To save that idol, reputation. If the familiarities of our loves had produced that consequence of which you were apprehensive, where could you have fixed a father's name with credit but on a husband? I knew Fainall to be a man lavish of his morals, an interested and professing friend, a false and a designing lover, yet one whose wit and outward fair behavior have gained a reputation with the town enough to make that woman stand excused who has suffered herself to be won by his addresses. A better man ought not to have been sacrificed to the occasion, a worse had not answered to the purpose. When you are weary of him, you know your remedy.

MRS. FAINALL. I ought to stand in some degree of credit with you, Mirabell.

MIRABELL. In justice to you, I have made you privy to my whole design, and put it in your power to ruin or advance my fortune.

MRS. FAINALL. Whom have you instructed to represent your pretended uncle?

MIRABELL. Waitwell, my servant.

MRS. FAINALL. He is an humble servant[2] to Foible, my mother's woman, and may win her to your interest.

MIRABELL. Care is taken for that—she is won and worn by this time. They were married this morning.

MRS. FAINALL. Who?

MIRABELL. Waitwell and Foible. I would not tempt my servant to betray me by trusting him too far. If your mother, in hopes to ruin me, should consent to marry my pretended uncle, he might, like Mosca in *The Fox*,[3] stand upon terms; so I made him sure beforehand.

MRS. FAINALL. So if my poor mother is caught in a contract, you will discover the imposture betimes, and release her by producing a certificate of her gallant's former marriage.

MIRABELL. Yes, upon condition that she consent to my marriage with her niece, and surrender the moiety of her fortune in her possession.

MRS. FAINALL. She talked last night of endeavoring at a match between Millamant and your uncle.

MIRABELL. That was by Foible's direction and my instruction, that she might seem to carry it more privately.

MRS. FAINALL. Well, I have an opinion of your success; for I believe my lady will do anything to get a husband; and when she has this which you have provided for her, I suppose she will submit to anything to get rid of him.

MIRABELL. Yes, I think the good lady would marry anything that resembled a man, though 'twere no more than what a butler could pinch out of a napkin.

MRS. FAINALL. Female frailty! We must all come to it if we live to be old and feel the craving of a false appetite when the true is decayed.

MIRABELL. An old woman's appetite is depraved like that of a girl— 'tis the green sickness of a second childhood, and, like the faint offer of a latter spring, serves but to usher in the fall, and withers in an affected bloom.

MRS. FAINALL. Here's your mistress.

[2] Suitor.   [3] Mosca is the parasite in Ben Jonson's *Volpone* (1605).

Enter MRS. MILLAMANT, WITWOUD, *and* MINCING

MIRABELL. Here she comes, i'faith, full sail, with her fan spread and her streamers out, and a shoal of fools for tenders. Ha, no, I cry her mercy!

MRS. FAINALL. I see but one poor empty sculler, and he tows her woman after him.

MIRABELL. [*To* MRS. MILLAMANT] You seem to be unattended, madam. You used to have the *beau monde*[4] throng after you, and a flock of gay fine perukes hovering round you.

WITWOUD. Like moths about a candle. — I had like to have lost my comparison for want of breath.

MRS. MILLAMANT. Oh, I have denied myself airs to-day. I have walked as fast through the crowd —

WITWOUD. As a favorite just disgraced, and with as few followers.

MRS. MILLAMANT. Dear Mr. Witwoud, truce with your similitudes; for I'm as sick of 'em —

WITWOUD. As a physician of a good air. — I cannot help it, madam, though 'tis against myself.

MRS. MILLAMANT. Yet again! Mincing, stand between me and his wit.

WITWOUD. Do, Mrs. Mincing, like a screen before a great fire. — I confess I do blaze to-day; I am too bright.

MRS. FAINALL. But, dear Millamant, why were you so long?

MRS. MILLAMANT. Long! Lord, have I not made violent haste? I have asked every living thing I met for you; I have inquired after you as after a new fashion.

WITWOUD. Madam, truce with your similitudes. — No, you met her husband, and did not ask him for her.

MRS. MILLAMANT. By your leave, Witwoud, that were like inquiring after an old fashion, to ask a husband for his wife.

WITWOUD. Hum, a hit! a hit! a palpable hit! I confess it.

MRS. FAINALL. You were dressed before I came abroad.

MRS. MILLAMANT. Aye, that's true. — Oh, but then I had — Mincing, what had I? Why was I so long?

MINCING. O mem, your la'ship stayed to peruse a pecquet[5] of letters.

MRS. MILLAMANT. Oh, aye, letters — I had letters — I am persecuted with letters — I hate letters. — Nobody knows how to write letters — and yet one has 'em, one does not know why. They serve one to pin up one's hair.

WITWOUD. Is that the way? Pray, madam, do you pin up your hair with all your letters? I find I must keep copies.

---

[4] The world of fashion.
[5] Packet. Mrs. Mincing's pronunciation is ignorantly affected.

MRS. MILLAMANT. Only with those in verse, Mr. Witwoud; I never pin up my hair with prose. I think I tried once, Mincing.

MINCING. O mem, I shall never forget it.

MRS. MILLAMANT. Aye, poor Mincing tift and tift[6] all the morning.

MINCING. Till I had the cremp in my fingers, I'll vow, mem; and all to no purpose. But when your la'ship pins it up with poetry, it sits so pleasant the next day as anything, and is so pure and so crips.

WITWOUD. Indeed, so "crips"?

MINCING. You're such a critic, Mr. Witwoud.

MRS. MILLAMANT. Mirabell, did you take exceptions last night? Oh, aye, and went away. Now I think on't I'm angry — No, now I think on't I'm pleased — for I believe I gave you some pain.

MIRABELL. Does that please you?

MRS. MILLAMANT. Infinitely; I love to give pain.

MIRABELL. You would affect a cruelty which is not in your nature; your true vanity is in the power of pleasing.

MRS. MILLAMANT. Oh, I ask your pardon for that — one's cruelty is one's power; and when one parts with one's cruelty, one parts with one's power; and when one has parted with that, I fancy one's old and ugly.

MIRABELL. Aye, aye, suffer your cruelty to ruin the object of your power, to destroy your lover — and then how vain, how lost a thing you'll be! Nay, 'tis true: you are no longer handsome when you've lost your lover; your beauty dies upon the instant, for beauty is the lover's gift. 'Tis he bestows your charms — your glass is all a cheat. The ugly and the old, whom the looking-glass mortifies, yet after commendation can be flattered by it and discover beauties in it; for that reflects our praises, rather than your face.

MRS. MILLAMANT. Oh, the vanity of these men! Fainall, d'ye hear him? If they did not commend us, we were not handsome! Now you must know they could not commend one, if one was not handsome. Beauty the lover's gift! — Lord, what is a lover, that it can give? Why, one makes lovers as fast as one pleases, and they live as long as one pleases, and they die as soon as one pleases: and then, if one pleases, one makes more.

WITWOUD. Very pretty. Why, you make no more of making of lovers, madam, than of making so many card-matches.

MRS. MILLAMANT. One no more owes one's beauty to a lover, than one's wit to an echo. They can but reflect what we look and say — vain empty things if we are silent or unseen, and want a being.

MIRABELL. Yet to those two vain empty things you owe two the greatest pleasures of your life.

MRS. MILLAMANT. How so?

---

[6] Set in order; arranged.

MIRABELL. To your lover you owe the pleasure of hearing yourselves praised, and to an echo the pleasure of hearing yourselves talk.

WITWOUD. But I know a lady that loves talking so incessantly, she won't give an echo fair play; she has that everlasting rotation of tongue, that an echo must wait till she dies before it can catch her last words.

MRS. MILLAMANT. Oh, fiction! — Fainall, let us leave these men.

MIRABELL. (Aside to MRS. FAINALL) Draw off Witwoud.

MRS. FAINALL. Immediately. — [Aloud] I have a word or two for Mr. Witwoud.   Exeunt WITWOUD and MRS. FAINALL

MIRABELL. [To MRS. MILLAMANT] I would beg a little private audience too. — You had the tyranny to deny me last night, though you knew I came to impart a secret to you that concerned my love.

MRS. MILLAMANT. You saw I was engaged.

MIRABELL. Unkind! You had the leisure to entertain a herd of fools — things who visit you from their excessive idleness, bestowing on your easiness that time which is the encumbrance of their lives. How can you find delight in such society? It is impossible they should admire you; they are not capable — or if they were, it should be to you as a mortification, for sure to please a fool is some degree of folly.

MRS. MILLAMANT. I please myself. Besides, sometimes to converse with fools is for my health.

MIRABELL. Your health! Is there a worse disease than the conversation of fools?

MRS. MILLAMANT. Yes, the vapors; fools are physic for it, next to asafoetida.

MIRABELL. You are not in a course of fools?

MRS. MILLAMANT. Mirabell, if you persist in this offensive freedom, you'll displease me. I think I must resolve, after all, not to have you. We shan't agree.

MIRABELL. Not in our physic, it may be.

MRS. MILLAMANT. And yet our distemper, in all likelihood, will be the same; for we shall be sick of one another. I shan't endure to be reprimanded nor instructed; 'tis so dull to act always by advice, and so tedious to be told of one's faults — I can't bear it. Well, I won't have you, Mirabell, — I'm resolved — I think — you may go. — Ha, ha, ha! What would you give that you could help loving me?

MIRABELL. I would give something that you did not know I could not help it.

MRS. MILLIMANT. Come, don't look grave, then. Well, what do you say to me?

MIRABELL. I say that a man may as soon make a friend by his wit, or a fortune by his honesty, as win a woman with plain dealing and sincerity.

MRS. MILLAMANT. Sententious Mirabell! Prithee, don't look with

that violent and inflexible wise face, like Solomon at the dividing of
the child in an old tapestry hanging.

MIRABELL. You are merry, madam, but I would persuade you for a
moment to be serious.

MRS. MILLAMANT. What, with that face? No, if you keep your
countenance, 'tis impossible I should hold mine. Well, after all, there
is something very moving in a lovesick face. Ha, ha, ha! — Well, I
won't laugh; don't be peevish — Heigho! now I'll be melancholy — as
melancholy as a watch-light.[7] Well, Mirabell, if ever you will win me,
woo me now. — Nay, if you are so tedious, fare you well; I see they
are walking away.

MIRABELL. Can you not find in the variety of your disposition one
moment —

MRS. MILLAMANT. To hear you tell me Foible's married, and your
plot like to speed? No.

MIRABELL. But how came you to know it?

MRS. MILLAMANT. Without the help of the devil, you can't imagine
— unless she should tell me herself. Which of the two it may have
been I will leave you to consider; and when you have done thinking of
that, think of me.   [*Exit* MRS. MILLAMANT]

MIRABELL. I have something more — Gone! — Think of you? To
think of a whirlwind, though 'twere in a whirlwind, were a case of
more steady contemplation — a very tranquillity of mind and mansion.
A fellow that lives in a windmill, has not a more whimsical dwelling
than the heart of a man that is lodged in a woman. There is no point
of the compass to which they cannot turn, and by which they are not
turned; and by one as well as another. For motion, not method, is their
occupation. To know this, and yet continue to be in love, is to be
made wise from the dictates of reason, and yet persevere to play the
fool by the force of instinct. — Oh, here come my pair of turtles! —
What, billing so sweetly! Is not Valentine's Day over with you yet?

Enter WAITWELL and FOIBLE

Sirrah Waitwell; why, sure you think you were married for your own
recreation, and not for my conveniency.

WAITWELL. Your pardon, sir. With submission, we have indeed
been solacing in lawful delights; but still with an eye to business, sir.
I have instructed her as well as I could. If she can take your directions
as readily as my instructions, sir, your affairs are in a prosperous way.

MIRABELL. Give you joy, Mrs. Foible.

FOIBLE. Oh, 'las, sir, I'm so ashamed! — I'm afraid my lady has
been in a thousand inquietudes for me. But I protest, sir, I made as
much haste as I could.

---

[7] A night light in a sick room.

WAITWELL. That she did indeed, sir. It was my fault that she did not make more.

MIRABELL. That I believe.

FOIBLE. But I told my lady as you instructed me, sir, that I had a prospect of seeing Sir Rowland, your uncle; and that I would put her ladyship's picture in my pocket to show him, which I'll be sure to say has made him so enamored of her beauty, that he burns with impatience to lie at her ladyship's feet and worship the original.

MIRABELL. Excellent Foible! Matrimony has made you eloquent in love.

WAITWELL. I think she has profited, sir; I think so.

FOIBLE. You have seen Madam Millamant, sir?

MIRABELL. Yes.

FOIBLE. I told her, sir, because I did not know that you might find an opportunity; she had so much company last night.

MIRABELL. Your diligence will merit more — in the meantime —

(Gives [her] money)

FOIBLE. O dear sir, your humble servant!

WAITWELL. Spouse.

MIRABELL. Stand off, sir, not a penny! — Go on and prosper, Foible. The lease shall be made good and the farm stocked if we succeed.

FOIBLE. I don't question your generosity, sir, and you need not doubt of success. If you have no more commands, sir, I'll be gone; I'm sure my lady is at her toilet, and can't dress till I come. — Oh, dear, (Looking out) I'm sure that was Mrs. Marwood that went by in a mask! If she has seen me with you, I'm sure she'll tell my lady. I'll make haste home and prevent her. Your servant, sir. — B'w'y, Waitwell. [Exit FOIBLE]

WAITWELL. Sir Rowland, if you please. — The jade's so pert upon her preferment she forgets herself.

MIRABELL. Come, sir, will you endeavor to forget yourself, and transform into Sir Rowland?

WAITWELL. Why, sir, it will be impossible I should remember myself. — Married, knighted, and attended all in one day! 'tis enough to make any man forget himself. The difficulty will be how to recover my acquaintance and familiarity with my former self, and fall from my transformation to a reformation into Waitwell. Nay, I shan't be quite the same Waitwell neither; for now I remember me, I'm married and can't be my own man again.

Aye, there's the grief; that's the sad change of life,
To lose my title, and yet keep my wife. Exeunt

ACT III

SCENE I. A *room in* LADY WISHFORT'S *house*
LADY WISHFORT *at her toilet,* PEG *waiting*

LADY WISHFORT. Merciful! no news of Foible yet?

PEG. No, madam.

LADY WISHFORT. I have no more patience. If I have not fretted my-self till I am pale again, there's no veracity in me! Fetch me the red — the red, do you hear, sweetheart? An arrant ash-color, as I'm a person! Look you how this wench stirs! Why dost thou not fetch me a little red? Didst thou not hear me, Mopus?[1]

PEG. The red ratafia, does your ladyship mean, or the cherry-brandy?

LADY WISHFORT. Ratafia, fool! No, fool. Not the ratafia, fool — grant me patience! — I mean the Spanish paper,[2] idiot — complexion, darling. Paint, paint, paint! — dost thou understand that, changeling, dangling thy hands like bobbins before thee? Why dost thou not stir, puppet? Thou wooden thing upon wires!

PEG. Lord, madam, your ladyship is so impatient! — I cannot come at the paint, madam; Mrs. Foible has locked it up and carried the key with her.

LADY WISHFORT. A pox take you both! Fetch me the cherry-brandy then. (*Exit* PEG) I'm as pale and as faint, I look like Mrs. Qualmsick, the curate's wife, that's always breeding. — Wench! Come, come, wench, what art thou doing? Sipping? Tasting? Save thee, dost thou not know the bottle?

Enter PEG *with a bottle and china cup*

PEG. Madam, I was looking for a cup.

LADY WISHFORT. A cup, save thee! and what a cup hast thou brought! Dost thou take me for a fairy, to drink out of an acorn? Why didst thou not bring thy thimble? Hast thou ne'er a brass thimble clinking in thy pocket with a bit of nutmeg? — I warrant thee. Come, fill, fill! — So — again. — (*One knocks*) — See who that is. Set down the bottle first. Here, here, under the table. What, wouldst thou go with the bottle in thy hand, like a tapster? As I'm a person, this wench has lived in an inn upon the road before she came to me, like Maritornes[3] the Asturian in *Don Quixote!* — No Foible yet?

PEG. No, madam, Mrs. Marwood.

[1] Mope, dull person.

[2] Used for cosmetic purposes.

[3] *Don Quixote*, Part I, xvi; or Lady Wishfort may have been thinking of D'Urfey's *The Comical History of Don Quixote* (1694), Part I, II, i.

LADY WISHFORT. Oh, Marwood; let her come in. — Come in, good
Marwood.

Enter MRS. MARWOOD

MRS. MARWOOD. I'm surprised to find your ladyship in dishabille at
this time of day.

LADY WISHFORT. Foible's a lost thing — has been abroad since morning, and never heard of since.

MRS. MARWOOD. I saw her but now as I came masked through the
park, in conference with Mirabell.

LADY WISHFORT. With Mirabell! You call my blood into my face,
with mentioning that traitor. She durst not have the confidence! I
sent her to negotiate an affair in which, if I'm detected, I'm undone.
If that wheedling villain has wrought upon Foible to detect me, I'm
ruined. Oh, my dear friend, I'm a wretch of wretches if I'm detected.

MRS. MARWOOD. O madam, you cannot suspect Mrs. Foible's integrity.

LADY WISHFORT. Oh, he carries poison in his tongue that would
corrupt integrity itself! If she has given him an opportunity, she has
as good as put her integrity into his hands. Ah, dear Marwood, what's
integrity to an opportunity? — Hark! I hear her! [*To* PEG] Go, you
thing, and send her in. *Exit* PEG
[*To* MRS. MARWOOD] Dear friend, retire into my closet, that I may
examine her with more freedom. — You'll pardon me, dear friend; I
can make bold with you. There are books over the chimney — Quarles
and Prynne, and *The Short View of the Stage*, with Bunyan's works,
to entertain you.[4] *Exit* MRS. MARWOOD

Enter FOIBLE

LADY WISHFORT. O Foible, where hast thou been? What hast thou
been doing?

FOIBLE. Madam, I have seen the party.

LADY WISHFORT. But what hast thou done?

FOIBLE. Nay, 'tis your ladyship has done, and are to do; I have only
promised. But a man so enamored — so transported! — Well, if
worshipping of pictures be a sin — poor Sir Rowland, I say.

LADY WISHFORT. The miniature has been counted like — but hast
thou not betrayed me, Foible? Hast thou not detected me to that
faithless Mirabell? — What hadst thou to do with him in the Park?
Answer me; has he got nothing out of thee?

FOIBLE. [*Aside*] So the devil has been beforehand with me. What
shall I say? — [*Aloud*] — Alas, madam, could I help it if I met that

---

[4] Possibly Francis Quarles' *Divine Emblems* (1635), William Prynne's
Histrio-Mastix (1633), and Jeremy Collier's A *Short View of the Immorality
and Profaneness of the English Stage* (1698).

confident thing? Was I in fault? If you had heard how he used me, and all upon your ladyship's account, I'm sure you would not suspect my fidelity. Nay, if that had been the worst, I could have borne; but he had a fling at your ladyship too, and then I could not hold; but i'faith I gave him his own.

LADY WISHFORT. Me? What did the filthy fellow say?

FOIBLE. Oh, madam! 'tis a shame to say what he said — with his taunts and his fleers, tossing up his nose. Humh! (says he) what, you are a hatching some plot (says he), you are so early abroad, or catering (says he), ferreting for some disbanded officer, I warrant. — Half-pay is but thin subsistence (says he) — well, what pension does your lady propose? Let me see (says he); what, she must come down pretty deep now, she's superannuated (says he) and —

LADY WISHFORT. Odds my life, I'll have him — I'll have him murdered! I'll have him poisoned! Where does he eat? — I'll marry a drawer to have him poisoned in his wine. I'll send for Robin from Locket's[5] immediately.

FOIBLE. Poison him! poisoning's too good for him. Starve him, madam, starve him: marry Sir Rowland, and get him disinherited. Oh, you would bless yourself to hear what he said!

LADY WISHFORT. A villain! Superannuated!

FOIBLE. Humh (says he), I hear you are laying designs against me too (says he), and Mrs. Millamant is to marry my uncle (he does not suspect a word of your ladyship); but (says he) I'll fit you for that, I warrant you (says he), I'll hamper you for that (says he) — you and your old frippery[6] too (says he); I'll handle you —

LADY WISHFORT. Audacious villain! Handle me, would he durst! — Frippery? old frippery! Was there ever such a foul-mouthed fellow? I'll be married to-morrow; I'll be contracted to-night.

FOIBLE. The sooner the better, madam. ·

LADY WISHFORT. Will Sir Rowland be here, sayest thou? When, Foible?

FOIBLE. Incontinently, madam. No new sheriff's wife expects the return of her husband after knighthood with that impatience in which Sir Rowland burns for the dear hour of kissing your ladyship's hand after dinner.

LADY WISHFORT. Frippery! superannuated frippery! I'll frippery the villain; I'll reduce him to frippery and rags! a tatterdemalion! I hope to see him hung with tatters, like a Long Lane penthouse[7] or a gibbet thief. A slander-mouthed railer! I warrant the spendthrift prodigal's

---

[5] The fashionable tavern at Charing Cross. Robin may have been a real tapster or the generic name for any drawer or waiter in a tavern.

[6] Tawdry finery.

[7] An old-clothes' dealer's stall in Long Lane, Smithfield.

in debt as much as the million lottery,[8] or the whole Court upon a birthday. I'll spoil his credit with his tailor. Yes, he shall have my niece with her fortune, he shall.

FOIBLE. He! I hope to see him lodge in Ludgate[9] first, and angle into Blackfriars for brass farthings with an old mitten.

LADY WISHFORT. Aye, dear Foible; thank thee for that, dear Foible. He has put me out of all patience. I shall never recompose my features to receive Sir Rowland with any economy of face. This wretch has fretted me that I am absolutely decayed. Look, Foible.

FOIBLE. Your ladyship has frowned a little too rashly, indeed, madam. There are some cracks discernible in the white varnish.

LADY WISHFORT. Let me see the glass. — Cracks, sayest thou? — why, I am arrantly flayed — I look like an old peeled wall. Thou must repair me, Foible, before Sir Rowland comes, or I shall never keep up to my picture.

FOIBLE. I warrant you, madam, a little art once made your picture like you, and now a little of the same art must make you like your picture. Your picture must sit for you, madam.

LADY WISHFORT. But art thou sure Sir Rowland will not fail to come? Or will he not fail when he does come? Will he be importunate, Foible, and push? For if he should not be importunate, I shall never break decorums — I shall die with confusion if I am forced to advance. — Oh, no, I can never advance! — I shall swoon if he should expect advances. No, I hope Sir Rowland is better bred than to put a lady to the necessity of breaking her forms. I won't be too coy, neither.— I won't give him despair — but a little disdain is not amiss, a little scorn is alluring.

FOIBLE. A little scorn becomes your ladyship.

LADY WISHFORT. Yes, but tenderness becomes me best — a sort of dyingness — you see that picture has a sort of a — ha, Foible? a swimmingness in the eyes — yes, I'll look so. — My niece affects it, but she wants features. Is Sir Rowland handsome? Let my toilet be removed — I'll dress above. I'll receive Sir Rowland here. — Is he handsome? Don't answer me. I won't know; I'll be surprised. I'll be taken by surprise.

FOIBLE. By storm, madam. Sir Rowland's a brisk man.

LADY WISHFORT. Is he? Oh, then he'll importune, if he's a brisk man. I shall save decorums if Sir Rowland importunes. I have a mortal terror at the apprehension of offending against decorums. Oh, I'm glad he's a brisk man! — Let my things be removed, good Foible.

[*Exit* LADY WISHFORT]

---

[8] A government lottery in 1694.
[9] The Fleet Prison for debtors.

Enter MRS. FAINALL.[10]

MRS. FAINALL. Oh, Foible, I have been in a fright lest I should come too late! That devil Marwood saw you in the Park with Mirabell, and I'm afraid will discover it to my lady.

FOIBLE. Discover what, madam?

MRS. FAINALL. Nay, nay, put not on that strange face! I am privy to the whole design and know that Waitwell, to whom thou wert this morning married, is to personate Mirabell's uncle, and as such, winning my lady, to involve her in those difficulties from which Mirabell only must release her, by his making his conditions to have my cousin and her fortune left to her own disposal.

FOIBLE. Oh, dear madam, I beg your pardon. It was not my confidence in your ladyship that was deficient, but I thought the former good correspondence between your ladyship and Mr. Mirabell might have hindered his communicating this secret.

MRS. FAINALL. Dear Foible, forget that.

FOIBLE. O dear madam, Mr. Mirabell is such a sweet, winning gentleman — but your ladyship is the pattern of generosity. Sweet lady, to be so good! Mr. Mirabell cannot choose but be grateful. I find your ladyship has his heart still. Now, madam, I can safely tell your ladyship our success; Mrs. Marwood has told my lady, but I warrant I managed myself. I turned it all for the better. I told my lady that Mr. Mirabell railed at her; I laid horrid things to his charge, I'll vow; and my lady is so incensed that she'll be contracted to Sir Rowland tonight, she says. I warrant I worked her up, that he may have her for asking for, as they say of a Welsh maidenhead.

MRS. FAINALL. O rare Foible!

FOIBLE. Madam, I beg your ladyship to acquaint Mr. Mirabell of his success. I would be seen as little as possible to speak to him; besides, I believe Madam Marwood watches me. — She has a month's mind;[11] but I know Mr. Mirabell can't abide her. — [*Enter Footman*] John, remove my lady's toilet. — Madam, your servant; my lady is so impatient I fear she'll come for me if I stay.

MRS. FAINALL. I'll go with you up the back stairs lest I should meet her.   *Exeunt*

Enter MRS. MARWOOD

MRS. MARWOOD. Indeed, Mrs. Engine, is it thus with you? Are you become a go-between of this importance? — Yes, I shall watch you. Why, this wench is the *passe-partout*, a very master-key to everybody's strong-box. My friend Fainall, have you carried it so swimmingly? I thought there was something in it, but it seems it's over with you.

10 It should be understood that Mrs. Marwood overhears the following conversation. Probably her face would appear throughout at one of the stage doors.
11 An eager desire for Mirabell.

Your loathing is not from a want of appetite, then, but from a surfeit. Else you could never be so cool to fall from a principal to be an assistant, — to procure for him! A pattern of generosity, that, I confess. Well, Mr. Fainall, you have met with your match. — O man, man! Woman, woman! The devil's an ass; if I were a painter, I would draw him like an idiot, a driveller with a bib and bells. Man should have his head and horns,[12] and woman the rest of him. Poor simple fiend! — "Madam Marwood has a month's mind, but he can't abide her." — 'Twere better for him you had not been his confessor in that affair, without you could have kept his counsel closer. I shall not prove another pattern of generosity; he has not obliged me to that with those excesses of himself! And now I'll have none of him. — Here comes the good lady, panting ripe, with a heart full of hope, and a head full of care, like any chemist upon the day of projection.[13]

Enter LADY WISHFORT

LADY WISHFORT. Oh, dear Marwood, what shall I say for this rude forgetfulness? — but my dear friend is all goodness.

MRS. MARWOOD. No apologies, dear madam; I have been very well entertained.

LADY WISHFORT. As I'm a person, I am in a very chaos to think I should so forget myself: but I have such an olio of affairs, really I know not what to do. — [*Calls*] Foible! — I expect my nephew, Sir Wilfull, every moment, too. — [*Calls again*] Why, Foible! — He means to travel for improvement.

MRS. MARWOOD. Methinks Sir Wilfull should rather think of marrying than travelling, at his years. I hear he is turned of forty.

LADY WISHFORT. Oh, he's in less danger of being spoiled by his travels. I am against my nephew's marrying too young. It will be time enough when he comes back and has acquired discretion to choose for himself.

MRS. MARWOOD. Methinks Mrs. Millamant and he would make a very fit match. He may travel afterwards. 'Tis a thing very usual with young gentlemen.

LADY WISHFORT. I promise you I have thought on't — and since 'tis your judgment, I'll think on't again. I assure you I will. I value your judgment extremely. On my word, I'll propose it.

Enter FOIBLE

LADY WISHFORT. Come, come, Foible — I had forgot my nephew will be here before dinner. I must make haste.

FOIBLE. Mr. Witwoud and Mr. Petulant are come to dine with your ladyship.

---

[12] Horns were the symbols of a cuckold.
[13] The day on which an alchemist cast into his crucible the element which he hoped would transmute base metal to gold.

LADY WISHFORT. Oh, dear, I can't appear till I'm dressed! Dear Marwood, shall I be free with you again, and beg you to entertain 'em? I'll make all imaginable haste. Dear friend, excuse me.

[*Exeunt* LADY WISHFORT *and* FOIBLE]

Enter MRS. MILLAMANT *and* MINCING

MRS. MILLAMANT. Sure never anything was so unbred as that odious man! — Marwood, your servant.

MRS. MARWOOD. You have a color; what's the matter?

MRS. MILLAMANT. That horrid fellow, Petulant, has provoked me into a flame. I have broken my fan. — Mincing, lend me yours. Is not all the powder out of my hair?

MRS. MARWOOD. No. What has he done?

MRS. MILLAMANT. Nay, he has done nothing; he has only talked — nay, he has said nothing neither, but he has contradicted everything that has been said. For my part, I thought Witwoud and he would have quarrelled.

MINCING. I vow, mem, I thought once they would have fit.

MRS. MILLAMANT. Well, 'tis a lamentable thing, I swear, that one has not the liberty of choosing one's acquaintance as one does one's clothes.

MRS. MARWOOD. If we had that liberty, we should be as weary of one set of acquaintance, though never so good, as we are of one suit, though never so fine. A fool and a doily stuff[14] would now and then find days of grace, and be worn for variety.

MRS. MILLAMANT. I could consent to wear 'em if they would wear alike; but fools never wear out — they are such *drap-de-Berry*[15] things. Without one could give 'em to one's chambermaid after a day or two!

MRS. MARWOOD. 'Twere better so indeed. Or what think you of the playhouse? A fine, gay, glossy fool should be given there, like a new masking habit, after the masquerade is over and we have done with the disguise. For a fool's visit is always a disguise, and never admitted by a woman of wit but to blind her affair with a lover of sense. If you would but appear barefaced now, and own Mirabell, you might as easily put off Petulant and Witwoud as your hood and scarf. And indeed, 'tis time, for the town has found it; the secret is grown too big for the pretence. 'Tis like Mrs. Primly's great belly; she may lace it down before, but it burnishes on her hips. Indeed, Millamant, you can no more conceal it than my Lady Strammel can her face — that goodly face, which, in defiance of her Rhenish-wine tea,[16] will not be comprehended in a mask.

14 A cheap woolen cloth.
15 Heavy, hard-finished woolens.
16 White Rhenish wine, supposed to be good for the figure and the complexion.

MRS. MILLAMANT. I'll take my death, Marwood, you are more censorious than a decayed beauty or a discarded toast. — Mincing, tell the
men they may come up. — My aunt is not dressing here; their folly
is less provoking than your malice.   *Exit* MINCING
— The town has found it! what has it found? That Mirabell loves me
is no more a secret than it is a secret that you discovered it to my
aunt, or than the reason why you discovered it is a secret.

MRS. MARWOOD. You are nettled.

MRS. MILLAMANT. You're mistaken. Ridiculous!

MRS. MARWOOD. Indeed, my dear, you'll tear another fan if you
don't mitigate those violent airs.

MRS. MILLAMANT. Oh, silly! ha, ha, ha! I could laugh immoder-
ately. Poor Mirabell! His constancy to me has quite destroyed his
complaisance for all the world beside. I swear, I never enjoined it him
to be so coy. If I had the vanity to think he would obey me, I would
command him to show more gallantry — 'tis hardly well-bred to be so
particular on one hand, and so insensible on the other. But I despair
to prevail, and so let him follow his own way. Ha, ha, ha! Pardon me,
dear creature, I must laugh — ha, ha, ha! — though I grant you 'tis a
little barbarous — ha, ha, ha!

MRS. MARWOOD. What pity 'tis, so much fine raillery and delivered
with so significant gesture, should be so unhappily directed to miscarry.

MRS. MILLAMANT. Ha? Dear creature, I ask your pardon. I swear,
I did not mind you.

MRS. MARWOOD. Mr. Mirabell and you both may think it a thing
impossible, when I shall tell him by telling you —

MRS. MILLAMANT. Oh dear, what? for it is the same thing if I hear
it — ha, ha, ha!

MRS. MARWOOD. That I detest him, hate him, madam.

MRS. MILLAMANT. O, madam! why, so do I — and yet the creature
loves me — ha, ha, ha! How can one forbear laughing to think of it.
I am a sibyl if I am not amazed to think what he can see in me. I'll
take my death, I think you are handsomer — and within a year or two
as young; if you could but stay for me, I should overtake you — but
that cannot be. Well, that thought makes me melancholic. Now I'll
be sad.

MRS. MARWOOD. Your merry note may be changed sooner than you
think.

MRS. MILLAMANT. D'ye say so? Then I'm resolved I'll have a song
to keep up my spirits.

Enter MINCING

MINCING. The gentlemen stay but to comb, madam, and will wait
on you.

MRS. MILLAMANT. Desire Mrs. —— that is in the next room to

sing the song I would have learned yesterday. — You shall hear it, madam — not that there's any great matter in it, but 'tis agreeable to my humor.

SONG
Set by Mr. John Eccles, and sung by Mrs. Hodgson

1
Love's but the frailty of the mind,
When 'tis not with ambition joined;
A sickly flame, which, if not fed, expires,
And feeding, wastes in self-consuming fires.

2
'Tis not to wound a wanton boy
Or amorous youth, that gives the joy;
But 'tis the glory to have pierced a swain,
For whom inferior beauties sighed in vain.

3
Then I alone the conquest prize,
When I insult a rival's eyes:
If there's delight in love, 'tis when I see
That heart, which others bleed for, bleed for me.

Enter PETULANT *and* WITWOUD

MRS. MILLAMANT. Is your animosity composed, gentlemen?

WITWOUD. Raillery, raillery, madam; we have no animosity — we hit off a little wit now and then, but no animosity. The falling out of wits is like the falling out of lovers. We agree in the main, like treble and bass. Ha, Petulant?

PETULANT. Aye, in the main — but when I have a humor to contradict —

WITWOUD. Aye, when he has a humor to contradict, then I contradict, too. What! I know my cue. Then we contradict one another like two battledores; for contradictions beget one another like Jews.

PETULANT. If he says black's black — if I have a humor to say 'tis blue — let that pass — all's one for that. If I have a humor to prove it, it must be granted.

WITWOUD. Not positively must — but it may — it may.

PETULANT. Yes, it positively must, upon proof positive.

WITWOUD. Aye, upon proof positive it must; but upon proof presumptive it only may. — That's a logical distinction now, madam.

MRS. MARWOOD. I perceive your debates are of importance and very learnedly handled.

PETULANT. Importance is one thing, and learning's another. But a debate's a debate; that I assert.

WITWOUD. Petulant's an enemy to learning; he relies altogether on his parts.

PETULANT. No, I'm no enemy to learning. It hurts not me.

MRS. MARWOOD. That's a sign indeed 'tis no enemy to you.

PETULANT. No, no, 'tis no enemy to anybody but them that have it.

MRS. MILLAMANT. Well, an illiterate man's my aversion. I wonder at the impudence of any illiterate man to offer to make love.

WITWOUD. That I confess I wonder at, too.

MRS. MILLAMANT. Ah! to marry an ignorant that can hardly read or write!

PETULANT. Why should a man be any further from being married, though he can't read, than he is from being hanged? The ordinary's[17] paid for setting the psalm, and the parish priest for reading the ceremony. And for the rest which is to follow in both cases, a man may do it without book — so all's one for that.

MRS. MILLAMANT. D'ye hear the creature? — Lord, here's company, I'll be gone.

Exeunt MRS. MILLAMANT *and* MINCING]

Enter SIR WILFULL WITWOUD *in a country riding habit, and Servant to*
LADY WISHFORT

WITWOUD. In the name of Bartlemew and his fair,[18] what have we here?

MRS. MARWOOD. 'Tis your brother, I fancy. Don't you know him?

WITWOUD. Not I. Yes, I think it is he — I've almost forgot him; I have not seen him since the Revolution.[19]

SERVANT. [*To Sir* WILFULL] Sir, my lady's dressing. Here's company; if you please to walk in, in the meantime.

SIR WILFULL. Dressing! What, 'tis but morning here I warrant, with you in London; we should count it towards afternoon in our parts, down in Shropshire. Why, then belike, my aunt han't dined yet, — ha, friend?

SERVANT. Your aunt, sir?

SIR WILFULL. My aunt, sir! Yes, my aunt, sir, and your lady, sir; your lady is my aunt, sir. — Why, what! Dost thou not know me, friend? Why, then send somebody hither that does. How long hast thou lived with thy lady, fellow, ha?

SERVANT. A week, sir — longer than anybody in the house, except my lady's woman.

SIR WILFULL. Why, then belike thou dost not know thy lady, if thou seest her, ha, friend?

SERVANT. Why, truly, sir, I cannot safely swear to her face in a morning, before she is dressed. 'Tis like I may give a shrewd guess at her by this time.

---

17 Prison chaplain who read a psalm before an execution.
18 Bartholomew Fair in Smithfield, about August 24.
19 Of 1688, when James II was dethroned.

SIR WILFULL. Well, prithee try what thou canst do; if thou canst not guess, inquire her out, dost hear, fellow? And tell her, her nephew, Sir Wilfull Witwoud, is in the house.

SERVANT. I shall, sir.

SIR WILFULL. Hold ye; hear me, friend; a word with you in your ear. Prithee, who are these gallants?

SERVANT. Really, sir, I can't tell; here come so many here, 'tis hard to know 'em all.   [*Exit Servant*]

SIR WILFULL. Oons,[20] this fellow knows less than a starling; I don't think a' knows his own name.

MRS. MARWOOD. Mr. Witwoud, your brother is not behindhand in forgetfulness — I fancy he has forgot you too.

WITWOUD. I hope so — the devil take him that remembers first, I say.

SIR WILFULL. Save you, gentlemen and lady!

MRS. MARWOOD. For shame, Mr. Witwoud; why don't you speak to him? And you, sir.

WITWOUD. Petulant, speak.

PETULANT. And you, sir.

SIR WILFULL. No offense, I hope.   (*Salutes*[21] MRS. MARWOOD)

MRS. MARWOOD. No, sure, sir.

WITWOUD. [*Aside*] This is a vile dog, I see that already. No offence! ha, ha, ha! — To him; to him, Petulant, smoke him.[22]

PETULANT. [*Surveying him round*] It seems as if you had come a journey, sir; — hem, hem.

SIR WILFULL. Very likely, sir, that it may seem so.

PETULANT. No offence, I hope, sir.

WITWOUD. [*Aside*] Smoke the boots, the boots, Petulant, the boots! Ha, ha, ha!

SIR WILFULL. May be not, sir; thereafter, as 'tis meant, sir.

PETULANT. Sir, I presume upon the information of your boots.

SIR WILFULL. Why, 'tis like you may, sir; if you are not satisfied with the information of my boots, sir, if you will step to the stable, you may inquire further of my horse, sir.

PETULANT. Your horse, sir? your horse is an ass, sir!

SIR WILFULL. Do you speak by way of offence, sir?

MRS. MARWOOD. The gentleman's merry, that's all, sir. —(*Aside*) 'Slife, we shall have a quarrel betwixt an horse and an ass before they find one another out. — (*Aloud*) You must not take anything amiss from your friends, sir. You are among your friends here, though it may be you don't know it. If I am not mistaken, you are Sir Wilfull Witwoud.

20 Contraction of "God's wounds."
21 Kisses her.
22 Banter him.

SIR WILFULL. Right, lady; I am Sir Wilfull Witwoud — so I write myself. No offence to anybody, I hope — and nephew to the Lady Wishfort of this mansion.

MRS. MARWOOD. Don't you know this gentleman, sir?

SIR WILLFUL. Hum! What, sure 'tis not — yea, by'r Lady, but 'tis — 'sheart, I know not whether 'tis or no — yea, but 'tis, by the Wrekin[23] Brother Anthony   What, Tony, i'faith! — what, dost thou not know me? By'r Lady, nor I thee, thou art so be-cravated, and so be-periwigged! — 'Sheart, why dost not speak? art thou overjoyed?

WITWOUD. Odso, brother, is it you? Your servant, brother.

SIR WILFULL. Your servant! — why yours, sir. Your servant again — 'sheart, and your friend and servant to that — and a (*puff*) — and a — flap-dragon for your service, sir! and a hare's foot and a hare's scut for your service, sir! an you be so cold and so courtly.

WITWOUD. No offence, I hope, brother.

SIR WILFULL. 'Sheart, sir, but there is, and much offence! — A pox, is this your Inns o' Court[24] breeding, not to know your friends and your relations, your elders, and your betters?

WITWOUD. Why, brother Wilfull of Salop, you may be as short as a Shrewsbury-cake,[25] if you please. But I tell you 'tis not modish to know relations in town. You think you're in the country, where great lubberly brothers slabber and kiss one another when they meet, like a call of sergeants[26] — 'tis not the fashion here; 'tis not indeed, dear brother.

SIR WILFULL. The fashion's a fool; and you're a fop, dear brother. 'Sheart, I've suspected this — by'r Lady, I conjectured you were a fop since you began to change the style of your letters, and write in a scrap of paper gilt round the edges, no bigger than a *subpoena*. I might expect this when you left off "Honored Brother," and "hoping you are in good health," and so forth — to begin with a "Rat me, knight, I'm so sick of a last night's debauch — 'ods heart," and then tell a familiar tale of a cock and a bull, and a whore and a bottle, and so conclude. — You could write news before you were out of your time, when you lived with honest Pumple Nose, the attorney of Furnival's Inn — you could entreat to be remembered then to your friends round the Wrekin. We could have gazettes, then, and Dawks's Letter, and the Weekly Bill,[27] till of late days.

PETULANT. 'Slife, Witwoud, were you ever an attorney's clerk? of the family of the Furnivals? Ha, ha, ha!

WITWOUD. Aye, aye, but that was but for a while — not long, not

---

[23] A hill in Shropshire.
[24] Witwoud had once been a law student.
[25] A short-cake.
[26] Lawyers newly appointed serjeants-at-law.
[27] Dawk's News-letter, a weekly summary, and the London list of deaths.

long. Pshaw! I was not in my own power then; an orphan, and this
fellow was my guardian. Aye, aye, I was glad to consent to that man
to come to London. He had the disposal of me then. If I had not
agreed to that, I might have been bound 'prentice to a felt-maker in
Shrewsbury; this fellow would have bound me to a maker of felts.

SIR WILFULL. 'Sheart, and better than to be bound to a maker of
fops — where, I suppose, you have served your time, and now you may
set up for yourself.

MRS. MARWOOD. You intend to travel, sir, as I'm informed.

SIR WILFULL. Belike I may, madam. I may chance to sail upon the
salt seas, if my mind hold.

PETULANT. And the wind serve.

SIR WILFULL. Serve or not serve, I shan't ask licence of you, sir; nor
the weathercock your companion. I direct my discourse to the lady, sir.
— 'Tis like my aunt may have told you, madam — yes, I have settled
my concerns, I may say now, and am minded to see foreign parts —
if an' how that the peace holds, whereby, that is, taxes abate.

MRS. MARWOOD. I thought you had designed for France at all adventures.

SIR WILFULL. I can't tell that; 'tis like I may, and 'tis like I may not.
I am somewhat dainty in making a resolution because when I make it
I keep it. I don't stand shill I, shall I, then; if I say't, I'll do't. But I
have thoughts to tarry a small matter in town to learn somewhat of
your lingo first, before I cross the seas. I'd gladly have a spice of your
French, as they say, whereby to hold discourse in foreign countries.

MRS. MARWOOD. Here's an academy in town for that use.

SIR WILFULL. There is? 'Tis like there may.

MRS. MARWOOD. No doubt you will return very much improved.

WITWOUD. Yes, refined, like a Dutch skipper from a whale-fishing.

Enter LADY WISHFORT *and* FAINALL

LADY WISHFORT. Nephew, you are welcome.

SIR WILFULL. Aunt, your servant.

FAINALL. Sir Wilfull, your most faithful servant.

SIR WILFULL. Cousin Fainall, give me your hand.

LADY WISHFORT. Cousin Witwoud, your servant; Mr. Petulant, your
servant. — Nephew, you are welcome again. Will you drink anything
after your journey, nephew, before you eat? Dinner's almost ready.

SIR WILFULL. I'm very well, I thank you, aunt — however, I thank
you for your courteous offer. 'Sheart, I was afraid you would have been
in the fashion, too, and have remembered to have forgot your relations.
Here's your cousin Tony; belike, I mayn't call him brother for fear of
offence.

LADY WISHFORT. Oh, he's a rallier, nephew — my cousin's a wit.

And your great wits always rally their best friends to choose. When you have been abroad, nephew, you'll understand raillery better.

(FAINALL *and* MRS. MARWOOD *talk apart*)

SIR WILFULL. When then, let him hold his tongue in the meantime, and rail when that day comes.

Enter MINCING

MINCING. Mem, I am come to acquaint your la'ship that dinner is impatient.

SIR WILFULL. Impatient! why, then, belike it won't stay till I pull off my boots. — Sweetheart, can you help me to a pair of slippers? — My man's with his horses, I warrant.

LADY WISHFORT. Fie, fie, nephew! you would not pull off your boots here! Go down into the hall — dinner shall stay for you.

[*Exit* SIR WILFULL]

My nephew's a little unbred; you'll pardon him, madam. — Gentlemen, will you walk? Marwood?

MRS. MARWOOD. I'll follow you, madam — before Sir Wilfull is ready.

Manent MRS. MARWOOD *and* FAINALL

FAINALL. Why then, Foible's a bawd, an arrant, rank, match-making bawd. And I, it seems, am a husband, a rank husband; and my wife a very errant, rank wife — all in the way of the world. 'Sdeath, to be an anticipated cuckold, a cuckold in embryo! Sure, I was born with budding antlers, like a young satyr or a citizen's child. 'Sdeath! to be outwitted, to be out-jilted — out-matrimony'd! — If I had kept my speed like a stag, 'twere somewhat — but to crawl after with my horns like a snail, and be outstripped by my wife — 'tis scurvy wedlock.

MRS. MARWOOD. Then shake it off. You have often wished for an opportunity to part, and now you have it. But first prevent their plot — the half of Millamant's fortune is too considerable to be parted with to a foe, to Mirabell.

FAINALL. Damn him! that had been mine, had you not made that fond discovery. — That had been forfeited, had they been married. My wife had added lustre to my horns by that increase of fortune; I could have worn 'em tipped with gold, though my forehead had been furnished like a deputy-lieutenant's hall.[28]

MRS. MARWOOD. They may prove a cap of maintenance[29] to you still, if you can away[30] with your wife. And she's no worse than when you had her — I dare swear she had given up her game before she was married.

[28] I.e., with many sets of antlers.
[29] A term in heraldry: a pointed cap.
[30] Put up with.

FAINALL. Hum! that may be. She might throw up her cards, but I'll be hanged if she did not put pam[31] in her pocket.

MRS. MARWOOD. You married her to keep you; and if you can contrive to have her keep you better than you expected, why should you not keep her longer than you intended?

FAINALL. The means, the means?

MRS. MARWOOD. Discover to my lady your wife's conduct; threaten to part with her! My lady loves her, and will come to any composition to save her reputation. Take the opportunity of breaking it just upon the discovery of this imposture. My lady will be enraged beyond bounds, and sacrifice niece, and fortune, and all, at that conjuncture. And let me alone to keep her warm; if she should flag in her part, I will not fail to prompt her.

FAINALL. Faith, this has an appearance.

MRS. MARWOOD. I'm sorry I hinted to my lady to endeavor a match between Millamant and Sir Wilfull; that may be an obstacle.

FAINALL. Oh, for that matter, leave me to manage him. I'll disable him for that; he will drink like a Dane. After dinner I'll set his hand in.[32]

MRS. MARWOOD. Well, how do you stand affected towards your lady?

FAINALL. Why, faith, I'm thinking of it. — Let me see — I am married already, so that's over. My wife has played the jade with me — well, that's over, too. I never loved her, or if I had, why, that would have been over, too, by this time. Jealous of her I cannot be, for I am certain; so there's an end of jealousy. Weary of her I am, and shall be — no, there's no end of that — no, no, that were too much to hope. Thus far concerning my repose; now for my reputation. As to my own, I married not for it, so that's out of the question; and as to my part in my wife's — why, she had parted with hers before; so bringing none to me, she can take none from me. 'Tis against all rule of play that I should lose to one who has not wherewithal to stake.

MRS. MARWOOD. Besides, you forgot marriage is honorable.

FAINALL. Hum, faith, and that's well thought on. Marriage is honorable, as you say; and if so, wherefore should cuckoldom be a discredit, being derived from so honorable a root?

MRS. MARWOOD. Nay, I know not; if the root be honorable, why not the branches?

FAINALL. So, so; why, this point's clear. — Well, how do we proceed?

MRS. MARWOOD. I will contrive a letter which shall be delivered to my lady at the time when that rascal who is to act Sir Rowland is with her. It shall come as from an unknown hand—for the less I appear to know of the truth, the better I can play the incendiary. Besides,

---

[31] The Jack of clubs, the highest trump in the fashionable card game, loo.
[32] Start him in the game.

I would not have Foible provoked if I could help it—because you know she knows some passages—nay, I expect all will come out. But let the mine be sprung first, and then I care not if I am discovered.

FAINALL. If the worst come to the worst, I'll turn my wife to grass. I have already a deed of settlement of the best part of her estate, which I wheedled out of her, and that you shall partake at least.

MRS. MARWOOD. I hope you are convinced that I hate Mirabell. Now you'll be no more jealous?

FAINALL. Jealous! No, by this kiss. Let husbands be jealous, but let the lover still believe; or, if he doubt, let it be only to endear his pleasure, and prepare the joy that follows when he proves his mistress true. But let husbands' doubts convert to endless jealousy; or, if they have belief, let it corrupt to superstition and blind credulity. I am single, and will herd no more with 'em. True, I wear the badge, but I'll disown the order. And since I take my leave of 'em, I care not if I leave 'em a common motto to their common crest:

> All husbands must or pain or shame endure;
> The wise too jealous are, fools too secure.

Exeunt

ACT IV

SCENE I. [*Scene continues*]

Enter LADY WISHFORT and FOIBLE

LADY WISHFORT. Is Sir Rowland coming, sayest thou Foible? And are things in order?

FOIBLE. Yes, madam, I have put wax lights in the sconces, and placed the footmen in a row in the hall, in their best liveries, with the coachman and postilion to fill up the equipage.

LADY WISHFORT. Have you pulvilled[1] the coachman and postilion, that they may not stink of the stable when Sir Rowland comes by?

FOIBLE. Yes, madam.

LADY WISHFORT. And are the dancers and the music ready, that he may be entertained in all points with correspondence to his passion?

FOIBLE. All is ready, madam.

LADY WISHFORT. And—well—how do I look, Foible?

FOIBLE. Most killing well, madam.

LADY WISHFORT. Well, and how shall I receive him? in what figure shall I give his heart the first impression? There is a great deal in the first impression. Shall I sit?—no, I won't sit—I'll walk—aye, I'll walk from the door upon his entrance, and then turn full upon him—no,

---

[1] Powdered with a scented powder.

that will be too sudden. I'll lie,—aye, I'll lie down—I'll receive him in my little dressing-room; there's a couch—yes, yes, I'll give the first impression on a couch. I won't lie neither, but loll and lean upon one elbow with one foot a little dangling off, jogging in a thoughtful way— yes—and then as soon as he appears, start, aye, start and be surprised, and rise to meet him in a pretty disorder—yes. Oh, nothing is more alluring than a levee from a couch, in some confusion; it shows the foot to advantage, and furnishes with blushes and recomposing airs beyond comparison. Hark! there's a coach.

FOIBLE. 'Tis he, madam.

LADY WISHFORT. Oh, dear, has my nephew made his addresses to Millamant? I ordered him.

FOIBLE. Sir Wilfull is set to in drinking, madam, in the parlor.

LADY WISHFORT. Odds my life, I'll send him to her. Call her down, Foible; bring her hither. I'll send him as I go. When they are together, then come to me, Foible, that I may not be too long alone with Sir Rowland. [*Exit* LADY WISHFORT]

Enter MRS. MILLAMANT *and* MRS. FAINALL

FOIBLE. Madam, I stayed here to tell your ladyship that Mr. Mirabell has waited this half-hour for an opportunity to talk with you— though my lady's orders were to leave you and Sir Wilfull together. Shall I tell Mr. Mirabell that you are at leisure?

MRS. MILLAMANT. No. What would the dear man have? I am thoughtful, and would amuse myself. Bid him come another time.

(*Repeating, and walking about*)

There never yet was woman made
Nor shall, but to be cursed.[2]

That's hard!

MRS. FAINALL. You are very fond of Sir John Suckling to-day, Millamant, and the poets.

MRS. MILLAMANT. He? Aye, and filthy verses—so I am.

FOIBLE. Sir Wilfull is coming, madam. Shall I send Mr. Mirabell away?

MRS. MILLAMANT. Aye, if you please, Foible, send him away, or send him hither—just as you will, dear Foible. I think I'll see him—shall I? Aye, let the wretch come. [*Exit* FOIBLE]

(*Repeating*)

Thyrsis, a youth of the inspired train.[3]

Dear Fainall, entertain Sir Wilfull—thou hast philosophy to undergo a fool. Thou art married and hast patience. I would confer with my own thoughts.

---

[2] The quotation is from Sir John Suckling. See his *Works*, ed. W. C. Hazlitt, I, 19.

[3] From Waller's "The Story of Phoebus and Daphne, Applied."

MRS. FAINALL. I am obliged to you that you would make me your proxy in this affair, but I have business of my own.

Enter SIR WILFULL

O Sir Wilfull, you are come at the critical instant. There's your mistress up to the ears in love and contemplation; pursue your point now or never.

SIR WILFULL. Yes; my aunt will have it so. I would gladly have been encouraged with a bottle or two, because I'm somewhat wary at first before I am acquainted. (*This while* MILLAMANT *walks about repeating to herself*)—But I hope, after a time, I shall break my mind —that is, upon further acquaintance. So for the present, cousin, I'll take my leave. If so be you'll be so kind to make my excuse, I'll return to my company—

MRS. FAINALL. Oh, fie, Sir Wilfull! What! You must not be daunted.

SIR WILFULL. Daunted! No, that's not it; it is not so much for that—for if it so be that I set on't, I'll do't. But only for the present, 'tis sufficient till further acquaintance, that's all—your servant.

MRS. FAINALL. Nay, I'll swear you shall never lose so favorable an opportunity if I can help it. I'll leave you together, and lock the door.

Exit

SIR WILFULL. Nay, nay, cousin—I have forgot my gloves!—What d'ye do?—'Sheart, a' has locked the door indeed, I think. Nay, Cousin Fainall, open the door! Pshaw, what a vixen trick is this?—Nay, now a' has seen me too.—Cousin, I made bold to pass through as it were— I think this door's enchanted!

MRS. MILLAMANT. (*Repeating*)

> I prithee spare me, gentle boy,
> Press me no more for that slight toy.[4]

SIR WILFULL. Anan?[5] Cousin, your servant.
MRS. MILLAMANT.

> — That foolish trifle of a heart. —

Sir Wilfull!

SIR WILFULL. Yes—your servant. No offence, I hope, cousin.
MRS. MILLAMANT. (*Repeating*)

> I swear it will not do its part,
> Though thou dost thine, employ'st thy power and art.

Natural, easy Suckling!

---

[4] See Suckling's *Works*, ed. cit., I, 22.
[5] What's that?

SIR WILFULL. Anan? Suckling? No such suckling neither, cousin, nor stripling; I thank heaven, I'm no minor.

MRS. MILLAMANT. Ah, rustic, ruder than Gothic!

SIR WILFULL. Well, well, I shall understand your lingo one of these days, cousin; in the meanwhile I must answer in plain English.

MRS. MILLAMANT. Have you any business with me, Sir Wilfull?

SIR WILFULL. Not at present, cousin.—Yes, I made bold to see, to come and know if that how you were disposed to fetch a walk this evening; if so be that I might not be troublesome, I would have sought a walk with you.

MRS. MILLAMANT. A walk! what then?

SIR WILFULL. Nay, nothing—only for the walk's sake, that's all.

MRS. MILLAMANT. I nauseate walking; 'tis a country diversion. I loathe the country and everything that relates to it.

SIR WILFULL. Indeed! ha! Look ye, look ye—you do? Nay, 'tis like you may—here are choice of pastimes here in town, as plays and the like; that must be confessed, indeed.

MRS. MILLAMANT. Ah, *l'étourdie!*[6] I hate the town too.

SIR WILFULL. Dear heart, that's much—ha! that you should hate 'em both! Ha! 'tis like you may; there are some can't relish the town, and others can't away with the country—'tis like you may be one of those, cousin.

MRS. MILLAMANT. Ha, ha, ha! yes, 'tis like I may. You have nothing further to say to me?

SIR WILFULL. Not at present, cousin. 'Tis like when I have an opportunity to be more private, I may break my mind in some measure—I conjecture you partly guess—however, that's as time shall try—but spare to speak and spare to speed, as they say.

MRS. MILLAMANT. If it is of no great importance, Sir Wilfull, you will oblige me to leave me; I have just now a little business—

SIR WILFULL. Enough, enough, cousin; yes, yes, all a case.—When you're disposed, when you're disposed. Now's as well as another time, and another time as well as now. All's one for that—Yes, yes, if your concerns call you, there's no haste; it will keep cold, as they say. Cousin, your servant.—I think this door's locked.

MRS. MILLAMANT. You may go this way, sir.

SIR WILFULL. Your servant; then with your leave I'll return to my company.

MRS. MILLAMANT. Aye, aye; ha, ha, ha!

　　　　　Like Phœbus sung the no less amorous boy.[7]

　　　　　　　　　　　　　　　　　　　　　　　　　　　Exit

---

[6] Thoughtless.

[7] From the Waller poem cited above. Mirabell caps the quotation in the following line.

Enter MIRABELL

MIRABELL. "Like Daphne she, as lovely and as coy." Do you lock yourself up from me to make my search more curious, or is this pretty artifice contrived to signify that here the chase must end, and my pursuit be crowned? For you can fly no further.

MRS. MILLAMANT. Vanity! No—I'll fly and be followed to the last moment. Though I am upon the very verge of matrimony, I expect you should solicit me as much as if I were wavering at the grate of a monastery, with one foot over the threshold. I'll be solicited to the very last—nay, and afterwards.

MIRABELL. What, after the last?

MRS. MILLAMANT. Oh, I should think I was poor and had nothing to bestow, if I were reduced to an inglorious ease and freed from the agreeable fatigues of solicitation.

MIRABELL. But do not know that when favors are conferred upon instant[8] and tedious solicitation, that they diminish in their value, and that both the giver loses the grace, and the receiver lessens his pleasure?

MRS. MILLAMANT. It may be in things of common application; but never, sure, in love. Oh, I hate a lover that can dare to think he draws a moment's air, independent of the bounty of his mistress. There is not so impudent a thing in nature as the saucy look of an assured man, confident of success. The pedantic arrogance of a very husband has not so pragmatical an air. Ah! I'll never marry unless I am first made sure of my will and pleasure.

MIRABELL. Would you have 'em both before marriage? or will you be contented with the first now, and stay for the other till after grace?

MRS. MILLAMANT. Ah! don't be impertinent.—My dear liberty, shall I leave thee? my faithful solitude, my darling contemplation, must I bid you then adieu? Ay-h adieu—my morning thoughts, agreeable wakings, indolent slumbers, all ye *douceurs*, ye *sommeils du matin*,[9] adieu.—I can't do't, 'tis more than impossible.—Positively, Mirabell, I'll lie abed in a morning as long as I please.

MIRABELL. Then I'll get up in a morning as early as I please.

MRS. MILLAMANT. Ah? Idle creature, get up when you will—and d'ye hear, I won't be called names after I'm married; positively, I won't be called names.

MIRABELL. Names!

MRS. MILLAMANT. Aye, as wife, spouse, my dear, joy, jewel, love, sweetheart, and the rest of that nauseous cant, in which men and their wives are so fulsomely familiar—I shall never bear that. Good Mirabell, don't let us be familiar or fond, nor kiss before folks, like my Lady Fadler and Sir Francis; nor go to Hyde Park together the first Sunday

8 Urgent.
9 Sweetnesses, morning slumbers.

in a new chariot, to provoke eyes and whispers, and then never be seen there together again, as if we were proud of one another the first week, and ashamed of one another ever after. Let us never visit together, nor go to a play together; but let us be very strange and well-bred. Let us be as strange as if we had been married a great while, and as well-bred as if we were not married at all.

MIRABELL. Have you any more conditions to offer? Hitherto your demands are pretty reasonable.

MRS. MILLAMANT. Trifles—as liberty to pay and receive visits to and from whom I please; to write and receive letters, without interrogatories or wry faces on your part; to wear what I please, and choose conversation with regard only to my own taste; to have no obligation upon me to converse with wits that I don't like, because they are your acquaintance; or to be intimate with fools, because they may be your relations. Come to dinner when I please; dine in my dressing-room when I'm out of humor, without giving a reason. To have my closet inviolate; to be sole empress of my tea-table, which you must never presume to approach without first asking leave. And lastly, wherever I am, you shall always knock at the door before you come in. These articles subscribed, if I continue to endure you a little longer, I may by degrees dwindle into a wife.

MIRABELL. Your bill of fare is something advanced in this latter account. Well, have I liberty to offer conditions—that when you are dwindled into a wife, I may not be beyond measure enlarged into a husband?

MRS. MILLAMANT. You have free leave. Propose your utmost; speak and spare not.

MIRABELL. I thank you.—*Imprimis* then, I covenant that your acquaintance be general; that you admit no sworn confidante or intimate of your own sex—no she-friend to screen her affairs under your countenance, and tempt you to make trial of a mutual secrecy. No decoy-duck to wheedle you a fop-scrambling to the play in a mask,[10] then bring you home in a pretended fright, when you think you shall be found out, and rail at me for missing the play and disappointing the frolic which you had, to pick me up and prove my constancy.

MRS. MILLAMANT. Detestable *imprimis!* I go to the play in a mask!

MIRABELL. *Item*, I article that you continue to like your own face as long as I shall; and while it passes current with me, that you endeavor not to new-coin it. To which end, together with all vizards for the day, I prohibit all masks for the night, made of oiled-skins and I know not what—hog's bones, hare's gall, pig-water, and the marrow of a roasted cat. In short, I forbid all commerce with the gentlewoman in what-d'ye-call-it Court. *Item*, I shut my doors against all

---

[10] Wheedle you to the theater to scramble after a fop.

bawds with baskets, and pennyworths of muslin, china, fans, atlases,[11] etc.—*Item*, when you shall be breeding—

MRS. MILLAMANT. Ah! name it not.

MIRABELL. Which may be presumed, with a blessing on our endeavors—

MRS. MILLAMANT. Odious endeavors!

MIRABELL. I denounce against all strait lacing, squeezing for a shape, till you mould my boy's head like a sugar-loaf, and instead of a man-child, make me father to a crooked billet. Lastly, to the dominion of the tea-table I submit—but with proviso, that you exceed not in your province, but restrain yourself to native and simple tea-table drinks, as tea, chocolate, and coffee; as likewise to genuine and authorized tea-table talk—such as mending of fashions, spoiling reputations, railing at absent friends, and so forth—but that on no account you encroach upon the men's prerogative, and presume to drink healths, or toast fellows; for prevention of which I banish all foreign forces, all auxiliaries to the tea-table, as orange-brandy, all aniseed, cinnamon, citron, and Barbadoes waters, together with ratafia, and the most noble spirit of clary,[12] but for cowslip wine, poppy water, and all dormitives, those I allow. These provisos admitted, in other things I may prove a tractable and complying husband.

MRS. MILLAMANT. O horrid provisos! filthy strong-waters! I toast fellows! odious men! I hate your odious provisos.

MIRABELL. Then we're agreed. Shall I kiss your hand upon the contract? And here comes one to be a witness to the sealing of the deed.

Enter MRS. FAINALL

MRS. MILLAMANT. Fainall, what shall I do? Shall I have him? I think I must have him.

MRS. FAINALL. Aye, aye, take him, take him; what should you do?

MRS. MILLAMANT. Well then—I'll take my death, I'm in a horrid fright.—Fainall, I shall never say it—well—I think—I'll endure you.

MRS. FAINALL. Fie! fie! Have him, have him, and tell him so in plain terms; for I am sure you have a mind to him.

MRS. MILLAMANT. Are you? I think I have—and the horrid man looks as if he thought so too. Well, you ridiculous thing you, I'll have you—I won't be kissed, nor I won't be thanked—here, kiss my hand though.—So, hold your tongue now; don't say a word.

MRS. FAINALL. Mirabell, there's a necessity for your obedience; you have neither time to talk nor stay. My mother is coming, and in my conscience if she should see you, would fall into fits, and maybe not recover time enough to return to Sir Rowland, who, as Foible tells me,

---

[11] An atlas is a variety of satin.
[12] These beverages were all strongly alcoholic.

is in a fair way to succeed. Therefore spare your ecstasies for another occasion, and slip down the backstairs, where Foible waits to consult you.

MRS. MILLAMANT. Aye, go, go. In the meantime I suppose you have said something to please me.

MIRABELL. I am all obedience.

[*Exit* MIRABELL]

MRS. FAINALL. Yonder, Sir Wilfull's drunk, and so noisy that my mother has been forced to leave Sir Rowland to appease him; but he answers her only with singing and drinking. What they may have done by this time I know not, but Petulant and he were upon quarrelling as I came by.

MRS. MILLAMANT. Well, if Mirabell should not make a good husband, I am a lost thing, for I find I love him violently.

MRS. FAINALL. So it seems, for you mind not what's said to you.—If you doubt him, you had best take up with Sir Wilfull.

MRS. MILLAMANT. How can you name that superannuated lubber? Foh!

Enter WITWOUD *from drinking*

MRS. FAINALL. So! Is the fray made up, that you have left 'em?

WITWOUD. Left 'em? I could stay no longer. I have laughed like ten christ'nings—I am tipsy with laughing. If I had stayed any longer I should have burst—I must have been let out and pieced in the sides like an unsized camlet.[13]—Yes, yes, the fray is composed; my lady came in like a *nolle prosequi*,[14] and stopped their proceedings.

MRS. MILLAMANT. What was the dispute?

WITWOUD. That's the jest; there was no dispute. They could neither of 'em speak for rage, and so fell a sputtering at one another like two roasting apples.

Enter PETULANT, *drunk*

Now, Petulant, all's over, all's well. Gad, my head begins to whim it about—Why dost thou not speak? Thou art both as drunk and mute as a fish.

PETULANT. Look you, Mrs. Millamant—if you can love me, dear nymph, say it—and that's the conclusion. Pass on, or pass off—that's all.

WITWOUD. Thou hast uttered volumes, folios, in less than *decimo sexto*,[15] my dear *Lacedemonian*.[16] Sirrah Petulant, thou art an epitomizer of words.

13 Unsized (i.e., unstiffened) material.
14 Legal term: unwilling to prosecute.
15 Sixteenmo; a very small size for a book.
16 The Lacedemonians or Spartans were noted for their terse speech.

PETULANT. Witwoud—you are an annihilator of sense.

WITWOUD. Thou art a retailer of phrases, and dost deal in remnants of remnants, like a maker of pincushions—thou art in truth (metaphorically speaking) a speaker of shorthand.

PETULANT. Thou art (without a figure) just one-half of an ass, and Baldwin[17] yonder, thy half-brother, is the rest.—A Gemini[18] of asses split would make just four of you.

WITWOUD. Thou dost bite, my dear mustard seed; kiss me for that.

PETULANT. Stand off!—I'll kiss no more males—I have kissed your twin yonder in a humor of reconciliation, till he (*hiccup*) rises upon my stomach like a radish.

MRS. MILLAMANT. Eh! filthy creature! What was the quarrel?

PETULANT. There was no quarrel—there might have been a quarrel.

WITWOUD. If there had been words enow between 'em to have expressed provocation, they had gone together by the ears like a pair of castanets.

PETULANT. You were the quarrel.

MRS. MILLAMANT. Me!

PETULANT. If I have a humor to quarrel, I can make less matters conclude premises.—If you are not handsome, what then, if I have a humor to prove it? If I shall have my reward, say so; if not, fight for your face the next time yourself. I'll go sleep.

WITWOUD. Do; wrap thyself up like a wood-louse, and dream revenge—and hear me; if thou canst learn to write by tomorrow morning, pen me a challenge.—I'll carry it for thee.

PETULANT. Carry your mistress's monkey a spider!—Go, flea dogs, and read romances!—I'll go to bed to my maid.

Exit [PETULANT]

MRS. FAINALL. He's horridly drunk. How came you all in this pickle?

WITWOUD. A plot, a plot, to get rid of the knight—your husband's advice, but he sneaked off.

Enter LADY [WISHFORT], *and* SIR WILFULL, *drunk*

LADY WISHFORT. Out upon't, out upon't! At years of discretion, and comport yourself at this rantipole[19] rate!

SIR WILFULL. No offence, aunt.

LADY WISHFORT. Offence! as I'm a person, I'm ashamed of you. Foh! how you stink of wine! D'ye think my niece will ever endure such a borachio! you're an absolute borachio.[20]

SIR WILFULL. Borachio?

---

[17] The ass in *Reynard the Fox.*
[18] Twins.
[19] Ill-mannered.
[20] A Spanish word for winebag; hence, drunkard.

LADY WISHFORT. At a time when you should commence an amour and put your best foot foremost—

SIR WILFULL. 'Sheart, an you grutch[21] me your liquor, make a bill — give me more drink, and take my purse — (*Sings*)

> Prithee fill me the glass,
>   Till it laugh in my face,
> With ale that is potent and mellow;
>   He that whines for a lass,
>   Is an ignorant ass,
> For a bumper has not its fellow.

But if you would have me marry my cousin—say the word, and I'll do't. Wilfull will do't; that's the word. Wilfull will do't; that's my crest. My motto I have forgot.

LADY WISHFORT. [*To* MRS. MILLAMANT] My nephew's a little overtaken, cousin, but 'tis with drinking your health. O' my word, you are obliged to him.

SIR WILFULL. *In vino veritas*,[22] aunt.—If I drunk your health to-day, cousin, I am a borachio. But if you have a mind to be married, say the word, and send for the piper; Wilfull will do't. If not, dust it away, and let's have t'other round.—Tony?—Odds heart, where's Tony?— Tony's an honest fellow; but he spits after a bumper, and that's a fault. (*Sings*)

> We'll drink, and we'll never ha' done, boys,
>   Put the glass then around with the sun, boys,
> Let Apollo's example invite us;
>   For he's drunk every night,
>   And that makes him so bright,
> That he's able next morning to light us.

The sun's a good pimple,[23] an honest soaker; he has a cellar at your Antipodes. If I travel, aunt, I touch at your Antipodes.—Your Antipodes are a good, rascally sort of topsy-turvy fellow: if I had a bumper, I'd stand upon my head and drink a health to 'em.—A match or no match, cousin with the hard name—Aunt, Wilfull will do't. If she has her maidenhead, let he look to't; if she has not, let her keep her own counsel in the meantime, and cry out at the nine months' end.

MRS. MILLAMANT. Your pardon, madam, I can stay no longer—Sir Wilfull grows very powerful. Eh! how he smells! I shall be overcome, if I stay. Come, cousin.

Exeunt MRS. MILLAMANT *and* MRS. FAINALL

LADY WISHFORT. Smells! He would poison a tallow-chandler and his family! Beastly creature, I know not what to do with him! Travel, quotha! Aye, travel, travel—get thee gone; get thee gone; get thee but

---

[21] Grudge.
[22] There is truth in wine.
[23] Boon companion.

far enough, to the Saracens, or the Tartars, or the Turks—for thou art not fit to live in a Christian commonwealth, thou beastly pagan!

SIR WILFULL. Turks? No; no Turks, aunt. Your Turks are infidels, and believe not in the grape. Your Mahometan, your Mussulman, is a dry stinkard—no offence, aunt. My map says that your Turk is not so honest a man as your Christian. I cannot find by the map that your Mufti is orthodox—whereby it is a plain case that orthodox is a hard word, aunt, and (hiccup)—Greek for claret.—

(Sings)

> To drink is a Christian diversion,
> Unknown to the Turk or the Persian:
> Let Mahometan fools
> Live by heathenish rules,
> And be damned over tea-cups and coffee.
> But let British lads sing,
> Crown a health to the king,
> And a fig for your sultan and sophy! [24]

Ah, Tony!

Enter FOIBLE, *and whispers* [to] LADY WISHFORT

LADY WISHFORT. *(Aside to* FOIBLE*)* Sir Rowland impatient? Good lack! what shall I do with this beastly tumbril?—*(Aloud)* Go lie down and sleep, you sot!—or, as I'm a person, I'll have you bastinadoed with broomsticks.—Call up the wenches.

Exit FOIBLE

SIR WILFULL. Ahey! wenches; where are the wenches?

LADY WISHFORT. Dear Cousin Witwoud, get him away, and you will bind me to you inviolably. I have an affair of moment that invades me with some precipitation. You will oblige me to all futurity.

WITWOUD. Come, knight.—Pox on him, I don't know what to say to him.—Will you go to a cock-match?

SIR WILFULL. With a wench, Tony? Is she a shakebag, sirrah? Let me bite your cheek for that.

WITWOUD. Horrible! he has a breath like a bagpipe—Aye, aye; come, will you march, my Salopian?[25]

SIR WILFULL. Lead on, little Tony—I'll follow thee, my Anthony, my Tantony. Sirrah, thou shalt be my Tantony, and I'll be thy pig.[26]

(Sings)

> And a fig for your sultan and sophy.

Exit singing with WITWOUD

LADY WISHFORT. This will never do. It will never make a match— at least before he has been abroad.

[24] The Shah of Persia.
[25] Native of Shropshire.
[26] St. Antony was the patron of swineherds.

Enter WAITWELL, *disguised as* SIR ROWLAND

LADY WISHFORT. Dear Sir Rowland, I am confounded with confusion at the retrospection of my own rudeness! I have more pardons to ask than the pope distributes in the year of jubilee. But I hope, where there is likely to be so near an alliance, we may unbend the severity of decorum and dispense with a little ceremony.

WAITWELL. My impatience, madam, is the effect of my transport; and till I have the possession of your adorable person, I am tantalized on the rack; and do but hang, madam, on the tenter of expectation.

LADY WISHFORT. You have excess of gallantry, Sir Rowland, and press things to a conclusion with a most prevailing vehemence.—But a day or two for decency of marriage—

WAITWELL. For decency of funeral, madam! The delay will break my heart—or, if that should fail, I shall be poisoned. My nephew will get an inkling of my designs, and poison me; and I would willingly starve him before I die—I would gladly go out of the world with that satisfaction.—That would be some comfort to me, if I could but live so long as to be revenged on that unnatural viper!

LADY WISHFORT. Is he so unnatural, say you? Truly, I would contribute much, both to the saving of your life and the accomplishment of your revenge—not that I respect myself, though he has been a perfidious wretch to me.

WAITWELL. Perfidious to you!

LADY WISHFORT. O Sir Rowland, the hours that he has died away at my feet, the tears that he has shed, the oaths that he has sworn, the palpitations that he has left, the trances and the tremblings, the ardors and the ecstasies, the kneelings and the risings, the heart-heavings and the handgrippings, the pangs and the pathetic regards of his protesting eyes! Oh, no memory can register!

WAITWELL. What, my rival! Is the rebel my rival?—a' dies!

LADY WISHFORT. No, don't kill him at once, Sir Rowland; starve him gradually, inch by inch.

WAITWELL. I'll do't. In three weeks he shall be barefoot; in a month out at knees with begging an alms. He shall starve upward and upward, till he has nothing living but his head, and then go out in a stink like a candle's end upon a save-all.[27]

LADY WISHFORT. Well, Sir Rowland, you have the way—you are no novice in the labyrinth of love; you have the clue. But as I am a person, Sir Rowland, you must not attribute my yielding to any sinister appetite, or indigestion of widowhood; nor impute my complacency to any lethargy of continence. I hope you do not think me prone to any iteration of nuptials—

WAITWELL. Far be it from me—

[27] A device for holding a candle end so that it will burn.

LADY WISHFORT. If you do, I protest I must recede—or think that I have made a prostitution of decorums; but in the vehemence of compassion, and to save the life of a person of so much importance—

WAITWELL. I esteem it so—

LADY WISHFORT. Or else you wrong my condescension.

WAITWELL. I do not, I do not—

LADY WISHFORT. Indeed you do.

WAITWELL. I do not, fair shrine of virtue!

LADY WISHFORT. If you think the least scruple of carnality was an ingredient,—

WAITWELL. Dear madam, no. You are all camphire and frankincense, all chastity and odor.

LADY WISHFORT. Or that—

Enter FOIBLE

FOIBLE. Madam, the dancers are ready; and there's one with a letter, who must deliver it into your own hands.

LADY WISHFORT. Sir Rowland, will you give me leave? Think favorably, judge candidly, and conclude you have found a person who would suffer racks in honor's cause, dear Sir Rowland, and will wait on you incessantly. [*Exit* LADY WISHFORT]

WAITWELL. Fie, fie!—What a slavery have I undergone! Spouse, hast thou any cordial? I want spirits.

FOIBLE. What a washy rogue art thou, to pant thus for a quarter of an hour's lying and swearing to a fine lady!

WAITWELL. Oh, she is the antidote to desire! Spouse, thou wilt fare the worse for't—I shall have no appetite to iteration of nuptials this eight-and-forty hours. By this hand I'd rather be a chairman in the dog-days than act Sir Rowland till this time to-morrow!

Enter LADY WISHFORT, *with a letter*

LADY WISHFORT. Call in the dancers.—Sir Rowland, we'll sit, if you please, and see the entertainment. (*A dance*) Now, with your permission, Sir Rowland, I will peruse my letter. I would open it in your presence, because I would not make you uneasy. If it should make you uneasy. I would burn it. Speak, if it does—but you may see the superscription is like a woman's hand.

FOIBLE. (*Aside to* WAITWELL) By heaven! Mrs. Marwood's, I know it. My heart aches—get it from her.

WAITWELL. A woman's hand? No, madam, that's no woman's hand; I see that already. That's somebody whose throat must be cut.

LADY WISHFORT. Nay, Sir Rowland, since you give me a proof of your passion by your jealousy, I promise you I'll make a return by a frank communication. You shall see it—we'll open it together—look you here.—(*Reads*)—"Madam, though unknown to you" —Look you there, 'tis from nobody that I know—"I have that honor for your character, that I think myself obliged to let you know you are abused. He who pretends to be Sir Rowland, is a cheat and a rascal." —Oh, heavens! what's this?

FOIBLE. (*Aside*) Unfortunate, all's ruined!

WAITWELL. How, how! Let me see, let me see!—(*Reads*) "A rascal, and disguised and suborned for that imposture,"—O villainy! O villainy!—"by the contrivance of—"

LADY WISHFORT. I shall faint! I shall die!—Oh!

FOIBLE. (*Aside to* WAITWELL) Say 'tis your nephew's hand—quickly, his plot,—swear swear it!

WAITWELL. Here's a villain! Madam, don't you perceive it? Don't you see it?

LADY WISHFORT. Too well, too well! I have seen too much.

WAITWELL. I told you at first I knew the hand.—A woman's hand! The rascal writes a sort of a large hand—your Roman hand.—I saw there was a throat to be cut presently. If he were my son, as he is my nephew, I'd pistol him!

FOIBLE. O treachery!—But are you sure, Sir Rowland, it is his writing?

WAITWELL. Sure? Am I here? Do I live? Do I love this pearl of India? I have twenty letters in my pocket from him in the same character.

LADY WISHFORT. How!

FOIBLE. Oh, what luck it is, Sir Rowland, that you were present at this juncture! This was the business that brought Mr. Mirabell disguised to Madam Millamant this afternoon. I thought something was contriving when he stole by me and would have hid his face.

LADY WISHFORT. How, how!—I heard the villain was in the house, indeed; and now I remember, my niece went away abruptly when Sir Wilfull was to have made his addresses.

FOIBLE. Then, then, madam, Mr. Mirabell waited for her in her chamber; but I would not tell your ladyship to discompose you when you were to receive Sir Rowland.

WAITWELL. Enough; his date is short.

FOIBLE. No, good Sir Rowland, don't incur the law.

WAITWELL. Law! I care not for law. I can but die and 'tis in a good cause. My lady shall be satisfied of my truth and innocence, though it cost me my life.

LADY WISHFORT. No, dear Sir Rowland, don't fight. If you should be killed, I must never show my face; or hanged—oh, consider my reputation, Sir Rowland!—No, you shan't fight.—I'll go in and examine my niece; I'll make her confess. I conjure you, Sir Rowland, by all your love, not to fight.

WAITWELL. I am charmed, madam; I obey. But some proof you

must let me give you; I'll go for a black box which contains the writings of my whole estate, and deliver that into your hands.

LADY WISHFORT. Aye, dear Sir Rowland, that will be some comfort. Bring the black box.

WAITWELL. And may I presume to bring a contract to be signed this night? May I hope so far?

LADY WISHFORT. Bring what you will, but come alive, pray, come alive! Oh, this is a happy discovery!

WAITWELL. Dead or alive I'll come—and married we will be in spite of treachery; aye, and get an heir that shall defeat the last remaining glimpse of hope in my abandoned nephew. Come, my buxom widow:

> Ere long you shall substantial proofs receive,
> That I'm an errant knight—

FOIBLE. (*Aside*) Or arrant knave.

Exeunt

ACT V

SCENE I. [*Scene continues*]

[*Enter*] LADY WISHFORT *and* FOIBLE

LADY WISHFORT. Out of my house! Out of my house, thou viper, thou serpent, that I have fostered! thou bosom traitress, that I raised from nothing!—Begone, begone, begone, go! go!—That I took from washing of old gauze and weaving of dead hair,[1] with a bleak blue nose over a chafing-dish of starved embers, and dining behind a traverse rag, in a shop no bigger than a bird-cage!—Go, go! Starve again! Do, do!

FOIBLE. Dear madam, I'll beg pardon on my knees.

LADY WISHFORT. Away! out, out!—Go, set up for yourself again! —Do, drive a trade, do, with your three-pennyworth of small ware, flaunting upon a packthread under a brandy-seller's bulk,[2] or against a dead wall by a ballad-monger! Go, hang out an old Frisoneer gorget,[3] with a yard of yellow colbertine again, do! An old gnawed mask, two rows of pins, and a child's fiddle; a glass necklace with the beads broken, and a quilted night-cap with one ear! Go, go, drive a trade! —These were your commodities, you treacherous trull! this was the merchandise you dealt in when I took you into my house, placed you next myself, and made you governante[4] of my whole family! You have forgot this, have you, now you have feathered your nest?

---

[1] I.e., making wigs.
[2] Stall.
[3] A gorget or wimple made of cheap cloth and decorated with cheap lace.
[4] Housekeeper.

FOIBLE. No, no, dear madam. Do but hear me; have but a moment's patience. I'll confess all. Mr. Mirabell seduced me. I am not the first he has wheedled with his dissembling tongue; your ladyship's own wisdom has been deluded by him—then how should I, a poor ignorant, defend myself? O madam, if you knew but what he promised me, and how he assured me your ladyship should come to no damage!—Or else the wealth of the Indies should not have bribed me to conspire against so good, so sweet, so kind a lady as you have been to me.

LADY WISHFORT. No damage! What, to betray me, and marry me to a cast serving-man! to make me a receptacle, an hospital for a decayed pimp! No damage! O thou frontless[5] impudence, more than a big-bellied actress!

FOIBLE. Pray, do but hear me, madam! He could not marry your ladyship, madam. — No, indeed; his marriage was to have been void in law, for he was married to me first, to secure your ladyship. He could not have bedded your ladyship; for if he had consummated with your ladyship, he must have run the risk of the law, and been put upon his clergy.[6] — Yes, indeed, I inquired of the law in that case before I would meddle or make.

LADY WISHFORT. What, then I have been your property, have I? I have been convenient to you, it seems! — while you were catering for Mirabell, I have been broker for you! What, have you made a passive bawd of me? — This exceeds all precedent! I am brought to fine uses, to become a botcher of second-hand marriages between Abigails and Andrews.[7] I'll couple you! Yes, I'll baste you together, you and your Philander.[8] I'll Duke's-place you, as I'm a person! Your turtle is in custody already: you shall coo in the same cage if there be a constable or warrant in the parish.   *Exit* LADY WISHFORT

FOIBLE. Oh, that ever I was born! Oh, that I was ever married! — A bride! — aye, I shall be a Bridewell-bride.[9] — Oh!

Enter MRS. FAINALL

MRS. FAINALL. Poor Foible, what's the matter?

FOIBLE. O madam, my lady's gone for a constable! I shall be had to a justice and put to Bridewell to beat hemp. Poor Waitwell's gone to prison already.

MRS. FAINALL. Have a good heart, Foible; Mirabell's gone to give security for him. This is all Marwood's and my husband's doing.

FOIBLE. Yes, yes; I know it, madam. She was in my lady's closet, and overheard all that you said to me before dinner. She sent the

---

[5] Shameless.
[6] Required to prove his ability to read in order to escape hanging.
[7] Generic names for servants.
[8] Lover.
[9] A prison famous as a house of correction, especially for harlots.

letter to my lady, and that missing effect, Mr. Fainall laid this plot to arrest Waitwell when he pretended to go for the papers, and in the meantime Mrs. Marwood declared all to my lady.

MRS. FAINALL. Was there no mention made of me in the letter? My mother does not suspect my being in the confederacy? I fancy Marwood has not told her, though she has told my husband.

FOIBLE. Yes, madam, but my lady did not see that part; we stifled the letter before she read so far. Has that mischievous devil told Mr. Fainall of your ladyship, then?

MRS. FAINALL. Aye, all's out, my affair with Mirabell —·everything discovered. This is the last day of our living together, that's my comfort.

FOIBLE. Indeed, madam; and so 'tis a comfort if you knew all — he has been even with your ladyship, which I could have told you long enough since, but I love to keep peace and quietness by my goodwill. I had rather bring friends together than set 'em at distance. But Mrs. Marwood and he are nearer related than ever their parents thought for.

MRS. FAINALL. Sayest thou so, Foible? Canst thou prove this?

FOIBLE. I can take my oath of it, madam; so can Mrs. Mincing. We have had many a fair word from Madam Marwood, to conceal something that passed in our chamber one evening when you were at Hyde Park, and we were thought to have gone a-walking, but we went up unawares — though we were sworn to secrecy, too; Madam Marwood took a book and swore us upon it, but it was but a book of poems. So long as it was not a Bible oath, we may break it with a safe conscience.

MRS. FAINALL. This discovery is the most opportune thing I could wish. — Now, Mincing!

Enter MINCING

MINCING. My lady would speak with Mrs. Foible, mem. Mr. Mirabell is with her; he has set your spouse at liberty, Mrs. Foible, and would have you hide yourself in my lady's closet till my old lady's anger is abated. Oh, my old lady is in a perilous passion at something Mr. Fainall has said; he swears, and my old lady cries. There's a fearful hurricane, I vow. He says, mem, how that he'll have my lady's fortune made over to him, or he'll be divorced.

MRS. FAINALL. Does your lady or Mirabell know that?

MINCING. Yes, mem; they have sent me to see if Sir Wilfull be sober, and to bring him to them. My lady is resolved to have him, I think, rather than lose such a vast sum as six thousand pound. — Oh, come, Mrs. Foible, I hear my old lady.

MRS. FAINALL. Foible, you must tell Mincing that she must prepare to vouch when I call her.

FOIBLE. Yes, yes, madam.

MINCING. Oh, yes! mem, I'll vouch anything for your ladyship's service, be what it will.   [*Exeunt* MINCING *and* FOIBLE]

Enter LADY WISHFORT *and* MRS. MARWOOD

LADY WISHFORT. Oh, my dear friend, how can I enumerate the benefits that I have received from your goodness! To you I owe the timely discovery of the false vows of Mirabell; to you I owe the detection of the imposter Sir Rowland. And now you are become an intercessor with my son-in-law, to save the honor of my house and compound for the frailties of my daughter. Well, friend, you are enough to reconcile me to the bad world, or else I would retire to deserts and solitudes, and feed harmless sheep by groves and purling streams. Dear Marwood, let us leave the world, and retire by ourselves and be shepherdesses.

MRS. MARWOOD. Let us first dispatch the affair in hand, madam. We shall have leisure to think of retirement afterwards. Here is one who is concerned in the treaty.

LADY WISHFORT. Oh, daughter, daughter! is it possible thou shouldst be my child, bone of my bone, and flesh of my flesh, and, as I may say, another me, and yet transgress the most minute particle of severe virtue? Is it possible you should lean aside to iniquity, who have been cast in the direct mould of virtue? I have not only been a mould but a pattern for you and a model for you, after you were brought into the world.

MRS. FAINALL. I don't understand your ladyship.

LADY WISHFORT. Not understand? Why, have you not been naught? have you not been sophisticated? Not understand! here I am ruined to compound for your caprices and your cuckoldoms. I must pawn my plate and my jewels, and ruin my niece, and all little enough —

MRS. FAINALL. I am wronged and abused, and so are you. 'Tis a false accusation — as false as hell, as false as your friend there, aye, or your friend's friend, my false husband!

MRS. MARWOOD. My friend, Mrs. Fainall! Your husband my friend? What do you mean?

MRS. FAINALL. I know what I mean, madam, and so do you; and so shall the world at a time convenient.

MRS. MARWOOD. I am sorry to see you so passionate, madam. More temper would look more like innocence. But I have done. I am sorry my zeal to serve your ladyship and family should admit of misconstruction, or make me liable to affronts. You will pardon me, madam, if I meddle no more with an affair in which I am not personally concerned.

LADY WISHFORT. O dear friend, I am so ashamed that you should meet with such returns! — [*To* MRS. FAINALL] You ought to ask pardon on your knees, ungrateful creature; she deserves more from you than all your life can accomplish. — [*To* MRS. MARWOOD] Oh, don't leave me destitute in this perplexity! No, stick to me, my good genius.

MRS. FAINALL. I tell you, madam, you're abused. — Stick to you! aye, like a leech, to suck your best blood — she'll drop off when she's full. Madam, you shan't pawn a bodkin, nor part with a brass counter, in composition for me. I defy 'em all. Let 'em prove their aspersions; I know my own innocence, and dare stand a trial.

[*Exit* MRS. FAINALL]

LADY WISHFORT. Why, if she should be innocent, if she should be wronged after all, ha? I don't know what to think — and I promise you her education has been unexceptionable — I may say it; for I chiefly made it my own care to initiate her very infancy in the rudiments of virtue, and to impress upon her tender years a young odium and aversion to the very sight of men. Aye, friend, she would ha' shrieked if she had but seen a man, till she was in her teens. As I am a person, 'tis true — she was never suffered to play with a male child, though but in coats; nay, her very babies[10] were of the feminine gender. Oh, she never looked a man in the face but her own father, or the chaplain, and him we made a shift to put upon her for a woman, by the help of his long garments and his sleek face, till she was going in her fifteen.

MRS. MARWOOD. 'Twas much she should be deceived so long.

LADY WISHFORT. I warrant you, or she would never have borne to have been catechized by him; and have heard his long lectures against singing and dancing, and such debaucheries; and going to filthy plays, and profane music-meetings, where the lewd trebles squeak nothing but bawdy, and the basses roar blasphemy. Oh, she would have swooned at the sight or name of an obscene play-book! — and can I think, after all this, that my daughter can be naught? What, a whore? and thought it excommunication to set her foot within the door of a playhouse! O dear friend, I can't believe it. No, no! As she says, let him prove it — let him prove it.

MRS. MARWOOD. Prove it, madam? What, and have your name prostituted in a public court — yours and your daughter's reputation worried at the bar by a pack of bawling lawyers? To be ushered in with an "O yez" of scandal, and have your case opened by an old fumbling lecher in a quoif[11] like a man-midwife; to bring your daughter's infamy to light; to be a theme for legal punsters and quibblers by the statute; and become a jest against a rule of court, where there is no precedent for a jest in any record — not even in Domesday Book; to discompose the gravity of the bench, and provoke naughty interrogatories in more naughty law Latin; while the good judge, tickled with the proceeding, simpers under a grey beard, and figes[12] off and on his cushion as if he had swallowed cantharides, or sat upon cow-itch.

---

[10] Dolls.   [11] White head-dress worn by lawyers.   [12] Fidgets.

LADY WISHFORT. Oh, 'tis very hard!

MRS. MARWOOD. And then to have my young revellers of the Temple take notes, like 'prentices at a conventicle, and after, talk it all over again in commons, or before drawers in an eating-house.

LADY WISHFORT. Worse and worse!

MRS. MARWOOD. Nay, this is nothing; if it would end here, 'twere well. But it must after this be consigned by the shorthand writers to the public press; and from thence be transferred to the hands, nay, into the throats and lungs of hawkers, with voices more licentious than the loud flounder-man's, or the woman that cries grey peas. And this you must hear till you are stunned — nay, you must hear nothing else for some days.

LADY WISHFORT. Oh, 'tis insupportable! No, no, dear friend, make it up, make it up; aye, aye, I'll compound. I'll give up all, myself and my all, my niece and her all — anything, everything for composition.

MRS. MARWOOD. Nay, madam, I advise nothing; I only lay before you, as a friend, the inconveniences which perhaps you have overseen. Here comes Mr. Fainall. If he will be satisfied to huddle up all in silence, I shall be glad. You must think I would rather congratulate than condole with you.

LADY WISHFORT. Aye, aye, I do not doubt it, dear Marwood; no, no, I do not doubt it.

Enter FAINALL

FAINALL. Well, madam, I have suffered myself to be overcome by the importunity of this lady, your friend; and am content you shall enjoy your own proper estate during life, on condition you oblige yourself never to marry, under such penalty as I think convenient.

LADY WISHFORT. Never to marry!

FAINALL. No more Sir Rowlands; the next imposture may not be so timely detected.

MRS. MARWOOD. That condition, I dare answer, my lady will consent to without difficulty; she has already but too much experienced the perfidiousness of men. — Besides, madam, when we retire to our pastoral solitude we shall bid adieu to all other thoughts.

LADY WISHFORT. Aye, that's true; but in case of necessity, as of health, or some such emergency —

FAINALL. Oh, if you are prescribed marriage, you shall be considered; I only will reserve to myself the power to choose for you. If your physic be wholesome, it matters not who is your apothecary. Next, my wife shall settle on me the remainder of her fortune not made over already, and for her maintenance depend entirely on my discretion.

LADY WISHFORT. This is most inhumanly savage, exceeding the barbarity of a Muscovite husband.

FAINALL. I learned it from his Czarish majesty's[13] retinue, in a winter evening's conference over brandy and pepper, amongst other secrets of matrimony and policy as they are at present practised in the northern hemisphere. But this must be agreed unto, and that positively. Lastly, I will be endowed, in right of my wife, with that six thousand pounds which is the moiety of Mrs. Millamant's fortune in your possession, and which she has forfeited (as will appear by the last will and testament of your deceased husband, Sir Jonathan Wishfort) by her disobedience in contracting herself against your consent or knowledge and by refusing the offered match with Sir Wilfull Witwoud, which you, like a careful aunt, had provided for her.

LADY WISHFORT. My nephew was *non compos*,[14] and could not make his addresses.

FAINALL. I come to make demands — I'll hear no objections.

LADY WISHFORT. You will grant me time to consider?

FAINALL. Yes, while the instrument is drawing, to which you must set your hand till more sufficient deeds can be perfected, which I will take care shall be done with all possible speed. In the meanwhile I will go for the said instrument, and till my return you may balance this matter in your own discretion. [*Exit* FAINALL]

LADY WISHFORT. This insolence is beyond all precedent, all parallel. Must I be subject to this merciless villain?

MRS. MARWOOD. 'Tis severe indeed, madam, that you should smart for your daughter's wantonness.

LADY WISHFORT. 'Twas against my consent that she married this barbarian, but she would have him, though her year[15] was not out. — Ah! her first husband, my son Languish, would not have carried it thus! Well, that was my choice, this is hers: she is matched now with a witness. — I shall be mad! — Dear friend, is there no comfort for me? must I live to be confiscated at this rebel-rate?[16] — Here come two more of my Egyptian plagues too.

Enter MRS. MILLAMANT *and* SIR WILFULL WITWOUD

SIR WILFULL. Aunt, your servant.

LADY WISHFORT. Out, caterpillar! Call not me aunt! I know thee not!

SIR WILFULL. I confess I have been a little in disguise,[17] as they say. — 'Sheart! and I'm sorry for't. What would you have? I hope I committed no offence, aunt — and if I did I am willing to make satisfaction; and what can a man say fairer? If I have broke anything, I'll pay

[13] Peter the Great visited England in 1698.
[14] Not in his right mind.
[15] Of mourning.
[16] As the property of rebels is confiscated.
[17] Drunk.

for't, an it cost a pound. And so let that content for what's past, and make no more words. For what's to come, to pleasure you I'm willing to marry my cousin; so pray let's all be friends. She and I are agreed upon the matter before a witness.

LADY WISHFORT. How's this, dear niece? Have I any comfort? Can this be true?

MRS. MILLAMANT. I am content to be a sacrifice to your repose, madam; and to convince you that I had no hand in the plot, as you were misinformed, I have laid my commands on Mirabell to come in person and be a witness that I give my hand to this flower of knighthood; and for the contract that passed between Mirabell and me, I have obliged him to make a resignation of it in your ladyship's presence. He is without, and waits your leave for admittance.

LADY WISHFORT. Well, I'll swear I am something revived at this testimony of your obedience, but I cannot admit that traitor — I fear I cannot fortify myself to support his appearance. He is as terrible to me as a gorgon, if I see him I fear I shall turn to stone, petrify incessantly.

MRS. MILLAMANT. If you disoblige him, he may resent your refusal and insist upon the contract still. Then 'tis the last time he will be offensive to you.

LADY WISHFORT. Are you sure it will be the last time? — If I were sure of that — shall I never see him again?

MRS. MILLAMANT. Sir Wilfull, you and he are to travel together, are you not?

SIR WILFULL. 'Sheart, the gentleman's a civil gentleman, aunt; let him come in. Why, we are sworn brothers and fellow-travellers. — We are to be Pylades and Orestes,[18] he and I. He is to be my interpreter in foreign parts. He has been overseas once already, and with proviso that I marry my cousin, will cross 'em once again only to bear me company. — 'Sheart, I'll call him in. An I set on't once, he shall come in; and see who'll hinder him.   [*Exit* SIR WILFULL]

MRS. MARWOOD. This is precious fooling, if it would pass; but I'll know the bottom of it.

LADY WISHFORT. O dear Marwood, you are not going?

MRS. MARWOOD. Not far, madam; I'll return immediately.

[*Exit* MRS. MARWOOD]

Re-enter SIR WILFULL *and* MIRABELL

SIR WILFULL. Look up, man, I'll stand by you. 'Sbud, an she do frown, she can't kill you; besides — harkee, she dare not frown desperately, because her face is none of her own. 'Sheart, an she should, her forehead would wrinkle like the coat of a cream-cheese; but mum for that, fellow-traveller.

[18] Types of faithful friends from Greek legend.

MIRABELL. If a deep sense of the many injuries I have offered to so good a lady, with a sincere remorse and a hearty contrition, can but obtain the least glance of compassion, I am too happy. Ah, madam, there was a time! — but let it be forgotten — I confess I have deservedly forfeited the high place I once held, of sighing at your feet. Nay, kill me not by turning from me in disdain. I come not to plead for favor — nay, not for pardon; I am a suppliant only for your pity. I am going where I never shall behold you more —

SIR WILFULL. How, fellow-traveller! you shall go by yourself then.

MIRABELL. Let me be pitied first, and afterwards forgotten. I ask no more.

SIR WILFULL. By'r Lady, a very reasonable request, and will cost you nothing, aunt! Come, come, forgive and forget, aunt. Why, you must, an you are a Christian.

MIRABELL. Consider, madam, in reality you could not receive much prejudice. It was an innocent device; though I confess it had a face of guiltiness, it was at most an artifice which love contrived — and errors which love produces have ever been accounted venial. At least think it is punishment enough that I have lost what in my heart I hold most dear, that to your cruel indignation I have offered up this beauty, and with her my peace and quiet — nay, all my hopes of future comfort.

SIR WILFULL. An he does not move me, would I may never be o' the quorum! An it were not as good a deed as to drink, to give her to him again, I would I might never take shipping! — Aunt, if you don't forgive quickly, I shall melt, I can tell you that. My contract went no farther than a little mouth glue, and that's hardly dry — one doleful sigh more from my fellow-traveller, and 'tis dissolved.

LADY WISHFORT. Well, nephew, upon your account — Ah, he has a false insinuating tongue! — Well, sir, I will stifle my just resentment at my nephew's request. I will endeavor what I can to forget, but on proviso that you resign the contract with my niece immediately.

MIRABELL. It is in writing, and with papers of concern; but I have sent my servant for it, and will deliver it to you with all acknowledgments for your transcendent goodness.

LADY WISHFORT. (*Aside*) Oh, he has witchcraft in his eyes and tongue! When I did not see him, I could have bribed a villain to his assassination; but his appearance rakes the embers which have so long lain smothered in my breast.

Enter FAINALL *and* MRS. MARWOOD

FAINALL. Your date of deliberation, madam, is expired. Here is the instrument; are you prepared to sign?

LADY WISHFORT. If I were prepared, I am not impowered. My niece exerts a lawful claim, having matched herself by my direction to Sir Wilfull.

FAINALL. That sham is too gross to pass on me — though 'tis imposed on you, madam.

MRS. MILLAMANT. Sir, I have given my consent.

MIRABELL. And, sir, I have resigned my pretensions.

SIR WILFULL. And, sir, I assert my right and will maintain it in defiance of you, sir, and of your instrument. 'Sheart, an you talk of an instrument, sir, I have an old fox [19] by my thigh shall hack your instrument of ram vellum [20] to shreds, sir! It shall not be sufficient for a mittimus [21] or a tailor's measure. Therefore withdraw your instrument, sir, or by'r Lady, I shall draw mine.

LADY WISHFORT. Hold, nephew, hold!

MRS. MILLAMANT. Good Sir Wilfull, respite your valor!

FAINALL. Indeed! Are you provided of a guard, with your single beef-eater [22] there? But I'm prepared for you, and insist upon my first proposal. You shall submit your own estate to my management, and absolutely make over my wife's to my sole use, as pursuant to the purport and tenor of this other covenant. — [*To* MRS. MILLAMANT] I suppose, madam, your consent is not requisite in this case; nor, Mr. Mirabell, your resignation; nor, Sir Wilfull, your right. — You may draw your fox if you please, sir, and make a bear-garden flourish somewhere else, for here it will not avail. This, my Lady Wishfort, must be subscribed, or your darling daughter's turned adrift, like a leaky hulk, to sink or swim, as she and the current of this lewd town can agree.

LADY WISHFORT. Is there no means, no remedy to stop my ruin? Ungrateful wretch! dost thou not owe thy being, thy subsistence, to my daughter's fortune?

FAINALL. I'll answer you when I have the rest of it in my possession.

MIRABELL. But that you would not accept of a remedy from my hands — I own I have not deserved you should owe any obligation to me; or else perhaps I could advise —

LADY WISHFORT. Oh, what? — what? To save me and my child from ruin, from want, I'll forgive all that's past; nay, I'll consent to anything to come, to be delivered from this tyranny.

MIRABELL. Aye, madam, but that is too late; my reward is intercepted. You have disposed of her who only could have made me a compensation for all my services. But be it as it may, I am resolved I'll serve you! You shall not be wronged in this savage manner.

LADY WISHFORT. How! Dear Mr. Mirabell, can you be so generous at last? But it is not possible. Harkee, I'll break my nephew's match; you shall have my niece yet, and all her fortune, if you can but save me from this imminent danger.

[19] Sword.
[20] Legal documents were written on sheepskin.
[21] Writ of commitment to prison.
[22] A warder of the Tower of London.

MIRABELL. Will you? I'll take you at your word. I ask no more. I must have leave for two criminals to appear.

LADY WISHFORT. Aye, aye; anybody, anybody!

MIRABELL. Foible is one, and a penitent.

Enter MRS. FAINALL, FOIBLE, *and* MINCING

MRS. MARWOOD. [*Aside*] Oh, my shame! (*To* FAINALL) These corrupt things are brought hither to expose me.

(MIRABELL *and* LADY WISHFORT *go to* MRS. FAINALL *and* FOIBLE)

FAINALL. If it must all come out, why let 'em know it; 'tis but the way of the world. That shall not urge me to relinquish or abate one tittle of my terms; no, I will insist the more.

FOIBLE. Yes, indeed, madam, I'll take my Bible oath of it.

MINCING. And so will I, mem.

LADY WISHFORT. O Marwood, Marwood, art thou false? My friend deceive me? Hast thou been a wicked accomplice with that profligate man?

MRS. MARWOOD. Have you so much ingratitude and injustice to give credit against your friend to the aspersions of two such mercenary trulls?

MINCING. Mercenary, mem? I scorn your words. 'Tis true we found you and Mr. Fainall in the blue garret; by the same token, you swore us to secrecy upon Messalina's poems.[23] Mercenary? No, if we would have been mercenary, we should have held our tongues; you would have bribed us sufficiently.

FAINALL. Go, you are an insignificant thing! — Well, what are you the better for this? Is this Mr. Mirabell's expedient? I'll be put off no longer. — You, thing that was a wife, shall smart for this! I will not leave thee wherewithal to hide thy shame; your body shall be naked as your reputation.

MRS. FAINALL. I despise you and defy your malice! You have aspersed me wrongfully — I have proved your falsehood! Go, you and your treacherous — I will not name it, but, starve together. Perish!

FAINALL. Not while you are worth a groat, indeed, my dear. Madam, I'll be fooled no longer.

LADY WISHFORT. Ah, Mr. Mirabell, this is small comfort, the detection of this affair.

MIRABELL. Oh, in good time. Your leave for the other offender and penitent to appear, madam.

Enter WAITWELL *with a box of writings*

LADY WISHFORT. O Sir Rowland! — Well, rascal!

WAITWELL. What your ladyship pleases. I have brought the black box at last, madam.

[23] Possibly a humorous mispronunciation of *miscellany*.

MIRABELL. Give it me. Madam, you remember your promise?

LADY WISHFORT. Aye, dear sir.

MIRABELL. Where are the gentlemen?

WAITWELL. At hand, sir, rubbing their eyes — just risen from sleep.

FAINALL. 'Sdeath, what's this to me? I'll not wait your private concerns.

Enter PETULANT *and* WITWOUD

PETULANT. How now! What's the matter? Whose hand's out?

WITWOUD. Heyday! What, are you all got together like players at the end of the last act?

MIRABELL. You may remember, gentlemen, I once requested your hands as witnesses to a certain parchment.

WITWOUD. Aye, I do; my hand I remember — Petulant set his mark.

MIRABELL. You wrong him. His name is fairly written, as shall appear. — (*Undoing the box*) You do not remember, gentlemen, anything of what that parchment contained?

WITWOUD. No.

PETULANT. Not I; I writ, I read nothing.

MIRABELL. Very well, now you shall know. — Madam, your promise.

LADY WISHFORT. Aye, aye, sir, upon my honor.

MIRABELL. Mr. Fainall, it is now time that you should know that your lady, while she was at her own disposal, and before you had by your insinuations wheedled her out of a pretended settlement of the greatest part of her fortune —

FAINALL. Sir! pretended!

MIRABELL. Yes, sir. I say that this lady while a widow, having, it seems, received some cautions respecting your inconstancy and tyranny of temper, which from her own partial opinion and fondness of you she could never have suspected — she did, I say, by the wholesome advice of friends and of sages learned in the laws of this land, deliver this same as her act and deed to me in trust, and to the uses within mentioned. You may read if you please —(*Holding out the parchment*) though perhaps what is written on the back may serve your occasions.

FAINALL. Very likely, sir. What's here? — Damnation! (*Reads*) "A deed of conveyance of the whole estate real of Arabella Languish, widow, in trust to Edward Mirabell." — Confusion!

MIRABELL. Even so, sir; 'tis the way of the world, sir, — of the widows of the world. I suppose this deed may bear an elder date than what you have obtained from your lady?

FAINALL. Perfidious fiend! then thus I'll be revenged.

(*Offers to run at* MRS. FAINALL)

SIR WILFULL. Hold, sir! Now you may make your bear-garden flourish somewhere else, sir.

FAINALL. Mirabell, you shall hear of this, sir, be sure you shall. — Let me pass, oaf! [*Exit* FAINALL]

MRS. FAINALL. Madam, you seem to stifle your resentment; you had better give it vent.

MRS. MARWOOD. Yes, it shall have vent — and to your confusion, or I'll perish in the attempt. [*Exit* MRS. MARWOOD]

LADY WISHFORT. O daughter, daughter! 'Tis plain thou hast inherited thy mother's prudence.

MRS. FAINALL. Thank Mr. Mirabell, a cautious friend, to whose advice all is owing.

LADY WISHFORT. Well, Mr. Mirabell, you have kept your promise — and I must perform mine. First, I pardon, for your sake, Sir Rowland there, and Foible. The next thing is to break the matter to my nephew — and how to do that —

MIRABELL. For that, madam, give yourself no trouble; let me have your consent. Sir Wilfull is my friend. He has had compassion upon lovers, and generously engaged a volunteer in this action for our service, and now designs to prosecute his travels.

SIR WILFULL. 'Sheart, aunt, I have no mind to marry. My cousin's a fine lady, and the gentleman loves her, and she loves him, and they deserve one another. My resolution is to see foreign parts — I have set on't — and when I'm set on't I must do't. And if these two gentlemen would travel too, I think they may be spared.

PETULANT. For my part, I say little — I think things are best off or on.

WITWOUD. 'Ygad, I understand nothing of the matter; I'm in a maze yet, like a dog in a dancing-school.

LADY WISHFORT. Well, sir, take her, and with her all the joy I can give you.

MRS. MILLAMANT. Why does not the man take me? Would you have me give myself to you over again?

MIRABELL. Aye, and over and over again; (*Kisses her hand*) I would have you as often as possibly I can. Well, Heaven grant I love you not too well; that's all my fear.

SIR WILFULL. 'Sheart, you'll have time enough to toy after you're married; or if you will toy now, let us have a dance in the meantime, that we who are not lovers may have some other employment besides looking on.

MIRABELL. With all my heart, dear Sir Wilfull. What shall we do for music?

FOIBLE. Oh, sir, some that were provided for Sir Rowland's entertainment are yet within call. (*A dance*)

LADY WISHFORT. As I am a person, I can hold out no longer. I have wasted my spirits so to-day already, that I am ready to sink under the fatigue, and I cannot but have some fears upon me yet, that my son Fainall will pursue some desperate course.

MIRABELL. Madam, disquiet not yourself on that account; to my knowledge his circumstances are such he must of force comply. For my part, I will contribute all that in me lies to a reunion; in the meantime, madam — (To MRS. FAINALL) let me before these witnesses restore to you this deed of trust. It may be a means, well-managed, to make you live easily together.

> From hence let those be warned who mean to wed,
> Lest mutual falsehood stain the bridal bed;
> For each deceiver to his cost may find
> That marriage-frauds too oft are paid in kind.

Exeunt omnes

EPILOGUE

Spoken by Mrs. Bracegirdle

After our epilogue this crowd dismisses,
I'm thinking how this play'll be pulled to pieces;
But pray consider, ere you doom its fall,
How hard a thing 'twould be to please you all.
There are some critics so with spleen diseased,
They scarcely come inclining to be pleased;
And sure he must have more than mortal skill,
Who pleases anyone against his will.
Then all bad poets, we are sure, are foes,
And how their number's swelled the town well knows;
In shoals I've marked 'em judging in the pit;
Though they're on no pretense for judgment fit,
But that they have been damned for want of wit.
Since then, they by their own offenses taught,
Set up for spies on plays, and finding fault.
Others there are whose malice we'd prevent;
Such who watch plays with scurrilous intent
To mark out who by characters are meant;
And though no perfect likeness they can trace,
Yet each pretends to know the copied face.
These with false glosses[1] feed their own ill nature,
And turn to libel what was meant a satire.
May such malicious fops this fortune find,
To think themselves alone the fools designed,
If any are so arrogantly vain,
To think they singly can support a scene,
And furnish fool enough to entertain.
For well the learn'd and the judicious know
That satire scorns to stoop so meanly low
As any one abstracted fop to show.
For, as when painters form a matchless face,
They from each fair one catch some different grace,
And shining features in one portrait blend,
To which no single beauty must pretend,
So poets oft do in one piece expose
Whole *belles- assemblées*[2] of coquettes and beaux.

---

[1] Interpretations.
[2] Polite gatherings.

THE BEAUX STRATAGEM

A

COMEDY

As it is Acted at the Queen's Theatre
in the Hay-market
by Her Majesty's Sworn Comedians

Written by Mr. Farquhar

Author of the Recruiting-Officer

LONDON:

Printed for Bernard Lintott, at the Cross-Keys
next Nando's Coffee-House in Fleetstreet. [1707]

THE BEAUX' STRATAGEM

George Farquhar

THE YOUNG Irishman who came to London in 1697 to win fame as an actor, and stayed to win it as a playwright, wrote some of the pleasantest comedies in the English language. Farquhar was only twenty-one when he wrote his first play, *Love and a Bottle* (1698); in the following nine years he turned out seven more plays, most of them at least moderately successful, and some so popular that they dominated the stage, to the mortification of rival playwrights. Two of his comedies, *The Recruiting Officer* (1705) and *The Beaux' Stratagem* (1707) are minor classics, lively, diverting, well-plotted, and gay.

If he is the last of the Restoration dramatists, Farquhar is also one of the first of the eighteenth-century writers of sentimental comedy. The cynical and the sentimental are mingled in *The Beaux' Stratagem*: one rake remains true to his libertine principles, while the other, in a burst of sentiment, reforms. The sad plight of Mrs. Sullen, married to a drunken country squire from whom she longs to be freed, is designed to arouse pity as well as laughter. (The focus on the problem of divorce may well be a reflection of the author's own unhappy marital situation.) On the other hand, the affair of Archer and Mrs. Sullen, which so narrowly escapes consummation, is a clever variant on the familiar seduction theme; and the "low" characters, Sullen, Foigard, Boniface, Scrub, and the comic-opera highwaymen, are broadly humorous. There is little wit in the play, but much brisk repartee; while the plot is full of surprises and sudden turns of fortune. The play, in short, conforms to Farquhar's own definition of a comedy: "a well-framed tale handsomely told, as an agreeable vehicle for counsel or reproof."

The Beaux' Stratagem was first produced at the magnificent new Haymarket Theatre on March 8, 1707, while the author lay stricken by the disease which caused his death on April 29. Mr. Robert Wilks, Farquhar's old friend (and formerly his fellow actor at the Smock Alley Theatre in Dublin), saw to the production and played the leading role of Archer in his usual polished, debonaire style. Opposite him, as Mrs. Sullen, was beautiful Anne Oldfield, whom Farquhar had "discovered" and brought on the stage. She was rapidly becoming the reigning favorite in comedy. Tall, melodious-voiced John Mills played Aimwell opposite pretty Lucretia Bradshaw (a woman of unblemished reputation) as Dorinda. Mrs. Mary Bicknell, a dancer, played romantic Cherry; Jack Verbruggen, a rough diamond, made the part of Squire Sullen something more than a mere country blockhead; hatchet-faced Colley Cibber brought his comic talents to the role of Gibbet; and little Henry ("Jubilee Dicky") Norris made the most of the low-comedy role of Scrub. The play was a vast success, and was often revived throughout the eighteenth century.

See *The Complete Works of George Farquhar*, ed. George Stonehill, 1930; John Palmer, *The Comedy of Manners*, 1913; Bonamy Dobrée, *Restoration Comedy*, 1924; and Willard Connely, *Young George Farquhar*, 1949.

Dramatis Personae

AIMWELL	two gentlemen of broken fortunes,	MR. MILLS
ARCHER	the first as master, and the second as servant	MR. WILKS

COUNT BELLAIR, a *French* officer,   MR. BOWMAN
prisoner at Lichfield

SULLEN, a country blockhead,   MR. VERBRUGGEN
brutal to his wife

FREEMAN, a gentleman from London   MR. KEEN

FOIGARD, a priest, chaplain to the French officers   MR. BOWEN

GIBBET, a highwayman   MR. CIBBER

HOUNSLOW } his companions
BAGSHOT

BONIFACE, landlord of the inn   MR. BULLOCK

SCRUB, servant to Mr. Sullen   MR. NORRIS

LADY BOUNTIFUL, an old, civil, country gentle-   MRS. POWELL
woman, that cures all her neighbors of all
distempers, and foolishly fond of her son
Sullen

DORINDA, *Lady Bountiful's daughter*   MRS. BRADSHAW

MRS. SULLEN, *her daughter-in-law*   MRS. OLDFIELD

GIPSY, maid to the ladies   MRS. MILLS

CHERRY, the landlord's daughter in the inn   MRS. BICKNELL

Scene: Lichfield

ADVERTISEMENT. — The reader may find some faults in this play, which my illness prevented the amending of, but there is great amends made in the representation, which cannot be matched, no more than the friendly and indefatigable care of Mr. Wilks, to whom I chiefly owe the success of the play.

GEORGE FARQUHAR.

PROLOGUE

Spoken by Mr. Wilks

When strife disturbs, or sloth corrupts an age,
Keen satire is the business of the stage.
When the Plain Dealer[1] writ, he lashed those crimes
Which then infected most the modish times;
But now, when faction sleeps, and sloth is fled,
And all our youth in active fields are bred;[2]
When through Great Britain's fair extensive round,
The trumps of fame the notes of Union[3] sound;
When Anna's sceptre points the laws their course,
And her example gives her precepts force,
There scarce is room for satire; all our lays
Must be or songs of triumph or of praise.
But as in grounds best cultivated, tares
And poppies rise among the golden ears,
Our products so, fit for the field or school,
Must mix with Nature's favorite plant — a fool;
A weed that has to twenty summers ran,
Shoots up in stalk, and vegetates to man.
Simpling,[4] our author goes from field to field,
And culls such fools as may diversion yield;
And, thanks to Nature, there's no want of those,
For, rain or shine, the thriving coxcomb grows.
Follies tonight we show ne'er lashed before,
Yet such as Nature shows you every hour;
Nor can the pictures give a just offense,
For fools are made for jests to men of sense.

---

[1] William Wycherly, so-called after his play, *The Plain Dealer*, 1676.
[2] I.e., in fields of war, specifically the War of the Spanish Succession.
[3] The union of England and Scotland, March 6, 1707.
[4] Collecting herbs, simples; with a pun on simpletons.

ACT I

SCENE I. *An Inn*

Enter BONIFACE *running*

BONIFACE. Chamberlain! maid! Cherry! daughter Cherry! all asleep? all dead?

Enter CHERRY *running*

CHERRY. Here! here! Why d'ye bawl so, father? d'ye think we have no ears?

BONIFACE. You deserve to have none, you young minx! The company of the Warrington[1] coach has stood in the hall this hour, and nobody to show them to their chambers.

CHERRY. And let 'em wait, father; there's neither redcoat in the coach, nor footman behind it.

BONIFACE. But they threaten to go to another inn to-night.

CHERRY. That they dare not, for fear the coachman should overturn them to-morrow. — Coming! coming! — Here's the London coach arrived.

Enter several People with trunks, bandboxes, and other luggage, and cross the stage

BONIFACE. Welcome, ladies!

CHERRY. Very welcome, gentlemen! — Chamberlain, show the Lion and the Rose.[2] *Exit with the company*

Enter AIMWELL *in riding habit,* ARCHER *as Footman, carrying a portmantle[3]*

BONIFACE. This way, this way, gentlemen!

AIMWELL. (*To* ARCHER) Set down the things; go to the stable, and see my horses well rubbed.

ARCHER. I shall, sir. *Exit*

AIMWELL. You're my landlord, I suppose?

BONIFACE. Yes, sir; I'm old Will Boniface, pretty well known upon this road, as the saying is.

AIMWELL. O Mr. Boniface, your servant!

---

[1] On the Mersey, near Liverpool.
[2] Rooms in inns were named, not numbered.
[3] Portmanteau, traveling bag.

BONIFACE. O sir! — What will your honor please to drink, as the saying is.

AIMWELL. I have heard your town of Lichfield much famed for ale; I think I'll taste that.

BONIFACE. Sir, I have now in my cellar ten tun of the best ale in Staffordshire; 'tis smooth as oil, sweet as milk, clear as amber, and strong as brandy; and will be just fourteen year old the fifth day of next March, old style.[4]

AIMWELL. You're very exact, I find, in the age of your ale.

BONIFACE. As punctual, sir, as I am in the age of my children. I'll show you such ale! — Here, tapster, broach number 1706, as the saying is. — Sir, you shall taste my *Anno Domini*.[5] — I have lived in Lichfield, man and boy, above eight-and-fifty years, and, I believe, have not consumed eight-and-fifty ounces of meat.

AIMWELL. At a meal, you mean, if one may guess your sense by your bulk.

BONIFACE. Not in my life, sir. I have fed purely upon ale. I have eat my ale, drank my ale, and I always sleep upon ale.

Enter TAPSTER *with a bottle and glass[es, and exit]*

Now, sir, you shall see! — (*Filling it out*) Your worship's health. — Ha! delicious, delicious! fancy it burgundy, only fancy it, and 'tis worth ten shillings a quart.

AIMWELL. (*Drinks*) 'Tis confounded strong!

BONIFACE. Strong! It must be so, or how should we be strong that drink it?

AIMWELL. And have you lived so long upon this ale, landlord?

BONIFACE. Eight-and-fifty years, upon my credit, sir; but it killed my wife, poor woman, as the saying is.

AIMWELL. How came that to pass?

BONIFACE. I don't know how, sir; she would not let the ale take its natural course, sir; she was for qualifying it every now and then with a dram,[6] as the saying is; and an honest gentleman that came this way from Ireland made her a present of a dozen bottles of usquebaugh — but the poor woman was never well after. But, howe'er, I was obliged to the gentleman, you know.

AIMWELL. Why, was it the usquebaugh that killed her?

BONIFACE. My Lady Bountiful said so. She, good lady, did what could be done; she cured her of three tympanies, but the fourth carried her off. But she's happy, and I'm contented, as the saying is.

AIMWELL. Who's that Lady Bountiful you mentioned?

BONIFACE. Od's my life, sir, we'll drink her health. — (*Drinks*)

---

[4] According to the Julian Calendar, used in England until 1752.

[5] Simple code to the tapster to draw the ale brewed the previous autumn.

[6] Of brandy or usquebaugh (whiskey).

My Lady Bountiful is one of the best of women. Her last husband, Sir Charles Bountiful, left her worth a thousand pound a year; and, I believe, she lays out one-half on't in charitable uses for the good of her neighbors. She cures rheumatisms, ruptures, and broken shins in men; green sickness, obstructions, and fits of the mother,[7] in women; the king's evil, chincough,[8] and chilblains, in children. In short, she has cured more people in and about Lichfield within ten years than the doctors have killed in twenty; and that's a bold word.

AIMWELL. Has the lady been any other way useful in her generation?

BONIFACE. Yes, sir; she has a daughter by Sir Charles, the finest woman in all our country, and the greatest fortune. She has a son too, by her first husband, Squire Sullen, who married a fine lady from London t'other day; if you please, sir, we'll drink his health.

AIMWELL. What sort of a man is he?

BONIFACE. Why, sir, the man's well enough; says little, thinks less, and does—nothing at all, faith. But he's a man of great estate, and values nobody.

AIMWELL. A sportsman, I suppose?

BONIFACE. Yes, sir, he's a man of pleasure; he plays at whisk[9] and smokes his pipe eight-and-forty hours together sometimes.

AIMWELL. And married, you say?

BONIFACE. Ay, and to a curious woman, sir. But he's a—he wants it; here, sir. *(Pointing to his forehead)*

AIMWELL. He has it there, you mean?[10]

BONIFACE. That's none of my business; he's my landlord, and so a man, you know, would not—But—icod, he's no better than—Sir, my humble service to you.—*(Drinks)* Though I value not a farthing what he can do to me; I pay him his rent at quarter-day, I have a good running trade, I have but one daughter, and I can give her—but no matter for that.

AIMWELL. You're very happy, Mr. Boniface. Pray, what other company have you in town?

BONIFACE. A power of fine ladies; and then we have the French officers.[11]

AIMWELL. Oh, that's right, you have a good many of those gentlemen. Pray, how do you like their company?

BONIFACE. So well, as the saying is, that I could wish we had as many more of 'em; they're full of money, and pay double for everything they have. They know, sir, that we paid good round taxes for the taking of 'em, and so they are willing to reimburse us a little. One of 'em lodges in my house.

---

[7] Hysterics. [8] Whooping-cough. [9] Whist.

[10] I.e., he has the horns of a cuckold.

[11] Captured in the War of the Spanish Succession and paroled in England.

Re-enter ARCHER

ARCHER. Landlord, there are some French gentlemen below that ask for you.

BONIFACE. I'll wait on 'em.—(*Aside to* ARCHER) Does your master stay long in town, as the saying is?

ARCHER. I can't tell, as the saying is.

BONIFACE. Come from London?

ARCHER. No.

BONIFACE. Going to London, mayhap?

ARCHER. No.

BONIFACE. (*Aside*) An odd fellow this.—(*To* AIMWELL) I beg your worship's pardon, I'll wait on you in half a minute.   *Exit*

AIMWELL. The coast's clear, I see.—Now, my dear Archer, welcome to Lichfield.

ARCHER. I thank thee, my dear brother in iniquity.

AIMWELL. Iniquity! prithee, leave canting; you need not change your style with your dress.

ARCHER. Don't mistake me, Aimwell, for 'tis still my maxim, that there is no scandal like rags, nor any crime so shameful as poverty.

AIMWELL. The world confesses it every day in its practice, though men won't own it for their opinion. Who did that worthy lord, my brother, single out of the side-box[12] to sup with him t'other night?

ARCHER. Jack Handycraft, a handsome, well-dressed, mannerly, sharping rogue, who keeps the best company in town.

AIMWELL. Right! And, pray, who married my Lady Manslaughter t'other day, the great fortune?

ARCHER. Why, Nick Marrabone,[13] a professed pickpocket, and a good bowler; but he makes a handsome figure, and rides in his coach, that he formerly used to ride behind.

AIMWELL. But did you observe poor Jack Generous in the Park[14] last week?

ARCHER. Yes, with his autumnal periwig shading his melancholy face, his coat older than anything but its fashion, with one hand idle in his pocket, and with the other picking his useless teeth; and, though the Mall was crowded with company, yet was poor Jack as single and solitary as a lion in a desert.

AIMWELL. And as much avoided, for no crime upon earth but the want of money.

ARCHER. And that's enough. Men must not be poor; idleness is the root of all evil; the world's wide enough, let 'em bustle. Fortune has

---

[12] At the theater.

[13] A corruption of "Marylebone," a district noted for gambling and bowling.

[14] St. James's Park.

taken the weak under her protection, but men of sense are left to their industry.

AIMWELL. Upon which topic we proceed, and I think luckily hitherto. Would not any man swear, now, that I am a man of quality, and you my servant; when if our intrinsic value were known—

ARCHER. Come, come, we are the men of intrinsic value, who can strike our fortunes out of ourselves, whose worth is independent of accidents in life, or revolutions in government; we have heads to get money and hearts to spend it.

AIMWELL. As to our hearts, I grant ye, they are as willing tits as any within twenty degrees; but I can have no great opinion of our heads from the service they have done us hitherto, unless it be that they have brought us from London hither to Lichfield, made me a lord, and you my servant.

ARCHER. That's more than you could expect already. But what money have we left?

AIMWELL. But two hundred pound.

ARCHER. And our horses, clothes, rings, &c.—Why, we have very good fortunes now for moderate people; and, let me tell you besides, that this two hundred pound, with the experience that we are now masters of is a better estate than the ten thousand we have spent. Our friends, indeed, began to suspect that our pockets were low; but we came off with flying colors, showed no signs of want either in word or deed—

AIMWELL. Ay, and our going to Brussels was a good pretence enough for our sudden disappearing; and, I warrant you, our friends imagine that we are gone a-volunteering.

ARCHER. Why, faith, if this prospect fails, it must e'en come to that. I am for venturing one of the hundreds, if you will, upon this knight-errantry; but, in case it should fail, we'll reserve the t'other to carry us to some counterscarp,[15] where we may die, as we lived, in a blaze.

AIMWELL. With all my heart; and we have lived justly, Archer; we can't say that we have spent our fortunes, but that we have enjoyed 'em.

ARCHER. Right! So much pleasure for so much money, we have had our pennyworths; and, had I millions, I would go to the same market again.—Oh London! London!—Well, we have had our share, and let us be thankful; past pleasures, for aught I know, are best, such as we are sure of; those to come may disappoint us.

AIMWELL. It has often grieved the heart of me to see how some inhuman wretches murder their kind fortunes; those that, by sacrificing all to one appetite, shall starve all the rest. You shall have some that live only in their palates, and in their sense of tasting shall drown the other four. Others are only epicures in appearances, such who

15 The outer slope of a fortification.

shall starve their nights to make a figure a-days, and famish their own to feed the eyes of others. A contrary sort confine their pleasures to the dark, and contract their spacious acres to the circuit of a muffstring.

ARCHER. Right; but they find the Indies in that spot where they consume 'em. And I think your kind keepers[16] have much the best on't; for they indulge the most senses by one expense. There's the seeing, hearing, and feeling, amply gratified; and some philosophers will tell you that from such a commerce there arises a sixth sense, that gives infinitely more pleasure than the other five put together.

AIMWELL. And to pass to the other extremity, of all keepers I think those the worst that keep their money.

ARCHER. Those are the most miserable wights in being: they destroy the rights of nature, and disappoint the blessings of Providence. Give me a man that keeps his five senses keen and bright as his sword; that has 'em always drawn out in their just order and strength, with his reason as commander at the head of 'em; that detaches 'em by turns upon whatever party of pleasure agreeably offers, and commands 'em to retreat upon the least appearance of disadvantage or danger! For my part, I can stick to my bottle while my wine, my company, and my reason, holds good; I can be charmed with Sappho's singing without falling in love with her face; I love hunting, but would not, like Actaeon, be eaten up by my own dogs; I love a fine house, but let another keep it; and just so I love a fine woman.

AIMWELL. In that last particular you have the better of me.

ARCHER. Ay, you're such an amorous puppy that I'm afraid you'll spoil our sport; you can't counterfeit the passion without feeling it.

AIMWELL. Though the whining part be out of doors[17] in town, 'tis still in force with the country ladies; and let me tell you, Frank, the fool in that passion shall outdo the knave at any time.

ARCHER. Well, I won't dispute it now; you command for the day, and so I submit. At Nottingham, you know, I am to be master.

AIMWELL. And at Lincoln, I again.

ARCHER. Then at Norwich I mount, which I think shall be our last stage; for, if we fail there, we'll embark for Holland, bid adieu to Venus, and welcome Mars.

AIMWELL. A match!—Mum!

Enter BONIFACE

BONIFACE. What will your worship please to have for supper?

AIMWELL. What have you got?

BONIFACE. Sir, we have a delicate piece of beef in the pot, and a pig at the fire.

AIMWELL. Good supper-meat, I must confess. I can't eat beef, landlord.

[16] Of mistresses.   [17] Out of fashion.

ARCHER. And I hate pig.

AIMWELL. Hold your prating, sirrah! Do you know who you are?

BONIFACE. Please to bespeak something else; I have everything in the house.

AIMWELL. Have you any veal?

BONIFACE. Veal, sir! We had a delicate loin of veal on Wednesday last.

AIMWELL. Have you got any fish or wild-fowl?

BONIFACE. As for fish, truly, sir, we are an inland town and indifferently provided with fish, that's the truth on't; and then for wild-fowl—we have a delicate couple of rabbits.

AIMWELL. Get me the rabbits fricasseed.

BONIFACE. Fricasseed! Lard, sir, they'll eat much better smothered with onions.

ARCHER. Psha! damn your onions!

AIMWELL. Again, sirrah!—Well, landlord, what you please. But hold—I have a small charge of money, and your house is so full of strangers, that I believe it may be safer in your custody than mine; for when this fellow of mine gets drunk he minds nothing.—Here, sirrah, reach me the strong-box.

ARCHER. Yes, sir.—(*Aside*) This will give us a reputation.

(*Brings the box*)

AIMWELL. Here, landlord; the locks are sealed down both for your security and mine; it holds somewhat above two hundred pound; if you doubt it, I'll count it to you after supper. But be sure you lay it where I may have it at a minute's warning; for my affairs are a little dubious at present; perhaps I may be gone in half an hour, perhaps I may be your guest till the best part of that be spent; and pray order your ostler to keep my horses always saddled. But one thing above the rest I must beg, that you would let this fellow have none of your Anno Domini, as you call it; for he's the most insufferable sot.—Here, sirrah, light me to my chamber.   *Exit, lighted by* ARCHER

BONIFACE. Cherry! daughter Cherry!

Re-enter CHERRY

CHERRY. D'ye call, father?

BONIFACE. Ay, child, you must lay by this box for the gentleman; 'tis full of money.

CHERRY. Money! all that money! why, sure, father, the gentleman comes to be chosen parliament-man. Who is he?

BONIFACE. I don't know what to make of him; he talks of keeping his horses ready saddled, and of going perhaps at a minute's warning, or staying perhaps till the best part of this be spent.

CHERRY. Ay, ten to one, father, he's a highwayman.

BONIFACE. A highwayman! upon my life, girl, you have hit it, and this box is some new-purchased booty. Now could we find him out, the money were ours.

CHERRY. He don't belong to our gang.

BONIFACE. What horses have they?

CHERRY. The master rides upon a black.

BONIFACE. A black! ten to one the man upon the black mare! And since he don't belong to our fraternity, we may betray him with a safe conscience; I don't think it lawful to harbor any rogues but my own. Look'ee, child, as the saying is, we must go cunningly to work: proofs we must have. The gentleman's servant loves drink, I'll ply him that way; and ten to one loves a wench—you must work him t'other way.

CHERRY. Father, would you have me give my secret for his?

BONIFACE. Consider, child, there's two hundred pound to boot.— (*Ringing without*) Coming!—coming!—Child, mind your business.

Exit

CHERRY. What a rogue is my father! My father? I deny it. My mother was a good, generous, free-hearted woman, and I can't tell how far her good-nature might have extended for the good of her children. This landlord of mine, for I think I can call him no more, would betray his guest, and debauch his daughter into the bargain—by a footman, too!

Enter ARCHER

ARCHER. What footman, pray, mistress, is so happy as to be the subject of your contemplation?

CHERRY. Whoever he is, friend, he'll be but little the better for't.

ARCHER. I hope so, for I'm sure you did not think of me.

CHERRY. Suppose I had?

ARCHER. Why then you're but even with me; for the minute I came in, I was a-considering in what manner I should make love to you.

CHERRY. Love to me, friend!

ARCHER. Yes, child.

CHERRY. Child! manners!—If you kept a little more distance, friend, it would become you much better.

ARCHER. Distance! Good-night, sauce-box.　　　　　　　　　*Going*

CHERRY. (*Aside*) A pretty fellow. I like his pride.—Sir, pray, sir, you see, sir, (ARCHER *returns*) I have the credit to be entrusted with your master's fortune here, which sets me a degree above his footman; I hope, sir, you an't affronted?

ARCHER. Let me look you full in the face, and I'll tell you whether you can affront me or no.—'Sdeath, child, you have a pair of delicate eyes, and you don't know what to do with 'em!

CHERRY. Why, sir, don't I see everybody?

ARCHER. Ay, but if some women had 'em, they would kill everybody. Prithee, instruct me, I would fain make love to you, but I don't know what to say.

CHERRY. Why, did you never make love to anybody before?

ARCHER. Never to a person of your figure, I can assure you, madam. My addresses have been always confined to people within my own sphere; I never aspired so high before. (A song)

> But you look so bright,
> And are dressed so tight,
> That a man would swear you're right,[18]
> As arm was e'er laid over.
> Such an air
> You freely wear
> To ensnare,
> As makes each guest a lover!
>
> Since then, my dear, I'm your guest,
> Prithee give me of the best
> Of what is ready dressed;
> Since then, my dear, etc.

CHERRY. (Aside) What can I think of this man?—Will you give me that song, sir?

ARCHER. Ay, my dear, take it while 'tis warm.—(Kisses her) Death and fire! her lips are honeycombs.

CHERRY. And I wish there had been bees too, to have stung you for your impudence.

ARCHER. There's a swarm of Cupids, my little Venus, that has done the business much better.

CHERRY. (Aside) This fellow is misbegotten as well as I.—What's your name, sir?

ARCHER. (Aside) Name! igad, I have forgot it.—Oh! Martin.

CHERRY. Where were you born?

ARCHER. In St. Martin's parish.

CHERRY. What was your father?

ARCHER. St. Martin's parish.

CHERRY. Then, friend, good night.

ARCHER. I hope not.

CHERRY. You may depend upon't.

ARCHER. Upon what?

CHERRY. That you're very impudent.

ARCHER. That you're very handsome.

CHERRY. That you're a footman.

ARCHER. That you're an angel.

CHERRY. I shall be rude.

---

[18] Slang for a woman of easy virtue.

ARCHER. So shall I.

CHERRY. Let go my hand.

ARCHER. Give me a kiss.   (*Kisses her*)

(*Call without*) Cherry! Cherry!

CHERRY. I'mm—my father calls; you plaguy devil, how durst you stop my breath so? Offer to follow me one step, if you dare.   *Exit*

ARCHER. A fair challenge, by this light! This is a pretty fair opening of an adventure; but we are knight-errants, and so Fortune be our guide.   *Exit*

ACT II

SCENE I. A *Gallery in* LADY BOUNTIFUL's *House*

MRS. SULLEN *and* DORINDA, *meeting*

DORINDA. Morrow, my dear sister; are you for church this morning?

MRS. SULLEN. Anywhere to pray; for Heaven alone can help me. But I think, Dorinda, there's no form of prayer in the liturgy against bad husbands.

DORINDA. But there's a form of law in Doctors-Commons;[1] and I swear, sister Sullen, rather than see you thus continually discontented, I would advise you to apply to that; for besides the part that I bear in your vexatious broils, as being sister to the husband, and friend to the wife, your example gives me such an impression of matrimony, that I shall be apt to condemn my person to a long vacation all its life. But supposing, madam, that you brought it to a case of separation, what can you urge against your husband? My brother is, first, the most constant man alive.

MRS. SULLEN. The most constant husband, I grant ye.

DORINDA. He never sleeps from you.

MRS. SULLEN. No; he always sleeps with me.

DORINDA. He allows you a maintenance suitable to your quality.

MRS. SULLEN. A maintenance! do you take me, madam, for an hospital child, that I must sit down, and bless my benefactors for meat, drink, and clothes? As I take it, madam, I brought your brother ten thousand pounds, out of which I might expect some pretty things, called pleasures.

DORINDA. You share in all the pleasures that the country affords.

MRS. SULLEN. Country pleasures! racks and torments! Dost think, child, that my limbs were made for leaping of ditches, and clambering over stiles? or that my parents, wisely foreseeing my future happiness in country pleasures, had early instructed me in the rural accomplish-

---

[1] Lawyers enabled to plead suits for separation or divorce in the ecclesiastical courts.

ments of drinking fat[2] ale, playing at whisk, and smoking tobacco with my husband? or of spreading of plasters, brewing of diet-drinks, and stilling rosemary-water, with the good old gentlewoman my mother-in-law?

DORINDA. I'm sorry, madam, that it is not more in our power to divert you; I could wish, indeed, that our entertainments were a little more polite, or your taste a little less refined. But, pray, madam, how came the poets and philosophers, that labored so much in hunting after pleasure, to place it at last in a country life?

MRS. SULLEN. Because they wanted money, child, to find out the pleasures of the town. Did you ever see a poet or philosopher worth ten thousand pound? If you can show me such a man, I'll lay you fifty pound you'll find him somewhere within the weekly bills.[3] Not that I disapprove rural pleasures, as the poets have painted them; in their landscape, every Phillis has her Corydon, every murmuring stream, and every flowery mead, gives fresh alarms to love. Besides, you'll find that their couples were never married.—But yonder I see my Corydon, and a sweet swain it is, Heaven knows! Come, Dorinda, don't be angry; he's my husband, and your brother; and between both, is he not a sad brute?

DORINDA. I have nothing to say to your part of him—you're the best judge.

MRS. SULLEN. O sister, sister! if ever you marry, beware of a sullen, silent sot, one that's always musing, but never thinks. There's some diversion in a talking blockhead; and since a woman must wear chains, I would have the pleasure of hearing 'em rattle a little. Now you shall see— but take this by the way: he came home this morning at his usual hour of four, wakened me out of a sweet dream of something else by tumbling over the tea-table, which he broke all to pieces; after his man and he had rolled about the room, like sick passengers in a storm, he comes flounce into bed, dead as a salmon into a fishmonger's basket; his feet cold as ice, his breath hot as a furnace, and his hands and his face as greasy as his flannel nightcap. O matrimony! He tosses up the clothes with a barbarous swing over his shoulders, disorders the whole economy of my bed, leaves me half naked, and my whole night's comfort is the tuneable serenade of that wakeful nightingale, his nose! Oh, the pleasure of counting the melancholy clock by a snoring husband! But now, sister, you shall see how handsomely, being a well-bred man, he will beg my pardon.

Enter SULLEN

SQUIRE SULLEN. My head aches consumedly.

MRS. SULLEN. Will you be pleased, my dear, to drink tea with us this morning? It may do your head good.

[2] Full-bodied.   [3] The Bills of Mortality for the city of London.

SQUIRE SULLEN. No.

DORINDA. Coffee, brother?

SQUIRE SULLEN. Pshaw!

MRS. SULLEN. Will you please to dress, and go to church with me? The air may help you.

SQUIRE SULLEN. Scrub!

Enter SCRUB

SCRUB. Sir!

SQUIRE SULLEN. What day o' th'week is this?

SCRUB. Sunday, an't please your worship.

SQUIRE SULLEN. Sunday! Bring me a dram; and d'ye hear, set out the venison-pasty, and a tankard of strong beer upon the hall-table; I'll go to breakfast.   (*Going*)

DORINDA. Stay, stay, brother, you shan't get off so; you were very naughty last night, and must make your wife reparation; come, come, brother, won't you ask pardon?

SQUIRE SULLEN. For what?

DORINDA. For being drunk last night.

SQUIRE SULLEN. I can afford it, can't I?

MRS. SULLEN. But I can't, sir.

SQUIRE SULLEN. Then you may let it alone.

MRS. SULLEN. But I must tell you, sir that this is not to be borne.

SQUIRE SULLEN. I'm glad on't.

MRS. SULLEN. What is the reason, sir, that you use me thus inhumanly?

SQUIRE SULLEN. Scrub!

SCRUB. Sir!

SQUIRE SULLEN. Get things ready to shave my head.

Exit [*with* SCRUB]

MRS. SULLEN. Have a care of coming near his temples, Scrub, for fear you meet something there that may turn the edge of your razor.— Inveterate stupidity! Did you ever know so hard, so obstinate a spleen as his? O sister, sister! I shall never ha' good of the beast till I get him to town; London, dear London, is the place for managing and breaking a husband.

DORINDA. And has not a husband the same opportunities there for humbling a wife?

MRS. SULLEN. No, no, child; 'tis a standing maxim in conjugal discipline, that when a man would enslave his wife, he hurries her into the country; and when a lady would be arbitrary with her husband she wheedles her booby up to town. A man dare not play the tyrant in London, because there are so many examples to encourage the subject to rebel. O Dorinda! Dorinda! a fine woman may do anything in

London: o' my conscience, she may raise an army of forty thousand men.

DORINDA. I fancy, sister, you have a mind to be trying your power that way here in Lichfield; you have drawn the French count to your colors already.

MRS. SULLEN. The French are a people that can't live without their gallantries.

DORINDA. And some English that I know, sister, are not averse to such amusements.

MRS. SULLEN. Well, sister, since the truth must be out, it may do as well now as hereafter; I think one way to rouse my lethargic, sottish husband is to give him a rival. Security begets negligence in all people, and men must be alarmed to make 'em alert in their duty. Women are like pictures, of no value in the hands of a fool, till he hears men of sense bid high for the purchase.

DORINDA. This might do, sister, if my brother's understanding were to be convinced into a passion for you; but I fancy there's a natural aversion of his side; and I fancy, sister, that you don't come much behind him, if you dealt fairly.

MRS. SULLEN. I own it, we are united contradictions, fire and water: but I could be contented, with a great many other wives, to humor the censorious mob, and give the world an appearance of living well with my husband, could I bring him but to dissemble a little kindness to keep me in countenance.

DORINDA. But how do you know, sister, but that, instead of rousing your husband by this artifice to a counterfeit kindness, he should awake in a real fury?

MRS. SULLEN. Let him; if I can't entice him to the one, I would provoke him to the other.

DORINDA. But how must I behave myself between ye?

MRS. SULLEN. You must assist me.

DORINDA. What, against my own brother?

MRS. SULLEN. He's but half a brother, and I'm your entire friend. If I go a step beyond the bounds of honor, leave me; till then, I expect you should go along with me in everything; while I trust my honor in your hands, you must trust your brother's in mine. The count is to dine here to-day.

DORINDA. 'Tis a strange thing, sister, that I can't like that man.

MRS. SULLEN. You like nothing; your time is not come; love and death have their fatalities, and strike home one time or other. You'll pay for all one day, I warrant ye. But come, my lady's tea is ready, and 'tis almost church time. *Exeunt*

SCENE II. *The Inn*

Enter AIMWELL *dressed, and* ARCHER

AIMWELL. And was she the daughter of the house?

ARCHER. The landlord is so blind as to think so; but I dare swear she has better blood in her veins.

AIMWELL. Why dost think so?

ARCHER. Because the baggage has a pert *je ne sais quoi;*[4] she reads plays, keeps a monkey, and is troubled with vapors.[5]

AIMWELL. By which discoveries I guess that you know more of her.

ARCHER. Not yet, faith; the lady gives herself airs; forsooth, nothing under a gentleman!

AIMWELL. Let me take her in hand.

ARCHER. Say one word more o'that, and I'll declare myself, spoil your sport there and everywhere else; look ye, Aimwell, every man in his own sphere.

AIMWELL. Right; and therefore you must pimp for your master.

ARCHER. In the usual forms, good sir, after I have served myself.— But to our business. You are so well dressed, Tom, and make so handsome a figure, that I fancy you may do execution in a country church; the exterior part strikes first, and you're in the right to make that impression favorable.

AIMWELL. There's something in that which may turn to advantage. The appearance of a stranger in a country church draws as many gazers as a blazing star; no sooner he comes into the cathedral, but a train of whispers runs buzzing round the congregation in a moment: Who is he? Whence comes he? Do you know him? Then I, sir, tips me the verger with half-a-crown; he pockets the simony, and inducts me into the best pew in the church. I pull out my snuff-box, turn myself round, bow to the bishop or the dean, if he be the commanding officer; single out a beauty, rivet both my eyes to hers, set my nose a-bleeding by the strength of imagination, and show the whole church my concern by my endeavoring to hide it. After the sermon, the whole town gives me to her for a lover; and by persuading the lady that I am a-dying for her, the tables are turned, and she in good earnest falls in love with me.

ARCHER. There's nothing in this, Tom, without a precedent; but instead of riveting your eyes to a beauty, try and fix 'em upon a fortune; that's our business at present.

AIMWELL. Pshaw! no woman can be a beauty without a fortune. Let me alone, for I am a marksman.

[4] Something undescribable; "I don't know what."   [5] Melancholia.

ARCHER. Tom!

AIMWELL. Ay.

ARCHER. When were you at church before, pray?

AIMWELL. Um—I was there at the coronation.[6]

ARCHER. And how can you expect a blessing by going to church now?

AIMWELL. Blessing! nay, Frank, I ask but for a wife.   *Exit*

ARCHER. Truly, the man is not very unreasonable in his demands.

Exit at the opposite door

Enter BONIFACE *and* CHERRY

BONIFACE. Well, daughter, as the saying is, have you brought Martin to confess?

CHERRY. Pray, father, don't put me upon getting anything out of a man; I'm but young, you know, father, and I don't understand wheedling.

BONIFACE. Young! why, you jade, as the saying is, can any woman wheedle that is not young? Your mother was useless at five-and-twenty. Not wheedle! would you make your mother a whore, and me a cuckold, as the saying is? I tell you, his silence confesses it; and his master spends his money so freely, and is so much a gentleman every manner of way, that he must be a highwayman.

Enter GIBBET, *in a cloak*

GIBBET. Landlord, landlord, is the coast clear?

BONIFACE. O Mr. Gibbet, what's the news?

GIBBET. No matter, ask no questions, all fair and honorable.— Here, my dear Cherry.—(*Gives her a bag*) Two hundred sterling pounds, as good as any that ever hanged or saved a rogue; lay 'em by with the rest; and here—three wedding or mourning rings, 'tis much the same, you know—here, two silver-hilted swords; I took those from fellows that never show any part of their swords but the hilts—here is a diamond necklace which the lady hid in the privatest place in the coach, but I found it out—this gold watch I took from a pawn-broker's wife; it was left in her hands by a person of quality, there's the arms upon the case.

CHERRY. But who had you the money from?

GIBBET. Ah! poor woman! I pitied her; from a poor lady just eloped from her husband. She had made up her cargo, and was bound for Ireland, as hard as she could drive; she told me of her husband's barbarous usage, and so I left her half a crown. But I had almost forgot, my dear Cherry, I have a present for you.

CHERRY. What is't?

[6] Of Queen Anne in 1702.

GIBBET. A pot of ceruse, my child, that I took out of a lady's under-pocket.

CHERRY. What, Mr. Gibbet, do you think that I paint?

GIBBET. Why, you jade, your betters do; I'm sure the lady that I took it from had a coronet upon her handkerchief. Here, take my cloak, and go, secure the premises.

CHERRY. I will secure 'em.   *Exit*

BONIFACE. But, heark'ee, where's Hounslow and Bagshot?[7]

GIBBET. They'll be here to-night.

BONIFACE. D'ye know of any other gentlemen o' the pad on this road?

GIBBET. No.

BONIFACE. I fancy that I have two that lodge in the house just now.

GIBBET. The devil! How d'ye smoke 'em?

BONIFACE. Why, the one is gone to church.

GIBBET. That's suspicious, I must confess.

BONIFACE. And the other is now in his master's chamber; he pretends to be servant to the other. We'll call him out and pump him a little.

GIBBET. With all my heart.

BONIFACE. Mr. Martin! Mr. Martin!

Enter ARCHER, *combing a periwig and singing*

GIBBET. The roads are consumed deep, I'm as dirty as old Brentford[8] at Christmas.—A good pretty fellow that. Whose servant are you, friend?

ARCHER. My master's.

GIBBET. Really!

ARCHER. Really.

GIBBET. That's much. [*Aside to* BONIFACE] The fellow has been at the bar, by his evasions.—But, pray, sir, what is your master's name?

ARCHER. Tall, all, dall!—(*Sings and combs the periwig*) This is the most obstinate curl—

GIBBET. I ask you his name?

ARCHER. Name, sir—*tall, all, dall!*—I never asked him his name in my life.—*Tall, all, dall!*

BONIFACE. (*Aside to* GIBBET) What think you now?

GIBBET. (*Aside to* BONIFACE) Plain, plain; he talks now as if he were before a judge.—But, pray, friend, which way does your master travel?

ARCHER. A-horseback.

GIBBET. (*Aside*) Very well again, an old offender, right.—But, I

[7] The names of two heaths near London famous as haunts of highwaymen.

[8] Brentford, a market town in Middlesex, was proverbially muddy, especially in mid-winter.

mean, does he go upwards or downwards

ARCHER. Downwards, I fear, sir.—*Tall, all!*

GIBBET. I'm afraid my fate will be a contrary way.

BONIFACE. Ha, ha, ha! Mr. Martin, you're very arch. This gentle-man is only travelling towards Chester, and would be glad of your company, that's all.—Come, Captain, you'll stay to-night, I suppose? I'll show you a chamber—come, Captain.

GIBBET. Farewell, friend! *Exit [with* BONIFACE]

ARCHER. Captain, your servant.—Captain! a pretty fellow! 'Sdeath, I wonder that the officers of the army don't conspire to beat all scoundrels in red but their own.

Enter CHERRY

CHERRY. (*Aside*) Gone! and Martin here! I hope he did not listen; I would have the merit of the discovery all my own, because I would oblige him to love me.—(*Aloud*) Mr. Martin, who was that man with my father?

ARCHER. Some recruiting sergeant, or whipped-out trooper, I suppose.

CHERRY. (*Aside*) All's safe, I find.

ARCHER. Come, my dear, have you conned over the catechise I taught you last night?

CHERRY. Come, question me.

ARCHER. What is love?

CHERRY. Love is I know not what, it comes I know not how, and goes I know not when.

ARCHER. Very well, an apt scholar.—(*Chucks her under the chin*) Where does love enter?

CHERRY. Into the eyes.

ARCHER. And where go out?

CHERRY. I won't tell ye.

ARCHER. What are the objects of that passion?

CHERRY. Youth, beauty, and clean linen.

ARCHER. The reason?

CHERRY. The two first are fashionable in nature, and the third at court.

ARCHER. That's my dear.—What are the signs and tokens of that passion?

CHERRY. A stealing look, a stammering tongue, words improbable, designs impossible, and actions impracticable.

ARCHER. That's my good child, kiss me.—What must a lover do to obtain his mistress?

CHERRY. He must adore the person that disdains him, he must bribe the chambermaid that betrays him, and court the footman that laughs at him. He must—he must—

ARCHER. Nay, child, I must whip you if you don't mind your lesson; he must treat his —

CHERRY. O ay! — he must treat his enemies with respect, his friends with indifference, and all the world with contempt; he must suffer much, and fear more; he must desire much, and hope little; in short, he must embrace his ruin, and throw himself away.

ARCHER. Had ever man so hopeful a pupil as mine! — Come, my dear, why is Love called a riddle?

CHERRY. Because, being blind, he leads those that see, and, though a child, he governs a man.

ARCHER. Mighty well! — And why is Love pictured blind?

CHERRY. Because the painters out of the weakness or privilege of their art chose to hide those eyes that they could not draw.

ARCHER. That's my dear little scholar, kiss me again. — And why should Love, that's a child, govern a man?

CHERRY. Because that a child is the end of love.

ARCHER. And so ends Love's catechism. — And now, my dear, we'll go in and make my master's bed.

CHERRY. Hold, hold, Mr. Martin! You have taken a great deal of pains to instruct me, and what d'ye think I have learned by it?

ARCHER. What?

CHERRY. That your discourse and your habit are contradictions, and it would be nonsense in me to believe you a footman any longer.

ARCHER. 'Oons, what a witch it is!

CHERRY. Depend upon this, sir, nothing in this garb shall ever tempt me; for, though I was born to servitude, I hate it. Own your condition, swear you love me, and then —

ARCHER. And then we shall go make the bed?

CHERRY. Yes.

ARCHER. You must know then, that I am born a gentleman, my education was liberal; but I went to London, a younger brother, fell into the hands of sharpers, who stripped me of my money, my friends disowned me, and now my necessity brings me to what you see.

CHERRY. Then take my hand — promise to marry me before you sleep, and I'll make you master of two thousand pounds.

ARCHER. How!

CHERRY. Two thousand pounds that I have this minute in my own custody; so, throw off your livery this instant, and I'll go find a parson.

ARCHER. What said you? a parson!

CHERRY. What! do you scruple?

ARCHER. Scruple! no, no, but — Two thousand pound, you say?

CHERRY. And better.

ARCHER. (*Aside*) 'Sdeath, what shall I do? — But hark'ee, child, what need you make me master of yourself and money, when you may have the same pleasure out of me, and still keep your fortune in your hands.

CHERRY. Then you won't marry me?

ARCHER. I would marry you, but —

CHERRY. O, sweet sir, I'm your humble servant, you're fairly caught! Would you persuade me that any gentleman who could bear the scandal of wearing a livery would refuse two thousand pound, let the condition be what it would? No, no, sir. But I hope you'll pardon the freedom I have taken, since it was only to inform myself of the respect that I ought to pay you.

ARCHER. (Aside) Fairly hit, by Jupiter! — Hold! hold! — And have you actually two thousand pounds?

CHERRY. Sir, I have my secrets as well as you; when you please to be more open I shall be more free; and be assured that I have discoveries that will match yours, be what they will. In the meanwhile, be satisfied that no discovery I make shall ever hurt you; but beware of my father! *Exit*

ARCHER. So! we're likely to have as many adventures in our inn as Don Quixote[9] had in his. Let me see — two thousand pounds! — If the wench would promise to die when the money were spent, igad, one would marry her; but the fortune may go off in a year or two, and the wife may live — Lord knows how long. Then an innkeeper's daughter; ay, that's the devil — there my pride brings me off.

> For whatsoe'er the sages charge on pride,
> The angels' fall, and twenty faults beside,
> On earth, I'm sure, 'mong us of mortal calling,
> Pride saves man oft, and woman too, from falling. *Exit*

ACT III

SCENE I. [*The Gallery in* LADY BOUNTIFUL'S *House*]

Enter MRS. SULLEN, DORINDA

MRS. SULLEN. Ha, ha, ha! my dear sister, let me embrace thee! Now we are friends indeed; for I shall have a secret of yours as a pledge for mine — now you'll be good for something; I shall have you conversable in the subjects of the sex.

DORINDA. But do you think that I am so weak as to fall in love with a fellow at first sight?

MRS. SULLEN. Pshaw! now you spoil all; why should not we be as free in our friendships as the men? I warrant you the gentleman has got to his confidant already, has avowed his passion, toasted your health, called you ten thousand angels, has run over your lips, eyes, neck, shape, air, and everything, in a description that warms their mirth to a second enjoyment.

---

[9] See *Don Quixote*, Part I, Book I, chapters ii and iii.

DORINDA. Your hand, sister, I an't well.

MRS. SULLEN. So — she's breeding already! Come, child, up with it — hem a little — so — now tell me, don't you like the gentleman that we saw at church just now?

DORINDA. The man's well enough.

MRS. SULLEN. Well enough! is he not a demigod, a Narcissus, a star, the man i'the moon?

DORINDA. O sister, I'm extremely ill!

MRS. SULLEN. Shall I send to your mother, child, for a little of her cephalic plaster[1] to put to the soles of your feet, or shall I send to the gentleman for something for you? Come, unlace your stays, unbosom yourself. The man is perfectly a pretty fellow; I saw him when he first came into church.

DORINDA. I saw him too, sister, and with an air that shone, methought, like rays about his person.

MRS. SULLEN. Well said, up with it!

DORINDA. No forward coquet behavior, no airs to set him off, no studied looks nor artful posture, — but nature did it all —

MRS. SULLEN. Better and better! — one touch more — come!

DORINDA. But then his looks — did you observe his eyes?

MRS. SULLEN. Yes, yes, I did — his eyes — well, what of his eyes?

DORINDA. Sprightly, but not wandering; they seemed to view, but never gazed on anything but me. — And then his looks so humble were, and yet so noble, that they aimed to tell me that he could with pride die at my feet, though he scorned slavery anywhere else.

MRS. SULLEN. The physic works purely! — How d'ye find yourself now, my dear?

DORINDA. Hem! much better, my dear. — Oh, here comes our Mercury! (*Enter* SCRUB) — Well Scrub, what news of the gentleman?

SCRUB. Madam, I have brought you a packet of news.

DORINDA. Open it quickly, come.

SCRUB. In the first place I inquired who the gentleman was; they told me he was a stranger. Secondly, I asked what the gentleman was; they answered and said, that they never saw him before. Thirdly, I inquired what countryman he was; they replied, 'twas more than they knew. Fourthly, I demanded whence he came; their answer was, they could not tell. And fifthly, I asked whither he went; and they replied, they knew nothing of the matter, — and this is all I could learn.

MRS. SULLEN. But what do the people say? Can't they guess?

SCRUB. Why, some think he's a spy, some guess he's a mountebank, some say one thing, some another; but for my own part, I believe he's a Jesuit.[2]

---

[1] Supposed to cure by drawing "humours" from the head.

[2] Jesuits were suspected at this time of plotting against the Hanoverian succession.

DORINDA. A Jesuit! Why a Jesuit?

SCRUB. Because he keeps his horses always ready saddled, and his footman talks French.

MRS. SULLEN. His footman!

SCRUB. Ay, he and the Count's footman were gabbering French like two intriguing ducks in a mill-pond; and I believe they talked of me, for they laughed consumedly.

DORINDA. What sort of livery has the footman?

SCRUB. Livery! Lord, madam, I took him for a captain, he's so bedizened with lace! And then he has tops on his shoes up to his mid leg, a silver-headed cane dangling at his knuckles; he carries his hands in his pockets just so — (*Walks in the French air*) and has a fine long periwig tied up in a bag. Lord, madam, he's clear another sort of man than I!

MRS. SULLEN. That may easily be. — But what shall we do now, sister?

DORINDA. I have it! This fellow has a world of simplicity, and some cunning; the first hides the latter by abundance. — Scrub!

SCRUB. Madam!

DORINDA. We have a great mind to know who this gentleman is, only for our satisfaction.

SCRUB. Yes, madam, it would be a satisfaction, no doubt.

DORINDA. You must go and get acquainted with his footman, and invite him hither to drink a bottle of your ale, because you're butler to-day.

SCRUB. Yes, madam, I am butler every Sunday.

MRS. SULLEN. O brave! Sister, o' my conscience, you understand the mathematics already. 'Tis the best plot in the world; your mother, you know, will be gone to church,[3] my spouse will be got to the ale-house with his scoundrels, and the house will be our own — so we drop in by accident, and ask the fellow some questions ourselves. In the country, you know, any stranger is company, and we're glad to take up with the butler in a country dance, and happy if he'll do us the favor.

SCRUB. O madam, you wrong me! I never refused your ladyship the favor in my life.

Enter GIPSY

GIPSY. Ladies, dinner's upon table.

DORINDA. Scrub, we'll excuse your waiting — go where we ordered you.

SCRUB. I shall. *Exeunt*

---

[3] For the afternoon sermon.

[SCENE II.] *Scene changes to the Inn.*

Enter AIMWELL *and* ARCHER

ARCHER. Well, Tom, I find you're a marksman.

AIMWELL. A marksman! who so blind could be as not discern a swan among the ravens?

ARCHER. Well, but hark'ee, Aimwell —

AIMWELL. Aimwell! call me Oroondates, Cesario, Amadis,[4] all that romance can in a lover paint, and then I'll answer. O Archer! I read her thousands in her looks, she looked like Ceres in her harvest: corn, wine and oil, milk and honey, gardens, groves, and purling streams, played on her plenteous face.

ARCHER. Her face! her pocket, you mean; the corn, wine and oil, lies there. In short, she has ten thousand pound, that's the English on't.

AIMWELL. Her eyes —

ARCHER. Are demi-cannons, to be sure; so I won't stand their battery.
(*Going*)

AIMWELL. Pray excuse me, my passion must have vent.

ARCHER. Passion! what a plague, d'ye think these romantic airs will do our business? Were my temper as extravagant as yours, my adventures have something more romantic by half.

AIMWELL. Your adventures!

ARCHER. Yes,

> The nymph that with her twice ten hundred pounds,
> With brazen engine[5] hot, and quoif[6] clear starched,
> Can fire the guest in warming of the bed —

There's a touch of sublime Milton for you, and the subject but an inn-keeper's daughter! I can play with a girl as an angler does with his fish; he keeps it at the end of his line, runs it up the stream, and down the stream, till at last he brings it to hand, tickles[7] the trout, and so whips it into his basket.

Enter BONIFACE

BONIFACE. Mr. Martin, as the saying is — yonder's an honest fellow below, my Lady Bountiful's butler, who begs the honor that you would go home with him and see his cellar.

ARCHER. Do my *baise-mains*[8] to the gentleman, and tell him I will do myself the honor to wait on him immediately.   *Exit* BONIFACE

---

[4] Heroes of French and Spanish romances.

[5] Warming pan.

[6] Cap.

[7] Strokes it until it is quiet.

[8] Give my respects.

AIMWELL. What do I hear? Soft Orpheus play, and fair Toftida[9] sing!

ARCHER. Pshaw! damn your raptures; I tell you, here's a pump going to be put into the vessel, and the ship will get into harbor, my life on't. You say, there's another lady very handsome there?

AIMWELL. Yes, faith.

ARCHER. I'm in love with her already.

AIMWELL. Can't you give me a bill upon Cherry in the meantime?

ARCHER. No, no, friend, all her corn, wine and oil, is ingrossed to my market. And once more I warn you to keep your anchorage clear of mine; for if you fall foul of me, by this light you shall go to the bottom! What! make prize of my little frigate, while I am upon the cruise for you! —

AIMWELL. Well, well, I won't. *Exit* [ARCHER]

Enter BONIFACE

Landlord, have you any tolerable company in the house? I don't care for dining alone.

BONIFACE. Yes, sir, there's a captain below, as the saying is, that arrived about an hour ago.

AIMWELL. Gentlemen of his coat are welcome everywhere; will you make him a compliment from me, and tell him I should be glad of his company?

BONIFACE. Who shall I tell him, sir, would —

AIMWELL. (*Aside*) Ha! that stroke was well thrown in! — [*Aloud*] I'm only a traveller like himself, and would be glad of his company, that's all.

BONIFACE. I obey your commands, as the saying is. *Exit*

Enter ARCHER

ARCHER. 'Sdeath! I had forgot; what title will you give yourself?

AIMWELL. My brother's, to be sure; he would never give me anything else, so I'll make bold with his honor this bout! — You know the rest of your cue.

ARCHER. Ay, ay. *Exit*

Enter GIBBET

GIBBET. Sir, I'm yours.

AIMWELL. 'Tis more than I deserve, sir, for I don't know you.

GIBBET. I don't wonder at that, sir, for you never saw me before. — (*Aside*) I hope.

AIMWELL. And pray, sir, how came I by the honor of seeing you now?

---

[9] Katherine Tofts, a well-known opera singer.

GIBBET. Sir, I scorn to intrude upon any gentleman — but my land-lord —

AIMWELL. O sir, I ask your pardon; you're the captain he told me of?

GIBBET. At your service, sir.

AIMWELL. What regiment, may I be so bold?

GIBBET. A marching regiment, sir, an old corps.

AIMWELL. (*Aside*) Very old, if your coat be regimental. — You have served abroad, sir?

GIBBET. Yes, sir, in the plantations;[10] 'twas my lot to be sent into the worst service. I would have quitted it indeed, but a man of honor, you know — Besides, 'twas for the good of my country that I should be abroad. Anything for the good of one's country — I'm a Roman for that.

AIMWELL. (*Aside*) One of the first, I'll lay my life. — You found the West Indies very hot, sir?

GIBBET. Ay, sir, too hot for me.

AIMWELL. Pray, sir, han't I seen your face at Will's coffeehouse?

GIBBET. Yes, sir, and at White's too.[11]

AIMWELL. And where is your company now, Captain?

GIBBET. They an't come yet.

AIMWELL. Why, d'ye expect 'em here?

GIBBET. They'll be here to-night, sir.

AIMWELL. Which way do they march?

GIBBET. Across the country. — (*Aside*) The devil's in't, if I han't said enough to encourage him to declare! But I'm afraid he's not right, I must tack about.

AIMWELL. Is your company to quarter in Lichfield?

GIBBET. In this house, sir.

AIMWELL. What! all?

GIBBET. My company's but thin, ha, ha, ha! we are but three, ha, ha, ha!

AIMWELL. You're merry, sir.

GIBBET. Ay, sir, you must excuse me, sir, I understand the world, especially the art of travelling: I don't care, sir, for answering questions directly upon the road — for I generally ride with a charge[12] about me.

AIMWELL. (*Aside*) Three or four, I believe.

GIBBET. I am credibly informed that there are highwaymen upon this quarter. Not, sir, that I could suspect a gentleman of your figure — but truly, sir, I have got such a way of evasion upon the road, that I don't care for speaking truth to any man.

---

[10] No doubt Gibbet had been a felon sentenced to transportation.

[11] Literary men resorted to Will's, gamblers to White's.

[12] Gibbet means money; Aimwell in his next speech puns upon "charge" — powder and shot for pistols.

AIMWELL. Your caution may be necessary. — Then I presume you're no captain?

GIBBET. Not I, sir. Captain is a good travelling name, and so I take it; it stops a great many foolish inquiries that are generally made about gentlemen that travel, it gives a man an air of something, and makes the drawers obedient; and thus far I am a captain, and no farther.

AIMWELL. And pray, sir, what is your true profession?

GIBBET. O sir, you must excuse me! — upon my word, sir, I don't think it safe to tell you.

AIMWELL. Ha, ha, ha! upon my word, I commend you.

Enter BONIFACE

Well, Mr. Boniface, what's the news?

BONIFACE. There's another gentleman below, as the saying is, that hearing you were but two, would be glad to make the third man, if you would give him leave.

AIMWELL. What is he?

BONIFACE. A clergyman, as the saying is.

AIMWELL. A clergyman! Is he really a clergyman? or is it only his travelling name, as my friend the captain has it?

BONIFACE. O sir, he's a priest, and chaplain to the French officers in town.

AIMWELL. Is he a Frenchman?

BONIFACE. Yes, sir, born at Brussels.

GIBBET. A Frenchman, and a priest! I won't be seen in his company, sir; I have a value for my reputation, sir.

AIMWELL. Nay, but, captain, since we are by ourselves — Can he speak English, landlord?

BONIFACE. Very well, sir; you may know him, as the saying is, to be a foreigner by his accent, and that's all.

AIMWELL. Then he has been in England before?

BONIFACE. Never, sir; but he's a master of languages, as the saying is; he talks Latin — It does me good to hear him talk Latin.

AIMWELL. Then you understand Latin, Mr. Boniface?

BONIFACE. Not I, sir, as the saying is; but he talks it so very fast, that I'm sure it must be good.

AIMWELL. Pray, desire him to walk up.

BONIFACE. Here he is, as the saying is.

Enter FOIGARD

FOIGARD. Save you, gentlemens, both.

AIMWELL. (Aside) A Frenchman! — [To FOIGARD] Sir, your most humble servant.

FOIGARD. Och, dear joy,[13] I am your most faithful shervant, and yours alsho.

GIBBET. Doctor, you talk very good English, but you have a mighty twang of the foreigner.

FOIGARD. My English is very vell for the vords, but we foreigners, you know, cannot bring our tongues about the pronunciation so soon.

AIMWELL. (*Aside*) A foreigner! a downright Teague,[14] by this light! — Were you born in France, doctor?

FOIGARD. I was educated in France, but I was borned at Brussels; I am a subject of the King of Spain, joy.

GIBBET. What King of Spain, sir? Speak![15]

FOIGARD. Upon my shoul, joy, I cannot tell you as yet.

AIMWELL. Nay, captain, that was too hard upon the doctor; he's a stranger.

FOIGARD. Oh, let him alone, dear joy, I am of a nation that is not easily put out of countenance.

AIMWELL. Come, gentlemen, I'll end the dispute. — Here, landlord, is dinner ready?

BONIFACE. Upon the table, as the saying is.

AIMWELL. Gentlemen — pray — that door —

FOIGARD. No, no, fait, the captain must lead.

AIMWELL. No, doctor, the church is our guide.

GIBBET. Ay, ay, so it is —   *Exit foremost, they follow*

[SCENE III.] *Scene changes to a gallery in* LADY BOUNTIFUL'*s house*

Enter ARCHER *and* SCRUB *singing, and hugging one another,* SCRUB *with a tankard in his hand.* GIPSY *listening at a distance*

SCRUB. *Tall, all, dall!* — Come, my dear boy, let's have that song once more.

ARCHER. No, no, we shall disturb the family. — But will you be sure to keep the secret?

SCRUB. Pho! upon my honor, as I'm a gentleman.

ARCHER. 'Tis enough. You must know then, that my master is the Lord Viscount Aimwell; he fought a duel t'other day in London, wounded his man so dangerously that he thinks fit to withdraw till he hears whether the gentleman's wounds be mortal or not. He never was in this part of England before, so he chose to retire to this place — that's all.

GIPSY. [*Aside*] And that's enough for me.   *Exit*

---

13 A term of friendly address. Foigard's accent is Irish.

14 An Irishman.

15 The Spanish succession was unsettled until the Treaty of Utrecht in 1713.

SCRUB. And where were you when your master fought?

ARCHER. We never know of our masters' quarrels.

SCRUB. No! If our masters in the country here receive a challenge, the first thing they do is to tell their wives; the wife tells the servants, the servants alarm the tenants, and in half an hour you shall have the whole county in arms.

ARCHER. To hinder two men from doing what they have no mind for. — But if you should chance to talk now of my business?

SCRUB. Talk! ay, sir, had I not learned the knack of holding my tongue, I had never lived so long in a great family.

ARCHER. Ay, ay, to be sure there are secrets in all families.

SCRUB. Secrets! ay; — but I'll say no more. Come, sit down, we'll make an end of our tankard; here —

ARCHER. With all my heart; who knows but you and I may come to be better acquainted, eh? Here's your ladies' healths; you have three, I think, and to be sure there must be secrets among 'em.

SCRUB. Secrets! ay, friend. — I wish I had a friend —

ARCHER. Am not I your friend? Come, you and I will be sworn brothers.

SCRUB. Shall we?

ARCHER. From this minute. Give me a kiss — and now, brother Scrub —

SCRUB. And now, brother Martin, I will tell you a secret that will make your hair stand on end. You must know that I am consumedly in love.

ARCHER. That's a terrible secret, that's the truth on't.

SCRUB. That jade, Gipsy, that was with us just now in the cellar, is the arrantest whore that ever wore a petticoat; and I'm dying for love of her.

ARCHER. Ha, ha, ha! — Are you in love with her person or her virtue, brother Scrub?

SCRUB. I should like virtue best, because it is more durable than beauty; for virtue holds good with some women long, and many a day after they have lost it.

ARCHER. In the country, I grant ye, where no woman's virtue is lost till a bastard be found.

SCRUB. Ay, could I bring her to a bastard, I should have her all to myself; but I dare not put it upon that lay, for fear of being sent for a soldier. Pray, brother, how do you gentlemen in London like that same Pressing Act?[16]

ARCHER. Very ill, brother Scrub; 'tis the worst that ever was made for us. Formerly I remember the good days, when we could dun our masters for our wages, and if they refused to pay us, we could have a

---

[16] An act authorizing the impressment of men into military service.

warrant to carry 'em before a justice; but now if we talk of eating, they have a warrant for us, and carry us before three justices.

SCRUB. And to be sure we go, if we talk of eating; for the justices won't give their own servants a bad example. Now this is my misfortune — I dare not speak in the house, while that jade Gipsy dings about like a fury. — Once I had the better end of the staff.

ARCHER. And how comes the change now?

SCRUB. Why, the mother of all this mischief is a priest!

ARCHER. A priest!

SCRUB. Ay, a damned son of a whore of Babylon, that came over hither to say grace to the French officers, and eat up our provisions. There's not a day goes over his head without a dinner or supper in this house.

ARCHER. How came he so familiar in the family?

SCRUB. Because he speaks English as if he had lived here all his life, and tells lies as if he had been a traveller from his cradle.

ARCHER. And this priest, I'm afraid, has converted the affections of your Gipsy.

SCRUB. Converted! ay, and perverted, my dear friend; for, I'm afraid, he had made her a whore and a papist! But this is not all; there's the French count and Mrs. Sullen, they're in the confederacy, and for some private ends of their own, to be sure.

ARCHER. A very hopeful family yours, brother Scrub! I suppose the maiden lady has her lover too?

SCRUB. Not that I know. She's the best on 'em, that's the truth on't. But they take care to prevent my curiosity by giving me so much business that I'm a perfect slave. What d'ye think is my place in this family?

ARCHER. Butler, I suppose.

SCRUB. Ah, Lord help you! I'll tell you. Of a Monday I drive the coach; of a Tuesday I drive the plough; on Wednesday I follow the hounds; a Thursday I dun the tenants; on Friday I go to market; on Saturday I draw warrants; and a Sunday I draw beer.

ARCHER. Ha, ha, ha! if variety be a pleasure in life, you have enough on't, my dear brother. But what ladies are those?

SCRUB. Ours, ours; that upon the right hand is Mrs. Sullen, and the other is Mrs. Dorinda. Don't mind 'em, sit still, man.

Enter MRS. SULLEN *and* DORINDA

MRS. SULLEN. I have heard my brother talk of my Lord Aimwell; but they say that his brother is the finer gentleman.

DORINDA. That's impossible, sister.

MRS. SULLEN. He's vastly rich, but very close, they say.

DORINDA. No matter for that; if I can creep into his heart, I'll open his breast, I warrant him. I have heard say, that people may be guessed at by the behavior of their servants; I could wish we might talk to that fellow.

MRS. SULLEN. So do I; for I think he's a very pretty fellow. Come this way, I'll throw out a lure for him presently.

(*They walk towards the opposite side of the stage*)

ARCHER. (*Aside*) Corn, wine, and oil indeed! But I think the wife has the greatest plenty of flesh and blood; she should be my choice. — Ah, a — say you so! — (MRS. SULLEN *drops her glove,* ARCHER *runs, takes it up, and gives it to her*) Madam — your ladyship's glove.

MRS. SULLEN. O sir, I thank you! — (*To* DORINDA) What a handsome bow the fellow has!

DORINDA. Bow! why I have known several footmen come down from London set up here for dancing masters, and carry off the best fortunes in the country.

ARCHER. (*Aside*) That project, for aught I know, had been better than ours. — Brother Scrub, why don't you introduce me?

SCRUB. Ladies, this is the strange gentleman's servant that you see at church to-day; I understood he came from London, and so I invited him to the cellar, that he might show me the newest flourish in whetting my knives.

DORINDA. And I hope you have made much of him?

ARCHER. O yes, madam; but the strength of your ladyship's liquor is a little too potent for the constitution of your humble servant.

MRS. SULLEN. What! then you don't usually drink ale?

ARCHER. No, madam; my constant drink is tea, or a little wine and water. 'Tis prescribed me by the physician for a remedy against the spleen.

SCRUB. O la! O la! a footman have the spleen!

MRS. SULLEN. I thought that distemper had been only proper to people of quality?

ARCHER. Madam, like all other fashions it wears out, and so descends to their servants; though in a great many of us, I believe, it proceeds from some melancholy particles in the blood, occasioned by the stagnation of wages.

DORINDA. [*Aside to* MRS. SULLEN] How affectedly the fellow talks! — How long, pray, have you served your present master?

ARCHER. Not long; my life has been mostly spent in the service of the ladies.

MRS. SULLEN. And pray, which service do you like best?

ARCHER. Madam, the ladies pay best; the honor of serving them is sufficient wages; there is a charm in their looks that delivers a pleasure with their commands, and gives our duty the wings of inclination.

MRS. SULLEN. [*Aside*] That flight was above the pitch of a livery. — And, sir, would not you be satisfied to serve a lady again?

ARCHER. As a groom of the chamber, madam, but not as a footman.

MRS. SULLEN. I suppose you served as footman before?

ARCHER. For that reason I would not serve in that post again; for my memory is too weak for the load of messages that the ladies lay upon their servants in London. My Lady Howd'ye, the last mistress I served, called me up one morning, and told me: Martin, go to my Lady Allnight with my humble service; tell her I was to wait on her ladyship yesterday, and left word with Mrs. Rebecca, that the preliminaries of the affair she knows of are stopped till we know the concurrence of the person that I know of, for which there are circumstances wanting which we shall accommodate at the old place; but that in the meantime there is a person about her ladyship, that, from several hints and surmises, was accessory at a certain time to the disappointments that naturally attend things, that to her knowledge are of more importance —

MRS. SULLEN and DORINDA. Ha, ha, ha! where are you going, sir?

ARCHER. Why, I han't half done! — The whole howd'ye was about half an hour long; so I happened to misplace two syllables, and was turned off, and rendered incapable.

DORINDA. [*Aside to* MRS SULLEN] The pleasantest fellow, sister, I ever saw! — But, friend, if your master be married, I presume you still serve a lady?

ARCHER. No, madam, I take care never to come into a married family; the commands of the master and the mistress are always so contrary, that 'tis impossible to please both.

DORINDA. (*Aside*) There's a main point gained: my lord is not married, I find.

MRS. SULLEN. But I wonder, friend, that in so many good services, you had not a better provision made for you.

ARCHER. I don't know how, madam. I had a lieutenancy offered me three or four times; but that is not bread, madam — I live much better as I do.

SCRUB. Madam, he sings rarely! I was thought to do pretty well here in the country till he came; but alack a day, I'm nothing to my brother Martin!

DORINDA. Does he? — Pray, sir, will you oblige us with a song?

ARCHER. Are you for passion or humor?

SCRUB. O la! he has the purest ballad about a trifle —

MRS. SULLEN. A trifle! pray, sir, let's have it.

ARCHER. I'm ashamed to offer you a trifle, madam; but since you command me — (*Sings to the tune of "Sir Simon the King"*)

> A trifling song you shall hear,
> Begun with a trifle and ended;
> All trifling people draw near,
> And I shall be nobly attended.

Were it not for trifles a few,
That lately have come into play,
The men would want something to do,
And the women want something to say.

What makes men trifle in dressing?
Because the ladies (they know)
Admire, by often possessing,
That eminent trifle, a beau.

When the lover his moments has trifled,
The trifle of trifles to gain,
No sooner the virgin is rifled,
But a trifle shall part 'em again.

What mortal man would be able
At White's half-an-hour to sit,
Or who could bear a tea-table,
Without talking of trifles for wit?

The Court is from trifles secure,
Gold keys are no trifles, we see!
White rods are no trifles, I'm sure,
Whatever their bearers may be.

But if you will go to the place,
Where trifles abundantly breed,
The levee will show you his Grace
Makes promises trifles indeed.

A coach with six footmen behind,
I count neither trifle nor sin:
But, ye gods! how oft do we find
A scandalous trifle within.

A flask of champagne, people think it
A trifle, or something as bad:
But if you'll contrive how to drink it,
You'll find it no trifle, egad!

A parson's a trifle at sea,
A widow's a trifle in sorrow,
A peace is a trifle to-day,
Who knows what may happen to-morrow!

A black coat a trifle may cloak,
Or to hide it the red may endeavor:
But if once the army is broke,
We shall have more trifles than ever.

The stage is a trifle, they say,
The reason, pray carry along,
Because at every new play,
The house they with trifles so throng.

But with people's malice to trifle,
And to set us all on a foot:
The author of this is a trifle,
And his song is a trifle to boot.

MRS. SULLEN. Very well, sir, we're obliged to you. — Something for a pair of gloves.   (*Offering him money*)

ARCHER. I humbly beg leave to be excused. My master, madam, pays me; nor dare I take money from any other hand, without injuring his honor, and disobeying his commands.   *Exit* [*with* SCRUB]

DORINDA. This is surprising! Did you ever see so pretty a well-bred fellow?

MRS. SULLEN. The devil take him for wearing that livery!

DORINDA. I fancy, sister, he may be some gentleman, a friend of my lord's, that his lordship has pitched upon for his courage, fidelity, and discretion, to bear him company in this dress — and who, ten to one, was his second too.

MRS. SULLEN. It is so, it must be so, and it shall be so! — for I like him.

DORINDA. What! better than the count?

MRS. SULLEN. The count happened to be the most agreeable man upon the place; and so I chose him to serve me in my design upon my husband. But I should like this fellow better in a design upon myself.

DORINDA. But now, sister, for an interview with this lord and this gentleman; how shall we bring that about?

MRS. SULLEN. Patience! you country ladies give no quarter if once you be entered. Would you prevent their desires, and give the fellows no wishing-time? Look'ee, Dorinda, if my Lord Aimwell loves you or deserves you, he'll find a way to see you, and there we must leave it. — My business comes now upon the tapis. Have you prepared your brother?

DORINDA. Yes, yes.

MRS. SULLEN. And how did he relish it?

DORINDA. He said little, mumbled something to himself, promised to be guided by me — but here he comes.

Enter SULLEN

SQUIRE SULLEN. What singing was that I heard just now?

MRS. SULLEN. The singing in your head, my dear; you complained of it all day.

SQUIRE SULLEN. You're impertinent.

MRS. SULLEN. I was ever so, since I became one flesh with you.

SQUIRE SULLEN. One flesh! rather two carcasses joined unnaturally together.

MRS. SULLEN. Or rather a living soul coupled to a dead body.

DORINDA. So, this is fine encouragement for me!

SQUIRE SULLEN. Yes, my wife shows you what you must do.

MRS. SULLEN. And my husband shows you what you must suffer.

SQUIRE SULLEN. 'Sdeath, why can't you be silent?

MRS. SULLEN. 'Sdeath, why can't you talk?

SQUIRE SULLEN. Do you talk to any purpose?

MRS. SULLEN. Do you think to any purpose?

SQUIRE SULLEN. Sister, heark'ye! — (*Whispers*) [*Aloud*] I shan't be home till it be late. *Exit*

MRS. SULLEN. What did he whisper to ye?

DORINDA. That he would go round the back way, come into the closet, and listen as I directed him. But let me beg you once more, dear sister, to drop this project; for as I told you before, instead of awaking him to kindness, you may provoke him to a rage; and then who knows how far his brutality may carry him?

MRS. SULLEN. I'm provided to receive him, I warrant you. But here comes the Count, vanish! *Exit* DORINDA

Enter COUNT BELLAIR

Don't you wonder, Monsieur le Count, that I was not at church this afternoon?

COUNT BELLAIR. I more wonder, madam, that you go dere at all, or how you dare to lift those eyes to heaven that are guilty of so much killing.

MRS. SULLEN. If Heaven, sir, has given to my eyes, with the power of killing, the virtue of making a cure, I hope the one may atone for the other.

COUNT BELLAIR. Oh, largely, madam, would your ladyship be as ready to apply the remedy as to give the wound. Consider, madam, I am doubly a prisoner; first to the arms of your general, then to your more conquering eyes. My first chains are easy, there a ransom may redeem me; but from your fetters I never shall get free.

MRS. SULLEN. Alas, sir! why should you complain to me of your captivity, who am in chains myself? You know, sir, that I am bound, nay, must be tied up in that particular that might give you ease. I am like you, a prisoner of war, — of war, indeed! I have given my parole of honor; would you break yours to gain your liberty?

COUNT BELLAIR. Most certainly I would, were I a prisoner among the Turks; dis is your case; you're a slave, madam, slave to the worst of Turks, a husband.

MRS. SULLEN. There lies my foible, I confess; no fortifications, no courage, conduct, nor vigilancy, can pretend to defend a place, where the cruelty of the governor forces the garrison to mutiny.

COUNT BELLAIR. And where de besieger is resolved to die before de place. — Here will I fix; — (*Kneels*) with tears, vows, and prayers assault your heart, and never rise till you surrender; or if I must storm — Love and St. Michael! — And so I begin the attack —

MRS. SULLEN. Stand off! — (*Aside*) Sure he hears me not! — And I could almost wish he — did not! — The fellow makes love very prettily. — But, sir, why should you put such a value upon my person, when you see it despised by one that knows it so much better?

COUNT BELLAIR. He knows it not, though he possesses it; if he but knew the value of the jewel he is master of, he would always wear it next his heart, and sleep with it in his arms.

MRS. SULLEN. But since he throws me unregarded from him —

COUNT BELLAIR. And one that knows your value well comes by and takes you up, is it not justice?   (*Goes to lay hold on her*)

Enter SULLEN *with his sword drawn*

SQUIRE SULLEN. Hold, villain, hold!

MRS. SULLEN. (*Presenting a pistol*) Do you hold!

SQUIRE SULLEN. What! murther your husband, to defend your bully!

MRS. SULLEN. Bully! for shame, Mr. Sullen! Bullies wear long swords, the gentleman has none, he's a prisoner, you know. I was aware of your outrage, and prepared this to recieve your violence; and, if occasion were, to preserve myself against the force of this other gentleman.

COUNT BELLAIR. O madam, your eyes be bettre firearms than your pistol; they nevre miss.

SQUIRE SULLEN. What! court my wife to my face!

MRS. SULLEN. Pray, Mr. Sullen, put up; suspend your fury for a minute.

SQUIRE SULLEN. To give you time to invent an excuse!

MRS. SULLEN. I need none.

SQUIRE SULLEN. No, for I heard every syllable of your discourse.

COUNT BELLAIR. Ay! and begar, I tink de dialogue was vera pretty.

MRS. SULLEN. Then I suppose, sir, you heard something of your own barbarity?

SQUIRE SULLEN. Barbarity! Oons, what does the woman call barbarity? Do I ever meddle with you?

MRS. SULLEN. No.

SQUIRE SULLEN. As for you, sir, I shall take another time.

COUNT BELLAIR. Ah, begar, and so must I.

SQUIRE SULLEN. Look'ee, madam, don't think that my anger proceeds from any concern I have for your honor, but for my own; and if you can contrive any way of being a whore without making me a cuckold, do it and welcome.

MRS. SULLEN. Sir, I thank you kindly; you would allow me the sin but rob me of the pleasure. No, no, I'm resolved never to venture upon the crime without the satisfaction of seeing you punished for't.

SQUIRE SULLEN. Then will you grant me this, my dear? Let anybody else do you the favor but that Frenchman, for I mortally hate his whole generation.   *Exit*

COUNT BELLAIR. Ah, sir, that be ungrateful, for begar, I love some of yours. Madam — (*Approaching her*)

MRS. SULLEN. No, sir.

COUNT BELLAIR. No, sir! Garzoon, madam, I am not your husband.

MRS. SULLEN. 'Tis time to undeceive you, sir. I believed your addresses to me were no more than an amusement, and I hope you will think the same of my complaisance; and to convince you that you ought, you must know that I brought you hither only to make you instrumental in setting me right with my husband, for he was planted to listen by my appointment.

COUNT BELLAIR. By your appointment?

MRS. SULLEN. Certainly.

COUNT BELLAIR. And so, madam, while I was telling twenty stories to part you from your husband, begar, I was bringing you together all the while?

MRS. SULLEN. I ask your pardon, sir, but I hope this will give you a taste of the virtue of the English ladies.

COUNT BELLAIR. Begar, madam, your virtue be vera great, but garzoon, your honeste be vera little.

Enter DORINDA

MRS. SULLEN. Nay, now, you're angry, sir.

COUNT BELLAIR. Angry! — Fair Dorinda (*Sings* DORINDA *the Opera Tune,*[17] *and addresses to* DORINDA) Madam, when your ladyship want a fool, send for me. *Fair Dorinda, Revenge, &c.* Exit

MRS. SULLEN. There goes the true humor of his nation — resentment with good manners, and the height of anger in a song! Well, sister, you must be judge, for you have heard the trial.

DORINDA. And I bring in my brother guilty.

MRS. SULLEN. But I must bear the punishment. 'Tis hard, sister.

DORINDA. I own it; but you must have patience.

MRS. SULLEN. Patience! the cant of custom — Providence sends no evil without a remedy. Should I lie groaning under a yoke I can shake off, I were accessory to my ruin, and my patience were no better than self-murder.[18]

DORINDA. But how can you shake off the yoke? Your divisions don't come within the reach of the law for a divorce.

MRS. SULLEN. Law! what law can search into the remote abyss of nature? What evidence can prove the unaccountable disaffections of wedlock? Can a jury sum up the endless aversions that are rooted in our souls, or can a bench give judgment upon antipathies?

[17] Possibly the opera *Camilla*, by M. A. Buononcini (D.L., March 30, 1706).

[18] This, and Mrs. Sullen's following speeches, echo Milton's *Doctrine and Discipline of Divorce*, Book II.

DORINDA. They never pretended, sister; they never meddle, but in case of uncleanness.

MRS. SULLEN. Uncleanness! O sister! casual violation is a transient injury, and may possibly be repaired; but can radical hatreds be ever reconciled? No, no, sister; Nature is the first lawgiver; and when she has set tempers opposite, not all the golden links of wedlock nor iron manacles of law can keep 'em fast.

> Wedlock we own ordained by Heaven's decree,
> But such as Heaven ordained it first to be —
> Concurring tempers in the man and wife
> As mutual helps to draw the load of life.
> View all the works of Providence above:
> The stars with harmony and concord move;
> View all the works of Providence below: ⎫
> The fire, the water, earth and air, we know, ⎬
> All in one plant agree to make it grow. ⎭
> Must man, the chiefest work of art divine,
> Be doomed in endless discord to repine?
> No, we should injure Heaven by that surmise:
> Omnipotence is just, were man but wise.   *Exeunt*

ACT IV

[SCENE I.]   *Scene continues*

Enter MRS. SULLEN

MRS. SULLEN. Were I born an humble Turk, where women have no soul nor property, there I must sit contented. But in England, a country whose women are its glory, must women be abused? Where women rule, must women be enslaved? Nay, cheated into slavery, mocked by a promise of comfortable society into a wilderness of solitude! I dare not keep the thought about me. Oh, here comes something to divert me.

Enter a COUNTRY WOMAN

WOMAN. I come, an't please your ladyship — you're my Lady Bountiful, an't ye?

MRS. SULLEN. Well, good woman, go on.

WOMAN. I come seventeen long mail to have a cure for my husband's sore leg.

MRS. SULLEN. Your husband! what, woman, cure your husband!

WOMAN. Ay, poor man, for his sore leg won't let him stir from home.

MRS. SULLEN. There, I confess, you have given me a reason. Well, good woman, I'll tell you what you must do. You must lay your husband's leg upon a table, and with a chopping-knife you must lay it open as broad as you can; then you must take out the bone, and beat the flesh soundly with a rolling pin; then take salt, pepper, cloves, mace and ginger, some sweet herbs, and season it very well; then roll it up like brawn, and put it into the oven for two hours.

WOMAN. Heavens reward your ladyship! I have two little babies too that are piteous bad with the graips, an't please ye.

MRS. SULLEN. Put a little pepper and salt in their bellies, good woman. (Enter LADY BOUNTIFUL) I beg your ladyship's pardon for taking your business out of your hands; I have been a-tampering here a little with one of your patients.

LADY BOUNTIFUL. Come, good woman, don't mind this mad creature; I am the person that you want, I suppose. What would you have, woman?

MRS. SULLEN. She wants something for her husband's sore leg.

LADY BOUNTIFUL. What's the matter with his leg, goody?

WOMAN. It comes first, as one might say, with a sort of dizziness in his foot, then he had a kind of laziness in his joints, and then his leg broke out, and then it swelled, and then it closed again, and then it broke out again, and then it festered, and then it grew better, and then it grew worse again.

MRS. SULLEN. Ha, ha, ha!

LADY BOUNTIFUL. How can you be merry with the misfortunes of other people?

MRS. SULLEN. Because my own make me sad, madam.

LADY BOUNTIFUL. The worst reason in the world, daughter; your own misfortunes should teach you to pity others.

MRS. SULLEN. But the woman's misfortunes and mine are nothing alike; her husband is sick, and mine, alas! is in health.

LADY BOUNTIFUL. What! would you wish your husband sick?

MRS. SULLEN. Not of a sore leg, of all things.

LADY BOUNTIFUL. Well, good woman, go to the pantry, get your bellyful of victuals, then I'll give you a receipt of diet-drink for your husband. But d'ye hear, goody, you must not let your husband move too much.

WOMAN. No, no, madam, the poor man's inclinable enough to lie still. *Exit*

LADY BOUNTIFUL. Well, daughter Sullen, though you laugh, I have done miracles about the country here with my receipts.

MRS. SULLEN. Miracles indeed, if they have cured anybody; but I believe, madam, the patient's faith goes farther toward the miracle than your prescription.

LADY BOUNTIFUL. Fancy helps in some cases; but there's your husband, who has as little fancy as anybody, I brought him from death's door.

MRS. SULLEN. I suppose, madam, you made him drink plentifully of ass's milk.

Enter DORINDA, *runs to* MRS. SULLEN

DORINDA. News, dear sister! news! news!

Enter ARCHER, *running*

ARCHER. Where, where is my Lady Bountiful? — Pray, which is the old lady of you three?

LADY BOUNTIFUL. I am.

ARCHER. O madam, the fame of your ladyship's charity, goodness, benevolence, skill and ability, have drawn me hither to implore your ladyship's help in behalf of my unfortunate master, who is this moment breathing his last.

LADY BOUNTIFUL. Your master! where is he?

ARCHER. At your gate, madam. Drawn by the appearance of your handsome house to view it nearer, and walking up the avenue, within five paces of the courtyard, he was taken ill of a sudden with a sort of I know not what, but down he fell, and there he lies.

LADY BOUNTIFUL. Here, Scrub, Gipsy, all run, get my easy chair downstairs, put the gentleman in it, and bring him in quickly! quickly!

ARCHER. Heaven will reward your ladyship for this charitable act.

LADY BOUNTIFUL. Is your master used to these fits?

ARCHER. O yes, madam, frequently; I have known him have five or six of a night.

LADY BOUNTIFUL. What's his name?

ARCHER. Lord, madam, he's a-dying! a minute's care or neglect may save or destroy his life.

LADY BOUNTIFUL. Ah, poor gentleman! — Come, friend, show me the way; I'll see him brought in myself.   *Exit with* ARCHER

DORINDA. O sister, my heart flutters about strangely! I can hardly forbear running to his assistance.

MRS. SULLEN. And I'll lay my life he deserves your assistance more than he wants[1] it. Did not I tell you that my lord would find a way to come at you? Love's his distemper, and you must be the physician; put on all your charms, summon all your fire into your eyes, plant the whole artillery of your looks against his breast, and down with him.

DORINDA. O sister! I'm but a young gunner; I shall be afraid to shoot, for fear the piece should recoil, and hurt myself.

MRS. SULLEN. Never fear! You shall see me shoot before you, if you will.

DORINDA. No, no, dear sister; you have missed your mark so unfortunately, that I shan't care for being instructed by you.

---

[1] Needs.

Enter AIMWELL, *in a chair, carried by* ARCHER *and* SCRUB:
LADY BOUNTIFUL [and] GIPSY: AIMWELL *counterfeiting*
a swoon

LADY BOUNTIFUL. Here, here, let's see the hartshorn drops. — Gipsy, a glass of fair water! His fit's very strong. — Bless me, how his hands are clenched!

ARCHER. For shame, ladies, what d'ye do? why don't you help us? — (*To* DORINDA) Pray, madam, take his hand and open it, if you can, whilst I hold his head. (DORINDA *takes his hand*)

DORINDA. Poor gentleman! — Oh! — he has got my hand within his, and he squeezes it unmercifully —

LADY BOUNTIFUL. 'Tis the violence of his convulsion, child.

ARCHER. Oh, madam, he's perfectly possessed in these cases — he'll bite you if you don't have a care.

DORINDA. Oh, my hand! my hand!

LADY BOUNTIFUL. What's the matter with the foolish girl? I have got this hand open you see with a great deal of ease.

ARCHER. Ay, but, madam, your daughter's hand is somewhat warmer than your ladyship's, and the heat of it draws the force of the spirits that way.

MRS. SULLEN. I find, friend, you're very learned in these sorts of fits.

ARCHER. 'Tis no wonder, madam, for I'm often troubled with them myself; I find myself extremely ill at this minute.

(*Looking hard at* MRS. SULLEN)

MRS. SULLEN. (*Aside*) I fancy I could find a way to cure you.

LADY BOUNTIFUL. His fit holds him very long.

ARCHER. Longer than usual, madam. — Pray, young lady, open his breast, and give him air.

LADY BOUNTIFUL. Where did his illness take him first, pray?

ARCHER. To-day, at church, madam.

LADY BOUNTIFUL. In what manner was he taken?

ARCHER. Very strangely, my lady. He was of a sudden touched with something in his eyes, which, at the first, he only felt, but could not tell whether 'twas pain or pleasure.

LADY BOUNTIFUL. Wind, nothing but wind!

ARCHER. By soft degrees it grew and mounted to his brain; there his fancy caught it, there formed it so beautiful, and dressed it up in such gay, pleasing colors, that his transported appetite seized the fair idea, and straight conveyed it to his heart. That hospitable seat of life sent all its sanguine spirits forth to meet, and opened all its sluicy gates to take the stranger in.

LADY BOUNTIFUL. Your master should never go without a bottle to smell to. — Oh, — he recovers! — The lavender water — some feathers to burn under his nose — Hungary water to rub his temples. — Oh, he

comes to himself! — Hem a little, sir, hem. — Gipsy! bring the cordial-
water.

(AIMWELL *seems to awake in amaze*)

DORINDA. How d'ye, sir?

AIMWELL. Where am I?   (*Rising*)

Sure I have pass'd the gulf of silent death,
And now I land on the Elysian shore! —
Behold the goddess of those happy plains,
Fair Proserpine — Let me adore thy bright divinity.

(*Kneels to* DORINDA, *and kisses her hand*)

MRS. SULLEN. So, so, so! I knew where the fit would end!

AIMWELL. Eurydice perhaps —
How could thy Orpheus keep his word,
And not look back upon thee?
No treasure but thyself could sure have bribed him
To look one minute off thee.

LADY BOUNTIFUL. Delirious, poor gentleman!

ARCHER. Very delirious, madam, very delirious.

AIMWELL. Martin's voice, I think.

ARCHER. Yes, my lord. — How does your lordship?

LADY BOUNTIFUL. Lord! did you mind that, girls?

AIMWELL. Where am I?

ARCHER. In very good hands, sir. You were taken just now with one
of your old fits, under the trees, just by this good lady's house; her
ladyship had you taken in, and has miraculously brought you to yourself, as you see —

AIMWELL. I am so confounded with shame, madam, that I can now
only beg pardon, and refer my acknowledgments for your ladyship's
care till an opportunity offers of making some amends. I dare be no
longer troublesome. — Martin, give two guineas to the servants.

(*Going*)

DORINDA. Sir, you may catch cold by going so soon into the air; you
don't look, sir, as if you were perfectly recovered.

(*Here* ARCHER *talks to* LADY BOUNTIFUL *in dumb show*)

AIMWELL. That I shall never be, madam; my present illness is so
rooted that I must expect to carry it to my grave.

MRS. SULLEN. Don't despair, sir; I have known several in your distemper shake it off with a fortnight's physic.

LADY BOUNTIFUL. Come, sir, your servant has been telling me that
you're apt to relapse if you go into the air. Your good manners sha'n't
get the better of ours — you shall sit down again, sir. Come, sir, we
don't mind ceremonies in the country. Here, sir, my service t'ye. —
You shall taste my water; 'tis a cordial I can assure you, and of my
own making — drink it off, sir. — (AIMWELL *drinks*) And how d'ye
find yourself now, sir?

AIMWELL. Somewhat better — though very faint still.

LADY BOUNTIFUL. Ay, ay, people are always faint after these fits. — Come, girls, you shall show the gentleman the house. — 'Tis but an old family building, sir; but you had better walk about, and cool by degrees, than venture immediately into the air. You'll find some tolerable pictures. — Dorinda, show the gentleman the way. I must go to the poor woman below. *Exit*

DORINDA. This way, sir.

AIMWELL. Ladies, shall I beg leave for my servant to wait on you, for he understands pictures very well?

MRS. SULLEN. Sir, we understand originals[2] as well as he does pictures, so he may come along.

Exeunt DORINDA, MRS. SULLEN, AIMWELL, ARCHER.
AIMWELL *leads* DORINDA.

Enter FOIGARD *and* SCRUB, *meeting*

FOIGARD. Save you, Master Scrub!

SCRUB. Sir, I won't be saved your way — I hate a priest, I abhor the French, and I defy the devil. Sir, I'm a bold Briton, and will spill the last drop of my blood to keep out popery and slavery.

FOIGARD. Master Scrub, you would put me down in politics, and so I would be speaking with Mrs. Gipsy.

SCRUB. Good Mr. Priest, you can't speak with her; she's sick, sir, she's gone abroad, sir, she's — dead two months ago, sir.

Enter GIPSY

GIPSY. How now, impudence! how dare you talk so saucily to the doctor? — Pray, sir, don't take it ill; for the common people of England are not so civil to strangers, as —

SCRUB. You lie! you lie! 'tis the common people that are civilest to strangers.

GIPSY. Sirrah, I have a good mind to — get you out, I say!

SCRUB. I won't.

GIPSY. You won't, sauce-box! — Pray, doctor, what is the captain's name that came to your inn last night?

SCRUB. [*Aside*] The captain! ah, the devil, there she hampers me again; the captain has me on one side, and the priest on t'other: so between the gown and the sword, I have a fine time on't. — But, *Cedunt arma togae*.[3] (*Going*)

GIPSY. What, sirrah, won't you march?

SCRUB. No my dear, I won't march — but I'll walk. — [*Aside*] And I'll make bold to listen a little too.

(*Goes behind the side-scene, and listens*)

[2] Odd or eccentric people.
[3] A famous phrase from Cicero: Let arms yield to the gown.

GIPSY. Indeed, doctor, the count has been barbarously treated, that's the truth on't.

FOIGARD. Ah, Mrs. Gipsy, upon my shoul, now, gra,[4] his complainings would mollify the marrow in your bones, and move the bowels of your commiseration! He veeps, and he dances, and he fistles, and he swears, and he laughs, and he stamps, and he sings: in conclusion, joy, he's afflicted *à la française*[5] and a stranger would not know whider to cry or to laugh with him.

GIPSY. What would you have me do, doctor?

FOIGARD. Noting, joy, but only hide the count in Mrs. Sullen's closet when it is dark.

GIPSY. Nothing! is that nothing? It would be both a sin ánd a shame, doctor.

FOIGARD. Here is twenty louis d'ors, joy, for your shame; and I will give you an absolution for the shin.

GIPSY. But won't that money look like a bribe?

FOIGARD. Dat is according as you shall tauk it. If you receive the money beforehand, 'twill be, *logicè*, a bribe; but if you stay till afterwards, 'twill be only a gratification.

GIPSY. Well, doctor, I'll take it *logicè*. But what must I do with my conscience, sir?

FOIGARD. Leave dat wid me, joy; I am your priest, gra; and your conscience is under my hands.

GIPSY. But should I put the count into the closet—

FOIGARD. Vel, is dere any shin for a man's being in a closhet? One may go to prayers in a closhet.

GIPSY. But if the lady should come into her chamber, and go to bed?

FOIGARD. Vel, and is dere any shin in going to bed, joy?

GIPSY. Ay, but if the parties should meet, doctor?

FOIGARD. Vel den—the parties must be responsible. Do you be after putting the count in the closhet, and leave the shins wid themselves. I will come with the count to instruct you in your chamber.

GIPSY. Well, doctor, your religion is so pure! Methinks I'm so easy after an absolution, and can sin afresh with so much security, that I'm resolved to die a martyr to't. Here's the key of the garden door, come in the back way when 'tis late. I'll be ready to receive you; but don't so much as whisper, only take hold of my hand; I'll lead you, and do you lead the count and follow me.   *Exeunt*

Enter SCRUB

SCRUB. What witchcraft now have these two imps of the devil been a-hatching here? There's twenty louis d'ors; I heard that, and saw the purse.—But I must give room to my betters.   *Exit*

---

[4] Dear.   [5] In the French fashion.

Enter AIMWELL, *leading* DORINDA, *and making love in dumb show;*
MRS. SULLEN *and* ARCHER

MRS. SULLEN. (*To* ARCHER) Pray, sir, how d'ye like that piece?

ARCHER. Oh, 'tis Leda! You find, madam, how Jupiter comes disguised to make love—

MRS. SULLEN. But what think you there of Alexander's battles?

ARCHER. We want only a Le Brun,[6] madam, to draw greater battles, and a greater general[7] of our own. The Danube, madam, would make a greater figure in a picture than the Granicus; and we have our Ramilies to match their Arbela.[8]

MRS. SULLEN. Pray, sir, what head is that in the corner there?

ARCHER. O madam, 'tis poor Ovid in his exile.

MRS. SULLEN. What was he banished for?

ARCHER. His ambitious love, madam.—(*Bowing*) His misfortune touches me.

MRS. SULLEN. Was he successful in his amours?

ARCHER. There he has left us in the dark.—He was too much a gentleman to tell.

MRS. SULLEN. If he were secret, I pity him.

ARCHER. And if he were successful, I envy him.

MRS. SULLEN. How d'ye like that Venus over the chimney?

ARCHER. Venus! I protest, madam, I took it for your picture; but now I look again, 'tis not handsome enough.

MRS. SULLEN. Oh, what a charm is flattery! If you would see my picture, there it is, over that cabinet. How d'ye like it?

ARCHER. I must admire anything, madam, that has the least resemblance of you. But, methinks, madam—(*He looks at the picture and* MRS. SULLEN *three or four times, by turns*) Pray, madam, who drew it?

MRS. SULLEN. A famous hand, sir.

(*Here* AIMWELL *and* DORINDA *go off*)

ARCHER. A famous hand, madam!—Your eyes, indeed, are featured there; but where's the sparkling moisture, shining fluid, in which they swim? The picture, indeed, has your dimples; but where's the swarm of killing Cupids that should ambush there? The lips too are figured out; but where's the carnation dew, the pouting ripeness, that tempts the taste in the original?

MRS. SULLEN. [*Aside*] Had it been my lot to have matched with such a man!

ARCHER. Your breasts too—presumptuous man! what, paint Heaven! —A propos, madam, in the very next picture is Salmoneus, that was

---

[6] Charles Le Brun (1619-90), Court painter of Louis XIV.
[7] The Duke of Marlborough.
[8] Victories of Marlborough and Alexander.

struck dead with lightning for offering to imitate Jove's thunder; I hope
you served the painter so, madam?

MRS. SULLEN. Had my eyes the power of thunder, they should
employ their lightning better.

ARCHER. There's the finest bed in that room, madam! I suppose
'tis your ladyship's bed-chamber.

MRS. SULLEN. And what then, sir?

ARCHER. I think the quilt is the richest that ever I saw. I can't
at this distance, madam, distinguish the figures of the embroidery; will
you give me leave, madam—?   [*Goes toward the door*]

MRS. SULLEN. The devil take his impudence!—Sure, if I gave him
an opportunity, he durst not offer it?—I have a great mind to try.—
(*Going; returns*) S'death, what am I doing?—And alone, too!—
Sister! sister!   (*Runs out*)

ARCHER. I'll follow her close —

>   For where a Frenchman durst attempt to storm,
>   A Briton sure may well the work perform.   (*Going*)

Enter SCRUB

SCRUB. Martin! brother Martin!

ARCHER. O brother Scrub, I beg your pardon, I was not a-going;
here's a guinea my master ordered you.

SCRUB. A guinea! hi! hi! hi! a guinea! eh—by this light, it is a
guinea! But I suppose you expect one and twenty shillings in change?

ARCHER. Not at all; I have another for Gipsy.

SCRUB. A guinea for her! Faggot and fire for the witch! Sir, give
me that guinea, and I'll discover a plot.

ARCHER. A plot!

SCRUB. Ay, sir, a plot, horrid plot! First, it must be a plot, because
there's a woman in't; secondly, it must be a plot, because there's a
priest in't; thirdly, it must be a plot, because there's French gold in't;
and fourthly, it must be a plot, because I don't know what to make
on't.

ARCHER. Nor anybody else, I'm afraid, brother Scrub.

SCRUB. Truly, I'm afraid so too; for where there's a priest and a
woman, there's always a mystery and a riddle. This I know, that
here has been the doctor with a temptation in one hand and an
absolution in the other, and Gipsy has sold herself to the devil; I
saw the price paid down, my eyes shall take their oath on't.

ARCHER. And is all this bustle about Gipsy?

SCRUB. That's not all; I could hear but a word here and there; but
I remember they mentioned a count, a closet, a back-door, and a key.

ARCHER. The count!—Did you hear nothing of Mrs. Sullen?

SCRUB. I did hear some word that sounded that way; but whether
it was Sullen or Dorinda, I could not distinguish.

ARCHER. You have told this matter to nobody, brother?

SCRUB. Told! no, sir, I thank you for that; I'm resolved never to speak one word, pro nor con, till we have a peace.

ARCHER. You're i'the right, brother Scrub. Here's a treaty afoot between the count and the lady; the priest and the chambermaid are the plenipotentiaries. It shall go hard but I find a way to be included in the treaty.—Where's the doctor now?

SCRUB. He and Gipsy are this moment devouring my lady's marmalade in the closet.

AIMWELL. (*From without*) Martin! Martin!

ARCHER. I come, sir, I come.

SCRUB. But you forgot the other guinea, brother Martin.

ARCHER. Here, I give it with all my heart.

SCRUB. And I take it with all my soul.—[*Exit* ARCHER] Ecod, I'll spoil your plotting, Mrs. Gipsy! and if you should set the captain upon me, these two guineas will buy me off. *Exit*

Enter MRS. SULLEN *and* DORINDA, *meeting*

MRS. SULLEN. Well, sister!

DORINDA. And well, sister!

MRS. SULLEN. What's become of my lord?

DORINDA. What's become of his servant?

MRS. SULLEN. Servant! he's a prettier fellow, and a finer gentleman by fifty degrees, than his master.

DORINDA. O' my conscience, I fancy you could beg that fellow at the gallows-foot![9]

MRS. SULLEN. O' my conscience I could, provided I could put a friend of yours in his room.

DORINDA. You desired me, sister, to leave you when you transgressed the bounds of honor.

MRS. SULLEN. Thou dear censorious country girl! what dost mean? You can't think of the man without the bedfellow, I find.

DORINDA. I don't find anything unnatural in that thought: while the mind is conversant with flesh and blood, it must conform to the humors of the company.

MRS. SULLEN. How a little love and good company improves a woman! Why, child, you begin to live—you never spoke before.

DORINDA. Because I was never spoke to.—My lord has told me that I have more wit and beauty than any of my sex; and truly I begin to think the man in sincere.

MRS. SULLEN. You're in the right, Dorinda; pride is the life of a woman, and flattery is our daily bread; and she's a fool that won't believe a man there, as much as she that believes him in anything else.

[9] Try to save his life by offering to marry him. Occasionally such attempts succeeded.

But I'll lay you a guinea that I had finer things said to me than you had.

DORINDA. Done! What did your fellow say to ye?

MRS. SULLEN. My fellow took the picture of Venus for mine.

DORINDA. But my lover took me for Venus herself.

MRS. SULLEN. Common cant! Had my spark called me a Venus directly, I should have believed him a footman in good earnest.

DORINDA. But my lover was upon his knees to me.

MRS. SULLEN. And mine was upon his tip-toes to me.

DORINDA. Mine vowed to die for me.

MRS. SULLEN. Mine swore to die with me.

DORINDA. Mine spoke the softest moving things.

MRS. SULLEN. Mine had his moving things too.

DORINDA. Mine kissed my hand ten thousand times.

MRS. SULLEN. Mine has all that pleasure to come.

DORINDA. Mine offered marriage.

MRS. SULLEN. O Lard! d'ye call that a moving thing?

DORINDA. The sharpest arrow in his quiver, my dear sister! Why, my ten thousand pounds may lie brooding here this seven years, and hatch nothing at last but some ill-natured clown like yours! Whereas, if I marry my Lord Aimwell, there will be title, place, and precedence, the Park, the play, and the drawing-room, splendor, equipage, noise, and flambeaux.—Hey, my Lady Aimwell's servants there!—Lights, lights to the stairs!— My Lady Aimwell's coach put forward!—Stand by, make room for her ladyship!—Are not these things moving?— What! melancholy of a sudden?

MRS. SULLEN. Happy, happy sister! your angel has been watchful for your happiness, whilst mine has slept, regardless of his charge. Long smiling years of circling joys for you, but not one hour for me!

(*Weeps*)

DORINDA. Come, my dear, we'll talk of something else.

MRS. SULLEN. O Dorinda! I own myself a woman, full of my sex; a gentle, generous soul, easy and yielding to soft desires; a spacious heart, where love and all his train might lodge. And must the fair apartment of my breast be made a stable for a brute to lie in?

DORINDA. Meaning your husband, I suppose?

MRS. SULLEN. Husband! no; even husband is too soft a name for him.—But, come, I expect my brother here to-night or to-morrow; he was abroad when my father married me; perhaps he'll find a way to make me easy.

DORINDA. Will you promise not to make yourself easy in the meantime with my lord's friend?

MRS. SULLEN. You mistake me, sister. It happens with us as among the men, the greatest talkers are the greatest cowards; and there's a reason for it; those spirits evaporate in prattle, which might do more

mischief if they took another course.—Though, to confess the truth,
I do love that fellow;—and if I met him dressed as he should be, and
I undressed as I should be—look'ye, sister, I have no supernatural
gifts—I can't swear I could resist the temptation; though I can safely
promise to avoid it; and that's as much as the best of us can do.

Exeunt

[SCENE II. *The Inn*]

Enter AIMWELL *and* ARCHER, *laughing*

ARCHER. And the awkward kindness of the good motherly old
gentlewoman—

AIMWELL. And the coming easiness of the young one—'Sdeath,
'tis pity to deceive her!

ARCHER. Nay, if you adhere to those principles, stop where you
are.

AIMWELL. I can't stop, for I love her to distraction.

ARCHER. 'Sdeath, if you love her a hair's breadth beyond discretion,
you must go no farther.

AIMWELL. Well, well, anything to deliver us from sauntering away
our idle evenings at White's, Tom's or Will's,[10] and be stinted to bare
looking at our old acquaintance, the cards, because our impotent
pockets can't afford us a guinea for the mercenary drabs.

ARCHER. Or be obliged to some purse-proud coxcomb for a scandalous bottle, where we must not pretend to our share of the discourse,
because we can't pay our club o'th' reckoning.—Damn it, I had rather
sponge upon Morris, and sup upon a dish of bohea scored behind the
door![11]

AIMWELL. And there expose our want of sense by talking criticisms,
as we should our want of money by railing at the government.

ARCHER. Or be obliged to sneak into the side-box, and between both
houses steal two acts of a play, and because we han't money to see the
other three, we come away discontented, and damn the whole five.[12]

AIMWELL. And ten thousand such rascally tricks—had we outlived
our fortunes among our acquaintance.—But now—

ARCHER. Ay, now is the time to prevent all this. Strike while the
iron is hot.—This priest is the luckiest part of our adventure; he shall
marry you, and pimp for me.

AIMWELL. But I should not like a woman that can be so fond of a
Frenchman.

ARCHER. Alas, sir, necessity has no law. The lady may be in distress;
perhaps she has a confounded husband, and her revenge may carry

10 Fashionable London coffee-houses.
11 I.e., run up an account at Morris's coffee-house in the Strand.
12 Persons who left the theater after one act paid nothing.

her farther than her love. Igad, I have so good an opinion of her, and of myself, that I begin to fancy strange things; and we must say this for the honor of our women, and indeed of ourselves, that they do stick to their men as they do to their *Magna Charta*. If the plot lies as I suspect, I must put on the gentleman.—But here comes the doctor —I shall be ready.　　　　　　　　　　　　　　　　　　*Exit*

Enter FOIGARD

FOIGARD. Sauve you, noble friend.

AIMWELL. O sir, your servant! Pray, doctor, may I crave your name?

FOIGARD. Fat naam is upon me! My naam is Foigard, joy.

AIMWELL. Foigard! A very good name for a clergyman.[13] Pray, Doctor Foigard, were you ever in Ireland?

FOIGARD. Ireland! No joy. Fat sort of plaace is dat saam Ireland? Dey say de people are catched dere when dey are young.

AIMWELL. And some of 'em when they're old—as for example.— (*Takes* FOIGARD *by the shoulder*) Sir, I arrest you as a traitor against the government; you're a subject of England, and this morning showed me a commission, by which you served as chaplain in the French army. This is death by our law, and your reverence must hang for't.

FOIGARD. Upon my shoul, noble friend, dis is strange news you tell me! Fader Foigard a subject of England! de son of a burgomaster of Brussels a subject of England! Ubooboo—

AIMWELL. The son of a bog-trotter in Ireland! Sir, your tongue will condemn you before any bench in the kingdom.

FOIGARD. And is my tongue all your evidensh, joy?

AIMWELL. That's enough.

FOIGARD. No, no, joy, for I vil never spake English no more.

AIMWELL. Sir, I have other evidence.—Here, Martin!

Enter ARCHER

You know this fellow?

ARCHER. (*In a brogue*) Saave you, my dear cussen, how does your health?

FOIGARD. (*Aside*) Ah! upon my shoul dere is my countryman, and his brogue will hang mine.—Mynhr, Ick wet neat watt hey zacht, Ick universton ewe neat, sacramant![14]

AIMWELL. Altering your language won't do, sir; this fellow knows your person, and will swear to your face.

FOIGARD. Faash! fey, is dere a brogue upon my faash too?

---

13 Since it means "defender of the faith."

14 Presumably intended to represent Flemish: "Sir, I do not know what he says; I understand you not, on my word."

ARCHER. Upon my soulvation, dere ish, joy!—But cussen Mackshane, vil you not put a remembrance upon me?

FOIGARD. (*Aside*) Mackshane! by St. Patrick, dat ish naame sure enough.

AIMWELL. [*Aside to* ARCHER] I fancy, Archer, you have it.

FOIGARD. The devil hang you, joy! by fat acquaintance are you my cussen?

ARCHER. Oh, de devil hang yourshelf, joy! you know we were little boys togeder upon de school, and your fostermoder's son was married upon my nurse's chister, joy, and so we are Irish cussens.

FOIGARD. De devil taak de relation! Vel, joy, and fat school was it?

ARCHER. I tinks it vas—aay,—'twas Tipperary.

FOIGARD. No, no, joy; it vas Kilkenny.

AIMWELL. That's enough for us—self-confession. Come, sir, we must deliver you into the hands of the next magistrate.

ARCHER. He sends you to jail, you're tried next assizes, and away you go swing into purgatory.

FOIGARD. And is it so wid you, cussen?

ARCHER. It vil be sho wid you, cussen, if you don't immediately confess the secret between you and Mrs. Gipsy. Look'ee, sir, the gallows or the secret, take your choice.

FOIGARD. The gallows! upon my shoul I hate that saame gallow, for it is a diseash dat is fatal to our family. Vel den, dere is nothing, shentlemens, but Mrs. Shullen would spaak wid the count in her chamber at midnight, and dere is no harm, joy, for I am to conduct the count to the plash myshelf.

ARCHER. As I guessed.—Have you communicated the matter to the count?

FOIGARD. I have not sheen him since.

ARCHER. Right again! Why then, doctor—you shall conduct me to the lady instead of the count.

FOIGARD. Fat, my cussen to the lady! upon my shoul, gra, dat is too much upon the brogue.

ARCHER. Come, come, doctor; consider we have got a rope about your neck, and if you offer to squeak, we'll stop your windpipe, most certainly. We shall have another job for you in a day or two, I hope.

AIMWELL. Here's company, coming this way; let's into my chamber, and there concert our affair farther.

ARCHER. Come, my dear cussen, come along.   *Exeunt*

Enter BONIFACE, HOUNSLOW *and* BAGSHOT *at one door,*
GIBBET at the opposite

GIBBET. Well, gentlemen, 'tis a fine night for our enterprise.

HOUNSLOW. Dark as hell.

BAGSHOT. And blows like the devil; our landlord here has showed us the window where we must break in, and tells us the plate stands in the wainscot cupboard in the parlor.

BONIFACE. Ay, ay, Mr. Bagshot, as the saying is, knives and forks, and cups and cans, and tumblers and tankards. There's one tankard, as the saying is, that's near upon as big as me; it was a present to the squire from his godmother, and smells of nutmeg and toast like an East-India ship.

HOUNSLOW. Then you say we must divide at the stair-head?

BONIFACE. Yes, Mr. Hounslow, as the saying is. At one end of that gallery lies my Lady Bountiful and her daughter, and at the other Mrs. Sullen. As for the squire—

GIBBET. He's safe enough, I have fairly entered him, and he's more than half seas over already. But such a parcel of scoundrels are got about him now, that, egad, I was ashamed to be seen in their company.

BONIFACE. 'Tis now twelve, as the saying is—gentlemen, you must set out at one.

GIBBET. Hounslow, do you and Bagshot see our arms fixed and I'll come to you presently.

HOUNSLOW and BAGSHOT. We will.   *Exeunt*

GIBBET. Well, my dear Bonny, you assure me that Scrub is a coward?

BONIFACE. A chicken, as the saying is. You'll have no creature to deal with but the ladies.

GIBBET. And I can assure you, friend, there's a great deal of address and good manners in robbing a lady; I am the most a gentleman that way that ever travelled the road.—But, my dear Bonny, this prize will be a galleon, a Vigo business.[15]—I warrant you we shall bring off three or four thousand pound.

BONIFACE. In plate, jewels, and money, as the saying is, you may.

GIBBET. Why then, Tyburn, I defy thee! I'll get up to town, sell off my horse and arms, buy myself some pretty employment in the household, and be as snug and as honest as any courtier of 'em all.

BONIFACE. And what think you then of my daughter Cherry for a wife?

GIBBET. Look'ee, my dear Bonny—Cherry "is the Goddess I adore," as the song goes; but it is a maxim that man and wife should never have it in their power to hang one another; for if they should, the Lord have mercy on 'um both!   *Exeunt*

[15] The capture of Spanish treasure ships by the English and Dutch in 1702.

ACT V

[SCENE I.] *Scene continues*

Knocking without, enter BONIFACE

BONIFACE. Coming! coming!—A coach and six foaming horses at this time o'night! Some great man, as the saying is, for he scorns to travel with other people.

Enter SIR CHARLES FREEMAN

SIR CHARLES. What, fellow! a public house, and abed when other people sleep!

BONIFACE. Sir, I an't abed, as the saying is.

SIR CHARLES. Is Mr. Sullen's family abed, think'ee?

BONIFACE. All but the squire himself, sir, as the saying is—he's in the house.

SIR CHARLES. What company has he?

BONIFACE. Why, sir, there's the constable, Mr. Gage, the exciseman, the hunchbacked barber, and two or three other gentlemen.

SIR CHARLES. [*Aside*] I find my sister's letters gave me the true picture of her spouse.

Enter SULLEN, *drunk*

BONIFACE. Sir, here's the squire.

SQUIRE SULLEN. The puppies left me asleep—Sir!

SIR CHARLES. Well, sir.

SQUIRE SULLEN. Sir, I'm an unfortunate man—I have three thousand pound a year, and I can't get a man to drink a cup of ale with me.

SIR CHARLES. That's very hard.

SQUIRE SULLEN. Ay, sir; and unless you have pity upon me, and smoke one pipe with me, I must e'en go home to my wife, and I had rather go to the devil by half.

SIR CHARLES. But, I presume, sir, you won't see your wife tonight; she'll be gone to bed. You don't use to lie with your wife in that pickle?

SQUIRE SULLEN. What! not lie with my wife! Why sir, do you take me for an atheist or a rake?

SIR CHARLES. If you hate her, sir, I think you had better lie from her.

SQUIRE SULLEN. I think so too, friend. But I'm a justice of peace, and must do nothing against the law.

SIR CHARLES. Law! As I take it, Mr. Justice, nobody observes law for law's sake, only for the good of those for whom it was made.

SQUIRE SULLEN. But, if the law orders me to send you to jail, you must lie there, my friend.

SIR CHARLES. Not unless I commit a crime to deserve it.

SQUIRE SULLEN. A crime! oons, an't I married?

SIR CHARLES. Nay, sir, if you call marriage a crime, you must disown it for a law.

SQUIRE SULLEN. Eh! I must be acquainted with you sir.—But, sir, I should be very glad to know the truth of this matter.

SIR CHARLES. Truth, sir, is a profound sea, and few there be that dare wade deep enough to find out the bottom on't. Besides, sir, I'm afraid the line of your understanding mayn't be long enough.

SQUIRE SULLEN. Look'ee, sir, I have nothing to say to your sea of truth, but if a good parcel of land can entitle a man to a little truth, I have as much as any he in the country.

BONIFACE. I never heard your worship, as the saying is, talk so much before.

SQUIRE SULLEN. Because I never met with a man that I liked before.

BONIFACE. Pray, sir, as the saying is, let me ask you one question: art not man and wife one flesh?

SIR CHARLES. You and your wife, Mr. Guts, may be one flesh, because ye are nothing else; but rational creatures have minds that must be united.

SQUIRE SULLEN. Minds!

SIR CHARLES. Ay, minds, sir: don't you think that the mind takes place of[1] the body?

SQUIRE SULLEN. In some people.

SIR CHARLES. Then the interest of the master must be consulted before that of his servant.

SQUIRE SULLEN. Sir, you shall dine with me to-morrow!—Oons, I always thought that we were naturally one.

SIR CHARLES. Sir, I know that my two hands are naturally one, because they love one another, kiss one another, help one another in all the actions of life; but I could not say so much if they were always at cuffs.

SQUIRE SULLEN. Then 'tis plain that we are two.

SIR CHARLES. Why don't you part with her, sir?

SQUIRE SULLEN. Will you take her, sir?

SIR CHARLES. With all my heart.

SQUIRE SULLEN. You shall have her to-morrow morning, and a venison-pasty into the bargain.

SIR CHARLES. You'll let me have her fortune too?

SQUIRE SULLEN. Fortune! why sir, I have no quarrel at her fortune; I only hate the woman, sir, and none but the woman shall go.

SIR CHARLES. But her fortune, sir—

1 Takes precedence.

SQUIRE SULLEN. Can you play at whisk, sir?

SIR CHARLES. No, truly, sir.

SQUIRE SULLEN. Not at all-fours?

SIR CHARLES. Neither.

SQUIRE SULLEN. (*Aside*) Oons! where was this man bred?—Burn me, sir! I can't go home, 'tis but two a clock.

SIR CHARLES. For half an hour, sir, if you please; but you must consider, 'tis late.

SQUIRE SULLEN. Late! that's the reason I can't go to bed—Come sir! *Exeunt*

Enter CHERRY, *runs across the stage, and knocks at*
AIMWELL's *chamber-door. Enter* AIMWELL
in his nightcap and gown

AIMWELL. What's the matter? You tremble, child, you're frighted.

CHERRY. No wonder, sir.—But, in short, sir, this very minute a gang of rogues are gone to rob my Lady Bountiful's house.

AIMWELL. How!

CHERRY. I dogged 'em to the very door, and left 'em breaking in.

AIMWELL. Have you alarmed anybody else with the news?

CHERRY. No, no, sir, I wanted to have discovered the whole plot, and twenty other things, to your man Martin; but I have searched the whole house, and can't find him! Where is he?

AIMWELL. No matter, child; will you guide me immediately to the house?

CHERRY. With all my heart, sir; my Lady Bountiful is my godmother, and I love Mrs. Dorinda so well—

AIMWELL. Dorinda! the name inspires me! The glory and the danger shall be all my own.—Come, my life, let me but get my sword. *Exeunt*

[SCENE II.] *Scene changes to a bedchamber in* LADY BOUNTIFUL's *house*

Enter MRS. SULLEN *and* DORINDA *undressed.*[2]

A table and lights

DORINDA. 'Tis very late, sister—no news of your spouse yet?

MRS. SULLEN. No, I'm condemned to be alone till towards four, and then perhaps I may be executed with his company.

DORINDA. Well, my dear, I'll leave you to your rest. You'll go directly to bed, I suppose?

MRS. SULLEN. I don't know what to do.—Heigh-ho!

DORINDA. That's a desiring sigh, sister.

[2] I.e., in dressing-gowns.

MRS. SULLEN. This is a languishing hour, sister.

DORINDA. And might prove a critical minute, if the pretty fellow were here.

MRS. SULLEN. Here! what, in my bed-chamber at two o'clock o'th' morning, I undressed, the family asleep, my hated husband abroad, and my lovely fellow at my feet!—O 'gad sister!

DORINDA. Thoughts are free, sister, and them I allow you.—So, my dear, good night.

MRS. SULLEN. A good rest to my dear Dorinda!—[*Exit* DORINDA] Thoughts free! are they so? Why, then, suppose him here, dressed like a youthful, gay, and burning bridegroom. (*Here* ARCHER *steals out of the closet*) with tongue enchanting, eyes bewitching, knees imploring.—(*Turns a little one side and sees* ARCHER *in the posture she describes*)—Ah!—(*Shrieks and runs to the other side of the stage*) Have my thoughts raised a spirit?—What are you, sir?—a man or a devil?

ARCHER. A man, a man, madam.   (*Rising*)

MRS. SULLEN. How shall I be sure of it?

ARCHER. Madam, I'll give you demonstration this minute.

                                        (*Takes her hand*)

MRS. SULLEN. What, sir! do you intend to be rude?

ARCHER. Yes, madam, if you please.

MRS. SULLEN. In the name of wonder, whence came ye?

ARCHER. From the skies, madam—I'm a Jupiter in love, and you shall be my Alcmena.

MRS. SULLEN. How came you in?

ARCHER. I flew in at the window, madam; your cousin Cupid lent me his wings, and your sister Venus opened the casement.

MRS. SULLEN. I'm struck dumb with admiration!

ARCHER. And I—with wonder.   (*Looks passionately at her*)

MRS. SULLEN. What will become of me?

ARCHER. How beautiful she looks!—The teeming jolly Spring smiles in her blooming face, and, when she was conceived, her mother smelt to roses, looked on lilies—

> Lilies unfold their white, their fragrant charms,
> When the warm sun thus darts into their arms.

                                        (*Runs to her*)

MRS. SULLEN. Ah! (*Shrieks*)

ARCHER. Oons, madam, what d'ye mean? You'll raise the house.

MRS. SULLEN. Sir, I'll wake the dead before I bear this!—What! approach me with the freedoms of a keeper! I'm glad on't, your impudence has cured me.

ARCHER. If this be impudence,—(*Kneels*) I leave to your partial self; no panting pilgrim, after a tedious, painful voyage, e'er bowed before his saint with more devotion.

MRS. SULLEN. (*Aside*) Now, now, I'm ruined if he kneels!—Rise, thou prostrate engineer, not all thy undermining skill shall reach my heart.—Rise, and know, I am a woman without my sex; I can love to all the tenderness of wishes, sighs, and tears—but go no farther. Still to convince you that I'm more than woman, I can speak my frailty, confess my weakness even for you—but—

ARCHER. For me! (*Going to lay hold on her*)

MRS. SULLEN. Hold sir! build not upon that; for my most mortal hatred follows if you disobey what I command you now.—Leave me this minute.—(*Aside*) If he denies I'm lost.

ARCHER. Then you'll promise—

MRS. SULLEN. Anything another time.

ARCHER. When shall I come?

MRS. SULLEN. To-morrow when you will.

ARCHER. Your lips must seal the promise.

MRS. SULLEN. Pshaw!

ARCHER. They must! they must!—(*Kisses her*) Raptures and paradise!—And why not now, my angel? the time, the place, silence, and secrecy, all conspire—And the now conscious stars have preordained this moment for my happiness.   (*Takes her in his arms*)

MRS. SULLEN. You will not! cannot, sure!

ARCHER. If the sun rides fast, and disappoints not mortals of to-morrow's dawn, this night shall crown my joys.

MRS. SULLEN. My sex's pride assist me!

ARCHER. My sex's strength help me!

MRS. SULLEN. You shall kill me first!

ARCHER. I'll die with you.   (*Carrying her off*)

MRS. SULLEN. Thieves! thieves! murther!—

Enter SCRUB *in his breeches and one shoe*

MRS. SULLEN. Thieves! thieves! murther!—

SCRUB. Thieves! thieves! murther! popery!

ARCHER. Ha! the very timorous stag will kill in rutting time.

                    (*Draws and offers to stab* SCRUB)

SCRUB. (*Kneeling*) O pray, sir, spare all I have, and take my life!

MRS. SULLEN. (*Holding* ARCHER's *hand*) What does the fellow mean?

SCRUB. O madam, down upon your knees, your marrowbones!—he's one of 'em.

ARCHER. Of whom?

SCRUB. One of the rogues—I beg your pardon, sir, one of the honest gentlemen that just now are broke into the house.

ARCHER. How!

MRS. SULLEN. I hope you did not come to rob me?

ARCHER. Indeed I did, madam, but I would have taken nothing

but what you might ha' spared; but your crying "Thieves" has waked this dreaming fool, and so he takes 'em for granted.

SCRUB. Granted! 'tis granted, sir, take all we have.

MRS. SULLEN. The fellow looks as if he were broke out of Bedlam.

SCRUB. Oons, madam, they're broke into the house with fire and sword! I saw them, heard them, they'll be here this minute.

ARCHER. What, thieves?

SCRUB. Under favor, sir, I think so.

MRS. SULLEN. What shall we do, sir?

ARCHER. Madam, I wish your ladyship a good night.

MRS. SULLEN. Will you leave me?

ARCHER. Leave you! Lord, madam, did not you command me to be gone just now, upon pain of your immortal hatred?

MRS. SULLEN. Nay, but pray, sir—   (*Takes hold of him*)

ARCHER. Ha, ha, ha! now comes my turn to be ravished.—You see now, madam, you must use men one way or other; but take this by the way, good madam, that none but a fool will give you the benefit of his courage, unless you'll take his love along with it.—How are they armed, friend?

SCRUB. With sword and pistol, sir.

ARCHER. Hush!—I see a dark lantern coming through the gallery.—Madam, be assured I will protect you, or lose my life.

MRS. SULLEN. Your life! no sir, they can rob me of nothing that I value half so much; therefore, now, sir, let me entreat you to be gone.

ARCHER. No, madam, I'll consult my own safety for the sake of yours; I'll work by stratagem. Have you courage enough to stand the appearance of 'em!

MRS. SULLEN. Yes, yes, since I have 'scaped your hands, I can face anything.

ARCHER. Come hither, brother Scrub! don't you know me?

SCRUB. Eh, my dear brother, let me kiss thee.   (*Kisses* ARCHER)

ARCHER. This way—here—

(ARCHER *and* SCRUB *hide behind the bed*)

Enter GIBBET, *with a dark lantern in one hand,*
and a pistol in t'other

GIBBET. Ay, ay, this is the chamber, and the lady alone.

MRS. SULLEN. Who are you, sir? what would you have? d'ye come to rob me?

GIBBET. Rob you! alack a day, madam, I'm only a younger brother, madam; and so, madam, if you make a noise, I'll shoot you through the head; but don't be afraid, madam,—(*Laying his lantern and pistol upon the table*) These rings, madam—don't be concerned, madam, I have a profound respect for you, madam! Your keys, madam—don't be frighted, madam, I'm the most of a gentleman.—(*Searching her*

pockets) This necklace, madam—I never was rude to any lady.—
I have a veneration—for this necklace—

> (*Here* ARCHER *having come round and seized the pistol,
> takes* GIBBET *by the collar, trips up his heels, and claps
> the pistol to his breast*)

ARCHER. Hold, profane villain, and take the reward of thy sacrilege!

GIBBET. Oh! pray, sir, don't kill me; I an't prepared.

ARCHER. How many is there of 'em, Scrub?

SCRUB. Five-and-forty, sir.

ARCHER. Then I must kill the villain, to have him out of the way.

GIBBET. Hold, hold, sir; we are but three, upon my honor.

ARCHER. Scrub, will you undertake to secure him?

SCRUB. Not I, sir; kill him, kill him!

ARCHER. Run to Gipsy's chamber, there you'll find the doctor; bring
him hither presently.—(*Exit* SCRUB, *running*) Come, rogue, if you
have a short prayer, say it.

GIBBET. Sir, I have no prayer at all; the government has provided
a chaplain to say prayers for us on these occasions.

MRS. SULLEN. Pray, sir, don't kill him; you fright me as much as him.

ARCHER. The dog shall die, madam, for being the occasion of my
disappointment.—Sirrah, this moment is your last.

GIBBET. Sir, I'll give you two hundred pound to spare my life.

ARCHER. Have you no more, rascal?

GIBBET. Yes, sir, I can command four hundred, but I must reserve
two of 'em to save my life at the sessions.

Enter SCRUB *and* FOIGARD

ARCHER. Here, doctor—I suppose Scrub and you between you may
manage him. Lay hold of him, doctor.

> (FOIGARD *lays hold of* GIBBET)

GIBBET. What! turned over to the priest already!—Look'ye, doctor, you come before your time; I an't condemned yet, I thank ye.

FOIGARD. Come, my dear joy, I vill secure your body and your
shoul too; I will make you a good Catholic, and give you an absolution.

GIBBET. Absolution! Can you procure me a pardon, doctor?

FOIGARD. No, joy.

GIBBET. Then you and your absolution may go to the devil!

ARCHER. Convey him into the cellar, there bind him—take the
pistol, and if he offers to resist, shoot him through the head—and come
back to us with all the speed you can.

SCRUB. Ay, ay; come, doctor—do you hold him fast, and I'll guard
him.   [*Exit* FOIGARD *with* GIBBET, SCRUB *following*]

MRS. SULLEN. But how came the doctor?

ARCHER. In short, madam—(*Shrieking without*) 'Sdeath! the rogues
are at work with the other ladies—I'm vexed I parted with the pistol;

but I must fly to their assistance.—Will you stay here, madam, or venture yourself with me?

MRS. SULLEN. Oh, with you, dear sir, with you.

Takes him by the arm, and exeunt

[SCENE III.] *Scene changes to another apartment in the same house*

Enter HOUNSLOW *dragging in* LADY BOUNTIFUL, *and*
BAGSHOT *hauling in* DORINDA; *the rogues with swords drawn*

HOUNSLOW. Come, come, your jewels, mistress!

BAGSHOT. Your keys, your keys, old gentlewoman!

Enter AIMWELL *and* CHERRY

AIMWELL. Turn this way, villains! I durst engage an army in such a cause.   (*He engages 'em both*)

DORINDA. O madam, had I but a sword to help the brave man!

LADY BOUNTIFUL. There's three or four hanging up in the hall; but they won't draw. I'll go fetch one, however.   *Exit*

Enter ARCHER *and* MRS. SULLEN

ARCHER. Hold, hold, my lord! every man his bird, pray. (*They engage man to man, the rogues are thrown and disarmed*)

CHERRY. [*Aside*] What! the rogues taken! then they'll impeach my father; I must give him timely notice.   (*Runs out*)

ARCHER. Shall we kill the rogues?

AIMWELL. No, no, we'll bind them.

ARCHER. Ay, ay. — (*To* MRS. SULLEN *who stands by him*) Here, madam, lend me your garter.

MRS. SULLEN. [*Aside*] The devil's in this fellow! he fights, loves, and banters, all in a breath. — Here's a cord that the rogues brought with 'em, I suppose.

ARCHER. Right, right, the rogue's destiny, a rope to hang himself. — Come, my lord — this is but a scandalous sort of an office, (*Binding the rogues together*) if our adventures should end in this sort of hangman-work; but I hope there is something in prospect, that —

Enter SCRUB

Well, Scrub, have you secured your Tartar?

SCRUB. Yes, sir, I left the priest and him disputing about religion.

AIMWELL. And pray carry these gentlemen to reap the benefit of the controversy.   (*Delivers the prisoners to* SCRUB, *who leads 'em out*)

MRS. SULLEN. Pray, sister, how came my lord here?

DORLNDA. And pray how came the gentleman here?

MRS. SULLEN. I'll tell you the greatest piece of villainy —

(They talk in dumb show)

AIMWELL. I fancy, Archer, you have been more successful in your adventures than the housebreakers.

ARCHER. No matter for my adventure, yours is the principal. Press her this minute to marry you — now while she's hurried between the palpitation of her fear and the joy of her deliverance, now, while the tide of her spirits are at high-flood — throw yourself at her feet, speak some romantic nonsense or other — address her like Alexander in the height of his victory, confound her senses, bear down her reason, and away with her. The priest is now in the cellar, and dare not refuse to do the work.

Enter LADY BOUNTIFUL

AIMWELL. But how shall I get off without being observed?

ARCHER. You a lover, and not find a way to get off! — Let me see —

AIMWELL. You bleed, Archer.

ARCHER. 'Sdeath, I'm glad on't; this wound will do the business. I'll amuse the old lady and Mrs. Sullen about dressing my wound, while you carry off Dorinda.

LADY BOUNTIFUL. Gentlemen, could we understand how you would be gratified for the services —

ARCHER. Come, come, my lady, this is no time for compliments; I'm wounded, madam.

LADY BOUNTIFUL AND MRS. SULLEN. How! Wounded!

DORINDA. [*To* AIMWELL] I hope, sir, you have received no hurt.

AIMWELL. None but what you may cure. —

(Makes love in dumb show)

LADY BOUNTIFUL. Let me see your arm, sir — I must have some powder-sugar to stop the blood. — O me! an ugly gash, upon my word, sir! You must go into bed.

ARCHER. Ay, my lady, a bed would do very well. — (*To* MRS. SUL-LEN) Madam, will you do me the favor to conduct me to a chamber?

LADY BOUNTIFUL. Do, do, daughter — while I get the lint and the probe and the plaster ready.

(Runs out one way, AIMWELL *carries off* DORINDA *another)*

ARCHER. Come, madam, why don't you obey your mother's commands?

MRS. SULLEN. How can you, after what is passed, have the confidence to ask me?

ARCHER. And if you go to that, how can you, after what is passed, have the confidence to deny me? Was not this blood shed in your defence, and my life exposed for your protection? Look'ye, madam, I'm none of your romantic fools, that fight giants and monsters for nothing; my valor is downright Swiss;[3] I'm a soldier of fortune, and must be paid.

MRS. SULLEN. 'Tis ungenerous in you, sir, to upbraid me with your services!

ARCHER. 'Tis ungenerous in you, madam, not to reward 'em.

MRS. SULLEN. How! at the expense of my honor?

ARCHER. Honor! can honor consist with ingratitude? If you would deal like a woman of honor, do like a man of honor. D'ye think I would deny you in such a case?

Enter a Servant

SERVANT. Madam, my lady ordered me to tell you that your brother in below at the gate.   [*Exit*]

MRS. SULLEN. My brother! Heavens be praised! — Sir, he shall thank you for your services, he has it in his power.

ARCHER. Who is your brother, madam?

MRS. SULLEN. Sir Charles Freeman. — You'll excuse me, sir; I must go and receive him.   [*Exit*]

ARCHER. Sir Charles Freeman! 'Sdeath and hell! my old acquaintance! Now unless Aimwell has made good use of his time, all our fair machine goes souse into the sea like the Eddystone.[4]

[SCENE IV.] *Scene changes to the gallery in the same house*

Enter AIMWELL *and* DORINDA

DORINDA. Well, well, my lord, you have conquered; your late generous action will, I hope, plead for my easy yielding; though I must own your lordship had a friend in the fort before.

AIMWELL. The sweets of Hybla dwell upon her tongue! — Here, doctor —

Enter FOIGARD, *with a book*

FOIGARD. Are you prepared boat?

DORINDA. I'm ready. But first, my lord, one word — I have a frightful example of a hasty marriage in my own family; when I reflect upon't, it shocks me. Pray, my lord, consider a little —

AIMWELL. Consider! do you doubt my honor or my love?

DORINDA. Neither; I do believe you equally just as brave, and were your whole sex drawn out for me to choose, I should not cast a look upon the multitude if you were absent. But, my lord, I'm a woman; colors, concealments may hide a thousand faults in me — therefore

---

[3] Mercenary soldiers.

[4] The first Eddystone lighthouse was destroyed in a storm in 1703.

know me better first. I hardly dare affirm I know myself, in anything except my love.

AIMWELL. (*Aside*) Such goodness who could injure! I find myself unequal to the task of villain; she has gained my soul, and made it honest like her own — I cannot, cannot hurt her. — Doctor, retire. —
(*Exit* FOIGARD)
Madam, behold your lover and your proselyte, and judge of my passion by my conversion! — I'm all a lie, nor dare I give a fiction to your arms; I'm all counterfeit, except my passion.

DORINDA. Forbid it, Heaven! a counterfeit!

AIMWELL. I am no lord, but a poor needy man, come with a mean, a scandalous design to prey upon your fortune; but the beauties of your mind and person have so won me from myself that, like a trusty servant, I prefer the interest of my mistress to my own.

DORINDA. Sure I have had the dream of some poor mariner, a sleepy image of a welcome port, and wake involved in storms! — Pray, sir, who are you?

AIMWELL. Brother to the man whose title I usurped, but stranger to his honor or his fortune.

DORINDA. Matchless honesty! — Once I was proud, sir, of your wealth and title, but now am prouder that you want it; now I can show my love was justly levelled, and had no aim but love. — Doctor, come in.

Enter FOIGARD *at one door,* GIPSY *at another, who whispers* DORINDA

[*To* FOIGARD] Your pardon, sir, we sha'not want you now. — [*To* AIMWELL] Sir, you must excuse me — I'll wait on you presently.
Exit with GIPSY
FOIGARD. Upon my shoul, now, dis is foolish. *Exit*
AIMWELL. Gone! and bid the priest depart! — It has an ominous look.

Enter ARCHER

ARCHER. Courage, Tom! — Shall I wish you joy?
AIMWELL. No.
ARCHER. Oons, man, what ha' you been doing?
AIMWELL. O Archer! my honesty, I fear, has ruined me.
ARCHER. How!
AIMWELL. I have discovered myself.
ARCHER. Discovered! and without my consent? What! have I embarked my small remains in the same bottom with yours, and you dispose of all without my partnership?
AIMWELL. O Archer! I own my fault.
ARCHER. After conviction — 'tis then too late for pardon. You may

remember, Mr. Aimwell, that you proposed this folly; as you begun, so end it. Henceforth I'll hunt my fortune single — so farewell!

AIMWELL. Stay, my dear Archer, but a minute.

ARCHER. Stay! what, to be despised, exposed, and laughed at! No, I would sooner change conditions with the worst of the rogues we just now bound, than bear one scornful smile from the proud knight that once I treated as my equal.

AIMWELL. What knight?

ARCHER. Sir Charles Freeman, brother to the lady that I had almost — but no matter for that, 'tis a cursed night's work, and so I leave you to make the best on't.   (*Going*)

AIMWELL. Freeman! — One word, Archer. Still I have hopes; methought she received my confession with pleasure.

ARCHER. 'Sdeath, who doubts it?

AIMWELL. She consented after to the match; and still I dare believe she will be just.

ARCHER. To herself, I warrant her, as you should have been.

AIMWELL. By all my hopes, she comes, and smiling comes!

Enter DORINDA *mighty gay*

DORINDA. Come, my dear lord — I fly with impatience to your arms — the minutes of my absence was a tedious year. Where's this tedious priest?

Enter FOIGARD

ARCHER. Oons, a brave girl!

DORINDA. I suppose, my lord, this gentleman is privy to our affairs?

ARCHER. Yes, yes, madam; I'm to be your father.

DORINDA. Come, priest, do your office.

ARCHER. Make haste, make haste, couple 'em any way. — (*Takes* AIMWELL's *hand*) Come, madam, I'm to give you —

DORINDA. My mind's altered; I won't.

ARCHER. Eh! —

AIMWELL. I'm confounded!

FOIGARD. Upon my shoul, and sho is myshelf.

ARCHER. What's the matter now, madam?

DORINDA. Look'ye, sir, one generous action deserves another. — This gentleman's honor obliged him to hide nothing from me; my justice engages me to conceal nothing from him. In short, sir, you are the person that you thought you counterfeited; you are the true Lord Viscount Aimwell, and I wish your lordship joy. — Now, priest, you may be gone; if my lord is pleased now with the match, let his lordship marry me in the face of the world.

AIMWELL *and* ARCHER. What does she mean?

DORINDA. Here's a witness for my truth.

Enter SIR CHARLES FREEMAN *and* MRS. SULLEN

SIR CHARLES. My dear Lord Aimwell, I wish you joy.

AIMWELL. Of what?

SIR CHARLES. Of your honor and estate. Your brother died the day before I left London; and all your friends have writ after you to Brussels; among the rest I did myself the honor.

ARCHER. Hark'ye, sir knight, don't you banter now?

SIR CHARLES. 'Tis truth, upon my honor.

AIMWELL. Thanks to the pregnant stars that formed this accident!

ARCHER. Thanks to the womb of time that brought it forth! — away with it!

AIMWELL. Thanks to my guardian angel that led me to the prize.

(*Taking* DORINDA'*s hand*)

ARCHER. And double thanks to the noble Sir Charles Freeman. — My lord, I wish you joy. — My lady, I wish you joy. — Egad, Sir Freeman, you're the honestest fellow living! — 'Sdeath, I'm grown strange airy upon this matter. — My lord, how d'ye? — A word, my lord; don't you remember something of a previous agreement, that entitles me to the moiety of this lady's fortune, which I think will amount to five thousand pound?

AIMWELL. Not a penny, Archer; you would ha' cut my throat just now, because I would not deceive this lady.

ARCHER. Ay, and I'll cut your throat again, if you should deceive her now.

AIMWELL. That's what I expected; and to end the dispute, the lady's fortune is ten thousand pounds, we'll divide stakes: take the ten thousand pounds or the lady.

DORINDA. How! is your lordship so indifferent?

ARCHER. No, no, no, madam! his lordship knows very well that I'll take the money; I leave you to his lordship, and so we're both provided for.

Enter COUNT BELLAIR

COUNT BELLAIR. Mesdames et Messieurs, I am your servant trice humble! I hear you be rob here.

AIMWELL. The ladies have been in some danger, sir.

COUNT BELLAIR. And, begar, our inn be rob too!

AIMWELL. Our inn! by whom?

COUNT BELLAIR. By the landlord, begar! — Garzoon, he has rob himself, and run away?

ARCHER. Robbed himself?

COUNT BELLAIR. Ay, begar, and me too of a hundre pound.

ARCHER. A hundred pound,

COUNT BELLAIR. Yes, that I owed him.

AIMWELL. Our money's gone, Frank.

ARCHER. Rot the money! my wench is gone. — (*To* COUNT BELLAIR) *Savez-vous quelque chose de Mademoiselle Cherry?*[5]

Enter a Fellow with a strong box and a letter

FELLOW. Is there one Martin here?

ARCHER. Ay, ay — who wants him?

FELLOW. I have a box here, and letter for him. [*Gives the box and letter to* ARCHER *and exit*]

ARCHER. Ha, ha, ha! what's here? Legerdemain! — By this light, my lord, our money again! — But this unfolds the riddle. — (*Opening the letter, reads*) Hum, hum, hum! — Oh, 'tis for the public good, and must be communicated to the company. [*Reads*]

MR. MARTIN,

My father being afraid of an impeachment by the rogues that are taken to-night, is gone off; but if you can procure him a pardon, he will make great discoveries that may be useful to the country. Could I have met you instead of your master to-night, I would have delivered myself into your hands, with a sum that much exceeds that in your strong-box, which I have sent you, with an assurance to my dear Martin that I shall ever be his most faithful friend till death.

CHERRY BONIFACE

There's a billet-doux for you! As for the father, I think he ought to be encouraged; and for the daughter — pray, my lord, persuade your bride to take her into her service instead of Gipsy.

AIMWELL. I can assure you, madam, your deliverance was owing to her discovery.

DORINDA. Your command, my lord, will do without the obligation. I'll take care of her.

SIR CHARLES. This good company meets opportunely in favor of a design I have in behalf of my unfortunate sister. I intend to part her from her husband — gentlemen, will you assist me?

ARCHER. Assist you! 'sdeath, who would not?

COUNT BELLAIR. Assist! garzoon, we all assist!

Enter SULLEN

SQUIRE SULLEN. What's all this? They tell me, spouse, that you had like to have been robbed.

MRS. SULLEN. Truly, spouse, I was pretty near it — had not these two gentlemen interposed.

SQUIRE SULLEN. How came these gentlemen here?

MRS. SULLEN. That's his way of returning thanks, you must know.

COUNT BELLAIR. Garzoon, the question be àpropos for all dat.

---

[5] Do you know anything about Miss Cherry?

SIR CHARLES. You promised last night, sir, that you would deliver your lady to me this morning.

SQUIRE SULLEN. Humph!

ARCHER. Humph! what do you mean by humph? Sir, you shall deliver her! In short, sir, we have saved you and your family; and if you are not civil, we'll unbind the rogues, join with 'em, and set fire to your house. What does the man mean? not part with his wife!

COUNT BELLAIR. Ay, garzoon, de man no understan common justice.

MRS. SULLEN. Hold, gentlemen! All things here must move by consent; compulsion would spoil us. Let my dear and I talk the matter over, and you shall judge it between us.

SQUIRE SULLEN. Let me know first who are to be our judges. Pray, sir, who are you?

SIR CHARLES I am Sir Charles Freeman, come to take away your wife.

SQUIRE SULLEN. And you, good sir?

AIMWELL. [Thomas], Viscount Aimwell, come to take away your sister.

SQUIRE SULLEN. And you, pray, sir?

ARCHER. Francis Archer, esquire, come —

SQUIRE SULLEN. To take away my mother, I hope. Gentlemen, you're heartily welcome; I never met with three more obliging people since I was born! — And now, my dear, if you please, you shall have the first word.

ARCHER. And the last, for five pound!

MRS. SULLEN. Spouse!

SQUIRE SULLEN. Rib!

MRS. SULLEN. How long have we been married?

SQUIRE SULLEN. By the almanac, fourteen months, but by my account, fourteen years.

MRS. SULLEN. 'Tis thereabout by my reckoning.

COUNT BELLAIR. Garzoon, their account will agree.

MRS. SULLEN. Pray, spouse, what did you marry for?

SQUIRE SULLEN. To get an heir to my estate.

SIR CHARLES And have you succeeded?

SQUIRE SULLEN. No.

ARCHER. The condition fails of his side. — Pray, madam, what did you marry for?

MR. SULLEN. To support the weakness of my sex by the strength of his, and to enjoy the pleasures of an agreeable society.

SIR CHARLES. Are your expectations answered?

MRS. SULLEN. No.

COUNT BELLAIR. A clear case! a clear case!

SIR CHARLES. What are the bars to your mutual contentment?

MRS. SULLEN. In the first place, I can't drink ale with him.

SQUIRE SULLEN. Nor can I drink tea with her.

MRS. SULLEN. I can't hunt with you.

SQUIRE SULLEN. Nor can I dance with you.

MRS. SULLEN. I hate cocking and racing.

SQUIRE SULLEN. And I abhor ombre and piquet.[6]

MRS. SULLEN. Your silence is intolerable.

SQUIRE SULLEN. Your prating is worse.

MRS. SULLEN. Have we not been a perpetual offence to each other? a gnawing vulture at the heart?

SQUIRE SULLEN. A frightful goblin to the sight?

MRS. SULLEN. A porcupine to the feeling?

SQUIRE SULLEN. Perpetual wormwood to the taste?

MRS. SULLEN. Is there on earth a thing we could agree in?

SQUIRE SULLEN. Yes — to part.

MRS. SULLEN. With all my heart.

SQUIRE SULLEN. Your hand.

MRS. SULLEN. Here.

SQUIRE SULLEN. These hands joined us, these shall part us. — Away!

MRS. SULLEN. North.

SQUIRE SULLEN. South.

MRS. SULLEN. East.

SQUIRE SULLEN. West — far as the poles asunder.

COUNT BELLAIR. Begar, the ceremony be very pretty.

SIR CHARLES. Now, Mr. Sullen, there wants only my sister's fortune to make us easy.

SQUIRE SULLEN. Sir Charles, you love your sister, and I love her fortune; every one to his fancy.

ARCHER. Then you won't refund?

SQUIRE SULLEN. Not a stiver.

ARCHER. Then I find, madam, you must e'en go to your prison again.

COUNT BELLAIR. What is the portion?

SIR CHARLES. Ten thousand pound, sir.

COUNT BELLAIR. Garzoon, I'll pay it, and she shall go home wid me.

ARCHER. Ha, ha, ha! French all over. — Do you know, sir, what ten thousand pound English is?

COUNT BELLAIR. No, begar, not *justement*.[7]

ARCHER. Why, sir, 'tis a hundred thousand livres.

COUNT BELLAIR. A hundre tousand livres! A garzoon, me canno' do't! Your beauties and their fortunes are both too much for me.

ARCHER. Then I will. This night's adventure has proved strangely lucky to us all — for Captain Gibbet in his walk had made bold, Mr. Sullen, with your study and escritoire, and had taken out all the writings of your estate, all the articles of marriage with your lady, bills,

---

[6] Card games.
[7] Exactly.

bonds, leases, receipts to an infinite value; I took 'em from him, and I deliver 'em to Sir Charles.

(*Gives him a parcel of papers and parchments*)

SQUIRE SULLEN. How, my writings! — my head aches consumedly. — Well, gentlemen, you shall have her fortune, but I can't talk. If you have a mind, Sir Charles, to be merry, and celebrate my sister's wedding and my divorce, you may command my house — but my head aches consumedly. — Scrub, bring me a dram.

ARCHER. (*To* MRS. SULLEN) Madam, there's a country dance to the trifle that I sung to-day; your hand, and we'll lead it up.

Here a Dance

ARCHER. 'Twould be hard to guess which of these parties is the better pleased, the couple joined, or the couple parted; the one rejoicing in hopes of an untasted happiness, and the other in their deliverance from an experienced misery.

> Both happy in their several states we find,
> Those parted by consent, and those conjoined.
> Consent, if mutual, saves the lawyer's fee —
> Consent is law enough to set you free.

EPILOGUE

Designed to be spoke in "The Beaux' Stratagem"

If to our play your judgment can't be kind,
Let its expiring author pity find;
Survey his mournful case with melting eyes,
Nor let the bard be damned before he dies.[1]
Forbear, you fair, on his last scene to frown,
But his true exit with a plaudit crown;
Then shall the dying poet cease to fear
The dreadful knell, while your applause he hears.
At Leuctra so the conquering Theban died,[2]
Claimed his friends' praises, but their tears denied;
Pleased in the pangs of death, he greatly thought
Conquest with loss of life but cheaply bought.
The difference this — the Greek was one would fight,
As brave, though not so gay, as Serjeant Kite.[3]
Ye sons of Will's,[4] what's that to those who write?
To Thebes alone the Grecian owed his bays;
You may the bard above the hero raise,
Since yours is greater than Athenian praise.

[1] Farquhar died (probably of tuberculosis) about two months after the production of the play.

[2] Epaminondas, Theban general, who died, not at the battle of Leuctra, but nine years later, at the battle of Mantincia.

[3] Hero of Farquhar's *The Recruiting Officer*.

[4] Men of letters who congregated at Will's Coffee House.

RIVERSIDE EDITIONS

* In preparation